The X Window System

Programming
and Applications
with Xt
OPEN LOOK® Edition

W9-BUU-473

Douglas A. Young

Silicon Graphics, Inc.
Mountain View, California

John A. Pew

Vivid Solutions
San Jose, California

PRENTICE HALL, Englewood Cliffs, New Jersey 07632

oging-in-Publication Data

YOUNG, D

    The X Window System : programming and applications with Xt /
Douglas A. Young, John A. Pew. — Open Look ed.
      p.   cm.
    Includes bibliographical references and index.
    ISBN 0-13-982992-X
    1. X Window System (Computer system) I. Pew, John A. II. Title.
QA76.76.W56Y67 1992
005.4'3—dc20   91-22212
                                               CIP

Cover design: *Bruce Kenselaar*
Pre-press buyer: *Mary Elizabeth McCartney*
Manufacturing buyer: *Susan Brunke*
Acquisition editor: *Gregory G. Doench*

© 1992 by Prentice-Hall, Inc.
A Division of Simon & Schuster
Englewood Cliffs, New Jersey 07632

The publisher offers discounts on this book when ordered in bulk quantities. For more information, write: Special Sales/Professional Marketing, Prentice Hall, Professional & Technical Reference Division, Englewood Cliffs, NJ 07632.

Printed in the United States of America

10 9 8 7 6 5 4 3 2 1

ISBN   0-13-982992-X

PRENTICE-HALL INTERNATIONAL (UK) LIMITED, *London*
PRENTICE-HALL OF AUSTRALIA PTY. LIMITED, *Sydney*
PRENTICE-HALL CANADA INC., *Toronto*
PRENTICE-HALL HISPANOAMERICANA, S.A., *Mexico*
PRENTICE-HALL OF INDIA PRIVATE LIMITED, *New Delhi*
PRENTICE-HALL OF JAPAN, INC., *Tokyo*
SIMON & SCHUSTER ASIA PTE. LTD., *Singapore*
EDITORA PRENTICE-HALL DO BRASIL, LTDA., *Rio de Janeiro*

To Teri and D.C.

D.Y.

*To Renée, Douglas, Brian,
Jeffrey, and Bradley*

J.P.

CONTENTS

PREFACE

The original version of this book was conceived in 1987 and was completed in late 1988. At that time, X was a relatively new technology. There were few X-based commercial applications, and nearly all X applications were based on Xlib. The Xt Intrinsics was beginning to stabilize, but there were few Xt-based applications. One reason for this was the lack of a standard widget set. Writing a complete application using only Xlib was, and still is, a challenging task. There were many competing widget sets, including both public domain software and commercial products. The X server, along with Xlib, provided a standard base, but above that level it was much harder to determine what toolkit, if any, would emerge as a preferred common platform for writing applications.

In the past few years that picture has changed significantly. Today, we have a wealth of applications based on X, most of which are based on the Xt Intrinsics. Instead of struggling to choose between many different user interface toolkits, most programmers who base their applications on the Xt Intrinsics can choose between two principle widget sets. These are the Motif widget set, developed by the Open Software Foundation, and the OPEN LOOK widget set (also known as OLIT), developed by AT&T and Sun Microsystems. An earlier version of this book used the Motif widget set in all examples. This version is intended for those who prefer to use the OPEN LOOK widget set.

The availability of professional-quality user interface toolkits like Motif and OLIT has had a significant impact on the quality of X applications. Only a few years ago, users were happy to have an X application that was simply functional. Today, the expectations tend to be much higher. Applications are now supposed to be visually attractive, easy to use, and have consistent, predictable behavior. (And of course they still have to provide raw functionality as well.) OLIT supports this trend by providing a widget set that implements the OPEN LOOK user interface style. Developing an application with good interactive user interface is a non-trivial task. Starting with a user interface toolkit that supports a well thought-out interface style and provides a pleasing appearance is an essential first step.

From the beginning, the approach taken by this book was to treat X, Xt, and a widget set as a unified toolkit as much as possible. Instead of focusing on each as a separate topic, this book simply focuses on how to write applications, viewing the X Window System as a whole. Examples in this book use the Xt Intrinsics as the framework of all programs, the OLIT widget set as the application's primary user interface components, and Xlib functions, when needed, to complete the task. This book seeks to strike a balance between the somewhat overwhelming amount of information represented by Xlib, Xt, and OLIT, and introduces the material programmers will need to get started writing typical applications as quickly as possible.

The information in this book is based on the X11R4 release of Xlib and the Xt Intrinsics, and version 3.0 of OLIT. Like most large software systems, X is an evolving system, and some details will necessarily evolve over time. In fact, as we go to press X11R5 is expected "soon". By emphasizing fundamental concepts, this book tries to provide the reader with a foundation that is relatively independent of these minor changes.

ACKNOWLEDGMENTS

We are indebted to many people who helped to improve this book. In addition to those who helped by reviewing the previous Motif edition, many people contributed to the success of this version. Our thanks to the members of the OLIT team at Sun Microsystems: Ramy Akras, Larry Cable, Yi-Ming Chou, John Cooper, Dave Curley, John Litt, John Mani, Debbie Stevenson, K. S. Suryanarayanan, and Steven Tom. Their many suggestions and reviews contributed greatly to this book. Others also contributed with reviews including: Darren Austin, Alice Kemp, Stuart Marks, and Amy Moore. A special thanks to Brian Stell for introducing the two of us to each other. Thanks to Keoki Williams for designing the screen shot for the book cover. We appreciate the cooperation of Frame Technology Corporation for providing an early version of FrameMaker 3.0. This entire book was produced using FrameMaker which greatly facilitated our efforts. We also thank the management of Sun Microsystems and Prentice Hall for their encouragement and support. Lastly, our deepest gratitude for the support of our wives and families. They have cheerfully endured the many long nights and weekends at the keyboard. We could not have completed this book without them.

John Pew
Douglas Young

1

AN INTRODUCTION TO
THE X WINDOW SYSTEM

The X Window System is an industry-standard software system that allows programmers to develop portable graphical user interfaces. One of the most important features of X is its device-independent architecture. X allows programs to display windows containing text and graphics on any hardware that supports the X protocol without modifying, recompiling, or relinking the application. This device independence, along with X's position as an industry standard, allows X-based applications to function in a heterogeneous environment consisting of mainframes, workstations, and personal computers.

X was developed at the Massachusetts Institute of Technology (MIT), with support from the Digital Equipment Corporation (DEC). The name, X, as well as some initial design ideas were derived from an earlier window system named W, developed at Stanford University. X was designed at MIT's Laboratory for Computer Science for Project Athena to fulfill that project's need for a distributed, hardware-independent user interface platform. Early versions of X were used primarily within MIT and DEC, but with the release of version 10, many manufacturers expressed interest in X as a commercial product. The early versions of X were designed and implemented primarily by Robert Scheifler and Ron Newman from MIT and Jim Gettys from DEC, although many additional people contributed to X, Version 11. Version 11 of the X Window System is supported by a consortium of hardware and software vendors who have made a commitment to X as a standard base for user interfaces across each of their product lines. The X Consortium supports and controls the standard specification of the X Window System. X is available on most UNIX systems, Digital's VAX/VMS operating system, and also many personal computers. Many companies have also begun to produce hardware specifically designed to support the X protocol.

One important difference between X and many other window systems is that X does not define any particular user interface style. X provides *mechanisms* to support many interface styles rather than enforcing any one *policy*. Many window systems — the one used by Apple's MacIntosh, or Microsoft Windows, for example — support a particular style of user interface. In contrast, X provides a flexible set of primitive window operations, but carefully avoids dictating the look or feel of any particular application's user interface. Instead, X provides a device-independent layer that serves as a base for a variety of interface styles. Therefore, the basic X Window System does not provide user interface components such as scrollbars, menus, or dialog boxes often found in other window systems. Most applications depend on higher level libraries built on top of the basic X protocol to provide these components.

1.1   THE CLIENT-SERVER MODEL

The architecture of the X Window System is based on a *client-server* model. A single process, known as the *server,* is responsible for all input and output devices. The server creates and manipulates windows on the screen, produces text and graphics, and handles input devices such as a keyboard and mouse. The server provides a portable layer between all applications and the display hardware. The X server typically runs on a workstation or personal computer with a graphics display, although some vendors offer dedicated X terminals that implement all or part of the X server in hardware or firmware.

An application that uses the facilities provided by the X server is known as a *client.* A client communicates with the X server via a network connection using an asynchronous byte-stream protocol. X supports many network protocols, including TCP/IP, DECnet, and Chaos. Multiple clients can connect to a single server concurrently, and an individual client can also connect to multiple servers.

The X architecture hides most of the details of the device-dependent implementation of the server and the hardware it controls from clients. Any client can communicate with any server, provided both the client and the server obey the X protocol.

In addition to providing device independence, the distributed architecture of X allows the server and clients to run on separate machines located anywhere on a network.[1] This feature has many potential applications. For example, imagine an interactive teaching program executing on a school's main computer that can display information on inexpensive personal computers located at each student's desk. In this scenario, the teaching program is a client that communicates with multiple servers, one for each student's display. Each student interacts with the program concurrently through a window on his or her local machine. The same program is also connected to another display located at the teacher's desk, allowing the teacher to check the progress of any individual student or the class as a whole. While one window on each of the student's machines

---

[1]The server and client(s) often run on separate machines within a local area network. However, X can also handle not-so-local configurations transparently. I once had an interesting opportunity to use this feature to read my electronic mail during a trip to Europe. The X-based mail program (the client) ran on my workstation in Palo Alto, California, while the X server ran on a workstation in Bristol, England! Although the response of the system suffered slightly from the satellite transmission time, X worked perfectly. The mail program was completely unaware that I was interacting with it from a location several thousand miles away.

provides an interface to the remote teaching program, other windows on a student's machine can provide interfaces to other clients. For example, each student can use a window to interact with an electronic mail system running on a central mail server. Still another window can provide an interface to an editor running locally on the student's machine.

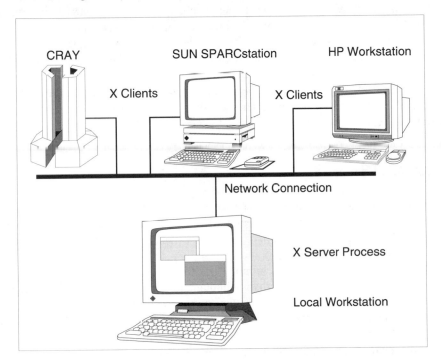

Figure 1.1 The client-server model.

1.2 DISPLAYS AND SCREENS

The terms display and screen are often used interchangeably to refer to a cathode ray tube (CRT) used by the computer to display text and/or graphics. However, X uses the term display to mean a single X server process, while a screen is a single hardware output device. A single X display can support many screens. X uses the terms display and server interchangeably. There is normally only one server per central processing unit (CPU).

Before a client can communicate with the X server it must open a connection to the server. Once a client establishes this connection, it can use any of the screens controlled by the server. X provides a security mechanism that allows a server to deny clients executing on other hosts the right to connect to a display. This mechanism works on a per-host basis.

1.3 RESOURCES

The X server controls all *resources* used by the window system. Resources include windows, bitmaps, fonts, colors, and other data structures used by an application. The X server maintains these resources privately within the server, to enable clients to use and share these data structures transparently. Client programs access each resource through a *resource identifier*, usually referred to simply as an ID. A resource ID is a unique identifier assigned by the X server.

The X server usually creates and destroys resources at the request of a client. Also, the server usually destroys most resources automatically when the client that requested them disconnects from the server. X allows clients to specify the *shutdown mode* of a resource. The shutdown mode controls the lifetime of a resource. The default mode destroys all resources allocated for a client when that client breaks its connection with the server.

1.4 REQUESTS

When a client application needs to use a service provided by the X server, the client issues a *request* to the server. Clients typically request the server to create, destroy, or reconfigure windows, or to display text or graphics in a window. Clients can also request information about the current state of windows or other resources.

The X server normally runs asynchronously with respect to its clients and all clients run asynchronously with respect to each other. Although the server processes requests from each particular application in the order in which they arrive, requests are not necessarily processed immediately. Requests from clients are placed in a queue until the server is able to process them, and clients do not wait for the server to respond to requests. Applications can request the server to handle requests synchronously, but this usually results in poorer performance, because each request to the server suffers a round-trip over the network connection.

1.5 BASIC WINDOW CONCEPTS

The most fundamental resource in X is the *window*. A window simply represents a rectangular section of the screen. Unlike windows in some other window systems, an X window has no title bar, scroll bar or other decorations. An X window appears as a rectangle with a background color or pattern. Each window also has a border. Applications can combine two or more windows to create scroll bars, title bars, and other higher-level user interface components.

The X server creates windows in response to requests from clients. The server stores and maintains the data structure representing a window, while clients refer to the window using the window's ID. Clients can issue requests to the server to alter the window's size, position, color, or other characteristics, and can also request the server to place text in a window or perform graphical operations on a window. Although the server creates each window at the request of a specific client, any client can request the server to manipulate any window, provided it has access to the window's ID. For example, X window managers use this feature to control the position of all windows on the screen.

1.5.1   The Window Hierarchy

X organizes windows as a hierarchy, referred to as the *window tree*. The top window in this window tree is known as the *root window*. The X server automatically creates a root window for each screen it controls. The root window occupies an entire physical screen, and cannot be moved or resized. Every window except the root window has a *parent* window (also known as an *ancestor*) and can also have *children* (also known as *descendents* or *subwindows*). Windows that share the same parent are known as *siblings*.

Figure 1.2 and Figure 1.3 illustrate this hierarchical model and show the relationship between several windows. Figure 1.2 illustrates how a set of windows might appear on the screen, while Figure 1.3 shows the window tree formed by these windows. Windows A and B are children of the root window, while Windows C and E are children of Window A. Window G is a child of Window E. Similarly, windows D and F are children of Window B and Window H is a child of Window F.

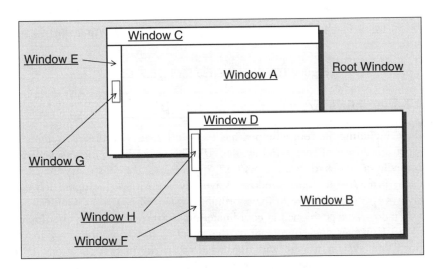

Figure 1.2 A typical window hierarchy.

X places few restrictions on the size or location of a window. One of the restrictions it does enforce is that only the portion of a window that lies within the bounds of its parent is visible; the server *clips* the remaining portions to the boundaries of the parent window. This means that Windows A and B are not completely visible because their children windows lie on top of them. For example, Window C covers the top portion of Window A. In other words, the upper left hand corners of Window C and Window A are the same point.

X allows siblings to overlap in a way that resembles a collection of papers on a desk. The *stacking order* determines which windows or portions of windows appear to be on top (and therefore are visible). If two windows occupy overlapping regions on the screen, the window that is higher in the stacking order completely or partially *obscures* the lower window. For example, in Figure 1.2, Window B is higher in the stacking order than Window A. Clients can request the X server to alter a window's position in the stacking order (for example, raising a window above all other windows). A window's stacking order can only be altered relative to its siblings. Therefore, from a user's viewpoint, a window's descendants raise and lower with the window.

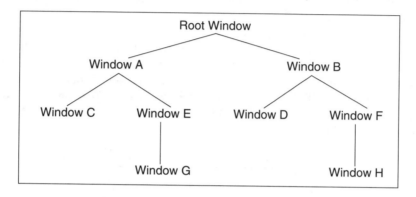

Figure 1.3 Window tree for Figure 1.2.

1.5.2   The X Coordinate System

Each X window, including the root window, has its own integer coordinate system. The coordinate of the upper left corner of each window is *(0, 0)*. The *x* coordinate increases toward the right and the *y* coordinate increases toward the bottom. Applications always specify the coordinate of a point on the screen relative to some window. A window's position (the upper left corner of the window) is always specified relative to the coordinate system of its parent window. For example, in Figure 1.4, Window A is positioned at coordinate *(50, 100)* relative to the coordinate system of the root window. However, the coordinate of this point is *(0, 0)* relative to Window A. Each window's coordinate system moves with the window, permitting applications to place text, graphics, or sub-windows in a window without regard to the window's location.

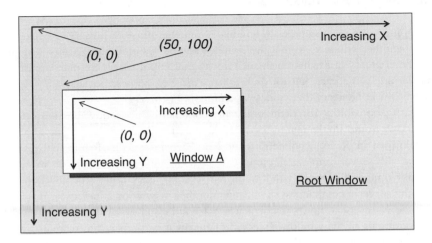

Figure 1.4 The X coordinate system.

1.5.3   Mapping and Window Visibility

Although each X window is associated with a rectangular region on the screen, windows are not necessarily visible to the user all the time. When the server creates a window, it allocates and initializes the data structures that represent the window within the server, but does not invoke the hardware-dependent routines that display the window on the screen. Clients can request the server to display a window by issuing a *map* request. Although a window is considered to be *mapped* if a client has issued a map request for that window, it still might not be visible for any of the following reasons:

- The window is completely *obscured* by another window on the screen. The window becomes visible only if it or the obscuring window is moved such that the window is no longer obscured, the obscuring window is removed from the screen, or the stacking order of the two windows changes so that the obscuring window is lower in the stacking order than the other window.

- An ancestor of the window is not mapped. Before a window can appear on the screen, every ancestor of the window must be mapped. A window that is mapped, but has an ancestor that is not mapped, is said to be *unviewable*. The window automatically becomes *viewable* when all ancestors are mapped.

- The window is completely clipped by an ancestor. If a window is located completely outside the visible boundaries of any ancestor, it is not visible on the screen. The window becomes visible if the ancestor or ancestors are resized to include the region occupied by the window, or if the window is moved to lie within the visible boundaries of all ancestors.

1.5.4   Maintaining Window Contents

In an overlapping window system, each window's contents must be preserved when that window is covered by another window, so that the contents can be restored later. Many systems maintain and restore the contents of a window in such a way that applications are unaware of the process. Such windows are sometimes known as *retained-raster* windows, because the window system generally saves the contents of the window as a *bitmap*, or *raster*.

In X, the responsibility for maintaining the contents of a window lies with the client that uses the window. Some implementations of X support retained rasters, or *backing store* as this technique is known in X, but applications must not depend on this feature because there is no guarantee that all server implementations can provide this service for all windows. Saving complete raster images for every window on the screen places a huge demand on the memory resources of the server's computer system as the number of windows increases. It is usually more efficient for the X server to notify a client when a window is *exposed*, and rely on the client to redisplay the contents of the window. Every X client must be prepared to recreate the contents of its windows at any time. This places some additional burden on the application programmer, although this is seldom a problem because most applications maintain internal representations of the contents of their windows anyway. The backing store feature is best used to support computationally-intensive applications that have difficulty recreating their output quickly. For servers that do not support backing store, such applications must usually resort to saving the current contents of its windows as an off-screen image.

Many X servers also support *save-unders*. A save-under is a technique of saving the image on the screen, *under* a particular window, so that the image can be restored when the window is moved to a new location or removed from the screen. This is done by taking a snapshot of an area of the screen just before this area is covered by a window. For save-unders to work, the state of the screen and all windows on the screen must be held constant between the time the snapshot is taken and the time the image is restored. Save-unders are used primarily when creating popup menus and other small transitory windows to achieve a smooth visual effect.

1.6 EVENTS

The X server communicates with clients by sending *events* to the client applications. The server generates events as a direct or indirect result of a user action (for example, pressing a key on the keyboard, moving the mouse, or pressing a mouse button). The server also generates events to notify the client of changes in the state of its windows. For example, the server sends a client an **Expose** event when a window's contents needs to be restored. X supports thirty-three types of events, and provides a mechanism that allows clients to define additional event types.

The server sends events to a client by placing the event on a first-in, first-out (FIFO) queue that can be read by the client. Each event consists of a packet that reports the type of event, the window in which the event occurred, and other data specific to the particular type of event.

Most X applications are completely *event-driven* and are designed to wait until an event occurs, respond to the event, and then wait for the next event. The event-driven approach provides a natural model for interactive applications. Chapter 5 discusses events and the event-driven model in detail.

1.7 INPUT DEVICES

X supports a variety of input devices. Depending on the implementation, a server can support tablets, track balls, scanners, and other data input and pointing devices. The most common input devices are the keyboard, used for textual input, and the mouse, which serves as both a pointing device and a selection device.

1.7.1 The Mouse

A mouse is a device that allows the user to point to locations on the screen and also to issue commands by pressing buttons. The user points to a screen location by controlling the position of an image on the screen known as the *pointer*.

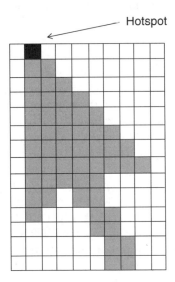

Figure 1.5 A typical mouse cursor.

The pointer is sometimes referred to as the *mouse cursor* or *sprite* although X usually uses the term pointer. The user controls the location of the pointer by moving the mouse on the user's desk.[2] The server maintains the pointer and tracks the location of the mouse. Clients can ask the server to report events when the pointer enters or leaves a window, changes position, or when the

---

[2] Because of the close relationship between the motion of the mouse and the motion of the pointer on the screen, users often talk of the position of the mouse when they really mean the position of the pointer. For example, someone might say "the mouse is in the window." Of course the mouse is really on the desk; the pointer is in the window.

user presses or releases a mouse button. Clients can also query the server to determine the current position of the pointer, and can change the size and appearance of the pointer as well. This feature is often used to indicate the current task or state of the application. For example, the mouse cursor might assume the shape of a diagonal arrow (see Figure 1.5) when the user points to a location on the screen, change to a vertical arrow when the user uses a scroll bar, and change to an hourglass when the application is busy.

Every mouse cursor has a *hotspot*. A hotspot is the point within the mouse cursor that defines the precise location of the pointer on the screen. The pointer is said to be *contained* by a window if the mouse cursor's hotspot is inside the visible region of the window, or one of its sub-windows. The pointer is *in* the smallest window that contains the hotspot.

1.7.2   The Keyboard

The server generates an event each time a key changes state. The information in the event structure includes a code identifying the key that was pressed or released. The client can translate this code into an ASCII character code if desired. The key code is independent of any particular keyboard arrangement to allow applications to handle a variety of keyboards made by different manufacturers.

1.8   WINDOW MANAGEMENT

A *window manager* allows the user to control the size and location of windows on the screen. In many window systems, the window manager is inseparable from the rest of the window system. In X, a window manager is an ordinary client application. However, X provides some features intended to allow window managers to control the size and placement of windows. For example, window managers can request that the X server *redirect* requests dealing with the structure of a window to the window manager rather than acting on the requests directly. If an application issues a map request for a window and a window manager has requested that such events be redirected, the X server sends a `MapRequest` event to the window manager. The window manager then has the opportunity to take some action before mapping the window, or can even refuse to map the window. Some window managers use this feature to place or resize windows according to a set of layout rules. For example, a *tiling* window manager might first rearrange or resize other windows already on the screen to ensure that no windows overlap. Many window managers use this feature to add a frame or title bar to the window before mapping it.

Window management is a complex subject that affects not only how users interact with a system, but also how applications interact with each other and with the X server. The *InterClient Communications Conventions Manual* (ICCCM) defines the protocol all window managers and applications should follow to interact properly with each other. In practice, these guidelines are of the most concern to those few programmers who design window managers[3] and user interface toolkits, or those programmers who choose to program directly with the Xlib C library.

1.9   THE APPLICATION PROGRAMMER'S INTERFACE TO X

Although the X server protocol is defined at the level of network packets and byte-streams, programmers generally base applications on libraries that provide an interface to the base window system. The most widely used low-level interface to X is the standard C language library known as Xlib.[4] Xlib defines an extensive set of functions that provide complete access and control over the display, windows, and input devices. Similar libraries also exist for LISP and ADA.

Although programmers can (and do) use Xlib to build applications, this relatively low-level library can be tedious and difficult to use correctly. Just handling the window manager conventions can require hundreds of lines of code. Many programmers prefer to use one of the higher-level toolkits designed to be used with X. In addition to the X Toolkit discussed in this book, there is InterViews (built at Stanford University), Andrew (from Carnegie Mellon), and XView (developed by Sun Microsystems), to name just a few. These toolkits are based on Xlib and are generally easier to use and hide many implementation details from the programmer.

This book discusses a standard toolkit known as the X Toolkit. The X Toolkit consists of two parts: a layer known as the Xt Intrinsics, and a set of user interface components known as widgets. The Xt Intrinsics supports many different widget sets. The examples in this book use the widgets from the OPEN LOOK Intrinsics Toolkit (OLIT). Other popular widget sets include Motif (from the Open Software Foundation (OSF)), and Athena (freely distributed with the MIT X distribution). From an application programmer's viewpoint, most widget sets provide similar capabilities. A programmer who is familiar with one widget set should be able to quickly learn to use any other widget set. Both the Xt Intrinsics and the OLIT widget set are written in C and are built on top of Xlib. The OLIT widget set implements user interface components, including scroll bars, menus, and buttons, while the Xt Intrinsics provides a framework that allows the programmer to combine these components to produce a complete user interface. Figure 1.6 shows the architecture of an application based on a widget set and the Xt Intrinsics.

The Xt Intrinsics and the OLIT widget set are smoothly integrated with Xlib, so applications that use the facilities of the higher level library can also use the functions provided by Xlib when needed. This book shows how the application programmer can use Xlib, the Xt Intrinsics, and the OLIT widget set as a complete system for constructing user interfaces.

---

[3]   Developing new window managers has been a popular activity among X programmers. Many programmers gained their initial understanding of X by writing new window managers. Consequently, X users have had the benefit of the many window managers that are available in the public domain. One early X window manager was simply named *wm*. This window manager was intended only for early X11 developers, not for public use. The source to wm was kept primarily in a file named "test.c"! In spite of the implications of this file name, wm served early developers well, and provided a model for some other window managers. The second wave of X window managers were more powerful, but did not comply with the as-yet-to-be written ICCCM. These window managers included *uwm* (Ultrix Window Manager), *awm* (Ardent Window Manager), *twm* (Tom's Window Manager), and a tiled window manager, *rtl* (which took its name from the Siemens Research Technology Laboratory). The third generation of window managers now conform to the ICCCM. These include a newer ICCCM-compliant version of *twm*, *mwm* (The OSF/Motif window manager), *gwm* (The Gnu Window Manager) and others. This book shows the OPEN LOOK window manager, *olwm* which is also an ICCCM-compliant window manager.

[4]   The X Consortium recognizes two types of standards, *exclusive* and *non-exclusive*. Xlib is an example of an exclusive standard. The Consortium will not recognize or adopt any other C-language interface to the underlying X protocol as a standard. Non-exclusive standards such as the Xt Intrinsics are considered part of the X Window System, but the Consortium may recognize other similar interfaces as well.

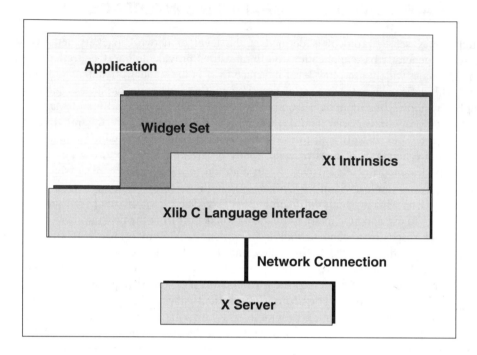

Figure 1.6 Programmer's view of the complete X Window System.

1.10 SUMMARY

This chapter presented the overall architecture of the X Window System and introduced some basic terminology. X provides a powerful platform that allows programmers to develop sophisticated user interfaces that are portable to any system that supports the X protocol. X is based on a network-transparent client-server model. The X server creates and manipulates windows in response to requests from clients, and sends events to notify clients of user input or changes in a window's state.

X does not support any particular interface style, and strives to be policy-free. Applications are free to use the X primitives to define their own type of user interface, although it is easier for an application to fit into an existing environment if the application follows a few guidelines. The easiest way for a programmer to follow these basic guidelines is to use a higher level toolkit, such as the Xt Intrinsics.

Some window systems refer to the entire system as a "window manager." In X, a window manager is a client, no different from any other client, that allows the user to move and manipulate windows. Users can choose from a variety of window managers, and therefore the programmer should not design an X application in such a way that it depends on a particular window manager. For the most part, X applications should function properly even when there is no window manager at all, although the ICCCM protocol forces applications to rely on the exist-ence of an ICCCM-compliant window manager for some services.

Most programmers find it easiest to base their applications on a toolkit, such as the X Toolkit. The Intrinsics layer of the X Toolkit defines an architecture for combining user interface components known as widgets. Widgets are user interface components that can be combined to create complex user interfaces. The following chapters use Xlib, the Xt Intrinsics, and the OLIT widget set to build examples that demonstrate many of the features of X. Chapter 2 introduces the Xt Intrinsics and demonstrates a simple X-based application.

2

PROGRAMMING WITH THE Xt INTRINSICS

This chapter introduces the application programmer's interface to the X Window System, concentrating on the Xt Intrinsics (sometimes referred to as simply "Xt"). Following the same philosophy as Xlib, the Xt Intrinsics library attempts to remain policy-free, and provides only those mechanisms that do not affect the look or feel of an application's user interface. Xt serves as a framework that allows programmers to create user interfaces by combining an extensible set of user interface components. These components are known as *widgets*, and include *scrollbars*, *buttons*, *menus*, and *dialog boxes*. Widgets consist of an X window along with some procedures that operate on the window. The Intrinsics provide a small core set of widgets, although most of these cannot be used directly in applications. Additional widgets are available from many sources.

Most programmers use a combination of Xlib, the Xt Intrinsics, and a widget set to write X-based applications. We refer to these programmers as *application programmers*. The Xt Intrinsics define an architectural model for widgets that also allows programmers to extend the toolkit by creating new types of widgets. We refer to a programmer who creates new widgets as a *widget programmer*.

This book describes the Xt Intrinsics and the OPEN LOOK Intrinsics Toolkit (OLIT) widget set. As of the time of this writing, the current release of OLIT from Sun Microsystems is version 3[1] which is based on the X11R4 release of the Xt Intrinsics. This chapter introduces a few of the basic functions included in the Xt Intrinsics layer and presents a simple application using the Xt Intrinsics and a simple widget.

---

[1] The OPEN LOOK widget set originates from AT&T. AT&T and Sun use different numbering schemes. The current version of the OPEN LOOK widget set from AT&T is version 4. These two products start from a common code base but have diverged slightly.

2.1 NAMING CONVENTIONS

Each layer of the application programmer's interface to X follows its own naming conventions. The names of all Xlib functions and user-accessible data structures begin with the capital letter **X**, and use a mixed case convention. When function names are composed of more than one word, the first letter of each word is capitalized. For example:

```
XCreateWindow()
XDrawString()
```

All Xlib macros also follow this mixed case convention, but do not begin with the letter **X**. For example:

```
DisplayWidth()
ButtonPressMask
```

Xlib also follows some conventions intended to make it easier to remember the argument order used by each Xlib function. The first argument to nearly every Xlib function is a pointer to a **Display** structure. If the function requires a resource identifier as an argument, the resource ID immediately follows the display argument. *Drawable*s precede all other resources. A *drawable* is any resource that can be the object of a graphics request. In X, this can be either a window or a pixmap. Whenever a function requires both a *source* and a *destination* drawable, the source argument always precedes the destination. When the function parameters include size and location specifications, *x* always precedes *y, width* always precedes *height*, and the *x, y* pair always precedes the *width, height* pair. For example, consider the argument order of the following Xlib function:

```
XDrawRectangle(display, drawable, gc, x, y, width, height)
```

As specified by the argument ordering conventions, the first argument to this function is a pointer to a **Display** structure. The next two arguments are resources. The first of these is a drawable, and must precede the second resource (a graphics context). Finally, the *x, y* location precedes the width and height of the rectangle.

The Xt Intrinsics use naming conventions similar to those used by Xlib. All functions and macros use mixed case and begin with the letters **Xt**. Unlike Xlib, the Intrinsics layer does not distinguish between functions and macros. For example:

```
XtCreateWidget() /* Function */
XtSetArg()       /* Macro    */
```

The Xt Intrinsics also use string constants to specify names of resources. Defining strings as constants promotes consistency and also assists the programmer by allowing the compiler to detect spelling errors. These resource strings fall into three categories: resource *name strings*, resource *class strings*, and resource *representation strings*. Chapter 3 discusses the meaning of these terms. By convention, Xt defines resource name string constants by adding the prefix **XtN** to the string. For example:

```
#define XtNwidth    "width"
```

Resource class strings use the prefix **XtC**:

```
#define XtCBackground    "Background"
```

A resource representation string is defined by adding the prefix **XtR** to the string:

```
#define XtRInt    "Int"
```

Different widget sets often follow their own conventions for naming functions, types, and variables. For example, most external symbols and functions in OLIT start with the letters **Ol**:

```
OlWarning
OlTextFieldGetString()
```

The class names of OLIT widgets use a mixed case convention without a prefix. For example:

```
AbbrevMenuButton
OblongButton
```

By convention, each widget class pointer consists of the name of the widget class followed by the word **WidgetClass**. In the OLIT widget set, widget class pointers begin with a lowercase letter. For example:

```
abbrevMenuButtonWidgetClass
oblongButtonWidgetClass
```

The first time a function is used in this book, the syntax of the function is given as it is used in a program. For example, the first time we discuss the function **XtNextEvent()** it is shown as:

```
XtNextEvent(&event)
```

To differentiate functions and variables defined by the examples presented in this book from those defined by Xlib, the Xt Intrinsics, or OLIT, all functions and variables defined by examples use a combination of lowercase letters and underscores. For example:

```
refresh_screen()
main_window
```

This book builds a small library of useful routines as we present examples of the various features of X, the Intrinsics, and the OLIT widget set. To distinguish these reusable library functions, all functions and symbols in this library begin with the letters **xs_**. For example:

```
xs_create_quit_button()
xs_concat_words()
```

2.2 THE X TOOLKIT PROGRAMMING MODEL

The X Toolkit provides application programmers with a specific model for writing applications. All X applications are normally designed to be event-driven. However, the X Toolkit builds on this event model to create something we might call a dispatch-driven programming model. Xlib applications usually have a switch statement inside an event loop. The **switch** statement looks at the type of each event and performs some action based on the information in the event. If the application uses multiple windows, the program also has to determine in which window the event occurred and take that into consideration.

For applications with many windows, the **switch** statement can become quite long and very complex. The X Toolkit hides this process and *dispatches* all events to the appropriate user interface component. So, instead of writing one large switch statement to handle the logic of the program, programmers who use the X Toolkit write small functions to deal with specific events that occur within each component. This approach allows programs to be written in a much more declarative style (when A happens, do B) that greatly simplifies the logic of most applications. With this model, most applications that use the Xt Intrinsics follow a similar format, and every X Toolkit application performs several basic steps. These are:

1. **Initialize the Intrinsics.** This step establishes a connection to the X server, allocates resources, and initializes the Intrinsics layer.

2. **Create widgets.** Every program creates one or more widgets to construct the program's user interface.

3. **Register callbacks and event handlers.** Callbacks and event handlers are application-defined functions that respond to user actions and events that occur within each widget.

4. **Realize all widgets.** Realizing a widget creates the X window used by the widget.

5. **Enter the event loop.** The event loop retrieves events from the X event queue and dispatches the event to the appropriate event handler or callback function associated with the widget in which the event occurred.

Within this basic framework, the details of individual applications may vary widely, of course. However, most applications differ primarily in how they organize widgets and what callbacks and event handlers they define. Section 2.4 presents a simple example that demonstrates these steps. But first, the following section looks at the Xt functions that implement each of these steps.

2.3 BASIC Xt INTRINSICS FUNCTIONS

Before looking at an example application, this section briefly discusses a few of the fundamental Intrinsics functions that implement each step of the programming model outlined in the previous section. Besides implementing the X Toolkit programming model, these Intrinsics functions provide the primary application programmer's interface to all widgets.

2.3.1 Initialization

All applications must begin by establishing a connection to the X server. Application that use the X Toolkit must also perform some initialization of the Xt Intrinsics before calling any other Intrinsics function. The OLIT toolkit must also be initialized before creating any OLIT widget.s The simplest way to do this is to call the function:

```
OlInitialize(name, class, options, noptions, &argc, argv)²
```

This function establishes a connection between the client and the X server and then initializes the resource database used by the X resource manager. The first two arguments to **OlInitialize()** specify the *name* and the *class* of the application. The **name** argument specifies the name by which the program was invoked, for example "emacs", while the **class** argument indicates the more general category to which the application belongs, for example, "Editor".

Although this is the basic intent of application names and classes, this is not precisely the convention that has evolved. By convention, the class name of an application is the same as the name of the application, with the first letter changed to upper-case, unless the name of the application starts with the letter X, in which case the first two letters are changed to upper case. So the class name of a program named "emacs" is "Emacs", but the class name of a program named "xterm" is "XTerm".

The X resource manager uses the name and class of an application to determine what resources the program uses. It also extracts resources from the application's command-line arguments. Xt recognizes several common command-line arguments by default. These are destructively removed from the program's **argv** array and placed in a resource data base. The value of **argc** is decremented accordingly. Notice that **OlInitialize()** requires the address of **argc**. This allows the function to decrement the value of the actual **argc**, rather than a copy. The third and fourth arguments allow an application to specify how the Intrinsics should interpret application-specific command-line arguments and are discussed in Chapter 3.

After initializing the Intrinsics layer, **OlInitialize()** creates and returns an ApplicationShell widget. This widget serves as a container for all other widgets in the calling application.

2.3.2   Creating Widgets

Rather than dealing directly with windows, applications built using the Xt Intrinsics use *widgets*. A widget is a complex data structure that combines an X window with a set of procedures that perform actions on that window. In addition to the ID of the X window used by the widget, the widget structure contains additional data needed by these procedures. Chapter 12 examines the internal structure of a widget in detail. However, application programmers usually only need to understand a widget's external, public interface to use the widget in a program. This public interface consists primarily of the functions discussed in this chapter, along with the customizable resources supported by the widget.

Widgets form a hierarchy similar to the X window tree, known as a *widget tree*. The root of every widget tree must be a special type of widget known as a *shell* widget. Shell widgets must have exactly one child widget. The shell widget serves as a wrapper around its child, providing an interface between the child widget and the window manager. The window used by a shell widget is created as a child of the root window of the display.³ **OlInitialize()** creates an initial shell

---

² The function **OlInitialize()** is used in OLIT applications as a replacement for the standard Xt function **XtInitialize()**. **OlInitialize()** takes exactly the same arguments as **XtInitialize()**, and in fact calls **XtInitialize()**, but does some additional initialization required by OLIT.

³ Most X11 window managers re-parent application's top-level windows so that they are no longer a direct child of the root window. However, shell widgets are initially created as children of the root window.

widget. Applications that use multiple, independent windows must create an additional shell widget for each top-level window.

The function

```
XtCreateWidget(name, class, parent, args, nargs)
```

provides the general mechanism for creating all widgets except shell widgets. The **name** argument is an arbitrary string that identifies the widget. Widget names do not need to be unique, although it is often useful if they are. (See the discussion of the resource manager in Chapter 3). The **class** argument is a widget class pointer that specifies the type of widget to be created. For example,

```
scrollbarWidgetClass
```

specifies a Scrollbar widget. Each widget class provides a header file that exports the widget's class pointer. This file must be included in any application that uses the widget class. For example, an application that creates an OLIT Scrollbar widget must include the file Scrollbar.h, which contains the declaration of **scrollbarWidgetClass**. This book assumes the header files for the OLIT widgets are located in the directory **$OPENWINHOME**/include/Xol.

The **parent** argument to **XtCreateWidget()** must be a widget that already exists. This widget can be a shell widget or any other type of widget that allows children. The arguments **args** and **nargs** specify values for resources used by the widget. If the application does not need to specify any widget resources, **args** can be given as NULL. **XtCreateWidget()** creates and returns a widget, which must be declared as type **Widget** by the program.

For example, the following function creates and returns a Scrollbar widget named "scroller" as a child of another widget.

```
Widget
create_scroll_bar(parent)
  Widget parent;
{
  Widget scroll_bar;

  scroll_bar = XtCreateWidget("scroller",scrollbarWidgetClass,
                              parent, NULL, 0);
  return(scroll_bar);
}
```

XtCreateWidget() allocates and initializes many of the data structures associated with the widget, but does not create the window associated with the widget. The function

```
XtRealizeWidget(widget)
```

creates a window for the widget. Once **XtRealizeWidget()** is called for a particular widget, the widget is said to be *realized*. If a widget has children, **XtRealizeWidget()** also realizes its children. Applications can use the function

```
XtIsRealized(widget)
```

to check if a widget is realized. Notice that it is an error to realize a widget if its parent is unrealized, because the window owned by the parent widget must exist before the child's window can be created. Normally, applications simply call **XtRealizeWidget()** only once, giving the top level shell widget as an argument.

The function

```
XtDestroyWidget(widget)
```

destroys a widget and its children, and frees the server resources used by the widget. The X server also automatically frees all resources used by an application, including the window used by each widget when the program exits or otherwise breaks its connection to the server.

Most Xt Intrinsics functions require a widget as the first argument. However, Xlib functions cannot deal directly with widgets, and instead require a pointer to a **Display** structure, window IDs, and so on, which are normally hidden from the programmer by the Intrinsics. The Intrinsics define several functions that are useful when combining Xlib and Xt Intrinsics functions. These functions retrieve the data structures and resource IDs required by Xlib functions from a widget.

The function

```
XtDisplay(widget)
```

returns a pointer to the Xlib **Display** structure used by the widget, while

```
XtScreen(widget)
```

returns a pointer to the Xlib **Screen** structure used by the widget. The function

```
XtWindow(widget)
```

retrieves the ID of the window used by the widget. This window ID will be **NULL** if the widget has not yet been realized. The display pointer and screen structure can be retrieved as soon as the widget has been created.

2.3.3 Managing Widgets

Except for shell widgets, all widgets must be *managed* by a parent widget. A widget's parent manages the widget's size and location, determines whether or not the widget is mapped, and also controls input to the widget by controlling the input focus. For example, some widgets arrange their children into rows and columns, while others group their children in scrollable lists, and still others allow the user or the programmer to specify the location of each child widget.

To add a widget to its parent's managed set, the application must use the function:

```
XtManageChild(widget)
```

The child widget is managed by the parent widget specified in **XtCreateWidget()**. The Intrinsics also provide a convenient function that creates a widget and then calls **XtManageChild()** automatically:

```
XtCreateManagedWidget(name, class, parent, args, nargs)
```

This function is convenient for the programmer, but is not always the best way to create and manage widgets. When a widget is managed, its parent is notified. Often the parent widget must perform some calculation or rearrange its other children to handle the new widget properly. Many times it is more efficient to create a group of widgets first, and then manage them at the same time, by passing an array of widgets to the function:

```
XtManageChildren(widgetlist, num_widgets)
```

This reduces the work a parent widget must do, because the widget can compute the layout of all children at once rather than as each individual widget is managed. The reduction in the number of requests made to the server, by eliminating repeated shuffling and resizing of windows, can be dramatic. In general, finding ways to reduce the number of server requests results in a more efficient program.

2.3.4   Event Dispatching

When an application uses Xlib directly, it must look at each event and perform an action based on the type of the event. If the application uses multiple windows, the information in the event structure must also be examined to determine the window in which the event occurred. If an application has many windows, using a **switch** statement to handle events can become complicated.

The Xt Intrinsics provide a much simpler and cleaner way to handle input events. Xt looks up the widget corresponding to the window in which each event occurs and looks for an *event handler*, a function registered by the application or by the widget itself to respond to a specific X event in a particular widget. If Xt finds an event handler registered with the widget in which the event occurred,[4] it invokes the function automatically. The procedure of finding the proper widget and invoking the appropriate handler for an event is known as *dispatching* the event. The function

```
XtDispatchEvent(&event)
```

dispatches a single event. Applications can use the function

```
XtNextEvent(&event)
```

to obtain the next event from the X event queue. This function waits until an event is available in the application's event queue. When an event is available, the function returns after copying the event at the head of the queue into an event structure supplied by the application. **XtNextEvent()** also removes the event from the queue. Because most X applications are entirely event driven, the heart of nearly every X application is a loop that gets events from the X event queue and then uses **XtDispatchEvent()** to invoke an event handler for that event. This event loop can be written as:

---

[4] Strictly speaking, an event never occurs within a widget. Events can only occur relative to a window. However, since there is normally a one-to-one correspondence between a widget and the window created and controlled by a widget, there should be no confusion if we talk about events as if they occur within a widget.

```
while(TRUE) {
  XEvent event;
  XtNextEvent(&event);
  XtDispatchEvent(&event);
}
```

Since this section of code is almost always identical in every X application, Xt provides it as a function:

```
XtMainLoop()
```

Notice that there is no way to exit this loop. We must arrange another way for the application to exit.

2.3.5   Setting Widget Resources

Most widgets allow the programmer to affect the way the widget appears or behaves by specifying values for resources used by the widget. Here, the term *resource* simply means any data used by the widget. Resources are discussed in greater detail in Chapter 3. The function **XtCreateWidget()** allows the programmer to pass an array specifying these resources. Resources are specified using an **Arg** data structure defined as:

```
typedef struct {
  String    name;
  XtArgVal value;
} Arg, *ArgList;
```

The **name** member is a string that indicates the name of a resource to be set to the value stored in the **value** member. If the size of the resource stored in the **value** member is less than or equal to the size of **XtArgVal** (the definition of which is system-dependent), the value is stored directly in the structure. Otherwise the **value** member represents a pointer to the resource.

Resources are often specified using a static array of **Arg** structures. For example, the width and height of a widget can be specified by creating an argument list, such as:

```
static Arg wargs[ ] = {
  { XtNwidth,   300 },
  { XtNheight, 400 },
};
```

Then, passing the **Arg** list as an argument to **XtCreateWidget()**, with a statement like

```
XtCreateWidget("sample", oblongButtonWidgetClass,
               parent, wargs, XtNumber(wargs));
```

creates a widget 300 pixels wide and 400 pixels high[5]. The macro **XtNumber()** determines the length of a fixed-size array. Using **XtNumber()** allows the programmer to change the size of the

---

[5]   To actually create an OblongButton of a size other than the calculated default you must set the **XtNrecomputeSize** resource to **FALSE**.

Arg array easily and eliminates the use of "magic numbers" in the code to indicate the length of the array.

It is often more convenient for the programmer to use the macro

```
XtSetArg(arg, name, value)
```

to set a single value in a previously allocated argument list. For example:

```
Arg args[10]; /* Allocate enough space for future arguments */
int n = 0;

XtSetArg(args[n], XtNwidth,  300); n++;
XtSetArg(args[n], XtNheight, 400); n++;
XtCreateWidget("sample", oblongButtonWidgetClass,
               parent, args, n);
```

Because **XtSetArg()** is a macro that references its first argument twice, the variable used as an index to the **Arg** array cannot be auto-incremented inside **XtSetArg()**.[6]

The **XtSetArg()** approach has one primary advantage over the technique shown earlier: it allows the programmer to place the values of the resources used by a widget close to the point in the program where the widget is created. This often produces programs that are easier to understand because it is easier to see which resources have been specified for each widget. On the other hand, using this approach with lengthy lists of options makes a program longer and hides the structure of a program.

Another way to specify resources is to use the **XtVaCreateWidget()** function. This function is a variation of **XtCreateWidget()** which allows a variable number of arguments. The resources are included as arguments to the function and are terminated by a NULL argument. For example:

```
XtVaCreateWidget("sample", oblongButtonWidgetClass,
                 parent,
                 XtNwidth,  (XtArgVal) 300,
                 XtNheight, (XtArgVal) 400,
                 NULL);
```

The last two arguments of the **XtCreateWidget()** function are replaced with the argument list. It is important to note that the last argument is NULL. This argument is essential in that it indicates that the argument list end has been reached.

Functions that take a variable number of arguments are called *varargs* routines. Any Xt function that takes an argument lists as parameters has a varargs version of the routine. All varargs functions have the same name as their counterpart function with the characters **Va** immediately following the **Xt**.

Most of the examples in this book use **XtSetArg()** to set resources, primarily because none of the examples set more than a few resources in the program. Some of the examples use the varargs versions of the function calls to demonstrate their usage and behavior.

---

[6] If this bothers you, it is simple to define a new macro that allows the index to be auto-incremented:
    #define SETARG(arg, n, v)   { Arg *tmp_ap = &(arg) ; tmp_ap->name = (n) ; tmp_ap->value = (XtArgVal) (v) ;}

Applications can also use the function

```
XtSetValues(widget, arglist, nargs)
```

to alter the resources used by a widget after it is created. For example, the following code segment does not provide an argument list when the widget is created. In this case, **XtCreateWidget()** creates the widget using default values specified by the widget and resources set in the user's resource files (see Chapter 3). After the widget has been created, we can use **XtSetValues()** to alter the widget's width and height.

```
Arg   args[10];
int   n = 0;

widget = XtCreateWidget("sample", oblongButtonWidgetClass,
                        parent, NULL, 0);
XtSetArg(args[n], XtNwidth,  300); n++;
XtSetArg(args[n], XtNheight, 400); n++;
XtSetValues(widget, args, n);
```

We could accomplish the same thing using **XtVaSetValues()** which is the varargs version of **XtSetValues()**.

```
widget = XtCreateWidget("sample", oblongButtonWidgetClass,
                        parent, NULL, 0);
XtVaSetValues(widget,
              XtNwidth,   (XtArgVal) 300,
              XtNheight,  (XtArgVal) 400,
              NULL);
```

Xt also allows programmers to retrieve the current value of most widget resources, using the function:

```
XtGetValues(widget, arglist, nargs)
```

The argument **arglist** must be an **Arg** array that specifies pairs of resource names and addresses of variables allocated by the calling function. **XtGetValues()** retrieves the named resources from the specified widget and copies the data into the given address if the size of the resource is less than the size of **XtArgVal**. Otherwise, **XtGetValues()** stores a pointer to the resource in the location specified by the application.

For example, the following code fragment retrieves the width and height of a widget, and also a character string kept in the **XtNlabel** resource:

```
Arg         args[10];
Dimension   width, height;
String      str;
int         n = 0;

XtSetArg(args[n], XtNwidth,  &width); n++;
```

```
XtSetArg(args[n], XtNheight, &height); n++;
XtSetArg(args[n], XtNlabel, &str); n++;
XtGetValues(widget, args, n);
```

When **XtGetValues()** returns, **width** and **height** contain copies of the widget's **XtNwidth** and **XtNheight** resources. Notice that **width** and **height** are declared as type **Dimension**. Declaring variables as the wrong type when retrieving resources is a common error that can result in subtle bugs because Xt copies the data bitwise into the provided address. The most common error is to request the width, height, or position of a widget as an **int**. The width and height of all widgets should be retrieved as type **Dimension**, while a widget's x, y position must be requested as type **Position**.

Although **width** and **height** contain copies of the widget's resources, the variable **str** contains a *pointer* to the widget's **XtNlabel** resource. This is because the size of **Dimension** is smaller than or equal to the size of **XtArgVal**, but the size of the entire character string is greater than the size of **XtArgVal**. Instead of copying the entire string, **XtGetValues()** copies the *address* of the resource into **str**. If the calling application intends to modify this string, it should allocate space for the string and copy it. In all cases, the calling application is responsible for allocating and deallocating resources retrieved using **XtGetValues()**.

2.4   AN EXAMPLE: memo

We have now introduced enough basic functions to examine a simple application that uses the X Toolkit. This first example, memo, is a simple program that displays any command-line arguments not recognized by the Intrinsics in a window. It is useful for displaying brief notes or memos on the screen. The example illustrates each of the steps in the Xt Intrinsics programming model discussed in Section 2.2, except that this example defines no event handlers or callbacks.

```
/*************************************************
 * memo.c: Display a message in a window
 ***********************************************/
#include <X11/Intrinsic.h>
#include <X11/StringDefs.h>
#include <Xol/OpenLook.h>
#include <Xol/StaticText.h>
#include "libXs.h"

main(argc, argv)
  int   argc;
  char *argv[];
{
  Widget      toplevel, msg_widget;
  Arg         wargs[1];
  int         n;
  String      message;
```

```
/*
 * Initialize the Intrinsics
 */
toplevel = OlInitialize(argv[0], "Memo", NULL, 0, &argc, argv);
/*
 * If a message is given on the command line,
 * use it as the StaticText argument for the widget
 */
n = 0;
if ((message = xs_concat_words(argc-1, &argv[1])) != NULL) {
  XtSetArg(wargs[n], XtNstring, message); n++;
}
/*
 * Create the StaticText widget.
 */
msg_widget = XtCreateManagedWidget("msg", staticTextWidgetClass,
                                   toplevel, wargs, n);
/*
 * Realize the widgets and enter the event loop.
 */
XtRealizeWidget(toplevel);
XtMainLoop();
}
```

All X applications must include some standard header files. Every application that uses the Intrinsics must include the file Intrinsic.h and most also require StringDefs.h. OLIT applications must include OpenLook.h before any widget header files. The header file StaticText.h includes definitions required to use the StaticText widget.

Let's look at each step of this program. The first executable line of the example initializes the Intrinsics, and creates an ApplicationShell widget.

```
toplevel = OlInitialize(argv[0], "Memo", NULL, 0, &argc, argv);
```

The name of the program is specified by **argv[0]**, while the class name of this application is **Memo**. Both **argc** and **argv** are modified by **OlInitialize()**. The function removes any command-line arguments recognized by the toolkit from **argv** and decrements **argc** accordingly.

Next, **memo** calls the application-defined function **xs_concat_words()**. This function concatenates the command-line arguments contained in the array **argv[]** into a single string. The first member of **argv** is not passed, because, by UNIX convention, it contains the name of the program. If the command-line contains a message, the lines

```
n = 0;
if ((message = xs_concat_words (argc - 1, &argv[1])) != NULL){
  XtSetArg (wargs[n], XtNlabel, message); n++;
}
```

set an entry in an **Arg** array to the string containing the message to be displayed. This array is then used as an argument to **XtCreateManagedWidget()**.

```
msg_widget = XtCreateManagedWidget("msg", staticTextWidgetClass,
                                   toplevel, wargs, n);
```

This statement creates a StaticText widget to display the string retrieved from the command line. The widget class pointer is specified as **staticTextWidgetClass**, and the widget's name is "**msg**". The widget is a managed child of the **toplevel** shell widget created by **OlInitialize()**.

The next step is to realize the top level shell widget. Realizing a widget also causes the widget's children, in this case the StaticText widget, to be realized. Finally, the program enters the main event loop. **XtMainLoop()** never returns. At this point, the message window appears on the screen and the program loops endlessly, processing events. The StaticText widget automatically handles all resize and exposure events generated by the server.

This example also requires an auxiliary function, **xs_concat_words()**, which can be written as:

```
/******************************************************
 * concat.c: utility function to concatenate
 *           an array of strings into a single
 *           string with spaces between words.
 ******************************************************/
#include <X11/Intrinsic.h>
#include <X11/StringDefs.h>
#include <stdio.h>

String
xs_concat_words(n, words)
  int     n;
  char *words[];
{
  int i, len;
  String s;
  /*
   * If there are no arguments other than the program
   * name, just return an empty string.
   */
  if (n <= 0)
    return ((String)NULL);

  len = 0;
  for (i = 0; i < n; i++)
    len += strlen(words[i])+1;
  s = XtMalloc(len);
  s[0] = '\0';
  for (i = 0; i < n; i++)  {
    if(i > 0)
      strcat(s, " ");
    strcat(s, words[i]);
```

```
    }
    return(s);
}
```

This function takes each null-terminated character string in the **words** argument and concatenates them into one *String*. If the **words** array is empty, **xs_concat_words()** returns an empty String.

Figure 2.1 shows the widget tree formed by the **memo** example. The figure shows each widget's name above its class name (shown in italics). Most, but not all, widget trees directly correspond to the X window tree created by the application. This widget tree is very simple, but later examples will produce much more complex widget trees. This figure shows the root of the widget tree as the program name and class, with the top level shell widget implied, but not shown.

Figure 2.1 The widget tree created by memo.

2.4.1   Building and Using memo

The **memo** example can be compiled and linked with the X libraries with the UNIX shell command:

```
% cc -I$OPENWINHOME/include -o memo memo.c concat.c \
        -L$OPENWINHOME/lib -lXol -lXt -lX11
```

This compiles the files memo.c and concat.c and links the OLIT, Xt Intrinsics, and Xlib libraries with the program. The **-I$OPENWINHOME/include** tells the compiler where to look for the header files. The **-L$OPENWINHOME/lib** tells the linker where to find the libraries. These options are necessary since the OLIT header files and libraries are not kept in directories the compiler searches by default. The ordering of the libraries is significant. All widget libraries must precede the Intrinsics library, which must precede the Xlib library.

We can now invoke **memo** from a UNIX shell, for example:

```
% memo Hello World
```

This produces the message window shown in Figure 2.2.

Hello World

Figure 2.2 memo's message window.

Depending on the window manager you use, **memo** might appear complete with a title bar and other decorations added by the window manager. Figure 2.3 shows the **memo** window with a title bar and the decorations added by the OPEN LOOK window manager, **olwm**.

Figure 2.3 memo's window with window manager decorations.

One practical application of **memo** is to invoke it from a *makefile*. A makefile is a script used by the UNIX make utility, which manages compilation of applications. For example, consider a basic makefile that can be used to build **memo**:

```
##############################
# Makefile for memo.c
##############################
CFLAGS = -I$$OPENWINHOME/include
LIBS   = -L$$OPENWINHOME/lib -lXol -lXt -lX11
memo:memo.o concat.o
        cc $(CFLAGS) -o memo memo.o concat.o $(LIBS)
        memo Program Compiled Successfully
```

Now, the shell command

```
make memo
```

builds **memo** and uses **memo** itself to announce the successful compilation.

One obvious problem with **memo** is that there is no explicit way to exit the program orderly. In fact, **memo** provides no way to handle user input of any kind. The rest of this chapter discusses several ways to handle user input, including event handlers, callbacks, and action procedures.

2.4.2   Creating a Utilities Library

As we demonstrate different parts of X, this book occasionally presents functions and utilities that are useful in more than one program. Some of these functions combine widgets to perform some higher level task, while others have little to do with X, but are useful nevertheless. For example, the function **xs_concat_words()** is a simple, self-contained procedure that we will use again in other examples. It is convenient to place these functions in a library where applications can use them by linking the library with the program. Libraries are useful for grouping collections of small functions into a single module that can be linked with any program needing any of the functions. A library also serves a second purpose in this book, by reducing the number of times a simple function used by multiple examples must be presented.

The first time such a reusable function is defined, we will add it to our library. Then, when we discuss examples that use the same function, we can simply refer to the library. We can start a library used by nearly all examples in this book with the function **xs_concat_words()**. We will name this library libXs. (The letters "Xs" stand for "X-sample library".) The library consists of an archive file that stores the relocatable compiled functions, and a header file containing definitions and declarations needed to use the library. At this point the file libXs.h contains only the following lines:

```
/**************************************************
 * libXs.h: Header file for X-sample library
 **************************************************/
extern String xs_concat_words();
```

We will add to this library throughout this book, as we find other useful functions. Refer to Appendix D for the complete libXs.h header file.

We can create a library containing **xs_concat_words()** with the commands:

```
cc -I$OPENWINHOME/include -c concat.c
ar ruv libXs.a concat.o
```

These commands compile concat.c into an object file, and then archive the file into the library file libXs.a. It is common practice to place library files in some standard location such as

```
/usr/lib
/usr/local/lib
```

where they can be found by the linker. Assuming this is done, we can build **memo** with the command:

```
cc -I$OPENWINHOME/include -o memo memo.c \
      -L$OPENWINHOME/lib -lXs -lXol -lXt -lX11
```

This command compiles the file memo.c and links the resulting object file with the libXs library as well as the OLIT and X libraries.

2.4.3   Event Handlers

An event handler is a procedure invoked by the Intrinsics when a specific type of event occurs within a widget. The widget programmer can define event handlers to handle some, all, or none of the X events. The application programmer can also use the function

```
XtAddEventHandler(widget, eventmask, nonmaskable,
                  handler, client_data)
```

to register additional event handlers for events that occur in a widget. This function registers an application-defined function specified by the argument **handler** as an event handler for the event or events specified in the **eventmask**. The argument **eventmask** must be one of the standard X event masks defined in the file X.h. The event handler can also be registered for more than one event by specifying the inclusive-OR of two or more event masks. Xt automatically invokes the given handler function when one of the event types specified by **eventmask** occurs within the widget's window.

Applications can register multiple event handlers for the same event type and the same widget. When an event occurs, each handler registered for that event type is called. However, the Intrinsics do not guarantee the order in which event handlers registered with **XtAddEventHandler()** are invoked. If this order is important, the function **XtInsertEventHandler()** can be used to either prepend or append the specified handler to the list of existing handlers for that event. Some X events that applications need to handle have no event mask. These events are said to be *nonmaskable* because they are sent to all applications whether an application selects them or not.[7] To register an event handler for a nonmaskable event, the argument **nonmaskable** must be set to **TRUE**. Since nonmaskable events have no event mask, the **mask** argument must be specified as **NoEventMask**.

Applications can use the argument **client_data** to specify some data to be passed as a parameter to the event handler. This argument can be given as **NULL** if the event handler does not require any application specific data.

The form of every event handler is:

```
void handler(w, client_data, event, continue_to_dispatch)
   Widget      w;
   XtPointer   client_data;
   XEvent      *event;
   Boolean     *continue_to_dispatch;
```

Every event handler is called with four arguments. The first argument is the widget in whose window the event occurred. The second argument is the client data specified by the application when registering the event handler. The event handler usually coerces this argument to the expected data type.[8] In C, this can be done by simply declaring the **client_data** argument to be the expected type in the definition of the event handler. However, the preferred method is to declare **client_data** as **XtPointer** and then cast it to the appropriate type when it is assigned to the respective variable.

The third argument is a pointer to the event that caused this function to be invoked. The last argument is initialized by the Intrinsics to point to **TRUE**. Setting this value to **FALSE** will abort further processing of any remaining event handlers for the given event. Extreme caution should be used when aborting event handling because the Intrinsics and/or OLIT may install event handlers that you are unaware of. Aborting event handling could cause the internal state of the toolkit to become corrupted as a result. Event handlers never return a useful value, and should be declared to be of type **void**.

We can use an event handler to provide a way to exit from the **memo** program. First we must define an event handler that simply exits when it is called. Before calling **exit()**, it is a good idea to close the application's connection to the X server. This isn't absolutely necessary, because

---

[7] The nonmaskable event types are ClientMessage, MappingNotify, SelectionNotify, SelectionClear, and SelectionRequest. Most of these events are used for interclient communication, and are discussed in Chapter 11.

[8] The Xt Intrinsics library uses the type **XtPointer** to indicate an untyped pointer. The actual definition of **XtPointer** is compiler dependent and may either be:
```
   typedef char * XtPointer;
        or
 typedef void * XtPointer;
```

the server will notice that the connection has been lost when the client exits. However, it is cleaner to request the server to close the connection and perform cleanup of the application's resources, using the function:

```
XtCloseDisplay(display)
```

The **quit()** event handler can be written as:

```
void
quit(w, client_data, event, continue_to_dispatch)
  Widget      w;
  XtPointer   client_data;
  XEvent      *event;
  Boolean     *continue_to_dispatch;
{
   XtCloseDisplay(XtDisplay(w));
   exit(0);
}
```

Next, we must register the event handler with the Xt Intrinsics so that the function can be called when the appropriate event occurs. For example, let's redesign the **memo** program to exit when the user presses a mouse button in the message window. The new version of **memo** simply adds the line

```
XtAddEventHandler(msg_widget, ButtonPressMask, FALSE, quit, NULL);
```

to register the **quit()** event handler for **ButtonPress** events. Notice that this version of **memo** includes the header file libXs.h (see Section 2.4.2) and must be linked with the libXs library which contains the **xs_concat_words()** function. The new version of **memo** can be written as:

```
/***********************************************
 * memo.c: Adding an event handler
 ***********************************************/
#include <X11/Intrinsic.h>
#include <X11/StringDefs.h>
#include <Xol/OpenLook.h>
#include <Xol/StaticText.h>
#include "libXs.h"

main(argc, argv)
  int    argc;
  char *argv[];
{
  Widget      toplevel, msg_widget;
  Arg         wargs[1];
  int         n;
  String      message;
  void        quit();
```

```
/*
 * Initialize the Intrinsics
 */
toplevel = OlInitialize(argv[0], "Memo", NULL, 0, &argc, argv);
/*
 * If a message is given on the command line,
 * use it as the StaticText argument for the widget
 */
n = 0;
if ((message = xs_concat_words(argc-1, &argv[1])) != NULL) {
  XtSetArg(wargs[n], XtNstring, message); n++;
}
/*
 * Create the staticText widget.
 */
msg_widget = XtCreateManagedWidget("msg", staticTextWidgetClass,
                                   toplevel, wargs, n);
/*
 * Register the event handler to be called when
 * a button is pressed
 */
XtAddEventHandler(msg_widget, ButtonPressMask, FALSE,
                  quit, NULL);
/*
 * Realize the widgets and enter the event loop.
 */
XtRealizeWidget(toplevel);
XtMainLoop();
}
```

2.4.4 Callback Functions

Some widgets provide hooks that allow applications to define procedures to be called when some widget-specific condition occurs. These hooks are known as *callback lists* and the application's procedures are known as *callback functions*, or simply *callbacks*, because the widget makes a "call back" to the application-defined function. Each widget maintains a callback list for each type of callback it supports. For example, every widget supports a **XtNdestroyCallback** callback list. Each callback on this callback list is invoked before the widget is destroyed.

Callbacks are different than event handlers because they are invoked by the widget rather than the Intrinsics, and are not necessarily tied to any particular event. Applications can add a callback to a widget's callback list with the function:

```
XtAddCallback(widget, callback_name, proc, client_data)
```

The argument, **callback_name**, specifies the callback list to which the callback function **proc** is to be added. The application can use the **client_data** argument to specify some application-defined data to be passed to the callback procedure by the Intrinsics when the callback is invoked.

The form of every callback procedure is:

```
void CallbackProcedure(widget, client_data, call_data)
  Widget     widget;
  XtPointer client_data;
  XtPointer call_data;
```

Like event handlers, callback functions do not return any useful value, and should be declared as type **void**. The first argument to every callback function is the widget for which the callback is registered. The second parameter is the **client_data** specified by the application in the call to **XtAddCallback()**. The last argument contains data provided by the widget. The type and purpose of this data can be determined by checking the documentation for the specific widget.

The **memo** example in Section 2.4.3 uses an event handler to exit the application when a **ButtonPress** event occurs. Another way to do this is to use a callback procedure. However, the StaticText widget used in the earlier versions of **memo** is limited in what callback lists it supports. To demonstrate callbacks, we must modify **memo** to use the OblongButton widget class, which supports an additional callback list:

> **XtNselect**

When the user presses the SELECT mouse button (the X "Button 1" by default, typically the left button) inside an OblongButton widget and releases it while still in the OblongButton, the functions on the **XtNselect** callback list are invoked. If the user moves the pointer out of the OblongButton widget's window before releasing the mouse button, the functions on the **XtNselect** list are not invoked.

We only need to change a few lines of code to use an **XtNselect** callback function instead of an event handler to exit the program. First, we must change the definition of **quit()** to the form used by a callback function.

```
void
quit(w, client_data, call_data)
  Widget     w;
  XtPointer client_data;
  XtPointer call_data;
{
  XtCloseDisplay(XtDisplay(w));
  exit(0);
}
```

Then we must replace the line

```
XtAddEventHandler(msg_widget,ButtonPressMask, FALSE, quit, NULL);
```

from the previous version of **memo** with the line:

```
XtAddCallback (msg_widget, XtNselect, quit, NULL);
```

We must also include the header file OblongButt.h, instead of StaticText.h and create the **msg_widget** as an OblongButton widget rather than a StaticText widget by replacing **static-TextWidgetClass** with **oblongButtonWidgetClass**. With these changes, the widget calls all functions on its **XtNselect** list, including **quit()**, when the user presses and releases the SELECT mouse button in the OblongButton window.

The difference between using the event handler and a callback may seem to be insignificant, since we accomplished the same task using both. However, there is at least one important advantage to using callback functions. With callbacks, the method used to exit the **memo** program is no longer tied directly to a specific X event, but instead is tied to a more abstract *action*, in this case the action of *selecting* the button widget. Further, the user can usually use the *translation manager* facility provided by the Xt Intrinsics to customize the action that invokes a callback. The next section discusses the translation manager, and shows yet another way that we can make **memo** respond to user actions.

2.4.5   Using The Translation Manager

The Xt Intrinsics's translation manager provides a mechanism that allows the user to specify a mapping between user actions and functions provided by a widget or an application. These functions are called *action procedures*. Widget sets can define their own action procedures that can be activated by the user without any additional programming. Widget-defined action procedures often correspond to the functionality of the particular widget, such as selecting a button.

The only action procedure that OLIT defines is a special procedure called **OlAction()**, which is used to implement OLIT *virtual events*. It is important to understand that the normal operation of many of the OLIT widgets is dependent on **OlAction()**. Care must be taken when defining an action procedure for a widget which relies on **OlAction()** to insure proper operation of the widget. Any additional action procedures are the responsibility of the application programmer to write.

The user can activate an action procedure via the translation manager by adding a line such as:

```
memo*OblongButton.translations:    <Key>q:    ActionProc()
```

to the .Xdefaults file. This specifies that the action procedure "**ActionProc()**" should be bound to the key sequence "**<Key>q**".

In its most basic form, a translation table consists of a list of expressions. Each expression has a left side and a right side, separated by a colon. The left side specifies the user event sequence that invokes the procedure given on the right side. The left side can specify modifier keys and also sequences of events. For example, we could specify that the **ActionProc()** function should be called after a mouse button has been pressed and released, by specifying:

```
*translations:<Btn1Down>,<Btn1Up>: ActionProc()
```

We can specify that a modifier key must also be held down while a mouse button is pressed, for example:

```
*translations: Ctrl<Btn1Down>:    ActionProc()
```

Multiple bindings can be specified in a single translation table. However, the more complex the translation table, the more chance there is for unwanted interaction between the entries. More specific events should always precede less specific events. For example, in the specification

```
# WRONG
*translations:   <Btn1Down>:     Proc1() \n\
                 Meta<Btn1Down>: Proc2()
```

the second button action overrides the first, because specifying no modifier keys is the same as specifying all modifier keys and the translation manager scans the translations for each event and uses the first match it finds. The correct way to specify that `<Btn1Down>` without the Meta key invokes the `Proc1()` procedure is:

```
# CORRECT
*StaticText*translations:  Meta<Btn1Down>: Proc2() \n\
                           <Btn1Down>:     Proc1()
```

When multiple translations are given, each specification must be separated by a newline character (`'\n'`). It is often convenient to use a backslash to break the translations across multiple lines.

To define the action procedures use:

```
XtAddActions(actions, num_actions)
```

The `actions` argument must be an array of type `XtActionsRec`. This structure consists of a string that defines the public name of the action procedure and a pointer to a procedure that performs the action. For example, we can register an action procedure `quit()` for the memo program as:

```
static XtActionsRec actionsTable [] = {
    {"bye",   quit},
};
```

The string, "`bye()`" is the name by which the action is known to the translation manager. The procedure `quit()`, which must be declared before referencing it, takes four arguments and can be written as:

```
void
quit(w, event, params, num_params)
  Widget    w;
  XEvent    *event;
  String    *params;
  Cardinal  *num_params;
{
  XtCloseDisplay(XtDisplay(w));
  exit(0);
}
```

The first argument specifies the widget in which the user action occurred, while `event` is a pointer to the X event that caused the procedure to be invoked. The `params` argument is a list of strings containing any arguments specified in the translation, while **num_params** indicates the length of this array.

If we use **XtAddActions()** to register this action list with the translation manager, the user can define a translation for the **bye()** action in the .Xdefaults file. For example:

```
memo*StaticText*translations: Ctrl<Key>q:    bye()
```

The **bye()** action is specified using a function-like syntax to allow parameters to be passed to the action procedure. For example, if the translation were defined as

```
memo*StaticText*translations: <Key>q:    bye(10, Goodbye)
```

the **quit()** procedure's **params** argument would contain two entries when the translation manager calls **quit()**, the string "10" and the string "Goodbye". It would be up to the action procedure to interpret these arguments.

Programmers often need to specify translations programmatically. This can be done using the function

```
XtAugmentTranslations(widget, translation_table)
```

or the function

```
XtOverrideTranslations(widget, translation_table)
```

Both of these functions register a translation table with a particular widget. **XtAugmentTranslations()** merges a list of translations with the list of current translations supported by the widget. It does not override existing translations specified by the widget or the user. **XtOverrideTranslations()** also merges the two lists, but replaces existing translations with entries from the new translation list whenever there is a conflict.

A translation table is a structure of type **XtTranslations**. The function

```
XtParseTranslationTable(source)
```

compiles a string containing a translation specification into a **XtTranslations** structure. For example, we can programmatically define translations for memo as:

```
static char defaultTranslations[] =  "<Key>q:  bye()";
```

In the body of the program, we must call **XtParseTranslationTable()** to compile this string. For example:

```
trans_table = XtParseTranslationTable(defaultTranslations);
```

Then we must add the translations to the existing translations for the message widget with:

```
XtOverrideTranslations(msg_widget, trans_table);
```

We can now write a new version of **memo** that uses the translation manager to exit. This version uses the StaticText widget to display the message.

```c
/********************************************************
 * memo.c: Defining application actions and translations
 ********************************************************/
#include <X11/Intrinsic.h>
#include <X11/StringDefs.h>
#include <Xol/OpenLook.h>
#include <Xol/StaticText.h>
#include "libXs.h"

void quit();

static XtActionsRec actionsTable [] = {
  {"bye",   quit},
};
static char defaultTranslations[] =  "<Key>q:  bye()";

main(argc, argv)
  int    argc;
  char *argv[];
{
  Widget         toplevel, msg_widget;
  Arg            wargs[1];
  int            n;
  String         message;
  XtTranslations trans_table;

  /*
   * Initialize the Intrinsics
   */
  toplevel = OlInitialize(argv[0], "Memo", NULL, 0, &argc, argv);
  /*
   * Register the new actions, and compile
   * translations table
   */
  XtAddActions(actionsTable, XtNumber(actionsTable));
  trans_table =
      XtParseTranslationTable(defaultTranslations);
  /*
   * If a message is given on the command-line,
   * use it as the XtNstring argument for the widget
   */
  n = 0;
  if ((message = xs_concat_words(argc-1, &argv[1])) != NULL) {
    XtSetArg(wargs[n], XtNstring, message); n++;
  }
  /*
   * Create the staticText widget.
```

```
    */
  msg_widget = XtCreateManagedWidget("msg", staticTextWidgetClass,
                                   toplevel, wargs, n);
  /*
   * Merge the program-defined translations with
   * existing translations.
   */
  XtOverrideTranslations(msg_widget, trans_table);
  /*
   * Realize the widgets and enter the event loop.
   */
  XtRealizeWidget(toplevel);
  XtMainLoop();
}
```

Action procedures in OLIT require some special attention. As mentioned earlier, the `OlAction()` function is declared as an action procedure for many of the OLIT widgets. For example, the OblongButton widget defines `OlAction()` as the action procedure for eight events: FocusIn, FocusOut, Key, BtnDown, BtnUp, Enter, Leave, and BtnMotion. Some of the most basic functionality of the OblongButton is dependent on `OlAction()` and it is therefore important that this function be called. Therefore, if an action procedure is to be set up for a particular event associated with a widget which requires `OlAction()`, then `OlAction()` must be specified as one of the action procedures to be invoked.

To illustrate this concept let's rewrite **memo** once again. We'll go back to the version that used a callback and an OblongButton widget. In this version we will also use the translation manager to set up an action procedure for a `<BtnDown>` event. The callback function `quit()` will still have the same functionality it did in the callback procedure example: it will close the server connection and exit the program. The action procedure will simply print a message to the terminal screen. OLIT defines `OlAction()` as the action procedure for the OblongButton associated with a `<BtnDown>` event. This means that a call to `XtAugmentTranslations()` would have no effect, so we call `XtOverrideTranslations()`.

```
/**********************************************************
 * memo.c: Defining application actions and translations
 **********************************************************/
#include <X11/Intrinsic.h>
#include <X11/StringDefs.h>
#include <Xol/OpenLook.h>
#include <Xol/OblongButt.h>
#include "libXs.h"

void quit();
void printit();

static XtActionsRec actionsTable [] = {
  {"hi",    printit},
};
```

```
                                      /* Imcomplete, need OlAction() */
static char defaultTranslations[] =  "<BtnDown>:  hi()";

main(argc, argv)
  int    argc;
  char *argv[];
{
  Widget          toplevel, msg_widget;
  Arg             wargs[1];
  int             n;
  String          message;
  XtTranslations  trans_table;

  /*
   * Initialize Intrinsics
   */
  toplevel = OlInitialize(argv[0], "Memo", NULL, 0, &argc, argv);
  /*
   * Register the new actions, and compile
   * translations table
   */
  XtAddActions(actionsTable, XtNumber(actionsTable));
  trans_table =
      XtParseTranslationTable(defaultTranslations);
  /*
   * If a message is given on the command-line,
   * use it as the XtNstring argument for the widget
   */
  n = 0;
  if ((message = xs_concat_words(argc-1, &argv[1])) != NULL){
    XtSetArg(wargs[n], XtNlabel, message); n++;
  }
  /*
   * Create the OblongButton widget.
   */
  msg_widget = XtCreateManagedWidget("msg", oblongButtonWidgetClass,
                                      toplevel, wargs, n);
  /*
   * Register the callback to be called when
   * a button is pressed
   */
  XtAddCallback(msg_widget, XtNselect, quit, NULL);
  /*
   * Merge the program-defined translations with
   * existing translations.
   */
```

```
    XtOverrideTranslations(msg_widget, trans_table);
    /*
     * Realize all widgets and enter the event loop.
     */
    XtRealizeWidget(toplevel);
    XtMainLoop();
}
```

The `quit()` function is unchanged from the earlier example that demonstrated callback procedures. We add a new action procedure, `printit()`, which is activated by the translation manager.

```
void
printit(w, event, params, num_params)
    Widget      w;
    XEvent      *event;
    String      *params;
    Cardinal    *num_params;
{
    printf("hello\n");
}
```

The problem with this program is that the action procedure we have defined overrides any other action procedures defined in the widget. This means that `OlAction()` is no longer being called when a button press occurs on the OblongButton widget. If you compile and run this program you will see that the `printit()` action procedure gets called when you press the SELECT mouse button, but the `XtNselect` callback procedure does not get called. As a matter of fact the button no longer appears to be *pressed* when you press the mouse button. In order for the OblongButton to perform as normally expected we must be sure to include `OlAction()` in the list of action procedures that get called for this particular event. If we redefine `defaultTranslations` to include `OlAction()` then both the action procedure and the callback function will be invoked.

```
    static char defaultTranslations[] =  "<BtnDown>:  OlAction() hi()";
```

It is unnecessary to add `OlAction()` to the `actionsTable` because OLIT registers the `OlAction()` action procedure with the translation manager at initialization time.

If the translation for the action procedure is going to be defined in a resource file, such as .Xdefaults, then a similar procedure must be followed. The program must still call `XtAddActions()` but the functions `XtParseTranslationTable()` and `XtOverrideTranslations()` are no longer used. The resources file, however, must include `OlAction()` and the `#override` directive. For example, to register the `hi()` function with the translation manager for `<BtnDown>` and still allow `OlAction()` to be called would require the following entry:

```
Memo*msg*translations: #override \n\
                <BtnDown>: OlAction() hi()
```

Using the translation manager to map between action procedures and events provides a flexible way for programmers to design customizable applications. It also provides a simple way for the application programmer to extend the behavior of any widget.

2.5   APPLICATION CONTEXTS

Most of the Xt Intrinsics functions described in this chapter are convenience routines. These functions are adequate for most applications and are also compatible with the earlier versions of the Intrinsics. However, most of these functions simply call other routines that require an additional parameter, known as an *application context*. Application contexts reduce re-entrancy problems in the toolkit, and also allow applications to use multiple displays. Each application context maintains a list of displays opened by the function **XtOpenDisplay()**. As of X11R4 programmers are encouraged to use the application context versions of the convenience routines.

Applications can create a unique application context using the convenience function:

```
XtAppInitialize(&app_context,
                class, options, noptions, &argc, argv
                fallback_resources, args, nargs)
```

The first argument, **app_context**, is used to return an application context. This application context must be used as the first argument to the application context function calls. The next five arguments correspond exactly to arguments two through six passed to **OlInitialize()** discussed earlier in this chapter. The **fallback_resources** argument allows the programmer to specify default resources that will be set if the application resource file does not exist. Chapter 3 discusses resource in more detail. The **args** argument is used to specify resource values for the created shell widget and **nargs** specifies the number of entries in **args**. Most programs do not need to set the last three arguments. They can safely be set to NULL. Table 2.1 shows the convenience functions that use the default application context, and the corresponding application context versions.

Table 2.1 Xt Intrinsics convenience functions

Convenience Routine	Application Context Version
XtMainLoop()	XtAppMainLoop()
XtNextEvent()	XtAppNextEvent()
XtProcessEvent()	XtAppProcessEvent()
XtPeekEvent()	XtAppPeekEvent()
XtPending()	XtAppPending()
XtAddInput()	XtAppAddInput()
XtAddTimeOut()	XtAppAddTimeOut()
XtAddWorkProc()	XtAppAddWorkProc()
XtCreateApplicationShell()	XtAppCreateShell()
XtInitialize()	XtAppInitialize()
XtAddConverter()	XtAppAddConverter()

The **XtAppInitialize()** function initializes the Intrinsics but not the OLIT toolkit. A new function that initializes the OLIT toolkit is now available:

```
OlToolkitInitialize(param)
```

The **param** argument is reserved for future used and should be set to NULL.

Together, these two functions, **OlToolkitInitialize()** and **XtAppInitialize()** initialize OLIT and the Intrinsics and are the preferred method of initialization in OLIT applications.[9]

Let's look at the **memo** program, rewritten using application contexts:

```
/*****************************************************************
 * memo.c: The Application Context version of the memo program
 *****************************************************************/
#include <X11/Intrinsic.h>
#include <X11/StringDefs.h>
#include <Xol/OpenLook.h>
#include <Xol/StaticText.h>
#include "libXs.h"

main(argc, argv)
  int    argc;
  char *argv[];
{
  Widget        toplevel, msg_widget;
  Arg           wargs[1];
  int           n;
  String        message;
  XtAppContext app;

  /*
   * Initialize OLIT
   */
  OlToolkitInitialize((XtPointer)NULL);
  toplevel = XtAppInitialize(&app, "Memo", (XrmOptionDescList)NULL,
                             0, &argc, argv, (String *) NULL,
                             (ArgList) NULL, 0);
  /*
   * If a message is given on the command line,
   * use it as the StaticText argument for the widget
   */
  n = 0;
  if ((message = xs_concat_words(argc-1, &argv[1])) != NULL) {
    XtSetArg(wargs[n], XtNstring, message); n++;
  }
```

---

[9] Unfortunately, the **OlToolkitInitialize()** function became available only a few days before this book went to press. Due to lack of time, the example programs were not modified to use **OlToolkitInitialize()** and **XtAppInitialize()** and the corresponding application context functions.

```
    /*
     * Create the StaticText widget.
     */
    msg_widget = XtCreateManagedWidget("msg", staticTextWidgetClass,
                                     toplevel, wargs, n);
    /*
     * Realize the widgets and enter the event loop.
     */
    XtRealizeWidget(toplevel);
    XtAppMainLoop(app);
}
```

2.6 SUMMARY

This chapter briefly introduced the key concepts of the Xt Intrinsics layer. We learned how to create and display a widget on the screen, explored four implementations of a simple X application, and introduced event handlers, callbacks, and the translation manager. Using the Xt Intrinsics and a widget set has many advantages over using Xlib directly:

- Using a higher level library reduces the amount of code that must be written by the application programmer, and helps make an application easier to understand and modify.

- The customization facilities provided by the Xt Intrinsics allow the end user to modify the behavior of applications in a consistent way.

- Standard widgets that provide essential components needed by many applications are available, eliminating the need for each programmer to re-implement these components for each application, and providing a consistent look-and-feel.

- A project with unique user interface requirements can create new widgets that can be used alone or mixed with an existing widget set. When many applications need to work together, using a common set of widgets is an excellent way to ensure consistency across all applications.

One major advantage offered by the Xt Intrinsics is the degree to which the Intrinsics are integrated with Xlib. Using the Intrinsics and a widget set does not prevent the programmer from calling Xlib functions directly. Most applications use a combination of the Xt Intrinsics framework, a set of widgets, and Xlib functions. Whenever an appropriate widget set is available, it is generally better to use these higher level facilities than to program directly with Xlib. However, when writing callbacks and event handlers, the programmer often needs to use Xlib functions as well.

The following chapter introduces the X resource manager, a facility that provides a simple and consistent way for users to customize applications. Chapter 4 introduces the OLIT widget set and shows how to combine widgets to create more complex interfaces.

3

THE X RESOURCE MANAGER

Managing resources is an important part of programming with X. It is difficult to write or even use any significant X Toolkit application without understanding the X resource management facilities. This chapter explains what resources are and shows how both the programmer and the user can use the resource manager to customize applications. It also explains how to take advantage of OLIT's dynamic resource handling feature, which allows users to dynamically customize an application while the application is running.

3.1 WHAT IS A RESOURCE?

X programmers often use the word *resource* to mean different things, depending on the context in which they use the word. For example, the Xlib documentation refers to windows, graphics contexts, and fonts as resources. These types of resources are maintained by the X server and accessed by clients through a resource ID. Widget programmers generally refer to any internal data required by the widget as a resource. The Xt Intrinsics also allow applications to manage user-customizable data, using the same mechanisms used by widgets. Therefore, we might say that a resource is any user-customizable data. In this broader sense, resources include window IDs, colors, fonts, images, text, names of windows or widgets, positions and sizes of windows, or any customizable parameter that affects the behavior of the application.

By convention, X applications allow the end user to specify most or all resources used by a program. Application programmers should always provide reasonable defaults for all resources required by a program, but should allow the end user to override these defaults whenever possible. It is important to allow the user to customize an application because no matter how well the program-

45

mer tries to anticipate the needs of the end user, there is always someone who wishes to alter the behavior of a program.

The X resource manager facility encourages programmers to write customizable applications by providing an easy-to-use mechanism for determining user customizations and specifying default values used by applications. The basic resource manager facilities provided by Xlib allow applications to store and retrieve information from a resource database. The Xt Intrinsics provide a higher level interface, built on the Xlib resource manager, that makes it easy for the application programmer to access the user's options and blend them with the program-defined defaults.

3.2 SPECIFYING RESOURCES

X maintains a database of resources containing user preferences as well as application defaults. The application can determine the proper value of a given resource at run time by querying the database. Traditional databases contain information that is completely and precisely specified. Users of such a database search for information by making imprecise queries. You might, for example, query a bibliographical database for books about the X Window System by requesting information on "windows." This query would return a possibly large list of books about "windows."

The X resource manager uses a slightly different model. In X, the database contains general information about the resources used by applications. For example, a user can specify that "All buttons should be red," or "All terminal-emulator windows should be 24 characters high and 80 characters wide." Applications query the database to determine the value of a specific resource for a specific application: "What color should the mail program's quit button be?" or "How wide should the command window be?"

3.2.1 Names and Classes

The resource manager requires that every X application and resource have both a name and a class. The class indicates the general category to which each of these entities belongs, while the name identifies the specific entity. For example, a program named "emacs" might belong to the general class "Editor". Similarly, the resource "destroyCallback" names a specific callback list. The class name of this resource, "Callback", identifies all callback lists.

Both resource names and resource class names are strings. The header file, StringDefs.h, contains a set of resource names commonly used by the Xt Intrinsics. Programmers can define additional resource names as needed, although they should not create new resource names unnecessarily. Choosing standard resource names and classes whenever possible promotes consistency between applications.

By convention, resource names generally begin with a lowercase letter, while class names begin with a capital letter. Resource names are often identical to the corresponding resource class names, except for the capitalization. For example, the resource name used to specify a foreground color is "foreground" and the resource class name is "Foreground".

A widget's class name can be an arbitrary string, but is usually related to its function. The class name of every widget is determined by the widget programmer who designs the widget, while the application programmer determines the widget's name. For example, the class name of the widget used to display a string in the previous chapter is "StaticText". The **memo** program specified the widget's name as "msg".

As we noted earlier, an application queries the resource database using a complete specification of the desired resource. Resources are completely specified by two strings that together uniquely identify a resource for a particular window or widget. The first string consists of the name of the application, followed by the names of each widget in the application's widget tree between the top widget and the widget using the resource, followed by the name of the resource. Each name in the string is separated by a dot ("."). The second string is similar except that it uses class names instead of resource names. Together, these strings (sometimes referred to as resource lists) specify a unique path through the application's widget tree.

Figure 3.1 and Figure 3.2 show the widget layout and hierarchy of a hypothetical graphics editor named "draw." By convention, the programmer has chosen the class name of the application as "Draw". Figure 3.2 shows the widget tree corresponding to the widget layout in Figure 3.1, with the class name of each widget in parentheses below the widget's name. We can specify the foreground color of the widget named in the upper portion of the window with a string containing the resource names

```
draw.panel.commands.button1.foreground
```

and a string containing the resource class names

```
Draw.Form.Nonexclusives.RectButton.Foreground
```

Notice that the resource name string uniquely identifies **button1**, differentiating it from the other children of the **commands** widget, and also from any other button with the same name but in a different widget hierarchy (such as the **button1** in the **options** widget). The class string, however, can potentially apply to many buttons. In this example, the class string specifies the foreground color of all RectButton widgets managed by both the **commands** widget and the **options** widget. This class string also applies to buttons in any other application that contains this exact widget tree.

A resource database consists of a set of associations between resource names or class names and the value of a resource. The user can specify these associations in a resource file, such as the .Xdefaults file in the user's home directory. Each association consists of a string containing resource names or class names, followed by a colon, zero or more spaces or tabs, and a value. For example, we can specify that the foreground color of **button1** in the **commands** panel should be red by adding the line

```
draw.panel.commands.button1.foreground: red
```

to a resource file. We can specify the color of all buttons in this application with the line:

```
Draw.Form.Nonexclusives.RectButton.Foreground: red
```

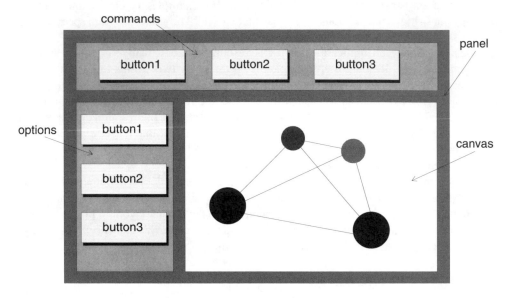

Figure 3.1 An example widget layout.

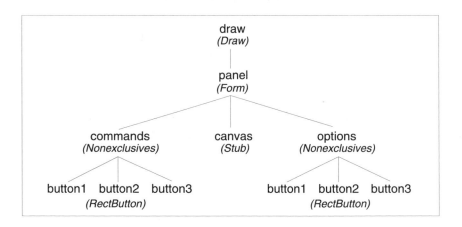

Figure 3.2 Widget tree forFigure 3.1.

Although this example specifies resources relative to widgets, we can use the same mechanism to specify resources unrelated to any particular widget or window by using the program name and the resource name. For example,

```
draw.bufsize:     100
```

specifies the value of some resource named "bufsize" used by the application.

3.2.2   The Resource Manager's Matching Algorithm

It is often inconvenient to specify the value of every resource using the complete name or class list as in the previous examples. Instead, the resource manager allows us to use an asterisk "*" as a wild card character to represent any number of resource names or class names. For example, continuing to use the widget tree in Figure 3.1 and Figure 3.2, we can specify the foreground color of a button named **button1** with:

```
draw*button1*foreground:    red
```

Notice, however, that there are two buttons in this example named **button1**. This resource specification applies to both buttons, because the asterisk matches both **options** and **commands**. We can be more specific and indicate the foreground color of **button1** in the **commands** widget with

```
draw*commands*button1*foreground:    red
```

We can also be more general, and specify all foreground colors used by the application with:

```
draw*foreground:    red
```

Or we can specify the foreground color of the **options** widget and all its children with:

```
draw*options*foreground:    red
```

Partial resource specifications can also consist of any combination of resource names and class names. For example, we can specify that the foreground color of all widgets belonging to class Rect-Button should be green, regardless of the application, with the line

```
*RectButton.foreground:    green
```

Although the user can specify resources using incomplete name and class lists, applications must query the database using both the complete name list and the complete class list. At the lowest level, the Xlib function

```
XrmGetResource(db, name, class, &type, &value)
```

is used to query the database. It returns the value and type of the resource that best matches the complete resource name and class name specification. The resource manager uses a matching algorithm to determine if any entry in the resource database matches the requested resource and returns a type and a value for the query. If no match is found, the returned value is **NULL**.

The matching algorithm uses several precedence rules to arbitrate between multiple matching entries in the resource database. These rules are:

1. Either the resource name or the class name of each item in the query must match the corresponding item in the database entry. For example, a query for the foreground color of **button1**, using the resource name and class name specifications

    ```
    draw.panel.commands.button1.foreground
    Draw.Form.Nonexclusives.RectButton.Foreground
    ```

    matches the resource database entry

```
draw.Form.commands.button1.Foreground: Blue
```

but not

```
draw.Form.commands.button1.Highlight:  Yes
```

because the class name **Foreground**, specified in the query, does not match the class name, **Highlight**, in the database.

2. Entries in the database prefixed by a dot ("."") are more specific than (and therefore have precedence over) those prefixed by an asterisk ("*"). Therefore, the database entry

```
*commands.Background:   green
```

has precedence over

```
*commands*Background:   red
```

If both these specifications are in the user's resource database, the **commands** widget will have a green background. However, all children of the **commands** widget (here, **button1**, **button2**, and **button3**) will have a red background.

3. Resource names always have precedence over class names. Therefore

```
*button1.Foreground:   red
```

has precedence over

```
*RectButton.Foreground:   green
```

because the name **button1** is more specific than the class RectButton.

4. Both resource names and class names have precedence over an asterisk. So

```
Draw*Form*RectButton*Foreground: red
```

has precedence over

```
Draw*Form*foreground: green
```

because the first entry more completely identifies the path through the widget tree.

5. The resource manager compares database entries left to right, and the first items in a resource specification have precedence over successive items. For example, when determining the foreground color of the buttons in Figure 3.1,

```
draw*Form*foreground: green
```

has precedence over

```
draw*Form*foreground: red
```

Specifying resources takes practice and is often a matter of trial and error, particularly as the size of the user's resource files grows and the potential for accidental interactions increases.

3.3 MANAGING APPLICATION RESOURCES

Individual widgets usually manage their own resources and require no action from the application programmer. However, programmers often need to obtain application level resources that have nothing to do with widgets and perhaps little to do with the application's user interface. The resource manager provides the programmer with a consistent mechanism for retrieving all options and resources used by applications. Although Xlib provides the basic resource manager facilities, the Xt Intrinsics provide a higher level interface that is much easier to use. This section demonstrates how the application programmer can use the resource manager facilities provided by the Xt Intrinsics.

3.3.1 Loading the Resource Database

Every OLIT application must begin by initializing the Xt Intrinsics and opening a connection to the X server, normally using the convenience function `OlInitialize()`. This procedure also creates a resource database and loads it with the resource specifications in the user's resource files. `OlInitialize()` also extracts options specified on the command line and adds them to the resource database. Because the command-line arguments are added last, they override the corresponding values specified in all resource files. X applications usually do not need to parse command-line arguments themselves, but instead use the resource manager interface to obtain command-line arguments.

   `OlInitialize()` loads the resource database with specifications from four distinct places. These are the *application defaults file*, the *per-user application defaults file*, the *user's defaults*, and the *user's per-host defaults*.

   By default, Xt first loads *application resources* by searching for a file whose path is identified by the environment variable `XFILESEARCHPATH`. On systems running Open Windows, `XFILESEARCHPATH` is set to

   $OPENWINHOME/lib/%T/%N%S

If this environment variable does not exist, the following default value is used:

   /usr/lib/X11/%L/%T/%N%S:/usr/lib/X11/%l/%T/%N%S:/usr/lib/X11/%T/%N%S

   The Xt Intrinsics substitute various values for the %<X> characters to resolve this path. The %L field is replaced by the value of the **LANG** environment variable. This allows a system to be set up with resource files for one or more different languages. Each language may have its own directory, allowing the user to specify a preferred language by setting the **LANG** environment variable. If the **LANG** variable is not set then **$LANG** collapses to an empty string.

   The %T field represents a file type and allows Xt's underlying mechanism for resolving pathnames to be used to locate many types of files. In the context of this discussion, the type field is always assumed to be "app-defaults".

   Finally, the %N and %S fields represent a name and a file suffix. For resource files the suffix is ignored, while the name field is replaced by the class name of the application.

   If **$LANG** is not set, this complex-sounding search algorithm collapses to the path

   /usr/lib/X11/app-defaults/<class>   or $OPENWINHOME/lib/app-defaults/<class>

where <class> is the class of the application as given to `OlInitialize()`.

Next, the resource manager searches for *a per-user application* resource file. If the UNIX environment variable **XUSERFILESEARCHPATH** is set, it is expected to specify a directory containing application specific resources files. This resource file is found using a search strategy similar to that used when loading the per-application resource file. If **XUSERFILESEARCHPATH** is not set, the default search path is

$XAPPLRESDIR/%L/%N:$XAPPLRESDIR/%l/%N/$XAPPLERESDIR/%N:$HOME/%N

Here, the various %<X> fields have the same meaning as before, and **$XAPPLRESDIR** is replaced by the value of that environment variable, if it exists. If **$XAPPLRESDIR** does not exist, the default path becomes:

$HOME/%L/%N:$HOME/%l/%N:$HOME/%N

Next, the resource manager loads the *user's defaults*. If the root window has a **RESOURCE_MANAGER** property, the resource manager assumes that this property contains the user's defaults. If this property doesn't exist, the resources in the file named .Xdefaults in the user's home directory are merged into the database.

Next, the *user's per-host defaults* are loaded. If the environment variable **XENVIRONMENT** is defined, the resource manager loads the contents of the file. If this environment variable does not exist, the resource manager loads the file .Xdefaults-<*host*>, where <*host*> is the name of the machine on which the client is running.

We will refer to any of these files as *resource files*. All resource files use the same format as the .Xdefaults file, discussed in Section 3.2.2. After processing all resource files, Xt also merges any recognized options from the application's command line into the resource database. **OlInitialize()** removes all recognized options from **argv** and leaves unrecognized options for the application to process.

The Xt Intrinsics support a standard set of options to ensure that all applications recognize the same command-line arguments. Table 3.1 lists these standard command-line options along with the corresponding resource name used to set the option in a resource file. Each application can also define additional options, which are passed in the **option** argument to **OlInitialize()**. Section 3.3.3 discusses the format of these options.

Notice that Xt simply recognizes these standard command line options and places the appropriate value in the application's resource database. This has nothing to do with whether or not the application actually uses or responds to these resources. For example, OLIT widgets use the "fontColor" resource to determine the color of the font used for displaying text. Other widget sets use the "foreground" resource to determine the font color. So, while the Intrinsics recognize the "-foreground" command-line option, and will place the corresponding value in the resource database, there is no guarantee that the OLIT widget set or any other widget set will use that resource at all, or as expected.

The "-xrm" command-line flag allows users to specify an arbitrary string to be placed in the resource database. This flag can be used to specify any resource on the command line, using the same syntax as a resource file

Table 3.1 Standard command-line options.

Flag	Resource Name	Type	Example of Effect
+rv	*reverseVideo	None	sets resource to "off"
+synchronous	*synchronous	None	sets resource to "off"
-background	*background	String	-background Black
-bd	*borderColor	String	-bd Black
-bordercolor	*borderColor	String	-bordercolor Black
-bg	*background	String	-bg Red
-borderwidth	.borderWidth	Integer	-borderwidth 2
-bw	.borderWidth	Integer	-bw 2
-display	.display	String	-display expo:0.1
-fg	*foreground	String	-fg Blue
-foreground	*foreground	String	-foreground Blue
-fn	*font	String	-fn 6x13
-font	*font	String	-font 6x13
-geometry	.geometry	String	-geometry =80x24
-iconic	.iconic	None	sets resource to "on"
-name	.name	String	-name Console
-reverse	*reverseVideo	None	sets resource to "on"
-rv	*reverseVideo	None	sets resource to "on"
-selectionTimeout	.selectionTimeout	Integer	-selectionTimeout 5
-synchronous	*synchronous	Nonc	sets resource to "on"
-title	.title	String	-title Console
-xnllanguage	.xnlLanguage	String	sets language
-xrm	N.A.	String	-xrm "*background: blue"

3.3.2   Retrieving Application Resources

Widgets retrieve their resources automatically when they are created. However, applications can also use the resource manager to retrieve the user's application level options and resources, by using an **XtResource** structure to specify the resources to be retrieved from the database. This structure is defined in the header file Intrinsic.h as:

```
typedef struct _XtResource {
   String       resource_name;   /* Resource name            */
   String       resource_class;  /* Resource class           */
   String       resource_type;   /* Desired type             */
   Cardinal     resource_size;   /* Size in bytes            */
   Cardinal     resource_offset;/* Offset from base          */
   String       default_type;    /* Type of specified default */
   XtPointer    default_addr;    /* Address of default resource*/
} XtResource;
```

The **resource_name** member is a string that specifies the name of the resource being retrieved. For example, to retrieve a foreground color, an application uses the string "**foreground**". Whenever possible, the constants defined in the header file Stringdefs.h should be used. This not only encourages consistency between applications, but also allows the compiler to catch spelling errors. For example, StringDefs.h defines the string "foreground" as the constant **XtNforeground**.

The **resource_class** member specifies the class of the resource, and is used by the resource manager's matching algorithm. For a foreground color, the class name is "**Foreground**", or the predefined constant **XtCForeground**. The **resource_type** member is a string that specifies the desired type of the resource. This type can be any valid data type, including any application-defined type. For example, an application might reasonably ask for a color by name (a string) or ask for the pixel value (an integer) that represents the color.

The file StringDefs.h also contains definitions of common resource types. By convention, a resource type consists of the name of the type preceded by the letters **XtR**, for example **XtRString** or **XtRPixel**. The **resource_size** member indicates the size, in bytes, of the resource to be retrieved. The **resource_offset** member of the **XtResource** structure indicates a relative address where the resource value should be placed. The Xt Intrinsics provide a utility macro

```
XtOffset(type *, field)
```

which determines the byte offset of a member of a C struct and provides a convenient way to specify relative addresses. The last members of the **XtResource** structure specify a default value for the resource and the type of the default value. The resource manager uses this default if it does not find a match in the user's resource database. This provides a simple way for the application programmer to specify default values for all resources.

Applications can use the function

```
XtGetApplicationResources(widget, base, resources,
                          nresources, args, nargs)
```

to retrieve the resources specified in an array of type **XtResource** from the database. The **widget** argument should specify the top-level shell widget that identifies the name and class of the application. The **base** argument specifies the base address of a data structure where the resource manager is to store the retrieved values. If the offsets specified in the **XtResource** list are absolute addresses, rather than offsets within a structure, the **base** argument can be specified as zero. The next argument, **resources**, is an **XtResource** list, while **nresources** indicates the length of the **resource** list.

The last arguments, **args** and **nargs** provide a way for the application to override values in the database. The **args** parameter must be an array of type **Arg** containing resource names and values while **nargs** indicates the number of resources in the array.

Let's look at an example to see how an application can use this mechanism. A simple test program, named **rmtest**, retrieves and prints the value of six parameters. The program supplies default values for these resources, but the user can also use the resource manager to customize the parameters. The six parameters are: **foreground** (color), **background** (color), a **delay** parameter, a **verbose** flag, and an **x** and **y** position. First we must include the header files Intrinsic.h and StringDefs.h.

```
/***************************************************
 * rmtest.c: simple test of the resource manager
 ***********************************************/
#include <X11/Intrinsic.h>
#include <X11/StringDefs.h>
#include <Xol/OpenLook.h>
```

Next, we define a single data structure to store the six parameters:

```
typedef struct {
    Pixel    fg, bg;
    int      delay;
    Boolean  verbose;
    Position x, y;
} ApplicationData, *ApplicationDataPtr;
```

Then we define an **XtResource** array that specifies how the resource manager should retrieve these resources from the database.

```
static XtResource resources[] = {
{ XtNforeground, XtCForeground, XtRPixel, sizeof (Pixel),
  XtOffset(ApplicationDataPtr, fg), XtRString, "Black" },
{ XtNbackground, XtCBackground, XtRPixel, sizeof (Pixel),
  XtOffset(ApplicationDataPtr, bg), XtRString, "White" },
{ "delay", "Delay", XtRInt, sizeof (int),
  XtOffset(ApplicationDataPtr, delay),
  XtRImmediate, (XtPointer) 2},
{ "verbose", "Verbose", XtRBoolean, sizeof (Boolean),
  XtOffset(ApplicationDataPtr, verbose), XtRString, "FALSE"},
{ XtNx, XtCX, XtRPosition, sizeof (Position),
  XtOffset(ApplicationDataPtr, x), XtRImmediate, (XtPointer)25 },
{ XtNy, XtCY, XtRPosition, sizeof (Position),
  XtOffset(ApplicationDataPtr, y), XtRImmediate, (XtPointer)33 },
};
```

The first line of this declaration specifies that the value of a resource with name **XtNforeground** and class **XtCForeground** should be retrieved from the resource database. The function **XtOffset()** determines the offset within the **ApplicationData** structure where the resource manager is to store the retrieved value. This line also specifies that the value should be retrieved as type **XtRPixel**. If the value in the resource database is some type other than **XtRPixel**, the resource manager automatically converts the data to the requested type (See Section 3.3.4). If the resource database does not contain a foreground color specification, the resource manager uses the default value, "Black". Similarly, this resource list specifies that the background color should be retrieved as type **XtPixel**, **delay** as type **XtRInt**, the flag **verbose** as a **XtRBoolean** and **x** and **y** as type **XtRPosition**.

The specification of the **delay**, **x**, and **y** resources illustrates the use of the **XtRImmediate** type, which allows the default value to be specified directly, rather than as a string to be converted to the expected type.

The body of **rmtest** uses **XtGetApplicationResources()** to retrieve the resources and then prints each value before exiting. Notice that this example specifies the address of the **ApplicationData** structure, **data**, as the base address relative to which the function **XtGetApplicationResources()** is to store the values retrieved from the resource data base.

```
main(argc, argv)
  int     argc;
  char   *argv[];
{
  Widget           toplevel;
  ApplicationData data;

  toplevel = OlInitialize(argv[0], "Rmtest", NULL, 0, &argc, argv);
  /*
   * Retrieve the application resources.
   */
  XtGetApplicationResources(toplevel, &data, resources,
                        XtNumber(resources), NULL, 0);
  /*
   * Print the results.
   */
  printf("fg=%d, bg=%d, delay=%d, verbose=%d, x=%d, y=%d\n",
         data.fg, data.bg, data.delay, data.verbose,
         data.x, data.y);
}
```

If none of the resources in the application's resource list are specified in the user's resource files, the resource manager uses the default values in the **XtResource** list. So, with no matching entries in any resource file, running the program gives the following output:

```
% rmtest
fg=0, bg=1, delay=2, verbose=0, x=25, y=33
%
```

Notice that the resource manager converts the foreground and background values from the colors named "Black" and "White" to the pixel values one and zero. These are pixel indexes commonly used by X graphics functions that correspond to the named colors. (Chapter 6 discusses the color model used by X.) Also notice that the resource manager converts the value of **verbose** from the string "FALSE" to the boolean value zero used by convention in C to mean **FALSE**.

Since the class name of this program is "Rmtest", resources can be specified in an application resource file such as Rmtest. Let's create an application resource file containing the following lines:

```
*foreground: Red
*delay:      10
*verbose:    TRUE
```

Now, if we run the program rmtest from a shell, we should see:

```
% rmtest
fg=9, bg=1, delay=10, verbose=1, x=25, y=33
%
```

Again, the pixel values of the foreground and background colors may vary because of X's color model. However, it should be clear that, in this case, the resource manager obtained the values of **foreground**, **delay**, and **verbose** from the application resource file rather than from the application-defined defaults. However, the background color and the **x** and **y** values still reflect the default values specified by the application, because the application resource file does not specify a background color nor a value for **x** or **y**.

End users of an application can selectively override any or all resource specifications specified in the application resource file in their own .Xdefaults file. Suppose we place the lines

```
*background: Blue
*delay:      20
*x:          35
```

in the file **$HOME**/.Xdefaults. Remember that if the root window has a **RESOURCE_MANAGER** property, the resource manager assumes that this property contains the user's defaults and the .Xdefaults file is not searched. To install the contents of the .Xdefaults in the **RESOURCE_MANAGER** property use the **xrdb** command. The **-m** option stands for merge, which means merge the resources specified with the existing resources installed in the **RESOURCE_MANAGER** property.

```
% xrdb -m $HOME/.Xdefaults
```

Now, if we run this program we should see:

```
% rmtest
fg=9, bg=13, delay=20, verbose=1, x=35, y=33
%
```

In this example, the resource manager obtains the values for **foreground** and **verbose** from the application resource file, and retrieves the values of **delay**, **background** and **x** from the user's **RESOURCE_MANAGER** property. The value of **y** still reflects the default value specified by the application.

3.3.3   Retrieving Resources from the Command Line

It is usually more convenient to specify options using resource files than to use the conventional UNIX command-line argument mechanism, because resource files allow defaults to be specified once in a file rather than each time the application is run. Resource files also allow users to specify general defaults to be used by all applications rather than specifying every option to every program on the command line. In addition, in a window-based environment, applications are less likely to be invoked from a UNIX command shell and more likely to be started from a menu or some type of applications browser.

In spite of this, there are many cases where it is convenient or necessary to specify arguments on a command line. One situation where this is necessary is when the user needs to specify options on a per-process basis. For example, a user cannot use a resource file to run one **xterm** (an X terminal emulator program) with a red foreground and another **xterm** with a blue foreground. As one solution to this problem, Xlib and the Xt Intrinsics provide mechanisms for parsing the command-line arguments and placing the contents into the resource database. This allows applications to use the same retrieval mechanism discussed in the previous section to determine the value of command-line arguments.

Applications can use the **options** argument to **OlInitialize()** or **XtOpenDisplay()** to define additional command-line arguments. The **options** argument, which must be an array of type **XrmOptionDescList**, specifies how additional command-line arguments should be parsed and loaded into the resource database. The **XrmOptionDescList** structure is defined as:

```
typedef struct {
    char            *option;       /* argv abbreviation */
    char            *specifier;    /* Resource specifier*/
    XrmOptionKind   argKind;       /* Style of option   */
    caddr_t         value;         /* Default Value     */
} XrmOptionDescRec, *XrmOptionDescList;
```

The **option** member of this structure is the name by which the resource is recognized on the command line, while the **specifier** is the name by which the resource is known in the resource database. The field **argKind** specifies the format of the command-line arguments and must be one of the values shown in Table 3.2.

Table 3.2 Command-line parsing options.

Argument Style	Meaning
XrmoptionNoArg	Value is specified in **OptionDescRec.value**
XrmoptionIsArg	Value is the option string itself
XrmoptionStickyArg	Value immediately follows the option - no space
XrmoptionSepArg	Value is next argument in **argv**
XrmoptionResArg	A resource and value are in the next argument in **argv**
XrmoptionSkipArg	Ignore this option and the next argument in **argv**
XrmoptionSkipLine	Ignore this option and the rest of **argv**
XrmoptionSkipNArgs	Ignore this option and the next **OptionDescRes.value** **arguments** in **argv**

Let's see how this works by adding some command-line arguments to the **rmtest** program from the previous section. The command-line options -fg and -bg are predefined by the Xt Intrinsics (see Section 3.3.1) so they are recognized automatically. We can specify command-line arguments corresponding to the other resources with:

```
static XrmOptionDescRec options[] = {
  {"-verbose", "*verbose", XrmoptionNoArg, "TRUE"},
  {"-delay",   "*delay",   XrmoptionSepArg, NULL }
};
```

The **verbose** resource is parsed as type **XrmoptionNoArg**, which means that if this option is present, its value is given by the fourth argument in the **XrmOptionsDescRec**. The Xt Intrinsics will extract the **delay** resource from the command line as type **XrmoptionSepArg**, which means that the value of the resource is given by the next argument in **argv**.

We must add these lines to the file rmtest.c and also change the first line of the program to:

```
toplevel = OlInitialize(argv[0], "Rmtest", options,
                        XtNumber(options), &argc, argv);
```

After making these changes to the **rmtest** program, we can try the new command-line options. Let's assume the contents of the application resource file and .Xdefaults file are the same as at the end of the previous section. We can now override the values in all resource files using command-line arguments. For example:

```
% rmtest2 -fg green -delay 15
fg=14, bg=13, delay=15, verbose=1, x=35, y=33
```

Now the resource manager retrieves the value of **verbose** from the application resource file and the value of **background** and **x** from the .Xdefaults file. However, the values of **foreground** and **delay** are specified by the command-line arguments.

Occasionally a programmer needs to override the values in the resource database, possibly because of a calculated condition that makes that option invalid. The resources obtained using **XtGetApplicationResources()** can be overridden by specifying a list of resource names and values as the **args** argument to the function.

3.3.4   Type Conversion

In each of the previous examples, the resource manager automatically converted the requested resources from one data type to another. The resource manager performs these conversions using functions known as *type-converters*. The most common type-converters convert from a string to some other data type, because resource files specify resources as strings. However, type-converters can be used to convert between any two data types, including application-defined types. Table 3.3 lists the standard type-converter conversions defined by the Xt Intrinsics, while Table 3.4 lists the additional type converters provided by OLIT.

Table 3.3 Type converters defined by the Xt Intrinsics.

From	To	From	To	From	To
String	Boolean	String	Bool	String	short
String	unsigned char	String	Font	String	LongBoolean
String	Fontstruct	String	Cursor	String	int
String	Display	String	Pixel	String	File
XColor	Pixel	int	Boolean	int	Bool
int	Short	int	Pixel	int	Pixmap
int	XColor	Pixel	XColor	String	Accelerators
String	Atom	String	Float	String	Geometry

Table 3.3 Type converters defined by the Xt Intrinsics.

From	To	From	To	From	To
String	InitialState	String	Translations	String	Visual
XColor	Pixel				

Table 3.4 Type converters defined by OLIT

From	To	From	To
String	Position	String	Gravity
String	Cardinal	String	OlDefine
String	Modifiers	String	FlatItemFields
String	FlatItems	String	Dimension
Visual	Colormap		

Applications can define additional type conversions by writing a type-converter function and registering it with the resource manager. A type converter is a procedure that has the form:

```
void Converter(args, nargs, fromVal toVal)
      XrmValue    *args;
      Cardinal    *nargs;
      XrmValue    *fromVal;
      XrmValue    *toVal;
```

The arguments **args**, **fromVal** and **toVal** are pointers to structures of type **XrmValue**, which is defined as:

```
typedef struct {
  unsigned int  size;
  XtPointer     *addr;
} XrmValue, *XrmValuePtr;
```

This structure holds a pointer to a value, and the size of the value. The last two parameters of a type converter provide the original data and a way to return the converted value. The type-converter is expected to convert the data in the **fromVal** structure and fill in the **toVal** structure with the result. The **args** parameter is an array of type **XrmValue** containing any additional data required by the converter.

Before the resource manager can use a type converter, the function must be registered with the resource manager. The function

```
XtSetTypeConverter(from_type, to_type, converter, args,
                   nargs, cache_type, destructor)
```

registers a type converter with the resource manager. The arguments **from_type** and **to_type** must be strings indicating the data types. Whenever appropriate, the standard names defined in StringDefs.h should be used for consistency. The **converter** argument specifies the address of the type-converter function, while **args** and **nargs** specify any additional arguments that should be passed to the type converter when it is called. The **cache_type** argument indicates how caching should be handled and must be one of the constants:

XtCacheNone	XtCacheAll	XtCacheByDisplay

Any of the above values may be OR'd together with **XtCacheRefCount** which specifies that a reference count will be kept of the cached value. When the reference count equals zero, the **destructor** function is called.

The **args** parameter must be an array of type **XtConvertArgList**, which is defined as:

```
typedef struct {
    XtAddressMode    address_mode;
    caddr_t          address_id;
    Cardinal         size;
} XtConvertArgRec, *XtConvertArgList;
```

The **address_mode** indicates the type of the data provided and may be one of the constants:

XtAddress	XtBaseOffset	XtWindowObjBaseOffset
XtImmediate	XtResourceString	XtResourceQuark

The **address_id** member specifies the address of the additional data, while the member indicates the size of the resource in bytes. Many converter functions require no additional data and **args** is often given as **NULL**, and **nargs** as zero.

Let's see how this works by writing an example type converter. We create a custom type converter that converts a string to an enumerated type. This enumerated type is used to create different levels of verbosity and is defined as:

```
typedef enum {
  LEVEL1,
  LEVEL2,
  LEVEL3,
  LEVEL4,
} verlevel;
```

We then define the type converter as:

```
/*************************************************
 * str2ver.c: Convert a string to a verlevel.
 *************************************************/
#include <X11/Intrinsic.h>
#include <X11/StringDefs.h>
#include "libXs.h"

Boolean
xs_cvt_str_to_verlevel(dpy, args, nargs, fromVal, toVal, data)
  Display    *dpy;
  XrmValuePtr  args;
  Cardinal   *nargs;
  XrmValuePtr  fromVal, toVal;
  XtPointer  *data;
```

```
{
  static verlevel result;
  /*
   * Make sure the number of args is correct.
   */
  if (*nargs != 0)
    XtWarning("String to verlevel conversion needs no args");
  /*
   * Convert the string in the fromVal to a verlevel pt.
   */
  if(!strcmp(fromVal->addr, "LEVEL1"))
    result =  LEVEL1;
  else if(!strcmp(fromVal->addr, "LEVEL2"))
    result =  LEVEL2;
  else if(!strcmp(fromVal->addr, "LEVEL3"))
    result =  LEVEL3;
  else if(!strcmp(fromVal->addr, "LEVEL4"))
    result =  LEVEL4;
  else {
    XtDisplayStringConversionWarning(dpy, fromVal->addr,
                                     "Verlevel");
    return FALSE;
  }
  /*
   * Make the toVal point to the result.
   */
  toVal->size = sizeof (verlevel);
  *(verlevel *)toVal->addr = result;
  return TRUE;
}
```

This type converter first checks how many **args** were given as parameters. Since no additional parameters are needed, the function uses the utility function

   XtWarning(message)

to print a warning if the number of arguments is not equal to zero. The type converter uses **strcmp()** to find the matching string. The **toVal** structure is then filled in with the size of a verlevel type and the address of the variable **result**. If no match is found, the function

   XtDisplayStringConversionWarning(dpy, from, to);

is used to issue a warning. This function takes three arguments indicating the display and the two data types involved in the conversion.

Notice that the variable **result**, which contains the value returned by the type converter, is declared as static. This is important because otherwise the address of **result** would be invalid after the function returns. Functions that call type converters must copy the returned value immediately, because the type converter reuses the same address each time it is called.

We can test this string-to-verlevel converter by modifying the **rmtest** program from Section 3.3.2. The example now defines the **verbose** member of the **ApplicationData** structure as type verlevel, rather than as Boolean as in the earlier version. We must also change the **XtResource** array to specify that the value of **verbose** should be retrieved as type **XtRVerlevel**. The Intrinsics library does not define **XtRVerlevel**, but we can easily add it to the libXs header file, defined as:

```
#define XtRVerlevel   "Verlevel"
```

We also modify the **options** structure to reflect the new type for **verbose**. The main difference in this version of **rmtest** is that the body of the test application registers the type-converter function before retrieving the application resources.

```
/*********************************************************
 * rmtest3.c: verlevel version.
 ********************************************************/
#include <X11/Intrinsic.h>
#include <X11/StringDefs.h>
#include <Xol/OpenLook.h>
#include "libXs.h"

static char *levels[] = { "LEVEL1", "LEVEL2", "LEVEL3", "LEVEL4" };

typedef struct {
   Pixel    fg, bg;
   float    delay;
   verlevel verbose;
   Position x, y;
} ApplicationData, *ApplicationDataPtr;

static XtResource resources[] = {
  { XtNforeground, XtCForeground, XtRPixel, sizeof (Pixel),
    XtOffset(ApplicationDataPtr, fg), XtRString, "Black" },
  { XtNbackground, XtCBackground, XtRPixel, sizeof (Pixel),
    XtOffset(ApplicationDataPtr, bg), XtRString, "White" },
  { "delay", "Delay", XtRFloat, sizeof (float),
    XtOffset(ApplicationDataPtr, delay), XtRString, "2.5" },
  { "verbose", "Verbose", XtRVerlevel, sizeof (verlevel),
    XtOffset(ApplicationDataPtr, verbose), XtRString, "LEVEL4"},
  { XtNx, XtCX, XtRPosition, sizeof (Position),
    XtOffset(ApplicationDataPtr, x), XtRImmediate, (XtPointer)25 },
  { XtNy, XtCY, XtRPosition, sizeof (Position),
    XtOffset(ApplicationDataPtr, y), XtRImmediate, (XtPointer)33 },
  };

static XrmOptionDescRec options[] = {
  {"-verbose", "*verbose", XrmoptionSepArg, NULL},
  {"-delay",   "*delay",   XrmoptionSepArg, NULL}
```

```
   };

main(argc, argv)
   int    argc;
   char *argv[];
{
   Widget          toplevel;
   ApplicationData data;

   toplevel = OlInitialize(argv[0], "Rmtest3", options,
                           XtNumber(options), &argc, argv);
   /*
    *   Add the string to Verlevel type-converter.
    */
   XtSetTypeConverter(XtRString, XtRVerlevel, xs_cvt_str_to_verlevel,
                      (XtConvertArgList)NULL, 0,
                      XtCacheAll, (XtDestructor)NULL);
   /*
    *  Retrieve the resources.
    */
   XtGetApplicationResources(toplevel, &data, resources,
                             XtNumber(resources), NULL, 0);
   /*
    * Print the result.
    */
   printf("fg=%d, bg=%d, delay=%.2f, verbose=%s, x=%d, y=%d\n",
          data.fg, data.bg, data.delay, levels[data.verbose],
          data.x, data.y);
}
```

We can test this version of **rmtest** using the following application resource file, or by specifying command line arguments.

```
*foreground:    Red
*background:    Blue
*verbose:       LEVEL3
```

Now, if we run this version of **rmtest** from a shell, we should see something like:

```
% rmtest3
fg=9, bg=1, delay=2, verbose=LEVEL3, x=25, y=33
% rmtest3 -verbose LEVEL1
fg=9, bg=1, delay=2, verbose=LEVEL1, x=25, y=33
```

3.3.5   Dynamic Resources

OLIT provides a facility to dynamically change resources. Some of the resources associated with particular widgets can be modified while an application is running. Those resources will be updated dynamically. Most of the resources which are built-in as dynamic resources are color related. The most common dynamic resources are:

Background	FontColor	InputFocusColor
Foreground	BorderColor	

Whenever the **RESOURCE_MANAGER** property is updated, OLIT is notified. For example, if a wdget's **XtNbackground** resource is modified while an application is running, the widget's background color will be updated immediately. We can also register our own callback functions to be called whenever the resource manager is updated by using the function

```
OlRegisterDynamicCallback(dcb, data)
```

The **dcb** argument specifies the callback function while **data** is the argument passed to the callback function. Each function registered with **OlRegisterDynamicCallback()** is called whenever the resource manager is updated. This gives us the flexibility to retrieve and update any resource dynamically. For example, we may want to be able to dynamically change the verbosity level of a running program. We do this by registering a dynamic callback which calls **XtGetApplicationResources()**. When the resource is changed, the application is notified immediately and the application can retrieve the new resource values.

We can demonstrate this technique by modifying rmtest once again. The new version is a more traditional Xt program: we will realize the widgets and call **XtMainLoop()**. This allows us to examine the state of resources as they change dynamically.

```
/*********************************************************
 * rmtest4.c: Dynamic resource version.
 *********************************************************/
#include <X11/Intrinsic.h>
#include <X11/StringDefs.h>
#include <Xol/OpenLook.h>
#include <Xol/StaticText.h>
#include "libXs.h"

static char *levels[] = { "LEVEL1", "LEVEL2", "LEVEL3", "LEVEL4" };

typedef struct {
    Pixel     fg, bg;
    float     delay;
    verlevel  verbose;
    Position  x, y;
} ApplicationData, *ApplicationDataPtr;

static XtResource resources[] = {
  { XtNforeground, XtCForeground, XtRPixel, sizeof (Pixel),
    XtOffset(ApplicationDataPtr, fg), XtRString, "Black" },
  { XtNbackground, XtCBackground, XtRPixel, sizeof (Pixel),
    XtOffset(ApplicationDataPtr, bg), XtRString, "White" },
  { "delay", "Delay", XtRFloat, sizeof (float),
    XtOffset(ApplicationDataPtr, delay), XtRString,"2.5" },
```

```
  { "verbose", "Verbose", XtRVerlevel, sizeof (verlevel),
    XtOffset(ApplicationDataPtr,verbose), XtRString, "LEVEL4"},
  { XtNx, XtCX, XtRPosition, sizeof (Position),
    XtOffset(ApplicationDataPtr, x), XtRImmediate, (XtPointer)25 },
  { XtNy, XtCY, XtRPosition, sizeof (Position),
    XtOffset(ApplicationDataPtr, y), XtRImmediate, (XtPointer)33 },
  };

static XrmOptionDescRec options[] = {
  {"-verbose", "*verbose", XrmoptionSepArg, NULL},
  {"-delay",   "*delay",   XrmoptionSepArg, NULL}
};

static Widget toplevel;

main(argc, argv)
  int    argc;
  char *argv[];
{
  Widget        msg_widget;
  int           n;
  Arg           wargs[1];
  void          dynamic_callback();
  ApplicationData data;

  toplevel = OlInitialize(argv[0], "Rmtest4", options,
                          XtNumber(options), &argc, argv);
  /*
   *   Add the string to float type-converter.
   */
  XtSetTypeConverter(XtRString, XtRVerlevel, xs_cvt_str_to_verlevel,
                     (XtConvertArgList)NULL, 0,
                     XtCacheAll, (XtDestructor)NULL);
  /*
   *  Retrieve the resources.
   */
  XtGetApplicationResources(toplevel, &data, resources,
                            XtNumber(resources), NULL, 0);
  /*
   * Print the result.
   */
  printf("fg=%d, bg=%d, delay=%.2f, verbose=%s, x=%d, y=%d\n",
         data.fg, data.bg, data.delay, levels[data.verbose],
         data.x, data.y);
  n = 0;
  XtSetArg(wargs[n], XtNstring, (XtArgVal) "MESSAGE"); n++;
  msg_widget = XtCreateManagedWidget("msgwidget",
```

```
                                staticTextWidgetClass,
                                toplevel, wargs, n);
    OlRegisterDynamicCallback(dynamic_callback, &data);
    XtRealizeWidget(toplevel);
    XtMainLoop();
}
```

The only difference in this version of rmtest is that we have added a StaticText widget and registered a dynamic callback. Having the StaticText widget allows us to demonstrate one of the built in dynamic resources. The callback function does nothing more than retrieve the application resources and report their current values.

```
void
dynamic_callback(datap)
   XtPointer datap;
{
    ApplicationDataPtr data = (ApplicationDataPtr)datap;

    XtGetApplicationResources(toplevel, data, resources,
                              XtNumber(resources), NULL, 0);
    printf("fg=%d, bg=%d, delay=%.2f, verbose=%s, x=%d, y=%d\n",
           data->fg, data->bg, data->delay, levels[data->verbose],
           data->x, data->y);
}
```

When we run this version of **rmtest** from a shell, we see a StaticText widget displayed with the string "MESSAGE". We also see a similar output as before except that the prompt is not returned until the program is terminated.

```
% rmtest4
fg=9, bg=1, delay=2, verbose=LEVEL3, x=25, y=33
```

We can use the **xrdb** program to change values for resources in the **RESOURCE_MANAGER** property. With the rmtest program running, go to another window running a shell and use **xrdb -m** to modify the relevant resources. The **-m** argument means to merge the specified resources with the existing database.

```
% xrdb -m
rmtest4.msgwidget.background: orange
^D
%
```

The background color of the StaticText widget should change to orange (Assuming you are using a color display). This demonstrates one of the built-in dynamic resources. Now, let's change the verbosity level. Changing an application's verbosity "on the fly" without restarting the application can be very useful for debugging or getting more information about some particular part of a program's execution.

```
% xrdb -m
rmtest4.verbose: LEVEL1
^D
%
```

Each time we run **xrdb**, the callback registered with **OlRegisterDynamicCallback()** is called. The callback function gets the application resources and prints the results. Returning to the window where **rmtest4** was invoked, you should now see three lines:

```
% rmtest4
fg=9, bg=1, delay=2, verbose=LEVEL3, x=25, y=33
fg=9, bg=1, delay=2, verbose=LEVEL3, x=25, y=33
fg=9, bg=1, delay=2, verbose=LEVEL1, x=25, y=33
```

The first line was printed from the **main()** of **rmtest4**. The last two lines were printed by the dynamic callback **dynamic_callback()**. The first time we invoked **xrdb** we set the background color of the StaticText widget. This changed a widget resource but did not change any application resources, so lines one and two of the **rmtest4** output are identical. The second time we invoked **xrdb** we changed the verbose application resource, and line three of the output reflects that change.

3.4 WIDGET RESOURCE CONVENTIONS

Widgets use the resource manager to retrieve the resources specified by the user when the widget is created. Applications can also set the value of a widget resource by passing an argument list to **XtCreateWidget()** or by using **XtSetValues()** to change the value after the widget is created. Because the resources specified by the programmer are applied *after* the user-specified resources are retrieved from the resource data base, they override the user's chosen options. It is sometimes difficult to determine when a widget resource should be set by an application programmer and when it should be left for the end user. The convention used in this book is as follows:

> *Application programmers should avoid specifying widget resource values in the program except where absolutely necessary to ensure that the application works correctly.*

Application programmers should think carefully whenever they are tempted to hard code resource values into an application. Whenever possible, the programmer should leave decisions regarding widget layout, fonts, labels, colors, and so on, to the end user. Applications that are customizable by the end user tend to be more portable. For example, the label displayed by a RectButton widget can be set by the user or the programmer. A programmer could probably justify hard coding the button labels for important functions to prevent the user from using the resource manager to mislabel them. But what if the labels are programmed in English, and the user reads only French? Labels that can be set in a resource data base can be changed easily and without access to source code.

Unfortunately, it is difficult to design a program to be customizable by the end user and still ensure that it works correctly. For example, if command labels can be redefined by the end user, there is nothing to prevent the labels of the buttons from being altered in a misleading way. Imagine a situation where the user has inadvertently switched the labels of the "Delete" and "Save" command buttons of an editor. The results could be disastrous. Documenting software that can be radically customized by the end user is also an enormous problem. Therefore, the approach advocated here is not without flaws.

One way to make programs customizable, while still providing useful defaults, is to provide an application resource file for every program. The programmer can use the application resource file to specify default resources that the user can override in the .Xdefaults file, if desired. The application resource file also provides a useful public place to document the resources and options recognized by an application. The programmer should exercise restraint even when providing an application resource file. For example, specifying colors in an app-default file is asking for trouble because the program may be displayed on different types of hardware.

Even when it is necessary to hard code some resources into a program, using a resource file while developing the application makes it easier for the application programmer to determine the best value for a resource. Rather than recompiling an application every time a resource needs to be changed, the programmer can simply change the appropriate entries in the resource file and run the program again until the proper value is determined. The examples in this book specify few resources in the source code, and many examples are accompanied by an application resource file containing the default resources used by the program.

The important point here is to use common sense when deciding how to control resources. The more customizable an application is, the more easily it can be made to fit the needs of the end user. However, an application that requires the user to do a great deal of setup to even try out the application is unlikely to please a new user.

3.5 SUMMARY

The resource manager provides a simple and powerful mechanism that allows the application programmer to create customizable applications easily. This chapter examined the basic principles of the Xlib resource manager and showed how applications can use the Xt Intrinsics resource facilities to manage application resources. Xt encourages consistency between all applications by providing a standard set of resource names recognized by all applications. Xt also assists the programmer by providing an easy-to-use mechanism for handling user-defined resources, command-line options, and programmer-defined defaults. In addition, OLIT accommodates the dynamic changing of resources.

We have now discussed the general architecture of X, the architecture of the Xt Intrinsics, and the resource manager. The following chapter introduces the widgets provided by the Xt Intrinsics and the OLIT widget set, and begins to put these pieces together as we explore more complex applications.

4

THE OLIT WIDGET SET

Chapter 2 introduced the Xt Intrinsics, a framework that allows programmers to combine user interface components known as widgets to create complete applications. Widgets are simply an X window along with some procedures that manipulate the window. Each widget maintains a data structure that stores additional information used by the widget's procedures. This chapter examines widgets more closely. We will explore the basic widgets provided by the Xt Intrinsics, discuss the widgets from the OPEN LOOK Intrinsics Toolkit (OLIT) widget set, and show how we can combine widgets to create a complete user interface for an application.

The X Consortium has not recognized any widget set as a standard part of the X Window System. However, several sets of widgets are freely available as contributed software, including the Athena widget set developed by M.I.T.'s Project Athena. Several proprietary widget sets are also available. AT&T and Sun Microsystems market OLIT, which includes a widget set that supports the OPEN LOOK interface style. The Open Software Foundation (OSF) and its member companies distribute the Motif widget set. The examples in this book use the OLIT widget set. Sun Microsystems also distributes the XView toolkit which is based on the OPEN LOOK interface style. XView, however, is not an Intrinsics based toolkit; it is based on Xlib.

Other widget sets provide different appearances or interaction styles, and may offer somewhat different functionality, but from the application programmer's viewpoint should be similar to the widgets used in this book. A programmer who understands the principles of the Xt Intrinsics and is familiar with one widget set can quickly learn to use any other widget set.

This book looks at each of the OLIT widgets in some detail. For an exhaustive study of each widget and the resources of that widget, refer to the reference manual that came with your product. In this chapter, we divide the widgets into several categories. The widgets are grouped by common functionality, purpose, or resources. Each widget is demonstrated with at least one example.

4.1 WIDGET CLASSES

The Xt Intrinsics define an object-oriented architecture that organizes widgets into *classes*.[1] In general, a class is a set of things that have similar characteristics. Individual things (objects) are always instances of some class. For example, an object-oriented drawing program might define a class named Rectangle. This class could define various attributes common to all rectangles: color, width, height, position, and so on. To display a particular rectangle on the screen, the program instantiates (creates an instance of) a rectangle. This rectangle has specific values for all its attributes, for example, color: red, width: 10, height: 20, x: 200, y: 325. In the Xt Intrinsics, the function **XtCreateWidget()** creates an instance of the widget class specified by the class argument. In the example in Chapter 2, the message window was an instance of the StaticText widget class.

Inheritance is another useful object-oriented concept supported by the Xt Intrinsics. In most object-oriented systems, a class can inherit some or all the characteristics of another class, in much the same way that people inherit characteristics from their parents. For example, the drawing program we discussed above could define a class named GraphicalObject that defines the attributes common to all objects that can be displayed on the screen. GraphicalObject might define position and color attributes. Next, we can define subclasses of GraphicalObject, such as Circle and Rectangle. The Circle class inherits the position and color attributes from its superclass, GraphicalObject and adds another attribute, radius. The Rectangle class also inherits the position and color attributes, but adds two more attributes, width and height.

The widget programmer (a programmer who designs new widgets) needs to understand these concepts to create new widget classes. Chapters 12, 13, and 14 discuss how the Xt Intrinsics implement classes and uses the architecture of the Xt Intrinsics to create several new widget classes. However, the application programmer should also understand these concepts because it is possible to characterize the behavior of a widget by knowing its class and its superclasses. For example, the OLIT widget set defines both OblongButton and RectButton as subclasses of the Button widget class. The Button widget class defines many of the features or resources that are inherited by both the OblongButton and the RectButton. The subclasses can then add unique options and resources appropriate for its class.

The characteristics that each widget class inherits from its superclass include all resources and all callback lists. For example, all widget classes are subclasses of the Core widget class provided by the Xt Intrinsics. Therefore, because the Core widget class provides a **XtNdestroy** callback list, all widget classes also support the **XtNdestroy** callback list. A widget can also inherit the procedures that define the widget's behavior, including the action list used by the translation manager. Each widget class has a class name used by the resource manager to retrieve resources, and also defines a pointer to a structure known as a widget class. The widget class pointer is used as an argument to **XtCreateWidget()**. For example, the widget class pointer for the Core widget is defined in Core.h as:

```
WidgetClass coreWidgetClass;
```

---

[1]   Object-oriented programming is a programming style that organizes systems according to the objects in the system, rather than the functions the system performs. An object is an abstraction that combines data and the operations that can be performed on that data in a single package.

Therefore,

```
XtCreateWidget("core", coreWidgetClass, parent, NULL, 0);
```

creates an instance of a widget belonging to the Core class.

4.2 INTRINSIC WIDGET CLASSES

The Xt Intrinsics define several basic widget classes that serve as superclasses for other widgets. These widget classes define the architecture used by all other widgets, and also provide some fundamental characteristics inherited by all other widget classes. The following sections discuss the fundamental widget classes provided by the Intrinsics.

4.2.1   The Core Widget Class

The Core widget class is the most fundamental widget class, and serves as the superclass for all other widget classes. The Core widget's class name is Core and its class pointer is **coreWidgetClass**.[2] The Core widget class provides some basic resources inherited by all widgets.

The Core widget class is an example of a *meta-class*. In the Xt Intrinsics, a meta-class is a class that serves only as a superclass to other widgets. Meta-classes are not designed to be used directly in applications. In spite of its intended purpose, the Core widget class *can* be instantiated, as illustrated by the following program:

```
/*********************************************************
 * generic.c: Test the Core widget class
 ********************************************************/
#include <X11/Intrinsic.h>

main(argc, argv)
  int    argc;
  char *argv[];
{
  Widget toplevel;
  /*
   * Initialize the Intrinsics.
   */
  toplevel = OlInitialize(argv[0], "Generic", NULL, 0,
                          &argc, argv);
  /*
   * Create a Core widget.
   */
  XtCreateManagedWidget("widget", coreWidgetClass,
                        toplevel, NULL, 0);
```

---

[2]   The remainder of this book simply refers to widgets by their class name, thereby avoiding any more statements like "the Core widget's class name is Core."

```
    XtRealizeWidget(toplevel);
    XtMainLoop();
}
```

   This program simply creates an empty window and displays it on the screen.[3] The application does nothing useful, but does obey all conventions of the X Window System. The program interacts correctly with window managers, and allows the end user to customize all resources supported by the Core widget class. Applications that need a basic window for displaying text or graphics can use the Core widget, although OLIT provides other widgets, the Stub, DrawArea, and ScrolledWindow widgets, which are more suitable for this purpose.

4.2.2   The Composite Widget Class

The Composite widget class is a subclass of the Core widget class and is also a meta-class. All subclasses of the Composite widget class are also known as composite widgets. Composite widgets serve primarily as containers for other widgets. A composite widget *manages* its children, which means that composite widgets are responsible for:

- Determining the physical layout of all managed children. Each composite widget has a geometry manager that controls the location of each child widget according to its management policy.

- Deallocating the memory used by all children when the composite widget is destroyed. When a composite widget is destroyed, all children are destroyed first.

- Mapping and unmapping its children's windows. By default, a widget's window is mapped when it is managed, and unmapped when it is unmanaged. This behavior can be altered by setting the widget's **XtNMappedWhenManaged** resource to **FALSE**.

- Controlling which child has the keyboard input focus. For example, a multiple field form editor might shift the input focus from one field to the next when the users enters a <RETURN> or a <TAB> key.

4.2.3   The Constraint Widget Class

The Constraint widget class is a subclass of the Composite widget class, and therefore can also manage children. Constraint widgets manage their children based on some additional information associated with each child. This information often takes the form of some constraint on the child's position or size. For example, children can be constrained to some minimum or maximum size, or they can be constrained to a particular location relative to another widget. The Constraint widget class is also a meta-class and is never instantiated directly. Section 4.3.3 discusses some constraint widgets.

---

[3]   The Core widget class uses a default size of 0 width by 0 height for its window. Since X does not allow zero width or height windows, this program will generate an error unless a geometry is specified on the command-line or in a resource file.

4.2.4   The Shell Widget Class

The Shell widget class is a subclass of the Composite widget class, but can have only one child. Shell widgets are special purpose widgets that provide an interface between other widgets and the window manager. A Shell widget negotiates the geometry of the application's top level window with the window manager, sets the properties required by the window manager, and generally handles the window manager protocol for the application, as defined by the ICCCM. The following sections briefly discuss several subclasses of the Shell widget class.

4.2.4.1   Application Shells

The ApplicationShell widget class is a subclass of the Shell widget class. `OlInitialize()` creates an ApplicationShell widget that applications usually use as their main top-level window. Applications that use multiple top-level windows can use the functions:

```
XtCreateApplicationShell(name, class, args, nargs)
XtAppCreateShell(context,classname,class,display,args, nargs)
```

to create additional shell widgets of the type specified by the `class` argument.

The following program is a modified version of the example from Section 4.2.1 that creates two independent top-level windows. Both windows can be manipulated independently, although both are created by the same client. Notice that applications must realize each top-level shell individually.

```
/*************************************************************
 * twoshells.c: Example of two independent top-level shells
 *************************************************************/
#include <X11/Intrinsic.h>
#include <X11/Shell.h>
#include <Xol/OpenLook.h>

main(argc, argv)
  int    argc;
  char *argv[];
{
  Widget toplevel, shell2;

  /*
   * Initialize the Intrinsics, create one ApplicationShell.
   */
  toplevel = OlInitialize(argv[0], "Generic", NULL, 0,
                          &argc, argv);
  /*
   * Create a second ApplicationShell widget.
   */
  shell2 = XtCreateApplicationShell("Window2",
                                    applicationShellWidgetClass,
```

```
                         NULL, 0);
     /*
      * Create a Core widget as a child of each shell.
      */
     XtCreateManagedWidget("Widget", coreWidgetClass, toplevel, NULL, 0);
     XtCreateManagedWidget("Widget2", coreWidgetClass, shell2, NULL, 0);
     /*
      * Realize both shell widgets.
      */
     XtRealizeWidget(toplevel);
     XtRealizeWidget(shell2);
     XtMainLoop();
 }
```

4.2.4.2   Transient Shells

Transient shells are similar to ApplicationShells except for the way in which they interact with window managers. Window managers are not supposed to iconify Transient shells separately. If an application's top-level window is iconified, the window manager should also iconify all Transient shells created by that application. Applications can create a transient shell by specifying the widget class pointer **transientShellWidgetClass** as an argument to **XtCreateApplication-Shell()** or to **XtCreatePopupShell()**.

4.2.4.3   Override Shells

The OverrideShell widget class is also similar to the ApplicationShell, except for the way in which it interacts with window managers. An OverrideShell widget sets the **override_redirect** attribute of its window to TRUE, which instructs the window manager to completely ignore it. OverrideShell widgets completely bypass the window manager and therefore have no added window manager decorations. OverrideShell widgets are often used for popup menus.

4.3   THE OLIT WIDGET CLASSES

The OLIT widget set contains many components, including scroll bars, menus, and buttons, that can be combined to create user interfaces. We can divide the widget classes that implement these components into several categories based on the general functionality they offer. For example, some widgets display information while others allow the user to select from a set of choices. Still others allow other widgets to be grouped together in various combinations.

Early versions of OLIT had strictly a two-dimensional appearance. The widget set now defaults to a three-dimensional look.[4] Many OLIT widgets include a border. The top and left sides of this border are set to a lighter color and the bottom and right sides are set to a darker color. This three-dimensional shading gives the effect of a light source existing in the upper left corner of the display. This effect is demonstrated in Figure 4.1. Notice that by making the top shadow lighter than the

---

[4]   The two-dimensional look is still available by setting the application resource **XtNthreeD** to FALSE.

background color and the bottom shadow darker, the widget appears to be coming out of the screen. Reversing these colors makes the widget appear to be recessed into the screen. The colors that create this three-dimensional effect are set automatically by OLIT. The colors used for the top and bottom shadow are calculated from the background color of the widget. These colors can be changed by setting the **XtNcolorTupleList** application resource.

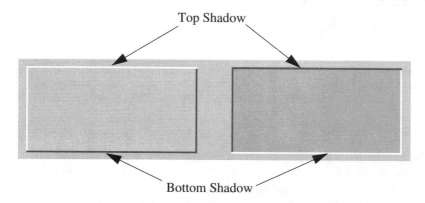

Figure 4.1 Three-dimensional shading in OPEN LOOK.

The OLIT widget set is also designed to encourage the programmer to follow the OPEN LOOK Graphical User Interface (GUI).[5] The OPEN LOOK GUI is a specification for the *look and feel* of a windowing environment. The widgets in the OLIT widget set are designed to encourage the OPEN LOOK style. The style is not, however, strictly enforced since the widgets in the OLIT widget set can be customized. However, programmers who want their applications to fit smoothly with other OPEN LOOK-based applications should follow the OPEN LOOK style as closely as possible.

4.3.1 OLIT Widget Meta-Classes

The OLIT widget set defines several additional meta-classes. The most basic of these is the Primitive widget class, which is a subclass of the Core widget class. The Primitive widget class is never instantiated, and serves only to define some standard resources inherited by its subclasses. The Manager widget class is another OLIT widget meta-class. It is a subclass of the Constraint widget class, and defines basic resources used by all composite and constraint widgets in the OLIT widget set.

The remainder of this chapter examines each of the OLIT widgets. We'll show example programs that demonstrate the widgets function, properties, and resources. The widgets are separated into five groups:

- Action Widgets
- Container Widgets
- Manager Widgets

---

[5]   For more information see the OPEN LOOK Graphical User Interface Application Style Guidelines.

- Text Control Widgets
- Popup Widgets

The widgets in each of these categories have some commonality: they either are subclassed off the same class or have similar functionality. Many of the widgets in the same category share common resources. Your widget reference manual probably lists all of the resources, resource types, defaults values, etc., for each widget. We will not attempt to be that complete. However, we will try to show a representative set of resources that may be commonly used.

The widget reference manual is an invaluable tool when developing applications. The list of resources described in this chapter is not complete. Appendix B contains a complete list of resources, their type, and their default value for each widget. However, providing a description of every resource is beyond the scope of this book. The widget reference manual provides this information.

All resources specified in this chapter begin with **XtN**. When resources are set in resource files, such as .Xdefaults, the **XtN** prefix is dropped. Resource values are also specified in this chapter for some widget resources. The value specified programmatically is not necessarily the same as the values specified in resource files. For example, to specify that a label is to be left justified the programmer would use **OL_LEFT** in their program, while the user would use **left** in a resources file. The convention used in this chapter is to present both versions separated by a slash:

```
OL_LEFT/"left"
```

The value enclosed in quotes is the one to use in a resource file.

4.3.2   Action Widgets

The OLIT widget set has ten *action* widgets.

OblongButton	RectButton	CheckBox
MenuButton	AbbrevMenuButton	Slider
Gauge	Scrollbar	DropTarget
Stub		

4.3.2.1   The OblongButton Widget

One of the simplest and most commonly used widgets is the OblongButton. When you "push" an OblongButton its three-dimensional appearance inverts, giving the illusion that the button has been pressed. The shading changes as shown in Figure 4.1, and the field on which the label is displayed becomes slightly darker as if a shadow covered it. When the button is released, color and shading return to normal.

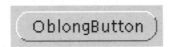

Figure 4.2 The OblongButton widget.

The OblongButton has numerous resources. Some of the more common resources provided by the OblongButton are:

- **XtNaccelerator**: The KeyPress event that will select the widget. When set the button label will include a string at the right side of the button which describes the accelerator, such as "Ctrl+q".

- **XtNacceleratorText**: The string displayed on the button associated with the **XtNaccelerator** resource.

- **XtNbackground**: The background color.

- **XtNborderWidth**: The width of the border surrounding the widget. The default value is 0.

- **XtNfont**: The font used to display the widget's label.

- **XtNfontColor**: The font color of the widget's label.

- **XtNheight, XtNwidth**: The height and width of the widget. Explicitly setting the widget's height and width only takes effect if **XtNrecomputSize** is FALSE.

- **XtNlabel**: The text displayed in the widget. When this resources is not set the label defaults to the *name* passed to **XtCreateWidget()**.

- **XtNlabelImage**: The image displayed in the widget. This takes the place of the label specified by **XtNlabel**. This resource is ignored unless **XtLabelType** is **OL_IMAGE**.

- **XtNlabelJustify**: The label justification. Labels can either be left justified or centered. Valid values are:
  - **OL_LEFT/"left"**: The label is left justified This is the default.
  - **OL_CENTER/"center"**: The label is centered.

- **XtNlabelType**: The label type. Valid values are:
  - **OL_STRING/"string"**: The label is a string. This is the default.
  - **OL_IMAGE/"image"**: The label is an image.
  - **Ol_POPUP/"popup"**: Three dots are added to the label when indicates that pressing this button will bring up a popup window.

- **XtNrecomputeSize**: The size computation policy. When TRUE (default) the size of the widget is calculated based on the size of the label and other constraints of its parent. When FALSE the size of the widget will be based on the **XtNwidth** and **XtNheight** resources.

- **XtNscale**: The scale of the widget. This resource controls the size of graphical elements of the widget. Valid scale values are 10, 12, 14, and 19.

- **XtNx, XtNy**: The X and Y-coordinate of the widget's upper left hand corner.

- **XtNselect**: The list of callbacks invoked when the widget is selected.

The most common use of the OblongButton is to activate a callback list. The **XtNselect** resource specifies the list of callbacks associated with the OblongButton.To activate the callback list, press and release the mouse button while the pointer is in the OblongButton. If you move the pointer out of the button area before you release the mouse button, the callback is not made.

Let's look at a simple example using the OblongButton widget and an **XtNselect** callback. This **oblong** program creates an OblongButton widget and registers a callback for it.The button is a child of a ControlArea widget. Section 4.3.3.2 discusses the ControlArea widget in more detail. We introduce the ControlArea widget here because action widgets are usually the children of some manager widget like the Form, BulletinBoard, or ControlArea. In addition, the **toplevel** widget returned by **OlInitialize()** can only parent one child which would be very limiting.

```
/***********************************************************
 * oblong.c: Demonstrate the OblongButton widget.
 ***********************************************************/
#include <X11/Intrinsic.h>
#include <X11/StringDefs.h>
#include <Xol/OpenLook.h>
#include <Xol/ControlAre.h>
#include <Xol/OblongButt.h>

main(argc, argv)
  int    argc;
  char *argv[];
{
  Widget  toplevel, con, but1;
  void button_callback();

  toplevel = OlInitialize(argv[0], "Oblong", NULL, 0, &argc, argv);
  con = XtCreateManagedWidget("control", controlAreaWidgetClass,
                              toplevel, NULL, 0);
  /*
   * Create the OblongButton widget.
   */
  but1 = XtCreateManagedWidget("button", oblongButtonWidgetClass,
                               con, NULL, 0);
  XtAddCallback(but1, XtNselect, button_callback, NULL);

  XtRealizeWidget(toplevel);
  XtMainLoop();
}
```

The callback function, **button_callback()** is registered via **XtAddCallback()**. Its only function is to print a message to the controlling terminal.

```
void
button_callback(w, client_data, call_data)
  Widget     w;
  XtPointer  client_data, call_data;
{
  printf("callback\n");
}
```

Now we can run the program to see how the button callback works. When the SELECT mouse button (left button by default) is pressed with the pointer over the button, the button's shadow colors are inverted to give it a three dimensional *pressed* look. Moving the pointer out of the button restore the button's appearance. When SELECT is pressed and released in the button the callback function is called. Figure 4.3 shows the appearance of the **oblong** program with the following resource:

```
Oblong*button.label:    OblongButton
```

Figure 4.3 A ControlArea with an OblongButton widget.

To demonstrate some of the OblongButton's resources we will set some additional resources and observe the changes in the appearance and behavior of the program. We change the background and fontColor resources to display different colors, change the font to a 19 point size, set the scale to 19, and change the button's label. Figure 4.4 shows the appearance of the **oblong** program with these resource settings:

```
Oblong*button.background:      gray60
Oblong*button.fontColor:       white
Oblong*scale:                  19
Oblong*button.font:            lucidasans-bold-19
Oblong*button.label:           Big Button
```

Figure 4.4 OblongButton resource settings demonstrated.

The OblongButton Gadget

In addition to widgets, the Intrinsics provide another user interface component known as a gadget. Gadgets are identical to widgets, except that they have no window of their own. A gadget must display text or graphics in the window provided by its parent, and must also rely on its parent for input. Because reducing the number of windows in an application reduces the number of server requests, using gadgets can make an application more efficient. From the application programmer's viewpoint, gadgets can be used exactly the same as their corresponding widgets, except for the following restrictions. Gadgets cannot support event handlers, translations, or popup children. They cannot do grabs (Section 5.3.2) or own or request selections (Section 11.4.2). Also, gadgets are not guaranteed to behave correctly if they are positioned so that they overlap. Gadgets can support callback functions and have the same appearance as the corresponding widgets. OLIT provides two gadget classes:

OblongButtonGadget   **MenuButtonGadget**

These gadgets correspond to the OblongButton widget and MenuButton widget.

Gadgets are created exactly the same way as widgets, using **XtCreateWidget()** or **XtCreateManagedWidget()**. For example, the OblongButton widget created in the previous example could be replaced with an OblongButton gadget by calling

XtCreateManagedWidget("button", oblongButtonGadgetClass, con, NULL, 0)

The behavior of an OblongButton gadget in that example would be identical.

4.3.2.2   The RectButton Widget

The RectButton is a toggle button. It can be in one of two possible states: set or not set. When a Rect-Button is "pushed" its three-dimensional appearance inverts, giving the illusion that the button has been pressed. This is the set state. The button remains in this state until it is pressed again or is unset.

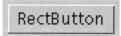

Figure 4.5 The RectButton Widget.

The RectButton has many of the same resources as the OblongButton. Some of its more common resources are:

- **XtNaccelerator**: The KeyPress event that will select the widget. When set the button label will include a string at the right side of the button which describes the accelerator, such as "Ctrl+q".
- **XtNacceleratorText**: The string displayed on the button associated with the **XtNaccelerator** resource.
- **XtNbackground**: The background color.
- **XtNborderWidth**: The width of the border surrounding the widget. The default value is 0.
- **XtNdim**: The RectButton is dimmed to represent an indeterminate state.
- **XtNfont**: The font used to display the widget's label.
- **XtNfontColor**: The font color of the widget's label.
- **XtNheight, XtNwidth**: The height and width of the widget. Explicitly setting the widget's height and width only takes effect if **XtNrecomputSize** is FALSE.

- **XtNlabel**: The text displayed in the widget. When this resources is not set the label defaults to the *name* passed to **XtCreateWidget()**.

- **XtNlabelImage**: The image displayed in the widget. This takes the place of the label specified by **XtNlabel**. This resource is ignored unless **XtLabelType** is **OL_IMAGE**.

- **XtNlabelJustify**: The label justification. Labels can either be left justified or centered. Valid values are:

  — **OL_LEFT/"left"**: The label is left justified This is the default.

  — **OL_CENTER/"center"**: The label is centered.

- **XtNlabelType**: The label type. Valid values are:

  — **OL_STRING/"string"**: The label is a string. This is the default.

  — **OL_IMAGE/"image"**: The label is an image.

- **XtNrecomputeSize**: The size computation policy. When TRUE (default) the size of the widget is calculated based on the size of the label and other constraints of its parent. When FALSE the size of the widget will be based on the **XtNwidth** and **XtNheight** resources.

- **XtNscale**: The scale of the widget. This resource controls the size of graphical elements of the widget. Valid scale values are 10, 12, 14, and 19.

- **XtNselect**: The list of callbacks invoked when the widget is set.

- **XtNset**: The current state of the button.

- **XtNx, XtNy**: The X and Y-coordinate of the widget's upper left hand corner.

- **XtNunselect**: The list of callbacks invoked when the widget is unset.

The RectButton has a callback list associated with each of its two states. The **XtNselect** resource specifies the list of callbacks associated with the button transitioning into the *set* state. The **XtNunselect** resources specifies the list of callbacks associated with the button transitioning into the *unset* state.

RectButtons are usually the children of either an Exclusives or Nonexclusives widget. These widgets are discussed in Section 4.3.5.2. There is no absolute requirement that RectButtons be the children of one of these two classes though their proper behavior is only guaranteed when they are. If a RectButton is the child of some other class of widget their behavior defaults to a nonexclusive behavior, meaning that its state can be set or unset regardless of the state of any other RectButton.

The **rectbutton** program demonstrates the usage of the RectButton. The program creates a RectButton and registers a callback for both **XtNselect** and **XtNunselect**.

```
/************************************************************
 * rectbutton.c: Demonstrate the RectButton widget.
 ************************************************************/
#include <X11/Intrinsic.h>
#include <X11/StringDefs.h>
#include <Xol/OpenLook.h>
#include <Xol/ControlAre.h>
#include <Xol/RectButton.h>
```

```
main(argc, argv)
  int     argc;
  char    *argv[];
{
  Widget  toplevel, con, button;
  int n;
  Arg wargs[2];
  void quit_callback(), button_callback();

  toplevel = OlInitialize(argv[0], "Rectbutton", NULL, 0,
                          &argc, argv);
  con = XtCreateManagedWidget("con", controlAreaWidgetClass,
                              toplevel, NULL, 0);
  /*
   * Create RectButton widget and add callbacks.
   */
  n = 0;
  XtSetArg(wargs[n], XtNlabel, "NOT Set"); n++;
  button = XtCreateManagedWidget("button",  rectButtonWidgetClass,
                                 con, wargs, n);
  XtAddCallback(button, XtNselect, button_callback, NULL);
  XtAddCallback(button, XtNunselect, button_callback, NULL);

  XtRealizeWidget(toplevel);
  XtMainLoop();
}
```

The callback function gets the current value of the **XtNset** resource and sets its label to reflect the current state of the button.

```
void
button_callback(w, client_data, call_data)
  Widget      w;
  XtPointer   client_data, call_data;
{
  Arg arg[1];
  char label[8];
  Boolean set;

  XtSetArg(arg[0], XtNset, &set);
  XtGetValues(w, arg, 1);
  sprintf(label, "%s", set ? "Set" : "NOT Set");
  XtSetArg(arg[0], XtNlabel, label);
  XtSetValues(w, arg, 1);
}
```

When the button is pressed its state is toggled and its label changes. Figure 4.6 shows the appearance of the **rectbutton** program.

Figure 4.6 The RectButton widget in the *unset* state.

We demonstrate some of the RectButton's resources by setting the font to a 19 point size font and adjusting the height and width. Notice that it is necessary to set **recomputeSize** to FALSE in order for the height and width to take effect. We also center the label. Figure 4.7 shows the appearance of the **rectbutton** program with these resource settings:

```
Rectbutton*font:                    lucidasans-bold-19
Rectbutton*button.width:            200
Rectbutton*button.height:           40
Rectbutton*button.recomputeSize:    FALSE
Rectbutton*button.labelJustify:     center
```

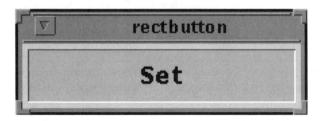

Figure 4.7 RectButton resource settings demonstrated.

4.3.2.3   The CheckBox Widget

The CheckBox widget is similar in functionality to the RectButton widget. It is most commonly used to implement a several-of-many selection and hence is created as the child of a Nonexclusives widget.

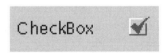

Figure 4.8 The CheckBox widget.

The CheckBox widget can be in one of two possible states: set or unset. Pressing the SELECT mouse button with the pointer over the box toggles the state of the CheckBox. A check mark appears in the box when the state is set and disappears when the state is unset. A callback is associated with each of the two states: **XtNselect** and **XtNunselect**.

- **XtNdim**: The CheckBox is dimmed to represent an indeterminate state.
- **XtNfont**: The font used to display the widget's label.
- **XtNfontColor**: The font color of the widget's label.
- **XtNlabel**: The text displayed in the widget. When this resources is not set the label defaults to the *name* passed to **XtCreateWidget()**.
- **XtNlabelJustify**: The label justification. Labels can either be left justified or centered. Valid values are:
  — **OL_LEFT/"left"**: The label is left justified This is the default.
  — **OL_RIGHT/"right"**: The label is right justified.
- **XtNposition**: The position of the label with respect to the CheckBox. Valid values are:
  — **OL_LEFT/"left"**: The label appears to the left of the CheckBox This is the default.
  — **OL_RIGHT/"right"**: The label appears to the right of the CheckBox.
- **XtNscale**: The scale of the widget. This resource controls the size of graphical elements of the widget. Valid scale values are 10, 12, 14, and 19.
- **XtNselect**: The list of callbacks invoked when the widget is set.
- **XtNset**: The current state of the CheckBox.
- **XtNx, XtNy**: The X and Y-coordinate of the widget's upper left hand corner.
- **XtNunselect**: The list of callbacks invoked when the widget is unset.

The **checkbox** example creates a CheckBox widget and registers a callback for **XtNselect** and **XtNunselect**.

```
/***********************************************************
 * checkbox.c: Demonstrate the CheckBox widget.
 ***********************************************************/
#include <X11/Intrinsic.h>
#include <X11/StringDefs.h>
#include <Xol/OpenLook.h>
#include <Xol/ControlAre.h>
#include <Xol/CheckBox.h>

main(argc, argv)
  int      argc;
  char     *argv[];
{
  Widget   toplevel, con, checkbox;
  int n;
```

```
    Arg wargs[2];
    void checkbox_callback();

    toplevel = OlInitialize(argv[0], "Checkbox", NULL, 0,
                            &argc, argv);
    con = XtCreateManagedWidget("con", controlAreaWidgetClass,
                                toplevel, NULL, 0);
    /*
     * Create checkbox widget.
     */
    n = 0;
    XtSetArg(wargs[n], XtNlabel, "OL_LEFT Position"); n++;
    checkbox = XtCreateManagedWidget("checkbox",  checkBoxWidgetClass,
                                     con, wargs, n);
    XtAddCallback(checkbox, XtNselect, checkbox_callback, NULL);
    XtAddCallback(checkbox, XtNunselect, checkbox_callback, NULL);

    XtRealizeWidget(toplevel);
    XtMainLoop();
}
```

The callback function, **checkbox_callback()**, checks the state of the CheckBox and sets the **XtNposition** resource to **OL_RIGHT** if the state is set, and **OL_LEFT** if the state is unset.

```
void
checkbox_callback(w, client_data, call_data)
  Widget      w;
  XtPointer   client_data, call_data;
{
  Arg warg[2];
  int n;
  Boolean set;

  n = 0;
  XtSetArg(warg[n], XtNset, &set); n++;
  XtGetValues(w, warg, n);
  n = 0;
  if(set == TRUE) {
      XtSetArg(warg[n], XtNlabel, "OL_RIGHT Position"); n++;
      XtSetArg(warg[n], XtNposition, OL_RIGHT); n++;
  } else {
      XtSetArg(warg[n], XtNlabel, "OL_LEFT Position"); n++;
      XtSetArg(warg[n], XtNposition, OL_LEFT); n++;
  }
  XtSetValues(w, warg, n);
}
```

Figure 4.9 shows the appearance of the **checkbox** program:

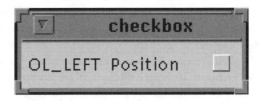

Figure 4.9 The CheckBox widget with **XtNposition** set to **OL_LEFT**.

When you SELECT the CheckBox the **XtNposition** resource is changed, which moves the label to the other side as shown is Figure 4.10.

Figure 4.10 The CheckBox widget with **XtNposition** set to **OL_RIGHT**.

4.3.2.4   The MenuButton Widget

The MenuButton widget is used to create a pop up menu. Its appearance is similar to the Oblong-Button widget with an additional mark near the right end of the button called the *menumark*.

Figure 4.11 The MenuButton widget.

When you press the MENU mouse button on the MenuButton, a menu pops up in the direction of the *menumark*. Typically, the pop-up menu will contain several objects, such as OblongButtons, from which you can make a selection. This pop-up menu is also called a *menu pane*. The menu pane can optionally have a *pushpin* associated with it. You can pin the menu by moving the pointer over the pushpin. When the pushpin is "in" the pop-up will stay pinned up. If the pushpin is left "out" the menu will pop down after you make a selection. Unpinning a menu will pop the menu down.

The MenuButton widget also lets you preview the default selection of the menu pane in the MenuButton. If the **selectDoesPreview** resource is set to true (default) then pressing the SE-LECT button over the MenuButton will display the default selection from the menu in the button, and upon release will activate the default selection from the menu pane.

The menu pane is created automatically when the MenuButton is created. A separate call to **XtCreateWidget()** is not necessary. The menu pane widget is obtained by getting the value of the **XtNmenuPane** resource after the MenuButton has been created. After getting the menu pane widget, it is then the responsibility of the application to populate the menu by creating other widgets such as OblongButtons or RectButtons as children of the menu pane. Menu panes can also be populated with other MenuButton widgets creating a *cascade* of MenuButtons.

Some of the more common resources for the MenuButton are:

- **XtNaccelerator**: The KeyPress event that will select the widget. When set the button label will include a string at the right side of the button which describes the accelerator, such as "Ctrl+q".

- **XtNacceleratorText**: The string displayed on the button associated with the **XtNaccelerator** resource.

- **XtNbackground**: The background color.

- **XtNdefault**: The default selection on the menu pane.

- **XtNfont**: The font used to display the widget's label.

- **XtNfontColor**: The font color of the widget's label.

- **XtNlabel**: The text displayed in the widget. When this resources is not set the label defaults to the *name* passed to **XtCreateWidget()**.

- **XtNmenuMark**: The direction of the menu arrow.
  - **OL_DOWN/"down"**: The menu mark points down. This is the default for top level MenuButtons.
  - **OL_RIGHT/"right"**: The menu mark points right. This is the default for MenuButtons that reside on a menu.

- **XtNmenuPane**: The menu pane widget. This resource can only be accessed after the MenuButton has been created.

- **XtNmnemonic**: The mnemonic that activates the widget. This resource is typically set on a widget which is a child of the menu pane.

- **XtNpushpin**: The menu pane's pushpin.There are two valid values:
  - **OL_NONE/"none"**: No pushpin will be included on the menu pane. This is the default.
  - **OL_OUT/"out"**: A pushpin will be included on the menu pane. Its initial state will be "out".

- **XtNscale**: The scale of the widget. This resource controls the size of graphical elements of the widget. Valid scale values are 10, 12, 14, and 19.

- **XtNtitle**: The menu pane title. This appears only when the menu is pinned.

The **menubutton** example program creates a MenuButton widget and retrieves the associated menu pane widget. Four buttons are then created as children of the menu pane. Each button has an **XtNselect** callback registered for it.

```c
/***********************************************************
 * menubutton.c: Demonstrate the MenuButton widget.
 **********************************************************/
#include <X11/Intrinsic.h>
#include <X11/StringDefs.h>
#include <Xol/OpenLook.h>
#include <Xol/ControlAre.h>
#include <Xol/OblongButt.h>
#include <Xol/MenuButton.h>

char *button_names[] = { "New", "Open", "Save", "Print" };

main(argc, argv)
  int     argc;
  char    *argv[];
{
  Widget  toplevel, con, menubutton, menu_pane,
          oblong[XtNumber(button_names)];
  int i, n;
  Arg wargs[2];
  void button_callback();

  toplevel = OlInitialize(argv[0], "Menubutton", NULL, 0,
                          &argc, argv);
  con = XtCreateManagedWidget("control", controlAreaWidgetClass,
                              toplevel, NULL, 0);
  /*
   * Create menubutton widget.
   */
  menubutton = XtCreateManagedWidget("File", menuButtonWidgetClass,
                                     con, NULL, 0);
  /*
   * Get the MenuPane widget
   */
  n = 0;
  XtSetArg(wargs[n], XtNmenuPane, &menu_pane); n++;
  XtGetValues(menubutton, wargs, n);
  /*
   * Create the buttons on the menu pane.
   */
  for(i=0;i<XtNumber(button_names);i++) {
    oblong[i] = XtCreateManagedWidget(button_names[i],
                                      oblongButtonWidgetClass,
                                      menu_pane, NULL, 0);
    XtAddCallback(oblong[i], XtNselect, button_callback,
                  button_names[i]);
  }
```

```
   XtRealizeWidget(toplevel);
   XtMainLoop();
}
```

The **button_callback()** callback function simply prints the **client_data** which, in this case, is the name of the button.

```
void
button_callback(w, client_data, call_data)
  Widget w;
  XtPointer client_data, call_data;
{
  printf("%s\n", (String)client_data);
}
```

Figure 4.12 shows two views of the **menubutton** program. Shown on the left is the result of pressing the MENU mouse button. The pop-up window appears. Shown on the right is the result of pressing the SELECT mouse button. When you press SELECT on the MenuButton you see that the first OblongButton label on the menu pane is previewed in the MenuButton. The first item on a menu is the default item if not specified otherwise.The default item has a border around it. You can select a default item by setting the **XtNdefault** resource for that item.

Figure 4.12 The menubutton program with a pop-up menu and previewing the default.

To demonstrate some of the MenuButton's resources we make a few changes to the resource settings. We change the default item to the Save button, add a pushpin, and change the menu mark to point to the right rather than down. We also add mnemonics and accelerators. Figure 4.13 shows the **menubutton** program with these resource settings:

```
Menubutton*Save.default:          TRUE
Menubutton*pushpin:               out
Menubutton*menuMark:              right
```

```
!
Menubutton*New.mnemonic:              n
Menubutton*Open.mnemonic:             o
Menubutton*Save.mnemonic:             s
Menubutton*Print.mnemonic:            p
!
Menubutton*New.accelerator:           c<n>
Menubutton*Open.accelerator:          c<o>
Menubutton*Save.accelerator:          c<s>
Menubutton*Print.accelerator:         c<p>
!
Menubutton*New.acceleratorText:       (^N)
Menubutton*Open.acceleratorText:      (^O)
Menubutton*Save.acceleratorText:      (^S)
Menubutton*Print.acceleratorText:     (^P)
```

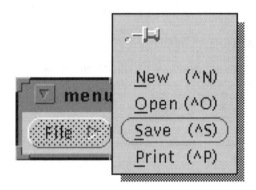

Figure 4.13 The menubutton program with a pushpin, accelerators, and mnemonics.

Both mnemonics and accelerators provide the ability to activate objects from the keyboard rather than using the mouse. The appearance and behavior of mnemonics and accelerators are slightly different.

Mnemonics are represented in the widget's label by underlining the character that acts as the mnemonic. For example, "N" is the mnemonic for the button labeled "New". Pressing "N" or "n" on the keyboard has the same effect as pressing the SELECT mouse button with the pointer positioned over the button. Typically, the first character of the label is used as the mnemonic. If the mnemonic chosen is not a character in the label of the widget then the character is enclosed in parentheses and added to the end of the widget's label. Each mnemonic on a given menu must be unique. However, the same mnemonic can be reused on other menus. The mnemonic can only be activated when the menu is popped up.

Accelerators are represented in the widget's label by a set of characters which are added to the right hand side of the widget's label. For example, if Control-N was set as the accelerator for a button, the text `Ctrl+n` would be displayed in the button's label. The text displayed on the objects label can be customized by setting the **XtNacceleratorText** resource. One advantage of accelerators is that they can be activated at any time, even if the accelerator is associated with an object which is on a pop-up menu. Mnemonics require the menu to be popped up, accelerators do not. However, all accelerators in an application must be unique, regardless of whether or not they exists on different popups.

The MenuButton Gadget

In addition to the MenuButton widget, OLIT supports a MenuButton gadget. The MenuButton gadget has the same functionality as the MenuButton widget with the same restrictions as all gadgets. Gadgets cannot support event handlers, translations, or popup children. They cannot do grabs (Section 5.3.2), or own or request selections (Section 11.4.2). Also, gadgets are not guaranteed to behave correctly if they are positioned so that they overlap.

The previous example could use a MenuButton gadget rather than a MenuButton widget. The behavior would be identical. The gadget is created by calling

```
XtCreateManagedWidget("file", menuButtonGadgetClass, con, NULL, 0)
```

4.3.2.5   The AbbrevMenuButton Widget

The AbbrevMenuButton widget is very similar to the MenuButton widget. Both widgets bring up a pop-up menu and allow previewing of a default item. The AbbrevMenuButton conserves screen space by taking less room than a MenuButton. Previewing is not handled by default but can be accommodated by selecting another widget as the *preview* widget.

Figure 4.14 The AbbrevMenuButton widget.

Some of the more common resources for the AbbrevMenuButton are:

- **XtNbackground**: The background color.
- **XtNdefault**: The default selection on the menu pane.
- **XtNmenuPane**: The menu pane widget. This resource can only be accessed after the MenuButton has been created.
- **XtNmnemonic**: The mnemonic that activates the widget. This resource is typically set on a widget which is a child of the menu pane.
- **XtNpreviewWidget**: The widget which will preview the default selection on the menu pane.
- **XtNpushpin**: The menu pane's pushpin.There are two valid values:
  - **OL_NONE/"none"**: No pushpin will be included on the menu pane. This is the default.
  - **OL_OUT/"out"**: A pushpin will be included on the menu pane. Its initial state will be "out".

- **XtNscale**: The scale of the widget. This resource controls the size of graphical elements of the widget. Valid scale values are 10, 12, 14, and 19.
- **XtNtitle**: Sets the title on the menu pane.

The AbbrevMenuButton has a menu pane associated with it just as does the MenuButton widget. The method of getting the menu pane is the same as with the MenuButton widget. Almost everything that applied to the MenuButton applies to the AbbrevMenuButton. One of the only differences is the handling of preview information. In the MenuButton, the previewing was done in the button itself. Since the AbbrevMenuButton does not have a suitable place in which it can display the default menu item, another widget can be specified as the *preview widget*. This is done by setting the **XtNpreviewWidget** resource.

The **abbrev** example creates an AbbrevMenuButton widget and two StaticText widgets: one to label the AbbrevMenuButton, and one to act as the preview widget. After the AbbrevMenuButton widget is created, the menu pane widget is retrieved and populated with four OblongButtons.

```
/*************************************************************
 * abbrev.c: Demonstrate the AbbrevMenuButton widget.
 *************************************************************/
#include <X11/Intrinsic.h>
#include <X11/StringDefs.h>
#include <Xol/OpenLook.h>
#include <Xol/ControlAre.h>
#include <Xol/AbbrevMenu.h>
#include <Xol/OblongButt.h>
#include <Xol/StaticText.h>
#include "libXs.h"

static Widget preview;
static char *us[] = { "Eastern", "Central", "Mountain", "Pacific" };

main(argc, argv)
  int     argc;
  char    *argv[];
{
  Widget  toplevel, con, abbrevmb, main_mp,
          buttons[XtNumber(us)], label;
  int i, j, n;
  Arg wargs[2];
  void menu_callback();

  toplevel = OlInitialize(argv[0], "Abbrev", NULL, 0, &argc, argv);
  con = XtCreateManagedWidget("control", controlAreaWidgetClass,
                              toplevel, NULL, 0);
  /*
   * Create statictext widget.
   */
```

```
      n = 0;
      XtSetArg(wargs[n], XtNstring, "Time Zone:"); n++;
      label = XtCreateManagedWidget("TZ", staticTextWidgetClass,
                              con, wargs, n);
      /*
       * Create AbbrevMenuButton widget.
       */
      abbrevmb = XtCreateManagedWidget("abbrevmb",
                                  abbrevMenuButtonWidgetClass,
                                  con, NULL, 0);
      n = 0;
      XtSetArg(wargs[n], XtNmenuPane, &main_mp); n++;
      XtGetValues(abbrevmb, wargs, n);
      /*
       * Create the statictext widget that will act as preview widget
       */
      n = 0;
      XtSetArg(wargs[n], XtNstring, "Eastern"); n++;
      preview = XtCreateManagedWidget("prev", staticTextWidgetClass,
                              con, wargs, n);
      n = 0;
      XtSetArg(wargs[n], XtNpreviewWidget, preview); n++;
      XtSetValues(abbrevmb, wargs, n);
      /*
       * Create menubutton widget.
       */
      for(i=0;i<XtNumber(us);i++) {
        buttons[i] = xs_create_button(main_mp, us[i], us[i]);
        XtAddCallback(buttons[i], XtNselect, menu_callback, us[i]);
      }

      XtRealizeWidget(toplevel);
      XtMainLoop();
  }
```

The callback function is where we set the new value for the preview widget. All of the buttons use this callback. The **client_data** argument contains the new string for the preview widget.

```
    void
    menu_callback(w, client_data, call_data)
      Widget w;
      XtPointer client_data, call_data;
    {
      Arg warg[1];

      XtSetArg(warg[0], XtNstring, client_data);
      XtSetValues(preview, warg, 1);
    }
```

Figure 4.15 show the output of the **abbrev** program with the following resource:

```
Abbrev*TZ.font:          lucidasans-bold
```

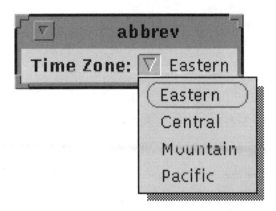

Figure 4.15 The abbrev program.

4.3.2.6   The Slider Widget

The Slider widget is used to set a numeric value. A Slider consists of a drag box, two end boxes (or anchors), and, optionally, tick marks and end labels. The Slider can be displayed horizontally or vertically; the default orientation is vertical.

The position of the Slider can be manipulated in several different ways. Pressing SELECT with the pointer on the drag box allows you to move the Slider to any position with the mouse. You can move the Slider to either end by pressing SELECT on one of the anchors. A third way to move the Slider is to click SELECT on the Slider bar. This moves the Slider in a given number of units in the direction of the pointer. The number of units moved depends on resource settings.

Figure 4.16 The Slider Widget.

Whenever the drag box on the Slider is moved, the callbacks associated with the **XtNsliderMoved** resource are called. The frequency with which the callbacks are called can be controlled by the **XtNdragCBType** resource. By default the callbacks are made continuously as the Slider changes positions. A granularity can be set so that the callbacks are made only when the drag box has moved a given number of units. This is set with the **XtNgranularity** resource and setting **XtNdragCBType** to **OL_GRANULARITY**. The callback list can also be set to be called only when the SELECT button is released by setting **XtNdragCBType** to **OL_RELEASE**.

Some of the more common resources for the Slider are:

- **XtNdragCBType**: The frequency with which the **XtNsliderMoved** callback functions are called. Valid values are:
  - — **OL_CONTINUOUS/"continuous"**: Callbacks are issued continuously. This is the default.
  - — **OL_GRANULARITY/"granularity"**: Callbacks are called only when the drag box crosses any granularity position.
  - — **OL_RELEASE/"release"**: Callbacks are called only when the drag box is released.
- **XtNendBoxes**: The existence of end boxes. If true, end boxes exist. If false, they do not. By default they are displayed.
- **XtNfont**: The font used to display the widget's label.
- **XtNfontColor**: The font color of the widget's label.
- **XtNgranularity**: The granularity with which the **XtNsliderMoved** callbacks are called. It also determines how far the drag box should move when clicking SELECT on the Slider bar.
- **XtNmaxLabel, XtNminLabel**: The labels placed at the ends of the Slider.
- **XtNorientation**: The orientation of the widget. Valid values are:
  - — **OL_HORIZONTAL/"horizontal"**: The widget is displayed horizontally.
  - — **OL_VERTICAL/"vertical"**: The widget is displayed vertically.
- **XtNscale**: The scale of the widget. This resource controls the size of graphical elements of the widget. Valid scale values are 10, 12, 14, and 19.
- **XtNsliderMin, XtNsliderMax**: The minimum and maximum values of the Slider. Default values are 0 and 100 respectively.
- **XtNsliderMoved**: The list of callbacks called when the Slider is moved. The **call_data** parameter of the callback function is a pointer to an integer value that represents the current value of the Slider.
- **XtNsliderValue**: The current value of the Slider.
- **XtNstopPosition**: The position at which the drag box can stop when being dragged. Valid values are:
  - — **OL_ALL/"all"**: Stops at all positions. This is the default.
  - — **OL_TICKMARK/"tickmark"**: Stops at nearest tick mark position.
  - — **OL_GRANULARITY/"granularity"**: Stops at the nearest granularity position.
- **XtNticks**: The distance between tick marks.
- **XtNtickUnit**: The tick mark units. This determines how tick marks are displayed. Valid values are:
  - — **OL_NONE/"none"**: No tick marks are displayed. This is the default.
  - — **OL_SLIDERVALUE/"slidervalue"**: The **XtNticks** resource value is interpreted in the same units as the Slider value.
  - — **OL_PERCENT/"percent"**: The **XtNticks** resource value is interpreted as a percent of the Slider range.

The **slider** program displays two Sliders. They are meant to specify a range of values with the Slider on the left specifying the lower boundary and the Slider on the right specifying the upper boundary. The Slider on the left cannot be set to a higher value than the Slider on the right. The Slider on the right cannot be set to a lower value than the Slider on the left. This is controlled by checking the values of both Sliders in the **XtNsliderMoved** callback.

```
/***********************************************************
 * slider.c: Demonstrate the Slider widget.
 ***********************************************************/
#include <X11/Intrinsic.h>
#include <X11/StringDefs.h>
#include <Xol/OpenLook.h>
#include <Xol/ControlAre.h>
#include <Xol/Slider.h>

main(argc, argv)
  int argc;
  char *argv[];
{
  void       slider_callback();
  Widget     toplevel, con, slider1, slider2;

  toplevel = OlInitialize(argv[0], "Slider", NULL, 0, &argc, argv);
  con = XtCreateManagedWidget("control", controlAreaWidgetClass,
                              toplevel, NULL, 0);
  /*
   * Create two slider widgets and their callbacks.
   */
  slider1 = XtCreateManagedWidget("slider1", sliderWidgetClass,
                                  con, NULL, 0);
  slider2 = XtCreateManagedWidget("slider2", sliderWidgetClass,
                                  con, NULL, 0);
  XtAddCallback(slider1, XtNsliderMoved, slider_callback, slider2);
  XtAddCallback(slider2, XtNsliderMoved, slider_callback, slider1);

  XtRealizeWidget(toplevel);
  XtMainLoop();
}
```

The **slider_callback()** callback function checks the values of both Sliders. The value of **slider2** must always be greater than or equal to the value of **slider1**. This callback function enforces that policy. It might have seemed more straightforward to use the same approach to get the value of both Sliders. Instead, we use the **call_data** to get one Slider value and **XtGetValues()** to get the other Slider value. The reason for this approach is that the result of calling **XtGetValues()** on the **XtNsliderValue** resource returns the previous position rather than the current position of the Slider. To get the current position of the Slider that invoked the callback, you must examine the **call_data** parameter.

```
void
slider_callback(w, client_data, call_data)
  Widget w;
  XtPointer client_data, call_data;
{
  int n;
  int s1val, s2val, tmp;
  Arg wargs[1];
  Widget otherslider = (Widget)client_data;

  n = 0;
  if(strcmp(XtName(w), "slider1") == NULL) {
    tmp = s1val = *(int *)call_data;
    XtSetArg(wargs[n], XtNsliderValue, &s2val); n++;
    XtGetValues(otherslider, wargs, n);
  } else {
    tmp = s2val = *(int *)call_data;
    XtSetArg(wargs[n], XtNsliderValue, &s1val); n++;
    XtGetValues(otherslider, wargs, n);
  }
  if(s1val > s2val) {
    n = 0;
    XtSetArg(wargs[n], XtNsliderValue, tmp); n++;
    XtSetValues(otherslider, wargs, n);
  }
}
```

Figure 4.17 shows the **slider** program with the following resources set:

```
Slider*Slider*height:         100
Slider*Slider*sliderMax:      200
Slider*slider1.maxLabel:      Max 1
Slider*slider2.maxLabel:      Max 2
```

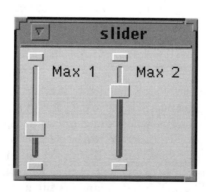

Figure 4.17 The slider program.

To demonstrate some of the Slider's resources we add some new resources and observe the differences. This time the Sliders are oriented horizontally. The granularity is set to 10 which means that clicking select on the Slider bar will move the Slider 10 units. Tick marks are added and the initial delay of each Slider is set to a different value. This resource represents the number of milliseconds delay that will be encountered when pressing SELECT on the Slider bar.

```
Slider*Slider*maxLabel:         200
Slider*Slider*granularity:      10
Slider*Slider*repeatRate:       10
Slider*Slider*minLabel:         0
Slider*Slider*width:            200
Slider*Slider*sliderMax:        200
Slider*Slider*tickUnit:         percent
Slider*Slider*ticks:            10
Slider*Slider*orientation:      horizontal
Slider*control.layoutType:      fixedcols
Slider*control.measure:         1
Slider*slider1.initialDelay:    1000
Slider*slider2.initialDelay:    10
```

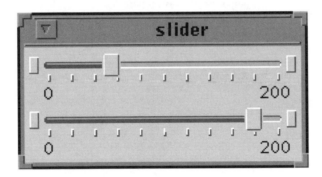

Figure 4.18 The slider program.

4.3.2.7   The Gauge Widget

The Gauge widget is much like the Slider widget except that it is a read-only widget. The Gauge widget can display a value but cannot take user input.

Figure 4.19 The Gauge widget.

Some of the more common resources for the Gauge are:

- **XtNmaxLabel**, **XtNminLabel**: The labels placed at the ends of the Gauge.
- **XtNorientation**: The orientation of the widget. Valid values are:
  - **OL_HORIZONTAL/"horizontal"**: The widget is displayed horizontally.
  - **OL_VERTICAL/"vertical"**: The widget is displayed vertically.
- **XtNscale**: The scale of the widget. This resource controls the size of graphical elements of the widget. Valid scale values are 10, 12, 14, and 19.
- **XtNsliderMin**, **XtNsliderMax**: The minimum and maximum values of the Gauge. Default values are 0 and 100 respectively.
- **XtNsliderValue**: The current value of the Gauge.
- **XtNticks**: The distance between tick marks.
- **XtNtickUnit**: The tick mark units. This determines how tick marks are displayed.

The **gauge** program implements a Celsius to Fahrenheit converter. Two widgets are created: a Slider and a Gauge. The Slider represents temperature in Celsius on a scale from 0 to 100. The Gauge widget displays the corresponding Fahrenheit temperature.

```
/************************************************************
 * gauge.c: Demonstrate the Gauge widget.
 ************************************************************/
#include <X11/Intrinsic.h>
#include <X11/StringDefs.h>
#include <Xol/OpenLook.h>
#include <Xol/ControlAre.h>
#include <Xol/Slider.h>
#include <Xol/Gauge.h>

main(argc, argv)
  int argc;
  char *argv[];
{
  void       slider_callback();
  Widget     toplevel, con, slider, gauge;

  toplevel = OlInitialize(argv[0], "Gauge", NULL, 0,
                      &argc, argv);
  con = XtCreateManagedWidget("control", controlAreaWidgetClass,
                            toplevel, NULL, 0);
  /*
   * Create a slider and a gauge widget
   */
  slider = XtCreateManagedWidget("slider", sliderWidgetClass,
                            con, NULL, 0);
  gauge = XtCreateManagedWidget("gauge", gaugeWidgetClass,
                            con, NULL, 0);
```

```
    XtAddCallback(slider, XtNsliderMoved, slider_callback, gauge);

    XtRealizeWidget(toplevel);
    XtMainLoop();
}
```

Whenever the Slider is moved the **slider_callback()** function is called. The callback does
some simple arithmetic to calculate the Celsius to Fahrenheit conversion and sets the Gauge accordingly. The Gauge value can be set by calling **XtSetValues()** on the **XtNsliderValue**
resource. However, the **OlSetGaugeValue()** function accomplishes the same result and is the
preferred method.

```
void
slider_callback(w, client_data, call_data)
   Widget w;
   XtPointer client_data, call_data;
{
   int     celsius, fahrenheit;
   Widget  gauge = (Widget)client_data;

   celsius = *(int *)call_data;
   fahrenheit = celsius * 9 / 5 + 32;
   OlSetGaugeValue(gauge, fahrenheit);
}
```

With the following set of resources the **gauge** program is displayed as shown in Figure 4.20.

```
Gauge*slider.height:        100
Gauge*slider.sliderMax:     100
Gauge*slider.maxLabel:      100
Gauge*slider.minLabel:      0
Gauge*slider.tickUnit:      slidervalue
Gauge*slider.ticks:         20
Gauge*gauge.height:         140
Gauge*gauge.sliderMax:      212
Gauge*gauge.sliderMin:      32
Gauge*gauge.sliderValue:    32
Gauge*gauge.maxLabel:       212
Gauge*gauge.minLabel:       32
Gauge*gauge.tickUnit:       slidervalue
Gauge*gauge.ticks:          20
```

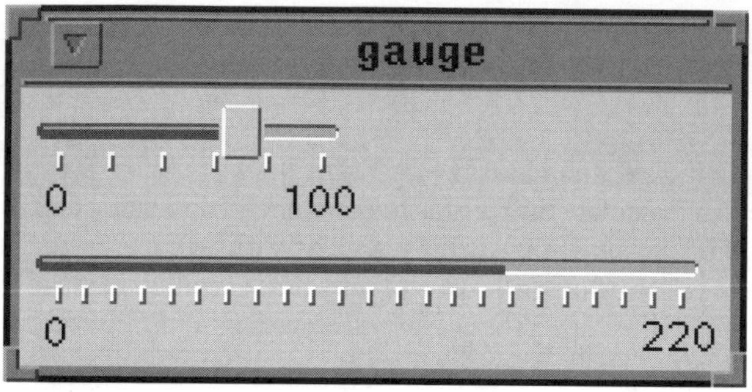

Figure 4.20 Celsius to Fahrenheit converter program.

4.3.2.8   The Scrollbar Widget

The Scrollbar widget is similar to the Slider widget but has some additional features. These features include directional arrows, a proportion indicator, and a page number. A popup menu is also associated with the Scrollbar widget. Pressing the MENU mouse button on the drag box pops up the menu. Use of the Scrollbar is especially appropriate when associated with a pane which displays text or graphics which are bigger than the visible viewing area.

Figure 4.21 The Scrollbar widget.

Like the Slider widget, the Scrollbar has an **XtNsliderMoved** callback. The **call_data** parameter of the Scrollbar is a pointer to an **OlScrollbarVerify** structure which is defined as:

```
typedef struct _OlScrollbarVerify {
        int     new_location;
        int     new_page;
        Boolean ok;
        int     slidermin;
        int     slidermax;
        int     delta;
        Boolean more_cb_pending;
} OlScrollbarVerify;
```

The **new_location** member of the structure reflects the current position of the Scrollbar. The **new_page** member is used to set the page number. The **ok** member can be used to disallow an attempted scroll. The **slidermin** and **slidermax** members contain the minimum and maximum value of the Scrollbar. The **delta** member indicates the change from the last position, and **more_cb_pending** is a Boolean which is true if more callbacks are pending.

Some of the more common resources associated with the Scrollbar widget include:

- **XtNcurrentPage**: The page number displayed when the **XtNshowPage** resource is set to **OL_RIGHT** or **OL_LEFT**.
- **XtNdragCBType**: The frequency with which the **XtNsliderMoved** callback functions are called. Valid values are:
  — **OL_CONTINUOUS/"continuous"**: Callbacks are issued continuously. This is the default.
  — **OL_GRANULARITY/"granularity"**: Callbacks are called only when the drag box crosses any granularity position.
  — **OL_RELEASE/"release"**: Callbacks are called only when the drag box is released.
- **XtNgranularity**: The granularity with which the **XtNsliderMoved** callbacks are called. It also determines how far the drag box should move when clicking SELECT on the cable.
- **XtNmenuPane**: The menu pane widget. This resource can only be accessed after the Scrollbar has been created.
- **XtNorientation**: The orientation of the widget. Valid values are:
  — **OL_HORIZONTAL/"horizontal"**: The widget is displayed horizontally.
  — **OL_VERTICAL/"vertical"**: The widget is displayed vertically.
- **XtNproportionLength**: The length of the proportional indicator.
- **XtNrepeatRate**: The time in milliseconds between repeated actions when SELECT is pressed on the cables or arrows.
- **XtNscale**: The scale of the widget. Valid scale values are 10, 12, 14, and 19.
- **XtNshowPage**: The page indicator. By default no page indicator is displayed. Valid values:
  — **OL_NONE/"none"**: The page indicator is not displayed. This is the default.
  — **OL_LEFT/"left"**: The page indicator is displayed to the left of the drag box.
  — **OL_RIGHT/"right"**: The page indicator is displayed to the right of the drag box.
- **XtNsliderMin, XtNsliderMax**: The minimum and maximum values of the Scrollbar. Default values are 0 and 100 respectively.
- **XtNsliderMoved**: The list of callbacks called when the Scrollbar is moved. The **call_data** parameter of the callback function is a pointer to an **OlScrollbarVerify** structure.
- **XtNsliderValue**: The current value of the Scrollbar.

The **scrollbar** program creates a Scrollbar widget and attaches an OblongButton to its menu pane. The **scrollbar_callback()** function is registered as the **XtNsliderMoved** callback. The **button_callback()** function is registered as the **XtNselect** callback for the OblongButton.

```
/**********************************************************
 * scrollbar.c: Demonstrate the Scrollbar widget.
 **********************************************************/
#include <X11/Intrinsic.h>
#include <X11/StringDefs.h>
#include <Xol/OpenLook.h>
#include <Xol/ControlAre.h>
#include <Xol/OblongButt.h>
#include <Xol/Scrollbar.h>

main(argc, argv)
  int argc;
  char *argv[];
{
  void    scrollbar_callback(), button_callback();
  Boolean verbose = FALSE;
  Widget  toplevel, con, menu_pane, scrollbar, button;
  int     n;
  Arg     wargs[2];


  toplevel = OlInitialize(argv[0], "Scrollbar", NULL, 0,
                          &argc, argv);
  con = XtCreateManagedWidget("control", controlAreaWidgetClass,
                              toplevel, NULL, 0);
  /*
   * Create the scrollbar widget.
   */
  scrollbar = XtCreateManagedWidget("scrollbar",
                                    scrollbarWidgetClass,
                                    con, NULL, 0);
  XtAddCallback(scrollbar, XtNsliderMoved, scrollbar_callback,
                &verbose);
  /*
   * Get the MenuPane widget
   */
  n = 0;
  XtSetArg(wargs[n], XtNmenuPane, &menu_pane); n++;
  XtGetValues(scrollbar, wargs, n);
  /*
   * Add a button to the MenuPane and set a mnemonic
   */
  n = 0;
  XtSetArg(wargs[n], XtNlabel, "Verify"); n++;
  XtSetArg(wargs[n], XtNmnemonic, 'V'); n++;
  button = XtCreateManagedWidget("button", oblongButtonWidgetClass,
                                 menu_pane, wargs, n);
```

```
   XtAddCallback(button, XtNselect, button_callback, &verbose);

   XtRealizeWidget(toplevel);
   XtMainLoop();
}
```

The **scrollbar_callback()** function prints the fields of the **OlScrollbarVerify** structure if the **verbose** flag is TRUE. The **button_callback()** toggles the value of the **verbose** flag.

```
void
scrollbar_callback(w, client_data, call_data)
   Widget w;
   XtPointer client_data, call_data;
{
   OlScrollbarVerify *sbv = (OlScrollbarVerify *)call_data;
   Boolean *verbose = (Boolean *)client_data;

   if(*verbose)
     printf("%s %3d, %s %d, %s %d, %s %d, %s %d, %s %4d,\n",
             "new_location", sbv->new_location,
             "new_page",     sbv->new_page,
             "ok",           sbv->ok,
             "slidermin",    sbv->slidermin,
             "slidermax",    sbv->slidermax,
             "delta",        sbv->delta);
}

void
button_callback(w, client_data, call_data)
   Widget w;
   XtPointer client_data, call_data;
{
   Boolean *verbose = (Boolean *)client_data;

   if(*verbose)
     *verbose = FALSE;
   else
     *verbose = TRUE;
}
```

Figure 4.22 shows the **scrollbar** program with the following resources set:

```
Scrollbar*scrollbar.width:              200
Scrollbar*scrollbar.sliderMax:          200
Scrollbar*scrollbar.orientation:        horizontal
Scrollbar*scrollbar.proportionLength:   20
Scrollbar*scrollbar.granularity:        10
```

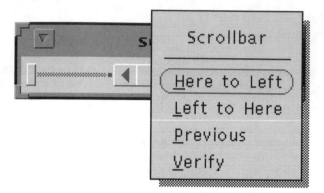

Figure 4.22 The Scrollbar widget with menu pane.

4.3.2.9   The DropTarget Widget

The DropTarget widget automatically handles much of the drag and drop transaction. The OLIT drag and drop mechanism allows the user to move data between applications by means of the mouse. Data can be selected and dragged from one DropTarget widget in a source application and dropped on a DropTarget widget in a destination application. Much of the drag and drop protocol is automated through the use of the DropTarget widget.

Figure 4.23 The DropTarget widget.

A detailed discussion of the drag and drop operation, with examples, is included in Chapter 11. The examples in Chapter 11 include two which use the DropTarget widget (Section 11.5.5).

4.3.2.10   The Stub Widget

The Stub widget provides a window on which an application can render images using Xlib calls and provides several convenient features especially useful for handling graphics. The Stub widget provides functions (similar to callbacks) for expose and resize events.

- **XtNexpose**: The function called when the widget receives an expose event.
- **XtNresize**: The function called when the widget receives a resize event.

Chapter 5 describes events and event handling in detail and also shows an example program using the Stub widget.

4.3.3   Manager Widgets

Most applications require a complex interface which combines many widgets. These widgets allow endless combinations of buttons, scroll bars, text fields, and so on, to be grouped together in an application. Widgets that control the layout of multiple children must be subclasses of the Composite widget class. In the OLIT widget set, widgets that control the layout of other widgets are also a subclass of the Manager meta-class. The OLIT Manager widgets are:

BulletinBoard	ControlArea	DrawArea
RubberTile	Form	FooterPanel

The following sections discuss each of these widgets.

4.3.3.1   The BulletinBoard Widget

The BulletinBoard widget class is a simple example of a container widget. The BulletinBoard widget allows children to be placed at absolute (x, y) coordinates within the widget. If no coordinates are provided for children of the BulletinBoard widget, the BulletinBoard widget places them all at location $(0, 0)$.

BulletinBoard resources include:

- **XtNlayout**: The layout policy of the BulletinBoard. Three values are supported:
  - **OL_MINIMIZE/"minimize"**: The BulletinBoard is just large enough to hold all its children. If children widgets are created or destroyed, the BulletinBoard will grow or shrink to the size just large enough to fit all its children. This is the default.
  - **OL_IGNORE/"ignore"**: The BulletinBoard ignores any changes in the size or number of its children. It will maintain its own size regardless of the attributes of any of its children.
  - **OL_MAXIMIZE/"miximize"**: The BulletinBoard grows in size when additional space is needed for its children, but it will not decrease in size.
- **XtNx, XtNy**: The X and Y-coordinate of the widget's upper left hand corner. This is used on the BulletinBoard's children widget to specify their position.

Let's look at a simple example that uses a BulletinBoard widget to display four OblongButton widgets. The **bboard** program creates a BulletinBoard widget as a child of the toplevel shell. It has four OblongButton children.

```
/***********************************************************
 * bboard.c: Demonstrate the BulletinBoard widget
 ***********************************************************/
#include <X11/Intrinsic.h>
#include <X11/StringDefs.h>
#include <Xol/OpenLook.h>
#include <Xol/OblongButt.h>
#include <Xol/BulletinBo.h>
#include "libXs.h"

main(argc, argv)
```

```
    int      argc;
    char    *argv[];
{
  Widget  toplevel, bulletinboard;
  Widget  button1, button2, button3, button4;

  toplevel = OlInitialize(argv[0], "Bboard", NULL, 0, &argc, argv);
  /*
   * Create the base area Bulletin Board widget.
   */
  bulletinboard = XtCreateManagedWidget("bulletinboard",
                                        bulletinBoardWidgetClass,
                                        toplevel, NULL, 0);
  /*
   * Create the four control buttons
   */
  button1 = xs_create_button(bulletinboard, "Button 1", "button1");
  button2 = xs_create_button(bulletinboard, "Button 2", "button2");
  button3 = xs_create_button(bulletinboard, "Button 3", "button3");
  button4 = xs_create_button(bulletinboard, "Button 4", "button4");

  XtRealizeWidget(toplevel);
  XtMainLoop();
}
```

The four OblongButtons are created by calling **xs_create_button()**. The function sets the name and the label. It returns the Widget created.

```
Widget
xs_create_button(parent, label, name)
  Widget parent;
  String label;
{
  Arg wargs[1];
  int n = 0;

  XtSetArg(wargs[n], XtNlabel, label); n++;
  return(XtCreateManagedWidget(name,  oblongButtonWidgetClass,
                               parent, wargs, n));
}
```

The program has little use other than to demonstrate the behavior of the BulletinBoard widget. Since this example does not specify any sizes or locations for the widgets, they will all appear at (*0, 0*), unless we specify the placement in a resources file. The following class resource file defines the widget layout show in Figure 4.24.

```
Bboard*button1.x:  0
Bboard*button1.y:  0
Bboard*button2.x:  100
Bboard*button2.y:  0
Bboard*button3.x:  0
Bboard*button3.y:  30
Bboard*button4.x:  100
Bboard*button4.y:  30
```

Figure 4.24 The bboard program.

4.3.3.2   The ControlArea Widget

The ControlArea widget organizes its children into rows and columns specified by resources. The number of rows and columns, as well as the overall height and width of the layout, is set by the ControlArea resources. The ControlArea does not resize its children. The ControlArea does resize itself to accommodate changes in its children's sizes. For example, if a new child widget is created or an existing child increases in size, the ControlArea will grow to the necessary size. Conversely, if an existing child is destroyed or shrinks in size, the ControlArea modifies its size accordingly.

Some of the more important resources of the ControlArea are:

- **XtNalignCaptions**: Controls whether Caption widgets, which are children of the ControlArea, will be aligned. (See Section 4.3.5.1)

- **XtNcenter**: Controls widget orientation within a column

- **XtNhPad, XtNvPad**: The amount of horizontal or vertical padding, in pixels, around the edges of the control area.

- **XtNhSpace, XtNvSpace**: The amount of horizontal or vertical padding, in pixels, to leave between controls.

- **XtNlayoutType**: The layout type of the ControlArea. Four values are supported:

  — **OL_FIXEDROWS/"fixedrows"**: The number of rows is fixed by the value of the **XtNmeasure** resource.

  — **OL_FIXEDCOLS/"fixedcols"**: The number of columns is fixed by the value of the **XtNmeasure** resource.

— **OL_FIXEDWIDTH**/**"fixedwidth"**: The width of the ControlArea is fixed by the value of the **XtNmeasure** resource.

— **OL_FIXEDHEIGHT**/**"fixedheight"**: The height of the ControlArea is fixed by the value of the **XtNmeasure** resource.

- **XtNmeasure**: The size of the ControlArea based on the **XtNlayoutType** resource.
- **XtNsameSize**: The width control. Determines which controls, if any, are forced to the same width.

The sample program, **control**, demonstrates some of the ControlArea's resources. The ControlArea is created as a child of the toplevel shell. It has six OblongButton children.

```
/***********************************************************
 * control.c: Demonstrate the ControlArea widget
 ***********************************************************/
#include <X11/Intrinsic.h>
#include <X11/StringDefs.h>
#include <Xol/OpenLook.h>
#include <Xol/OblongButt.h>
#include <Xol/ControlAre.h>
#include "libXs.h"

#define MAXBUTTONS 6

main(argc, argv)
  int     argc;
  char    *argv[];
{
  Widget  toplevel, ca;
  Widget  button[MAXBUTTONS];
  char    label[16];
  char    name[16];
  int     i;

  toplevel = OlInitialize(argv[0], "Control", NULL, 0, &argc, argv);
  /*
   * Create the base ControlArea widget.
   */
  ca = XtCreateManagedWidget("ca", controlAreaWidgetClass,
                             toplevel, NULL, 0);
  /*
   * Create some OblongButtons
   */
  for(i=0;i<MAXBUTTONS;i++) {
    sprintf(label,"But%d",i);
    sprintf(name, "button%d", i);
    button[i] = xs_create_button(ca, label, name);
```

```
    }

    XtRealizeWidget(toplevel);
    XtMainLoop();
}
```

We can see how the ControlArea widget manages the layout of its children. Child widgets are always placed in a unique position in the ControlArea, never overlapping. With no explicit resources set the **XtNlayoutType** resource defaults to **OL_FIXEDROWS** and the **XtNmeasure** resource defaults to 1. Figure 4.25 shows the layout.

Figure 4.25 A ControlArea widget in its default layout.

Let's change the **XtNlayoutType** and **XtNmeasure** resources and observe the changes. Figure 4.26 shows the new layout based on the following resources.

```
Control*ca.layoutType: fixedcols
Control*ca.measure:    2
```

Figure 4.26 A ControlArea widget with two columns.

Let's change the **XtNlayoutType** and **XtNmeasure** resources again, and add some vertical space between buttons. Figure 4.27 shows the new layout.

```
Control*ca.layoutType: fixedrows
Control*ca.measure:    4
Control*ca.vSpace:     20
```

Figure 4.27 A ControlArea widget with four rows and vertical spacing.

4.3.3.3   The DrawArea Widget

The DrawArea widget is a subclass of the BulletinBoard widget. Therefore, it inherits all the attributes of the BulletinBoard with some additional features. In particular, the DrawArea widget provides a window on which an application can render images using Xlib calls. The DrawArea can support a visual, depth, and colormap other than the default. This is especially useful when displaying on special hardware which supports simultaneous multiple visuals. Applications which require sophisticated graphics can use the DrawArea widget to render graphics in. The details of visuals, depth, and colormaps are discussed in Chapter 6.

Even if special hardware is not being used, the DrawArea widget provides several convenient features especially useful for handling graphics. The widget provides callbacks for three events: exposure, graphics exposure, and resize. Chapter 5 describes events and event handling.

Here are some of the resources supported by the DrawArea widget:

- **XtNcolormap**: Sets the colormap associated with the DrawArea widget. By default the DrawArea widget inherits its parent's colormap.

- **XtNdepth**: Sets the depth or number of bits used for each pixel of the window associated with the DrawArea widget. By default the DrawArea widget inherits its parent's depth.

- **XtNexposeCallback**: Indicates the procedure called whenever the DrawArea widget receives an **ExposeEvent**.

- **XtNgraphicsExposeCallback**: Indicates the procedure called whenever the DrawArea widget receives a **GraphicsExposeEvent**.

- **XtNlayout**: Controls the layout policy of the DrawArea. Identical to the **XtNlayout** resource of the BulletinBoard.

- **XtNresizeCallback**: Indicates the procedure called whenever the DrawArea widget is resized.

- **XtNvisual**: Sets the visual used to create the window associated with the DrawArea widget. By default the DrawArea widget inherits its parent's visual.

There are three functions which return information about an object's visual, depth, or colormap:

`OlVisualOfObject()`	Returns the visual associated with the object specified.
`OlDepthOfObject()`	Returns the depth associated with the object specified.
`OlColormapOfObject()`	Returns the colormap associated with the object specified.

The **XtNexposeCallback**, **XtNgraphicsExposeCallback**, and **XtNresize-Callback** each provide an identical **call_data** parameter when the callback function is invoked. The **call_data** is a pointer to a **OlDrawAreaCallbackStruct** which is defined as:

```
typedef struct {
    int         reason;
    XEvent      *event;
    Position    x;
    Position    y;
    Dimension   width;
    Dimension   height;
} OlDrawAreaCallbackStruct;
```

The **reason** field may be one of **OL_REASON_EXPOSE**, **OL_REASON_GRAPHICS_EX-POSE**, or **OL_REASON_RESIZE** indicating that the callback function was called as the result of an Expose event, GraphicsExpose event, or Resize request. The **event** field points to the XEvent that triggered the callback. The **event** field is only valid for Expose and GraphicsExpose events. The **x** and **y** fields indicate the upper left corner of the area. The **width** and **height** fields indicate the dimensions of the area.

Examples of the DrawArea widget are included in other chapters of this book:

`fileview`	Chapter 9
`fractal`	Chapter 10
`draw`	Chapter 10

4.3.3.4   The RubberTile Widget

The RubberTile widget manages children widgets in a single row or column. When the RubberTile widget is resized, it resizes its children according to the weight constraint given each child.

- **XtNorientation**: The orientation of the widget. Two values are supported:
  - **OL_VERTICAL/"vertical"**: The children of the RubberTile will be created in a single vertical column. This is the default.

— `OL_HORIZONTAL`/`"horizontal"`: The children of the RubberTile will be created in a single horizontal row.

- `XtNweight`: The relative weight given to each child when the RubberTile is resized. The default value is 1.

- `XtNspace`: The amount of space between children of the RubberTile.

It should be noted that the `XtNweight` resource does not effect the size of the child widget at creation time, only when the RubberTile is resized. When the RubberTile grows, it parcels out the additional size to each of its children based on the relative weight of each child. For example, if a RubberTile widget has three children and their respective weights are 2, 3, and 5, then the widgets will get 2/10th, 3/10th, and 5/10th, respectively, of the additional space created when the RubberTile is resized. Conversely, if the RubberTile shrinks, it will decrease the size of its children relative to their respective weights.

Let's look at a simple example that creates a matrix of nine RectButton widgets. A RubberTile is created as the child of the toplevel. It defaults to a vertical orientation. This top level RubberTile then has three RubberTile children, which are set to a horizontal orientation. Each of these three RubberTile widgets has three RectButton children. This gives us the effect of three rows and three columns.

```
/************************************************************
 * rubbertile.c: Demonstrate the RubberTile widget
 ************************************************************/
#include <X11/Intrinsic.h>
#include <X11/StringDefs.h>
#include <Xol/OpenLook.h>
#include <Xol/RubberTile.h>
#include <Xol/RectButton.h>
#include "libXs.h"

main(argc, argv)
   int     argc;
   char    *argv[];
{
   Widget  toplevel, base, rt[3], rb[9];
   Arg wargs[5];
   int n, i, j;
   char name[16];

   toplevel = OlInitialize(argv[0], "Rubbertile", NULL, 0,
                           &argc, argv);
   /*
    * Create the base RubberTile widget.
    */
   base = XtCreateManagedWidget("base", rubberTileWidgetClass,
                                toplevel, NULL, 0);
   /*
```

```
 * Create the 3 rubbertile widgets that are childen of base.
 */
for(i=0;i<3;i++) {
  n = 0;
  XtSetArg(wargs[n], XtNorientation, OL_HORIZONTAL); n++;
  sprintf(name, "rt%d", i + 1);
  rt[i] = XtCreateManagedWidget(name, rubberTileWidgetClass,
                                base, wargs, n);
  /*
   * Create 3 rectbutton widgets as children of each rubbertile.
   */
  for(j=0;j<3;j++) {
    sprintf(name, "rb%d", (i * 3) + j + 1);
    rb[(i * 3)+j] = XtCreateManagedWidget(name,
                                          rectButtonWidgetClass,
                                          rt[i], NULL, 0);
  }
}


XtRealizeWidget(toplevel);
XtMainLoop();
}
```

Without setting any weights on any of the RubberTiles or RectButtons, the weight defaults to 1. This means that each of the three RubberTiles that are children of the base RubberTile, will receive an equal portion of the size when the base RubberTile is resized vertically. It also means that as each of the three RubberTiles is resized horizontally, their RectButton children will receive an equal portion of the increased horizontal size. In other words, all the RectButtons will grow identically when the application is resized. Figure 4.28 shows the **rubbertile** program before any resizing occurs.

Figure 4.28 RubberTile widget.

At creation time, all the RectButtons are the identical size. Without any explicit weights set on the RectButtons, all the buttons will resize equally. If we add some different weights and resize the application we can see the how the RubberTile manages its children. Figure 4.29 shows the **rub-bertile** program after being resized with the following resources.

```
Rubbertile*rt1.weight: 1
Rubbertile*rt2.weight: 4
Rubbertile*rt3.weight: 20
!
Rubbertile*rb1.weight: 1
Rubbertile*rb2.weight: 4
Rubbertile*rb3.weight: 20
Rubbertile*rb4.weight: 1
Rubbertile*rb5.weight: 4
Rubbertile*rb6.weight: 20
Rubbertile*rb7.weight: 1
Rubbertile*rb8.weight: 4
Rubbertile*rb9.weight: 20
```

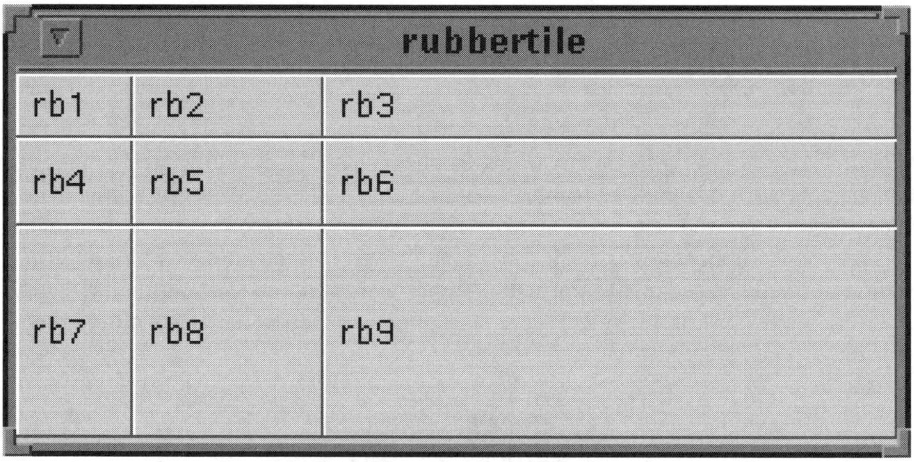

Figure 4.29 The RubberTile widget after being resized.

4.3.3.5   The Form Widget

The Form widget class is a sophisticated widget that manages its children based on constraints that specify the position of each widget relative to another widget, known as a *reference* widget. Each widget can have an x and y reference widget. By default, a widget attaches its left and top sides to its x and y reference widgets respectively. By carefully specifying the attachments and reference widgets, we can specify how the children of a Form widget are positioned, and also how those positions are affected when the Form widget is resized.

The Form widget attaches additional resources to each managed child that allow the programmer or the user to specify the constraints for each widget. These resources include:

- **XtNxAddWidth, XtNyAddHeight**: The position of the widget determined relative to the reference widget. When true, the width or height of the reference widget is added to determine the position.

- **XtNxAttachOffset, XtNyAttachOffset**: The separation between the widget and the form. The default is 0.

- **XtNxAttachRight, XtNyAttachBottom**: The attachment policy. If true the widget floats along the right or bottom of the form.

- **XtNxOffset, XtNyOffset**: The separation between the widget and the reference widget. The default is 0.

- **XtNxRefName, XtNyRefName**: The horizontal and vertical reference widget given by name.

- **XtNxRefWidget, XtNyRefWidget**: The horizontal and vertical reference widget given by widget ID.

- **XtNxResizable, XtNyResizable**: The resize policy. If true, the form resizes the widget in the x or y direction.

- **XtNxVaryOffset, XtNyVaryOffset**: The offset policy. If true the space between a widget and its reference widget can vary.

The **form** program is a simple example that creates four OblongButtons as children of a form widget.

```
/************************************************************
 * form.c: Demonstrate the Form widget
 ************************************************************/
#include <X11/Intrinsic.h>
#include <X11/StringDefs.h>
#include <Xol/OpenLook.h>
#include <Xol/OblongButt.h>
#include <Xol/Form.h>
#include "libXs.h"

#define MAXBUTTONS 4

main(argc, argv)
  int      argc;
  char     *argv[];
{
  Widget   toplevel, form;
  Widget   button[MAXBUTTONS];
  char     label[16];
  char     name[16];
  int      i;

  toplevel = OlInitialize(argv[0], "Form", NULL, 0, &argc, argv);
```

```
/*
 * Create the base Form widget.
 */
form = XtCreateManagedWidget("form", formWidgetClass,
                            toplevel, NULL, 0);
/*
 * Create some OblongButtons
 */
for(i=0;i<MAXBUTTONS;i++) {
  sprintf(label,"But%d", i);
  sprintf(name, "button%d", i);
  button[i] = xs_create_button(form, label, name);
}

XtRealizeWidget(toplevel);
XtMainLoop();
}
```

If we do not set any of the constraint resources on the OblongButtons they all end up occupying the same space. In our first attempt at layout we arrange the buttons in a single column and set them to be resizable in the x direction. All the buttons are attached to the right side of the form so that when the form is resized, the buttons will resize.

```
Form*xResizable:             TRUE
Form*xVaryOffset:            FALSE
Form*xAttachRight:           TRUE
Form*yAddHeight:             TRUE
Form*button1.yRefName:       button0
Form*button2.yRefName:       button1
Form*button3.yRefName:       button2
```

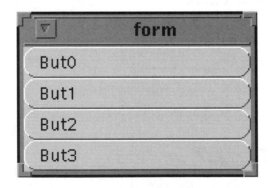

Figure 4.30 The form widget.

Let's try another example. We use the reference name resource to lay out the buttons in two rows and two columns. By setting the x and y vary offset resources to true and the attach right and bottom to true we can change the size of the form and have the buttons *float* along the right and bottom of the form. Figure 4.31 shows the **form** program with the following resources after it has been resized.

```
Form*xVaryOffset:              TRUE
Form*yVaryOffset:              TRUE
Form*button1.xRefName:         button0
Form*button1.xAddWidth:        TRUE
Form*button2.yRefName:         button0
Form*button2.yAddHeight:       TRUE
Form*button3.xRefName:         button2
Form*button3.xAddWidth:        TRUE
Form*button3.yRefName:         button1
Form*button3.yAddHeight:       TRUE
```

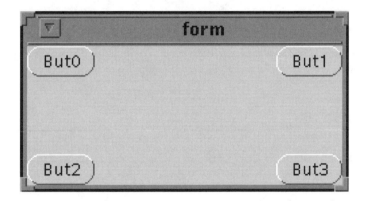

Figure 4.31 The form widget.

4.3.3.6   The FooterPanel Widget

The FooterPanel provides a convenient way to put a footer at the bottom of a window. The most common use of the FooterPanel is to display a message in the footer area. This message might reflect status or indicate an error.

The FooterPanel allows two children: a Top Child and a Footer Child. The order in which the children widgets are created determines which is the Top and which is the Footer. The first widget is the Top Child, the second widget is the Footer Child. The FooterPanel will accept only two children.

The FooterPanel attempts to always maintain the height of the Footer Child. When the Footer-Panel changes size, the Top Child's height is adjusted to absorb the change. The Footer Child maintains its original height. The only time the Footer Child changes size is when the FooterPanel is resized so small that the Top Child shrinks to a height of zero, and there is insufficient room for the Footer Child. In this case, the Footer Child is clipped.

The **footer** program demonstrates the features of the FooterPanel. The top child is a ControlArea, the bottom child is a Form. The ControlArea has two OblongButton children, the Form has two StaticText children. Each button activates one of the messages displayed in the bottom footer. The messages demonstrate the OPEN LOOK convention of using the left footer for status or error messages, and the right footer for state or mode.

```c
/************************************************************
 * footer.c: Demonstrate the FooterPanel widget.
 ************************************************************/
#include <X11/Intrinsic.h>
#include <X11/StringDefs.h>
#include <Xol/OpenLook.h>
#include <Xol/ControlAre.h>
#include <Xol/OblongButt.h>
#include <Xol/FooterPane.h>
#include <Xol/Form.h>
#include <Xol/StaticText.h>

typedef struct _footermessage {
  Widget w;
  int        index;
  char  **message;
} footermessage;

main(argc, argv)
  int argc;
  char *argv[];
{
  static char *leftmess[]  = { "Status Message", "Error Message", "" };
  static char *rightmess[] = { "State", "Mode", "" };
  void        button_callback();
  Widget      toplevel, footerpanel, con, form, status, state,
              st_left, st_right;
  static footermessage left  = { (Widget)0, 0, leftmess };
  static footermessage right = { (Widget)0, 0, rightmess };

  toplevel = OlInitialize(argv[0], "Footer", NULL, 0, &argc, argv);
  /*
   * Create the base FooterPanel widget.
   */
  footerpanel = XtCreateManagedWidget("footerpanel",
                                      footerPanelWidgetClass,
                                      toplevel, NULL, 0);
  /*
   * Create the Top Child, a ControlArea widget
```

```
    */
    con = XtCreateManagedWidget("control", controlAreaWidgetClass,
                                footerpanel, NULL, 0);
    /*
     * Create the Footer Child, a Form widget
     */
    form = XtCreateManagedWidget("form", formWidgetClass,
                                 footerpanel, NULL, 0);
    /*
     * Create the buttons and static text widgets
     */
    status = XtCreateManagedWidget("Status", oblongButtonWidgetClass,
                                   con, NULL, 0);
    state = XtCreateManagedWidget("State", oblongButtonWidgetClass,
                                  con, NULL, 0);
    st_left  = XtCreateManagedWidget("st_left", staticTextWidgetClass,
                                     form, NULL, 0);
    st_right  = XtCreateManagedWidget("st_right", staticTextWidgetClass,
                                      form, NULL, 0);
    left.w = st_left;
    right.w = st_right;
    XtAddCallback(status, XtNselect, button_callback, &left);
    XtAddCallback(state, XtNselect, button_callback, &right);

    XtRealizeWidget(toplevel);
    XtMainLoop();
}
```

The **button_callback()** callback cycles through the supplied messages and updates the corresponding StaticText widget.

```
void
button_callback(w, client_data, call_data)
  Widget w;
  XtPointer client_data, call_data;
{
  Arg       wargs[1];
  footermessage *fm = (footermessage *)client_data;

  XtSetArg(wargs[0], XtNstring, fm->message[fm->index]);
  XtSetValues(fm->w, wargs, 1);
  fm->index = fm->index == 2 ? 0 : fm->index + 1;
}
```

Figure 4.32 shows the layout of the **footer** program after being resized. Notice that as the application is resized the FooterPanel maintains the height of its bottom child and resizes the upper child.

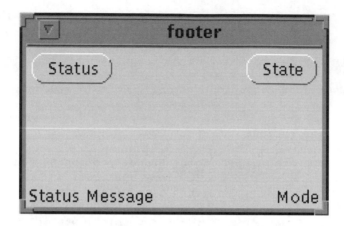

Figure 4.32 The footer program after being resized.

4.3.4 Text Control Widgets

Many applications require text to be entered by the user or to be displayed by the application. OLIT provides three text control widgets that allow input and output of text. The OLIT Text Control widgets are:

StaticText   TextField   TextEdit

The StaticText is a read-only widget. The TextField and TextEdit widget can be used for both display and user input. The TextField widget is for single line input. The TextEdit widget is a multi-line editor and provides a sophisticated set of text manipulation functions.The following sections discuss each of the OLIT Text Control widgets.

4.3.4.1 The StaticText Widget

The StaticText widget provides a way to display a single or multi-line read-only text. The layout of the text is controlled by a few simple layout features.We have already seen the StaticText widget in use earlier in the book. The **memo** program in Chapter 2 used a StaticText widget.

The StaticText will wrap its contents if there is insufficient room to display the entire string in the width provided. Wrapping normally occurs at word boundaries but this feature can also be modified via resources.

Some of the StaticText resources are:

- **XtNalignment**: The alignment to be applied to the text. There are three valid values:
  - **OL_LEFT/"left"**: The lines are aligned on the left. This is the default.
  - **OL_CENTER/"center"**: The lines are centered.
  - **OL_RIGHT/"right"**: The lines are aligned on the right.

- **XtNgravity**: The text gravity. When the width and height of the StaticText exceed the amount of space required to view the entire text, this resource determines where the text will be placed.
  - **CenterGravity/"center"**: The text is centered vertically and horizontally. This is the default.
  - **NorthGravity/"north"**: The text aligns along the top edge.
  - **SouthGravity/"south"**: The text aligns along the bottom edge.
  - **EastGravity/"east"**: The text aligns along the right edge.
  - **WestGravity/"west"**: The text aligns along the left edge.
  - **NorthWestGravity/"northwest"**: The text aligns along the upper left edge.
  - **NortEastGravity/"northeast"**: The text aligns along the upper right edge.
  - **SouthWestGravity/"southwest"**: The text aligns along the lower left edge.
  - **SouthEastGravity/"southeast"**: The text aligns along the lower right edge.
- **XtNlineSpace**: The distance between successive lines.
- **XtNstring**: The text displayed in the StaticText widget.
- **XtNstrip**: The stripping control. If true leading and trailing blanks are stripped.
- **XtNwrap**: The wrapping control. If true, the text will wrap, otherwise it is clipped.

The **statictext** program displays a StaticText widget in a RubberTile. As the application is re-sized the text in the StaticText widget is re-arranged according to the constraints set.

```
/**********************************************************
 * statictext.c: Demonstrate the StaticText widget.
 **********************************************************/
#include <X11/Intrinsic.h>
#include <X11/StringDefs.h>
#include <Xol/OpenLook.h>
#include <Xol/RubberTile.h>
#include <Xol/StaticText.h>

#define LONGSTRING "If the text is too long to fit in the \
width provided by the StaticText widget, the text may be \
\"wrapped\" if the application requests it."

main(argc, argv)
  int argc;
  char *argv[];
{
  Widget      toplevel, rt, st;
  Arg         wargs[2];
  int         n;
```

```
    toplevel = OlInitialize(argv[0], "Statictext", NULL, 0,
                            &argc, argv);
    rt = XtCreateManagedWidget("rt", rubberTileWidgetClass,
                               toplevel, NULL, 0);
    /*
     * Create the StaticText widget
     */
    n = 0;
    XtSetArg(wargs[n], XtNstring, LONGSTRING); n++;
    st = XtCreateManagedWidget("st", staticTextWidgetClass,
                               rt, wargs, n);
    XtRealizeWidget(toplevel);
    XtMainLoop();
}
```

Figure 4.33 shows the **statictext** program with the following resources set:

```
Statictext*rt.st.height:        120
Statictext*rt.st.width:         400
Statictext*rt.st.gravity:       south
```

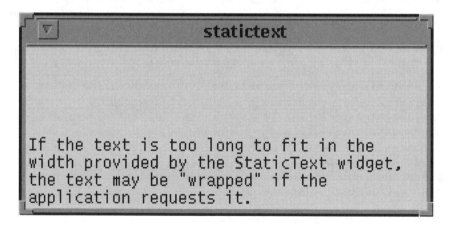

Figure 4.33 The statictext program.

To demonstrate some of the StaticText's resources we add some new resources and observe the differences. We set the gravity to north, the line spacing to 50 pixels, and the alignment to right. The results of setting these resources is shown in Figure 4.34.

```
Statictext*rt.st.height:        100
Statictext*rt.st.width:         300
Statictext*rt.st.gravity:       north
Statictext*rt.st.lineSpace:     50
Statictext*rt.st.alignment:     right
```

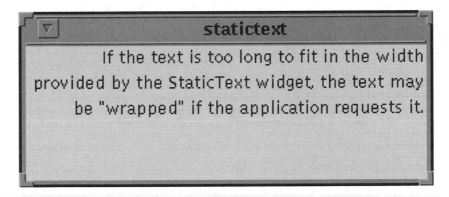

Figure 4.34 The statictext program.

4.3.4.2   The TextField Widget

The TextField widget provides a one-line text input field. The TextField contains a scrollable input line. When the string displayed or entered in the TextField is longer than the display area, left and/ or right arrows appear at either end of the TextField. These arrows indicate that there is more data. Pressing SELECT on the arrows causes the TextField contents to scroll.

The TextField widget is commonly used in an application when user input is required. For example, if a filename were required to be input by the user, it is likely that a TextField widget would be used to input the filename. For data typed at the keyboard to be received by the TextField widget it is necessary for it to have *input focus*. When a widget has input focus it means that keyboard input is received by that widget. When a TextField widget has the input focus, the input caret flashes.

Some of the TextField resources are:

- **XtNcharsVisible**: The number of characters visible. This overrides the **XtNwidth** resource. This resource can only be set at initialization time.
- **XtNinsertTab**: The policy regarding insertion of tabs into the TextField widget.
- **XtNmaximumSize**: The maximum number of character that can be entered into the TextField.
- **XtNstring**: The string of characters displayed in the TextField widget.
- **XtNtextEditWidget**: The TextEdit widget associated with the TextField widget.
- **XtNverification**: The callback list invoked when the user presses the RETURN or TAB key or moves the input focus out of the TextField widget.

The input area of a TextField widget is actually a TextEdit widget. Using the **XtNtextEdit-Widget** resource, you can retrieve the TextEdit widget associated with the TextField. Any resources available to a TextEdit widget can be applied or retrieved from the TextField's TextEdit widget.

When the **XtNverification** callback is invoked the **call_data** parameter is a pointer to an **OlTextFieldVerify** structure which is defines as:

```
typedef struct _OlTextFieldVerify {
  String string;
  Boolean ok;
  OlTextVerifyReason reason;
} OlTextFieldVerify, *OlTextFieldVerifyPointer;
```

The **string** field is a pointer to the TextField contents. It is a pointer to the internal buffer and should not be manipulated directly. Rather, a copy should be made if necessary. The **ok** field is unused. The **reason** field indicates the reason for the callback. Possible values for the reason field are:

OlTextFieldReturn   OlTextFieldNext   OlTextFieldPrevious

which correspond to the user entering RETURN, NEXTFIELD (TAB by default), or PREVFIELD (Shift TAB by default) respectively.

The **textfield** program displays three TextField widgets and three StaticText widgets in a ControlArea. The StaticText widgets act as labels for the TextFields. Each of the three TextField widgets registers an **XtNverification** callback.

```
/***********************************************************
 * textfield.c: Demonstrate the TextField widget.
 ***********************************************************/
#include <X11/Intrinsic.h>
#include <X11/StringDefs.h>
#include <Xol/OpenLook.h>
#include <Xol/ControlAre.h>
#include <Xol/StaticText.h>
#include <Xol/TextField.h>

main(argc, argv)
  int argc;
  char *argv[];
{
  Widget     toplevel, control, st[3], tf[3];
  void       verify_callback();
  char       name[8];
  int        i;

  toplevel = OlInitialize(argv[0], "Textfield", NULL, 0,
                          &argc, argv);
  control = XtCreateManagedWidget("control", controlAreaWidgetClass,
                                  toplevel, NULL, 0);
  /*
   * Create the StaticText and TextField widgets
   */
  for(i=0;i<3;i++) {
    sprintf(name, "st%d",i);
    st[i] = XtCreateManagedWidget(name, staticTextWidgetClass,
                                  control, NULL, 0);
```

```
      sprintf(name, "tf%d",i);
      tf[i] = XtCreateManagedWidget(name, textFieldWidgetClass,
                                    control, NULL, 0);
   }
   XtAddCallback(tf[0], XtNverification, verify_callback, tf[1]);
   XtAddCallback(tf[1], XtNverification, verify_callback, tf[2]);
   XtAddCallback(tf[2], XtNverification, verify_callback, tf[0]);

   XtRealizeWidget(toplevel);
   XtMainLoop();
}
```

The **verify_callback()** callback is registered for each of the three TextField widgets. The reason field of the **OlTextFieldVerify** structure is examined to determine the reason for the callback. If the callback was issued due to RETURN being entered, then we call

```
OlCallAcceptFocus(w, time)
```

The first argument, **w**, specifies the widget to which focus should be set. The **time** argument specifies the X server time of the event that initiated the accept focus request. **OlCallAcceptFocus()** moves the input focus to the widget specified by **w**. The default order in which input focus traverses is based on the order in which widgets are created.

```
void
verify_callback(w, client_data, call_data)
   Widget w;
   XtPointer client_data, call_data;
{
   OlTextFieldVerify *tfv = (OlTextFieldVerify *)call_data;
   Widget nextwid = (Widget)client_data;

   /*
    * If the user hits return, move focus to specified field
    */
   if(tfv->reason == OlTextFieldReturn)
     if(!OlCallAcceptFocus(nextwid, CurrentTime))
       printf("cannot set input focus\n");
}
```

There are several functions available for manipulating input focus. These include:

OlCallAcceptFocus()	Set input focus to widget specified.
OlGetCurrentFocusWidget()	Return widget which has current input focus.
OlHasFocus()	Returns TRUE is specified widget has input focus.
OlMoveFocus()	Moves input focus in the direction specified by parameters.

There are also two other functions for copying the string associated with the TextField widget:

```
OlTextFieldCopyString()       Copies string into user supplied String pointer.
OlTextFieldGetString()        Returns a pointer to the newly allocated copy of the
                              string associated with the TextField.
```

Figure 4.35 shows the **textfield** program with the following resources set:

```
Textfield*control.layoutType:      fixedcols
Textfield*control.measure:         2
Textfield*StaticText*width:        70
Textfield*StaticText*gravity:      east
Textfield*st0.string:              MAKE:
Textfield*st1.string:              MODEL:
Textfield*st2.string:              SERIAL #:
Textfield*TextField*charsVisible:  10
```

Figure 4.35 The textfield program.

4.3.4.3   The TextEdit Widget

The TextEdit widget provides a sophisticated multi-line text editing capability. The TextEdit widget displays its contents on a pane that scrolls to accommodate cursor motion. There are no scroll bars included with the widget but when the cursor is moved to a position that would be off the pane, the contents of the panel scroll up or down so that the cursor is always displayed in the pane.

The TextEdit widget supports two types of text wrapping: at word boundaries (white space) and at any character. Text wrapping can also be turned off. When it is turned off, lines that extend past the right margin are clipped. In this mode, moving the cursor past the right edge of the viewable line causes horizontal scrolling.

The TextEdit widget also supports both the cut and paste, and the drag and drop facilities. This is implemented via the X selection mechanism discussed in Chapter 11. These features allow the *selection* of a string of characters from the TextEdit widget with the ability to either cut or copy the characters and insert, or paste, them elsewhere. The movement of text can be from within one application (or one TextEdit widget), or between independent applications which both support the same mechanism.

Using cut and paste is accomplished by first selecting text. Selecting text from the TextEdit widget involves highlighting the desired text with the cursor. To select text, press the SELECT key at one boundary of the selection and then while holding down the SELECT key, drag the pointer to the other boundary of the desired selection. The characters between the two boundaries appear highlighted. Another way to select text is to click the SELECT key at one boundary and then click ADJUST (the middle button by default) at the other boundary. The highlighted text can then be either cut or copied. This is done by pressing MENU on the TextEdit. A menu pops-up with several choices including cut and copy. Once the selection has been cut or copied it can be pasted. Position the cursor where desired and choose paste from the pop-up menu. It's very likely that your keyboard includes keys which will accomplish the same actions as the pop-up menu actions.

The drag and drop facility also requires that text be selected as described above. After the text is selected, press the SELECT mouse button with the pointer on the selection and move the pointer to the desired insertion point. As the pointer is moved, the cursor changes to the shape of a *flying punchcard*. When the SELECT button is released the drop occurs.

The TextEdit widget can be used whenever there is need for user input. It is highly configurable. Some of its resources are:

- **XtNbottomMargin, XtNtopMargin, XtNleftMargin, XtNrightMargin**: The number of pixels used for the bottom, top, left, and right margins respectively.
- **XtNbuttons**: The callback list used when a mouse button is pressed in the TextEdit widget.
- **XtNcharsVisible**: The number of characters visible. This overrides the **XtNwidth** resource. This resource can only be set at initialization time.
- **XtNcursorPosition**: The position of the cursor in the text buffer.
- **XtNdisplayPosition**: The position in the text buffer that is displayed at the top of the pane.
- **XtNeditType**: The state of the source text buffer. Valid values are:
  - **OL_TEXT_READ/"textread"**: The text is read-only. It cannot be edited.
  - **OL_TEXT_EDIT/"textedit"**: The text is editable. This is the default.
- **XtNgrowMode**: The resize policy of the TextEdit widget. Valid values are:
  - **OL_GROW_OFF/"off"**: The widget does not grow either horizontally or vertically when text exceeds window boundaries. This is the default.
  - **OL_GROW_HORIZONTAL/"horizontal"**: The widget grows horizontally if text exceeds the window's width. **XtNwrapMode** must be **OL_WRAP_OFF**.
  - **OL_GROW_VERTICAL/"vertical"**: The widget grows vertically if text exceeds the window's height.
  - **OL_GROW_BOTH/"both"**: The widget grow both horizontally and vertically if text exceeds window's width and height. **XtNwrapMode** must be **OL_WRAP_OFF**.
- **XtNinsertTab**: The policy regarding insertion of tabs into the TextField widget.
  - **TRUE**: TAB characters are inserted into the text buffer.
  - **FALSE**: TAB characters are not inserted in the text buffer. Instead they are used to indicate traversal to the next input field.
- **XtNkeys**: The callback list used when a key is pressed in the TextEdit widget.

- **XtNlinesVisible**: The initial number of lines displayed in the TextEdit widget.
- **XtNmodifyVerification**: The callback list used when a modification to the text buffer is attempted.
- **XtNmotionVerification**: The callback list used when a the cursor position moves with the TextEdit widget.
- **XtNsource**: The source to be loaded into the text buffer.
- **XtNsourceType**: The type that the **XtNsource** resources specifies. Valid values are:
  — **OL_STRING_SOURCE/"stringsrc"**: The **XtNsource** resource is interpreted as the string of characters to load into the text buffer. This is the default.
  — **OL_DISK_SOURCE/"disksrc"**: The **XtNsource** resource is interpreted as the file name to load.
  — **OL_TEXT_BUFFER_SOURCE/"buffersrc"**: The **XtNsource** resource is interpreted as a pointer to a **TextBuffer** structure.
- **XtNwrapMode**: The wrapping policy enforced by the TextEdit widget. Valid values are:
  — **OL_WRAP_ANY/"wrapany"**: Wrap at any point when the character reaches the right margin.
  — **OL_WRAP_WHITE_SPACE/"wrapwhitespace"**: Wrap only at white space when the character reaches the right margin. This is the default.
  — **OL_WRAP_OFF/"wrapoff"**: Do not wrap.

The **textedit** example demonstrates a few of the TextEdit widget's features. Two buttons are included. One clears the contents of the TextEdit widget, the other extracts the contents of the widget and prints it on the screen. An **XtNmotionVerification** callback is registered. If the checkbox is set the callback prints the contents of the **OlTextMotionCallData** structure which is passed as **call_data**. This structure is defined as:

```
typedef struct {
    Boolean          ok;
    TextPosition     current_cursor;
    TextPosition     new_cursor;
    TextPosition     select_start;
    TextPosition     select_end;
} OlTextMotionCallData, *OlTextMotionCallDataPointer;
```

If the **ok** member is set to FALSE in the callback, the motion does not take effect. The other fields represent the position of the cursor and the selection.

The **textedit** program requires a filename be included on the command line. This file is then loaded into the TextEdit widget by setting **XtNsource** to the name of the command line argument. The **XtNsourceType** resource is set to **OL_DISK_SOURCE** to indicate the value of the **XtNsource** resource represents a file on disk.

```
/**********************************************************
 * textedit.c: Demonstrate the TextEdit widget.
 **********************************************************/
#include <X11/Intrinsic.h>
#include <X11/StringDefs.h>
#include <Xol/OpenLook.h>
#include <Xol/ControlAre.h>
#include <Xol/TextEdit.h>
#include <Xol/OblongButt.h>
#include <Xol/RubberTile.h>
#include <Xol/CheckBox.h>

main(argc, argv)
  int argc;
  char *argv[];
{
  Widget  toplevel, te, clear, retrieve, con, rt, cb;
  void    clear_callback(), insert_callback(),
          getbuffer_callback(), verify_callback(),
          motionverify_callback();
  String  filename = NULL;
  Arg     wargs[3];
  int     n;

  toplevel = OlInitialize(argv[0], "Textedit", NULL, 0, &argc, argv);
  if(argc < 2) {
    printf("Usage: textedit filename\n");
    exit(0);
  }
  /*
   * Create the RubberTile and ControlArea widgets.
   */
  rt = XtCreateManagedWidget("rt", rubberTileWidgetClass,
                                toplevel, NULL, 0);
  con = XtCreateManagedWidget("con", controlAreaWidgetClass,
                                rt, NULL, 0);
  /*
   * Get command line argument, if any, and create TextEdit widget
   */
  filename = argv[1];
  if(filename) {
    n = 0;
    XtSetArg(wargs[n], XtNsource, filename); n++;
    XtSetArg(wargs[n], XtNsourceType, OL_DISK_SOURCE); n++;
  }
  te = XtCreateManagedWidget("te", textEditWidgetClass,
                                rt, wargs, n);
```

```
      clear = XtCreateManagedWidget("clear", oblongButtonWidgetClass,
                                 con, NULL, 0);
      XtAddCallback(clear, XtNselect, clear_callback, te);
      retrieve = XtCreateManagedWidget("retrieve",
                                       oblongButtonWidgetClass,
                                       con, NULL, 0);
      XtAddCallback(retrieve, XtNselect, getbuffer_callback, te);
      cb = XtCreateManagedWidget("cb", checkBoxWidgetClass,
                                 con, NULL, 0);
      XtAddCallback(te, XtNmotionVerification, motionverify_callback, cb);

      XtRealizeWidget(toplevel);
      XtMainLoop();
  }
```

The **clear_callback()** callback calls **OlTextEditClearBuffer()** to clear the contents of the TextEdit widget.

```
  void
  clear_callback(w, client_data, call_data)
    Widget w;
    XtPointer client_data, call_data;
  {
    Widget te = (Widget)client_data;

    (void)OlTextEditClearBuffer(te);
  }
```

The **getbuffer_callback()** callback uses **OlTextEditCopybuffer()** to copy the contents of the TextEdit widget and print it to the screen. The widget allocates the storage to copy the buffer into, and leaves it to the application to free that storage.

```
  void
  getbuffer_callback(w, client_data, call_data)
    Widget w;
    XtPointer client_data, call_data;
  {
    Widget te = (Widget)client_data;
    Boolean retval;
    char *buffer;

    retval = OlTextEditCopyBuffer(te, &buffer);
    if(retval == FALSE) {
      printf("Unable to retrieve buffer\n");
      return;
    }
    printf("buffer = %s\n", buffer);
    XtFree(buffer);
  }
```

The `motionverify_callback()` callback procedure prints the contents of the `OlTextMotionCallData` structure if the CheckBox widget is set.

```
void
motionverify_callback(w, client_data, call_data)
  Widget w;
  XtPointer client_data, call_data;
{
  OlTextMotionCallData *tmcd = (OlTextMotionCallData *)call_data;
  Widget checkbox = (Widget)client_data;
  Arg wargs[1];
  Boolean set;

  XtSetArg(wargs[0], XtNset, &set);
  XtGetValues(checkbox, wargs, 1);
  if(set)
    printf("%s %d, %s = %d, %s = %d, %s = %d, %s = %d\n",
            "ok", tmcd->ok,
            "current_cursor", tmcd->current_cursor,
            "new_cursor", tmcd->new_cursor,
            "select_start", tmcd->select_start,
            "select_end", tmcd->select_end);
}
```

Figure 4.36 shows the `textedit` program with the following resources set:

```
! TextEdit
Textedit*te.background:       white
Textedit*te.borderWidth:      1
Textedit*te.font:             lucidasans-typewriter
! OblongButtons
Textedit*clear.label:         Clear
Textedit*retrieve.label:      Retrieve
! CheckBox motion
Textedit*cb.label:            Print Motion:
Textedit*cb.font:             lucidasans-bold
!
Textedit*con.weight:          0
```

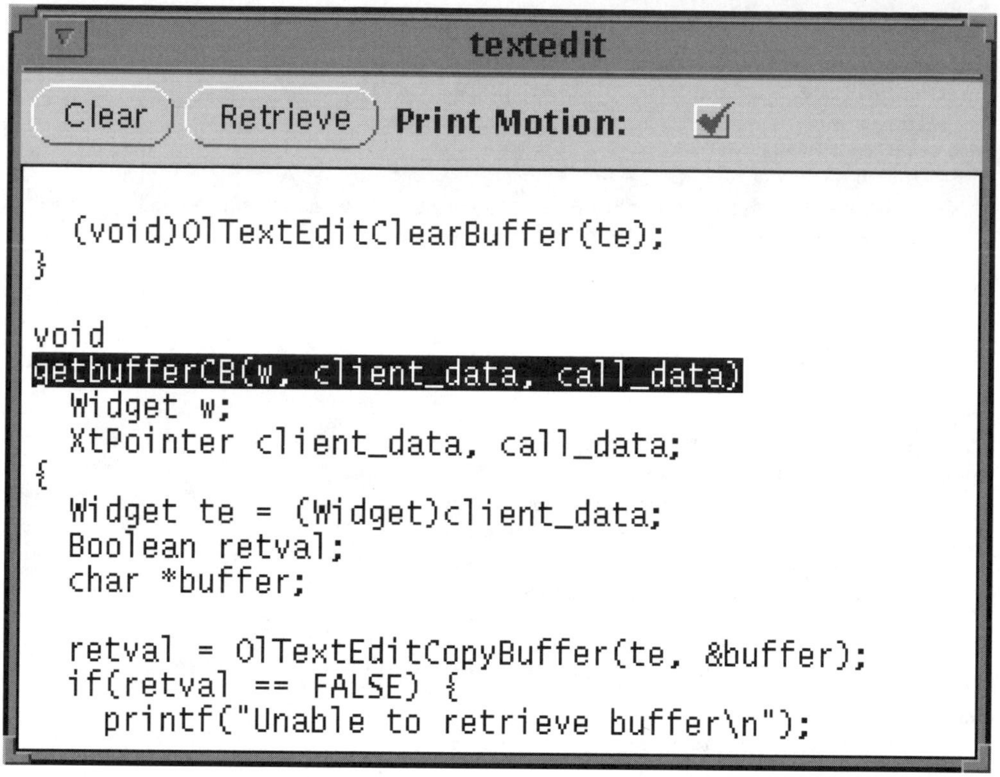

Figure 4.36 The textedit program with text selected.

Some of the other functions available for operation on the TextEdit widget are:

`OlTextEditClearBuffer()`	Clears the TextEdit buffer.
`OlTextEditCopyBuffer()`	Copies the TextEdit buffer.
`OlTextEditCopySelection()`	Copies the current selection.
`OlTextEditRedraw()`	Refreshes the TextEdit display.
`OlTextEditGetCursorPosition()`	Returns the cursor position.
`OlTextEditSetCursorPosition()`	Set the cursor position.
`OlTextEditInsert()`	Inserts a string in the TextEdit widget.
`OlTextEditPaste()`	Paste the contents of the CLIPBOARD.

4.3.5   Container Widgets

The Container widgets, like the Manager widgets discussed in the last section, are a subclass of the Manager meta-class. The Container widgets manage one or more children but are usually not used for managing the layout of an entire application as would the Form or ControlArea.The Container widgets generally manage their children in order to create a desired behavior or layout of a specific set of children widgets. The OLIT Container widgets are:

Caption	Exclusives	Nonexclusives
FlatExclusives	FlatNonexclusives	FlatCheckBox
ScrolledWindow	ScrollingList	

The following sections discuss each of these OLIT Container widgets.

4.3.5.1   The Caption Widget

The Caption widget is used to create a label for any child widget. The position and alignment of the label is determined by the Caption resources. Multiple Caption labels can also be aligned with each other when used in conjunction with a ControlArea. The ControlArea includes the `XtNalignCaptions` resource which aligns the labels of all child Caption widgets.

Some of the more common resources for the Caption are:

- `XtNalignment`: The alignment of the label with respect to its child widget. Valid values are:
  - `OL_LEFT`/`"left"`: The left edge of the label is aligned with the left edge of the child.
  - `OL_TOP`/`"top"`: The top edge of the label is aligned with the top edge of the child.
  - `OL_CENTER`/`"center"`: The center of the label is aligned with the center of the child. This is the default.
  - `OL_RIGHT`/`"right"`: The right edge of the label is aligned with the right edge of the child.
  - `OL_BOTTOM`/`"bottom"`: The bottom edge of the label is aligned with the bottom edge of the child.
- `XtNlabel`: The string used as the label.
- `XtNposition`: The position that the label is placed in. Valid values are:.
  - `OL_LEFT`/`"left"`: The label is placed to the left of the child widget. This is the default.
  - `OL_TOP`/`"top"`: The label is placed above the child widget.
  - `OL_RIGHT`/`"right"`: The label is placed to the right of the child widget.
  - `OL_BOTTOM`/`"bottom"`: The label is placed below the child widget.
- `XtNspace`: The distance between the label and the child widget.

The `caption` program demonstrates the Caption widget. We reuse the Celsius to Fahrenheit converter program from Section 4.3.2.7. This time we create two Caption widgets. The Slider and Gauge widgets will each be a child of one of the Caption widgets.

```
/************************************************************
 * caption.c: Demonstrate the Caption widget.
 ************************************************************/
#include <X11/Intrinsic.h>
#include <X11/StringDefs.h>
#include <Xol/OpenLook.h>
```

```
#include <Xol/ControlAre.h>
#include <Xol/Slider.h>
#include <Xol/Gauge.h>
#include <Xol/Caption.h>

main(argc, argv)
  int argc;
  char *argv[];
{
  void      slider_callback();
  Widget    toplevel, con, slider, gauge, cap_slider, cap_gauge;

  toplevel = OlInitialize(argv[0], "Caption", NULL, 0, &argc, argv);
  con = XtCreateManagedWidget("control", controlAreaWidgetClass,
                              toplevel, NULL, 0);
  /*
   * Create the caption widgets
   */
  cap_slider = XtCreateManagedWidget("cap_slider", captionWidgetClass,
                                     con, NULL, 0);
  cap_gauge = XtCreateManagedWidget("cap_gauge", captionWidgetClass,
                                    con, NULL, 0);
  /*
   * Create a slider and a gauge widget
   */
  slider = XtCreateManagedWidget("slider", sliderWidgetClass,
                                 cap_slider, NULL, 0);
  gauge = XtCreateManagedWidget("gauge", gaugeWidgetClass,
                                cap_gauge, NULL, 0);
  XtAddCallback(slider, XtNsliderMoved, slider_callback, gauge);

  XtRealizeWidget(toplevel);
  XtMainLoop();
}
```

The **slider_callback()** callback is identical to the one shown in Section 4.3.2.7, so it is not repeated here. We set the resources on the Caption so that the label is placed on the left of the child widget (default) and is aligned with the top of the child widget. Notice that the **XtNalignCaptions** resource of the ControlArea is set to TRUE which aligns the right edge of each Caption label. With the following set of resources the **caption** program is displayed as shown in Figure 4.38.

```
Caption*Caption.font:           lucidasans-bold
Caption*Control*alignCaptions:  TRUE
Caption*cap_slider.label:       Celsius:
Caption*cap_gauge.label:        Fahrenheit:
Caption*Caption*alignment:      top
Caption*orientation:            horizontal
```

```
Caption*control.layoutType:        fixedcols
Caption*control.measure:           1
Caption*control.sameSize:          none
!
Caption*slider.width:              100
Caption*slider.sliderMax:          100
Caption*slider.maxLabel:           100
Caption*slider.minLabel:           0
Caption*slider.tickUnit:           slidervalue
Caption*slider.ticks:              20
Caption*slider.endBoxes:           FALSE
Caption*gauge.width:               212
Caption*gauge.sliderMax:           220
Caption*gauge.sliderMin:           0
Caption*gauge.sliderValue:         32
Caption*gauge.maxLabel:            220
Caption*gauge.minLabel:            0
Caption*gauge.tickUnit:            slidervalue
Caption*gauge.ticks:               10
```

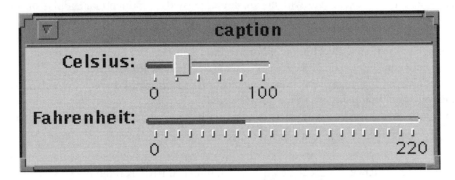

Figure 4.37 Celsius to Fahrenheit converter program with Captions

Changing the Captions to be above their children and centering the ControlArea's children results in the layout shown in Figure 4.38.

```
Caption*Caption*position:          top
Caption*control.center:            TRUE
!The rest of the resources the same as above
...
```

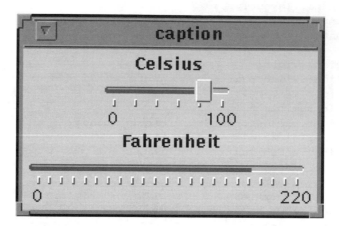

Figure 4.38 Caption program with labels centered and above children.

4.3.5.2   The Exclusives and Nonexclusives Widgets

The Exclusives and Nonexclusives widgets are container widgets which manage one or more Rect-Button or CheckBox widgets. The Exclusives widget manages RectButton widgets and provides a one-of-many button selection mechanism. Only one of the buttons parented by the Exclusives widget may be selected at once. RectButton children of an Exclusives widget are laid out such that there is no space between them. The Nonexclusives widget manages RectButton or CheckBox widgets and provides a several-of-many selection mechanism. RectButton children of a Nonexclusives widget are laid out such that there is a space between each.

The layout of the children widgets is handled with the same resources as the ControlArea:

- **XtNlayoutType**: The layout type of the Exclusives or Nonexclusives. Four values are supported:
  - **OL_FIXEDROWS/"fixedrows"**: The number of rows is fixed by **XtNmeasure**.
  - **OL_FIXEDCOLS/"fixedcols"**: The number of columns is fixed by **XtNmeasure**.
  - **OL_FIXEDWIDTH/"fixedwidth"**: The width is fixed by **XtNmeasure**.
  - **OL_FIXEDHEIGHT/"fixedheight"**: The height is fixed by **XtNmeasure**.
- **XtNmeasure**: The size of the Exclusives or Nonexclusives based on the **XtNlayoutType** resource.

The Exclusives widget also provides one other resources of interest which controls whether a button is required to be set.

- **XtNnoneSet**: The policy controlling whether a button can be unset directly.
  - **TRUE**: The Exclusives widget may have children, none of which is set.
  - **FALSE**: The Exclusives widget must have exactly one of its children set at all times.

The **fontchooser** program uses both Exclusives and Nonexclusives widgets. A font type, colors, and scale can be selected via RectButtons contained in an Exclusives widget. A Nonexclusives widget manages two buttons which control the italics and bold features of the font displayed.

In this example we use the varargs versions of the Intrinsics calls such as **XtVaCreateManagedWidget()** and **XtVaSetValues()**. These functions are particularly useful when setting colors and fonts because they handle automatic type conversion. Nearly all of the resources for this application are set programmatically to illustrate how to use the varargs functions.

The file fontchooser.h defines the strings used to specify fonts and declares the **fontchoice** structure.

```
/***********************************************************
 * fontchooser.h: Header file for fontchooser.c
 ***********************************************************/
char *fonts[]  = { "lucidasans", "rockwell", "gillsans" };
char *styles[] = { "bold", "italic" };
char *colors[] = { "white", "black", "red", "green",
                   "blue", "yellow" };
char *scales[] = { "10", "12", "14", "18", "24", "36" };

#define BOLDINDEX 0
#define ITALICINDEX 1

typedef struct Fontchoice {
  String font;
  Boolean bold;
  Boolean italic;
  String fontcolor;
  String bgcolor;
  String scale;
} fontchoice;
```

The file fontchooser.c contains the main body of the program. It calls **create_ex_nonex()** which creates either an Exclusives or Nonexclusives widget depending on the arguments passed. A StaticText widget is used to display the current font choice.

```
/***********************************************************
 * fontchooser.c: Demonstrate the Exclusives and
 *                Nonexclusives widgets.
 ***********************************************************/
#include <X11/Intrinsic.h>
#include <X11/StringDefs.h>
#include <Xol/OpenLook.h>
#include <Xol/ControlAre.h>
#include <Xol/Exclusives.h>
#include <Xol/Nonexclusi.h>
```

```
#include <Xol/Caption.h>
#include <Xol/RectButton.h>
#include <Xol/StaticText.h>
#include "fontchooser.h"

static Widget st, font, style, fontcolor, bgcolor, scale;
static fontchoice *fc;

main(argc, argv)
  int argc;
  char *argv[];
{
  Widget       toplevel, con, font_rb[4], style_rb[2],
               fc_rb[6], bg_rb[6], scale_rb[6];
  void         font_callback(), scale_callback(),
               fontcolor_callback(), bgcolor_callback(),
               style_callback(), create_ex_nonex(),
               default_choice(), set_font();

  /*
   * Initialize the fontchoice structure
   */
  fc      = (fontchoice *)XtMalloc(sizeof(fontchoice));
  default_choice(fc);
  toplevel = OlInitialize(argv[0], "Fontchooser", NULL, 0,
                          &argc, argv);
  con = XtVaCreateManagedWidget("control",
                                controlAreaWidgetClass,
                                toplevel,
                                XtNalignCaptions, TRUE,
                                XtNlayoutType,    OL_FIXEDCOLS,
                                XtNmeasure,       1,
                                NULL);
  /*
   * Create Exclusives and Nonexclusives widgets
   */
  create_ex_nonex(con, font_rb, fonts, XtNumber(fonts),
                  "Font:", exclusivesWidgetClass,
                  font_callback);
  create_ex_nonex(con, style_rb, styles, XtNumber(styles),
                  "Style:", nonexclusivesWidgetClass,
                  style_callback);
  create_ex_nonex(con, fc_rb, colors, XtNumber(colors),
                  "Font Color:", exclusivesWidgetClass,
                  fontcolor_callback);
  create_ex_nonex(con, bg_rb, colors, XtNumber(colors),
                  "Background Color:", exclusivesWidgetClass,
```

```
                          bgcolor_callback);
    create_ex_nonex(con, scale_rb, scales, XtNumber(scales),
                    "Scale:", exclusivesWidgetClass,
                    scale_callback);
    /*
     * Create the StaticText widget used to display the font
     */
    st = XtVaCreateManagedWidget("st", staticTextWidgetClass,
                                 con,
                                 XtNborderWidth, 4,
                                 NULL);

    set_font(st);
    XtRealizeWidget(toplevel);
    XtMainLoop();
}
```

The **create_ex_nonex()** function creates either an Exclusives or Nonexclusives widget depending on the **class** argument. Because a layout type is not specified, the layout of the Exclusives and Nonexclusives defaults to arranging its children in a single row. The function first creates a Caption widget followed by either the Exclusives or Nonexclusives widget. Then the RectButtons are created and the callbacks registered. For each of the RectButtons, the client data passed to its callback is the name used for the label. This string is used to construct the font name.

```
void
create_ex_nonex(parent, buttons, names, number,
                        label, class, callback)
  Widget       parent, buttons[];
  char         *names[];
  int          number;
  String       label;
  WidgetClass  class;
  void         (*callback)();
{
  Widget caption, ex_nonex;
  int    i;

  /* Create Exclusives or Nonexclusives widgets */
  caption = XtVaCreateManagedWidget("", captionWidgetClass,
                          parent,
                          XtNlabel, label,
                          NULL);
  ex_nonex = XtVaCreateManagedWidget("", class,
                          caption, NULL);
  for(i=0;i<number;i++) {
    buttons[i] = XtVaCreateManagedWidget(names[i],
                          rectButtonWidgetClass,
                          ex_nonex, NULL);

    if(callback != NULL)
```

```
        XtAddCallback(buttons[i], XtNselect, callback, names[i]);
      if(class == nonexclusivesWidgetClass)
        XtAddCallback(buttons[i], XtNunselect, callback,
                      names[i]);
    }
  }
```

Each of the callback functions sets a field in the **fontchoice** structure and calls the **set_font()** function. The **set_font()** function updates the StaticText widget which displays the font selections.

```
void
font_callback(w, client_data, call_data)
  Widget    w;
  XtPointer client_data, call_data;
{
  void set_font();

  fc->font = (String)client_data;
  set_font(st);
}

void
scale_callback(w, client_data, call_data)
  Widget w;
  XtPointer client_data, call_data;
{
  void set_font();

  fc->scale = (String)client_data;
  set_font(st);
}

void
fontcolor_callback(w, client_data, call_data)
  Widget    w;
  XtPointer client_data, call_data;
{
  void set_font();

  fc->fontcolor = (String)client_data;
  set_font(st);
}

void
bgcolor_callback(w, client_data, call_data)
  Widget    w;
  XtPointer client_data, call_data;
```

```
{
  void set_font();

  fc->bgcolor = (String)client_data;
  set_font(st);
}
```

The **style_callback()** function must do some extra checking because it is the callback for the Nonexclusives widget. This function is registered for both the **XtNselect** and **XtNunselect** action. The state of the button is retrieved and then the **fontchoice** structure updated.

```
void
style_callback(w, client_data, call_data)
  Widget     w;
  XtPointer client_data, call_data;
{
  static Boolean italic = FALSE, bold = FALSE;
  void set_font();

  /*
   * Get the current state of the buttons
   */
  if(strcmp(client_data, "italic") == NULL)
    XtVaGetValues(w, XtNset, &italic, NULL);
  if(strcmp(client_data, "bold") == NULL)
    XtVaGetValues(w, XtNset, &bold, NULL);
  fc->italic = italic;
  fc->bold = bold;
  set_font(st);
}
```

The **default_font()** function is called from the main to initialize the **fontchoice** structure.

```
void
default_choice(fchoice)
  fontchoice *fchoice;
{
  fchoice->font       = fonts[0];
  fchoice->bold       = FALSE;
  fchoice->italic     = FALSE;
  fchoice->fontcolor  = colors[0];
  fchoice->bgcolor    = colors[0];
  fchoice->scale      = scales[0];
}
```

The **set_font()** function updates the StaticText display that shows the font, style, color, and scale. The call to **XtVaSetValues()** uses the **XtVaTypedArg** parameter to handle the conversion of a string to font, and string to color. This technique is very convenient when doing conversions. The **XtVaTypedArg** is followed by the resource name, the type to convert it to, the name, and finally the size. The call to **XtVaSetValues()** in this procedures contains three such conversions: one for font and two for color.

```
void
set_font(w)
  Widget w;
{
  char    fontname[64];

  /*
   * Create the string for the font name
   */
  sprintf(fontname, "%s%s%s%s-%s",
                  fc->font,
                  ((fc->bold || fc->italic) ? "-" : ""),
                  (fc->bold ? "bold" : ""),
                  (fc->italic ? "italic" : ""),
                  fc->scale);
  /*
   * Set the values from the fontchoice structure
   */
  XtVaSetValues(w,
                  XtNstring, fontname,
                  XtVaTypedArg, XtNfont, XtRString,
                  fontname, strlen(fontname)+1,
                  XtVaTypedArg, XtNfontColor, XtRString,
                  fc->fontcolor, strlen(fc->fontcolor)+1,
                  XtVaTypedArg, XtNbackground, XtRString,
                  fc->bgcolor, strlen(fc->bgcolor)+1,
                  NULL);
}
```

We set just one resource in our resources file to set the font for all Captions. With this resource set the program is displayed as shown in Figure 4.39.

```
Fontchooser*Caption.font:        lucidasans-bold
```

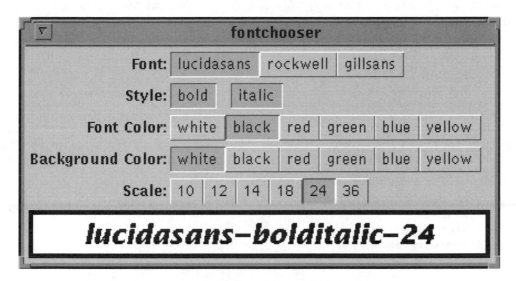

Figure 4.39 The `fontchooser` program.

4.3.5.3   The Flat Widgets

Flat widgets are designed to provide the identical functionality to the Exclusives and Nonexclusives widgets. Rather than creating individual RectButton or CheckBox widgets as children of a container widget, the Flat widgets create *sub-objects* that have the same behavior as either RectButtons or CheckBoxes. Flat widgets are especially useful when managing a large number of sub-objects. Fewer widgets need be created which implies fewer resources and better performance.

There are three types of Flat widgets: FlatCheckBox, FlatExclusives, and FlatNonexclusives. The behavior of these three widgets is identical to: 1) a Nonexclusives managing CheckBox widgets, 2) an Exclusives managing RectButtons, and 3) a Nonexclusives managing RectButtons, respectively. The programmatic interface for the three Flat widgets is nearly identical. There are only a very few differences between the Flat widgets, one of which is that FlatExclusives supports an **XtNnoneSet** resource and the other two do not.

One of the advantages of using Flat widgets is the savings in memory. Each widget created consumes resources that can affect performance. For example, one Flat widget can take the place of an Exclusives and several RectButton children. The example in the last section created 1 Nonexclusives, 4 Exclusives, and 23 RectButton widgets for a total of 28 widgets. In this section we recreate the **fontchooser** program, replacing 28 widgets with 5 Flat widgets. A Flat widget does allocate some memory for each sub-object but much less than is allocated by a widget. As the number of widgets increases so does the potential savings by using Flat widgets.

The key to understanding the Flat widgets is the application defined data structures that must be created to indicate and set the resources for each sub-object. For example, if an application required that the label and font color resources be available for the Flat widgets sub-objects, and that a callback procedure be called when the sub-object is set, a structure identifying these elements would be required, such as:

```
typedef struct {
  XtArgVal label;
  XtArgVal fontColor;
  XtArgVal selectProc;
} FlatItems;
```

Each field of the structure represents one *item* or resource that the application can set for each sub-object. The **XtNitems** resource is set to the address of this structure. In addition, another data structure defines the list of resource names that correspond to the item fields. The **XtNitem-Fields** resources is set to the address of this list.

```
String FlatFields[] = {
  XtNlabel,
  XtNfontColor,
  XtNselectProc,
};
```

The order of the resources named in these two data structure must correspond.

Before the Flat widget is created the items list must be set to the appropriate resources. An array of item structures is usually declared:

```
FlatItems Items[6];
```

Each element of the array represents the resources for one sub-object of the Flat widget. After the array of items is initialized the Flat widget is created.

The Flat widgets have many resources. Many of them are familiar resources identical to those for RectButtons and CheckBoxes. Some of the resources that apply specifically to Flat widgets are:

- **XtNclientData**: The client data passed to the callback procedure.
- **XtNitems**: The list of sub-object items.
- **XtNitemFields**: The list of resource names that match the fields in the **XtNitems** list.
- **XtNitemsTouched**: Indicates that the list of sub-object items has been updated.
- **XtNnumItems**: The number of sub-object items specified by the **XtNitems** resource.
- **XtNnumItemFields**: The number of resource names specified by the **XtNitemsFields** resource.
- **XtNselectProc**: The callback procedure called when the sub-object is set.
- **XtNunselectProc**: The callback procedure called when the sub-object is unset.

The **flfontchooser** program is identical in operation to the **fontchooser** program shown in the previous section on Exclusives and Nonexclusives. It uses both FlatExclusives and FlatNonexclusives widgets. The resources of interest are **XtNlabel**, **XtNselectProc**, **XtNun-selectProc**, and **XtNclientData**. The **FlatItems** and **FlatFields** structures are designed to use these resources.

The file flfontchooser.h defines the strings used to specify fonts and declares the **fontchoice** structure. It also declares the **FlatItems** structure and the **FlatFields** strings that are used specifically with Flat widgets.

```
/***********************************************************
 * flfontchooser.h: Header file for flfontchooser.c
 ***********************************************************/
char *fonts[]  = { "lucidasans", "rockwell", "gillsans" };
char *styles[] = { "bold", "italic" };
char *colors[] = { "white", "black", "red", "green",
                   "blue", "yellow" };
char *scales[] = { "10", "12", "14", "18", "24", "36" };

#define BOLDINDEX 0
#define ITALICINDEX 1

typedef struct {
  XtArgVal label;
  XtArgVal selectProc;
  XtArgVal unselectProc;
  XtArgVal clientData;
} FlatItems;

FlatItems fontItems[3], styleItems[2], bgColorItems[6],
          fontColorItems[6], scaleItems[6];

String FlatFields[] = {
  XtNlabel,
  XtNselectProc,
  XtNunselectProc,
  XtNclientData,
};

typedef struct Fontchoice {
  String font;
  Boolean bold;
  Boolean italic;
  String fontcolor;
  String bgcolor;
  String scale;
} fontchoice;
```

The main body of the **flfontchooser** program is very similar to that of the **fontchooser** program from the previous section. One main difference is the call to **create_fl_ex_nonex()** which creates either a FlatExclusives or FlatNonexclusives widget.

```
/***********************************************************
 * flfontchooser.c: Demonstrate the FlatExclusives and
 *                  FlatNonexclusives widgets.
 ***********************************************************/
#include <X11/Intrinsic.h>
#include <X11/StringDefs.h>
#include <Xol/OpenLook.h>
#include <Xol/ControlAre.h>
#include <Xol/FExclusive.h>
#include <Xol/FNonexclus.h>
#include <Xol/Caption.h>
#include <Xol/RectButton.h>
#include <Xol/StaticText.h>
#include "flfontchooser.h"

static Widget st, font, style, fontcolor, bgcolor, scale;
static fontchoice *fc;

main(argc, argv)
  int argc;
  char *argv[];
{
  Widget     toplevel, con, create_fl_ex_nonex();
  void       font_callback(), scale_callback(),
             fontcolor_callback(), bgcolor_callback(),
             style_callback(), default_choice(), set_font();

  /*
   * Initialize the fontchoice structure
   */
  fc      = (fontchoice *)XtMalloc(sizeof(fontchoice));
  default_choice(fc);
  toplevel = OlInitialize(argv[0], "Flfontchooser", NULL, 0,
                          &argc, argv);
  con = XtVaCreateManagedWidget("control",
                                controlAreaWidgetClass,
                                toplevel,
                                XtNalignCaptions, TRUE,
                                XtNlayoutType,    OL_FIXEDCOLS,
                                XtNmeasure,       1,
                                NULL);
  /*
   * Create FlatExclusives and FlatNonexclusives widgets
   */
  font      = create_fl_ex_nonex(con, fontItems, fonts,
                XtNumber(fonts), "Font:",
                flatExclusivesWidgetClass, font_callback);
```

```
    style       = create_fl_ex_nonex(con, styleItems, styles,
                     XtNumber(styles), "Style:",
                     flatNonexclusivesWidgetClass, style_callback);
    fontcolor = create_fl_ex_nonex(con, fontColorItems,
                     colors, XtNumber(colors),
                     "Font Color:", flatExclusivesWidgetClass,
                     fontcolor_callback);
    bgcolor     = create_fl_ex_nonex(con, bgColorItems, colors,
                     XtNumber(colors), "Background Color:",
                     flatExclusivesWidgetClass, bgcolor_callback);
    scale       = create_fl_ex_nonex(con, scaleItems, scales,
                     XtNumber(scales),
                     "Scale:", flatExclusivesWidgetClass,
                     scale_callback);
    /*
     * Create the StaticText widget used to display the font
     */
    st = XtVaCreateManagedWidget("st", staticTextWidgetClass,
                                    con,
                                    XtNborderWidth, 4,
                                    NULL);
    set_font(st);
    XtRealizeWidget(toplevel);
    XtMainLoop();
}
```

The `create_fl_ex_nonex()` function creates either a FlatExclusives or FlatNonexclusives widget depending on the `class` argument. Before the Flat widget is created the `flitems` structure must be initialized with the appropriate resource values. Rather than calling `XtAddCallback()`, the `selectProc` field of the `flitems` structures is set to point to the callback function. The same procedure applies for the `unselectProc` field.

The `XtNitems` resource is set to `flitems` which includes the resources for all the sub-objects of this Flat widget. The `XtNnumItems` resources is set to the number of sub-objects that are to be created. The `XtNitemFields` resource is set to `FlatFields`, which is the structure that includes the resources names. The `XtNnumItemFields` is set to the number of elements in the `FlatFields` structure.

```
Widget
create_fl_ex_nonex(parent, flitems, names, number,
                                label, class, callback)
    Widget      parent;
    FlatItems   *flitems;
    char        *names[];
    int         number;
    String      label;
    WidgetClass class;
    void        (*callback)();
```

```
{
  Widget caption, fl_ex_nonex;
  int    i;

  /* Create Exclusives widgets */
  caption = XtVaCreateManagedWidget("", captionWidgetClass,
                     parent,
                     XtNlabel, label,
                     NULL);
  for(i=0;i<number;i++) {
    (flitems[i]).label = (XtArgVal)names[i];
    (flitems[i]).selectProc = (XtArgVal)callback;
    if(class == flatNonexclusivesWidgetClass)
      (flitems[i]).unselectProc = (XtArgVal)callback;
    else
      (flitems[i]).unselectProc = (XtArgVal)NULL;
    (flitems[i]).clientData = (XtArgVal)names[i];
  }
  fl_ex_nonex = XtVaCreateManagedWidget("", class, caption,
                     XtNitems, flitems,
                     XtNnumItems, number,
                     XtNitemFields, FlatFields,
                     XtNnumItemFields, XtNumber(FlatFields),
                     NULL);
  return(fl_ex_nonex);
}
```

The **font_callback()**, **fontColor_callback()**, **bgcolor_callback()**, and **scale_callback()** callback functions for the FlatExclusives widgets are identical to the version used for the Exclusives version in the previous section. The **default_choice()** and **set_font()** functions are also identical. The callback function for the FlatNonexclusives widget, **style_callback()**, must be slightly altered. This is necessary because the application cannot use **XtVaGetValues()** to retrieve a resource set on a sub-object. Instead, the function

```
OlFlatGetValues(widget, index, args, num_args)
```

is used to retrieve resource values from sub-objects. In this example, the varargs version is used:

```
OlVaFlatGetValues(widget, index, ... )
```

The arguments are identical to that of **XtGetValues()** and **XtVaGetValues()** with an additional argument which specifies the index of the sub-object to retrieve from.

The **style_callback()** function also demonstrates the use of the **call_data** which is a pointer to an **OlFlatCallData** structure. This is defined as:

```
typedef struct {
        Cardinal        item_index;   /* sub-object initiating callb. */
        XtPointer       items;        /* sub-object list              */
        Cardinal        num_items;    /* number of sub-objects        */
```

```
        String *       item_fields;    /* key of fields for list    */
        Cardinal       num_item_fields;/* number of item fields      */
        Cardinal       num_fields;     /* number of item fields      */
} OlFlatCallData;
```

The **OlFlatCallData** structure that **call_data** points to is the actual data passed to **XtCreateManagedWidget()** when the Flat widget was created. This data may be changed directly as long as the Flat widget is notified by setting the **XtNitemsTouched** resource to TRUE. In this example the **item_index** field of the **OlFlatCallData** is accessed to determine which button was pressed. This is compared with the previously defined constants **BOLDINDEX** and **ITALICINDEX**.

```
void
style_callback(w, client_data, call_data)
  Widget    w;
  XtPointer client_data, call_data;
{
  OlFlatCallData *olfcd = (OlFlatCallData *)call_data;
  static Boolean italic = FALSE, bold = FALSE;
  void set_font();

  /*
   * Get the current state of the buttons
   */
  if(olfcd->item_index == BOLDINDEX)
    OlVaFlatGetValues(w, BOLDINDEX, XtNset, &bold, NULL);
  if(olfcd->item_index == ITALICINDEX)
    OlVaFlatGetValues(w, ITALICINDEX, XtNset, &italic, NULL);
  fc->italic = italic;
  fc->bold = bold;
  set_font(st);
}
```

The application runs identically to the one created with Exclusives and Nonexclusives widgets in Section 4.3.5.2.

There are several functions for manipulating Flat widgets. These include:

OlFlatCallAcceptFocus()	Assign focus to specified sub-object.
OlFlatGetFocusItem()	Determine which sub-object has the focus.
OlFlatGetItemIndex()	Returns the sub-object that contains the given x and y coordinates.
OlFlatGetValues()	Similar to **XtGetvalues()** for Flat widgets.
OlFlatSetValues()	Similar to **XtSetvalues()** for Flat widgets.
OlVaFlatGetValues()	Similar to **XtVaGetvalues()** for Flat widgets.
OlVaFlatSetValues()	Similar to **XtVaSetvalues()** for Flat widgets.

4.3.5.4   The ScrolledWindow Widget

The ScrolledWindow widget provides a view of a text or graphics pane. The pane or contents of the ScrolledWindow can be larger than the viewing area. In this case, the ScrolledWindow provides horizontal and/or vertical scroll bars for panning the pane. The ScrolledWindow knows nothing inherently about its contents; it has no semantics regarding text or graphics. It simply provides a "window" into a larger widget.

The ScrolledWindow automatically creates or destroys horizontal and vertical scrollbars when needed. This is based on the size of the pane. For example, if the entire vertical height of the pane is displayed, then a vertical scrollbar is not needed. If the ScrolledWindow is resized such that part of the pane in the vertical direction is obscured, the ScrolledWindow displays a vertical scrollbar.

Some of the ScrolledWindow resources are:

- **XtNalignHorizontal, XtNalignVertical**: The placement of the scrollbars. By default the scrollbars are place at bottom and to the right.

- **XtNforceHorizontalSB, XtNforceVerticalSB**: Force attachment of scrollbars.

- **XtNinitialX, XtNinitialY**: The initial position of the upper left hand corner.

- **XtNviewWidth**: The preferred size of the view in pixels.

There are many other resources, most of which relate to the horizontal and vertical scrollbars.

The **textedit** program from Section 4.3.4.3 is a good candidate for including a Scrolled-Window. The new version, **scrolledwindow**, is nearly identical to **textedit** with the addition of a ScrolledWindow widget that serves as a parent to the TextEdit widget. One other change is to turn off wrapping on the TextEdit widget. If wrapping is not turned off, a horizontal scrollbar is never created. Little else in the program changes.

```
/***********************************************************
 * scrolledwindow.c: Demonstrate the ScrolledWindow widget.
 ***********************************************************/
#include <X11/Intrinsic.h>
#include <X11/StringDefs.h>
#include <Xol/OpenLook.h>
#include <Xol/ControlAre.h>
#include <Xol/TextEdit.h>
#include <Xol/StaticText.h>
#include <Xol/OblongButt.h>
#include <Xol/RubberTile.h>
#include <Xol/CheckBox.h>
#include <Xol/ScrolledWi.h>

main(argc, argv)
  int argc;
  char *argv[];
{
  Widget  toplevel, sw, te, clear, retrieve, con, rt, cb;
  void    clear_callback(), insert_callback(),
```

```
              getbuffer_callback(), verify_callback(),
              motionverify_callback();
String   filename = NULL;
Arg      wargs[3];
int      n;

toplevel = OlInitialize(argv[0], "Scrolledwindow", NULL, 0,
                        &argc, argv);
if(argc < 2) {
  printf("Usage: scrolledwindow filename\n");
  exit(0);
}
/*
 * Create the RubberTile and ControlArea widgets.
 */
rt = XtCreateManagedWidget("rt", rubberTileWidgetClass,
                           toplevel, NULL, 0);
con = XtCreateManagedWidget("con", controlAreaWidgetClass,
                            rt, NULL, 0);
/*
 * Get command line argument, if any, and create the
 * ScrolledWindow and TextEdit widgets
 */
sw = XtCreateManagedWidget("sw", scrolledWindowWidgetClass,
                           rt, NULL, 0);
filename = argv[1];
n = 0;
if(filename) {
  XtSetArg(wargs[n], XtNsource, filename); n++;
  XtSetArg(wargs[n], XtNsourceType, OL_DISK_SOURCE); n++;
}
XtSetArg(wargs[n], XtNwrapMode, OL_WRAP_OFF); n++;
te = XtCreateManagedWidget("te", textEditWidgetClass,
                           sw, wargs, n);

...
```

The remainder of the program is identical the to **textedit** program from Section 4.3.4.3. Figure 4.40 shows the layout of the **scrolledwindow** program using the resources as described in Section 4.3.4.3 with the exception that the class name **Textedit** is changed to **Scrolled-window**.

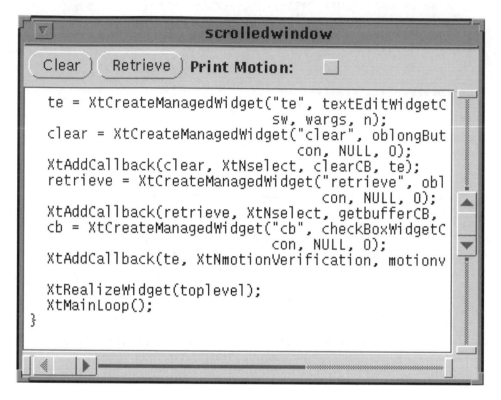

Figure 4.40 The ScrolledWindow widget with horizontal and vertical scrollbars.

4.3.5.5   The ScrollingList Widget

The ScrollingList widget displays a list of items in a scrollable pane and provides a sophisticated set of widget-defined functions for manipulating the items in the list. The key to understanding the ScrollingList is the set of widget-defined functions provided by the ScrollingList. These functions are used to do such things as add, delete, and edit items on the list. The functions are obtained by first creating the ScrollingList widget and then calling **XtGetValues()** on the resources which correspond to the functions. The seven widget-defined functions are retrieved by getting the values of the following resources:

XtNapplAddItem	XtNapplDeleteItem	XtNapplEditClose
XtNapplEditOpen	XtNapplTouchItem	XtNapplUpdateView
XtNapplViewItemf		

The value retrieved from **XtGetValues()** is a pointer to the widget-defined function. This value can then be used to call the appropriate function.

Each item that is added to the list requires an **OlListItem** structure, which is passed as an argument to the "AddItem" function. The **OlListItem** structure is defined as:

```
typedef struct _OlListItem {                    /* OPEN LOOK list item */
    OlDefine            label_type;
    XtPointer           label;
    XImage *            glyph;
    OlBitMask           attr;
    XtPointer           user_data;
    unsigned char       mnemonic;
} OlListItem;
```

The **label_type** field identifies what type of label is to be displayed in the list. Currently, the only type supported is **OL_STRING**. The **label** field contains the label to display in the list. The **glyph** field is unused. The **attr** field is a 32 bit field. The lower 16 bits are for application use and can be used by the application for any purpose. The upper 16 bits are used by the widget. When an item in the list is to be set, the application turns on the **OL_LIST_ATTR_CURRENT** bit in the **attr** field.

```
    Item->attr |= OL_LIST_ATTR_CURRENT;
```

The **OL_LIST_ATTR_CURRENT** constant corresponds to one of the bits in the upper 16 bits. This informs the widget that this item is set. The **user_data** field is available for any application-specific data, and finally, the **mnemonic** field is a single character that is used as a mnemonic accelerator. It is important to initialize all fields of the **OlListItem** structure before passing it to the "AddItem" function. Failure to do so can result in unwanted results.

It's important to understand the distinction between "setting" and "selecting" an item or items on a ScrollingList. Setting, or making an item current, is accomplished as shown above with the **OL_LIST_ATTR_CURRENT** bit of the **attr** field. The item on the list gives the appearance of being depressed like a RectButton. Setting an item is the responsibility of the application and is usually done in the **XtNuserMakeCurrent** callback procedure.

Selecting an item or items on a ScrollingList is equivalent to selecting text in a TextEdit widget. The text is highlighted and can then be cut or copied and pasted into another widget or application. This feature is handled by the widget and does not require intervention by the programmer. The ability to make items selectable can be turned off with the **XtNselectable** resource.

The "AddItem" function returns a "token" which uniquely identifies the item created. This token is usually stored in an application defined data structure. It is retrieved whenever an operation on that particular item is required.

The following is a list of some of the ScrollingList resources:

- **XtNapplAddItem**: The routine the application calls when it adds a new item to the list.

- **XtNapplDeleteItem**: The routine the application calls when it deletes an item from the list.

- **XtNapplEditClose**: The routine the application calls when the user finishes editing an item on the list.

- **XtNapplEditOpen**: The routine the application calls when the user begins editing an item on the list.

- **XtNapplTouchItem**: The routine the application calls when it changes an item on the list.

- **XtNapplUpdateView**: The routine the application calls to control whether changes made to the list are updated on the display immediately.
- **XtNapplViewItem**: The routine the application calls to adjust the list so that a set item is displayed in the view.
- **XtNselectable**: The selection policy. When TRUE items on the list can be selected with the SELECT and ADJUST keys and CUT or COPIED.
- **XtNtextField**: The TextField widget associated with the ScrollingList when editing an item.
- **XtNuserDeleteItems**: The callback list invoked when the user deletes items from the list via the selection mechanism.
- **XtNuserMakeCurrent**: The callback list invoked when the user presses SELECT over an item.
- **XtNviewHeight**: The number of items to display in the view area.

The **scrollinglist** program uses a ScrollingList widget to display the files in a directory specified on the command line. If a command line argument is not given, the application will examine the current directory. The application maintains a linked list of **file** structures that represent each file in the list.

```
typedef struct _file {
  String       filename;
  OlListToken   token;
  struct _file *next;
} file;
```

Any operation on an item in the list requires the **token** field which uniquely identifies the item. The token field is returned from the call to **(*AddItem)** which adds a new item to the list.

The **scrollinglist** program uses five of the widget-defined routines for manipulating items in the list. The application must first retrieve the pointers to these functions using **XtGetValues()**. For example, to get the **XtNapplAddItem** function the widget must first be created. Then **XtGetValues()** can be called on the **XtNapplAddItem** resource.

```
sl = XtCreateManagedWidget("sl", scrollingListWidgetClass,
                           rt, wargs, n);
n = 0;
XtSetArg(wargs[n], XtNapplAddItem, &AddItem); n++;
XtGetValues(sl, wargs, n);
```

The application uses a similar technique to get the other widget-defined functions. After the widget-defined functions are retrieved, an **XtNuserMakeCurrent** callback is registered and the other control buttons are created.

```
/************************************************************
 * scrollinglist.c: Demonstrate the ScrollingList widget.
 ************************************************************/
#include <X11/Intrinsic.h>
```

```
#include <X11/StringDefs.h>
#include <Xol/OpenLook.h>
#include <Xol/RubberTile.h>
#include <Xol/ScrollingL.h>
#include <Xol/ControlAre.h>
#include <Xol/OblongButt.h>
#include <sys/dirent.h>
#include <sys/dir.h>

OlListToken (*AddItem)();
void        (*DeleteItem)();
void        (*TouchItem)();
void        (*UpdateView)();
void        (*ViewItem)();

typedef struct _file {
  String        filename;
  OlListToken   token;
  struct _file *next;
} file;

file *head = NULL;      /* head of the list */
OlListToken lasttoken = NULL;

main(argc, argv)
  int argc;
  char *argv[];
{
  int       n;
  Arg       wargs[10];
  Widget    toplevel, rt, sl, ca, delete, findcurrent;
  String    directory;
  void      initList(), current_callback(), delete_callback();
  void      findcurrent_callback();

  toplevel = OlInitialize(argv[0], "Scrollinglist", NULL, 0,
                          &argc, argv);
  /*
   * Get the command line argument, if any
   */
  directory = argv[1];
  rt = XtCreateManagedWidget("rt", rubberTileWidgetClass,
                             toplevel, NULL, 0);
  /*
   * Create the ScrollingList widget
   */
  n = 0;
```

```
    XtSetArg(wargs[n], XtNviewHeight, 6); n++;
    XtSetArg(wargs[n], XtNselectable, FALSE); n++;
    sl = XtCreateManagedWidget("sl", scrollingListWidgetClass,
                                    rt, wargs, n);
    n = 0;
    XtSetArg(wargs[n], XtNapplAddItem,    &AddItem); n++;
    XtSetArg(wargs[n], XtNapplTouchItem,  &TouchItem); n++;
    XtSetArg(wargs[n], XtNapplUpdateView, &UpdateView); n++;
    XtSetArg(wargs[n], XtNapplDeleteItem, &DeleteItem); n++;
    XtSetArg(wargs[n], XtNapplViewItem,   &ViewItem); n++;
    XtGetValues(sl, wargs, n);
    XtAddCallback(sl, XtNuserMakeCurrent, current_callback, NULL);
    /*
     * Create the ControlArea and Buttons
     */
    ca = XtCreateManagedWidget("ca", controlAreaWidgetClass,
                                   rt, NULL, 0);
    delete = XtCreateManagedWidget("Delete",
                                      oblongButtonWidgetClass,
                                      ca, NULL, 0);
    XtAddCallback(delete, XtNselect, delete_callback, sl);
    findcurrent = XtCreateManagedWidget("Current",
                                          oblongButtonWidgetClass,
                                          ca, NULL, 0);
    XtAddCallback(findcurrent, XtNselect,
                    findcurrent_callback, sl);
    initList(sl, directory);

    XtRealizeWidget(toplevel);
    XtMainLoop();
}
```

The **initList()** function initializes the items in the ScrollingList. It reads the directory specified, or the current directory if none is specified, and adds each file to the list by filling in the **item** structure and calling

```
    (*AddItem)(sl, 0, 0, item);
```

for each file in the directory. The **(*AddItem)()** function returns a token which is stored in the linked list of **file** structures. This token uniquely identifies the item and is required when other widget-defined routines are called.

Before any of the items are added to the list, **(*UpdateView)()** is called with FALSE as a parameter. This turns off immediate redisplay of the ScrollingList. After all the items in the list have been added, another call to **(*UpdateView)()** with TRUE as a parameter refreshes the entire list with all the updates. This approach avoids flashing as the list is updated.

```
void
initList(sl, directory)
  Widget sl;
  String directory;
{
  OlListItem      item;
  short           count = 0;
  DIR             *dirp;
  struct direct *dp;
  file            *filep, *prevp;

  if(directory == NULL)
    directory = ".";
  dirp = opendir(directory);
  if(dirp == NULL) {
    perror(directory);
    exit(-1);
  }
  (*UpdateView)(sl, FALSE);
  for (dp = readdir(dirp); dp != NULL; dp = readdir(dirp)) {
    filep = (file *)XtCalloc(1, sizeof(file));
    if(head == NULL)
      head = prevp = filep;
    else {
      prevp->next = filep;
      prevp = filep;
    }
    filep->next = NULL;
    item.label_type = OL_STRING;
    item.attr = count;
    item.label = filep->filename = XtNewString(dp->d_name);
    item.mnemonic = NULL;
    filep->token = (*AddItem)(sl, 0, 0, item);
    count++;
  }
  closedir(dirp);
  (*UpdateView)(sl, TRUE);
}
```

The **current_callback()** function is invoked when the user clicks SELECT on an item in the list. The **call_data** is a pointer to an **OlListToken** which uniquely identifies the item in the list. The function

```
OlListItemPointer(OlListToken)
```

takes an **OlListToken** as an argument and returns a pointer to an **OlListItem** structure. This gives the programmer access to the data structure that controls list items. The **current_call-back()** function has been designed to implement an Exclusives style list with the ability to have no items set. When one item is set, any other set item is unset. This functionality is not an inherent part of the ScrollingList widget; it must be managed by the application. To implement a Nonexclusives type behavior the **current_callback()** function would have to be rewritten with that policy in mind.

```
void
current_callback(w, client_data, call_data)
  Widget w;
  XtPointer client_data, call_data;
{
  OlListToken token = (OlListToken)call_data;
  OlListItem *newItem = OlListItemPointer(token);
  OlListItem *lastItem;

  if(lasttoken == token) {        /* unset current choice */
    newItem->attr &= ~OL_LIST_ATTR_CURRENT;
    (*TouchItem)(w, token);
    lasttoken = NULL;
    return;
  }

  if(lasttoken) {
    lastItem = OlListItemPointer(lasttoken);
    if(lastItem->attr & OL_LIST_ATTR_CURRENT)
      lastItem->attr &= ~OL_LIST_ATTR_CURRENT;
    (*TouchItem)(w, lasttoken);
  }
  newItem->attr |= OL_LIST_ATTR_CURRENT;
  (*TouchItem)(w, token);
  lasttoken = token;
}
```

The **delete_callback()** function is invoked when the user presses the *delete* button. The entire list is scanned and any set item is deleted with a call to **(*DeleteItem)()**. A simpler approach would be to examine the **lasttoken** variable which is a global that indicates the token of the currently set item. Then all that would be required would be to re-adjust the pointers to maintain the linked list, and delete that particular item. That approach would certainly work for our implementation, however, it assumes that an Exclusives model is being used. The implementation illustrated in **delete_callback()** will work for an Exclusives or Nonexclusives model. Each item in the list is examined and if it is set, it is deleted.

```
void
delete_callback(w, client_data, call_data)
  Widget    w;
  XtPointer client_data, call_data;
{
  Widget       sl = (Widget)client_data;
```

```
file        *filep, *prevp;
OlListItem *fileItem;

filep = prevp = head;
while(filep) {
  fileItem = OlListItemPointer(filep->token);
  if(fileItem->attr & OL_LIST_ATTR_CURRENT) {
    (*DeleteItem)(sl, filep->token);
    if(filep == head) {
      head = filep->next;
      XtFree(filep);
      filep = prevp = head;
    } else {
      prevp->next = filep->next;
      XtFree(filep);
      filep = prevp->next;
    }
  } else {
    prevp = filep;
    filep = filep->next;
  }
}
lasttoken = NULL;
}
```

The `findcurrent_callback()` function is invoked when the user presses the *current* button. The `(*ViewItem)()` function is called, which brings the set item into the view area.

```
void
findcurrent_callback(w, client_data, call_data)
  Widget w;
  XtPointer client_data, call_data;
{
  Widget sl = (Widget)client_data;

  if(lasttoken)
    (*ViewItem)(sl, lasttoken);
}
```

We set just one resource in our resources file to set the weight of the ControlArea to zero. When the application is resized, only the ScrollingList resizes. With this resource set, the program is displayed as shown in Figure 4.39.

```
Scrollinglist*ca.weight:        0
```

Figure 4.41 The scrollinglist program.

4.3.6   Popup Widgets

The *popup* widgets create pop-up shells. These are used for a variety of purposes including notification, prompting for input, setting properties, etc. Popup widgets are all subclassed off the TransientShell class. The window manager treats Popup shells as independent applications with the exception that they cannot be iconified separately from the *parent* application. Popup widgets are created differently from other widgets discussed so far in this chapter. Rather than calling `XtCreateWidget()`, the function `XtCreatePopupShell()` is used. The arguments to these two functions are identical. The OLIT Popup widgets are:

      NoticeShell   MenuShell   PopupWindowShell

The following sections discuss each of these widgets.

4.3.6.1   The NoticeShell Widget

The NoticeShell widget creates a pop-up to notify the user. This notification might entail confirming a choice, or warning the user of a problem. When a NoticeShell widget is popped up, no other action can take place for that application until the NoticeShell is popped down.

The NoticeShell widget consists of two parts: a StaticText widget on top and a ControlArea widget below. The StaticText widget is intended to contain a message to the user. The ControlArea parents one of more children, usually OblongButtons.

Some of the more common resources for the NoticeShell are:

- **XtNcontrolArea**: The ControlArea widget that occupies the lower part of the Notice.
- **XtNemanateWidget**: The widget from which the Notice emanates. That widget is set busy.
- **XtNfocusWidget**: The widget that is to get the focus the next time this shell takes focus.
- **XtNpopdownCallback**: The callback list invoked when the Notice is popped down.
- **XtNpopupCallback**: The callback list invoked when the Notice is popped up.
- **XtNtextArea**: The StaticText widget that occupies the upper part of the Notice.

The **notice** program demonstrates the NoticeShell widget. A single OblongButton is created. The NoticeShell widget is created as a child of the "Print" OblongButton. After the NoticeShell is created the StaticText and ControlArea of the NoticeShell are retrieved.

```
/************************************************************
 * notice.c: Demonstrate the Notice widget.
 ***********************************************************/
#include <X11/Intrinsic.h>
#include <X11/StringDefs.h>
#include <Xol/OpenLook.h>
#include <Xol/ControlAre.h>
#include <Xol/OblongButt.h>
#include <Xol/Notice.h>

main(argc, argv)
  int    argc;
  char *argv[];
{
  Widget  toplevel, con, button, notice;
  Widget  n_controlarea, n_textarea, confirm, cancel;
  void    button_callback(), confirm_callback();
  Arg     wargs[3];
  int     n;

  toplevel = OlInitialize(argv[0], "Notice", NULL, 0, &argc, argv);
  con = XtCreateManagedWidget("control", controlAreaWidgetClass,
                              toplevel, NULL, 0);
  /*
   * Create the OblongButton widget.
   */
  button = XtCreateManagedWidget("Print", oblongButtonWidgetClass,
                              con, NULL, 0);
  /*
   * Create the notice widget
   * The notice widget emanates from the button widget.
   */
  n = 0;
  XtSetArg(wargs[n], XtNemanateWidget, button); n++;
  notice = XtCreatePopupShell("notice", noticeShellWidgetClass,
```

```
                                           button, wargs, n);
     /*
      * Retrieve the XtNtextArea and XtNcontrolArea widgets.
      */
     n = 0;
     XtSetArg(wargs[n], XtNtextArea, &n_textarea); n++;
     XtSetArg(wargs[n], XtNcontrolArea, &n_controlarea); n++;
     XtGetValues(notice, wargs, n);
     /*
      * Set the message and create the buttons on the notice pop-up.
      */
     XtSetArg(wargs[0], XtNstring, "Print Message?");
     XtSetValues(n_textarea, wargs, 1);
     confirm = XtCreateManagedWidget("Confirm", oblongButtonWidgetClass,
                                     n_controlarea, NULL, 0);
     cancel = XtCreateManagedWidget("Cancel", oblongButtonWidgetClass,
                                    n_controlarea, NULL, 0);
     XtAddCallback(confirm, XtNselect, confirm_callback, NULL);
     XtAddCallback(button, XtNselect, button_callback, notice);

     XtRealizeWidget(toplevel);
     XtMainLoop();
 }
```

It's important to understand that creating a pop-up from a callback is not like calling a subroutine. The callback function does not wait for the NoticeShell to return a value. This makes it impractical for the **button_callback()** to handle the printing of the message since it can't predict nor wait for the user's response. Therefore, the printing of the message must be moved out of the **button_callback()** function. It is put into the **confirm_callback()** function. The **button_callback()** callback simply pops up the NoticeShell by calling

```
    XtPopup(widget, grab_mode)
```

The **widget** argument must be a popup Shell. Sometimes popup shells pop up other shells, creating a *cascade* of popup shells. The **grab_mode** argument allows the programmer to specify how events are dispatched within a cascade of popups. If **XtNgrabNone** is specified, events are processed normally. If the **grab_mode** is **XtNGrabNonExclusive**, device events are sent to any widget in the popup cascade. If the **grab_mode** is **XtNGrabExclusive**, all device events are sent only to the last popup in the cascade. Since we are not using a cascade of popups we use **XtNGrabExclusive** for the grab mode.

```
    void
    button_callback(w, client_data, call_data)
      Widget     w;
      XtPointer  client_data, call_data;
    {
      Widget notice = (Widget)client_data;
```

```
    XtPopup(notice, XtGrabExclusive);
}
```

The **confirm_callback()** function is invoked if the user chooses "Confirm" from the popup. Its only function is to print a message.

```
void
confirm_callback(w, client_data, call_data)
    Widget     w;
    XtPointer  client_data, call_data;
{
    printf("Message\n");
}
```

Figure 4.42 shows the **notice** program.

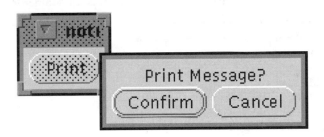

Figure 4.42 The **notice** program.

4.3.6.2   The MenuShell Widget

The MenuShell widget is similar to the MenuButton widget discussed in Section 4.3.2.4. The difference between the two widgets is that the MenuShell widget can be associated with any other widget. It does not have an inherent object associated with it like the MenuButton does. For example, you can create a MenuShell widget and associate it with a StaticText widget. When the user presses the MENU mouse button with the pointer in the StaticText widget, the menu pops up.

Typically, the pop-up menu will contain several objects, such as OblongButtons, from which the user can make a selection. This pop-up menu is also call a *menu pane*. The menu pane can optionally have a pushpin associated with it. When the pushpin is "in" the pop-up will stay pinned up. When the pushpin is "out" the menu will pop-down after a selection has been made.

The MenuShell widget is created by calling **XtCreatePopupShell()**. The parent argument to **XtCreatePopupShell()** is the object that will activate the menu when the user presses MENU. The menu pane is created automatically when the MenuShell is created. A separate call to **XtCreateWidget()** is not necessary. The menu pane widget is obtained by getting the value of the **XtNmenuPane** resource after the MenuShell has been created. After getting the menu pane widget, it is then the responsibility of the application to populate the menu by creating other widgets such as OblongButtons or RectButtons as children of the menu pane.

Some of the more common resources for the MenuShell are:

- **XtNfocusWidget**: The widget that is to get the focus the next time this shell takes focus.
- **XtNmenuPane**: The menu pane widget. This resource can only be accessed after the MenuShell has been created.
- **XtNpushpin**: The menu pane's pushpin. There are two valid values:
  - **OL_NONE/"none"**: No pushpin will be included on the menu pane. This is the default.
  - **OL_OUT/"out"**: A pushpin will be included on the menu pane. Its initial state will be out.
- **XtNpopdownCallback**: The callback list invoked when the MenuShell is popped down.
- **XtNpopupCallback**: The callback list invoked when the MenuShell is popped up.
- **XtNtitle**: The menu pane title.

The **menu** program demonstrates the MenuShell widget. It is very similar to the menubutton program described in Section 4.3.2.4 except that a MenuShell is used rather than a MenuButton.

```
/*************************************************************
 * menu.c: Demonstrate the Menu widget.
 *************************************************************/
#include <X11/Intrinsic.h>
#include <X11/StringDefs.h>
#include <Xol/OpenLook.h>
#include <Xol/ControlAre.h>
#include <Xol/OblongButt.h>
#include <Xol/StaticText.h>
#include <Xol/Menu.h>

static char *button_names[] = { "New", "Open", "Save", "Print" };

main(argc, argv)
  int     argc;
  char    *argv[];
{
  Widget  toplevel, con, menu, menu_pane, st,
          oblong[XtNumber(button_names)];
  int     i, n;
  Arg     wargs[2];
  void    button_callback();

  toplevel = OlInitialize(argv[0], "Menu", NULL, 0,
                          &argc, argv);
  con = XtCreateManagedWidget("control", controlAreaWidgetClass,
                              toplevel, NULL, 0);
  /*
   * Create a StaticText widget
   */
```

```
    st = XtCreateManagedWidget("st", staticTextWidgetClass,
                                con, NULL, 0);
    /*
     * Create menu widget.
     */
    menu = XtCreatePopupShell("popup", menuShellWidgetClass,
                                st, NULL, 0);
    /*
     * Get the MenuPane widget
     */
    n = 0;
    XtSetArg(wargs[n], XtNmenuPane, &menu_pane); n++;
    XtGetValues(menu, wargs, n);
    /*
     * Create the buttons on the menu pane.
     */
    for(i=0;i<XtNumber(button_names);i++) {
      oblong[i] = XtCreateManagedWidget(button_names[i],
                                        oblongButtonWidgetClass,
                                        menu_pane, NULL, 0);
      XtAddCallback(oblong[i], XtNselect, button_callback,
                    button_names[i]);

    }

    XtRealizeWidget(toplevel);
    XtMainLoop();
}
```

The **button_callback()** prints the name of the button that is pushed.

```
void
button_callback(w, client_data, call_data)
  Widget w;
  XtPointer client_data, call_data;
{
  printf("%s\n", (String)client_data);
}
```

Figure 4.43 shows the **menu** program with the following resources set:

```
Menu*st.string:              Press MENU here
Menu*pushpin:                out
!
Menu*New.mnemonic:           n
Menu*Save.mnemonic:          s
Menu*Print.mnemonic:         p
```

```
Menu*Open.mnemonic:              o
Menu*MenuShell.title:            Title
Menu*MenuShell*title.font:       lucidasans-bold
```

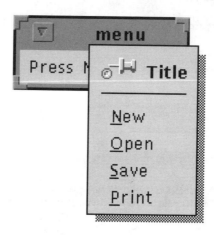

Figure 4.43 The menu program.

4.3.6.3   The PopupWindowShell Widget

The PopupWindowShell widget creates a pop-up that can be used to implement an OPEN LOOK property window or command window. The pop-up created includes an upper and lower ControlArea and a FooterPanel. The upper ControlArea is generally used for user input. The lower ControlArea is usually populated with buttons which specify an action. The FooterPanel is used to display a message to the user.

The PopupWindowShell supports automatic creation of four OblongButtons in its lower ControlArea. These buttons represent "Apply", "Reset", "Reset to Factory", and "Set Defaults". For example, setting the **XtNapply** resource automatically creates the "Apply" button. The **XtNapply** resource is set to an **XtCallbackRec** structure that specifies a list of callback functions and client data for each function. The list in NULL terminated. For example:

```
XtCallbackRec applycallback[] = {
  { Apply, client_data },
  { NULL, NULL },
}
```

specifies a callback function, **Apply()**, which passes client data **client_data**. This is very different from the way we have been creating objects and registering callback procedures, and it can be a bit confusing at first.

Setting the **XtNapply** resource to **applycallback** forces an "Apply" button to be created automatically, and the **Apply()** function to be registered as the **XtNselect** callback for that button. This same procedure is used to create each of the four buttons introduced above.

Some of the more common resources for the PopupWindowShell are:

- **XtNapply, XtNreset, XtNresetFactory, XtNsetDefaults**: The callback list for buttons in the lower ControlArea.
- **XtNapplyButton, XtNresetButton, XtNresetFactoryButton, XtNsetDefaultsButton**: The ID of the widgets created in the lower ControlArea.
- **XtNfocusWidget**: The widget that is to get the focus the next time this shell takes focus.
- **XtNfooterPanel**: The FooterPanel widget created automatically as part of the pop-up.
- **XtNlowerControlArea**: The lower ControlArea widget created automatically as part of the pop-up.
- **XtNupperControlArea**: The upper ControlArea widget created automatically as part of the pop-up.
- **XtNverify**: The callback list invoked before popping down the pop-up.
- **XtNpushpin**: The resource that indicates whether the pop-up should have a pushpin.

The **popupwindow** program demonstrates the PopupWindowShell widget. This program is a combination of two applications used earlier in this chapter: **scrolledwindow** and **fl-fontchooser**. The main window of the application contains a TextEdit widget in a ScrolledWindow. Two buttons are provided: "Load" and "Properties". Each of these buttons brings up a PopupWindowShell.

The "Load..." button brings up a command window. Figure 4.44 shows the layout of the command window. The user may enter the name of a file to be loaded into the TextEdit widget. When the user presses the "Load" button the file is loaded into the TextEdit widget.

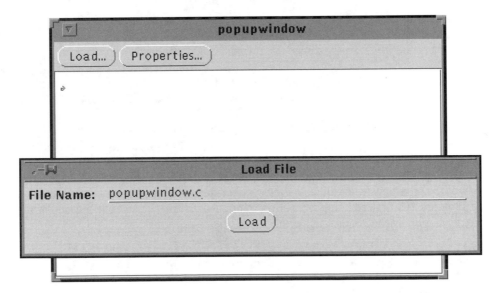

Figure 4.44 The **popupwindow** program with the Command widow.

The "Properties..." button brings up a property window. Figure 4.43 shows the layout of the property window. The user may choose the font, point size, colors, etc., to be displayed in the TextEdit widget. The property window includes three buttons: "Apply", "Reset", and "Reset To Factory". When the "Apply" button is pressed the user's selections are applied to the TextEdit widget. When the "Reset" button is pressed the buttons change to reflect the current selection displayed in the TextEdit window. When the "Reset To Factory" button is pressed the font choices are returned to their original values.

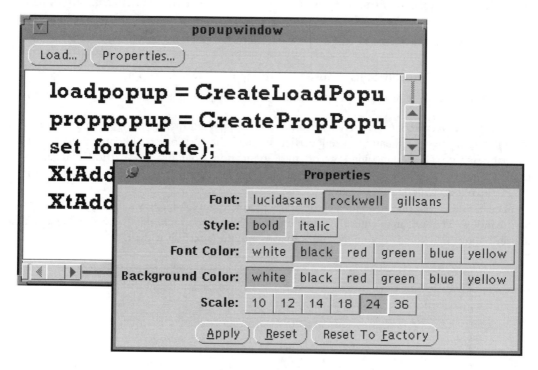

Figure 4.45 The **popupwindow** program with the Property widow.

The **popupwindow** program includes the flfontchooser.h header file from Section 4.3.5.3 which declares the appropriate structures for the Flat widgets which we reuse from that section. The main body of the program creates all the various widgets including the PopupWindowShell widgets and their children. The "Load" and "Properties" buttons each register a callback which will call **XtPopup()** to pop up the PopupWindowShell widgets.

```
/************************************************************
 * popupwindow.c: Demonstrate the PopupWindow widget.
 ************************************************************/
#include <X11/Intrinsic.h>
#include <X11/StringDefs.h>
#include <Xol/OpenLook.h>
```

```
#include <Xol/ControlAre.h>
#include <Xol/Form.h>
#include <Xol/TextEdit.h>
#include <Xol/TextField.h>
#include <Xol/StaticText.h>
#include <Xol/OblongButt.h>
#include <Xol/RubberTile.h>
#include <Xol/ScrolledWi.h>
#include <Xol/PopupWindo.h>
#include <Xol/Caption.h>
#include <Xol/FExclusive.h>
#include <Xol/FNonexclus.h>
#include <sys/types.h>
#include <sys/stat.h>
#include <errno.h>
#include <stdio.h>
#include "flfontchooser.h"

extern char *sys_errlist[];
extern int errno;

typedef struct Popupdata {
  Widget tf;      /* TextField */
  Widget te;      /* TextEdit */
  Widget st;      /* StaticText */
} popupdata;

typedef struct _choiceindex {
  int font, fontcolor, bgcolor, scale;
  Boolean styleb, stylei;
} choiceindex;

static Widget font, style, fontcolor, bgcolor, scale;
static Boolean popdown = TRUE;
static fontchoice *fc, *current;
static popupdata pd;
static choiceindex lastindex, currentindex;

main(argc, argv)
  int argc;
  char *argv[];
{
  Widget  toplevel, file, prop, ca, rt, sw,
          loadpopup, proppopup;
  Widget  CreateLoadPopup(), CreatePropPopup();
  void    popup_callback(), set_font(), default_choice();
```

```
    /*
     * Initialize the fontchoice structure
     */
    fc      = (fontchoice *)XtMalloc(sizeof(fontchoice));
    current = (fontchoice *)XtMalloc(sizeof(fontchoice));
    default_choice(fc);
    default_choice(current);
    toplevel = OlInitialize(argv[0], "Popupwindow", NULL, 0,
                            &argc, argv);
    /*
     * Create the RubberTile widget.
     */
    rt = XtVaCreateManagedWidget("rt", rubberTileWidgetClass,
                                    toplevel, NULL);
    /*
     * Create a ControlArea widget to hold the control buttons
     */
    ca = XtVaCreateManagedWidget("ca", controlAreaWidgetClass,
                                    rt, NULL);
    file = XtVaCreateManagedWidget("file",
                                        oblongButtonWidgetClass, ca,
                                        XtNlabelType, OL_POPUP,
                                        NULL);
    prop = XtVaCreateManagedWidget("prop",
                                        oblongButtonWidgetClass, ca,
                                        XtNlabelType, OL_POPUP,
                                        NULL);
    /*
     * Create ScrolledWindow and TextEdit widgets.
     */
    sw = XtVaCreateManagedWidget("sw", scrolledWindowWidgetClass,
                                    rt, NULL);
    pd.te = XtVaCreateManagedWidget("te", textEditWidgetClass,
                                        sw,
                                        XtNwrapMode, OL_WRAP_OFF,
                                        XtNsourceType, OL_DISK_SOURCE,
                                        NULL);
    loadpopup = CreateLoadPopup(file);
    proppopup = CreatePropPopup(prop);
    set_font(pd.te);
    XtAddCallback(file, XtNselect, popup_callback, loadpopup);
    XtAddCallback(prop, XtNselect, popup_callback, proppopup);

    XtRealizeWidget(toplevel);
    XtMainLoop();
}
```

The `CreateLoadPopup()` function creates a command window style PopupWindowShell. The pop-up contains a TextField widget in its upper ControlArea and an OblongButton in its lower ControlArea. The user is prompted for a filename to load into the TextEdit widget. The TextField and OblongButton, as well as the TextEdit widget, are maintained in the **popupdata** structure for use in the **load_callback()** callback function.

```
Widget
CreateLoadPopup(parent)
  Widget parent;
{
  Widget popup, upper, lower, footer, caption, tf, load, st;
  void load_callback(), verify_callback();
  static XtCallbackRec verify[] = {
      { (XtCallbackProc)verify_callback, (XtPointer)NULL },
      { NULL, NULL },
  };

  popup = XtVaCreatePopupShell("loadpopup",
                popupWindowShellWidgetClass,
                parent,
                XtNverify, verify,
                XtNtitle, "Load File",
                NULL);
  XtVaGetValues(popup,
                XtNupperControlArea, &upper,
                XtNlowerControlArea, &lower,
                XtNfooterPanel,      &footer,
                NULL);
  caption = XtVaCreateManagedWidget("popupcaption",
                captionWidgetClass,
                upper, NULL);
  pd.tf = XtVaCreateManagedWidget("popuptf",
                textFieldWidgetClass, caption,
                XtNwidth, 400,
                NULL);
  load = XtVaCreateManagedWidget("popupload",
                oblongButtonWidgetClass,
                lower,
                XtNlabel, "Load",
                NULL);
  pd.st = XtVaCreateManagedWidget("popupst",
                staticTextWidgetClass, footer,
                XtNstring, "",
                XtNgravity, WestGravity,
                XtNwrap, FALSE,
                NULL);
```

```
    XtAddCallback(load, XtNselect, load_callback, (XtPointer)&pd);
    return(popup);
}
```

The **CreatePropPopup()** function creates a property window style PopupWindowShell. The pop-up contains a series of FlatExclusives and FlatNonexclusives choices. These are identical to those created and used in the **flfontchooser** program from Section 4.3.5.3. The function first creates the pop-up and then populates it with Flat widgets by calling **create_fl_ex_nonex()**. This is the same function used to create Flat widgets in the **flfontchooser** program.

```
Widget
CreatePropPopup(parent)
  Widget parent;
{
  Widget   popup, upper, lower, footer;
  void     load_callback(), verify_callback(), apply_callback(),
           reset_callback(), resetFactory_callback(),
           set_button_defaults(), copy_index();
  Widget   create_fl_ex_nonex();
  void     font_callback(), style_callback(), fontcolor_callback(),
           bgcolor_callback(), scale_callback();

  static XtCallbackRec verify[] = {
      { (XtCallbackProc)verify_callback, (XtPointer)NULL },
      { NULL, NULL },
  };
  static XtCallbackRec apply[] = {
      { (XtCallbackProc)apply_callback, (XtPointer)NULL },
      { NULL, NULL },
  };
  static XtCallbackRec reset[] = {
      { (XtCallbackProc)reset_callback, (XtPointer)NULL },
      { NULL, NULL },
  };
  static XtCallbackRec resetFactory[] = {
      { (XtCallbackProc)resetFactory_callback, (XtPointer)NULL },
      { NULL, NULL },
  };

  popup = XtVaCreatePopupShell("proppopup",
                  popupWindowShellWidgetClass,
                  parent,
                  XtNapply, apply,
                  XtNreset, reset,
                  XtNresetFactory, resetFactory,
                  XtNverify, verify,
                  XtNtitle, "Properties",
                  NULL);
```

```
    XtVaGetValues(popup,
                XtNupperControlArea, &upper,
                XtNlowerControlArea, &lower,
                XtNfooterPanel,      &footer,
                NULL);
    /*
     * Create FlatExclusives and FlatNonexclusives widgets
     */
    font      = create_fl_ex_nonex(upper, fontItems, fonts,
                XtNumber(fonts), "Font:",
                flatExclusivesWidgetClass,
                font_callback);
    style     = create_fl_ex_nonex(upper, styleItems, styles,
                XtNumber(styles), "Style:",
                flatNonexclusivesWidgetClass,
                style_callback);
    fontcolor = create_fl_ex_nonex(upper, fontColorItems, colors,
                XtNumber(colors), "Font Color:",
                flatExclusivesWidgetClass, fontcolor_callback);
    bgcolor   = create_fl_ex_nonex(upper, bgColorItems, colors,
                XtNumber(colors), "Background Color:",
                flatExclusivesWidgetClass, bgcolor_callback);
    scale     = create_fl_ex_nonex(upper, scaleItems, scales,
                XtNumber(scales), "Scale:",
                flatExclusivesWidgetClass,
                scale_callback);
    /*
     * Set up the defaults
     */
    set_button_defaults(0, FALSE, FALSE, 1, 0, 1);
    copy_index(&lastindex, &currentindex);
    return(popup);
}
```

The **popup_callback()** callback function is invoked when the user presses the "Proper-ties..." button. It calls **XtPopup()** to pop up the properties window.

```
void
popup_callback(w, client_data, call_data)
  Widget w;
  XtPointer client_data, call_data;
{
  Widget popup = (Widget)client_data;
  XtPopup(popup, XtGrabNone);
}
```

The **verify_callback()** function is registered as the callback associated with the **Xt-Nverify** resource for each of the two pop-up windows. If the user enters a filename in the command window for a file that does not exist, the desired behavior is for the window to stay popped up. The `load_callback()` function sets the global variable **popdown** to FALSE which will be checked by **verify_callback()**. The **verify_callback()** function is called to verify that it is okay to pop down the PopupWindow. In the **verify_callback()** function the value of **popdown** is checked. If it equals FALSE, the `call_data` parameter is set to FALSE which prevents the pop-up from popping down. This is the desired action if the user inputs an invalid filename.

If the user presses the "Reset" button on the property window the **popdown** variable is set to FALSE to indicate that the window should not be popped down. Only when the user presses the "Apply" button is the window popped down

```
void
verify_callback(w, client_data, call_data)
  Widget w;
  XtPointer client_data, call_data;
{
  Boolean *popdownmenu = (Boolean *)call_data;

  /*
   * Determine if the pop-up should be popped down
   */
  if(popdown == FALSE)
    *popdownmenu = FALSE;
}
```

The `load_callback()` function is invoked when the user presses the "load" button on the command pop-up. The name of the file input by the user is retrieved from the TextField widget and checked to ensure that the file exists. If the file does exist, it is loaded into the TextEdit widget and the FooterPanel of the pop-up is cleared of any previously displayed error message. If the file does not exist, an error message is displayed in the pop-up's FooterPanel and the **popdown** variable is set to FALSE. The **popdown** variable is checked in the **verify_callback()** callback to determine if the pop-up should be allowed to pop down.

```
void
load_callback(w, client_data, call_data)
  Widget w;
  XtPointer client_data, call_data;
{
  popupdata *pd = (popupdata *)client_data;
  String filename;
  struct stat info;
  int size, retval;
  char errormsg[256];

  /*
   * read the filename
   */
  filename = OlTextFieldGetString(pd->tf, &size);
```

```
    retval = stat(filename, &info);
    if(retval == 0) {
      XtVaSetValues(pd->te, XtNsource, filename, NULL);
      XtVaSetValues(pd->st, XtNstring, "", NULL);
      popdown = TRUE;
    } else {
      /*
       * Put an error message in the footer
       */
      sprintf(errormsg, "%s: %s", filename, sys_errlist[errno]);
      XtVaSetValues(pd->st, XtNstring, errormsg, NULL);
      popdown = FALSE;
    }
}
```

The `apply_callback()` callback function is invoked when the user presses the "Apply" button on the property window. This function calls `set_font()` to set the font of the TextEdit widget. It also stores a copy of the current settings in the `lastindex` structure so that these values can be retrieved if the user chooses to "Reset" the selection. The pop-up window will automatically pop down if not pinned.

```
void
apply_callback(w, client_data, call_data)
  Widget w;
  XtPointer client_data, call_data;
{
  void set_font(), copy_index();

  /*
   * Store current settings so Reset
   * will know what values to use
   */
  copy_index(&lastindex, &currentindex);
  set_font(pd.te);
  popdown = TRUE;
}
```

The `reset_callback()` callback function is invoked when the user presses the "Reset" button on the property window. The function sets the button values back to the values saved during the last "Apply" which are stored in the `lastindex` structure. All buttons will reflect the current settings displayed in the TextEdit widget.

```
void
reset_callback(w, client_data, call_data)
  Widget w;
  XtPointer client_data, call_data;
{
  void set_button_defaults();
```

```
/*
 * Set the button defaults to whatever was set
 * during the last "apply"
 */
set_button_defaults(lastindex.font,    lastindex.styleb,
                     lastindex.stylei,  lastindex.fontcolor,
                     lastindex.bgcolor, lastindex.scale);
copy_index(&currentindex, &lastindex);
}
```

The **resetFactory_callback()** callback function is invoked when the user presses the "Reset To Factory" button on the property window. The function sets the default values back to their original initialization time values.

```
void
resetFactory_callback(w, client_data, call_data)
  Widget w;
  XtPointer client_data, call_data;
{
  void set_button_defaults(), default_choice();

  set_button_defaults(0, FALSE, FALSE, 1, 0, 1);
  default_choice(fc);
  popdown = FALSE;
}
```

The **set_button_defaults()** function sets all the Flat widgets to the values specified in the parameters by calling

```
OlActivateWidget(widget, action, data)
```

The **OlActivateWidget()** function executes the **action** on the specified **widget**. In this case the widgets being activated are Flat widgets and the action to take is **OL_SELECTKEY**. Because we are using Flat widgets we set the **data** parameter to indicate the index[6] of the sub-object that we want activated. This has the same effect as the user pressing the SELECT button on the widget specified. Each of the callbacks invoked as a result of calling **OlActivateWidget()** updates the **currentindex** structure so that it reflects the current settings.

```
void
set_button_defaults(fontd, stylebd, styleid, fontcolord,
                    bgcolord, scaled)
  int fontd, fontcolord, bgcolord, scaled;
  Boolean stylebd, styleid;
{
  Boolean bold, italic;
```

---

[6]   For this function, indexes of sub-object begin from 1 rather than 0.

```
  OlActivateWidget(font, OL_SELECTKEY, (XtPointer)(fontd+1));
  OlVaFlatGetValues(style, 0, XtNset, &bold, NULL);
  if(stylebd != bold)
    OlActivateWidget(style, OL_SELECTKEY, (XtPointer)(BOLDINDEX+1));
  OlVaFlatGetValues(style, 1, XtNset, &italic, NULL);
  if(styleid != italic)
    OlActivateWidget(style, OL_SELECTKEY, (XtPointer)(ITALICINDEX+1));
  OlActivateWidget(fontcolor, OL_SELECTKEY,(XtPointer)(fontcolord+1));
  OlActivateWidget(bgcolor, OL_SELECTKEY, (XtPointer)(bgcolord+1));
  OlActivateWidget(scale, OL_SELECTKEY, (XtPointer)(scaled+1));
}
```

The callbacks associated with the Flat widgets are identical to the ones used in the flfontchooser except that the set_font() function is not called from any of them. The set_font() function is only called when the "Apply" button is pressed.

```
void
font_callback(w, client_data, call_data)
  Widget    w;
  XtPointer client_data, call_data;
{
  OlFlatCallData *olfcd = (OlFlatCallData *)call_data;

  fc->font = (String)client_data;
  currentindex.font = olfcd->item_index;
}

void
style_callback(w, client_data, call_data)
  Widget    w;
  XtPointer client_data, call_data;
{
  OlFlatCallData *olfcd = (OlFlatCallData *)call_data;
  static Boolean italic = FALSE, bold = FALSE;

  /*
   * Get the current state of the buttons
   */
  if(olfcd->item_index == BOLDINDEX)
    OlVaFlatGetValues(w, BOLDINDEX, XtNset, &bold, NULL);
  if(olfcd->item_index == ITALICINDEX)
    OlVaFlatGetValues(w, ITALICINDEX, XtNset, &italic, NULL);
  currentindex.stylei = fc->italic = italic;
  currentindex.styleb = fc->bold = bold;
}

void
scale_callback(w, client_data, call_data)
```

```
   Widget w;
   XtPointer client_data, call_data;
{
   OlFlatCallData *olfcd = (OlFlatCallData *)call_data;

   fc->scale = (String)client_data;
   currentindex.scale = olfcd->item_index;
}

void
fontcolor_callback(w, client_data, call_data)
   Widget    w;
   XtPointer client_data, call_data;
{
   OlFlatCallData *olfcd = (OlFlatCallData *)call_data;

   fc->fontcolor = (String)client_data;
   currentindex.fontcolor = olfcd->item_index;
}

void
bgcolor_callback(w, client_data, call_data)
   Widget    w;
   XtPointer client_data, call_data;
{
   OlFlatCallData *olfcd = (OlFlatCallData *)call_data;

   fc->bgcolor = (String)client_data;
   currentindex.bgcolor = olfcd->item_index;
}
```

The `copy_index()` function is a utility to copy **choiceindex** structures.

```
void
copy_index(to, from)
   choiceindex *to, *from;
{
   to->font = from->font;
   to->styleb = from->styleb;
   to->stylei = from->stylei;
   to->fontcolor = from->fontcolor;
   to->bgcolor = from->bgcolor;
   to->scale = from->scale;
}
```

The `default_choice()` sets all the buttons to their original values.

```
void
default_choice(fchoice)
  fontchoice *fchoice;
{
  fchoice->font       = fonts[0];
  fchoice->bold       = FALSE;
  fchoice->italic     = FALSE;
  fchoice->fontcolor  = colors[1];
  fchoice->bgcolor    = colors[0];
  fchoice->scale      = scales[1];
}
```

Figure 4.43 and Figure 4.44 show the **popupwindow** program with the following resources set:

```
Popupwindow*te.background:      white
!Popupwindow*te.font:           lucidasans-typewriter
! Spacing
Popupwindow*OblongButton*xOffset:   5
Popupwindow*OblongButton*yOffset:   5
Popupwindow*StaticText*xOffset:     5
Popupwindow*StaticText*yOffset:     5
Popupwindow*TextField*xOffset:      5
Popupwindow*TextField*yOffset:      5
Popupwindow*ScrolledWindow*yOffset:     5
! OblongButtons
Popupwindow*file.label:         Load
Popupwindow*prop.label:         Properties
! Buttons
Popupwindow*file.string:        Load File:
! TextField
Popupwindow*prop.xRefName:      file
Popupwindow*prop.xAddWidth:     TRUE
! Form
Popupwindow*ca.weight:          0
! Popup Window widgets
*popupcaption.label:            File Name:
*popupcaption.font:             lucidasans-bold
Popupwindow*Caption.font:       lucidasans-bold
Popupwindow*Caption.space:      8
```

4.3.7   Registering Help

The OLIT widget set supports a mechanism which allows the programmer to define one or more help windows which can be associated with different objects in the application. When the user presses the "Help" key or "F1" key, the application pops up a window with the help information. This is enabled by calling

```
OlRegisterHelp(id_type, id, tag, source_type, source)
```

This function registers help for a widget, gadget, or class of widgets. The `id_type` parameter indicates the type of help to use. This can be one of

OL_WIDGET_HELP   OL_CLASS_HELP   OL_FLAT_HELP

If `OL_WIDGET_HELP` is used, then the `id` field must be a widget or gadget ID. If `OL_CLASS_HELP` is used, then the `id` field must be a widget or gadget class such as `oblongButtonWidgetClass`. If `OL_FLAT_HELP` is used, then the `id` field must a Flat widget. The `tag` parameter specifies the title to appear on the help pop-up window. The `source_type` parameter indicates the type of the `source` parameter and must be one of

OL_STRING_SOURCE   OL_DISK_SOURCE
OL_INDIRECT_SOURCE   OL_TRANSPARENT_SOURCE

If `OL_STRING_SOURCE` is used, then `source` must be a String. If `OL_DISK_SOURCE` is used then `source` must be the name of a file. If `OL_INDIRECT_SOURCE` or `OL_TRANSPARENT_SOURCE` is used, then `source` must point to an application defined routine which handles the help message.

Let's demonstrate the use of help by modifying the `oblong` program from Section 4.3.2.1. The new version, `help`, calls `OlRegisterHelp()` with `OL_STRING_SOURCE` as the `source_type`.

```
/*********************************************************
 * help.c: Demonstrate help.
 *********************************************************/
#include <X11/Intrinsic.h>
#include <X11/StringDefs.h>
#include <Xol/OpenLook.h>
#include <Xol/ControlAre.h>
#include <Xol/OblongButt.h>

static String HelpTitle = "OblongButton";
static String HelpMessage =
      "Pressing this button activates the callback function";

main(argc, argv)
  int   argc;
  char *argv[];
{
  Widget  toplevel, con, but1;
  void button_callback();

  toplevel = OlInitialize(argv[0], "Help", NULL, 0, &argc, argv);
  con = XtCreateManagedWidget("control", controlAreaWidgetClass,
                              toplevel, NULL, 0);
  /*
   * Create the OblongButton widget.
   */
  but1 = XtCreateManagedWidget("button", oblongButtonWidgetClass,
```

```
                              con, NULL, 0);
   XtAddCallback(but1, XtNselect, button_callback, NULL);
   OlRegisterHelp(OL_WIDGET_HELP, but1, HelpTitle,
                   OL_STRING_SOURCE, (XtPointer)HelpMessage);

   XtRealizeWidget(toplevel);
   XtMainLoop();
}

void
button_callback(w, client_data, call_data)
   Widget      w;
   XtPointer   client_data, call_data;
{
   printf("callback\n");
}
```

We could accomplish the same thing using **OL_DISK_SOURCE** by creating a file with the contents of the desired message and calling

```
   OlRegisterHelp(OL_WIDGET_HELP, but1, *HelpTitle,
                   OL_DISK_SOURCE, filename);
```

Setting the source_type to **OL_INDIRECT_SOURCE** requires that a function be created to handle creation of the help message. The user defined function is called with the following parameters:

```
   (*source_func)(id_type, id, src_x, src_y, &source_type, &source);
```

The **id_type** and **id** are identical to the values passed to **OlRegisterHelp()**. The **src_x** and **src_y** parameters indicate the x and y values of the position of the pointer at the time the user pressed the Help key. The **source_type** and **source** parameters are to be set by the function. They indicate the source and type of the message to be displayed in the help window. The following shows the code segment necessary to implement an **OL_INDIRECT_SOURCE** type help message.

```
   void do_help();
   . . .
   OlRegisterHelp(OL_WIDGET_HELP, con, HelpTitle,
                   OL_INDIRECT_SOURCE, do_help);
   . . .
   void
   do_help(id_type, id, src_x, src_y, source_type, source)
     OlDefine id_type;
     XtPointer id;
     int src_x, src_y;
     OlDefine *source_type;
     XtPointer *source;
   {
```

```
    *source_type = OL_STRING_SOURCE;
    *source = "This help is from the do_help function";
}
```

Setting the source_type to **OL_TRANPARENT_SOURCE** also requires that a function be provided. However, the application is expected to handle the HELP event completely.The user defined function is called with the following parameters:

```
(*source_func)(id_type, id, src_x, src_y);
```

The help message is display as shown in Figure 4.46.

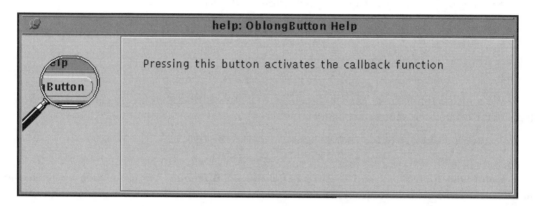

Figure 4.46 The help window.

4.4 SUMMARY

This chapter demonstrated how applications can combine various widgets to create a complete user interface. Widgets provide basic user interface components such as scroll bars, buttons, and menus. Applications can use composite and constraint widgets to group simple widgets together to form complex user interfaces.

The widgets in the OLIT widget set are powerful enough to meet most of the user interface needs of typical applications. These widgets allow the programmer to display and edit text and graphics, pop up menus and property windows, and display a variety of selection devices, such as buttons, sliders, and lists. For those applications that need functionality not addressed by existing widgets, the application programmer has two choices:

- Use a primitive widget class, such as the Core, Stub, or DrawArea widget class, as a window in which to display output. Such applications must use Xlib text and graphics functions to draw the contents of the window.

- Write a new widget to provide the needed function. This is quite feasible, although it requires a good understanding of the widget architecture. Chapters 12, 13, and 14 show how to write new widgets.

5

HANDLING EVENTS

The X server communicates with clients by sending events. The architecture of the Xt Intrinsics allows individual widgets to handle most common events automatically. For example, most widgets handle the **Expose** events sent by the server when the contents of a widget's window needs refreshed, and also handle configuration events generated by the server when a window is resized. Most widgets support callbacks for those situations that must be handled by the application. In spite of this, most programmers still find occasions when they must handle events directly, even when using the X Toolkit. Having a good understanding of the events generated by the X server also helps the programmer understand and use the Xt Intrinsics and widgets more effectively.

Chapter 2 provided a brief introduction to events and event handlers. This chapter examines events in more detail and provides examples that use features of the Intrinsics to handle events. The chapter first examines the events and event structures provided by X and Xlib and then looks at the event-handling mechanisms built on top of Xlib by the Xt Intrinsics. We also examine some applications that depend on input from sources other than X events. Events used for interclient communication are discussed in Chapter 11.

5.1 WHAT IS AN EVENT?

An *event* is a notification, sent by the X server to a client, that some condition has changed. The X server generates events as a result of some user input, or as a side effect of a request to the X server. The server sends each event to all interested clients, who determine what kind of event has occurred by looking at the *type* of the event. Applications do not receive events automatically. They must specifically request the X server to send the types of events in which they are interested. Events always occur relative to a window, known as the *source window* of the event. If no client has requested the event for the source window, the server propagates the event up the X window hierarchy until it finds a window for which some client has requested the event, or it finds a window that prohibits the event propagation. The server only propagates *device events* generated as a result of a key, mouse button, or pointer motion. If the server reaches the root of the window tree without finding a client interested in the event, the event is discarded. The window to which the server finally reports the event is known as the *event window*.

The X server places all events in an event queue. Clients usually remove events from the event queue using the Xt Intrinsics function, **XtNextEvent()**. This function fills in an **XEvent** structure allocated by the client. Each event type is defined as a C struct. The **XEvent** structure is a C union of all event types.

All events contain a core set of basic information, contained in the first five members of every event structure. This information specifies

- the **type** of the event,
- the **display** where the event occurred,
- the event **window**,
- the **serial** number of the last request processed by server, and
- a **send_event** flag that indicates if this event was generated by the server or if the event was sent by another client. The flag is **TRUE** if the event was sent by another client, and **FALSE** if it was sent by the server.

The structure **XAnyEvent** is defined to allow access to those members that are common to all event types. Clients can access this basic information in any event using the **xany** member of the **XEvent** union, for example:

```
event.xany.window
```

The type of every event can also be accessed directly using:

```
event.type
```

Each event contains additional information, specific to the type of the event, that must be accessed using the member of the union corresponding to that event type. For example, the width of a window can be extracted from an **XConfigureNotify** event with

```
event.xconfigure.width
```

5.2 EVENT MASKS

An X application must request the event types it wishes the server to report for each window by passing an *event mask* to the Xlib function **XSelectInput()**, or by registering an event handler for the event using the Xt Intrinsics function **XtAddEventHandler()**. For example, the statement

```
XSelectInput(display, window, ButtonPressMask | ButtonReleaseMask);
```

requests the server to generate events when a mouse button is pressed or released in the given window. There is not always a direct correlation between the masks clients use to request events and the types of events reported by the server. For example, a client that selects events with SubstructureNotifyMask may be sent the events CirculateNotify, ConfigureNotify, and CreateNotify, and others. On the other hand, clients requesting events using PointerMotionMask or ButtonMotionMask receive a MotionNotify event when either type of event occurs.

5.3   EVENT TYPES

We can group the events supported by X into several general categories. The following sections discuss each event category and examine the information contained in these events.

5.3.1   Keyboard Events

The server generates a **KeyPress** event whenever a key is pressed and generates a **KeyRelease** event when the key is released. All keys, including modifier keys, (the <SHIFT> key, for example) generate events. A client can request **KeyPress** events by specifying **KeyPressMask** as the event mask when calling **XSelectInput()** or when defining an event handler. Clients request **KeyRelease** events using **KeyReleaseMask**. The server reports both **KeyRelease** and **KeyPress** events using an **XKeyEvent** structure. In addition to the members common to all X events, the **XKeyEvent** structure contains some additional information:

```
Window         root;
Window         subwindow;
Time           time;
int            x, y;
int            x_root, y_root;
unsigned int   state;
unsigned int   keycode;
Bool           same_screen;
```

The **root** member reports the ID of the root window of the screen where the event occurred. If the source window is a descendent of the event window, the **subwindow** member indicates the ID of the immediate child of the event window that lies between the event window and the source window. For example, assume that a window named BaseWindow has a child named Channel, and that Channel has a child named Thumb, as shown in Figure 5.1 and Figure 5.2. Also assume that only window BaseWindow has selected **KeyPress** events. If a **KeyPress** event occurs in Rect-Button, the event propagates to BaseWindow. The source window is **RectButton**. The event received by BaseWindow indicates BaseWindow as the event window. The **subwindow** member of the event contains the ID of the Channel window.

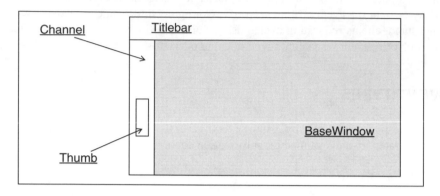

Figure 5.1 Event propagation.

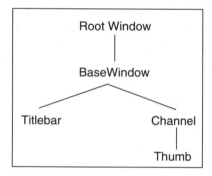

Figure 5.2 Window tree for Figure 5.1.

The **time** member of an **XKeyEvent** structure indicates the time in milliseconds since the server reset. This information is useful in preventing race conditions that can arise because the X server and its clients run asynchronously with respect to each other.

The **XKeyEvent** structure also contains the coordinates of the pointer relative to both the event window and the root window, as long as the event window is on the same screen as the root window. If this is not the case, the event reports the coordinates of the pointer as *(0, 0)*, relative to the root window.

The **XKeyEvent** structure contains a keycode that uniquely identifies the key that caused the event. Applications can use the Xlib function **XLookupString()** to map this keycode to the character string it represents. Xt also includes several functions for manipulating keycodes.

The **state** member of the event contains a mask indicating which, if any, modifier keys were depressed when this key was pressed. X supports many modifier keys including **<SHIFT>**, **<SHIFTLOCK>**, **<CONTROL>**, as well as up to five additional system-dependent modifier keys.

5.3.2   Pointer Events

The server generates **ButtonPress**, **ButtonRelease**, and **MotionNotify** events when the user presses or releases a mouse button or moves the pointer. The source window for pointer events is always the smallest window containing the pointer, unless some client has *grabbed* the pointer. When the pointer is grabbed, the server reports all pointer events to the window that initiated the grab.

The server reports **ButtonPress** and **ButtonRelease** events using an **XButtonEvent** structure. This event structure is similar to the **KeyPress** event structure, but instead of a key code, the **XButtonEvent** structure contains a **button** member which indicates what mouse button was pressed or released. X supports up to five mouse buttons, defined in the file X.h as **Button1**, **Button2**, **Button3**, **Button4**, and **Button5**. The mouse buttons can also be combined with a modifier key, such as the <SHIFT> or <META> key. The state of all modifier keys when the event occurred is indicated by the **state** member.

The server reports pointer motion events using an **XMotionEvent** structure. Clients can request the server to generate motion events whenever the user moves the pointer, or only when the user moves the pointer while holding down a particular button or combination of buttons. However, the server reports all motion events as type **MotionNotify**, using the **XMotionEvent** structure. Clients can determine the state of the mouse buttons (which buttons are up and which are down) by looking at the **state** member of the event.

By default, the server reports motion events continuously as the pointer moves. Clients can also request the server to *compress* motion events and generate events only when the pointer starts or stops moving. Most applications do not need continuous motion events and should request the server to compress pointer motion into *hints*, by requesting motion events with **PointerMotionHintMask**. The **is_hint** member of the **XMotionEvent** structure indicates whether an event indicates continuous motion or a hint. Other members of the event structure report the *(x, y)* position of the pointer relative to both the event window and the root window. The members of the **XMotionEvent** event structure include:

```
Window        root;
Window        subwindow;
Time          time;
int           x, y;
int           x_root, y_root;
unsigned int  state;
char          is_hint;
Bool          same_screen;
```

5.3.3   Crossing Events

The server generates crossing events whenever the pointer crosses the boundary of a window. The server sends an **EnterNotify** event to the window the pointer enters and a **LeaveNotify** event to the window the pointer leaves. The server also generates crossing events when the pointer enters a window because of a change in the window hierarchy. For example, if a window containing the pointer is lowered to the bottom of the window stack so that the pointer is now in another window, the first window receives a **LeaveNotify** event and the second window receives a **EnterNotify** event. Clients must request **EnterNotify** events using the mask **EnterWindowMask** and **LeaveNotify** events using the mask **LeaveWindowMask**. Both crossing events use the **XCrossingEvent** structure, which includes the members:

```
Window        root;
Window        subwindow;
Time          time;
int           x, y;
int           x_root, y_root;
int           mode;
int           detail;
Bool          same_screen;
Bool          focus;
unsigned int  state;
```

The **XCrossingEvent** structure always contains the final *(x, y)* coordinate of the pointer relative to both the event window and the root window. The **state** member of the event structure indicates the state of the mouse buttons immediately preceding the event.

Applications often need to determine the hierarchical relationship of the windows involved in a crossing event. For example, suppose we wish to write a program that highlights the border of its top-level window whenever the window contains the pointer. Highlighting the window border whenever the client receives an **EnterNotify** event, and unhighlighting the border whenever the client receives an **LeaveNotify** event, works correctly unless the window has subwindows. When the pointer enters a subwindow, the top-level window receives a **LeaveNotify** event, even though the pointer is still within the bounds of the window. There are several possible scenarios that can occur when the pointer moves between windows. To handle all possibilities correctly it is necessary to inspect the **detail** member of the event structure. The server sets this member to one of the constants **NotifyAncestor**, **NotifyVirtual**, **NotifyInferior**, **NotifyNonlinear**, or **NotifyNonlinearVirtual**, signifying the different types of window crossings that can occur.

Figure 5.3 through Figure 5.6 show the root window, and two children, Window A and Window B. Window A and Window B have subwindows Window C and Window D respectively. The vector in each figure represents a pointer movement starting in one window and ending in the window containing the arrow head. The text at the beginning and end of each line indicates the type of event generated in that window, with the value of the **detail** member of the event structure shown in parenthesis. Figure 5.3 illustrates the pointer moving from the root window into a child, Window B. The root window receives a **LeaveNotify** event with the **detail** member of the event set to **NotifyInferior**, while Window B receives an **EnterNotify** event, with the **detail** member set to **NotifyAncestor**.

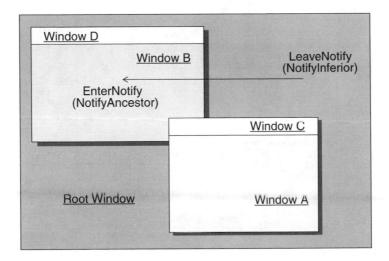

Figure 5.3 Crossing events.

Figure 5.4 illustrates the opposite situation, where the pointer moves from a window into the window's parent.

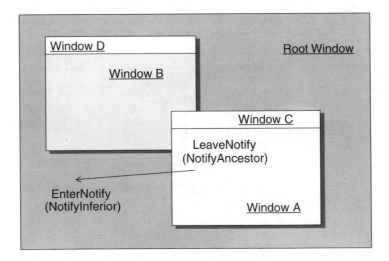

Figure 5.4 Crossing events.

Figure 5.5 illustrates movement of the pointer between two siblings. In this case, the server sets the `detail` member of each event to `NotifyNonlinear`.

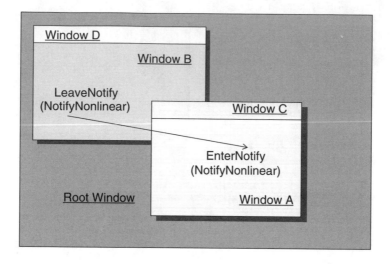

Figure 5.5 Crossing events.

Figure 5.6 shows the most complex situation, in which the pointer moves between two windows that are more than one level apart in the window hierarchy. In this case, Window C receives a `LeaveNotify` event and Window B receives an `EnterNotify` event. The `detail` member in both events is `NotifyNonlinear`. However, Window A also receives a `LeaveNotify` event, with the `detail` member set to `NotifyNonlinearVirtual`.

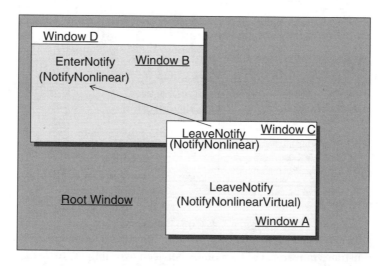

Figure 5.6 Crossing events.

The server also generates crossing events when an application grabs or ungrabs the pointer. When an application grabs the pointer, the server sends the window containing the pointer a **LeaveNotify** event with the **mode** member set to the constant **NotifyGrab**. When the grabbing application ungrabs the pointer, the server sends the window containing the pointer an **EnterNotify** event with the **mode** member set to **NotifyUngrab**. If the crossing event is not a result of a grab, the server sets the **mode** member of the event to **NotifyNormal**.

5.3.4   Focus Events

The window to which the X server sends keyboard events is known as the focus window. The server generates **FocusIn** and **FocusOut** events whenever the focus window changes, usually as a result of a window manager explicitly changing the focus window. Applications wishing to receive these events must select them using **FocusChangeMask**. Focus events are similar to **EnterNotify** and **LeaveNotify** events but are even more complex, because the pointer is not necessarily in any of the windows involved in the change of focus. Most applications that use the Xt Intrinsics do not need to handle focus events directly, because focus is handled by manager widgets.

5.3.5   Exposure Events

The server generates exposure events when a window or a portion of a window becomes visible. Clients must request exposure events using the **ExposureMask** event mask. There are three types of exposure events. The most common type, **Expose**, is generated when the contents of a region of a window are lost for any reason. The server sends a **GraphicsExpose** event when a client attempts to use **XCopyArea()** or **XCopyPlane()** to copy an obscured region of a window. **NoExpose** events can also be generated when copying areas between drawables. The server generates this event when an application requests **GraphicsExpose** events but no regions were obscured in the source that was copied. The server reports **Expose** events using an **XExposeEvent** structure, which includes the members:

```
int     x, y;
int     width, height;
int     count;
```

The **XExposeEvent** structure contains the x and y coordinates relative to the upper left corner of the window and the width and height of the rectangular region of the window that has been exposed. The event also contains a **count** member which indicates how many **Expose** events are still pending. If **count** is zero, there are no more **Expose** events pending for this window. However, if the **count** member is non-zero, then *at least* this many events are still pending.

Multiple **Expose** events occur primarily when an exposed region consists of more than one rectangular region. Applications that are not capable of redrawing arbitrary regions of windows can ignore **Expose** events with a non-zero **count** member, and redraw the entire contents of the window when the server generates an event whose **count** member is zero. The Xt Intrinsics allow widgets to request that multiple exposure events be *compressed* into a single **Expose** event. Xt automatically accumulates all **Expose** events until an event with **count** set to zero is received. The

Intrinsics then replace the coordinates in this last **Expose** event with the bounding box of the areas in all previous **Expose** events and invokes the widget's **Expose** event handler with the single **Expose** event.

5.3.6   Structure Control

The server reports structure control events to clients that ask for requests to be *redirected*. Window managers generally use event redirection to exercise control over application's windows. For example, if a window manager requests events using the mask **ResizeRedirectMask**, the X server ignores all requests from other applications to resize windows and instead sends a **ResizeRequest** event to the window manager. The window manager then has the opportunity to act on the request according to its screen management policy.

Requests that circulate a window's position in the stacking order, configure the window in any way, or map the window can also be redirected. If a window manager requests events using **SubstructureRedirectMask**, the X server generates **CirculateRequest**, **ConfigureRequest**, and **MapRequest** events instead of acting directly on these requests. Only one application can request the server to redirect events at any one time.

5.3.7   State Notification

Some applications need to be informed when its windows are reconfigured in any way. Clients can use the **StructureNotifyMask** event mask to request events when a window's configuration changes, or **SubstructureNotifyMask** to request notification of changes to a window's subwindows.

Clients that select events using the **StructureNotifyMask** can receive many different types of events, depending on what changes occur. When a window's position in the stacking order changes because of a call to the Xlib functions **XCirculateSubwindows()**, **XCirculateSubwindowsUp()**, or **XCirculateSubwindowsDown()**, the server generates a **CirculateNotify** event, which uses an **XCirculateEvent** structure. This structure includes the members:

```
Window event;
Window window;
int    place;
```

The **event** member of this structure indicates the event window. The **window** member is set to the ID of the window that was restacked. This window is not necessarily the same as the event window. The server also sets the **place** member of this event to the constant **PlaceOnBottom**, indicating the window is below all siblings, or the constant **PlaceOnTop**, indicating that the window is above all siblings.

The server generates **ConfigureNotify** events whenever a window's size, position, or border width changes. The server reports this event using an **XConfigureEvent** structure. **ConfigureNotify** events are also generated when a window's position in the stacking order changes because of a call to the Xlib functions **XLowerWindow()**, **XRaiseWindow()**,

`XRestackWindow()`, or `XRestackWindows()`. The members in the `XConfigureEvent` structure include:

```
Window   event;
Window   window;
int      x, y;
int      width, height;
int      border_width;
Window   above;
Bool     override_redirect;
```

The **event** member of the **XConfigureEvent** structure indicates the event window while the **window** member indicates the window that has changed. The **above** member contains the ID of the sibling window just below the window whose position in the stacking order has changed. If the window is on the bottom of the stacking order, the **above** member of the **XConfigureNotify** event is set to **None**.

The server generates **CreateNotify** and **DestroyNotify** events whenever a window is created or destroyed, respectively. Clients that wish to receive these events must request events for the window's parent using **SubstructureNotifyMask**. The event structure of the **CreateNotify** event contains the IDs of both the new window and the parent of the new window, and also the size and location of the window. The **DestroyNotify** event contains only the event window and the ID of the destroyed window.

Other types of structure notification events include **GravityNotify**, **MapNotify**, **ReparentNotify**, **UnmapNotify**, and **VisibilityNotify**. The application programmer seldom needs to deal with these events directly, because Xt normally handles them automatically.

5.3.8   Colormap Notification

Applications that need to know when a new color map is installed can request **ColormapNotify** events using the mask **ColormapChangeMask**. Color maps determine the colors available to an application, and are discussed in Chapter 6. The server reports **ColormapNotify** events using an **XColormapEvent** structure that contains the ID of the colormap, a boolean value that indicates whether an attribute of colormap has changed, and a **state** member set to one of the constants **ColormapInstalled** or **ColormapUninstalled**. The members of the **XColormapEvent** structure include:

```
Colormap colormap;
Bool     new;
int      state;
```

5.3.9   Communication Events

X also supports events that allow direct communication between applications, and events that provide a mechanism for exchanging and sharing data between applications. **ClientMessage** events can be used by applications to define additional events that can be sent between applications using the Xlib function:

```
XSendEvent(display, window, propagate, mask, event)
```

Applications cannot specifically request `ClientMessage` events. The server always sends `ClientMessage` events to the destination window. Chapter 11 discusses `ClientMessage` events and shows some examples of direct interclient communication.

The server generates `PropertyNotify` events when the value of a window *property* is modified. Applications interested in receiving `PropertyNotify` events must select the event using `PropertyChangeMask` as an argument to `XSelectInput()` or `XtAddEventHandler()`. Properties and `PropertyNotify` events are discussed in Chapter 11.

`SelectionClear`, `SelectionNotify`, and `SelectionRequest` events are used by the X selection mechanism for exchanging data between applications. Like `ClientMessage` events, selection events cannot be specifically selected by an application. Selections are also discussed in Chapter 11.

5.4 HANDLING EVENTS WITH THE Xt INTRINSICS

Xt hides many of the details of handing events from the programmer and allows widgets to handle many of the common X events automatically. As a result, many applications built using the X Toolkit do not need to deal directly with events at all. However, the Xt Intrinsics library does provide facilities that allow applications to receive and handle events if needed. Applications can request a specific type of event by defining a handler for that event. The **memo** example in Chapter 2 introduced the use of event handlers. That chapter also discussed the advantages of using callbacks and the translation manager instead of handling the events directly. There are situations, however, where applications need to handle events directly. The following sections explore some ways to use events and event handlers.

5.4.1 Using Event Handlers

This section presents two examples that use event handlers to handle `MotionNotify` events, `ButtonPress` events, and crossing events. These examples illustrate accessing and using the information in the event structures. Later examples demonstrate dynamically installing and removing event handlers.

The first example creates a module that tracks and reports the position of the pointer in an arbitrary widget. We will refer to this module as a *mouse tracker*. For purposes of demonstration, the mouse tracker displays the current position of the pointer in a StaticText widget, but you can probably imagine more practical uses for tracking the position of the pointer. Let's first examine the body of a simple driver program to test the mouse tracker, named **mousetracks**.

```
/************************************************************
 * mousetracks.c: Driver to test the mouse tracker module
 ************************************************************/
#include <X11/StringDefs.h>
#include <X11/Intrinsic.h>
#include <Xol/OpenLook.h>
```

```
#include <Xol/ControlAre.h>
#include <Xol/Stub.h>
#include "libXs.h"

main(argc, argv)
    int            argc;
    char           *argv[];
{
    Widget         toplevel, command, target;

    /*
     * Initialize the Intrinsics.
     */
    toplevel = OlInitialize(argv[0], "Mousetracks", NULL, 0,
                            &argc, argv);
    /*
     * Create a command widget to hold both the target area
     * and the mouse tracker display.
     */
    command = XtCreateManagedWidget("command",
                                    controlAreaWidgetClass,
                                    toplevel, NULL, 0);
    /*
     *  Create the widget in which we track the
     *  motion of the pointer.
     */
    target = XtCreateManagedWidget("target", stubWidgetClass,
                                    command, NULL, 0);
    /*
     * Create the mouse tracker.
     */
    create_mouse_tracker(command, target);
    XtRealizeWidget(toplevel);
    XtMainLoop();
}
```

This test driver initializes the Intrinsics and then creates a ControlArea widget that manages two children, a StaticText widget and a Stub widget. The Stub widget provides an empty window, used in this example as the window in which the pointer motion is tracked. The StaticText widget is used to display the mouse position. Figure 5.7 shows the widget tree formed by the widgets in this example.

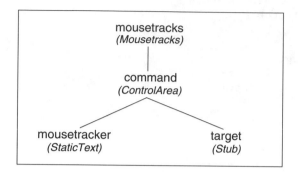

Figure 5.7 The mousetracks widget tree.

The function **create_mouse_tracker()** creates the mouse tracker module, and takes two arguments. The first indicates a parent widget that manages the StaticText widget created by the mouse tracker. The second specifies the widget in which the pointer position is to be tracked. The mouse tracker only reports the pointer position when the pointer is in this target widget.

The function **create_mouse_tracker()** is defined as:

```
create_mouse_tracker(parent, target)
  Widget    parent, target;
{
  extern void  clear_tracker();
  extern void  track_mouse_position();
  Widget        tracker;

  /*
   * Create the tracker widget and register event
   * handlers for the target widget.
   */
  tracker = XtCreateManagedWidget("mousetracker",
                             staticTextWidgetClass,
                             parent, NULL, 0);
  XtAddEventHandler(target, LeaveWindowMask, FALSE,
                   clear_tracker, tracker);
  XtAddEventHandler(target, PointerMotionMask, FALSE,
                   track_mouse_position, tracker);
}
```

This function creates a StaticText widget, **tracker**, as a child of the given parent widget and then registers two event handlers for the **target** widget. The first handles **PointerMotion** events while the other handles **LeaveNotify** events. The **tracker** widget is specified as client data for both event handlers.

Xt invokes the event handler **track_mouse_motion()** whenever the user moves the pointer within the **target** window. This function extracts the current pointer location from the event structure and displays it in the **tracker** widget. This event handler is defined as:

```
void
track_mouse_position(w, client_data, event, continue_to_dispatch)
  Widget    w;
  XtPointer client_data;
  XEvent    *event;
  Boolean   *continue_to_dispatch;
{
  Widget tracker = (Widget)client_data;

  /*
   * Extract the position of the pointer from the event
   * and display it in the tracker widget.
   */
  xs_wprintf(tracker, "X: %4d, Y: %4d",
             event->xmotion.x, event->xmotion.y);
}
```

The function **xs_wprintf()** is a simple routine that displays text in a widget using the same syntax as **printf()**. Let's wait to describe this function until we have finished describing the tracker module.

It is usually a bad idea to display status information when it is no longer valid, such as when the pointer is no longer in the target window. The **clear_tracker()** event handler clears the contents of the **tracker** widget when the pointer leaves the **target** widget's window.

```
void
clear_tracker(w, client_data, event, continue_to_dispatch)
  Widget    w;
  XtPointer client_data;
  XEvent    *event;
  Boolean   *continue_to_dispatch;
{
  Widget tracker = (Widget)client_data;

  /*
   * Display an empty string in the tracker widget.
   */
  xs_wprintf(tracker, "");
}
```

The mouse tracker could be added to nearly any application without interfering with the normal operation of the program. The Intrinsics library allows applications to define multiple event handlers for each event, so the event handlers added by **create_mouse_tracker()** are invoked in addition to any other handlers registered with the target widget for the same events.

This example uses event handlers in a very straightforward way, but we can create more complex variations of this example. For example, let's modify the mouse tracker to report the position of the pointer only while a mouse button is pressed. To do this, we first need to redefine the `create_mouse_tracker()` function.

```
create_mouse_tracker(parent, target)
  Widget      parent, target;
{
  extern void   clear_tracker();
  extern void   track_mouse_position();
  extern void   show_mouse_position();
  Widget        tracker;

  /*
   * Create the tracker widget.
   */
  tracker = XtCreateManagedWidget("mousetracker",
                                  staticTextWidgetClass,
                                  parent, NULL, 0);
  /*
   * Set up event handlers on target widget.
   */
  XtAddEventHandler(target, ButtonPressMask, FALSE,
                    show_mouse_position, tracker);
  XtAddEventHandler(target,
                    Button1MotionMask | Button2MotionMask,
                    FALSE, track_mouse_position, tracker);
  XtAddEventHandler(target, ButtonReleaseMask, FALSE,
                    clear_tracker, tracker);
}
```

This variation registers three event handlers for the **target** widget. The function **track_mouse_position()** (defined exactly as before) is registered as an event handler for both **Button1MotionMask** and **Button2MotionMask** events by passing the inclusive-OR of both event masks to **XtAddEventHandler()**. When a single function handles multiple types of events, the event handler can check the type member of the event to determine the event type. In this example **track_mouse_position()** performs the same action in either case. This function is only invoked if the user moves the pointer while holding down mouse button 1 or mouse button 2. It should also be noted that the **track_mouse_position()** event handler continues to be called when the pointer moves out of the target widget if the mouse button is continuously held down. This is because the server establishes a *passive grab* on the mouse button. For more details on grabs see section 10.2.

This version of the mouse tracker registers a new event handler for **ButtonPress** events. This function, **show_mouse_position()**, is defined as:

```
void
show_mouse_position(w, client_data, event, continue_to_dispatch)
  Widget    w;
  XtPointer client_data;
  XEvent    *event;
  Boolean   *continue_to_dispatch;
{
  Widget tracker = (Widget)client_data;

  /*
   * Extract the position of the pointer from the event
   * and display it in the tracker widget.
   */
  xs_wprintf(tracker, "X: %4d, Y: %4d",
             event->xbutton.x, event->xbutton.y);
}
```

This function is nearly the same as **track_mouse_position()**, except that it extracts the position of the pointer from the **XButtonPressedEvent** structure, using the **xbutton** member of the **XEvent** union rather than **xmotion**. We could use the same function to handle both of these events, because the definition of the **XButtonEvent** and **XMotionEvent** event structures are identical, except for the names. The expressions

```
event->xbutton.x
```

and

```
event->xmotion.x
```

both access the same member in the event structure. However it is not good programming practice to rely on such implementation-dependent details.

In this version of **create_mouse_tracker()**, the function **clear_tracker()** (also defined exactly as in the earlier version) is registered as an event handler for the **ButtonRelease** event.

The function **xs_wprintf()** is a useful function that uses **XtSetValues()** to change the string displayed in any subclass of the StaticText widget class. The function has a form similar to the C library function **fprintf()**, except that it displays its output in a widget. We will use this function again, so we will place it in the libXs library. The function uses the utility macros found in the UNIX header file /usr/include/varargs.h in combination with **vsprintf()** to handle a variable number of arguments.

```
/************************************************************
 * xs_wprintf: fprintf-like function for StaticText widgets
 ************************************************************/
#include <varargs.h>
#include <stdio.h>
#include <X11/Intrinsic.h>
#include <X11/StringDefs.h>
```

```
#include <Xol/OpenLook.h>
#include <Xol/StaticText.h>

void xs_wprintf(va_alist)
  va_dcl
{
  Widget    w;
  char      *format;
  va_list   args;
  char      str[1000];   /* DANGER: Fixed buffer size */
  Arg       wargs[1];

  /*
   * Init the variable length args list.
   */
  va_start(args);
  /*
   * Extract the destination widget.
   * Make sure it is a subclass of StaticText.
   */
  w = va_arg(args, Widget);
  if(!XtIsSubclass(w, staticTextWidgetClass))
     XtError("xs_wprintf() requires a StaticText Widget");
  /*
   * Extract the format to be used.
   */
  format = va_arg(args, char *);
  /*
   * Use vsprintf to format the string to be displayed in the
   * StaticText widget.
   */
  vsprintf(str, format, args);

  XtSetArg(wargs[0], XtNstring, str);
  XtSetValues(w, wargs, 1);

  va_end(args);
}
```

5.5 THE CONSUME EVENT CALLBACK

OLIT provides an alternative method of handling events. Rather than calling
`XtAddEventHandler()`, a callback can be added to the `XtNconsumeEvent` callback list
which is invoked when specified events occur. This is possible because the translation table action
procedure for all OLIT widgets is always `OlAction()`. `OlAction()` calls the procedures on the

XtNconsumeEvent callback list before allowing the toolkit or widgets to process the event. This gives the programmer a hook to modify or override normal operations. This feature takes advantage of OLIT's *virtual event* mechanism.

Virtual events are an abstraction built on top of the X event mechanism and are used extensively within the OLIT toolkit. An example of a virtual event is **OL_SELECT** which represents the SELECT mouse button. Virtual events can be used to re-map user actions. For example, we can change the SELECT mouse button from the left button (the default) to the right button and the MENU button from the right button (the default) to the left button. We do this by setting a resource that binds Button3 to the virtual event **OL_SELECT** and binds Button1 to the virtual event **OL_MENU**.

```
*selectBtn: <Button3>
*menuBtn:   <Button1>
```

Now the right mouse button is mapped as the SELECT button and the left mouse buttons is mapped as the MENU button. This is a button binding. An example of a key binding is:

```
*pageDownKey:  c<v>
```

This binds Control-V to the **OL_PAGEDOWN** virtual event. A widget such as the ScrolledWindow will now page down when Control-V is pressed. Binding keys and buttons to virtual events provides a convenient way to handle user configuration without having to re-program applications.

Let's modify the original version of the mouse tracker program using an **XtNconsumeEvent** callback rather than event handlers. We will only need one callback: **consume_callback()**.

```
#include <X11/StringDefs.h>
#include <X11/Intrinsic.h>
#include <Xol/OpenLook.h>
#include <Xol/StaticText.h>
#include "libXs.h"

create_mouse_tracker(parent, target)
  Widget    parent, target;
{
  extern void  clear_tracker();
  extern void  track_mouse_position();
  extern void  consume_callback();
  Widget        tracker;

  /*
   * Create the tracker widget and register event
   * handlers for the target widget.
   */
  tracker = XtCreateManagedWidget("mousetracker",
                                  staticTextWidgetClass,
                                  parent, NULL, 0);
  XtAddCallback(target, XtNconsumeEvent, consume_callback, tracker);
}
```

When `consume_callback()` is invoked, its `call_data` parameter is a pointer to an `OlVirtualEvent` structure. The members of the `OlVirtualEvent` structure include:

```
Boolean          consumed;
XEvent           *xevent;
OlVirtualName    virtual_name;
```

The **consumed** member is used to *consume* the event. Setting the **consumed** member of the structure to TRUE in the callback will consume the event. Consuming an event means that the event will not be dispatched further by the event processing mechanism. This prevents OLIT from acting on the event in any way. This is analogous to setting the **continue_to_dispatch** parameter of an event handler to FALSE. The **xevent** member of this structure is a pointer to the **XEvent** which caused the callback to be invoked. The **virtual_name** member is the name of the virtual event that occurred. (See APPENDIX C).

In the **consume_callback()** function we examine both the **virtual_name** and the **xevent** fields to determine the type of event that occurred and take the appropriate action. In this function, we are interested in both the **MotionNotify** X event and the **OL_SELECT** virtual event. If we receive both an **OL_SELECT** virtual event and a **MotionNotify** X event, then the position of the pointer is displayed. This means that the user must hold down the SELECT key while in the **tracker** widget for the position to be displayed.

```
void
consume_callback( w, client_data, call_data)
  Widget w;
  XtPointer client_data, call_data;
{
  OlVirtualEvent vevent = (OlVirtualEvent)call_data;
  XMotionEvent *event = (XMotionEvent *)vevent->xevent;
  Widget tracker = (Widget)client_data;

  if(vevent->virtual_name == OL_SELECT && event->type == MotionNotify)
    xs_wprintf(tracker, "X: %4d, Y: %4d", event->x, event->y);
  else
    xs_wprintf(tracker, "");
}
```

The **XtNconsumeEvent** callback is invoked for every event that occurs which has a translation defined for **OlAction()**. (See Section 2.4.5). Therefore, we ensure that a translation for **OlAction()** is defined by adding the following resource:

```
Mousetracks*Stub.translations: #augment \n\
        <Motion>: OlAction()
```

5.6   MANAGING THE EVENT QUEUE

Most applications use the function **XtMainLoop()** to remove events from the event queue and dispatch them to the appropriate widgets. However, occasionally an application needs to have more control over this process. Xlib provides many functions for examining and manipulating the event queue. These are seldom needed by applications that use the Intrinsics and widgets, although they can be used if needed. The Xt Intrinsics layer provides its own versions of the most common functions for examining the event queue,

```
XtPending()
```

and

```
XtPeekEvent(&event)
```

XtPending() returns a mask of type **XtInputMask** that indicates the type of input available or zero if the event queue is empty. The possible return values include **XtIMXEvent**, **XtIMTimer**, **XtIMAlternateInput**, and **XtIMAll**. **XtPeekEvent()** copies the event at the top of the event queue into the application-supplied event structure, but does not remove the event from the event queue. **XtPending()** is useful when an application needs to do other tasks whenever there are no events in the event queue. For example, we could write an application's main event loop as:

```
if(XtPending()) {
   XtNextEvent(&event);
   XtDispatchEvent (&event)
}
else{  /* Do something else for a while */
 }
```

Notice that this can result in many wasted CPU cycles because the application continuously polls for events. To prevent this, the loop should block for some length of time after the task is completed. This can be done using the UNIX function **select()** to watch for input from the X file descriptor, which can be retrieved from the display using the **ConnectionNumber()** macro:

```
while(TRUE){
  if(XtPending()) {  /* If an event is pending, get it and */
     XEvent event;  /* process it normally.              */
     XtNextEvent(&event);
     XtDispatchEvent (&event);
  }
  else{              /* Otherwise do a "background" task */
    struct timeval timeout;
    int readfds = 0;  /* Initialize arguments to select() */
    int maxfds = 1 + ConnectionNumber(XtDisplay(toplevel));
    timeout.tv_sec = 1; /* Set timeout for 1 second. */
    timeout.tv_usec = 0;
    /*
```

```
       * Do something else for a while - insert code here.
       */
      readfds = 1 << ConnectionNumber(XtDisplay(toplevel));
      /*
       * Block for tv.sec or until input is pending from X
       */
      if (select(maxfds, &readfds, NULL, NULL, &timeout) == -1){
        if (EINTR != errno)
            exit(1);
      }
    }
}
```

This approach assumes that the time required to perform the task when no events are available is short, so that the loop returns to process events in a reasonable time period. Sections 5.6 and 5.7 describe slightly different approaches for doing this.

5.7 HANDLING TIMEOUTS

Although many useful X applications only process events from the user, some applications need to perform other tasks as well. The next few sections explore facilities provided by the Xt Intrinsics that extend Xlib's notion of events to allow applications to use the event dispatching mechanism to perform these tasks. One such feature allows applications to register a callback procedure to be invoked by the Intrinsics when a specified interval has elapsed. Applications can use the function

```
XtAddTimeOut(interval, proc, client_data)
```

to register a timeout callback and specify the time delay before it is invoked. **XtAddTimeOut()** returns an ID of type **XtIntervalId** that uniquely identifies this timeout event. The first argument specifies the time interval, in milliseconds, until Xt invokes the callback function **proc**. The **data** parameter specifies some client data to be passed to the timeout callback function when it is called.

The form of a timeout callback is:

```
void proc(client_data, id)
   XtPointer      client_data;
   XtIntervalId  *id;
```

where **data** is the client data specified in the call to **XtAddTimeOut()** and **id** is a pointer to the **XtIntervalId** identifier of the timeout event. When a timeout event occurs, Xt invokes the corresponding callback and then automatically removes the callback. Therefore, timeout events are only invoked once. Clients can use the function

```
XtRemoveTimeOut(id)
```

to remove a timeout callback before the timeout occurs. The argument, **id**, must be the **XtIntervalId** of the timer event to be removed.

5.7.1   Using Timeouts as Alarms

Timeout events can be viewed as alarms that can be set to go off some time in the future. This section uses such an alarm to improve the original version of the mouse tracker example from Section 5.4.1. One problem with tracking and reporting all **MotionNotify** events is that both the X server and clients generally have trouble keeping up with the large number of events that can be generated. Moving the pointer across the mouse tracker's target window can slow the entire system because of the overhead involved in generating continuous motion events. This might be acceptable to someone actually using something like the mouse tracker, but what if the user accidently moves the pointer through the mouse tracker's target window on the way to another application's window? It can be frustrating to have the pointer slow down while it passes through the target area, when we are not really interested in the pointer position in the window.

We can solve this problem by using **XtAddTimeOut()** to set an alarm whenever the pointer enters the target window. We can then redesign the mouse tracker so that the position of the pointer is not reported (and no events are generated) until the alarm goes off. By setting the alarm interval appropriately, we can keep the mouse tracker from being activated when the pointer passes quickly through the target window.

In addition to demonstrating the use of timeout events, this version of the mouse tracker also demonstrates several other techniques for using event handlers. The previous examples defined and installed event handlers when the program began. This example dynamically adds and removes event handlers and callbacks within other event handlers. This example also exploits the ability to pass client-defined data to event handlers and callbacks to allow all event handlers access to some common data without resorting to global variables.

In this example, all data used by the mouse tracker and its event handlers is kept in a single data structure, defined as:

```
typedef struct {
    Widget          tracker;
    Widget          target;
    XtIntervalId    id;
    int             delay;
} track_data, *track_data_ptr;
```

The **tracker** member of this structure contains the mouse tracker's StaticText widget, while the **target** member indicates the widget in which mouse motion events are being monitored. The **id** member of this data structure contains the **XtIntervalId** identifier for the timeout event, and **delay** specifies the time, in milliseconds, that the pointer must remain in the target window before the pointer position is reported. In this example, this delay is set to one second. The function **create_mouse_tracker()** allocates and initializes this structure and then registers a single event handler for the target widget.

```
#define DELAY 1000

create_mouse_tracker(parent, target)
  Widget          parent, target;
{
```

```
    extern void        enter_window_handler();
    static track_data data;

    data.delay = DELAY;
    /*
     * Store the target and tracker widgets in the data.
     */
    data.target  = target;
    data.tracker = XtCreateManagedWidget("mousetracker",
                                          staticTextWidgetClass,
                                          parent, NULL, 0);
    /*
     * Start with a single event handler.
     */
    XtAddEventHandler(data.target, EnterWindowMask, FALSE,
                      enter_window_handler, &data);
}
```

The Intrinsics invoke the function **enter_window_handler()** when an **EnterNotify** event occurs. The client data for this event handler is a pointer to the **track_data** structure declared in the **create_mouse_tracker()** routine. This event handler does two things. First, it registers a new event handler, **disable_alarm()**. Xt calls this event handler when the pointer leaves the target window. Second, it adds a timeout callback, **start_tracking()**, to be invoked after the time specified by the **delay** member of the client data structure. Notice that the same client data is also given as the client data argument for the timeout callback.

```
static void
enter_window_handler(w, client_data, event, continue_to_dispatch)
  Widget     w;
  XtPointer client_data;
  XEvent    *event;
  Boolean   *continue_to_dispatch;
{
  track_data *data = (track_data *)client_data;
  extern void  start_tracking();
  extern void  disable_alarm();

  /*
   * When the pointer enters the window, install
   * a timeout callback, and start the count-down.
   */
  XtAddEventHandler(data->target, LeaveWindowMask, FALSE,
                    disable_alarm, data);
  data->id = XtAddTimeOut(data->delay, start_tracking, data);
}
```

So, what happens when the pointer quickly passes through the target window? First, the Intrinsics invoke the function **enter_window_handler()**. This function sets an alarm that causes the function **start_tracking()** to be invoked after the specified delay. However, if the pointer leaves the target window before the timeout event occurs, the event handler **disable_alarm()** is called. This event handler is defined as:

```
static void
disable_alarm(w, client_data, event, continue_to_dispatch)
  Widget    w;
  XtPointer client_data;
  XEvent    *event;
  Boolean   *continue_to_dispatch;
{
  track_data *data = (track_data *)client_data;

  /*
   * Remove the timeout callback and then remove
   * ourself as an event handler.
   */
  XtRemoveTimeOut(data->id);
  XtRemoveEventHandler(data->target, LeaveWindowMask, FALSE,
                       disable_alarm, data);
}
```

This function uses **XtRemoveTimeOut()** to remove the timeout callback before it is invoked and also uses **XtRemoveEventHandler()** to remove itself as an event handler. At this point, the mouse tracker is in the same state as before the pointer entered the window, and the only event handler registered is the **enter_window_handler()** function. Notice that in this scenario, no **MotionNotify** events are generated because the mouse tracker never requests motion events.

Now suppose the pointer is still within the target window when the timeout event occurs. In this case, the Intrinsics call the timeout callback **start_tracking()**. This callback does three things. First, it removes the **disable_alarm()** event handler, which is no longer needed because Xt removes timeout callbacks automatically when the timeout occurs. Next, it registers the function **track_mouse_position()** as an event handler for **MotionNotify** events, and last, it registers **leave_window_handler()** as an event handler for **LeaveNotify** events. This sets up the event handlers in the same way as the original example in Section 5.4.1.

```
static void
start_tracking(client_data, id)
  XtPointer       client_data;
  XtIntervalId    *id;
{
  track_data *data = (track_data *)client_data;
  extern void disable_alarm();
  extern void leave_window_handler();
  extern void track_mouse_position();

  /*
```

```
       * If this function was called, the alarm must have
       * gone off, so remove the disable_alarm event handler.
       */
     XtRemoveEventHandler(data->target, LeaveWindowMask,
                           FALSE, disable_alarm, data);
     /*
      * Now add event handlers to track the pointer motion
      * and clear the tracker when we leave the target window.
      */
     XtAddEventHandler(data->target, PointerMotionMask,
                       FALSE, track_mouse_position, data);
     XtAddEventHandler(data->target, LeaveWindowMask,
                       FALSE, leave_window_handler, data);
}
```

The function **track_mouse_position()** is similar to the previous version in Section 5.4.1, but extracts the tracker widget from the **track_data** structure passed as client data.

```
static void
track_mouse_position(w, client_data, event, continue_to_dispatch)
  Widget    w;
  XtPointer client_data;
  XEvent    *event;
  Boolean   *continue_to_dispatch;
{
  track_data *data = (track_data *)client_data;

  /*
   * Extract the position of the pointer from the event
   * and display it in the tracker widget.
   */
  xs_wprintf(data->tracker, "X: %4d, Y: %4d",
             event->xmotion.x, event->xmotion.y);
}
```

As long as the pointer remains in the target widget, the tracker widget displays the current position of the pointer. When the pointer leaves the target widget, the Intrinsics call the event handler **leave_window_handler()**. This function resets the mouse tracker to its initial state by removing the **track_mouse_position()** event handler, clearing the mouse tracker's display widget, and finally removing itself as an event handler.

```
static void
leave_window_handler(w, client_data, event, continue_to_dispatch)
  Widget    w;
  XtPointer client_data;
  XEvent    *event;
  Boolean   *continue_to_dispatch;
{
```

```
    track_data *data = (track_data *)client_data;
    extern void  track_mouse_position();

    /*
     * Clear the tracker widget display.
     */
    xs_wprintf(data->tracker, "");
    /*
     * Remove the dynamically installed event handlers.
     */
    XtRemoveEventHandler(data->target, PointerMotionMask, FALSE,
                         track_mouse_position, data);
    XtRemoveEventHandler(data->target, LeaveWindowMask, FALSE,
                         leave_window_handler, data);
}
```

5.7.2   Cyclic Timeouts

Applications often need to perform some action repeatedly at designated intervals. Although Xt automatically removes timeout callbacks when the timeout event occurs, applications can arrange for timeout callbacks to be invoked at regular intervals by designing the callback to re-install itself each time it is called. An obvious application of this technique is a clock. We can write a digital clock easily using an StaticText widget and a single timeout callback. The body of the clock program is:

```
/****************************************************
 * xclock.c : A simple digital clock
 ****************************************************/
#include <X11/Intrinsic.h>
#include <X11/StringDefs.h>
#include <Xol/OpenLook.h>
#include <Xol/StaticText.h>
#include <time.h>

void update_time();

main(argc, argv)
  int           argc;
  char          *argv[];
{
  Widget        toplevel, clock;

  /*
   * Create the widgets.
   */
  toplevel = OlInitialize(argv[0], "Clock", NULL, 0, &argc, argv);
  clock = XtCreateManagedWidget("face", staticTextWidgetClass,
                                toplevel, NULL, 0);
```

```
/*
 * Get the initial time.
 */
update_time(clock, NULL);
XtRealizeWidget(toplevel);
XtMainLoop();
}
```

Before entering the main loop, the program calls the function **update_time()** to display the initial time in the widget. This function uses the UNIX system call **time()** to determine the current time in seconds since 00:00:00 GMT (Greenwich Mean Time), Jan 1, 1970. After rounding the time to the nearest minute, the function calls the UNIX library routine **ctime()** to convert this value to a string representing the current time and date.

After displaying the string in the StaticText widget, the function registers itself as a timeout callback. Each time the callback is invoked, it re-registers itself. The delay until the next timeout event is calculated to occur on the next full minute, to keep the clock reasonably accurate in spite of any variations in the timeouts. The **update_time()** function is defined as:

```
void
update_time(client_data, id)
   XtPointer      client_data;
   XtIntervalId  *id;
{
   Widget w = (Widget)client_data;
   long   tloc, rounded_tloc, next_minute;
   char   thetime[256];

   /*
    * Ask Unix for the time.
    */
   time(&tloc);
   /*
    * Convert the time to a string and display it,
    * after rounding it down to the last minute.
    */
   rounded_tloc = tloc / 60 * 60;
   sprintf(thetime, "%s", ctime(&rounded_tloc));
   thetime[strlen(thetime)-1] = NULL;
   xs_wprintf(w, "%s", thetime);
   /*
    * Adjust the time to reflect the time till
    * the next round minute.
    */
   next_minute = (60 - tloc % 60) * 1000;
   /*
    * The Intrinsics removes timeouts when they occur,
    * so put ourselves back.
    */
```

```
    */
  XtAddTimeOut(next_minute, update_time, w);
}
```

Figure 5.8 shows the digital clock created by this example.

Figure 5.8 xclock: A digital clock.

5.8 USING WORK PROCEDURESS

The Xt Intrinsics support a type of callback function known as a work procedure that provides a limited form of background processing. This facility works in much the same way as the example using `select()` in Section 5.6. However, work procedures allow the programmer to register a callback and hides the details of the event processing from the programmer. A work procedure is a callback that is invoked by the Intrinsics whenever there are no events pending. A work procedure takes only a single argument, which is client-defined data. The procedure is expected to return **TRUE** if the callback should be removed after it is called, and **FALSE** otherwise.

Applications can register a work procedure using the function:

```
XtAddWorkProc(proc, client_data)
```

This function returns an ID that identifies the work procedure. The **client_data** argument specifies some application-defined data to be passed to the work procedure. Work procedures can be removed by calling the function

```
XtRemoveWorkProc(id)
```

where **id** is the identifier returned by **XtAddWorkProc()**. We can use work procedures to write a "stopwatch" variation on the clock program from the previous section that updates the time continuously. This example shows how work procedures allow a mixture of background processing and event handling.

In addition to a StaticText widget in which time is continuously displayed, this example creates two OblongButton widgets. One starts the stopwatch, the other stops the stopwatch. The main body of the program creates the OblongButton and StaticText widgets and registers a callback functions for each OblongButton widget.

```
/*****************************************************
 * stopwatch.c: A digital stopwatch using work procedures.
 *****************************************************/
#include <X11/Intrinsic.h>
#include <X11/StringDefs.h>
```

```
#include <Xol/OpenLook.h>
#include <Xol/StaticText.h>
#include <Xol/ControlAre.h>
#include <Xol/OblongButt.h>
#include <time.h>
#include "libXs.h"

Boolean update_time();
void    start_timing();
void    stop_timing();

long          start_time;
XtWorkProcId work_proc_id = NULL;

main(argc, argv)
  int       argc;
  char      *argv[];
{
  Widget    toplevel, panel, commands, start, stop, timer;

  toplevel = OlInitialize(argv[0], "Stopwatch", NULL, 0,
                          &argc, argv);
  /*
   * Create a ControlArea widget to hold everything.
   */
  panel = XtCreateManagedWidget("panel", controlAreaWidgetClass,
                                toplevel, NULL, 0);
  /*
   * A StaticText widget shows the current time.
   */
  timer = XtCreateManagedWidget("timer", staticTextWidgetClass,
                                panel, NULL, 0);
  /*
   * Add start and stop buttons and register callbacks.
   * Pass the timer widget to all callbacks.
   */
  commands = XtCreateManagedWidget("commands",
                                   controlAreaWidgetClass,
                                   panel, NULL, 0);
  start = XtCreateManagedWidget("start", oblongButtonWidgetClass,
                                commands, NULL, 0);
  XtAddCallback(start, XtNselect, start_timing, timer);
  stop = XtCreateManagedWidget("stop", oblongButtonWidgetClass,
                               commands, NULL, 0);
  XtAddCallback(stop, XtNselect, stop_timing, timer);
  xs_wprintf(timer, "%02d : %02d", 0, 0);
```

```
   XtRealizeWidget(toplevel);
   XtMainLoop();
}
```

The **start_timing()** callback function determines the initial time and registers a work procedure with the Intrinsics to update the stopwatch display. It uses **time()** to get the current time. Next, in case the user presses the start button multiple times, the function removes any previous work procedure before registering the function **update_time()** as a work procedure.

```
void
start_timing(w, client_data, call_data)
   Widget      w;
   XtPointer   client_data;
   XtPointer   call_data;
{
   Widget timer = (Widget)client_data;

   /*
    * Get the initial time, and save it in a global.
    */
   time(&start_time);
   /*
    * If a WorkProc has already been added, remove it.
    */
   if(work_proc_id)
     XtRemoveWorkProc(work_proc_id);
   /*
    * Register update_time() as a WorkProc.
    */
   work_proc_id = XtAddWorkProc(update_time, timer);
}
```

The **stop_timing()** callback function simply removes the work procedure, if one exists.

```
void
stop_timing(w, client_data, call_data)
   Widget      w;
   XtPointer client_data;
   XtPointer call_data;
{
   Widget timer = (Widget)client_data;

   if(work_proc_id)
     XtRemoveWorkProc(work_proc_id);
   work_proc_id = NULL;
}
```

The stopwatch display is updated by the work procedure, **update_time()**, which is called whenever no events are pending. The client data for this function specifies the StaticText widget in which the time is displayed. The function **update_time()** subtracts the initial time from the current time to obtain the elapsed time in seconds since the user pressed the start button, and then converts the time to minutes and seconds before displaying the elapsed time.

Because work procedures are called whenever there are no events pending, **update_time()** can be called more often than necessary. Therefore, this function remembers the elapsed time each time the display is updated, and if at least one second has not elapsed, it simply returns.

```
Boolean
update_time(w)
  Widget   w;
{
  static long elapsed_time, current_time, last_time = -1;
  int minutes, seconds;

  /*
   * Retrieve the current time and calculate the elapsed time.
   */
  time(&current_time);
  elapsed_time = current_time - start_time;
  /*
   * WorkProcs are irregularly called; don't update the
   * display if it's been less than a second since the last
   * time it was updated.
   */
  if(last_time == elapsed_time)
    return(FALSE);
  /*
   * If one or more seconds has elapsed, remember this time,
   * and convert the elapsed time to minutes and seconds.
   */
  last_time = elapsed_time;
  minutes = elapsed_time / 60;
  seconds = elapsed_time % 60;
  /*
   * Display the time as minutes and seconds.
   */
  xs_wprintf(w, "%02d : %02d", minutes, seconds);
  /*
   * Return FALSE so this WorkProc keeps getting called.
   */
  return(FALSE);
}
```

The layout for the stopwatch program shown in Figure 5.9 can be specified using the following resources.

```
Stopwatch*panel.layoutType: fixedrows
Stopwatch*panel.measure: 2
Stopwatch*commands.layoutType: fixedcols
Stopwatch*commands.measure: 2
Stopwatch*timer*background: white
Stopwatch*timer.borderWidth: 1
```

Figure 5.9 The stopwatch program.

5.9 HANDLING OTHER INPUT SOURCES

Many X applications require input from sources other than the X event queue. The Xt Intrinsics provide a simple way to handle additional input sources, such as a UNIX file. Applications can define input callbacks to be invoked when input is available from a specified file descriptor. The function

```
XtAddInput(source, condition, proc, client_data)
```

registers an input callback with the Intrinsics. The **source** argument must be a UNIX file number, while **condition** indicates under what circumstances the input callback should be invoked. The **condition** must be one of the constants:

XtInputNoneMask	XtInputReadMask
XtInputWriteMask	XtInputExceptMask

When the given condition occurs, the Intrinsics invoke the callback function specified by **proc**. The **client_data** parameter allows the application to provide some data to be passed to the callback function when it is called. **XtAddInput()** returns an identifier of type **XtInputId** that uniquely identifies this callback.

Input callback functions have the form:

```
void io_callback(client_data, file_num, id)
    XtPointer   client_data;
    int         *file_num;
    XtInputId   *id;
```

When the Intrinsics invoke an input callback, it passes the `client_data` provided by the application along with a pointer to the file number of the source responsible for the callback. It also provides a pointer to the `XtInputId` associated with this callback.

Input callbacks that are no longer needed can be removed using the function:

```
XtRemoveInput(id)
```

The argument, `id`, must be the `XtInputId` identifier for the input callback to be removed.

5.9.1   Using Input Callbacks

This section looks at an example that uses an input callback to read from a UNIX *pipe*. Pipes provide a way to connect the output of one UNIX program to the input of another. This example uses pipes to add a mouse-driven interface to a standard UNIX utility without modifying the code of the original application in any way. The example builds a simple interface for the UNIX calculator program **bc** that allows the user to input commands using the mouse and displays the results in a window. The resulting "desktop calculator," named **xbc**, communicates with **bc** using UNIX pipes. To keep this example simple, **xbc** provides only a few basic arithmetic functions, although it could be extended to take advantage of more advanced features of **bc**. Figure 5.10 shows the window-based interface to **bc**.

Figure 5.10 xbc: A mouse-driven calculator.

The body of the calculator program creates the widgets used as a keypad and the calculator display panel.

```
/****************************************************
 * xbc.c: An X interface to bc
 ****************************************************/
```

```
#include <stdio.h>
#include <ctype.h>
#include <X11/StringDefs.h>
#include <X11/Intrinsic.h>
#include <Xol/OpenLook.h>
#include <Xol/OblongButt.h>
#include <Xol/ControlAre.h>
#include <Xol/Form.h>
#include <Xol/TextEdit.h>
#include "libXs.h"

Widget      display;
Widget      create_button();
void        quit_bc();
void        get_from_bc();
void        send_to_bc();

main(argc, argv)
  int       argc;
  char      *argv[];
{
  Widget    toplevel, panel, keyboard, qbutton;
  Arg       wargs[10];
  int       n;

  toplevel = OlInitialize(argv[0], "Xbc", NULL, 0, &argc, argv);
  /*
   * Create a ControlArea widget as a base for the
   * rest of the calculator.
   */
  n = 0;
  XtSetArg(wargs[n], XtNlayoutType, OL_FIXEDCOLS); n++;
  XtSetArg(wargs[n], XtNmeasure, 1); n++;
  panel = XtCreateManagedWidget("panel",
                                 controlAreaWidgetClass,
                                 toplevel, wargs, n);
  /*
   * Create the calculator display.
   */
  n = 0;
  XtSetArg(wargs[n], XtNlinesVisible, (XtArgVal) 1); n++;
  XtSetArg(wargs[n], XtNborderWidth, (XtArgVal) 1); n++;
  display = XtCreateManagedWidget("display", textEditWidgetClass,
                                 panel, wargs, n);
  /*
   * Make the keyboard, which manages 4 columns of buttons
   */
```

```
    n = 0;
    XtSetArg(wargs[n], XtNlayoutType, OL_FIXEDCOLS); n++;
    XtSetArg(wargs[n], XtNsameSize, OL_ALL); n++;
    XtSetArg(wargs[n], XtNmeasure, 4); n++;
    keyboard = XtCreateManagedWidget("keyboard",
                                     controlAreaWidgetClass,
                                     panel, wargs, n);
    /*
     * Create the keyboard buttons. This order makes it
     * look like a typical desktop calculator.
     */
    create_button("1", keyboard);
    create_button("2", keyboard);
    create_button("3", keyboard);
    create_button("+", keyboard);
    create_button("4", keyboard);
    create_button("5", keyboard);
    create_button("6", keyboard);
    create_button("-", keyboard);
    create_button("7", keyboard);
    create_button("8", keyboard);
    create_button("9", keyboard);
    create_button("*", keyboard);
    create_button("0", keyboard);
    create_button(".", keyboard);
    create_button("=", keyboard);
    create_button("/", keyboard);
    /*
     *  Add a callback that tells bc to exit.
     */
    OlAddCallback(toplevel, XtNwmProtocol, quit_bc, NULL);
    /*
     * Add callback get_from_bc() --  invoked when input
     * is available from stdin.
     */
    XtAddInput(fileno(stdin), XtInputReadMask,
               get_from_bc, display);
    /*
     * Exec the program "bc" and set up pipes
     * between it and us.
     */
    xs_talkto("bc");

    XtRealizeWidget(toplevel);
    XtMainLoop();
}
```

Figure 5.11 shows the widget tree created by **xbc**. The calculator consists of a display area (a TextEdit widget) and a keyboard area (a ControlArea widget). Both of these widgets are managed by a ControlArea widget. The ControlArea widget which represents the keyboard area manages five rows of buttons used for input to the calculator.

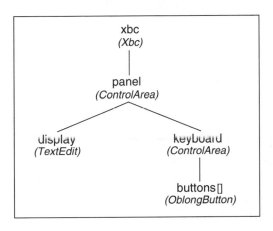

Figure 5.11 The xbc widget tree.[1]

The function **create_button()** takes two arguments, a label for the calculator key and the parent widget of the button. The function creates a single OblongButton widget and adds the callback **send_to_bc()** to the **XtNselect** list. The name of the widget is also given as client data, to be used as a string that is sent to **bc** when the user selects the button. This function is defined as:

```
Widget
create_button(name, parent)
  char    *name;
  Widget   parent;
{
  extern void send_to_bc();
  Widget       button;

  /*
   * Create a single button and attach an activate callback.
   */
  button = XtCreateManagedWidget(name, oblongButtonWidgetClass,
                             parent, NULL, 0);
  XtAddCallback(button, XtNselect, send_to_bc, name);
  return (button);
}
```

---

[1] The array-style brackets after the button widget in this figure signifies many button widgets.

The main program also adds a callback function to handle graceful termination of the **bc** program. This callback is registered by calling **OlAddCallback()** rather than **XtAddCallback()**. The use of **OlAddCallback()** is required for this particular callback due to internal requirements OLIT. The callback is registered on the **toplevel** widget that was returned from **OlInitialize()**. The callback is registered for the **XtNwmProtocol** callback list. When the callback function is invoked, the call data parameter is a pointer to an **OLWMProtocolVerify** structure which is defined as:

```
typedef struct {
  int     msgtype;
  XEvent *xevent;
} OLWMProtocolVerify;
```

The **xevent** field is a pointer to an **XEvent** structure. The **msgtype** is an integer constant indicating the type of protocol message which invoked the callback. Its value can be one of:

OL_WM_TAKE_FOCUS   **OL_WM_SAVE_YOURSELF**   **OL_WM_DELETE_WINDOW**

If its value is **OL_WM_DELETE_WINDOW** then the window manager is quitting the window.

The **quit_bc()** callback prints the string "**quit**" when the user activates the button, causing the **bc** process to exit before **xbc**.

```
void
quit_bc(w, client_data, call_data)
  Widget      w;
  XtPointer   client_data;
  XtPointer   call_data;
{
  OlWMProtocolVerify *olwmpv = (OlWMProtocolVerify *)call_data;

  if(olwmpv->msgtype == OL_WM_DELETE_WINDOW) {
    /*
     * Tell bc to quit.
     */
    fprintf(stdout, "quit\n");
    exit(0);
  }
}
```

The line

```
XtAddInput(fileno(stdin), XtInputReadMask, get_from_bc, display);
```

in the main program registers an input callback. Whenever input is pending from **stdin**, the Intrinsics call the function **get_from_bc()** with the **display** widget as client data. We will look at this function shortly, but first we must discuss how **xbc** communicates with **bc**.

Before entering **XtMainLoop()**, **xbc** calls the function **xs_talkto()**. This function starts up the program **bc** and establishes a two-way connection between **bc** and **xbc**, by creating two pipes that connect the **stdin** and **stdout** of the parent process (**xbc**) to the **stdout** and **st-**

din respectively the child process (**bc**). This function can be used to establish similar pipes between any two programs.

Initially, **xs_talkto()** creates two pipes and *forks* a new process. The **fork()** function is a UNIX system call that creates a duplicate of the calling process, and returns the *process id* of the newly created process to the parent. Both processes have access to the pipes created earlier. The calling process closes its **stdin** and **stdout** file descriptors and replaces them, using **dup()**, with one end of each pipe. Similarly, the forked process closes its input and output files and replaces them by the other end of the same pipes. Finally the forked process is overlaid by **cmd** by calling **execlp()**. Notice that this function is a bit over-simplified in that it performs no error checking.

```
#include <stdio.h>
void xs_talkto(cmd)
    char    *cmd;
{
  int    to_child[2], /* pipe descriptors from parent->child */
         to_parent[2];/* pipe descriptors from child->parent */
  int    pid;
  pipe(to_child);
  pipe(to_parent);
  if (pid = fork(), pid == 0){      /* in the child    */
     close(0);                      /* redirect stdin */
     dup(to_child[0]);
     close(1);                      /* redirect stdout*/
     dup(to_parent[1]);
     close(to_child[0]);            /* close pipes     */
     close(to_child[1]);
     close(to_parent[0]);
     close(to_parent[1]);
     execlp(cmd, cmd, NULL);        /* exec the new cmd */
  }
   else if (pid > 0){               /* in the parent   */
     close(0);                      /* redirect stdin */
     dup(to_parent[0]);
     close(1);                      /* redirect stdout  */
     dup(to_child[1]);
     setbuf(stdout, NULL);          /* no buffered output */
     close(to_child[0]);            /* close pipes */
     close(to_child[1]);
     close(to_parent[0]);
     close(to_parent[1]);
  }
   else {                           /* error!         */
     fprintf(stderr,"Couldn't fork process %s\n", cmd);
     exit(1);
  }
}
```

The UNIX standard I/O (stdio) package normally buffers its output. The function `setbuf()` turns off buffering so that all output from the parent process is sent to the child process immediately. Unfortunately, we can only unbuffer the output in the parent process. To avoid problems, both processes should use unbuffered output, but we do not have access to the child process.

After calling `xs_talkto()`, when **xbc** reads from `stdin`, it is really reading from the pipe connected to the output of **bc**. When **xbc** writes to `stdout` it is actually writing to a pipe connected to the input of **bc**. Notice that **bc** does not have to be modified in any way. As far as **bc** is concerned, it is reading from `stdin` and writing to `stdout`.

This approach can be used to create window-based interfaces to many UNIX applications. However, it is not always as simple as we might wish, partially because of inconsistencies in the output of UNIX commands. In spite of UNIX conventions that encourage small applications that can be piped together in various combinations, the output of UNIX applications is often inconsistent. For example, many applications add headers at the top of each page. Others format their output differently depending on the options specified on the command line. The same utility may also behave differently on different vendor's machines. Therefore, one of the difficulties in using existing UNIX applications this way is sending the correct input to the application and parsing the results.

The pipe mechanism itself can also cause other problems. Handling all the exceptions and error conditions that can occur when using two-way pipes can be difficult. For example, this version of `talkto()` neglects the problems that can arise when either process exits unexpectedly, and also does not attempt to do any signal handling. Problems can also occur if the maximum buffer size of a pipe is exceeded. This is usually not a problem for **xbc** because only a few digits pass through the pipes at any time.

The callback function `send_to_bc()`, invoked each time an **xbc** button is activated, sends a command to **bc**. As a first pass, we could define this function as:

```
/* INCOMPLETE VERSION */
void
send_to_bc(w, client_data, call_data)
  Widget     w;
  XtPointer  client_data;
  XtPointer  call_data;
{
  char *buffer = (char *)client_data;

  fprintf(stdout, "%s", buffer);  /* Not Good Enough! */
  xs_insert_string(display, buffer);
}
```

This simplified function prints the characters given as client data to `stdout`, (now attached to the input of **bc**), and calls `xs_insert_string()`, a yet-to-be-defined function that appends a string to the current contents of the `display` widget. Although this function shows the general idea, we must write a slightly more complex function to make **xbc** act like a real calculator and also send correct input to **bc**. The complete `send_to_bc()` function is:

```
void
send_to_bc(w, client_data, call_data)
  Widget    w;
  XtPointer client_data;
  XtPointer call_data;
{
  char *buffer = (char *)client_data;
  static int  start_new_entry = TRUE;
  char *copybuffer;

  /*
   * If this is the beginning of a new operand,
   * clear the display.
   */
  if(start_new_entry){
    reset_display();
    start_new_entry = FALSE;
  }
  switch (buffer[0]) {
  /*
   * If the user entered and '=', send bc a newline, clear
   * the display, and get ready for a new operand.
   */
  case '=':
    OlTextEditCopyBuffer(display, &copybuffer);
    fprintf(stdout, "%s", copybuffer);
    XtFree(copybuffer);
    fprintf(stdout, "\n");
    reset_display();
    start_new_entry = TRUE;
    break;
  /*
   * If this is an operator, get the previous operand
   * from the display buffer, and send it to bc before
   * sending the operand.
   */
  case '-':
  case '+':
  case '/':
  case '*':
  case '^':
    OlTextEditCopyBuffer(display, &copybuffer);
    fprintf(stdout, "%s", copybuffer);
    fprintf(stdout, "%c", buffer[0]);
    XtFree(copybuffer);
    reset_display();
    break;
```

```
      /*
       * Anything else must be a digit, so append it to the
       * display buffer.
       */
      default:
        xs_insert_string(display, buffer);
      }
      fflush(stdout);
    }
```

This function creates an interface between the input **bc** expects and the behavior we expect from a desktop calculator. A flag, **start_new_entry**, indicates when one calculation sequence has been completed and another one is beginning. If this flag is **TRUE**, the calculator display is cleared and reset using the function **reset_display()**.

Normally, a calculator displays the results of a calculation when the user presses the "=" key. However, **bc** evaluates an expression when a newline character is entered. The first case (**'='**) in the **switch** statement uses the function **OlTextEditCopyBuffer()** to retrieve the contents of the TextEdit widget, sends it to **bc** by printing it to **stdout**, and then prints a newline character to get **bc** to evaluate the expression. It also sets the flag **start_new_entry** to **TRUE** to signal the end of a calculation sequence, and calls **reset_display()** to clear the **display** widget.

Calculators display numbers as they are entered, but do not usually display math operators. Therefore, all operators are sent to **bc**, but not displayed. When an operator is selected, **send_to_bc()** prints the current contents of the **display** widget, followed by the operator. It then clears the **display** widget to prepare for the next operand.

The default case handles all digits and calls **xs_insert_string()** to insert the digit at the current position in the **display** widget. The digit is not sent to **bc** until the user presses an operator or the "=" button or any operand.

The function **xs_insert_string()** simply uses the function

```
    OlTextEditInsert(widget, buffer, length)
```

to insert **buffer** at the current cursor position in the TextEdit widget.

```
    /***********************************************************
     * xs_insert_string(): insert a string in a TextEdit widget
     ***********************************************************/
    #include <X11/Intrinsic.h>
    #include <Xol/OpenLook.h>
    void xs_insert_string(text_widget, buf)
      Widget    text_widget;
      char      *buf;
    {
      int retval;

      retval = OlTextEditInsert(text_widget, &buf[0], 1);
    }
```

The input callback **get_from_bc()** handles output from **bc**. This function reads from **stdin**, and, after adding a **NULL** to the end of the buffer, calls **xs_insert_string()** to display the string.

```
void
get_from_bc(client_data, fid, id)
   XtPointer     client_data;
   int           *fid;
   XtInputId     *id;
{
   Widget w = (Widget)client_data;
   char    buf[BUFSIZ];
   int     nbytes, i;
   /*
    * Get all pending input and append it to the display
    * widget. Discard lines that begin with a newline.
    */
   nbytes = read(*fid, buf, BUFSIZ);
   if (nbytes && buf[0] != '\n') {
   /*
    * Null terminate the string at the first newline,
    * or at the end of the bytes read.
    */
   for(i=0;i<nbytes;i++)
     if(buf[i] == '\n')
         buf[i] = '\0';
     buf[nbytes] = '\0';
     xs_insert_string(display, buf);
   }
}
```

The only complication here is that this function must handle the newline characters that **bc** prints after each result, by ignoring the data if the first character is a newline character and by stripping off any other newlines that appear in the buffer.

The last function, **reset_display()**, uses the function

```
OlTextEditClearBuffer(widget)
```

to clears the TextEdit widget **display**.

```
reset_display()
{
   /*
    * Clear the text buffer and go to position 1.
    */
   if(OlTextEditClearBuffer((TextEditWidget)display) == FALSE) {
     fprintf(stderr,"OlTextEditClearBuffer() failed\n");
   }
}
```

5.10 SUMMARY

This chapter examined many of the events supported by the X Window System and discussed the event-handling mechanisms provided by the Xt Intrinsics. Xlib reports events whenever any aspect of a window's environment changes. The Intrinsics provide a higher level interface to the X event mechanism and also adds the ability to handle input from sources other than the X server using a similar event handling mechanism. Timeout events and work procedures provide a simple way to perform tasks not directly related to user input.

This chapter did not discuss some of the most powerful and interesting events provided by X, communication events, which are discussed in Chapter 11.

6

USING COLOR

Previous chapters demonstrated some simple applications using the Xt Intrinsics and the OLIT widget set. In these programs, the widgets completely controlled how they displayed the information specified by an application. The next few chapters discuss Xlib facilities that allow applications to display text and graphics directly in windows. Discussing these facilities gives us a better understanding of X and allows us to write applications that cannot be built from existing widgets alone. Before discussing the Xlib text and graphics functions, we need to understand the color model used by X. This chapter discusses how X uses color, and presents a simple color editor as an example.

6.1 THE X COLOR MODEL

X uses a flexible color model that provides a common interface to many different types of display hardware. The color model allows a properly designed application to run equally well on a variety of monochrome and color screens.

It is particularly difficult to design a color model for a window system that supports multiple processes, because most color screens support a limited number of colors. For example, a typical color screen with eight bit planes of display memory supports only 256 colors at one time. Often, these 256 colors can be chosen from a large palette of available colors. One common configuration provides a palette of nearly 16 million different colors; however, on a screen with eight bit planes, only 256 of these colors can be displayed at any given time.

This might not be a serious problem for systems where one graphics application controls the entire screen. However, in a multiprocess window-based system, many applications are present on the screen at once, and therefore each application competes for the limited number of colors available.

One way to solve this problem is to support only a fixed set of colors used by all applications. Some low-cost personal computers use this approach by providing a small set of basic colors: red, green, blue, magenta, yellow, and so on. All applications must choose from one of these preset colors. Using a fixed palette of colors is not acceptable for X, because portability between many architectures was a basic design goal.

Instead, X uses a unique approach that allows each application to use as many colors as it needs, but also encourages applications to share colors. The approach used by X is based on an allocation scheme, in which an application requests the server to allocate only those colors it needs. If two applications request the same color, the server gives each application a pointer to the same color cell.

6.1.1   Colormaps

The X color model uses a *colormap*. A colormap, sometimes called a color lookup table, is an array of colors. Applications refer to colors using an index into the colormap. The colormap provides a level of indirection between the color index used by an application and the color displayed on the screen. Most displays provide a hardware colormap.

To draw a point on the screen, applications place a value in the appropriate location of the display's *frame buffer*. A frame buffer is a large contiguous area of memory. The frame buffer must contain at least one bit for each screen location (pixel) on the screen. The amount of memory corresponding to one bit per pixel is known as a *bit plane*. The number of colors that a screen can display at one time is determined by the number of bit planes in the frame buffer, according to the relation $colors = 2^{planes}$. For example, a frame buffer with three bit planes can support 8 different colors.

The value in each pixel of the frame buffer is used as an index into the colormap. The value stored in that location of the colormap is then used to determine the color and intensity of the color shown on the screen for that pixel. Figure 6.1 shows how a typical hardware display uses the colormap to convert a value in the frame buffer to a color on the screen. This figure illustrates a display with a 3 plane frame buffer. The hardware scans each cell, or pixel, in the frame buffer, and uses the combined value of all planes as an index to the colormap. The value stored in this location in the colormap is then converted to an intensity on the screen.

Figure 6.1 shows a 4 bit colormap for a monochrome display. A display with a single 4 bit colormap and a single color gun can display 16 levels of a single color. Typically, a colormap supports more color intensities by adding more bits to the lookup table. Also, color displays typically divide the colormap into different fields to control each of the red, green, and blue color components.

Each X window has a virtual colormap associated with it. Before the colors in this colormap are reflected on the screen, the colormap must be *installed* into the hardware colormap. Some hardware displays allow multiple colormaps to be installed at once, but many support only one colormap at a time. By convention, X window managers install the colormap of the current focus window, allowing the application using this window to be displayed using correct colors. However, when this approach is used, other applications on the screen are unlikely to be displayed in their true colors, because the colors stored in the hardware color map change, but the indexes used by applications do not.

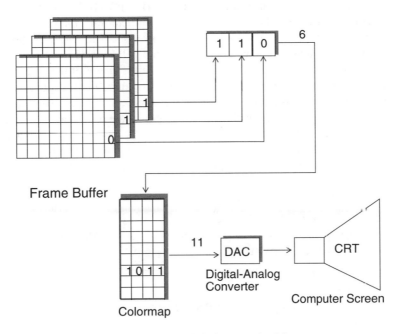

Figure 6.1 A Typical Colormap Architecture.

Applications can often share the same colormap. By default, windows inherit the colormap of their parent, and most applications can use the default colormap of the root window. Applications can use the macro

```
DefaultColormap(display, screen)
```

to access the default colormap of any screen. This default colormap is installed by the X server when the server is started. The server normally allocates two colors, black and white, from the default colormap. All other color cells can be allocated by clients. (See Section 6.1.2).

OLIT provides the ability to associate a colormap with each widget. To retrieve the colormap associated with a particular object use the function

```
OlColormapOfObject(widget)
```

This method is preferred over calling **DefaultColormap()** since it does not assume that the default colormap is the one the application is using.

Applications can also create their own colormaps. A programmer might consider creating a new colormap when an application needs many colors, requires colors to be placed in particular locations in the colormap, or wants to alter the contents of the colormap without affecting the default colormap. Applications can use the function

```
XCreateColormap(display, window, visual, alloc)
```

to create a colormap. This function returns a unique ID for the new colormap. **XCreateColormap()** uses the **window** argument only to determine the screen where the colormap is used, so this window does not need to be the window associated with the colormap, but only a window on the same screen as that on which the colormap will be used.

This function also requires the programmer to specify the *visual* of the screen. Every screen supports one or more visuals. A visual is represented by a structure, **Visual**, defined in the header file Xlib.h. This structure contains information about the screen, including how many colormap entries it supports, whether it supports monochrome, color, gray scale only, and so on. It is possible for a screen to support more than one visual. Although it is currently more common for hardware to support only one visual, hardware that supports multiple visual is becoming increasingly more available. The previous discussion of colormaps applies most directly to a screen whose visual class is **PseudoColor**.

The visual classes recognized by X are:

- **PseudoColor**. On a **PseudoColor** screen, pixel values index a colormap to produce independent, dynamically changeable red, green, and blue values. Most of the discussion in this chapter assumes a PseudoColor visual class.
- **StaticColor**. This type is similar to **PseudoColor**, except that the colormap contains predefined (fixed) values.
- **GrayScale**. This type is similar to **PseudoColor**, except that only shades of a single color (usually gray) are available.
- **StaticGray**. Screens with a **StaticGray** visual have a fixed, predetermined monochrome colormap.
- **DirectColor**. Screens that support **DirectColor** decompose the pixel values into separate red, green, and blue fields. Each component is then used as an index into a separate color lookup table.
- **TrueColor**. This visual class is similar to **DirectColor** except that the colormap contains pre-defined, fixed values.

The default visual structure for a particular screen can be obtained using the Xlib macro:

```
DefaultVisual(display, screen)
```

For hardware that supports multiple visuals, the default visual may not be the correct one to use. OLIT provides a function to obtain the visual class of a particular object:

```
OlVisualOfObject(widget)
```

If an application is running on a display that supports only one visual, the return value from **DefaultVisual()** and **OlVisualOfObject()** will be identical. However, if the application is run on a display which supports multiple visuals, and the application is run in a visual other than the default, **DefaultVisual()** will return the default visual of the screen rather than the visual being used by this application.

You can also get a valid visual using the Xlib function:

```
XMatchVisualInfo(display, screen, depth, class, &info)
```

This function returns a status of **TRUE** if it was able to find a visual to match the specified screen, depth, and class. It fills in the **info** argument, which is an **XVisualInfo** struct. This structure contains a variety of information about the visual. The **visual** member of the **XVisualInfo** structure is a pointer to a structure of type **Visual**. For example, if we wish to determine if a PseudoColor visual is available on a certain screen, we could write a code segment like:

```
Status          result;
Display         *dpy    = XtDisplay(widget);
int             screen = DefaultScreen(dpy);
XVisualInfo     info;
Visual          *my_visual;
result = XMatchVisualInfo(dpy, screen,
                          DefaultDepth(dpy, screen),
                          PseudoColor, &info))
if(result)
    my_visual = info.visual;
```

Colormaps contain no colors when first created. Before an application can store colors in a colormap, it must *allocate* color cells. The last argument to **XCreateColormap()** specifies how many entries in the colormap should be allocated initially. This argument must be one of the constants **AllocNone** or **AllocAll**. The value **AllocNone** must be used for static visuals.

The function

```
XInstallColormap(display, cmap)
```

installs a colormap as the current colormap used by the display. When a colormap is installed, the screen instantly reflects the colors in the new colormap, and the server sends a **ColormapNotify** event to all windows associated with the newly installed colormap. By convention, **XInstallColormap()** should not be used by applications. X window managers use this function to install the colormap associated with an application's top-level window when the application gets the input focus. By default, a window inherits its parent's colormap. It is common for applications to inherit the colormap of the root window. Applications that need to use a different colormap can use the function

```
XSetWindowColormap(display, window, cmap)
```

to associate a colormap with a window. The colormap and window must be created with the same visual. Applications that wish to use their own colormap can use this function to set the colormap of their top-level window and rely on the window manager to install it for them. OLIT applications can associate a colormap with an object by using the **XtNcolormap** resource.

```
XtSetArg(wargs[0], XtNcolormap, cmap);
XtSetValues(widget, wargs, 1);
```

Theoretically, each widget in an application could have its own colormap associated with it. A more common approach is to set the **XtNcolormap** resource on the toplevel shell. When a widget has a colormap associated with it, any children created subsequent to the colormap association inherit that colormap resource. If the colormap becomes associated with a widget via

XtSetValues() after it has created its children, the colormap resource does not propagate to those existing children.When the **XtNvisual** resource is used to associate a visual other than the default visual with a widget, a colormap is automatically created for that visual.

Applications can use the function

```
XFreeColormap(display, id)
```

to free a colormap when it is no longer needed. The **id** argument must specify a resource ID of a colormap.

6.1.2   Allocating Colors

Once an application has access to a colormap, it can allocate colors in that colormap. The Xlib functions that allocate colors make use of an **XColor** structure. This structure is defined as:

```
typedef struct {
  unsigned long  pixel;
  unsigned short red, green, blue;
  char           flags;
} XColor;
```

The **pixel** member identifies the colormap cell allocated for this particular color. Colors are specified by the intensity of each of their red, green, and blue (RGB) components. The **red**, **green**, and **blue** members represent the values of these components and can range from 0 to 65535. A value of 0 corresponds to the lowest intensity of a color component, and 65535 corresponds to the highest intensity. The X server scales these values to the range of color intensities supported by the hardware. Some functions require the **flags** member to be set to indicates which of the red, green, and blue field are to be used. The **flags** field can be set to one or more of **DoRed**, **DoGreen**, and **DoBlue**. When these three constants are ORed together it indicates that all three colors are to be used.

We can initialize an **XColor** structure representing bright white with:

```
XColor color;
color.red   = 65535;
color.green = 65535;
color.blue  = 65535;
```

We can initialize a color structure to represent bright red with:

```
XColor color;
color.red   = 65535;
color.green = 0;
color.blue  = 0;
```

Color cells of a colormap can be *read-only* or *read-write*. The color components in a read-only cell cannot be altered, and therefore can be shared between all applications that use the same colormap. Attempts to change the value of a read-only cell generate an error. A read-write cell cannot be shared between applications, because the application that allocated the cell can change it at any time.

The Xlib function

```
XAllocColor(display, cmap, &color)
```

allocates a read-only entry in a colormap. This function requires an **XColor** structure containing the RGB components of the color to be allocated. If some other application has already allocated the same color as a read-only cell, the same cell is reused and the **pixel** member of the **XColor** structure is set to the value of the existing colormap cell. Otherwise, **XAllocColor()** attempts to store the given color components in the next available cell of the colormap **cmap**. If successful, the function fills in the **pixel** member of the **XColor** structure to the newly allocated color cell and returns a status of **TRUE**.

To see how this function is used, let's write a function named **get_pixel()** that allocates a color cell from the colormap associated with a widget and loads it with a color. The function takes a widget and the red, green, and blue components of the desired color as input. It returns a pixel index that refers to the specified color.

```
Pixel
get_pixel(w, red, green, blue)
  Widget  w;
  unsigned short red, green, blue;
{
  Display *dpy =  XtDisplay(w);
  Colormap cmap = OlColormapOfObject(w);
  XColor    color;

  /*
   * Fill in the color structure.
   */
  color.red   = red;
  color.green = green;
  color.blue  = blue;
  /*
   * Try to allocate the color.
   */
  if(XAllocColor(dpy, cmap, &color))
     return (color.pixel);
  else {
     printf("Warning: Couldn't allocate requested color\n");
     return(OlBlackPixel(w));
  }
}
```

Whenever color allocation fails, applications should always be prepared to use one of the default values, usually black or white, available in all visual types. Applications can use the macros

```
BlackPixel(display, screen)
WhitePixel(display, screen)
```

to access the default pixels representing black and white in the default colormap of a particular screen. These functions are intended only for the default colormap of the screen. If you are using your own colormap, there is no guarantee that these functions will return the expected values. OLIT applications should use

```
OlBlackPixel(widget)
OlWhitePixel(widget)
```

to return the black and white pixels of the colormap associated with the specified widget. This insures that the correct pixel values are used.

Because new colors are allocated in the next available cell of the colormap, applications must not assume that the index representing a particular color in a shared colormap is the same each time the application runs. The exact index used to refer to a particular color depends on the order in which all applications request the colors.

Applications sometimes need to know the color components stored in any pixel index of a colormap. The function

```
XQueryColor(display, cmap, &color)
```

fills in the RGB components of the **color** structure corresponding to the **pixel** member of that structure. The function

```
XQueryColors(display, cmap, colors, ncolors)
```

fills in the RGB components of an array of colors.

Sometimes applications need to set up the colormap in a specific way, controlling the colors in each cell. Such applications should first allocate the number of color cells needed, using the function:

```
XAllocColorCells(display, cmap, contig, planes,
                 nplanes, cells, ncells)
```

This function allocates $ncells * 2^{nplanes}$ read-write color cells. Of course, this only works with visual types which support read-write color cells. Applications that do not need to control the bit planes of the screen can specify **nplanes** as zero.[1]

The function **XAllocColorCells()** allocates read-write color cells. If the application requires the color cells to be contiguous, it must set the **contig** argument to **TRUE**. Otherwise the planes and cells are allocated from wherever they are available. **XAllocColorCells()** fails and returns a status of **FALSE** if it cannot allocate the exact number of planes and cells. If the function is able to allocate the requested number of colors, it returns the allocated color cells in **cells**, which must be an array of type unsigned long, allocated by the application. If the application requests one or more planes, the **planes** argument, which must also be an array of type unsigned long, returns the allocated planes.

---

[1] A common mistake is to attempt to allocate all planes and all color cells. This generates more colors than the screen supports. For example, on a screen with 4 bit-planes (and therefore 16 colors), a request such as

```
XAllocColorCells(display, cmap, TRUE, planes, 4, cells, 16);
```

attempts to allocate $16 * 2^4$, or 256 colors.

Once color cells are allocated, applications can use the function

```
XStoreColor(display, cmap, &color)
```

to alter the values stored in each cell of the colormap. The **color** argument must be an **XColor** structure containing both the **pixel** value and the **red, green** and **blue** values to store in that cell. Let's see how this works by defining a function, **load_rgb()**, that loads the colors red, green, and blue into three consecutive color cells of the default colormap. In order for the new colors to be loaded into the colormap, the **flags** field of the **XColor** structure must be set to **DoRed | DoGreen | DoBlue**. The pixel indexes are assigned to the parameters **red, green,** and **blue.**

```
load_rgb(w, red, green, blue)
  Widget   w;
  unsigned short      *red, *green, *blue;
{
  Display *dpy  = XtDisplay(w);
  Colormap cmap = OlColormapOfObject(w);
  XColor   color;
  unsigned long       cells[3];

  /*
   *  Try to allocate three consecutive color cells.
   */
  if(XAllocColorCells(dpy, cmap, True, NULL, 0, cells, 3)) {
    /*
     *  If successful, store red in the first allocated cell,
     *  green in the second and blue in the third.
     */
    color.flags = DoRed | DoGreen | DoBlue;
    color.red = 65535;
    color.green = color.blue = 0;
    *red = color.pixel = cells[0];
    XStoreColor(dpy, cmap, &color);
    /*
     *  Store Green in the second cell.
     */
    color.green = 65535;
    color.red =   color.blue = 0;
    *green = color.pixel = cells[1];
    XStoreColor(dpy, cmap, &color);
    /*
     * Store Blue in the second cell.
     */
    color.blue = 65535;
    color.red = color.green = 0;
    *blue = color.pixel = cells[2];
    XStoreColor(dpy, cmap, &color);
  } else {
```

```
        printf("Warning:Couldn't allocate color cells\n");
        *blue = *red = *green = OlBlackPixel(w);
    }
}
```

The function

```
XStoreColors(display, colormap, colors, ncolors)
```

stores values in multiple color cells with a single request. The **colors** argument must be an array of **XColor** structures and **ncolors** indicates the number of colors in the array.

Xlib also provides functions that allow applications to refer to colors by their symbolic names. Color names are stored in a database along with their RGB components. The location and format of this database is operating-system-dependent. On most UNIX systems, the color database files are found in the directory /usr/lib/X11. On Sun systems, the color database files are found in the directory **$OPENWINHOME**/lib. The file rgb.txt contains a human-readable version of the database.

The color database distributed with X defines many common colors, and users can add additional colors. The function

```
XLookupColor(display, cmap, name, &color, &exact)
```

returns the color components corresponding to a named color in the color database. The **name** argument can be either a color name (such as **Red**) or a hexadecimal specification (such as **#bf22a3**). If the color exists in the database, **XLookupColor()** fills in the **red**, **green**, and **blue** members of the **XColor** structures **color** and **exact**. The **color** argument contains the closest color supported by the hardware, while **exact** indicates the precise value of color components specified in the color database. The **cmap** argument must specify a colormap ID. **XLookupColor()** uses this colormap only to determine the visual type of the screen on which the color is used. This function does not allocate or store the color in the colormap.

Applications can also allocate colors by name, using the function:

```
XAllocNamedColor(display, cmap, name, &color, &exact)
```

This function is similar to **XAllocColor()**, except that the color is specified by name only (not hexadecimal). Let's use **XAllocNamedColor()** to write a function called **get_pixel_by_name()**. This function is similar to the **get_pixel()** function described earlier, but it returns a pixel index for a named color.

```
Pixel
get_pixel_by_name(w, colorname)
  Widget w;
  char   *colorname;
{
  Display *dpy  = XtDisplay(w);
  Colormap cmap = OlColormapOfObject(w);
  XColor    color, ignore;

  /*
   * Allocate the named color.
```

```
    */
  if(XAllocNamedColor(dpy, cmap, colorname, &color, &ignore))
    return (color.pixel);
  else{
    printf("Warning: Couldn't allocate color %s\n", colorname);
    return (OlBlackPixel(w));
  }
}
```

6.2 EXAMPLE: A COLORMAP EDITOR

This section demonstrates how these Xlib color functions can be used in a program named **color-edit** that allows the user to edit a colormap interactively. The color editor allocates color cells in a colormap and allows the user to alter the red, green, and blue components stored in each cell. This program allows the user to change the colors used by other applications by installing a new colormap which duplicates the default colormap of the screen. Changes made to the colormap are only effective while the color editor has the input focus (and therefore has its colormap installed).

Figure 6.2 shows the window layout of the **coloredit** program.

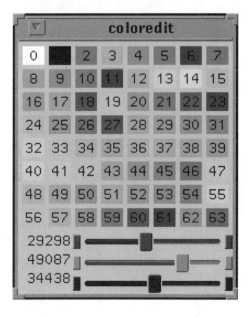

Figure 6.2 The coloredit program.

The matrix of widgets in the coloredit window display the colors available for editing. The user chooses a color cell to be edited by selecting one of these colors using the mouse. The selected color can then be edited using the three sliders located below the color pane. Each slider allows the user to set the intensity of one component of the current color. When the user selects a color, each of the three sliders moves to the position corresponding to the red, green, and blue values of the selected color. StaticText widgets also display the numeric values of the red, green, and blue components of the current color.

6.2.1   The Header File: coloredit.h

The file coloredit.h includes the Xt Intrinsics and OLIT header files for the widgets used by **col-oredit**, declares several callbacks, and defines the resources and global parameters used in the example.

```
/******************************************************
 * coloredit.h: Header file for coloredit
 ******************************************************/
#include <X11/StringDefs.h>
#include <X11/Intrinsic.h>
#include <Xol/OpenLook.h>
#include <Xol/StaticText.h>
#include <Xol/ControlAre.h>
#include <Xol/Form.h>
#include <Xol/Slider.h>
#include "libXs.h"

#define MAXCOLORS    64
#define RED          1
#define GREEN        2
#define BLUE         3

Display    *dpy;
Colormap    my_colormap;
XColor      current_color;
int         ncolors, ncells;

Widget      red_slider,
            blue_slider,
            green_slider,
            red_text,
            blue_text,
            green_text,
            toplevel,
            sliders,
            form;
void        slider_selected();
void        slider_moved();
void        set_current_color();
```

```
Widget        make_slider();
Widget        make_text();
Widget        create_color_bar();
```

The global variables, **ncells** and **ncolors**, store the total number of cells in the colormap and the number of colors available to be edited. **MAXCOLORS** determines the maximum number of colors the program can edit. The variable **my_colormap** stores the ID of an editable colormap, while **current_color** is an **XColor** structure used to set individual color cells.

6.2.2   The Source File, coloredit.c

The file coloredit.c contains the main body of the **coloredit** program. After initializing the Intrinsics, the program examines the **map_entries** field of the Visual structure returned by **OlVisualOfObject()** to determine the number of color cells in the associated colormap. If the number of color cells supported by the screen exceeds **MAXCOLORS**, the variable **ncolors** is limited to **MAXCOLORS**, otherwise, **ncolors** is set to the number of cells in the colormap. After creating the widgets used by the application, the program then initializes an array of **XColor** structures to represent each color cell in the toplevel widget's colormap. The color components in each cell of the toplevel widget's colormap are loaded into the **XColor** array using **XQueryColors()**. Then, we can make a copy of the colormap by creating a new color map and storing the colors that were retrieved using **XQueryColors()**. The new colormap contains the same colors as the toplevel widget's colormap, but all colors are writable by the **coloredit** program. Finally, **XtSetValues()** is called to set the **XtNcolormap** resource to the new colormap on the toplevel shell. This colormap is loaded when the focus moves to the toplevel shell's window.[2]

```
/*****************************************************
 * coloredit.c: A simple color editor.
 *****************************************************/
#include "coloredit.h"

main(argc, argv)
  int     argc;
  char    *argv[];
{
  Colormap  top_colormap;
  XColor    *Colors;
  int       i;
  Arg       wargs[1];
  Visual    *visual;

  /*
   * Initialize the Intrinsics and save pointer to the display.
```

---

[2] Caution! This requires an ICCCM-compliant window manager, such as OPEN LOOK's olwm. This program will not work without such a window manager.

```
*/
toplevel = OlInitialize(argv[0], "Coloredit", NULL, 0,
                        &argc, argv);
dpy = XtDisplay(toplevel);
visual = OlVisualOfObject(toplevel);
/*
 * If the application's colormap is readonly then
 * inform the user and exit
 */
switch(visual->class) {
case StaticGray:
case StaticColor:
case TrueColor:
  printf("Coloredit's colormap is non-writable, Exiting...\n");
  exit(1);
}
/*
 * Determine the number of colors to be edited.
 */
ncells = visual->map_entries;
if(ncells > MAXCOLORS)
  ncolors = MAXCOLORS;
else
  ncolors = ncells;
/*
 * Create a base Form widget to hold everything.
 */
form = XtCreateManagedWidget("base", formWidgetClass,
                              toplevel, NULL, 0);
/*
 * Create a grid of buttons, one for each
 * color to be edited.
 */
create_color_bar(form);
/*
 * Create a Form widget containing three Sliders,
 * and three StaticTexts, one for each color component.
 */
sliders = XtCreateManagedWidget("sliderpanel", formWidgetClass,
                                form, NULL, 0);
red_text     = make_text("redtext", sliders);
red_slider   = make_slider("red", sliders, RED);
green_text   = make_text("greentext", sliders);
green_slider = make_slider("green", sliders, GREEN);
blue_text    = make_text("bluetext", sliders);
blue_slider  = make_slider("blue",  sliders, BLUE);
/*
```

```
 * Get the ID of toplevel's colormap.
 */
top_colormap = OlColormapOfObject(toplevel);
Colors = (XColor *) XtMalloc(ncells * sizeof(XColor));
for( i = 0; i < ncells; i++ ) {
  Colors[i].pixel = i;
  Colors[i].flags = DoRed | DoGreen | DoBlue;
}
XQueryColors(dpy, top_colormap, Colors, ncells);
my_colormap = XCreateColormap(dpy,
                   RootWindowOfScreen(XtScreenOfObject(toplevel)),
                   visual, AllocAll);
XStoreColors(dpy, my_colormap, Colors, ncells);
/*
 * Initialize the pixel member of the global color struct
 * To the first editable color cell.
 */
current_color.pixel = 0;
XtSetArg(wargs[0], XtNcolormap, my_colormap);
XtSetValues(toplevel, wargs, 1);

XtRealizeWidget(toplevel);
XtMainLoop();
}
```

Figure 6.3 shows the widget tree created by the **coloredit** program.

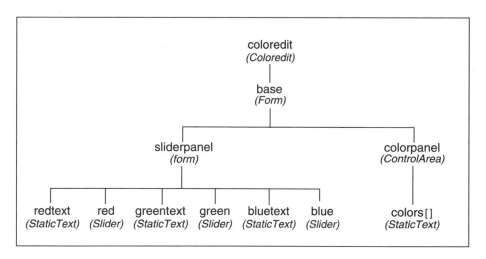

Figure 6.3 The coloredit widget tree.

The function **make_slider()** creates a Slider widget used to control one color component and assigns the associated callbacks. The range between the minimum and maximum values of the slider allows the program to map directly between the position of a slider and the color component controlled by the slider. The minimum value of the slider, zero, corresponds to zero contribution from that color component, while the maximum valuator position (65535) corresponds to a one hundred percent contribution from that component. The **slider_moved()** function is registered as the **XtNsliderMoved** callback function. It is invoked whenever the Slider moves.

```
Widget
make_slider(name, parent, color)
  char   *name;
  Widget parent;
  int    color;
{
  Widget  w;
  int     n;
  Arg     wargs[3];

  /*
   * Create a Slider widget.
   */
  n = 0;
  XtSetArg(wargs[n], XtNsliderMin, 0); n++;
  XtSetArg(wargs[n], XtNsliderMax, 65535); n++;
  w = XtCreateManagedWidget(name, sliderWidgetClass, parent, wargs, n);
  /*
   * Add callbacks to be invoked when the slider moves.
   */
  XtAddCallback(w, XtNsliderMoved, slider_moved, color);

  return(w);
}
```

The **make_text()** function creates a **StaticText** widget which is used to display the current value of a **Slider**. Each Slider has a separate StaticText widget in which to display its current value.

```
Widget
make_text(name, parent)
  char   *name;
  Widget parent;
{
  Widget  w;
  int     n;
  Arg     wargs[3];

  /*
   * Create a StaticText widget.
```

```
     */
    n = 0;
    XtSetArg(wargs[n], XtNstring, "0"); n++;
    w = XtCreateManagedWidget(name, staticTextWidgetClass,
                              parent, wargs, n);
    return(w);
}
```

The function **create_colorbar()** creates StaticText widgets, one for each color to be edited, managed by a ControlArea widget. This function sets the background color of each widget to one of the pixel values allocated for editing. An event handler is registered for **ButtonPress** events for each widget to set the current pixel index when a color is selected. It might seem as though it would be better to use OblongButton widgets for the colors, since buttons provide a callback that allows them to be activated by a button press. However, OLIT's automatic color generation gets in the way in this case. Because OblongButton widgets have top and bottom shadow colors, and OLIT generates these automatically from the background color of each widget, we cannot create a widget for each color supported by the screen. OLIT would automatically attempt to create up to three times as many colors as the screen supports. Using the StaticText widget, which has no shadowing effect, is one way to get around this problem.

```
Widget
create_color_bar(parent)
  Widget parent;
{
  Widget        panel;
  WidgetList    colors;
  int           i, n;
  char          name[10];
  Arg           wargs[3];

  colors = (WidgetList) XtMalloc( ncolors * sizeof(Widget));
  /*
   * Create the ControlArea manager to hold all color buttons.
   */
  n = 0;
  panel = XtCreateManagedWidget("colorpanel",
                                controlAreaWidgetClass,
                                parent, wargs, n);
  /*
   * Create ncolors widgets. Use the relative color cell
   * number as the name of each color. Add an event handler for
   * each cell with the color index as client_data.
   */
  for(i=0;i<ncolors;i++) {
    n = 0;
    XtSetArg(wargs[n], XtNbackground, i); n++;
    sprintf(name, "%d", i);
```

```
      XtSetArg(wargs[n], XtNstring, name); n++;
      colors[i] = XtCreateWidget(name, staticTextWidgetClass,
                                 panel, wargs, n);
      XtAddEventHandler(colors[i], ButtonPressMask, False,
                        set_current_color, i);
   }
   XtManageChildren(colors, ncolors);

   return(panel);
}
```

Whenever the user moves a slider, the slider's corresponding callback function is invoked. These functions set the corresponding member of the global **XColor** structure, **current_color**, to the value indicated by the current position of the slider, extracted from the Slider widget's call data. The **current_color** structure is used to update the color currently being edited and always contains the current value of each color component. When the user selects a color, the function **set_current_color()** sets the **pixel** member of **current_color**. Before each callback returns, the function **update_color()** is called to update the color components displayed in the StaticText widget. Each slider registers **slider_moved()** as its **XtNsliderMoved** callback. The **client_data** parameter identifies which slider invoked the callback.

```
void
slider_moved(w, client_data, call_data)
  Widget    w;
  XtPointer client_data;
  XtPointer call_data;
{
  int color = (int)client_data;
  /*
   * Set the red color components of  the global
   * current_color structure.
   */
  switch(color) {
  case RED:
      current_color.red = *(int *)call_data;
      update_color(red_text, current_color.red);
      break;
  case GREEN:
      current_color.green = *(int *)call_data;
      update_color(green_text, current_color.green);
      break;
  case BLUE:
      current_color.blue = *(int *)call_data;
      update_color(blue_text, current_color.blue);
      break;
  }
}
```

The function **update_color()** displays the values of each color component of the current color in the corresponding StaticText widget. It also uses **XStoreColor()** to update the current color in the application's colormap.

```
update_color(w, color)
  Widget w;
  unsigned short color;
{
  Arg  wargs[1];
  char str[25];

  /*
   * Update the digital display.
   */
  xs_wprintf(w, "%d", color);
  /*
   * Update the current color.
   */
  XStoreColor(dpy, my_colormap, &current_color);
}
```

The event handler **set_current_color()** is invoked when the user presses a mouse button in a widget in the color bar. This function sets the **pixel** member of the global **XColor** structure **current_color** to the pixel corresponding to the selected color. The **flags** member of the color structure is also set to the mask **DoRed | DoGreen | DoBlue**. The Xlib function **XQueryColor()** is used to initialize the **red**, **green**, and **blue** members of **current_color** to the components currently shown by the selected button. **XQueryColor()** fills in the existing RGB components of an **XColor** structure, given a pixel index. Finally, **set_current_color()** sets the position of each slider to correspond to the value of each color component.

```
void
set_current_color(w, client_data, event, continue_to_dispatch)
  Widget     w;
  XtPointer client_data;
  XEvent    *event;
  Boolean   *continue_to_dispatch;
{
  int number = (int)client_data;
  Arg wargs[2];

  current_color.flags = DoRed | DoGreen | DoBlue;
  /*
   * Get the current color components of the selected button.
   */
  current_color.pixel = number;
  XQueryColor(dpy, my_colormap, &current_color);
```

```
    /*
     * Use each color component to set the new
     * position of the corresponding slider.
     */
    XtSetArg(wargs[0], XtNsliderValue, current_color.red);
    XtSetValues(red_slider, wargs, 1);

    XtSetArg(wargs[0], XtNsliderValue, current_color.green);
    XtSetValues(green_slider, wargs, 1);

    XtSetArg(wargs[0], XtNsliderValue, current_color.blue);
    XtSetValues(blue_slider, wargs, 1);
    update_color(red_text, current_color.red);
    update_color(green_text, current_color.green);
    update_color(blue_text, current_color.blue);
}
```

6.2.3   The Class Resource File

Because the color editor uses the Form widget to manage the colors editor's controls, we need to specify the position of each widget relative to another widget in a resource file. Setting the **XtNx-AttachRight**, **XtNxVaryOffset**, and **XtNxResizable** resources of the Slider widgets allows the sliders to resize when the window is resized. The class resource file corresponding to the layout shown in Figure 6.2, contains:

```
!!!!!!!!!!!!!!!!!!!!!!!!!!!!!!!!!!!!!!!!!!!!!!!!!!!!!!!!
! Coloredit: Resources for the coloredit program
!!!!!!!!!!!!!!!!!!!!!!!!!!!!!!!!!!!!!!!!!!!!!!!!!!!!!!!!
!
! Layout the colorpanel in a 16x16 matrix
!
Coloredit*colorpanel*layoutType:        fixedcols
Coloredit*colorpanel*measure:           8
Coloredit*background:                   gray80
!
! Position the sliderpanel below the colorpanel
!
Coloredit*Slider.orientation:           horizontal
Coloredit*sliderpanel.yRefName:         colorpanel
Coloredit*sliderpanel.yAddHeight:       TRUE
Coloredit*sliderpanel.xRefName:         base
Coloredit*sliderpanel.xAttachRight:     TRUE
Coloredit*sliderpanel.xVaryOffset:      FALSE
Coloredit*sliderpanel.xResizable:       TRUE
!
! Slider resources
!
```

```
Coloredit*Slider.granularity:              1000
Coloredit*Slider.repeatRate:               10
Coloredit*Slider.xAddWidth:                TRUE
Coloredit*Slider.xVaryOffset:              FALSE
Coloredit*Slider.xAttachRight:             TRUE
Coloredit*Slider.xResizable:               TRUE
!
! Position the red StaticText and Slider
!
Coloredit*redtext.xRefName:                sliderpanel
Coloredit*redtext.width:                   50
Coloredit*redtext.recomputeSize:           FALSE
Coloredit*redtext.gravity:                 East

Coloredit*red.xRefName:                    redtext
Coloredit*red.background:                  red
!
! Position the green StaticText and Slider
!
Coloredit*greentext.yRefName:              redtext
Coloredit*greentext.yAddHeight:            TRUE
Coloredit*greentext.width:                 50
Coloredit*greentext.recomputeSize:         FALSE
Coloredit*greentext.gravity:               East

Coloredit*green.yRefName:                  red
Coloredit*green.yAddHeight:                TRUE
Coloredit*green.xRefName:                  greentext
Coloredit*green.background:                green
!
! Position the blue StaticText and Slider
!
Coloredit*bluetext.yRefName:               greentext
Coloredit*bluetext.yAddHeight:             TRUE
Coloredit*bluetext.width:                  50
Coloredit*bluetext.recomputeSize:          FALSE
Coloredit*bluetext.gravity:                East

Coloredit*blue.yRefName:                   green
Coloredit*blue.yAddHeight:                 TRUE
Coloredit*blue.xRefName:                   bluetext
Coloredit*blue.background:                 blue
```

Notice that the widgets in this program are organized so that the user can specify the location of functionally related groups of widgets, but cannot separate widgets that belong together. For example, all buttons used to select colors are grouped in a ControlArea widget. The user can control whether the buttons are arranged vertically in a single column, horizontally in a single row, or in a matrix. Similarly, the Slider widgets can be oriented horizontally or vertically, in rows or columns, anywhere within the applications control area. However, they cannot be completely separated. This is one way the programmer can allow the user to achieve drastically different layouts, while maintaining some control over the layout of the program's widgets. It is also easier for the user to customize such a configuration than if each widget had to be placed individually.

6.3 SUMMARY

This chapter introduced the use of color in the X Window System. X provides a uniform color model that supports the design of applications that are portable across many types of displays, from monochrome to "true color" displays. It is important for programmers to be aware of the X color model and use it correctly so that their applications function properly on as many display types as possible.

The number of colors available, and also how colors can be used, depends on visuals are supported by the hardware. One common visual class is **PseudoColor**, which allows applications to choose from a large number of colors, although only a subset of the available colors can be used at once.

X associates a colormap with each window. A colormap contains the colors potentially available to an application. At any given time, one or more colormaps are installed into the hardware, so that the colors can be displayed. Applications refer to colors in the color map using an index, or pixel. The server maintains the contents of each colormap. Applications can request the server to allocate private, read-write color cells in a colormap, or sharable, read-only cells. Xlib provides many functions for allocating and manipulating the colors in a colormap.

7

MANIPULATING RASTER IMAGES

X provides many functions for creating and manipulating images stored in off-screen memory in addition to those displayed on the screen. These images fall into three categories: *pixmaps, bitmaps*, and *XImages*. This chapter introduces the Xlib functions for creating and manipulating these images and briefly describes how they are used.

7.1 PIXMAPS

A pixmap is a chunk of memory similar to a rectangular region of the screen, except that pixmaps are stored in *off-screen memory* and therefore are not visible to the user. Pixmaps have a depth, which is often, but not necessarily, the same as the depth of the screen with which it is associated. The function

```
XCreatePixmap(display, drawable, width, height, depth)
```

creates a pixmap `width` by `height` pixels in size. Each pixel contains `depth` bits. The new pixmap is associated with the same screen as the specified `drawable`. The pixmap can be used only on this screen, or on a screen with the same visual type. Applications can deallocate pixmaps when they are no longer needed using the Xlib function:

```
XFreePixmap(display, pixmap)
```

Pixmaps are drawables and can be used as destinations for text and graphics operations in the same way as windows. Because data can also be copied between drawables, pixmaps can be used to store off-screen representations of windows. Pixmaps can be used to specify clipping regions for graphics operations and can also be combined with other graphics operations to create patterns used by many Xlib graphics primitives.

Pixmaps are often referred to as *tiles*, because they are often used as a repeating background or fill pattern. A pixmap referred to as a tile is usually small (16 by 16 pixels) to facilitate rapid duplication.

7.2 BITMAPS

A pixmap with a depth of one is referred to as a bitmap. Applications can create a bitmap by specifying a depth of one when calling the function **XCreatePixmap()**. However, Xlib also provides functions used specifically to create bitmaps. The function

```
XCreateBitmapFromData(display, drawable, data, width, height)
```

creates a bitmap of **width** by **height** from the specified **data**, which must be a series of bits that represent the value of each pixel in the bitmap. One way to generate the data for a bitmap is to create it interactively using the standard editor, **bitmap**, usually distributed with X. This program creates a file that can be included directly in a program. Another way to generate data for bitmaps is to use the **iconedit** program available on Sun systems.The directory

```
$OPENWINHOME/include/X11/bitmaps
```

contains some predefined bitmap files. For example, the file

```
$OPENWINHOME/include/X11/bitmaps/xlogo64
```

defines the data for a bitmap of the X logo shown in Figure 7.1.

Figure 7.1 A bitmap of the X logo.

7.3 COPYING BETWEEN DRAWABLES

The contents of a drawable (a window or a pixmap) may be copied to any other drawable that has the same depth using the function:

```
XCopyArea(display, src, dest, gc, src_x, src_y,
          width, height, dest_x, dest_y)
```

XCopyArea() copies the rectangular region of size **width** by **height**, starting at coordinate (**src_x, src_y**) in the **src** drawable, to (**dest_x, dest_y**) in the **dest** drawable. The graphics context, **gc**, controls how the bits from the source drawable are combined with the bits in the destination drawable. If the source and destination drawables do not have the same depth, the server generates a **BadMatch** error.

Applications can use the function

```
XCopyPlane(display, src, dest, gc, src_x, src_y,
           width, height, dest_x, dest_y, plane)
```

to copy data between drawables of different depths. **XCopyPlane()** copies the contents of a single plane of the specified region in the source drawable to the destination drawable. The graphics context determines the foreground and background color of the pattern in the destination drawable.

Let's examine a simple program named **xlogo** that uses bitmaps and pixmaps to display the X logo shown in Figure 7.1. The header portion of the program includes the widget header files, the xlogo64 bitmap file, and declares a pixmap and a graphics context used by the program. The body of the program creates a Stub widget in which to display the pixmap.

The function **redisplay()** is registered as the function to be invoked when the widget's window needs to be refreshed. The function **resize()** is registered as the function to be invoked when the widget's window is resized. The **create_logo()** function is then called to create and initialize a pixmap containing the X logo. The pixmap is stored along with a graphics context and the size of the pixmap in a structure. A pointer to the structure is stored in the Stub widget's **XtNuserData** resource so that it can be accessed in the expose and resize handlers.

```
/***********************************************
 * xlogo.c: Display the X logo
 ***********************************************/
#include <X11/StringDefs.h>
#include <X11/Intrinsic.h>
#include <Xol/OpenLook.h>
#include <Xol/Stub.h>
#include <X11/Xutil.h>
#include "xlogo64"

void      redisplay();
void      resize();
extern Pixmap create_logo();

typedef struct {
```

```
     Pixmap      pix;
     GC          gc;
     Dimension   width, height;
} pixmap_data;

main(argc, argv)
   int    argc;
   char *argv[];
{
   Widget         toplevel, canvas;
   Arg            wargs[3];
   int            n;
   XGCValues      values;
   pixmap_data    data;

   toplevel = OlInitialize(argv[0], "Xlogo", NULL, 0, &argc, argv);
   /*
    * Create a widget in which to display the logo.
    */
   n = 0;
   XtSetArg(wargs[n], XtNexpose, redisplay); n++;
   XtSetArg(wargs[n], XtNresize, resize); n++;
   XtSetArg(wargs[n], XtNuserData, &data); n++;
   canvas = XtCreateManagedWidget("canvas",
                                     stubWidgetClass,
                                     toplevel, wargs, n);
  /*
   * Use the foreground and background colors
   * of the canvas to create a graphics context.
   */
   n = 0;
   XtSetArg(wargs[n], XtNforeground, &values.foreground); n++;
   XtSetArg(wargs[n], XtNbackground, &values.background); n++;
   XtGetValues(canvas, wargs, n);
   data.gc = XtGetGC(canvas, GCForeground | GCBackground, &values);
   /*
    * Create the pixmap conatinign the X logo. Store the
    * pixmap, as well as the size of the pixmap in the struct.
    */
   data.width = xlogo64_width;
   data.height = xlogo64_height;
   data.pix = create_logo(canvas, data.gc, xlogo64_bits,
                          xlogo64_width, xlogo64_height );

   XtRealizeWidget(toplevel);
   XtMainLoop();
}
```

The function **create_logo()** creates and returns a pixmap representing the bit pattern passed to it. First, the function uses **XCreateBitmapFromData()** to create a bitmap from the data. Then, **XCreatePixmap()** creates a pixmap of the same width and height as the bitmap, but with the default depth of the screen used by the given widget. Finally, **XCopyPlane()** copies the contents of the bitmap from the single plane of the bitmap to the pixmap.[1] The graphics context determines the foreground and background colors of the pixmap. Since the bitmap is no longer needed, we can use **XFreePixmap()** to free it before returning the pixmap.

```
Pixmap
create_logo(w, gc, bits, width, height)
  Widget      w;
  GC          gc;
  char        *bits;
  Dimension width, height;
{
  Pixmap bitmap, pix;

  /*
   * Create a bitmap from the data.
   */
  bitmap=XCreateBitmapFromData(XtDisplay(w),
                      RootWindowOfScreen(XtScreen(w)),
                      bits, width, height);
  /*
   * Create a pixmap of the same depth as the default screen.
   */
  pix = XCreatePixmap(XtDisplay(w),
                      RootWindowOfScreen(XtScreen(w)),
                      width, height,
                      DefaultDepthOfScreen(XtScreen(w)));
  /*
   * Copy the contents of plane 1 of the bitmap to the
   * pixmap, using the widget's colors.
   */
  XCopyPlane(XtDisplay(w), bitmap, pix, gc, 0, 0,
             xlogo64_width, xlogo64_height, 0, 0, 1);
  /*
   * We don't need the bitmap anymore, so free it.
   */
  XFreePixmap(XtDisplay(w), bitmap);
  return(pix);
}
```

---

[1] This is an example of an area where many programmers introduce portability problems into their programs. A programmer using a single-plane system (black-and-white screen) can use XCopyArea() to copy the bitmap to the pixmap, or to a window, because both the bitmap and the destination drawable have the same depth. However, such a program will fail when run on a multiplane system.

The function **redisplay()** is registered as the function called when an exposure event occurs. The **redisplay()** function checks the current width and height of the widget and then uses **XCopyArea()** to transfer the contents of the pixmap passed in the client data structure to the center of the Stub widget's window.

```
void
redisplay (w, xevent, region)
  Widget        w;
  XEvent    *xevent;
  Region *region;
{
  Arg           wargs[3];
  int           n;
  Dimension     widget_width, widget_height;
  pixmap_data *data;

  /*
   * Get the current size of the widget window.
   */
  n = 0;
  XtSetArg(wargs[n], XtNwidth,  &widget_width); n++;
  XtSetArg(wargs[n], XtNheight, &widget_height); n++;
  XtSetArg(wargs[n], XtNuserData, &data); n++;
  XtGetValues(w, wargs, n);
  /*
   * Copy the contents of the pixmap to the
   * center of the window.
   */
  XCopyArea(XtDisplay(w), data->pix, XtWindow(w), data->gc,
            0, 0, data->width, data->height,
            (int)(widget_width  - data->width) / 2,
            (int)(widget_height - data->height) / 2);
}
```

The **resize()** function simply clears the Stub widget's window, if it is realized. It is important to check whether or not the widget is realized, because the **XtNexpose** function can be called when the widget is resized, even if the window does not yet exist. This function uses the Xlib function

```
XClearArea(display, window, x, y, width, height, exposures)
```

to clear the window. This function clears a rectangular area in a window. If the **width** is given as zero, it is replaced by the width of the window minus **x**. Similarly, if the **height** is given as zero, it is replaced by the height of the window minus **y**. The **exposures** parameter is a boolean value that indicates whether or not exposure events should be generated for the cleared area. With **exposures** set to **TRUE**, **XClearArea()** triggers an **Expose** event for the entire window every time the window is resized. This ensures that the **redisplay()** function will be invoked every time the window is resized.

```
void
resize (w)
  Widget w;
{
  if(XtIsRealized(w))
    XClearArea(XtDisplay(w), XtWindow(w), 0, 0, 0, 0, TRUE);
}
```

This example illustrates many of the Xlib functions that create and initialize bitmaps and pixmaps, and also shows how data can be transferred between bitmaps, pixmaps, and windows. However, you may have noticed that one step in this example is unnecessary. The **redisplay()** function could use **XCopyPlane()** to copy directly between the bitmap and the widget window, completely eliminating the need for the pixmap. Using this approach, we can define **create_logo()** as:

```
Pixmap
create_logo(w, gc, bits, width, height)
  Widget     w;
  char       *bits;
  Dimension width, height;
{
  Pixmap bitmap;
  /*
   * Create a bitmap containing the logo.
   */
  bitmap=XCreateBitmapFromData(XtDisplay(w),
                               RootWindowOfScreen(XtScreen(w)),
                               bits, width, height);
  return(bitmap);
}
```

Then, we can write the **redisplay()** function as:

```
void
redisplay (w, xevent, region)
  Widget       w;
  XEvent      *xevent;
  Region *region;
{
  Arg             wargs[3];
  int             n;
  Dimension       widget_width, widget_height;
  pixmap_data *data;

  /*
   * Get the current size of the widget window.
   */
  n = 0;
```

```
    XtSetArg(wargs[n], XtNwidth,   &widget_width); n++;
    XtSetArg(wargs[n], XtNheight, &widget_height); n++;
    XtSetArg(wargs[n], XtNuserData, &data); n++;
    XtGetValues(w, wargs, n);
    /*
     * Copy plane 1 of the bitmap to the center
     * of the window, using the widget's foreground
     * and background color.
     */
    XCopyPlane(XtDisplay(w), data->pix, XtWindow(w), data->gc,
            0, 0,  data->width, data->height,
            (int)(widget_width - data->width) / 2,
            (int)(widget_height - data->height) / 2, 1);
}
```

Another slight improvement in this example would be to have the **XtNresize** function detect changes in the width and height of the widget. This would a be a much cleaner and more efficient way to handle changes in size because the server already notifies the application of any size changes. We could eliminate the step of retrieving the widget's width and height every time the widget's window is exposed. It should be noted, however, that the purpose of the examples in this section is to demonstrate pixmaps and their related functions and not necessarily to show the easiest way to display the X logo. The easiest way to display a single pixmap such as the X logo, is to create the pixmap, as done by **create_logo()** and then use a StaticText widget, with the **XtNbackgroundPixmap** resource set to **data.pix** to display the pixmap.

7.4 IMAGES

X provides a way to transfer images between applications and the server using an **XImage** data structure. This structure stores data in a device-dependent format; therefore, applications should never access the data directly. The server handles byte-swapping and other data transformations that are sometimes necessary when exchanging images between applications running on different machines. The **XImage** data structure contains the pixel data representing the image as well as information about the format of the image.

7.4.1   Creating Images

Applications can allocate an **XImage** using the function

```
XCreateImage(display, visual, depth, format, offset, data,
             width, height, bitmap_pad, bytes_per_line)
```

This function requires a pointer to the **Visual** structure used by the display. The **data** argument must specify an array of bits representing the image. The size of this data is specified by the **width, height** and **depth**. The **format** specifies the byte order of the data and must be one of the constants **XYPixmap, XYBitmap**, or **ZPixmap**. In **XYPixmap** format, each byte of data specifies the values of 8 pixels along one plane of a raster, with one bit of the data corresponding to each pixel. **ZPixmap** format specifies the data *depth-first*. For example, in **XYPixmap** format, on a display with eight bit planes, each byte of data represents one pixel. The argument **bytes_per_line** specifies the number of bytes in one raster and must be a multiple of 8, 16, or 32 bits.

Images may also be extracted from a drawable using the function:

```
XGetImage(display, drawable, x, y, width, height,
          plane_mask, format)
```

XGetImage() creates an **XImage** structure, copies a rectangular region of a drawable into the image, and returns a pointer to the **XImage** structure. The argument **plane_mask** determines which planes in the drawable are included in the image, while the **format** argument determines whether the image is created in **XYPixmap** or **ZPixmap** format.

X also provides several other functions for manipulating images.

- **XSubImage()** creates a new image and copies the contents of a rectangular sub-region of an old image into the new image.
- **XDestroyImage()** frees an image.
- **XPutPixel()** sets the pixel value of an *(x, y)* location in an **XImage**.
- **XGetPixel()** retrieves the value of a pixel at a particular *(x, y)* location with an **XImage**.
- **XPutImage()** transfers an image to a drawable.

7.4.2   Displaying Images

Let's create a simple application that will act as a pattern browser. The browser allows the user to select from a list of patterns. For this example, the browser displays nine patterns that we define. OLIT does not have any pre-defined bitmaps, so our first task is to locate or create some bitmaps that we can use for displaying. We will use nine common bitmaps in the browser program. Each pattern is defined as a 32 by 32 bit array of 1's. As an example, the *vertical* bitmap looks like this:

```
#define vertical_width 32
#define vertical_height 32
static unsigned char vertical_bits[] = {
   0x88,0x88,0x88,0x88,0x88,0x88,0x88,0x88,0x88,0x88,0x88,0x88,
   0x88,0x88,0x88,0x88,0x88,0x88,0x88,0x88,0x88,0x88,0x88,0x88,
   0x88,0x88,0x88,0x88,0x88,0x88,0x88,0x88,0x88,0x88,0x88,0x88,
   0x88,0x88,0x88,0x88,0x88,0x88,0x88,0x88,0x88,0x88,0x88,0x88,
   0x88,0x88,0x88,0x88,0x88,0x88,0x88,0x88,0x88,0x88,0x88,0x88,
   0x88,0x88,0x88,0x88,0x88,0x88,0x88,0x88,0x88,0x88,0x88,0x88,
   0x88,0x88,0x88,0x88,0x88,0x88,0x88,0x88,0x88,0x88,0x88,0x88,
   0x88,0x88,0x88,0x88,0x88,0x88,0x88,0x88,0x88,0x88,0x88,0x88,
   0x88,0x88,0x88,0x88,0x88,0x88,0x88,0x88,0x88,0x88,0x88,0x88,
   0x88,0x88,0x88,0x88,0x88,0x88,0x88,0x88,0x88,0x88,0x88,0x88,
   0x88,0x88,0x88,0x88,0x88,0x88,0x88,0x88
};
```

Each of the other eight bitmaps has a similar format.[2] We put all nine of the bitmaps in an **xs_bitmap_struct** which is defined as:

```
typedef struct _bitmap_struct {
  char *bitmap;
  Dimension width;
  Dimension height;
} xs_bitmap_struct;
```

Each structure contains the bitmap and a width and height field. This information will be used to create an image.

The main body of the browser is very simple. The program calls **create_pixmap_browser()** with the **bitmaps** as an argument.

```
/****************************************************
 * browser.c : Display some tiling patterns
 ***************************************************/
#include <X11/StringDefs.h>
#include <X11/Intrinsic.h>
#include <Xol/OpenLook.h>
#include "xs_bitmaps.h"
#include "libXs.h"

xs_bitmap_struct bitmaps[] = {
  solid_bits,         solid_width,         solid_height,
  clear_bits,         clear_width,         clear_height,
  vertical_bits,      vertical_width,      vertical_height,
  horizontal_bits,    horizontal_width,    horizontal_height,
  slant_right_bits,   slant_right_width,   slant_right_height,
  slant_left_bits,    slant_left_width,    slant_left_height,
  fg50_bits,          fg50_width,          fg50_height,
  fg25_bits,          fg25_width,          fg25_height,
  cross_bits,         cross_width,         cross_height,
};

main(argc, argv)
  int    argc;
  char *argv[];
{
  Widget toplevel, browser;

  toplevel = OlInitialize(argv[0], "Browser", NULL, 0,
                          &argc, argv);
  /*
   * Create the browser.
```

---

[2]   All nine bitmaps are defined in xs_bitmaps.h which can be seen in Appendix E.

```
     */
    browser = xs_create_pixmap_browser(toplevel,bitmaps,
                                       XtNumber(bitmaps),
                                       NULL, NULL, NULL);
    XtManageChild(browser);
    XtRealizeWidget(toplevel);
    XtMainLoop();
}
```

The function **xs_create_pixmap_browser()** creates an Exclusives widget containing
a RectButton widget for each pixmap in the browser. The Exclusives widget ensures that only one
button is selected at any one time.

```
/************************************************************
 * xs create_pixmap_browser(): let the user select from a set
 *                             of patterns.
 ************************************************************/
#include <X11/StringDefs.h>
#include <X11/Intrinsic.h>
#include <X11/Xutil.h>
#include <Xol/OpenLook.h>
#include <Xol/Exclusives.h>
#include <Xol/RectButton.h>
#include "libXs.h"

Widget
xs_create_pixmap_browser (parent, bitmaps, n_bmaps,
                          callback, data, widgets)
    Widget       parent;          /* widget to manage the browser */
    xs_bitmap_struct *bitmaps;    /* list of bitmaps              */
    int          n_bmaps;         /* how many bitmaps             */
    void         (*callback)();   /* invoked when state changes   */
    XtPointer    data;            /* data to be passed to callback*/
    WidgetList   *widgets;        /* list of RectButton widgets   */
{
    Widget       browser;
    WidgetList   buttons;
    XImage       **images;
    int          i, n;
    Arg          wargs[3];

    /*
     * Malloc room for button widgets.
     */
    buttons = (WidgetList) XtMalloc(n_bmaps * sizeof(Widget));
    images = (XImage **) XtMalloc(n_bmaps * sizeof(XImage *));
    /*
     * Create an Exclusives widget.
```

```
   */
  n = 0;
  XtSetArg(wargs[n], XtNlayoutType, OL_FIXEDCOLS); n++;
  XtSetArg(wargs[n], XtNmeasure, 3); n++;
  browser = XtCreateManagedWidget("browser",
                                       exclusivesWidgetClass,
                                       parent, wargs, n);
  /*
   * Create a button for each tile. If a callback function
   * has been given, register it as an XtNselect
   */
  for(i=0;i< n_bmaps;i++) {
    images[i] = xs_create_image(parent, bitmaps[i].bitmap,
                                   bitmaps[i].width,
                                   bitmaps[i].height);

    buttons[i] = xs_create_pixmap_button(browser, images[i]);
    if(callback)
      XtAddCallback(buttons[i], XtNselect, callback, data);
  }
  /*
   * Manage all buttons and return the Exclusives widget
   */
  XtManageChildren(buttons, n_bmaps);
  if(widgets != NULL)
    *widgets = buttons;
  return(browser);
}
```

The function **xs_create_image()** creates an image from the supplied bitmap data by calling **XCreateImage()**. A pointer to the created **XImage** structure is returned.

```
XImage *
xs_create_image(w, bits, width, height)
  Widget      w;
  char        *bits;
  Dimension   width, height;
{
  XImage *image;
  image = XCreateImage(XtDisplay(w),
                         OlVisualOfObject(w),
                         1, XYBitmap, 0,
                         bits, width, height, 32, 0);
  return(image);
}
```

The function **xs_create_pixmap_button()** creates a RectButton widget to display the given pixmap pattern. The image is passed as an argument to **xs_create_pixmap_button()**.

To display an image in a RectButton widget, the widget's **XtNlabelType** resource must be set to **OL_IMAGE**, and the **XtNlabelImage** resource set to the image to be displayed. This function also sets the **XtNuserData** resource, supported by all OLIT widgets, to the image displayed in the widget. This resource can be used to store any data an application needs to associate with a widget. Storing the image as user data allows an application to retrieve the image from within a callback or event handler registered for the widget.

```
Widget
xs_create_pixmap_button(parent, image)
  Widget    parent;
  XImage    *image;
{
  Widget    button;
  Arg       wargs[10];
  int       n;

  /*
   * Display the XImage in the button and also store it
   * so it can be retrieved from the button later.
   */
  n = 0;
  XtSetArg(wargs[n], XtNlabelType,    OL_IMAGE); n++;
  XtSetArg(wargs[n], XtNlabelImage,  image); n++;
  XtSetArg(wargs[n], XtNuserData,    image); n++;
  button = XtCreateWidget("", rectButtonWidgetClass,
                          parent, wargs, n);
  /*
   * Return the unmanaged button.
   */
  return(button);
}
```

Figure 7.2 shows the pixmap browser created by this example. The functions described in this section are used again in Chapter 10, so they are placed in the libXs library for convenient reuse.

Figure 7.2 The pixmap browser.

7.5 SUMMARY

This chapter introduced the various types of raster images supported by X and the Xlib functions that manipulate them. X supports several types of image formats, bitmaps, pixmaps, and **XImage** struc-tures. Pixmaps, bitmaps, and tiles are drawables, and can be used as destinations for Xlib graphics operations. Pixmaps are stored in off-screen memory, and are useful for storing and manipulating raster images without displaying them on the screen. A bitmap is simply a single-plane pixmap. Tile is another name for pixmap, usually used to refer to a pixmap containing a repeating pattern.

Applications can store images in the server using the Xlib **XImage** structure and its related functions. The primary reason for using the **XImage** structure is to allow images to be transferred between clients running on different machines. Different machines sometimes store data in different formats, and the X server handles the byte swapping required to move images from one machine to another.

The following chapter discusses graphics contexts, a resource that controls how X graphics op-erations are performed. Graphics contexts affect how images are transferred between drawables such as pixmaps and bitmaps. Pixmaps are also used by graphics contexts as patterns to be combined with drawing operations.

8

GRAPHICS CONTEXTS

All graphics operations use attributes that determine the width of lines, foreground and background colors, fill patterns, fonts to be used when displaying text, and so on. X stores these attributes in an internal data structure known as a *graphics context*, often abbreviated as GC. This chapter discusses the attributes of GCs as well as the Xlib and Intrinsics functions that create and manipulate them. Chapters 9 and 10 show how to use graphics contexts with the X text and graphics functions.

8.1 CREATING GRAPHICS CONTEXTS

The Xlib function

```
XCreateGC(display, drawable, mask, &values)
```

creates a graphics context and returns a resource identifier that applications can use to refer to the GC. The X server maintains the data associated with the graphics context, and all clients must reference the graphics context by its ID. Graphics contexts can be used with any drawable that has the same depth, and is on the same screen, as the drawable specified when the GC is created.

Applications can specify the initial value of each component of a graphics context in the **values** argument when calling **XCreateGC()**. This argument must be a pointer to an **XGCValues** structure, which is defined as:

```
typedef struct {
    int           function;    /* logical operation      */
    unsigned long plane_mask;  /* plane mask             */
    unsigned long foreground;  /* foreground pixel       */
    unsigned long background;  /* background pixel       */
```

```
    int              line_width; /* line width (in pixels)    */
    int              line_style; /* LineSolid,
                                     LineOnOffDash, or
                                     LineDoubleDash            */
    int              cap_style;  /* CapNotLast, CapButt,
                                     CapRound, CapProjecting   */
    int              join_style; /* JoinMiter, JoinRound,
                                     or JoinBevel              */
    int              fill_style; /* FillSolid, FillTiled,
                                     FillStippled,
                                     or FillOpaqueStippled     */
    int              fill_rule;  /* EvenOddRule, WindingRule   */
    int              arc_mode;   /* ArcChord, ArcPieSlice      */
    Pixmap           tile;       /* tile pixmap for tiling     */
    Pixmap           stipple;    /* stipple 1 plane pixmap     */
    int              ts_x_origin;/* tile and stipple offset    */
    int              ts_y_origin;
    Font             font;       /* default text font          */
    int     subwindow_mode;      /* ClipByChildren, or
                                     IncludeInferiors          */
    Bool    graphics_exposures;  /* report graphics exposures?*/
    int     clip_x_origin;       /* clipping origin            */
    int     clip_y_origin;
    Pixmap  clip_mask;           /* bitmap clipping            */
    int     dash_offset;         /* line information           */
    char    dashes;
} XGCValues;
```

The **mask** argument to **XCreateGC()** specifies which members of the **XGCValues** structure contain valid information. If this mask is zero, the GC will be created with default values for all attributes. To override the default value for a particular field, the mask must include a constant corresponding to that field. Table 8.1 lists the GC attribute masks, along with the default values of each attribute.

Table 8.1 Masks used with graphics contexts.

Mask	Default Value of GC
GCFunction	GXCopy
GCPlaneMask	AllPlanes
GCForeground	0
GCBackground	1
GCLineWidth	0
GCLineStyle	LineSolid
GCCapStyle	CapButt
GCJoinStyle	JoinMiter
GCFillStyle	FillSolid

Table 8.1 (Continued) Masks used with graphics contexts.

Mask	Default Value of GC
GCFillRule	EvenOddRule
GCTile	Foreground
GCStipple	0
GCTileStipXOrigin	0
GCTileStipYOrigin	1
GCFont	Implementation-Dependent
GCSubwindowMode	ClipByChildren
GCGraphicsExposure	TRUE
GCClipXOrigin	0
GCClipYOrigin	0
GCClipMask	None
GCDashOffset	0
GCDashList	4
GCArcMode	ArcPieSlice

For example, the following code segment creates a graphics context, specifying the foreground pixel, background pixel, and line style:

```
XGCValues gcv;
GC        gc;
gcv.foreground = 1;
gcv.background = 2;
gcv.line_style = LineOnOffDash;
gc = XCreateGC(display, window,
               GCForeground | GCBackground | GCLineStyle,
               &gcv);
```

The Xt Intrinsics also provide a function for creating graphics contexts:

```
XtGetGC(widget, mask, values)
```

This function caches graphics contexts to allow sharing of GCs within an application. Therefore, applications must not modify GCs created with `XtGetGC()`.

8.2 MANIPULATING GRAPHICS CONTEXTS

After a GC is created, applications can use the function

```
XChangeGC(display, gc, mask, &values)
```

to modify any of the GCs attributes. The **mask** and **values** arguments serve the same function here as they do in **XCreateGC()**. Xlib also provides many convenience functions for modifying individual GC attributes. The following sections introduce many of these functions as we discuss the purpose of each of the attributes of a graphics context.

8.2.1   Display Functions

A graphics context's **GCFunction** attribute specifies a logical display function that determines how each pixel of a new image is combined with the current contents of a destination drawable. The new image, referred to as the *source*, could be copied from another drawable, or be generated by a graphics request. For example, when this attribute is set to **GXcopy**, the source image completely replaces the current contents of the affected region of the drawable. On the other hand, if the same figure is drawn using the **GXor** display function, the bits of the affected region of the drawable are set to the logical OR of the source and the previous contents of the destination.

Table 8.2 shows the display functions defined in X.h, along with their corresponding logical operations. The **src** parameter represents the bits being written and the **dst** parameter represents the current state of the bits in the drawable.

Table 8.1 Display functions.

Mask	Display Function
GXclear	0
GXand	src AND dst
GXandReverse	src AND (NOT dst)
	src
GXandInverted	(NOT src) AND dst
GXnoop	dst
GXxor	src XOR dst
GXor	src OR dst
GXnor	NOT (src OR dst)
GXequiv	(NOT src) XOR dst
GXinvert	NOT dst
GXorReverse	src OR (NOT dst)
GXcopyInverted	NOT src
GXorInverted	(NOT src) OR dst
GXnand	NOT (src AND dst)
GXset	1

On color screens, these logical operations are performed bit-wise on each pixel within the affected area. For example, let's see what happens if we draw a line using the **GXand** drawing function and a pixel index of 3 for the foreground color. If we draw the line in a drawable whose background color is pixel 10 on a display with 4 bit planes, the resulting line color is the represented by the pixel 2. This is easier to see if we examine the binary representation of these numbers:

$$3_{10} \text{ AND } 10_{10} = 2_{10}$$
$$0011_2 \text{ AND } 1010_2 = 0010_2$$

The *exclusive-OR* (XOR) function, specified by the constant **GXxor**, is a commonly used display function. The XOR function has the interesting property that drawing a figure twice in XOR mode restores the screen to its original state. This allows us to erase an image drawn in XOR mode simply by drawing it a second time. Contrast this with erasing an object on the screen by drawing the object in the background color of the window. In the latter case, the application must redraw the previous contents, if any, of the window. When an image is redrawn in XOR mode, the previous contents of the window are restored, as long as nothing else on the screen has changed.

The most common use of the **XOR** display function is for *rubber banding* operations, where an object on the screen, often a line or rectangle, is moved and stretched in response to mouse motion. The **XOR** mode allows the rubber band object to move across other objects on the screen without disturbing them. Chapter 10 presents an example that illustrates rubber banding.

The function

```
XSetFunction(display, gc, function)
```

provides an easy way for applications to alter a graphics context's display function. The default value is **GXcopy**.

8.2.2   Plane Mask

The value of the **GCPlaneMask** attribute determines which bit planes of a drawable are affected by a graphics operation. The plane mask contains a one in each bit that can be modified. The function

```
XSetPlaneMask(display, gc, mask)
```

sets the plane mask of a graphics context. For example, a line drawn with foreground pixel 6 would normally affect bit planes 2 and 3 ($6_{10} = 0110_2$). However, if the plane mask of the graphics context is set to 5_{10} (0101_2), drawing a line with a foreground pixel 6 affects only plane 3, and the resulting line is displayed in the color indicated by the pixel index 4. Applications can use the macro

```
AllPlanes
```

as the value for **mask** to indicate all planes supported by a screen. The default value of the **GCPlaneMask** attribute is **AllPlanes**.

8.2.3   Foreground and Background

The **GCForeground** and **GCBackground** attributes of a graphics context indicate the pixels used as foreground and background colors for graphics operations. The pixel index must be an integer between zero and *n - 1*, where *n* is the number of colors supported within the visual type used by the program. This index is usually obtained using the color allocation functions discussed in Chapter 6. The function

```
XSetForeground(display, gc, pixel)
```

sets the **GCForeground** attribute while the function

```
XSetBackground(display, gc, pixel)
```

sets the **GCBackground** attribute. The default value of **GCForeground** is 0 and the default value of **GCBackground** is 1.

8.2.4   Line Attributes

Several GC attributes determine how a line is drawn. The **GCLineWidth** controls the width, in pixels, of the line. The default width is 0. The server draws zero width lines one pixel wide using an implementation-dependent algorithm. On displays that have hardware support for line drawing, this is often the fastest way to draw lines. The **GCLineStyle** attribute can be one of the constants:

    LineSolid   LineOnOffDash   LineDoubleDash

Figure 8.1 shows each of these styles. The default value is **LineSolid**.

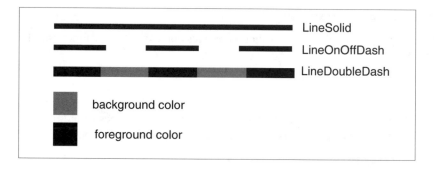

Figure 8.1 Line styles.

Graphics contexts also control how the server draws the ends of wide lines. The **GCCapStyle** of a line can be one of the constants:

    CapNotLast
    CapButt
    CapRound
    CapProjecting

The default value is **CapButt**. Figure 8.2 shows how X draws each of these styles.

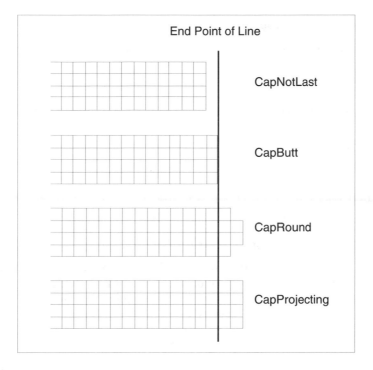

Figure 8.2 Line cap styles.

The graphics context also determines how the server draws connected lines. The style is determined by the **GCJoinStyle** attribute and can be one of the constants:

      JoinMiter   **JoinRound**   **JoinBevel**

Figure 8.3 illustrates each of these styles. The default style is **JoinMiter**.

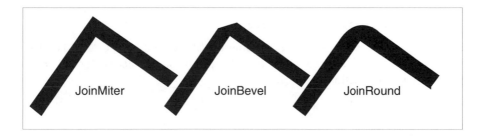

Figure 8.3 Line join styles.

The function

```
XSetLineAttributes(display, gc, width, style, cap_style, join_style)
```

sets each of a GC's line attributes.

8.2.5   Fill Styles

X allows graphics figures to be *filled* by some color or pattern. The **GCFillStyle** attribute determines how figures are filled and must be one of the constants:

```
FillSolid
FillTiled
FillStippled
FillOpaqueStippled
```

Applications can use the function

```
XSetFillStyle(display, gc, style)
```

to set the fill style of a graphics context. The default fill style, **FillSolid**, specifies that figures are to be filled with the current foreground color. The **FillTiled** style indicates that figures are to be filled with the pixmap pattern specified in the **tile** attribute. This pixmap must have the same depth and screen as the drawable with which the graphics context is used.

The function

```
XSetTile(display, gc, tile)
```

sets a graphics context's **GCTile** attribute. Setting the **GCFillStyle** to **FillStippled** or **FillOpaqueStippled** specifies that regions be filled with a *stipple*. A stipple is a repeating pattern produced by using a bitmap (a pixmap of depth 1) as a mask in the drawing operation. When **FillStippled** is specified, graphics operations only operate on those bits of the stipple pattern that are set to 1. When **FillOpaqueStippled** is specified, bits in the stipple pattern that contain a 1 are drawn using the foreground color of the graphics context and those that contain a zero are drawn using the background color.

The function

```
XSetStipple(display, gc, stipple)
```

sets a GC's stipple pattern. Graphics contexts also use a fill rule attribute, **GCFillRule**, to determine the algorithm used to fill a region. The fill rule must be one of the constants **EvenOddRule** or **WindingRule**. The function

```
XSetFillRule(display, gc, rule)
```

sets the fill rule for a graphics context.

Figure 8.4 shows how the fill rule affects the appearance of a filled polygon. If **EvenOddRule** is specified, the server sets a pixel at a particular point if an imaginary line drawn between the point and the outside of the figure crosses the figure an odd number of times. If **WindingRule** is specified, the server determines whether a point should be filled using an imaginary line between the point and a vertex of the figure. The line is rotated about the point so that it touches each vertex of the figure, in order, until it returns to the original position. If the line makes one or more complete rotations, the point is considered to be inside the figure, and the point is filled.

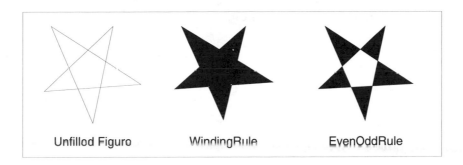

Figure 8.4 Comparison of EvenOddRule and WindingRule.

8.2.6   Fonts

The **GCFont** attribute of a graphics context determines the font used for all text operations. The function

```
XSetFont(display, gc, font_id)
```

sets a graphics context's font attribute. The default font is implementation-dependent. Chapter 9 discusses fonts and how they are used to display text in a window.

8.2.7   Clip Masks

The **GCClipMask** attribute specifies a bitmap as a clip mask for all drawing operations. If a graphics context has a clip mask, drawing operations affect only those pixels in the drawable that correspond to a 1 in the clip mask. The function

```
XSetClipMask(display, gc, bitmap)
```

sets the bitmap used as a clip mask. The default value is **None**, in which case no clipping against the bitmap is performed.

The function

```
XSetClipOrigin(display, gc, x, y)
```

alters the location of the clipmask relative to the origin of the drawable. A clipping region can also be specified as a list of rectangular areas, using the function:

```
XSetClipRectangles(display, gc, xoffset, yoffset,
                    rect, nrect, ordering)
```

The arguments **xoffset** and **yoffset** indicate an offset to be added to the origin of all rectangles. The **rect** argument must be an array of **XRectangle** structures. This structure is defined as:

```
typedef struct {
    short x, y;
    unsigned short width, height;
} XRectangle;
```

If the list of rectangles is given as **None**, no clipping is performed. Some X servers can perform clipping more efficiently if they know the order of the rectangles. The **ordering** argument must specify one of the constants **Unsorted, YSorted, YXSorted,** or **YXBanded** to indicate the order of the rectangles within the array.

8.3 GRAPHICS EXPOSURES

The server generates **GraphicsExpose** events when an **XCopyArea()** or **XCopyPlane()** function is unable to copy an area because the area is occluded by a window. The function

```
XSetGraphicsExposures(display, gc, flag)
```

enables or disables generation of these events for graphics operations that use the graphics context. **GraphicsExpose** events are enabled when **flag** is set to **TRUE**. The default value is **TRUE**.

8.4 REGIONS

Xlib provides a set of utility routines for representing and manipulating non-rectangular areas. For example, applications often need to determine whether an exposed area intersects with the area occupied by a particular object on the screen. To deal with such situations, X provides an *opaque*[1] data, **Region**, and a set of functions that operate on regions. Internally, a region consists of an array of rectangles. Applications cannot access the region data structure directly, but must use functions provided by Xlib to manipulate **Region**s. Functions that manipulate regions do not make requests to the server; all calculations are done locally in the client. Applications that use regions must include the header file Xutil.h.

Some widgets use regions when reporting exposure events. Widgets that request the Intrinsics to compress exposure events are passed a **Region** that defines the sum of all exposed areas after all expose events are received. Some widgets choose to pass the region on to the application in callbacks.

The function

```
XCreateRegion()
```

1 An opaque data structure is one whose true definition is hidden using data abstraction techniques. The public definition of the structure is just a pointer to an undefined structure. The true definition and the procedures that operate on the data are kept in a private file. This same technique is used by the Xt Intrinsics to hide the implementation of widgets, and is discussed in more detail in Chapter 12.

creates and returns a new, empty **Region**. The function

```
XPolygonRegion(points_array, npoints, fill_rule)
```

creates a **Region** representing the polygonal area defined by an array of **XPoint** structures. This structure is defined as:

```
typedef struct {
    short x, y;
} XPoint;
```

The **fill_rule** argument to **XPolygonRegion()** determines the algorithm used to convert the polygon to a region and may be one of the constants **EvenOddRule** or **WindingRule**. Chapter 10 describes the meaning of these terms.

The function

```
XDestroyRegion(region)
```

destroys a **Region** and frees the memory used by the **Region**. The function

```
XEqualRegion(r1, r2)
```

compares two Regions and returns **TRUE** if they are equal, or **FALSE** if they are not.

The function

```
XEmptyRegion(region)
```

returns **TRUE** if the given **Region** is empty. A new **Region** defined by the intersection of two **Regions** can be obtained using the function:

```
XIntersectRegion(region1, region2, result)
```

For example, we can use **XIntersectRegion()** to write a simple function that determines if two regions intersect:

```
does_intersect(region1, region2)
    Region region1, region2;
{
    int     is_empty;
    Region intersection;
    /*
     * Create the empty intersection region.
     */
    intersection = XCreateRegion();
    /*
     * Get the intersection of the two regions.
     */
    XIntersectRegion(region1, region2, intersection);
    /*
     * Check whether the result is an empty region.
     */
    is_empty = XEmptyRegion(intersection));
```

```
    /*
     * Free the region we created before returning the result.
     */
    XDestroyRegion(intersection);
    return (!is_empty);
}
```

The function

```
XPointInRegion(region, x, y)
```

returns **TRUE** if the given (*x, y*) point lies within the bounds of the region, while the function

```
XRectInRegion(region, x, y, width, height)
```

determines whether a rectangular area intersects a region. **XRectInRegion()** returns the constant **RectangleIn** if the rectangle is totally contained within the region, **RectangleOut** if the rectangle lies completely outside the region, and **RectanglePart** if the rectangle partially intersects the Region.

The smallest enclosing rectangle of a region can be obtained using the function:

```
XClipBox(region, &rect)
```

When this function returns, the **XRectangle** structure **rect** contains the bounding box of the specified region.

Applications can also use a **Region** as a clip mask in a graphics context. The function

```
XSetRegion(display, gc, region)
```

sets the clip mask of a graphics context to the given region. Xlib also includes many other useful functions that operate on **Region**s. These include functions that find the union of two regions, subtract regions, move regions, and so on.

The Xt Intrinsics also provide a useful function for converting the area reported in an **Expose** event to a region. The function

```
XtAddExposureToRegion(&event, region)
```

computes the union of the region and the rectangle contained in the **Expose** event and stores the result in the region.

8.5 SUMMARY

This chapter discussed graphics contexts and regions. Graphics contexts control color, style and other attributes used by the Xlib text and graphics primitives. Graphics contexts are maintained by the server and accessed by applications through a resource ID. Xlib provides functions to control the attributes of a graphics context, and the Xt Intrinsics provide a way to cache graphics contexts, so they can be shared within an application.

This chapter also discussed regions, which are often used by graphics applications to define clipping areas. Regions allow rectangular or non-rectangular areas to be represented, compared, and manipulated.

The following two chapters show how the topics discussed in this and the previous chapters (graphics contexts, raster images, regions, and color) are used in conjunction with the Xlib text and graphics operations.

9

TEXT AND FONTS

Xlib provides a set of primitive functions for drawing text in a window or pixmap. X draws characters on the screen using bitmaps that represent each character. A *font* is a collection of bitmapped characters. This chapter discusses fonts and presents the Xlib functions that draw text in a window. The chapter also presents examples that combine the elements of the last few chapters with the Xlib text-drawing functions.

9.1 FONTS

A font is a collection of *glyphs*, which are rectangular bitmaps representing an image. Although a glyph may contain any bit pattern, fonts usually contain textual characters. Before an application can use a font, it must load the font into the server. The function

```
XLoadFont(display, font_name)
```

finds and loads the named font, and returns a resource ID that refers to the font. It is common, but not necessary, for fonts to be kept in a file. However, this is an implementation-dependent detail that application programmers do not need to be concerned with.

The function

```
XQueryFont(display, font_ID)
```

returns a pointer to an **XFontStruct** structure that contains detailed information about the font. The function

```
XLoadQueryFont(display, name)
```

performs the equivalent of an **XLoadFont()** followed by an **XQueryFont()** and returns the **XFontStruct** information with a single server request. The information in the **XFontStruct** structure includes:

- **fid**: The resource ID used to refer to the font.
- **direction**: A flag that indicates whether the characters in the font are defined left to right or right to left. X supports only horizontally drawn text.
- **min_bounds**: An **XCharStruct** structure that contains the bounding box of the smallest character in the font.
- **max_bounds**: An **XCharStruct** structure that contains the bounding box of the largest character in the font.
- **ascent**: An integer that indicates how far the font extends above the baseline.
- **descent**: An integer that indicates how far the font extends below the baseline.
- **per_char**: An array containing an **XCharStruct** structure for each character in the font. X fonts can be *mono-spaced* (having the same width) or *proportional* (varying widths among characters).

The **XCharStruct** structure is defined in Xlib.h:

```
typedef struct {
    short           lbearing;
    short           rbearing;
    short           width;
    short           ascent;
    short           descent;
    unsigned short  attributes;
} XCharStruct;
```

This structure contains information about the size and location of a single character relative to the origin, as shown in Figure 9.1.

Xlib provides functions that calculate the size, in pixels, of character strings based on the font used. The function

```
XTextWidth(fontstruct, string, string_length)
```

calculates the pixel length of a character string for a particular font. The function

```
XTextExtents(font, string, string_length, &direction,
             &ascent, &descent, &overall)
```

provides additional information. This function returns the **direction, ascent,** and **descent** for the entire string, and also returns an **XCharStruct, overall,** containing the width, left bearing, and right bearing of the entire string.

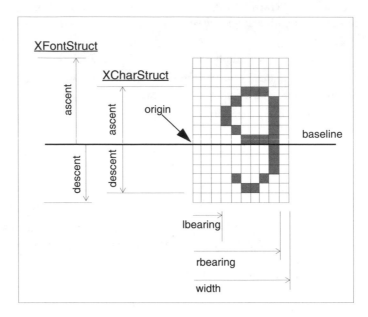

Figure 9.1 Bounding box of a character.

9.2 TEXT OPERATIONS

X displays text in a drawable by performing a fill operation on a region using the text font as a mask. Xlib provides two simple functions for displaying strings:

```
XDrawString(display, drawable, gc, x, y, str, length)
```

and

```
XDrawImageString(display, drawable, gc, x, y, str, length)
```

Both functions display a string in a drawable starting at the given position. The graphics context determines the foreground color, background color, the display function, the font, and the fill style. The graphics context also determines the stipple or tile pattern and clipping region used. **XDrawString()** draws only the foreground component of the text, while **XDrawImageString()** also fills the background region within each character's bounding box.

Xlib also includes drawing functions that draw lines of text using multiple fonts in a single operation. The function

```
XDrawText(display, drawable, gc, x, y, items, nitems)
```

draws **nitems** of text as specified in an array of type **XTextItem**. This structure is defined as:

```
typedef struct {
  char  *chars;    /* Character array               */
  int    nchars;   /* number of characters in string */
  int    delta;    /* distance from previous string  */
  Font   font;     /* Font for this string or None   */
} XTextItem;
```

XDrawText() processes each item in the array. If an entry in the array specifies the font as **None**, **XDrawText()** uses the font used by the previous item. The **delta** member of the structure specifies the distance along the *x* axis between the start of the current item and the end of the previous item.

9.3 EXAMPLE: A FILE VIEWER

This section uses some of the text and font functions discussed in the previous section to build a simple file viewer, called **fileview**. The viewer allows the user to view and scroll the contents of a text file in a window. The example uses a DrawArea widget as a drawing surface on which to display the text, and demonstrates how the Xlib text functions can be used with the Xt Intrinsics and OLIT widget set.[1]

The header of the **fileview** program includes the widget header files used by the program and defines the global variables and data structures used by the program.

```
/************************************************
 * fileview.h: declarations for fileview program
 ************************************************/
#include <stdio.h>
#include <X11/Intrinsic.h>
#include <X11/StringDefs.h>
#include <X11/Xutil.h>
#include <Xol/OpenLook.h>
#include <Xol/DrawArea.h>
#include <Xol/Scrollbar.h>
#include <Xol/RubberTile.h>
#include "libXs.h"

#define MAXLINESIZE  300
#define MAXLINES     2000
#define MIN(a,b)     (((a) < (b)) ? (a) : (b))
#define ABS(a)       (((a) >= 0) ? (a) : -(a))
#define MAX(a,b)     ((a > b) ? a : b)
#define MARGIN       5
```

---

[1] The approach used in this example is hardly the easiest way to write a file viewer. The most straightforward approach would simply use a TextEdit widget in a ScrolledWindow widget to display the file. The entire program would fit on a single page. However the point of this section is to demonstrate the Xlib text functions, so that we can use these functions when necessary (when writing a new widget that displays text, for example).

```
#define VERTMARGIN    3
#define DISPLAYLINES 50


typedef struct {
  char          *chars[MAXLINES];   /* Lines of text        */
  int           length[MAXLINES];   /* Length of each line  */
  int           rbearing[MAXLINES]; /* right bearing of line */
  int           descent;            /* descent below baseline*/
  XFontStruct   *font;              /* The font struct      */
  GC            gc;                 /* A read/write GC      */
  Widget        scrollbar;
  Widget        canvas;
  Dimension     canvas_height;      /* canvas dimensions    */
  Dimension     canvas_width;
  int           fontheight;         /* descent + ascent     */
  int           nitems;             /* number of text lines */
  int           top;                /* line at top of window */
} text_data, *text_data_ptr;

int           displaylines = DISPLAYLINES;
void          handle_exposures();
void          scroll_bar_moved ();
void          resize ();
void          graphics_exposure ();

static XtResource resources[] = {
  {XtNfont, XtCFont, XtRFontStruct, sizeof (XFontStruct *),
     XtOffset(text_data_ptr, font), XtRString, "Fixed"      },
};
```

This example limits the size of the file to 2000 lines, as defined by the constant **MAXLINES**; a more realistic implementation would allocate space based on the size of the file. The **text_data** structure contains two arrays. The **chars** member is an array of character strings, while **length** is an array that caches the length of each line of the file. The **nitems** member records the number of lines in the file, and **top** contains the index of the line displayed at the top of the window. The structure also contains other useful information that needs to be passed to the event handlers and call-backs in this example, including the font, the graphics context used to draw the text, and the widgets used by the application.

The **resources** structure is used by the resource manager to load the font information into the buffer data structure. The default font is specified as "Fixed".

The file viewer window contains both a DrawArea widget used to display the text and a Scroll-bar widget that scrolls the text in the DrawArea widget. These widgets are managed by a RubberTile widget. In this example, the RubberTile widget simply provides a convenient layout for the Scrollbar and the DrawArea widgets. The main body of the program creates all widgets, and calls other functions to load the file into the text buffer and initialize the global data structures defined in the header file.

```
/*****************************************************
 * fileview.c: A simple file viewer
 *****************************************************/
#include "fileview.h"

extern Widget create_scrollbar ();
short           large_rbearing = 0;

main (argc, argv)
  int        argc;
  char       *argv[];
{
  Widget       toplevel, rt, sb, sw;
  Arg          wargs[10];
  int          n;
  text_data    data;

  toplevel = OlInitialize(argv[0], "Fileview", NULL, 0,
                          &argc, argv);
  XtGetApplicationResources(toplevel, &data, resources,
                            XtNumber(resources), NULL, 0);
  /*
   * Read the file specified in argv[1] into the text buffer.
   */
  data.canvas_height = data.canvas_width = 0;
  load_file(&data, (argc == 2) ? argv[1] : NULL);
  /*
   * Create a RubberTile widget as a base.
   */
  n = 0;
  XtSetArg(wargs[n], XtNorientation, OL_HORIZONTAL); n++;
  rt = XtCreateManagedWidget("rt", rubberTileWidgetClass,
                             toplevel, wargs, n);
  /*
   * Create the drawing surface.
   */
  n = 0;
  XtSetArg(wargs[n], XtNborderWidth, 1); n++;
  XtSetArg(wargs[n], XtNwidth, large_rbearing+(MARGIN*2)); n++;
  XtSetArg(wargs[n], XtNheight,
           (data.fontheight*displaylines)+VERTMARGIN); n++;
  data.canvas= XtCreateManagedWidget("canvas", drawAreaWidgetClass,
                                     rt, wargs, n);
  /*
```

```
 * Determine the initial size of the canvas and store it
 */
n = 0;
XtSetArg(wargs[n], XtNheight, &data.canvas_height); n++;
XtSetArg(wargs[n], XtNwidth, &data.canvas_width); n++;
XtGetValues(data.canvas, wargs, n);
/*
 * Create the scrollbar
 */
data.scrollbar = create_scrollbar(rt, &data);
/*
 * Register callbacks for resizes and exposes.
 */
XtAddCallback(data.canvas, XtNexposeCallback,
              handle_exposures, &data);
XtAddCallback(data.canvas, XtNresizeCallback,
              resize, &data);
XtRealizeWidget(toplevel);
create_gc(&data);
XtMainLoop();
}
```

After calling **OlInitialize()**, the program retrieves the application resources that specify the font used to display the text. The function **load_file()** then reads the file into the text buffer. After creating the DrawArea and Scrollbar widgets, the program registers two callback functions with the DrawArea widget. The **XtNresizeCallback** function updates the data in the text buffer when the widget is resized, while the **XtNexposeCallback** function redraws the text when necessary. The function **create_gc()** creates the graphics context used by the program. Notice that the graphics context is not created until after the widgets have been realized. This is because we need to create a modifiable graphics context using the Xlib function **XCreateGC()**, which requires a valid window ID.

The function **load_file()** attempts to open a file. If successful, the function uses **fgets()** to read each line of the file and load it into the text buffer. Because the contents of the buffer cannot change once the file has been read, we can use **XTextExtents()** to calculate the bounding box of each line of the file as it is read, and store this information with the text buffer. When the entire file has been read, the function stores the number of lines in the file and initializes the line to be displayed at the top of the window to zero.

```
load_file(data, filename)
  text_data      *data;
  char           *filename;
{
  int            foreground, background, i, dir, ascent, desc;
  XCharStruct    char_info;
  FILE           *fp, *fopen();
  char           buf[MAXLINESIZE];
```

```
/*
 * Open the file.
 */
if((fp = fopen(filename, "r")) == NULL) {
  fprintf(stderr, "Unable to open %s\n", filename);
  exit(1);
}
/*
 * Read each line of the file into the buffer,
 * calculating and caching the extents of each line.
 */
i = 0;
while((fgets(buf, MAXLINESIZE, fp)) != NULL && i < MAXLINES) {
  data->chars[i] = XtMalloc(strlen(buf) + 1);
  buf[strlen(buf) - 1] = '\0';
  strcpy(data->chars[i], buf);
  data->length[i] = strlen(data->chars[i]);
  XTextExtents(data->font, data->chars[i], data->length[i],
               &dir, &ascent, &desc, &char_info);
  data->rbearing[i] = char_info.rbearing;
  if(large_rbearing < char_info.rbearing)
    large_rbearing = char_info.rbearing;
  data->descent    = desc;
  data->fontheight = ascent + desc;
  i++;
}
/*
 * Close the file.
 */
fclose(fp);
/*
 * Remember the number of lines, and initialize the
 * current line number to be 0.
 */
data->nitems = i;
data->top = 0;
}
```

The function **create_scrollbar()** creates a Scrollbar widget and defines a callback for the Scrollbar's **XtNsliderMoved** callback list. This function also sets the minimum position of the Scrollbar widget to zero and the maximum position to the number of lines in the file. This allows the current position of the scroll bar to correspond directly to the line number of the first line of text in the window. The function sets the proportion indicator of the Scrollbar by setting **XtNproportionLength** to the number of lines displayed in the DrawArea. The

XtNshowPage resource is also set to **OL_RIGHT** which turns on the page indicator during dragging.

```
Widget
create_scrollbar(parent, data)
  Widget        parent;
  text_data    *data;
{
  Arg    wargs[10];
  int    n = 0;
  Widget scrollbar;

  /*
   * Set the scrollbar so that movements are reported
   * in terms of lines of text. Set the scrolling
   * granularity to a single line, and the proportion
   * indicator to the size of the canvas widget.
   * Also turn on the page indicator.
   */
  n = 0;
  XtSetArg(wargs[n], XtNsliderMin, 0); n++;
  XtSetArg(wargs[n], XtNsliderMax, data->nitems); n++;
  XtSetArg(wargs[n], XtNgranularity, 1); n++;
  XtSetArg(wargs[n], XtNproportionLength, displaylines); n++;
  XtSetArg(wargs[n], XtNweight, 0); n++;
  XtSetArg(wargs[n], XtNshowPage, OL_RIGHT); n++;
  scrollbar = XtCreateManagedWidget("scrollbar",
                                    scrollbarWidgetClass,
                                    parent, wargs, n);

  XtAddCallback(scrollbar, XtNsliderMoved,
                   scroll_bar_moved, data);
  return(scrollbar);
}
```

The function **create_gc()** creates a graphics context using the foreground and background colors retrieved from the **canvas** widget and the font retrieved from the resource data base.

```
create_gc(data)
  text_data  *data;
{
  XGCValues  gcv;
  Display   *dpy  = XtDisplay(data->canvas);
  Window     w    = XtWindow(data->canvas);
  int        mask = GCFont | GCForeground | GCBackground;
  Arg        wargs[10];
  int        n;
```

```
/*
 * Create a GC using the colors of the canvas widget.
 */
n = 0;
XtSetArg(wargs[n], XtNbackground, &gcv.background); n++;
XtSetArg(wargs[n], XtNforeground, &gcv.foreground); n++;
XtGetValues(data->canvas, wargs, n);

gcv.font       = data->font->fid;
data->gc       = XCreateGC(dpy, w, mask, &gcv);
}
```

The DrawArea widget passes a pointer to a structure of type **OlDrawAreaCallback-Struct** as call data to functions registered as **XtNexposeCallback** and **XtNresizeCallback** callback functions. This structure is defined as:

```
typedef struct {
    int        reason;
    XEvent     *event;
    Position   x, y;
    Dimension  width, height;
} OlDrawAreaCallbackStruct;
```

The callback function **handle_exposures()** draws as many lines of text as the DrawArea widget's window can hold. This function uses the information contained in the call data structure to set the clip mask of the graphics context before redrawing the text to eliminate redrawing areas of the window outside the exposed region. To do this, the function creates a **Region** to represent the rectangular area reported by the **Expose** event. This allows us to use the Xlib region facilities to handle clipping. Once a valid region is available, this function uses **XSetRegion()** to set the clip mask of the GC to the area represented by the region.

Next, **handle_exposures()** draws each line in the text buffer, beginning with the line indexed by **data->top**, and continuing until either the text line lies outside the extent of the window, or the last line in the buffer has been drawn. The variable **yloc**, which determines the current y coordinate of the next line of text, is incremented by the height of the text each time through the while loop. Notice that **yloc** is incremented *before* each line is drawn, because **XDrawImageString()** draws text relative to the *lower* left corner of the bounding box. Therefore, the first line is drawn at **data->fontheight**.

Although setting the clipping region in the graphics contexts allows the server to clip the text to the region that needs to be redrawn, it is also somewhat inefficient to send the server requests for every line in the window, when only a few lines may need to be redrawn. A smart application should be able to redraw only those lines or portions of lines that are required, instead of relying on the server to do the clipping. The **fileview** example does this in a crude way, by using **XRectInRegion()** to determine whether or not a line intersects with the exposed region. By redrawing a line of text only if it intersects the exposed region, we can reduce the number of server requests and thereby improve the performance of the program. In this example, the performance gain is probably too small to be measured, but the basic principle of trying to reduce the number of server requests by drawing only what is necessary is applicable to more complex examples as well.

```
void
handle_exposures(w, client_data, call_data)
   Widget          w;
   XtPointer       client_data;
   XtPointer       call_data;
{
   text_data *data = (text_data *)client_data;
   int      yloc = 0, index = data->top;
   Region   region;
   OlDrawAreaCallbackStruct *cb =
                           (OlDrawAreaCallbackStruct *)call_data;

   /*
    * Create a region and add the contents of the event
    */
   region = XCreateRegion();
   XtAddExposureToRegion(cb->event, region);
   /*
    * Set the clip mask of the GC.
    */
   XSetRegion(XtDisplay(w), data->gc, region);
   /*
    * Loop through each line until the bottom of the
    * window is reached, or we run out of lines. Redraw any
    * lines that intersect the exposed region.
    */
   while(index < data->nitems && yloc < (int)data->canvas_height) {
     yloc += data->fontheight;
     if(XRectInRegion(region, MARGIN, yloc - data->fontheight,
                      data->rbearing[index],
                      data->fontheight) != RectangleOut)
        XDrawImageString(XtDisplay(w), XtWindow(w), data->gc,
                         MARGIN, yloc, data->chars[index],
                         data->length[index]);
     index++;
   }
   /*
    * Free the region.
    */
   XDestroyRegion(region);
}
```

To scroll the text in the window, all we have to do is change the value of **data->top** and redraw the entire buffer. The callback **scroll_bar_moved()** sets **data->top** to the current position of the scroll bar as reported in the **OlScrollbarVerify** structure, updates the

new_page field of the structure, and then calls **XClearArea()** to generate an **Expose** event for the entire window.

```
void
scroll_bar_moved(w, client_data, call_data)
  Widget          w;
  XtPointer       client_data;
  XtPointer       call_data;
{
  text_data *data = (text_data *)client_data;
  OlScrollbarVerify *cb = (OlScrollbarVerify *)call_data;

  data->top = cb->new_location;
  cb->new page = (cb->new_location/displaylines)+1;
  if(cb->delta)
      XClearArea(XtDisplay(w), XtWindow(data->canvas),
                 0, 0, 0, 0, TRUE);
}
```

The last function to discuss is the **resize()** callback function. This function simply updates the width and height information stored in the text buffer. We also reset the Scrollbar widget's proportion indicator resource to reflect the new size of the canvas widget. Because the server generates an **Expose** event after a resizing a window, no further action is required to display the new text.

```
void
resize(w, client_data, call_data)
  Widget          w;
  XtPointer       client_data;
  XtPointer       call_data;
{
  text_data *data = (text_data *)client_data;
  Arg   wargs[10];
  int   n;

  /*
   * Determine the new widget of the canvas widget.
   */
  n = 0;
  XtSetArg(wargs[n], XtNheight, &data->canvas_height);n++;
  XtSetArg(wargs[n], XtNwidth,  &data->canvas_width);n++;
  XtGetValues(w, wargs, n);
  displaylines = (int)data->canvas_height / data->fontheight;
  /*
   * Reset the scrollbar slider to indictae the relative
   * proportion of text displayed and also the new page size.
   */
  n = 0;
```

```
    XtSetArg(wargs[n], XtNproportionLength, displaylines); n++;
    XtSetValues(data->scrollbar, wargs, n);
}
```

Figure 9.2 shows the fileview program.

```
      gcv.foreground = BlackPixelOfScreen(XtScreen(data->canvas));;

      gcv.font       = data->font->fid;
      data->gc       = XCreateGC (dpy, w, mask, &gcv);
}

void
handle_exposures (w, client_data, call_data)
   Widget          w;
   XtPointer       client_data;
   XtPointer       call_data;
{
   text_data *data = (text_data *)client_data;
   int     yloc = 0, index = data->top;
   Region  region;
   OlExposeCallbackStruct *cb = (OlExposeCallbackStruct *)call_data;
   /*
    * Create a region and add the contents of the of the event
    */
   region = XCreateRegion();

   XtAddExposureToRegion(cb->event, region);
   /*
    * Set the clip mask of the GC.
    */
   XSetRegion (XtDisplay(w), data->gc, region);
   /*
    * Loop through each line until the bottom of the
    * window is reached, or we run out of lines. Redraw any
    * lines that intersect the exposed region.
    */
   while (index < data->nitems && yloc < data->canvas_height) {
      yloc += data->fontheight;
      if(XRectInRegion(region, MARGIN, yloc - data->fontheight,
                       data->rbearing[index],
                       data->fontheight) != RectangleOut)
         XDrawImageString(XtDisplay (w), XtWindow (w), data->gc,
                       MARGIN, yloc, data->chars[index],
                       data->length[index]);
      index++;
   }
   /*
    * Free the region.
    */
   XDestroyRegion(region);
}

void
scroll_bar_moved (w, client_data, call_data)
   Widget          w;
```

Figure 9.2   The fileview program.

9.3.1   Adding Smooth Scrolling

There are many optimizations and improvements that we can make to the file viewer example. For example, in the version in the previous section, each time the text is scrolled by even a single line, the entire window of text is redrawn. It is often better to copy the bitmapped image of some of the lines to their new location, and redraw only a few lines. Figure 9.3 illustrates this approach, which produces a smooth scrolling effect.

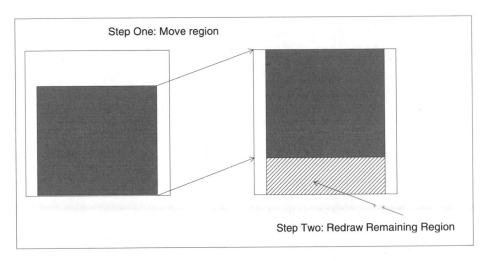

Figure 9.3 Using **XCopyArea()** to scroll the contents of a window.

To achieve a smooth scrolling effect, all we need to do is redesign the
scroll_bar_moved() callback function. All other parts of the program can remain the same.
The new **scroll_bar_moved()** function uses **XCopyArea()** to move as much text as possible. It also calculates the remaining region of the window that must be redrawn and clears that area.
The server will generate **Expose** events to redraw the cleared area.

```
void
scroll_bar_moved(w, client_data, call_data)
  Widget          w;
  XtPointer       client_data;
  XtPointer       call_data;
{
  text_data *data = (text_data *)client_data;
  OlScrollbarVerify *cb = (OlScrollbarVerify *)call_data;
  Arg     wargs[10];
  int     page;
  int     n = 0;
  int     sliderpos = cb->new_location;
  int     ysrc,  redraw_top, delta;

  page = (cb->new_location/displaylines)+1;
  cb->new_page = page;

  /*
   * Compute number of pixels the text needs to be moved.
   */
  delta = ABS((data->top - sliderpos) * data->fontheight);
```

```
    delta = MIN(delta, (int)data->canvas_height);
    /*
     * If we are scrolling down, we start at zero and simply
     * move by the delta. The portion that must be redrawn
     * is simply between zero and delta.
     */
    ysrc = redraw_top = 0;
    /*
     * If we are scrolling up, we start at the delta and move
     * to zero. The part to redraw lies between the bottom
     * of the window and the bottom - delta.
     */
    if(sliderpos >= data->top) {
      ysrc        = delta;
      redraw_top  = data->canvas_height - delta;
    }
    /*
     * Set the top line of the text buffer.
     */
    data->top = sliderpos;
    /*
     * Move the existing text to its new position.
     * Turn off any clipping on the GC first.
     */
    XSetClipMask(XtDisplay(w), data->gc, None);
    XCopyArea(XtDisplay(data->canvas), XtWindow(data->canvas),
                     XtWindow(data->canvas), data->gc,
                     0, ysrc,
                     data->canvas_width,
                     data->canvas_height - delta,
                     0,  delta - ysrc);
    /*
     * Clear the remaining area of any old text,
     * Request server to generate Expose events for the
     * area by setting exposures to TRUE.
     */
    XClearArea(XtDisplay(w), XtWindow(data->canvas),
               0, redraw_top,
               0, delta, TRUE);
}
```

If the slider position is less than the top line in the window, then we need to scroll the window's contents down. The current contents of the window must be copied to the position determined by the difference between the old top and the new top of the window. Since the indexes are in terms of characters, we must multiply them by the font height to convert to pixel dimensions. If the scrollbar position is greater than the top line in the window, the text must be scrolled up. This can be done by moving the text from the computed delta to the top of the window.

After calculating the coordinates of the areas of text to be moved and redrawn, `scroll_bar_moved()` sets **data->top** to its new value, and calls **XCopyArea()** to shift the bitmapped image in the window to its new position. The remaining area of the window is cleared to remove the old text, and also to generate an **Expose** event on the cleared area. The **Expose** event then causes the **handle_exposures()** event handler to be invoked, which redraws the newly exposed area of text.

With this technique, only a small portion of the window is redrawn, producing a much smoother effect. An even smoother effect could be obtained by eliminating the server round trip that generates the **Expose** event when scrolling. One way to do this is to redraw the new portion of the text directly in the **scroll_bar_moved()** callback. In this case, the callback should not request exposures in the call to **XClearArea()**. In addition to reducing the number of server requests, this approach eliminates a race condition that can occur when scrolling rapidly. It is quite possible to scroll the window fast enough so that the contents of the window have already been scrolled a second time before the server generates the first **Expose** event. To use this approach, we must replace the call to **XClearArea()** in the previous version with the following lines:

```
    /*
     * Clear the remaining area of any old text, and
     * redraw the area in that part of the window.
     */
    XClearArea(XtDisplay(w), XtWindow(data->canvas),
               0, redraw_top,
               0, delta, FALSE);
    {
      int      yloc = 0, index = data->top;
      while (index < data->nitems && yloc < data->canvas_height) {
        yloc += data->fontheight;
        if(yloc >= redraw_top
             && (yloc - data->fontheight) <= (redraw_top + delta))
           XDrawImageString(XtDisplay (w), XtWindow (data->canvas),
                            data->gc,
                            MARGIN, yloc, data->chars[index],
                            data->length[index]);
        index++;
      }
    }
```

9.4 SUMMARY

This chapter discussed the Xlib functions used to display text in a window as well as the fonts X uses to represent characters. X draws text by performing a fill operation on a rectangular region using a bitmap representing a character as a mask. A font is a collection of bitmapped characters. X provides several functions for drawing strings in windows or pixmaps. Because X treats text the same as any graphics operation, applications can combine Xlib text functions with clipping regions, graphics contexts, and raster operations.

The DrawArea widget is useful when combining Xlib drawing functions with the widgets and architecture of the Xt Intrinsics. Using this widget, the programmer can let the Intrinsics handle the low-level details of the X protocol, but still directly control the contents of the widget's window.

The following chapter discusses the primitive graphics functions provided by Xlib and continues to explore graphics contexts, regions, and related functions.

10

USING THE X
GRAPHICS PRIMITIVES

Previous chapters examined the X color model, graphics contexts, and regions. This chapter presents the graphics primitives provided by Xlib and demonstrates some of these features in examples. Xlib provides a set of simple two-dimensional graphics functions for drawing points, lines, arcs and rectangles. These drawing functions use the same integer coordinate system as the functions that operate on windows. Applications that require more complex graphics functions for panning, scaling, or three-dimensional graphics must usually implement these as a layer above the Xlib graphics functions. All graphics functions operate on a drawable, either a window or a pixmap.

10.1 DRAWING WITH POINTS

The simplest Xlib graphics function displays a single point in a drawable. The function

```
XDrawPoint(display, drawable, gc, x, y)
```

sets a single pixel at location x, y according to the specified GC. It is often more efficient to draw multiple points at once using the function:

```
XDrawPoints(display, drawable, gc, points, npoints, mode)
```

This function draws **npoints** points with a single server request. The **points** argument must be an array of **XPoint** structures. The **mode** argument determines how the server interprets the coordinates in this array and must be one of the constants **CoordModeOrigin** or **CoordModePrevious**. If **CoordModeOrigin** is specified, the server interprets each coordinate relative to the origin of the drawable. The constant **CoordModePrevious** specifies that each coordinate should be interpreted relative to the preceding point. The server always interprets the first point relative to the drawable's origin.

Several attributes of the graphics context affect how points are drawn. These are:

GCFunction	GCPlaneMask	GCForeground	GCClipYOrigin
GCSubwindowMode	GCClipMask	GCBackground	GCClipXOrigin

Let's look at a simple example that uses **XDrawPoint()** to illustrate the basic use of graphics functions in X. The program computes and displays a *fractal* image. Fractals are mathematical expressions based on complex numbers that produce interesting images from simple equations. This example displays a fractal image generated by repeatedly evaluating the expression

$$z = (z + k)^2$$

where both z and k are complex numbers. The value of z is initially set to *(0, 0)*, while k is initialized to the value of each *(x, y)* position in the window. After evaluating the expression some number of times for each point, we test the value of z to see how far it has moved from the *(x, y)* plane. If it is within some predetermined distance of the plane, the pixel is said to be part of the *Mandelbrot Set* and the color of the pixel is set to the same color as all other pixels in the Mandelbrot Set. Otherwise, some other color is chosen for the pixel. This example program bases the color on the distance of the point from the *(x, y)* plane.

The header file of this program includes the necessary X header files and defines a few data structures. The fractal program defines a **complex** structure to represent complex numbers, and also defines an **image_data** structure to store a graphics context, a pixmap (used to save the image once it is drawn), and some auxiliary data needed for the image calculation.

```
/***************************************************
 * fractal.h: declarations for the fractal program
 ***************************************************/
#include <X11/StringDefs.h>
#include <X11/Intrinsic.h>
#include <Xol/OpenLook.h>
#include <Xol/DrawArea.h>
#include <X11/Xutil.h>
#include "libXs.h"

void      resize();
void      redisplay();
void      create_image ();
/*
 * Structure to represent a complex number.
 */
typedef struct {
  float  real, imag;
} complex;
/*
 * Assorted information needed to generate and draw the image.
```

```
 */
typedef struct {
   int          depth, ncolors;
   float        range, max_distance;
   complex      origin;
   GC           gc;
   Pixmap       pix;
   Dimension    width, height;
} image_data, *image_data_ptr;
/*
 * Resource that affect the appearance of the fractal image.
 */
static XtResource resources[] = {
  {"depth", "Depth", XtRInt, sizeof (int),
    XtOffset(image_data_ptr, depth), XtRString, "20"          },
  {"real_origin", "RealOrigin", XtRFloat, sizeof (float),
    XtOffset(image_data_ptr, origin.real), XtRString, "-1.4" },
  {"imaginary_origin","ImaginaryOrigin",XtRFloat,sizeof(float),
    XtOffset(image_data_ptr, origin.imag), XtRString, "1.0"  },
  {"range", "Range", XtRFloat, sizeof(float),
    XtOffset(image_data_ptr,range), XtRString, "2.0"          },
  {"max_distance", "MaxDistance", XtRFloat, sizeof (float),
    XtOffset(image_data_ptr, max_distance),XtRString, "4.0"  }
};
```

The header file also defines an **XtResources** array used by the resource manager to initialize some of the members of the **image_data** struct. The **depth** member determines how many times the fractal expression is evaluated for each pixel, while the **real_origin** and **imaginary_origin** members allow the image to be *panned* to view different parts of the image. These are floating point coordinates because the example calculates the image in normalized floating coordinates. This allows us to generate the same image regardless of the size of the window that displays the image. The **range** parameter determines the width and height of the real coordinates of the image, and can be altered to *zoom* the image in and out, while the **max_distance** parameter controls the z distance considered to be "close" to the (x, y) plane.

The main body of the program creates a DrawArea widget used as a drawing canvas, and adds callbacks to handle exposures and resizes. Before entering the main event loop, the function **resize()** is called to trigger the creation of the initial image.

```
/***********************************************
 * fractal.c: A simple fractal generator
 ***********************************************/
#include "fractal.h"

main(argc, argv)
  int    argc;
  char *argv[];
{
```

```
    Widget       toplevel, canvas;
    image_data data;

    toplevel = OlInitialize(argv[0], "Fractal", NULL, 0,
                            &argc, argv);
    XtGetApplicationResources(toplevel, &data, resources,
                              XtNumber(resources), NULL, 0);
    /*
     * Create the widget to display the fractal and register
     * callbacks for resize and refresh.
     */
    canvas = XtCreateManagedWidget("canvas",
                                   drawAreaWidgetClass,
                                   toplevel, NULL, 0);
    XtAddCallback(canvas, XtNexposeCallback, redisplay, &data);
    XtAddCallback(canvas, XtNresizeCallback, resize, &data);
    init_data(canvas, &data);
    XtRealizeWidget(toplevel);
    resize(canvas, &data, NULL);
    XtMainLoop();
}
```

The function **init_data()** creates a graphics context, determines how many colors are supported by the display, and initializes the **pixmap** member of the **image_data** structure to NULL.

```
init_data(w, data)
  Widget       w;
  image_data *data;
{
  int y;
  Arg wargs[2];
  /*
   * Get the size of the drawing area.
   */
  XtSetArg(wargs[0], XtNwidth,  &data->width);
  XtSetArg(wargs[1], XtNheight, &data->height);
  XtGetValues(w, wargs,2);
  /*
   * Find out how many colors we have to work with, and
   * create a default, writable, graphics context.
   */
  data->ncolors = OlVisualOfObject(w)->map_entries;
  data->gc = XCreateGC(XtDisplay(w),
                       DefaultRootWindow(XtDisplay(w)),
                       NULL, NULL);
  /*
   *  Initialize the pixmap to NULL.
```

```
    */
  data->pix = NULL;
}
```

The fractal image is displayed when the window is exposed. However, the function **create_image**() actually generates the fractal. The function uses three nested **for** loops to evaluate the fractal expression. For each *(x, y)* coordinate, **create_image()** calculates the value of the expression repeatedly until either the maximum number of iterations are performed or until the *z* distance from the *(x, y)* plane exceeds the specified limit. If the point is still on the plane when all iterations are calculated, no point is drawn (which is equivalent to drawing the window's background color). If a point moves away from the plane before all iterations are calculated, the function draws a point on the screen. There are many ways to choose the color of each pixel. This example uses a straightforward method that achieves interesting results on color displays. The foreground color of the graphics context is determined by the *z* distance from the plane modulo the number of colors available.

Notice that **create_image()** draws each point twice: once in the DrawArea widget and once in a pixmap. This creates a duplicate of the image in off-screen memory. Depending on the size of the window, this image can take considerable time to draw. Storing the image in off-screen memory allows us to use **XCopyArea()** to restore the image rather than recalculating the entire image each time the window is exposed.[1] However, we also have to be careful to draw the point in the window only if the widget has been realized. This is because **create_image()** is called from the widget's **XtNresizeCallback** list, and it is possible for this procedure to be called before the widget is realized.

```
void create_image (w, data)
  Widget           w;
  image_data      *data;
{
  int   x, y, iteration;
  /*
   * For each pixel on the window....
   */
  for (y = 0; y < (int)data->height; y++) {
    for (x = 0; x < (int)data->width; x++) {
      complex z, k;
      /*
       * Initialize K to the normalized, floating coordinate
       * in the x, y plane. Init Z to (0.0, 0.0).
       */
      z.real =  z.imag = 0.0;
      k.real =  data->origin.real + (float) x /
                    (float) data->width * data->range;
```

---

[1] It isn't necessary to draw the point to the window at all. We could just store the image in the pixmap, then copy the image from the pixmap to the window. However, drawing the fractal image is time-consuming, and it is useful to provide some reassurance to the user that the program is making some progress by showing the preliminary image in the window as it is being created.

```
        k.imag =  data->origin.imag - (float) y /
                    (float) data->height * data->range;
    /*
     * Calculate z = (z + k) * (z + k) over and over.
     */
    for (iteration = 0; iteration < data->depth; iteration++) {
      float   distance, real_part, imag_part;

      real_part = z.real + k.real;
      imag_part = z.imag + k.imag;
      z.real = real_part * real_part - imag_part * imag_part;
      z.imag = 2 * real_part * imag_part;
      distance  = z.real * z.real + z.imag * z.imag;
      /*
       * If the z point has moved off the plane, set the
       * current foreground color to the distance (coerced to
       * an int and modulo the number of colors available),
       * and draw a point in both the window and the pixmap.
       */
      if (distance  >= data->max_distance) {
        int color = (int) distance % data->ncolors;

        XSetForeground(XtDisplay(w), data->gc, color);
        XDrawPoint (XtDisplay(w), data->pix, data->gc, x, y);
        if(XtIsRealized(w))
          XDrawPoint (XtDisplay(w), XtWindow(w), data->gc,x,y);
        break;
      }
    }
  }
 }
 }
}
```

The callback function **redisplay()** handles **Expose** events by copying the image from a region in the pixmap to the window. It uses **XCopyArea()** to copy the rectangular area defined by the **Expose** event in the call data from the pixmap to the window. Copying an image between a pixmap and a window is normally much faster than recomputing the image. This program is a good example of an application that could benefit from a server that provides backing store to automatically maintain a window's contents. However, using a pixmap to maintain the image works even with X servers that do not support this feature, as long as there is sufficient off-screen memory to support the pixmap.

```
    void
    redisplay (w, client_data, call_data)
      Widget        w;
      XtPointer       client_data;
      XtPointer       call_data;
```

```
{
  OlDrawAreaCallbackStruct *cb = (OlDrawAreaCallbackStruct *)call_data;
  image_data *data = (image_data *)client_data;
  /*
   * Extract the exposed area from the event and copy
   * from the saved pixmap to the window.
   */
  XCopyArea(XtDisplay(w), data->pix, XtWindow(w), data->gc,
            cb->x, cb->y, cb->width, cb->height, cb->x, cb->y);
}
```

The remaining function to be discussed is the **XtNresizeCallback** function **resize()**. This function frees the current pixmap, which no longer corresponds to the size of the window, and creates a new pixmap the same size as the window. The pixmap is cleared by calling **XFillRect-angle()** (see Section 10.3) with the default black pixel of the screen. It then calls **create_image()** to generate a new fractal scaled to the size of the new window.

```
void
resize (w, client_data, call_data)
  Widget         w;
  XtPointer      client_data;
  XtPointer      call_data;
{
  Arg wargs[2];
  image_data *data = (image_data *)client_data;
  /*
   *  Get the new window size.
   */
  XtSetArg(wargs[0], XtNwidth,  &data->width);
  XtSetArg(wargs[1], XtNheight, &data->height);
  XtGetValues(w, wargs, 2);
  /*
   * Clear the window.
   */
  if(XtIsRealized(w))
    XClearArea(XtDisplay(w), XtWindow(w), 0, 0, 0, 0, TRUE);
  /*
   *  Free the old pixmap and create a new pixmap
   *  the size of the window.
   */
  if(data->pix)
    XFreePixmap(XtDisplay(w), data->pix);
  data->pix= XCreatePixmap(XtDisplay(w),
                           DefaultRootWindow(XtDisplay(w)),
                           data->width, data->height,
                           OlDepthOfObject(w));
  XSetForeground(XtDisplay(w), data->gc, OlBlackPixel(w));
  XFillRectangle(XtDisplay(w), data->pix, data->gc, 0, 0,
```

```
                        data->width,  data->height);
    /*
     * Generate a new image.
     */
    create_image(w, data);
}
```

Figure 10.1 shows the fractal generated by this program.

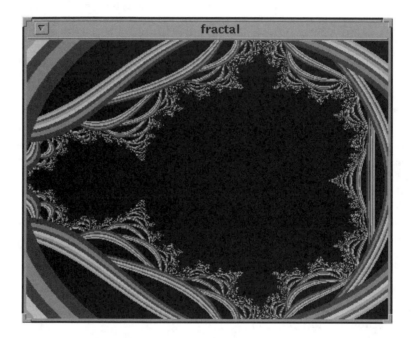

Figure 10.1 The Fractal Program

Although using a pixmap to store the fractal image in off-screen memory partially alleviates the problem of handling **Expose** events for a graphics-intensive image application, the initial time required to compute and draw the image still leaves something to be desired. The calculation itself is time consuming, although there is little we can do about that because fractals are inherently expensive to compute. We can, however, optimize the drawing of the image by reducing the number of server requests. The function **XDrawPoints()** draws multiple points with a single server request. All points use the same graphics context, but do not have to be contiguous. Using **XDrawPoints()** to reduce the number of server requests greatly increases the speed of the fractal program. The only part of the fractal program that must change is the function **create_image()**.

```
    void create_image (w, data)
      Widget          w;
      image_data      *data;
```

```
{
  int x, y, iteration;
  /*
   * We have to buffer all points of the same color, until
   * enough points are available to draw efficiently. Start
   * by zeroing all buffers.
   */
  init_buffer(data);
  /*
   * For each pixel on the window....
   */
  for (y = 0; y < (int)data->height; y++) {
    for (x = 0; x < (int)data->width; x++) {
      complex z, k;
      /*
       *  Initialize K to the normalized, floating coordinate in
       *  the x,y plane. Init Z to (0.0, 0.0).
       */
      z.real = z.imag = 0.0;
      k.real =  data->origin.real + (float) x /
                    (float) data->width * data->range;
      k.imag =  data->origin.imag - (float) y /
                    (float) data->height * data->range;
      /*
       * Calculate z = (z + k) * (z + k) over and over.
       */
      for (iteration = 0; iteration < data->depth; iteration++){
        float distance, real_part, imag_part;
        real_part = z.real + k.real;
        imag_part = z.imag + k.imag;
        z.real    = real_part * real_part - imag_part * imag_part;
        z.imag    = 2 * real_part * imag_part;
        distance  = z.real * z.real + z.imag * z.imag;
        /*
         * If the z point has moved off the plane, buffer the
         * point using the integerized distance (modulo the
         * number of colors we have) as the color.
         */
        if (distance  >= data->max_distance) {
          buffer_point(w, data, (int) distance % data->ncolors,
                    x, y);
          break;
        }
      }
    }
  }
  /*
```

```
     * Display all remaining points.
     */
    flush_buffer(w, data);
}
```

The primary difference between this version of **create_image()** and the previous version is that instead of calling **XDrawPoint()** directly, **create_image()** calls the function **buffer_point()**. This function stores points until they can be drawn as a group using **XDrawPoints()**. The function **init_buffer()** must be called before beginning the calculations to initialize the data structures used by the buffer routines and **flush_buffer()** must also be called to flush the buffer after all points are generated.

The buffering routines use a global data structure containing a two-dimensional array of **XPoint** structures. The array holds **MAXPOINTS** number of points for **MAXCOLOR** possible colors. The **points** structure also contains an array of integers that indicates how many points are stored in each of the point arrays.

```
#define MAXPOINTS 500
#define MAXCOLOR  256

struct {
   XPoint  data[MAXCOLOR][MAXPOINTS];
   int     npoints[MAXCOLOR];
} points;
```

The function **init_buffer()** initializes the number of points of each color to zero.

```
init_buffer(data)
  image_data *data;
{
  int i;
  if (data->ncolors > MAXCOLOR)
    XtError("This display has too many colors");
  for(i=0;i<MAXCOLOR;i++)
    points.npoints[i] = 0;
}
```

The **buffer_point()** routine first checks how many points of the given color are already stored in the buffer. If this number is equal to the maximum number that can be buffered, it uses **XDrawPoints()** to draw all points stored in the buffer in both the window and the pixmap. Then, it resets the number of points for the given color to zero, and stores the current point in the buffer.

```
buffer_point(w, data, color, x , y)
  Widget      w;
  image_data *data;
  int         color, x,y;
{
  if(points.npoints[color] == MAXPOINTS - 1) {
    /*
     * If the buffer is full, set the foreground color
```

```
     * of the graphics context and draw the points in both
     * the window and the pixmap.
     */
    XSetForeground(XtDisplay(w), data->gc, color);
    if(XtIsRealized(w))
      XDrawPoints (XtDisplay(w), XtWindow(w), data->gc,
                   points.data[color], points.npoints[color],
                   CoordModeOrigin);
    XDrawPoints (XtDisplay(w), data->pix, data->gc,
                 points.data[color], points.npoints[color],
                 CoordModeOrigin);
    /*
     * Reset the buffer.
     */
    points.npoints[color] = 0;
  }
  /*
   * Store the point in the buffer according to its color.
   */
  points.data[color][points.npoints[color]].x = x;
  points.data[color][points.npoints[color]].y = y;
  points.npoints[color] += 1;
}
```

The function **flush_buffer()** must be called when the image calculation is finished to draw any points remaining in the buffer. This function loops through all colors, drawing the remaining points in both the window and the pixmap.

```
flush_buffer(w, data)
  Widget       w;
  image_data *data;
{
  int i;
  /*
   * Check each buffer.
   */
  for(i=0;i<data->ncolors;i++)
    /*
     * If there are any points in this buffer, display them
     * in the window and the pixmap.
     */
    if(points.npoints[i]){
      XSetForeground(XtDisplay(w), data->gc, i);
      if(XtIsRealized(w))
        XDrawPoints (XtDisplay(w), XtWindow(w), data->gc,
                     points.data[i], points.npoints[i],
                     CoordModeOrigin);
      XDrawPoints (XtDisplay(w), data->pix, data->gc,
```

```
                              points.data[i], points.npoints[i],
                              CoordModeOrigin);
            points.npoints[i] = 0;
      }
  }
```

Although the image calculation itself is still time consuming, buffering the points provides a significant speedup. In addition to reducing the time initially required to draw the image, buffering the drawing requests reduces the load on the server, which reduces the degree to which the fractal program interferes with other applications using the server while the image is being generated. This buffering example was more complex than many applications might be because the Xlib functions for drawing multiple points and lines use only a single GC. A black and white version of this program would be much simpler.

10.2 DRAWING WITH LINES

The Xlib function

```
XDrawLine(display, drawable, gc, x1, y1, x2, y2)
```

draws a single line between two points. The way in which **XDrawLine()** draws lines is determined by the following attributes of the graphics context:

GCFunction	GCPlaneMask	GCLineWidth
GCLineStyle	GCCapStyle	GCFillStyle
GCSubwindowMode	GCClipXOrigin	GCClipYOrigin
GCClipMask		

The function

```
XDrawSegments(display, drawable, gc, segments, nsegments)
```

draws multiple, discontiguous line segments with a single request. The line segments are specified by an array of type XSegment, which includes the members:

```
short x1, y1, x2, y2;
```

Although the line segments do not need to be connected, **XDrawSegments()** draws all segments using the same graphics context. This function uses the same graphics context members as **XDrawLine()**.

The function

```
XDrawLines(display, drawable, gc, points, npoints, mode)
```

draws multiple connected lines. This function draws **npoints - 1** lines between the points in the **points** array. **XDrawLines()** draws all lines in the order in which the points appear in the array. The **mode** argument determines whether the points are interpreted relative to the origin of the drawable or relative to the last point drawn, and must be one of **CoordModeOrigin** or

CoordModePrevious. **XDrawLines()** uses the **GCJoinStyle** attribute of the graphics context, in addition to the graphics context members used by **XDrawLine()**.

We can demonstrate **XDrawLine()** in a simple program that uses a technique known as *rubber banding*. A rubber band line is usually drawn interactively by the user. The user first sets an initial endpoint, usually by pressing a mouse button. A line is then drawn between this endpoint and the current position of the pointer. As the user moves the pointer, the line appears to stretch as if it were a rubber band connected between the pointer and the initial position. The rubber banding ends in response to some user action, typically when the mouse button is released. This technique is commonly used to allow the user to define a beginning and ending coordinate for drawing lines or other figures interactively.

The example program, named **rubberband**, allows the user to draw rubber band lines in the window of a DrawArea widget. The **rubberband** program begins by defining a data structure, **rubberband_data**, that contains information used by the event handlers that perform the rubber banding.

```
/*************************************************
 * rubberband.c: rubberband line example
 *************************************************/
#include <X11/StringDefs.h>
#include <X11/Intrinsic.h>
#include <X11/cursorfont.h>
#include <Xol/OpenLook.h>
#include <Xol/DrawArea.h>
#include "libXs.h"

typedef struct {
    int start_x, start_y, last_x, last_y;
    GC  gc;
} rubber_band_data;

void start_rubber_band();
void end_rubber_band();
void track_rubber_band();
```

The body of the program simply creates a DrawArea widget and adds event handlers for **ButtonPress**, **ButtonRelease** and pointer motion events which work together to implement the rubber banding.

```
main(argc, argv)
  int    argc;
  char *argv[];
{
  Widget            toplevel, canvas;
  rubber_band_data data;

  toplevel = OlInitialize(argv[0], "Rubberband", NULL, 0,
                          &argc, argv);
```

```
    /*
     * Create a drawing surface, and add event handlers for
     * ButtonPress, ButtonRelease and MotionNotify events.
     */
    canvas = XtCreateManagedWidget("canvas",
                                        drawAreaWidgetClass,
                                        toplevel, NULL, 0);
    XtAddEventHandler(canvas, ButtonPressMask, FALSE,
                        start_rubber_band, &data);
    XtAddEventHandler(canvas, ButtonMotionMask, FALSE,
                        track_rubber_band, &data);
    XtAddEventHandler(canvas, ButtonReleaseMask,
                        FALSE, end_rubber_band, &data);
    XtRealizeWidget(toplevel);
    /*
     * Establish a passive grab, for any button press.
     * Force the pointer to stay within the canvas window, and
     * change the pointer to a cross_hair.
     */
    XGrabButton(XtDisplay(canvas), AnyButton, AnyModifier,
                XtWindow(canvas), TRUE,
                ButtonPressMask | ButtonMotionMask |
                ButtonReleaseMask,
                GrabModeAsync, GrabModeAsync,
                XtWindow(canvas),
                XCreateFontCursor(XtDisplay(canvas),
                                    XC_crosshair));
    /*
     * Create the GC used by the rubber banding functions.
     */
    data.gc = xs_create_xor_gc(canvas);
    XtMainLoop();
}
```

This example introduces some new Xlib and Intrinsics functions. The function

```
XGrabButton(display, button, modifiers, grab_window,
            owner_events, event_mask, pointer_mode,
            keyboard_mode, confine_to, cursor)
```

establishes a *passive grab* on the specified mouse button. A passive grab takes effect automatically when the user presses the specified mouse button. Once the pointer is grabbed, the server reports all mouse events to the grabbing client, even if the pointer leaves the window. This allows the server to track pointer motion more efficiently. **XGrabButton()** also allows us to constrain the pointer to stay within a particular window while the grab is in effect. In this example, the pointer is constrained to the **canvas** window as long as the grab is in effect. **XGrabButton()** also allows the programmer to specify the shape of the mouse cursor while the grab is in effect. In this example, the mouse cursor changes to a crosshair shape when the pointer is grabbed. The function

```
XCreateFontCursor(display, cursor_index)
```

retrieves a mouse cursor from a standard font. The file cursorfont.h defines a set of constants used as indexes into the cursor font. When the user releases the mouse button, the grab automatically terminates and the mouse cursor returns to its previous shape.

The function **xs_create_xor_gc()** creates a graphics context set to exclusive-OR mode which is used to draw the rubber band lines.

```
#include <X11/StringDefs.h>
#include <X11/Intrinsic.h>

GC
xs_create_xor_gc(w)
  Widget          w;
{
  XGCValues values;
  GC        gc;
  Arg       wargs[10];

  /*
   * Get the background and foreground colors.
   */
  XtSetArg(wargs[0], XtNforeground, &values.foreground);
  XtSetArg(wargs[1], XtNbackground, &values.background);
  XtGetValues(w, wargs, 2);
  /*
   * Set the fg to the XOR of the fg and bg, so if it is
   * XOR'ed with bg, the result will be fg and vice-versa.
   * This effectively achieves inverse video for the line.
   */
  values.foreground = values.foreground ^ values.background;
  /*
   * Set the rubber band gc to use XOR mode and draw
   * a dashed line.
   */
  values.line_style = LineOnOffDash;
  values.function   = GXxor;
  gc = XtGetGC(w, GCForeground | GCBackground |
               GCFunction | GCLineStyle, &values);
  return gc;
}
```

The graphics context is created using the foreground and background colors obtained from the widget's resources. In addition, the line style is set to **LineOnOffDash** and the drawing function is set to XOR mode.

The task of drawing the rubber band line is performed by three cooperating event handlers. When the user presses a mouse button, the Intrinsics call the first event handler, **start_rubber_band()**. This function stores the position of the pointer when the **Button-**

Press event occurs as the initial position of the line, and also sets the last position of the line to the same point. The function **XDrawLine()** is called to draw the initial line, which is simply a point, because the start and end points are the same.

```
void start_rubber_band(w, data, event)
  Widget               w;
  rubber_band_data     *data;
  XEvent               *event;
{
  data->last_x  =  data->start_x = event->xbutton.x;
  data->last_y  =  data->start_y = event->xbutton.y;
  XDrawLine(XtDisplay(w), XtWindow(w),
            data->gc, data->start_x,
            data->start_y, data->last_x, data->last_y);
}
```

The function **track_rubber_band()** is called each time the pointer moves. It draws a line between the initial position at which the user pressed the mouse button and the last recorded position of the pointer. Because the line is drawn in XOR mode, this erases the current line and restores the previous contents of the screen. The end points of the line are then updated to reflect the new pointer position and the line is drawn again.

```
void track_rubber_band(w, data, event)
   Widget               w;
   rubber_band_data    *data;
   XEvent              *event;
{
  /*
   * Draw once to clear the previous line.
   */
  XDrawLine(XtDisplay(w), XtWindow(w), data->gc,
            data->start_x,data->start_y,
            data->last_x, data->last_y);
  /*
   * Update the endpoints.
   */
  data->last_x  =  event->xbutton.x;
  data->last_y  =  event->xbutton.y;
  /*
   * Draw the new line.
   */
  XDrawLine(XtDisplay(w), XtWindow(w), data->gc,
            data->start_x, data->start_y,
            data->last_x, data->last_y);
}
```

When the user releases the mouse button, the event handler **end_rubber_band()** is invoked. This function draws the line one last time in XOR mode to erase the line. The function also stores the current position of the pointer in the client data structure where any interested routine can retrieve it.

```
void end_rubber_band(w, data, event)
  Widget              w;
  rubber_band_data *data;
  XEvent             *event;
{
 /*
  * Clear the current line and update the endpoint info.
  */
  XDrawLine(XtDisplay(w), XtWindow(w), data->gc,
          data->start_x, data->start_y,
          data->last_x, data->last_y);
  data->last_x  =  event->xbutton.x;
  data->last_y  =  event->xbutton.y;
}
```

10.3 DRAWING POLYGONS AND ARCS

Xlib also provides functions for drawing more complex figures, including filled and unfilled polygons, arcs, and circles. The function

```
XDrawRectangle(display, drawable, gc, x, y, width, height)
```

draws the outline of a rectangle, while the function

```
XDrawRectangles(display, drawable, gc, rectangles,nrectangles)
```

draws multiple rectangles. The argument **rectangles** must be an array of type **XRectangle**, which includes the members:

```
short          x, y;
unsigned short width, height;
```

An arc can be drawn using the function:

```
XDrawArc(display, drawable, gc, x, y, width, height,
       angle1, angle2)
```

This function draws an arc starting from **angle1**, relative to a three o'clock position, to **angle2**, within the bounding rectangle specified by the parameters **x**, **y**, **width**, **height**, as shown in Figure 10.2. The angles are specified in units of *(degrees * 64)*. For example, this function can be used to draw a circle or ellipse by specifying a starting angle of zero degrees and an ending angle of *(64 * 360)* degrees. Angles greater than *(64 * 360)* degrees are truncated.

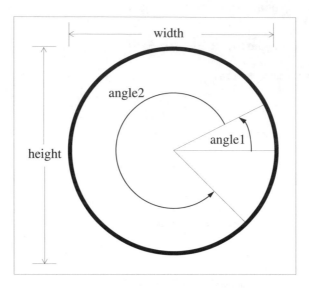

Figure 10.2 Dimensions of an Arc.

The function

```
XDrawArcs(display, drawable, gc, arcs, narcs)
```

draws multiple arcs with a single server request and uses an array of type **XArc** to define the parameters of each arc. The **XArc** structure contains the following members:

```
short          x, y;
unsigned short width, height;
short          angle1, angle2;
```

Xlib also provides functions for drawing polygons, rectangles, and arcs filled with a solid color or pattern. The function

```
XFillRectangle(display, drawable, gc, x, y, width, height)
```

draws a single rectangle filled as specified by the **GCForeground**, **GCBackground**, **GCTile**, and **GCStipple** attributes of the graphics context. The function

```
XFillRectangles(display, drawable, gc, rectangles,nrectangles)
```

draws multiple filled rectangles using an array of XRectangle structures. The function

```
XFillPolygon(display, drawable, gc, points, npoints,
             shape, mode)
```

draws a single polygon specified by an array of **XPoint** structures. If the path is not closed, **XFillPolygon()** automatically closes it before filling the figure. The shape parameter can be one of the constants **Complex**, **Convex**, or **Nonconvex**. The server can use this information to select the optimal drawing algorithm. The `mode` argument determines how the points are interpreted and must be one of the constants **CoordModeOrigin** or **CoordModePrevious**. The functions

```
XFillArc(display, drawable, gc, x, y, width, height, angle1, angle2)
```

and

```
XFillArcs(display, drawable, gc, arcs, narcs)
```

draw single and multiple filled arcs, respectively.

10.4 EXAMPLE: A SIMPLE DRAWING PROGRAM

This section concludes our discussion of the Xlib graphics functions by looking at a simple drawing program that uses many of the techniques and functions discussed in this chapter, as well as in the previous three chapters. The **draw** program shown in Figure 10.3 allows the user to select from several possible shapes, and then position and size them using the rubber banding techniques discussed in Section 10.2. The user can also select fill patterns from the pixmap browser functions we developed in Chapter 7.

The only resources set outside the **draw** program are:

```
Draw*canvas.background:   white
Draw*canvas.foreground:   black
Draw*canvas.borderWidth:  1
Draw*background:          gray84
Draw*canvas.width:        300
```

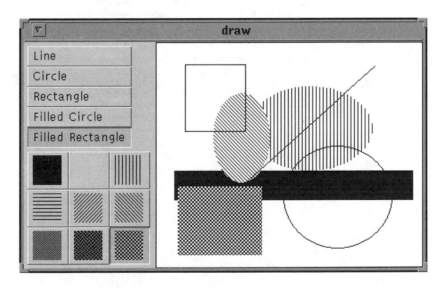

Figure 10.3 Using draw: A simple drawing program.

The header file, draw.h, includes the OLIT widget header files used in this example, and also contains forward declarations of the callbacks and other procedures used in the program. It also includes definitions of two data structures used by the program. An array of type **GBUFFER** serves as a graphics buffer. Each position in the buffer stores a pair of *(x, y)* points, a graphics context and a pointer to a function that draws the object. The second data structure provides a central location for all client data used by the callback procedures. It is similar to the data structure used by the rubber banding function in Section 10.2, but is expanded to include a pointer to the graphics buffer and also a pointer to a function used to draw the graphical objects.

```
/***********************************************
 * draw.h: declarations for the draw program
 ***********************************************/
#include <X11/StringDefs.h>
#include <X11/cursorfont.h>
#include <X11/Intrinsic.h>
#include <X11/Xutil.h>
#include <Xol/OpenLook.h>
#include <Xol/DrawArea.h>
#include <Xol/ControlAre.h>
#include <Xol/Form.h>
#include <Xol/RectButton.h>
#include <Xol/Exclusives.h>
#include "xs_bitmaps.h"
#include "libXs.h"

xs_bitmap_struct bitmaps[] = {
    solid_bits,         solid_width,         solid_height,
    clear_bits,         clear_width,         clear_height,
    vertical_bits,      vertical_width,      vertical_height,
    horizontal_bits,    horizontal_width,    horizontal_height,
    slant_right_bits,   slant_right_width,   slant_right_height,
    slant_left_bits,    slant_left_width,    slant_left_height,
    fg50_bits,          fg50_width,          fg50_height,
    fg25_bits,          fg25_width,          fg25_height,
    cross_bits,         cross_width,         cross_height,
};

#define MAXOBJECTS 1000

typedef struct {
    int  x1, y1, x2, y2;
    int  (*func) ();
    GC   gc;
} GBUFFER;

typedef struct {
    int             start_x, start_y, last_x, last_y;
```

```
GC              xorgc;
GC              gc;
int             (*current_func)();
int             foreground, background;
GBUFFER         buffer[MAXOBJECTS];
int             next_pos;
} graphics_data;

void  draw_line();
void  draw_circle();
void  draw_rectangle();
void  draw_filled_circle();
void  draw_filled_rectangle();

void  activate();
void  refresh();
void  set_stipple();
void  start_rubber_band();
void  track_rubber_band();
void  end_rubber_band();
void  set_fill_pattern();
void  create_drawing_commands();
```

The **draw** program uses a Form widget to manage a command pane built from a ControlArea widget and a drawing canvas (a DrawArea widget). Figure 10.4 shows the widget tree created by the **draw** program.

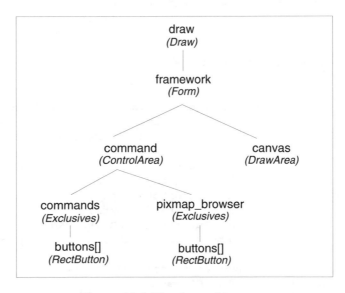

Figure 10.4 The draw widget tree.

The body of the program creates these widgets, initializes the graphics buffer and related data structures, and defines event handlers for the mouse buttons and pointer motion events.

```
/****************************************************
 * draw.c: a simple graphics drawing program.
 ***************************************************/
#include "draw.h"

main(argc, argv)
  int    argc;
  char *argv[];
{
  Widget         toplevel, canvas, framework, command, tiles;
  graphics_data data;
  int            n;
  Arg            wargs[10];

  toplevel = OlInitialize(argv[0], "Draw", NULL, 0, &argc, argv);
  framework = XtCreateManagedWidget("framework", formWidgetClass,
                                      toplevel, NULL, 0);
  /*
   * Create the column to hold the commands.
   */
  n = 0;
  XtSetArg(wargs[n], XtNlayoutType, OL_FIXEDCOLS);n++;
  XtSetArg(wargs[n], XtNmeasure, 1);n++;
  command = XtCreateManagedWidget("command",
                                    controlAreaWidgetClass,
                                    framework, wargs, n);
  /*
   * Create the drawing surface and add the
   * rubber banding callbacks.
   */
  canvas = XtCreateManagedWidget("canvas", drawAreaWidgetClass,
                                   framework, NULL, 0);
  XtAddCallback(canvas, XtNexposeCallback, refresh, &data);

  XtAddEventHandler(canvas, ButtonPressMask, FALSE,
                    start_rubber_band, &data);
  XtAddEventHandler(canvas, ButtonMotionMask, FALSE,
                    track_rubber_band, &data);
  XtAddEventHandler(canvas, ButtonReleaseMask, FALSE,
                    end_rubber_band, &data);
  n = 0;
  XtSetArg(wargs[n], XtNyAttachBottom, TRUE);n++;
  XtSetArg(wargs[n], XtNyVaryOffset,   FALSE);n++;
  XtSetArg(wargs[n], XtNyResizable,    TRUE);n++;
```

```
    XtSetArg(wargs[n], XtNxAttachRight,  TRUE);n++;
    XtSetArg(wargs[n], XtNxVaryOffset,   FALSE);n++;
    XtSetArg(wargs[n], XtNxResizable,    TRUE);n++;
    XtSetArg(wargs[n], XtNxRefWidget,    command);n++;
    XtSetArg(wargs[n], XtNxAddWidth,     TRUE);n++;
    XtSetValues(canvas, wargs, n);
    /*
     * Initialize the graphics buffer and other data.
     */
    init_data(canvas, &data);
    /*
     * Add the drawing command panel.
     */
    create_drawing_commands(command, &data);
    /*
     * Add a palette of fill patterns.
     */
    tiles = xs_create_pixmap_browser(command,bitmaps,
                                     XtNumber(bitmaps),
                                     set_fill_pattern, &data,
                                     NULL);
    XtManageChild(tiles);
    XtRealizeWidget(toplevel);
    /*
     * Establish a passive grab on the drawing canvas window.
     */
    XGrabButton(XtDisplay(canvas), AnyButton, AnyModifier,
                XtWindow(canvas), TRUE,
                ButtonPressMask | ButtonMotionMask |
                ButtonReleaseMask,
                GrabModeAsync, GrabModeAsync,
                XtWindow(canvas),
                XCreateFontCursor(XtDisplay(canvas),
                                  XC_crosshair));
    XtMainLoop();
}
```

The command panel contains a set of buttons used to set the current drawing function. The function **create_drawing_commands()** creates an Exclusives widget containing a set of RectButton widgets, which the user can use to select the current drawing function. The selected function remains in effect until the user selects a new drawing function. Notice that each callback shares the **data** structure containing the graphics buffer through the callback functions' **client_data** argument.

```
struct {
  char   *name;
  void   (*func)();
}  command_info[] = {
```

```
            "Line",              draw_line,
            "Circle",            draw_circle,
            "Rectangle",         draw_rectangle,
            "Filled Circle",     draw_filled_circle,
            "Filled Rectangle",  draw_filled_rectangle
};

void
create_drawing_commands(parent, data)
  Widget           parent;
  graphics_data *data;
{
  Widget   w, commands;
  Arg      wargs[2];
  int      i, n;
  /*
   * Group all commands in a column.
   */

  n = 0;
  XtSetArg(wargs[n], XtNlayoutType, OL_FIXEDCOLS); n++;
  XtSetArg(wargs[n], XtNmeasure, 1); n++;
  commands = XtCreateManagedWidget("commands",
                            exclusivesWidgetClass, parent,
                            wargs, n);
  /*
   * Create a button for each drawing function.
   */
  for(i=0;i < XtNumber(command_info); i++){
    XtSetArg(wargs[0], XtNuserData, command_info[i].func);
    w = XtCreateManagedWidget(command_info[i].name,
                            rectButtonWidgetClass,
                            commands, wargs, 1);
    XtAddCallback(w, XtNselect, activate, data);
    if(i == 0)
      XtCallCallbacks(w, XtNselect, NULL);
  }
}
```

Often, we can use the client data passed to callbacks and event handlers to associate a piece of data with a particular widget. However, only one piece of client data can be passed to any one function. In this example, we are using the client data to pass the data structure containing the graphics buffer between functions. However, in addition, the **activate()** function requires a pointer to a function to be installed as the current drawing function. Since the graphics buffer and its associated data is passed as client data, we must find some other way to associate a drawing function with a particular button. Fortunately OLIT allows us to attach an arbitrary data structure to any widget, using the **XtNuserData** resource. A pointer to the drawing function corresponding to each button is stored in the **XtNuserData** resource of each widget, where it can be retrieved by a callback function.

The next section of the command panel contains a menu of patterns that can be used as fill patterns for rectangles and circles. This pixmap browser is created by the functions described in Chapter 7. The callback function **set_fill_pattern()** is passed to the function **xs_create_pixmap_browser()**, to be invoked when one of the RectButton widgets in the pixmap browser is selected. It sets the GC to the color and fill pattern of the selected button.

```
void
set_fill_pattern(w, client_data, call_data)
  Widget        w;
  XtPointer      client_data;
  XtPointer      call_data;
{
  graphics_data *data = (graphics_data *)client_data;
  Pixmap     tile;
  XImage     *image;
  int        i;
  XGCValues values;
  Arg        wargs[1];
  GC         gc;

  static int mask = GCForeground | GCBackground |
                    GCTile | GCFillStyle;

  XtSetArg(wargs[0], XtNuserData, &image);
  XtGetValues(w, wargs, 1);
  tile = XCreatePixmap(XtDisplay(w),
                    DefaultRootWindow(XtDisplay(w)),
                    solid_width, solid_height,
                    OlDepthOfObject(w));

  values.foreground = data->foreground;
  values.background = data->background;
  gc = XCreateGC(XtDisplay(w), DefaultRootWindow(XtDisplay(w)),
              GCForeground | GCBackground, &values);
  XPutImage(XtDisplay(w), tile, gc, image,
          0, 0, 0, 0, solid_width, solid_height);
  /*
   * Get a GC using this tile pattern
   */
  values.foreground = data->foreground;
  values.background = data->background;
  values.fill_style = FillTiled;
  values.tile        = tile;
  data->gc = XtGetGC(w, mask, &values);
}
```

Now that we have seen how all the widgets used in this example are created, let's look at how the client data is initialized and used. The function **init_data()** initializes the current drawing function to NULL, sets the next available position in the graphics buffer to zero, and then creates two graphics contexts. One graphics context is used by the graphics objects, while the other graphics context is used by the rubber banding routines that position the objects.

```
init_data(w, data)
  Widget         w;
  graphics_data  *data;
{
  XGCValues values;
  Arg       wargs[5];
  data->current_func = NULL;
  data->next_pos     = 0;

  /*
   * Get the colors the user has set for the widget.
   */
  XtSetArg(wargs[0], XtNbackground, &data->background);
  XtSetArg(wargs[1], XtNforeground, &data->foreground);
  XtGetValues(w, wargs, 2);
  /*
   * Fill in the values structure
   */
  values.foreground = data->foreground;
  values.background = data->background;
  values.fill_style = FillTiled;
  /*
   * Get the GC used for drawing.
   */
  data->gc= XtGetGC(w, GCForeground | GCBackground |
                      GCFillStyle, &values);
  /*
   * Get a second GC in XOR mode for rubber banding.
   */
  data->xorgc = xs_create_xor_gc(w);
}
```

The three event handlers in this example draw objects using a rubber banding approach similar to that described in Section 10.2. However, instead of a hard-coded Xlib drawing function, these routines use the **current_function** member of the shared client data to draw the figures. This allows the same rubber banding functions to draw all types of figures. The function **start_rubber_band()** sets the initial anchor point of the rubber band figure when the user presses a mouse button.

```
void
start_rubber_band(w, data, event)
  Widget         w;
```

```
  graphics_data   *data;
  XEvent          *event;
{
  if(data->current_func){
    /*
     * Store the starting point and draw the initial figure.
     */
    data->last_x = data->start_x = event->xbutton.x;
    data->last_y = data->start_y = event->xbutton.y;
    (*(data->current_func))(w, data->xorgc,
                            data->start_x, data->start_y,
                            data->last_x, data->last_y);
  }
}
```

The function **track_rubber_band()** erases the previous figure by drawing it in XOR mode, updates the position, and redraws the figure each time the pointer moves.

```
void
track_rubber_band(w, data, event)
  Widget          w;
  graphics_data   *data;
  XEvent          *event;
{
  if(data->current_func){
    /*
     * Erase the previous figure.
     */
    (*(data->current_func))(w, data->xorgc,
                            data->start_x, data->start_y,
                            data->last_x, data->last_y);
    /*
     * Update the last point.
     */
    data->last_x  =  event->xbutton.x;
    data->last_y  =  event->xbutton.y;
    /*
     * Draw the figure in the new position.
     */
    (*(data->current_func))(w, data->xorgc,
                            data->start_x, data->start_y,
                            data->last_x, data->last_y);
  }
}
```

When the mouse button is released, the function **end_rubber_band()** erases the rubber banded figure, and redraws the figure using the current graphics context. After updating the position information in data, the function **store_object()** is called to record the new object in the graphics buffer.

```
void
end_rubber_band(w, data, event)
  Widget         w;
  graphics_data  *data;
  XEvent         *event;
{
  if(data->current_func){
    /*
     * Erase the XOR image.
     */
    (*(data->current_func))(w, data->xorgc,
                            data->start_x, data->start_y,
                            data->last_x, data->last_y);
    /*
     * Draw the figure using the normal GC.
     */
    (*(data->current_func))(w, data->gc,
                            data->start_x, data->start_y,
                            event->xbutton.x,
                            event->xbutton.y);
    /*
     * Update the data, and store the object in
     * the graphics buffer.
     */
    data->last_x  =  event->xbutton.x;
    data->last_y  =  event->xbutton.y;
    store_object(data);
  }
}
```

The key to using the same rubber band functions for all figures is to find a way to draw all figures using the same parameters. Although the various Xlib graphics functions are similar, they are not exactly the same. However, it is easy to define functions that require the same parameters. Each of the following functions takes a widget, a graphics context, and a pair of *(x, y)* points. The function **draw_line()** draws a line between two points.

```
void
draw_line(w, gc, x, y, x2, y2)
  Widget   w;
  GC       gc;
  Position x, y, x2, y2;
{
  Display *dpy = XtDisplay(w);
```

```
  Window    win = XtWindow(w);
  XDrawLine(dpy, win, gc, x, y, x2, y2);
}
```

The functions **draw_rectangle()** and **draw_filled_rectangle()** draw rectangles using the given points as the upper left and lower right corners of the rectangle. These functions are defined as:

```
void
draw_rectangle(w, gc, x, y, x2, y2)
  Widget    w;
  GC        gc;
  Position x, y, x2, y2;
{
  Display *dpy = XtDisplay(w);
  Window    win = XtWindow(w);

  check_points(&x, &y, &x2, &y2);
  XDrawRectangle(dpy, win, gc,  x, y, x2 - x, y2 - y);
}

void
draw_filled_rectangle(w, gc, x, y, x2, y2)
  Widget    w;
  GC        gc;
  Position  x, y, x2, y2;
{
  Display *dpy = XtDisplay(w);
  Window    win = XtWindow(w);

  check_points(&x, &y, &x2, &y2);
  XFillRectangle(dpy, win, gc, x, y, x2 - x, y2 - y);
}
```

Some X servers do not draw polygonal figures correctly if the second point is less than the first in either direction. The auxiliary function **check_points()** checks for this case and reverses the coordinates if necessary.

```
check_points(x, y, x2, y2)
  Position *x, *y, *x2, *y2;
{
  if(*x2 < *x){ Position tmp = *x; *x = *x2; *x2 = tmp;}
  if(*y2 < *y){ Position tmp = *y; *y = *y2; *y2 = tmp;}
}
```

The functions **draw_circle()** and **draw_filled_circle()** use the two points as the upper left and lower right corners of the bounding box of a circle. Theses functions are defined as:

```
void
draw_circle(w, gc, x, y, x2, y2)
  Widget    w;
  GC        gc;
  Position  x, y, x2, y2;
{
  Display *dpy = XtDisplay(w);
  Window   win = XtWindow(w);

  check_points(&x, &y, &x2, &y2);
  XDrawArc(dpy, win, gc, x, y, x2 - x, y2 - y, 0, 64 * 360);
}

void
draw_filled_circle(w, gc, x, y, x2, y2)
  Widget    w;
  GC        gc;
  Position  x, y, x2, y2;
{
  Display *dpy = XtDisplay(w);
  Window   win = XtWindow(w);

  check_points(&x, &y, &x2, &y2);
  XFillArc(dpy, win, gc, x, y, x2 - x, y2 - y, 0, 64 * 360);
}
```

These functions must be installed as the current drawing function when the user selects one of the drawing commands. Each RectButton widget in the command pane has a callback function which activates the corresponding drawing function by setting the **current_func** member of the shared client data structure. This function is retrieved from the widget's **XtNuserData** resource. The **activate()** function is defined as:

```
void
activate(w, client_data, call_data)
  Widget         w;
  XtPointer   client_data;
  XtPointer   call_data;
{
  graphics_data  *data = (graphics_data *)client_data;
  int (*func)();
  Arg wargs[5];

  XtSetArg(wargs[0], XtNuserData, &func);
  XtGetValues(w, wargs, 1);
  data->current_func = func;
}
```

We must save each figure the user draws in a buffer so we can redraw the image when the DrawArea widget is exposed. The function **store_object()** saves the size and location of the figure, the graphics context, and a pointer to the function used to draw the object in the next available slot of the graphics buffer array. It then increments the **next_pos** counter. If the graphics buffer is full, the function issues a warning and returns without storing the object.

```
store_object(data)
  graphics_data *data;
{
  /*
   * Check for space.
   */
  if(data->next_pos >= MAXOBJECTS) {
    printf("Warning: Graphics buffer is full\n");
    return;
  }
  /*
   * Save everything we need to draw this object again.
   */
  data->buffer[data->next_pos].x1 = data->start_x;
  data->buffer[data->next_pos].y1 = data->start_y;
  data->buffer[data->next_pos].x2 = data->last_x;
  data->buffer[data->next_pos].y2 = data->last_y;
  data->buffer[data->next_pos].func = data->current_func;
  data->buffer[data->next_pos].gc = data->gc;
  /*
   * Increment the next position index.
   */
  data->next_pos++;
}
```

When the DrawArea widget is exposed, Xt invokes the callback functions on the **XtNexposeCallback** list, including the **refresh()** callback function. This function loops through the graphics buffer, redrawing each object.

```
void refresh(w, client_data, call_data)
  Widget        w;
  XtPointer     client_data;
  XtPointer     call_data;
{
  graphics_data  *data = (graphics_data *)client_data;
  int i;
  for(i=0;i<data->next_pos;i++)
   (*(data->buffer[i].func))(w, data->buffer[i].gc, data->buffer[i].x1,
                             data->buffer[i].y1, data->buffer[i].x2,
                               data->buffer[i].y2);
}
```

This function could be improved by applying the techniques discussed in Chapter 9 for compressing **Expose** events and using a region to set the clip mask in the graphics context.

10.5 SUMMARY

This chapter explored the graphics facilities provided by Xlib, and demonstrated how they can be used with the Xt Intrinsics and widgets. X provides simple two-dimensional graphics primitives, although efforts are underway to provide more sophisticated three-dimensional capabilities. Various attributes of a graphics context control how the Xlib drawing functions affect a drawable and allow the programmer to produce various special effects such as drawing rubber band lines.

Because each graphics operation makes a server request, complex images can be time consuming. It is often necessary to take extra steps to reduce the number of server requests, such as caching and combining requests, or saving complete or partial renditions of images in off-screen pixmaps.

The following chapter leaves the topic of graphics operations and discusses ways to provide communication and data sharing between applications.

11

INTERCLIENT COMMUNICATION

X provides many facilities that allow applications to communicate with each other and to exchange and share data. Interclient communication involves the use of *atoms*, *properties*, and *client messages*. This chapter first describes atoms and shows how atoms are used to identify names and types of properties. Then a short example demonstrates how properties can be used to store data in the server, where the data can be shared by multiple clients. Next we discuss how applications can use client message events to communicate with each other. Finally, we look at the X *selection* mechanism and the OLIT *drag and drop* facility which are both used for exchanging typed data between applications.

11.1 ATOMS

An atom is a unique resource ID used to represent a string. The relationship is stored in the X server so that all clients connected to that server share the same ID for any particular string. Atoms are primarily used for efficiency; it is faster to compare two atoms (using ==) than to compare two strings (using `strcmp()`).

Creating an atom is referred to as *interning*. The function

```
XInternAtom(display, name, only_if_exists)
```

returns a unique atom corresponding to the string specified by name. When the Boolean `only_if_exists` is `TRUE`, `XInternAtom()` returns an atom ID if the atom already exists. If the atom does not exist, the function returns the constant `None`. When `only_if_exists` is `FALSE`, `XInternAtom()` always returns an atom ID, creating a new atom unless the atom already exists. All applications that request an atom for the same string from the same server receive the same ID. The string must match exactly, including the case.

Applications can create new atoms to represent any arbitrary string. For example, the statement

```
Atom NEWATOM = XInternAtom(display, "A New Atom", FALSE);
```

creates an atom, **NEWATOM**, representing the string

```
"A New Atom"
```

Once an atom is interned, it exists until the server is reset, even if the client that created the atom exits. The function

```
XGetAtomName(display, atom)
```

returns the string corresponding to **atom**.

OLIT provides a similar utility to intern atoms which provides caching.

```
OlInternAtom(display, name)
```

This function call returns an Atom just as does **XInternAtom()**. Calling **OlInternAtom()** is the same as calling **XInternAtom()** with the **only_if_exists** parameter set to FALSE. **OlInternAtom()** caches the atoms so that a request to the server is not necessary on subsequent requests for the same atom.

Atoms are useful whenever a unique identifier that must be shared and recognized by multiple applications is required. For example, atoms are used to identify the type of data stored in a property. X predefines a small set of atoms to identify common resource types such as **DRAWABLE**, **POINT**, **INTEGER**, **FONT**, and **PIXMAP**. The symbols for all predefined atoms are preceded by the letters "**XA_**" to avoid name clashes between client-defined atoms. For example, the atom that identifies the type **INTEGER** is defined by the symbol **XA_INTEGER**. X also predefines atoms intended for other uses, including selection types, property names, and font properties. Applications that use these predefined atoms must include the header file Xatom.h.

11.2 USING PROPERTIES

A property is a collection of named, typed data. Every property is associated with a window, and the data stored in the property is maintained by the server, where it can be accessed or altered by any client that has the window's ID and the name of the property. Properties are named and typed using atoms. The X server predefines some atoms commonly used as property names, including:

XA_CUT_BUFFER0	XA_RGB_RED_MAP	XA_WM_HINTS
XA_CUT_BUFFER1	XA_RESOURCE_MANAGER	XA_WM_ICON_NAME
XA_CUT_BUFFER2	XA_RGB_BEST_MAP	XA_WM_ICON_SIZE
XA_CUT_BUFFER3	XA_RGB_BLUE_MAP	XA_WM_NAME
XA_CUT_BUFFER4	XA_RGB_DEFAULT_MAP	XA_WM_NORMAL_HINTS
XA_CUT_BUFFER5	XA_RGB_GRAY_MAP	XA_WM_ZOOM_HINTS
XA_CUT_BUFFER6	XA_WM_CLASS	XA_WM_TRANSIENT_FOR

```
XA_CUT_BUFFER7          XA_WM_CLIENT_MACHINE
XA_RGB_GREEN_MAP        XA_WM_COMMAND
```

Although these property names are predefined by the server, the corresponding properties do not automatically exist, nor do they necessarily contain any data. Xlib predefines property names as a convenience so clients can use these properties without explicitly interning the atoms. Like all predefined atoms, predefined property names begin with the letters **XA_**. The data associated with a property is simply stored as a stream of bytes, and a second atom associated with the property identifies the type of the data. The server also predefines atoms to represent some common X data types, including:

```
XA_ARC                  XA_ATOM                 XA_BITMAP
XA_CARDINAL             XA_COLORMAP             XA_CURSOR
XA_DRAWABLE             XA_FONT                 XA_INTEGER
XA_PIXMAP               XA_POINT                XA_RGB_COLOR_MAP
XA_RECTANGLE            XA_STRING               XA_VISUALID
XA_WINDOW               XA_WM_HINTS             XA_WM_SIZE_HINTS
```

Applications can create new atoms to represent any data type, including client-defined structures. The server attaches no particular meaning to any atom.

The function

```
XChangeProperty(display, window, name, type,
                format, mode, &data, nelements)
```

stores the given data in a property of the specified window. The third and fourth arguments to **XChangeProperty()** must be atoms that specify the name of the property and the type of the data stored in the property. The **format** argument specifies whether the data consists of multiples of 8, 16, or 32 bits. This information allows the server to do byte swapping, if necessary, when data is transferred between clients running on different machines. The **mode** argument indicates whether the data is to replace any data already stored in the property or be added to the beginning or the end of any existing contents, and must be one of the constants **PropModeReplace**, **PropModePrepend**, or **PropModeAppend**. The **data** argument provides the address of the data to be stored while **nelements** specifies the length of the data in multiples of the unit given by the **format** argument.

Window properties are normally used to share information with other clients. For example, most X window managers expect some basic properties to be stored in properties on every application's top level window. Programmers who use the Xt Intrinsics do not usually need to be aware of this, because the Intrinsics set these properties automatically. One of these window manager properties, **XA_WM_NAME**, is expected to contain the name of a window. Xlib provides a convenient function,

```
XStoreName(display, window, name)
```

which stores a string, specified by the **name** argument, in the **XA_WM_NAME** property of the given window. This Xlib function provides an easy-to-use interface to the function **XChangeProperty()**, and is defined as:

```
XStoreName (dpy, w, name)
    Display  *dpy;
    Window   w;
    char     *name;
{
 XChangeProperty(dpy, w, XA_WM_NAME, XA_STRING,
                    8, PropModeReplace,
                    (unsigned char *)name,
                    name ? strlen(name) : 0);
}
```

Many other Xlib functions, including **XSetStandardProperties()** and **XSetWMHints()**, are implemented similarly.

A property exists until the window with which it is associated is destroyed, or until a client explicitly deletes the property. The lifetime of a property is not determined by the lifetime of the client that stores the property. The function

```
XDeleteProperty(display, window, property)
```

deletes a property from a window's property list.

Clients can retrieve the data stored in a property with the Xlib function:

```
XGetWindowProperty(display, window, name, offset, length,
                    delete, requested_type, &actual_type,
                    &actual_format, &nitems, &bytes_left,
                    &data);
```

This function returns the constant **Success**, defined in Xlib.h, if no error condition is encountered while executing the function. This does not imply that the property was found, or that any data was retrieved. The **name** argument must be an atom identifying the property containing the desired data. The **offset** argument specifies the starting point within the data stored in the property from which data should be returned. The offset is measured in 32-bit quantities from the beginning of the stored data. The **length** argument specifies how many 32-bit multiples of the data should be returned. The Boolean argument, **delete**, indicates whether or not the server should delete the data after it is retrieved. The **requested_type** must be either an atom identifying the desired type of the data or the constant **AnyPropertyType**. When **XGetWindowProperty()** returns, the argument **actual_type** is set to an atom representing the type of the data stored in the property, while **actual_format** contains the format of the stored data. If the property does not exist for the specified window, **actual_type** is set to **None**, and the **actual_format** is set to zero. The arguments **nitems** and **bytes_left** indicate the number of bytes retrieved and how many remaining bytes are stored in the property. This allows applications to retrieve large amounts of data by repeated calls to **XGetWindowProperty()**. If the function returns successfully, the **data** argument points to the bytes retrieved from the property. X allocates this data using **Xmalloc()**, and applications should free the data using **Xfree()** when the data is no longer needed.

The Xlib function

```
XFetchName(display, window, name)
```

uses **XGetProperty()** to retrieve the name of a window, stored in the **XA_WM_NAME** property. This function is the counterpart to **XStoreName()** and is defined by Xlib as:

```
Status XFetchName (dpy, w, name)
    Display *dpy;
    Window   w;
    char   **name;
{
  Atom              actual_type;
  int               actual_format;
  unsigned long   nitems;
  unsigned long   leftover;
  unsigned char *data = NULL;
  if (XGetWindowProperty(dpy, w, XA_WM_NAME, 0L, (long)BUFSIZ,
                         FALSE, XA_STRING, &actual_type,
                         &actual_format, &nitems,
                         &leftover, &data) != Success){
    *name = NULL;
    return (FALSE);
  }
  if ((actual_type == XA_STRING) && (actual_format == 8)){
    *name = (char *)data;
     return (TRUE);
  }
  if (data)
      Xfree ((char *)data);
 *name = NULL;
  return (FALSE);
}
```

If the call to **XGetWindowProperty()** is unsuccessful, **XFetchName()** returns **FALSE**, with **name** set to **NULL**. If the call is successful, **XGetWindowProperty()** returns **Success**, and **XFetchName()** checks whether the property type matches the requested type and also checks the format to ensure that the data is in 8-bit format. If these conditions are met, **XFetchName()** sets **name** to point to the retrieved data and returns **TRUE**. If the type and format of the data are incorrect, the function frees the retrieved data, using **Xfree()**, and returns **FALSE**.

11.2.1 Property Events

The X server notifies interested clients when any change occurs in a window's property list. The server generates a **PropertyNotify** event when the data stored in a property changes, when a property is initially created, or when a property is deleted. Clients must request **PropertyNotify** events using the event mask **PropertyChangeMask**. The server reports **PropertyNotify** events using an **XPropertyEvent** structure. In addition to the basic members included in all events, this structure contains the following members:

```
Atom        atom;
Time        time;
int         state;
```

The **atom** member contains the name of the modified property. The **state** member is set to the constant **NewValue** if the value of property has changed, or to **Deleted** if the property has been deleted. The **time** member is set to the server time when the property was modified.

11.2.2 Using Properties to Share Data

This section uses a simple example to demonstrate how properties and atoms can be used to allow two or more applications to share data. The first application, **controldata**, allows the user to control three parameters named **altitude**, **speed** and **direction**. The current values of these parameters are kept in a single data structure, stored in a property on the root window of the display. A second application, **monitordata**, displays the current value of this data. The monitoring application uses **PropertyNotify** events to detect changes in the data and update its display.

11.2.2.1   The controldata Program

First, let's examine the **controldata** program, which lets the user set some values using scroll bars. The program then stores these values in a property in the server.

Both **controldata** and **monitordata** use the same header file, data.h. This file includes the header files for the widgets used by both programs and also the definition of a data structure common to both programs. It also includes declarations of two new atoms used by both applications to identify a property and the data type stored in the property.

```
/*****************************************************
 *   data.h: declarations for shared data example
 *****************************************************/
#include <X11/StringDefs.h>
#include <X11/Intrinsic.h>
#include <Xol/OpenLook.h>
#include <Xol/Slider.h>
#include <Xol/ControlAre.h>
#include <Xol/Caption.h>
#include <Xol/OblongButt.h>
#include <Xol/StaticText.h>
#include "libXs.h"

/* Maximum settings */
#define MAX_SPEED 100
#define MAX_ANGLE 359
#define MAX_ALT   200
/*
 *   Data structure to be stored in a property
 */
typedef struct {
```

```
  int               speed;
  int               angle;
  float             altitude;
} flight_data;
/*
 * Atoms representing the property name and data type.
 */
Atom        FLIGHT_DATA, FLIGHT_DATA_TYPE;
```

The `flight_data` structure contains three parameters shared by the two programs. The user can position a slider to set the value of each member of this structure between zero and the maximum value determined by corresponding constant: **MAX_ALT**, **MAX_ANGLE**, or **MAX_SPEED**.

The source file, controldata.c, includes the file data.h and globally defines the widgets used by the program. The main program initializes each member of the `flight data` structure to zero, and creates the ScrollBar widgets that control each parameter. A ControlArea widget manages three columns, each containing a ScrollBar widget and a StaticText widget. The StaticText widget displays a label for the scroll bar.

```
/************************************************
 *   controldata.c: The data controller
 ***********************************************/
#include "data.h"

void        slider_moved();
Widget      speed_ctl, angle_ctl, temp_ctl;
Widget      create control();
Widget      make_controller();

main(argc, argv)
  int    argc;
  char *argv[];
{
  Widget          toplevel, cont_area;
  flight_data     data;

  data.speed = data.angle = data.altitude = 0;
  toplevel = OlInitialize(argv[0], "Controldata", NULL, 0,
                          &argc, argv);
  /*
   * Create the atoms to represent the properties
   * used to store the data.
   */
  create_atoms(toplevel);
  cont_area = XtCreateManagedWidget("panel", controlAreaWidgetClass,
                                    toplevel, NULL, 0);
  /*
   *  Make three columns, each containing a label and a
```

```
 *    slider control to control: speed, direction,
 *    and altitude.
 */
speed_ctl = make_controller("speed",     MAX_SPEED,
                               cont_area, &data);
angle_ctl = make_controller("direction", MAX_ANGLE,
                               cont_area, &data);
temp_ctl  = make_controller("altitude",  MAX_ALT,
                               cont_area, &data);

XtRealizeWidget(toplevel);
XtMainLoop();
}
```

The function **create_atoms()** creates two new atoms. The first is the name of the property in which the data is stored and the other represents the type of the data.

```
create_atoms(w)
  Widget w;
{
  Display       *dpy = XtDisplay(w);
  FLIGHT_DATA       = XInternAtom(dpy, "Flight Data",      0);
  FLIGHT_DATA_TYPE = XInternAtom(dpy, "Flight Data Type", 0);
}
```

The function **make_controller()** takes a name, a maximum value, a parent widget, and a pointer to some client data as arguments and creates a ControlArea widget containing a scroll bar and a label. It returns a pointer to the ScrollBar widget.

```
Widget
make_controller(name, max, parent, data)
  char          *name;
  int            max;
  Widget         parent;
  flight_data   *data;
{
  Widget rc, w;
  /*
   * Create a ControlArea widget to manage a single
   * control and a label.
   */
  rc = XtCreateManagedWidget(name, controlAreaWidgetClass,
                                parent, NULL, 0);
  XtCreateManagedWidget("label", staticTextWidgetClass,
                        rc, NULL, 0);
  w = create_control(rc, "control", 0, max, data);

  return (w);
}
```

The function **create_control()** creates an ScrollBar widget, defines minimum and maximum values for the scroll bar, and registers the callbacks that are invoked when the user moves the scroll bar slider.

```
Widget
create_control(parent, name, minimum, maximum, data)
  Widget        parent;
  char          *name;
  int           minimum, maximum;
  flight_data   *data;
{
  int   n;
  Arg   wargs[2];
  Widget w;

  /*
   * Create a slider with range minimum to maximum.
   */
  n = 0;
  XtSetArg(wargs[n], XtNsliderMin, minimum); n++;
  XtSetArg(wargs[n], XtNsliderMax, maximum); n++;
  w = XtCreateManagedWidget(name, sliderWidgetClass,
                            parent, wargs, n);
  /*
   * Register callback function for when the user moves the
   * slider.
   */
  XtAddCallback(w, XtNsliderMoved, slider_moved, data);
  return (w);
}
```

The **XtNsliderMoved** function **slider_moved()** updates the member of the **flight_data** structure corresponding to the slider that moved, and then calls **XChangeProperty()** to store the data in the **FLIGHT_DATA** property of the default root window of the display.

```
void
slider_moved(w, client_data, call_data)
  Widget        w;
  XtPointer     client_data;
  XtPointer     call_data;
{
  int   n;
  Arg   wargs[2];
  int max, min;
  flight_data   *data = (flight_data *)client_data;
  int value = *(int *)call_data;
```

```
        /*
         * Set the member of the flight_data corresponding to
         * the slider that invoked this callback.
         */
        n = 0;
        XtSetArg(wargs[n], XtNsliderMin, &min); n++;
        XtSetArg(wargs[n], XtNsliderMax, &max); n++;
        XtGetValues(w, wargs, n);
        if(w == angle_ctl)
          data->angle = value;
        else if(w == speed_ctl)
          data->speed = value;
        else if(w == temp_ctl)
          data->altitude = (float) value / 10.0;
        /*
         * Replace the previous contents of the property
         * with the new data.
         */
        XChangeProperty(XtDisplay(w),
                        DefaultRootWindow(XtDisplay(w)),
                        FLIGHT_DATA, FLIGHT_DATA_TYPE,
                        32, PropModeReplace,
                        (unsigned char *) data,
                        sizeof(flight_data) / 4);
    }
```

The class resource file contains the resources corresponding to the widget layout shown in Figure 11.1.

```
    Controldata*font:                       lucidasans-bold
    Controldata*panel*Control.layoutType:   fixedrows
    Controldata*panel*Control.measure:      2
    Controldata*Slider*orientation:         horizontal
    Controldata*Slider*width:               100
    Controldata*speed*label.string:         Speed
    Controldata*direction*label.string:     Direction
    Controldata*altitude*label.string:      Altitude
```

11.2.2.2   The monitordata Program

The **controldata** program allows a user to control the values represented by a complex data structure, and stores this data structure in a property of the root window. This section examines the **monitordata** program, which uses **PropertyNotify** events to retrieve and display the current value of this data whenever the program detects changes in the **FLIGHT_DATA** property.

The program includes the header file data.h, which contains the definition of the data structure used by both the **controldata** program and the **monitordata** program.

The first portion of the main program is similar to the **controldata** program, except that each of the three columns in the **monitordata** window consists of two StaticText widgets. One of these displays the current value of a member of the shared data structure, while the other is used as a label. The function **create_atoms()** is identical to the function used by the **controldata** program, and is not repeated here.

```
/***********************************************************
 *  monitordata.c: display the data set by controldata
 ***********************************************************/
#include "data.h"

Widget    make_display();

main(argc, argv)
  int    argc;
  char *argv[];
{
  Widget        toplevel, rc, speed, direction,  altitude;
  Window        root;
  XEvent        event;

  /*
   * Initialize the Intrinsics,saving the default root window.
   */
  toplevel = OlInitialize(argv[0], "Monitordata", NULL, 0,
                          &argc, argv);
  root =  DefaultRootWindow(XtDisplay(toplevel));
  /*
   * Initialize the Atoms used for the properties.
   */
  create_atoms(toplevel);
  rc = XtCreateManagedWidget("panel", controlAreaWidgetClass,
                             toplevel,  NULL, 0);
  /*
   * Create the display widgets.
   */
  speed      = make_display("speed",     rc);
  direction  = make_display("direction", rc);
  altitude   = make_display("altitude",  rc);

  XtRealizeWidget(toplevel);
  /*
   * Request property change event for the ROOT window.
   */
  XSelectInput(XtDisplay(toplevel), root, PropertyChangeMask);
  /*
   *  Get the initial value of the data.
```

```
      */
     update_data(speed, direction, altitude);
     /*
      * We must use our own event loop to get properties
      * events for the ROOT window.
      */
     while(TRUE){
       XtNextEvent(&event);
       /*
        * Check for property change events on the ROOT window
        * before dispatching the event through the Intrinsics.
        */
       switch (event.type){
         case PropertyNotify:
           if(event.xproperty.window == root &&
              event.xproperty.atom == FLIGHT_DATA)
            update_data(speed, direction, altitude);
           else
            XtDispatchEvent(&event);
           break;
         default:
           XtDispatchEvent(&event);
       }
     }
   }
```

The event loop for this program is quite different from previous examples. Because we are storing the property on the root window of the display, we cannot use **XtMainLoop()**. The Xt Intrinsics event handler mechanism allows applications to register event handlers to be invoked when a event occurs relative to a specific *widget*, but **monitordata** needs to be notified when an event occurs relative to the root window. Since the root window is not a widget, we cannot use the Intrinsics' dispatch mechanism to handle the event. Therefore, we must write our own event loop to intercept the event before it reaches the event dispatcher. Before entering the event loop, the program uses the Xlib function **XSelectInput()** to request **PropertyNotify** events for the root window. The default root window of the display is specified as the event window and the event mask is given as **PropertyChangeMask**. This requests the X server to send **PropertyNotify** events to **monitordata** when any property of the root window changes. The event loop uses **XtNextEvent()** to remove each event from the event queue. A switch statement checks the type of each event to determine if it is a **PropertyNotify** event. If it is, and the **property** member of the event is the atom **FLIGHT_DATA**, **update_data()** is called to retrieve the data stored in the property and update the values displayed in each StaticText widget. Otherwise, the function **XtDispatchEvent()** is called to dispatch events to the appropriate widget. **XtDispatchEvent()** is also called for event types other that **PropertyNotify**.

The function **update_data()** uses **XGetWindowProperty()** to retrieve the contents of the **FLIGHT_DATA** property. The requested number of bytes is determined by the size of the **flight_data** structure. The length of the data actually retrieved is returned in the variable

nitems, while **retdata** points to the contents of the property. If **XGetWindowProperty()** succeeds and the type of the property is **FLIGHT_DATA_TYPE**, the value of each field of the structure is converted to a string and displayed in the corresponding StaticText widget.

```
update_data(speed, direction, altitude)
  Widget speed, direction, altitude;
{
  int              format;
  unsigned long    nitems, left;
  flight_data      *retdata;
  char             str[100];
  Arg              wargs[1];
  Atom             type;

  /*
   * Retrieve the data from the root window property.
   */
  if(XGetWindowProperty(XtDisplay(speed),
                        DefaultRootWindow(XtDisplay(speed)),
                        FLIGHT_DATA, 0, sizeof(flight_data),
                        FALSE, FLIGHT_DATA_TYPE,
                        &type, &format, &nitems, &left,
                        (unsigned char **)&retdata) == Success &&
      type ==FLIGHT_DATA_TYPE){
    /*
     * If the data exists, display it.
     */
    xs_wprintf(speed,     "%2d",   retdata->speed);
    xs_wprintf(direction, "%2d",   retdata->angle);
    xs_wprintf(altitude,  "%2.1f", retdata->altitude + 0.05);
    XFree((XtPointer)retdata);
  }
}
```

The only **monitordata** function we have not discussed, **make_display()**, creates one row of StaticText widgets. One widget functions as a label for the data, while the other displays the value of the data.

```
Widget make_display(name, parent)
  char      *name;
  Widget    parent;
{
  Widget cap, w;

  /*
   * Create a ControlArea widget containing two
   * StaticText widgets.
   */
```

```
cap = XtCreateManagedWidget(name, staticTextWidgetClass,
                            parent, NULL, 0);
w = XtCreateManagedWidget("display", staticTextWidgetClass,
                            parent, NULL, 0);
return (w);
}
```

Figure 11.1. shows both the `monitordata` and `controldata` programs

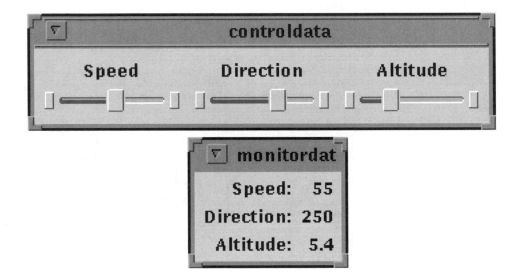

Figure 11.1 The monitordata and controldata programs.

This example illustrates how properties allow two separate applications to share data. **PropertyNotify** events allow multiple applications to be informed whenever a property changes. Properties and **PropertyNotify** events not only provide a way for applications to share data, but also provide a *trigger* mechanism that can be used to notify clients that data has changed and to synchronize multiple applications that use the data. Efficiency problems might arise if many applications use properties on the root window for such purposes, because **PropertyNotify** events cannot be requested for a particular property, only for all properties on a window's property list. However, the same effect can be achieved by having a set of related applications watch the properties on one common window instead of the root window.

The next section discusses a more direct way to provide communication between applications, using **ClientMessage** events.

11.3 COMMUNICATING WITH EVENTS

X allows applications to send events to any window. This feature can be used to forward events from one application to another, or to create and send new events. The function

```
XSendEvent(display, window, propagate, mask, &event)
```

sends an event to clients that have selected any of the events in **mask** for the specified window. **XSendEvent()** can be used to send any valid X event type. The **window** argument must be either a valid window ID on the given display, or the constant **PointerWindow**, in which case the event is sent to the window currently containing the pointer. The **window** argument can also be the constant **InputFocus**, requesting that the event be sent to the current focus window. If **InputFocus** is specified and the pointer is contained within the focus window, the event is sent to the smallest window or subwindow of the focus window containing the pointer. The boolean flag, **propagate**, determines whether the server should propagate the event to ancestors if the specified window has not selected the event type. **XSendEvent()** returns a non-zero value if the function executes correctly. Successful execution does not imply that the intended window received the event, only that no error condition occurred during the process of sending the event.

11.3.1 Client Message Events

One common use of **XSendEvent()** is to send client messages. **ClientMessage** events are never generated by the server. They are used by applications to define new events and provide the basis for one form of interclient communication. **ClientMessage** events have no corresponding event mask and cannot be specifically selected. They are always received by the client that owns the window to which the event is sent.[1] The **XClientMessageEvent** structure is defined in Xlib.h as:

```
typedef struct {
    int             type;
    unsigned long   serial;
    Bool            send_event;
    Display         *display;
    Window          window;
    Atom            message_type;
    int             format;
    union {
        char        b[20];
        short       s[10];
        long        l[5];
    } data;
} XClientMessageEvent;
```

---

[1]   The event is always received, in the sense that the server always places the event in the client's event queue. However, unless the client has defined an event handler for the event, the event will be ignored.

In addition to the first five members, which are common to all event types, the **ClientMessage** event structure contains a **message_type** field that identifies the subtype of the event. The subtype is specified by an atom whose meaning must be recognized by both the sending and the receiving applications. The X server does not interpret the field. The **format** member specifies the data format of the bytes in the **data** field, and must be one of 8, 16, or 32. The **data** field consists of 20 bytes, declared as a union of bytes, shorts, and longs. Clients are free to use this data field for any purpose.

Because **ClientMessage** events are *non-maskable* events, applications must specify **NoEventMask** (or 0) as the event mask when registering event handlers for **ClientMessage** events. For example, a function named **message_handler()** can be registered as an event handler for a widget with the statement:

```
XtAddEventHandler(w, NoEventMask, TRUE, message_handler, NULL);
```

The argument following the event mask must be **TRUE** to indicate that this is a non-maskable event.

11.3.2 An Example: xtalk

This section presents an example program that shows how **XSendEvent()** can be used to communicate between two applications. The program demonstrates **ClientMessage** events and also provides some additional examples of how properties and atoms can be used. The example, named **xtalk**, allows users on two different machines to communicate with each other, and is similar in spirit to the **talk** program found on most UNIX systems. First, let's look at Figure 11.2 and discuss how the program works from the user's viewpoint.

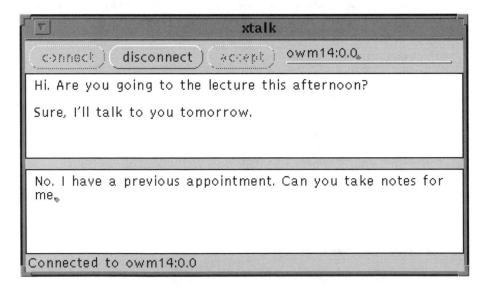

Figure 11.2 The xtalk program.

The main window of **xtalk** is divided into three primary areas: a command pane and two message panes. The user types into the top message pane, while messages from a remote **xtalk** program appear in the bottom message pane. The user can request a connection to another **xtalk** user by typing the name of the other user's display into the text field in the middle of the control pane, and then selecting the "connect" button. At this point, the message field on the right side of the command pane displays the message:

```
Waiting for a response
```

Assuming there is an **xtalk** program running on the requested display, the remote **xtalk** displays a message,

```
Connection requested from <machine>
```

where <machine> is the name of the first user's display.[2] If the user of the remote **xtalk** is willing to accept the talk request, he or she selects the "accept" button. Once a connection is established, the message field of each user's **xtalk** displays the message

```
Connected to <machine>
```

where <machine> is the name of the other user's machine. From this point on, until either user breaks the connection by selecting the disconnect button, everything typed in the top message pane of each **xtalk** is echoed in the bottom panel of the other **xtalk**.

The **xtalk** program uses **ClientMessage** events to make connection requests and to send "disconnect" and "accept" notifications between programs. In addition, the program uses **XSendEvent()** to forward each **KeyPress**, **ButtonPress**, and **MotionNotify** event that occurs in the top message pane of either **xtalk** to the lower text pane of the remote program. The **xtalk** program has several interesting aspects. First, the application must properly handle the atoms, properties, and window IDs on two different displays. Remembering when to use resources from the local display and when to use those of the remote display can be confusing, but interesting. This program also uses widget *sensitivity* to control what commands are available to the user at any given time, depending on the state of the program.[3] At any particular time, only the buttons that represent commands available to the user are sensitive to events. All other buttons are disabled.

The header file for **xtalk** includes the header files for each widget class used by the program. The header file also defines several atoms used as subtypes of **ClientMessage** events as well as some global variables used by the program. The file defines some strings as constants to eliminate the possibility of spelling the words differently in different parts of the program.

```
/***********************************************
 *   xtalk.h: declarations used by xtalk
 ***********************************************/
#include <stdio.h>
```

---

[2] For this program to work, each user must be able to open the display of the other user. Security in X is handled by the xhost program or the file /usr/lib/X0.hosts. Consult your local user's documentation for details.

[3] Every widget has an XtNsensitive resource that determines whether a widget responds to events. If a widget is insensitive, the Intrinsics do not dispatch device events for it or any of its children. Most widgets change their appearance, and are "grayed out" when they are in an insensitive state.

```
#include <X11/Intrinsic.h>
#include <X11/StringDefs.h>
#include <X11/Xatom.h>
#include <Xol/OpenLook.h>
#include <Xol/ControlAre.h>
#include <Xol/RubberTile.h>
#include <Xol/TextField.h>
#include <Xol/TextEdit.h>
#include <Xol/StaticText.h>
#include <Xol/OblongButt.h>
#include "libXs.h"
/*
 *    Atoms used for communication
 */
Atom        XTALK_WINDOW, CONNECTION_REQUEST,
            CONNECTION_ACCEPT, DISCONNECT_NOTIFY;
Display  *remote_display = NULL;
Display  *my_display;
Window     remote_talker_window;
/*
 *  Various widgets
 */
Widget     name_field, msg_field,
            connect_button, disconnect_button,
            accept_button;
char       *othermachine;
char       *my_displayname;
int         connection_accepted = FALSE;
/*
 *  Define the strings used to create atoms
 */
#define XtNdisconnect          "Disconnect Notify"
#define XtNconnectionAccept    "Connection Accept"
#define XtNconnectionRequest "Connection Request"
#define XtNtalkWindow          "XTalk Window"
/*
 * Declare the callbacks used in xtalk
 */
void     client_message_handler();
void     register_talker_window();
void     create_command_panel();
void     warn_wrong_pane();
void     accept_callback();
void     connect_callback();
void     disconnect_callback();
void     send_to_remote();
void     quit_callback();
```

The main body of the program uses **OlInitialize()** to initialize the toolkit and open the local X display, and then saves both the display and the name of the display for later use. Figure 11.3 shows the widget tree created by **xtalk**. A RubberTile widget manages the three panes of the **xtalk** window. The top pane, created by the function **create_command_panel()**, contains a row of OblongButton widgets used to issue commands. The lower two panes each contain a TextEdit widget. The upper pane, referred to as the *talk* pane, allows the user to enter text. The lower pane, referred to as the *listen* pane, displays the text sent from remote **xtalk** programs. The event handler **send_to_remote()**, registered for the talk pane, is invoked when a **KeyPress** event, any button event, or a **MotionNotify** event occurs in the talk pane. The listen pane has two event handlers defined, one for **KeyPress** events and the other for events with no event mask, which includes **ClientMessage** events. We will examine the purpose of these event handlers shortly.

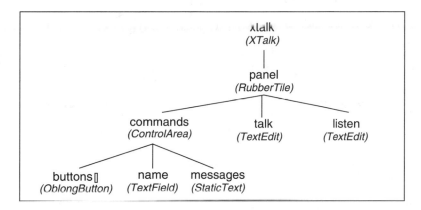

Figure 11.3 Widget tree for xtalk.

Finally, after realizing all widgets, the function **register_talker_window()** is called. This function stores the window ID of the listen pane in a property of the root window, where it can be accessed by other **xtalk** programs. This publicly announces the window ID to which remote **xtalk** programs can send connection requests. We cannot register the window ID until after the widget has been realized and the window actually exists.

```
/************************************************
 *   xtalk.c
 ************************************************/
#include "xtalk.h"

main(argc, argv)
  int    argc;
  char *argv[];
{
  Widget toplevel, vpane, talk, listen;
  Widget sw_listen, sw_talk;
  Arg    wargs[10];
```

```
    /*
     * Open display and save display and display name.
     */
    toplevel = OlInitialize(argv[0], "XTalk", NULL, 0,
                            &argc, argv);

    my_display = XtDisplay(toplevel);
    my_displayname = DisplayString(my_display);
    /*
     * Create a pane to hold all other widgets.
     */
    vpane = XtCreateManagedWidget("panel",
                                  rubberTileWidgetClass,
                                  toplevel, NULL,0);
    create_command_panel(vpane);
    /*
     * Create the text panes used to talk.
     */
    talk = XtCreateManagedWidget("talk", textEditWidgetClass,
                                 vpane, NULL, 0);
    XtAddEventHandler(talk, KeyPressMask | KeyReleaseMask,
                      FALSE, send_to_remote, NULL);
    listen = XtCreateManagedWidget("listen", textEditWidgetClass,
                                   vpane, NULL, 0);
    /*
     * Create the message area.
     */
    XtSetArg(wargs[0], XtNgravity, SouthWestGravity);
    msg_field = XtCreateManagedWidget("messages",
                                      staticTextWidgetClass,
                                      vpane, wargs, 1);
    xs_wprintf(msg_field, "No Current Connection");
    XtAddEventHandler(listen, KeyPressMask, FALSE,
                      warn_wrong_pane, NULL);
    XtAddEventHandler(listen, NoEventMask, TRUE,
                      client_message_handler, NULL);
    OlAddCallback(toplevel, XtNwmProtocol, quit_callback, NULL);
    XtRealizeWidget(toplevel);
    /*
     * Store the listen window ID in a public place.
     */
    register_talker_window(listen);
    XtMainLoop();
}
```

The function **create_command_panel()** creates a row of buttons and text widgets in the top pane of the **xtalk** window. Several of the buttons are initially made insensitive to input events. These buttons represent commands that are not currently available and are made sensitive when these commands can be issued. For example, the **accept_button** is enabled when a connection request is received and disabled again once the user has accepted a connection. The **disconnect_button** is enabled whenever a connection to another **xtalk** is established. The **name_field** widget provides a place where the user can enter the name of a remote display. Finally, a StaticText widget serves as a status message area.

```
void
create_command_panel(parent)
  Widget parent;
{
  Widget   command, quit;
  Arg      wargs[3];
  int      n;
  /*
   * Create a row widget to hold the command buttons.
   */
  command = XtCreateManagedWidget("command", controlAreaWidgetClass,
                                  parent, NULL, 0);

  quit = xs_create_quit_button (command);
  XtAddCallback(quit, XtNselect, quit_callback, NULL);
  /*
   * Create the buttons.
   */
  connect_button = XtCreateManagedWidget("connect",
                                         oblongButtonWidgetClass,
                                         command, NULL, 0);
  XtAddCallback(connect_button, XtNselect, connect_callback, NULL);
  XtSetArg(wargs[0], XtNsensitive, FALSE);
  disconnect_button =
     XtCreateManagedWidget("disconnect", oblongButtonWidgetClass,
                           command, wargs, 1);
  XtAddCallback(disconnect_button, XtNselect,
                disconnect_callback, NULL);
  XtSetArg(wargs[0], XtNsensitive, FALSE);
  accept_button = XtCreateManagedWidget("accept",
                                         oblongButtonWidgetClass,
                                         command, wargs, 1);
  XtAddCallback(accept_button, XtNselect, accept_callback, NULL);
  /*
   * Create a text field in which the user can
   * enter new machine names.
   */
  name_field = XtCreateManagedWidget("name", textFieldWidgetClass,
```

```
                                          command, NULL, 0);
    /*
     * Create the message area.
     */
    msg_field = XtCreateManagedWidget("messages",
                                      staticTextWidgetClass,
                                      command, NULL, 0);
    xs_wprintf(msg_field, "No Current Connection");
}
```

Before one **xtalk** program can send messages to another, it must have the window ID of the listen pane belonging to the other **xtalk**. The function **register_talker_window()** stores the window ID of the listen pane in a property of the root window, where it can be accessed by any other **xtalk** program. The function creates several atoms used by the program, and stores the listen window ID in the **XTALK_WINDOW** property.

```
void
register_talker_window(w)
  Widget w;
{
  Window    window = XtWindow(w);
  Display *dpy     = XtDisplay(w);

  /*
   * Intern the atoms used for communication.
   */
  XTALK_WINDOW        = XInternAtom(dpy, XtNtalkWindow, 0);
  CONNECTION_REQUEST = XInternAtom(dpy, XtNconnectionRequest, 0);
  CONNECTION_ACCEPT  = XInternAtom(dpy, XtNconnectionAccept, 0);
  DISCONNECT_NOTIFY  = XInternAtom(dpy, XtNdisconnect, 0);
  /*
   * Store the listen window ID on our root window.
   */
  XChangeProperty(dpy, DefaultRootWindow(dpy),
                  XTALK_WINDOW, XA_WINDOW,
                  32, PropModeReplace,
                  (unsigned char *)&window, 1);
}
```

To establish a connection with another **xtalk** program, the user must enter the name of a remote display in the **name_field** widget, and then select the **connect_button**. This action invokes the **connect_callback()** function, which attempts to open the display named by the string in the **name_field** widget. This function must make sure the string is not empty because **XOpenDisplay()** interprets an empty string as an instruction to open the display named by the environment variable **DISPLAY**, which is normally set to the local display. Therefore if the string is empty, **xtalk** would attempt to open a connection to itself. If the remote display is opened successfully, the function then retrieves the **XTALK_WINDOW** property from the remote display, and sends a connection request to the remote **xtalk** window.

```
void
connect_callback(w, client_data, call_data)
  Widget   w;
  XtPointer  client_data, call_data;
{
  int              format, fail;
  unsigned long  nitems, left;
  unsigned char *retdata;
  Arg            wargs[2];
  char           *msg;
  Atom           type, REMOTE_XTALK_WINDOW;
  int            size;

  /*
   * Get the name of the display to connect to.
   */
  othermachine = OlTextFieldGetString(name_field, &size);
  /*
   * Make sure the string isn't empty, so we don't connect
   * to ourselves.
   */
  if(strlen(othermachine) > 0) {
    xs_wprintf(msg_field, "%s", "Trying To Open Connection");
    /*
     * Attempt to open the remote display.
     */
    if((remote_display = XOpenDisplay(othermachine)) == NULL) {
        xs_wprintf(msg_field, "%s", "Connection Failed");
        return;
    }
    /*
     * Get the REMOTE property containing THEIR listen ID.
     */
    REMOTE_XTALK_WINDOW =
          XInternAtom(remote_display, XtNtalkWindow, 0);
    if(XGetWindowProperty(remote_display,
                          DefaultRootWindow(remote_display),
                          REMOTE_XTALK_WINDOW,
                          0, 4, FALSE, XA_WINDOW,
                          &type, &format, &nitems, &left,
                          &retdata) == Success &&
         type == XA_WINDOW) {
      remote_talker_window = *(Window *)retdata;
      /*
```

```
      *   If all went well, request a connection.
      */
     xs_wprintf(msg_field, "Waiting for a response");
     connection_accepted = FALSE;
     xs_send_message(remote_display, remote_talker_window,
                     XtNconnectionRequest, my_displayname);
   }
 /*
   *   If something went wrong, disconnect.
   */
   else
     disconnect_callback(disconnect_button, NULL, NULL);
 }
}
```

Notice how atoms and properties on the remote display are accessed in this example. In previous sections we noted that an atom is a unique identifier for a string, shared by all applications connected to a server. Here, we are connected to two servers, and there is no guarantee that any two servers use the same atom to represent the same string. Therefore, we must obtain the **XTALK_WINDOW** atom defined by the remote server before retrieving the contents of the **XTALK_WINDOW** property from the remote display. Also notice that the first argument to **XGetWindowProperty()** refers to the *remote* display.

The function **xs_send_message()** is a general purpose routine that can be used to send a **ClientMessage** event to a window on any display. This function is used by **xtalk** to send various requests to remote **xtalk** programs. The name of the atom representing the message type must be given as the **msg_name** argument, while the **data** argument is expected to be a character string, which cannot exceed 19 characters.

This function first determines the atom ID that represents the **message type** on the given display. It then fills in the members of an **XClientMessageEvent** structure with the display and the ID of the destination window and copies the given **data** into the event's **data** field before using **XSendEvent()** to send the event. After sending the event, this function calls **XFlush()**, an Xlib function that forces the server to process all requests in the request queue. This is seldom necessary, because **XtNextEvent()** flushes the queue each time it is called. However, **XtNextEvent()** flushes the local display, and this function may be sending an event to a remote display. Without the call to **XFlush()**, the **ClientMessage** event would remain in the remote server's request queue until enough requests had accumulated to cause it to process the request. Explicitly flushing the remote request queue ensures that the remote server handles the **XSendEvent()** request in a timely manner.

```
/********************************************************
 * xs_send_message(): send a client message
 ********************************************************/
#include <stdio.h>
#include <X11/Intrinsic.h>
#include <X11/StringDefs.h>
#include <X11/Xatom.h>
```

```
xs_send_message(display, window, msg_name, data)
  Display *display;
  Window   window;
  char    *msg_name;
  char    *data;
{
  XClientMessageEvent event;
  Atom                MSG_ATOM;

  /*
   * Get the atom used
   * by the display.
   */
  MSG_ATOM = XInternAtom(display, msg_name, FALSE);
  /*
   * Fill out the client message event structure.
   */
  event.display = display;
  event.window  = window;
  event.type    = ClientMessage;
  event.format  = 8;
  event.message_type = MSG_ATOM;
  strcpy(event.data.b, data);
  /*
   * Send it and flush.
   */
  XSendEvent(display, window,
             TRUE, (long)0, (XEvent *)&event);
  XFlush(display);
}
```

When **xtalk** receives a client message, the Intrinsics invoke the event handler **client_message_handler()**, which looks at the subtype of each client message, and acts on those that it recognizes. Because the atoms used to identify subtypes are not constants, we cannot use a **switch** statement. Instead, we must check the subtype using a series of **if** statements.[4] If the subtype of the client message is **CONNECTION_REQUEST**, the **client_message_handler()** rings the terminal bell and displays a message to notify the user of the incoming connection request. It then saves a copy of the name of the machine making the connection request and enables the **accept_button** widget.

Other types of client messages are handled similarly. When a remote **xtalk** accepts a connection, it sends a client message of subtype **CONNECTION_ACCEPT**. After displaying a message for the user, the **client_message_handler()** disables the **disconnect_button** widget and

---

[4] The atoms predefined by the X server are defined as constants, so this restriction applies only to atoms that are created by an application.

enables the **connect_button** widget. The function also sets the global flag **connection_accepted** to **TRUE**.

If the client message is of subtype **DISCONNECT_NOTIFY**, **xtalk** closes the display connection, resets various parameters and buttons to their initial state, and displays the message "Disconnected".

Notice that because **client_message_handler()** is registered for a non-maskable event we must check the event type to be sure this event is a **ClientMessage** event. This event handler would also be called if the application receives any other type of non-maskable event.

```
void
client_message_handler(w, client_data, event)
  Widget          w;
  XtPointer       client_data;
  XEvent          *event;
{
  Arg wargs[10];

  if(event->type != ClientMessage)
    return;
  if(event->xclient.message_type == CONNECTION_REQUEST) {
   /*
    * Notify the user of the incoming request and
    * enable the "accept" button.
    */
    XBell(XtDisplay(w), 0);
    othermachine = XtNewString(event->xclient.data.b);
    xs_wprintf(msg_field, "Connection Request from: %s",
                       othermachine);
    XtSetSensitive(accept_button, TRUE);
  } else if(event->xclient.message_type == CONNECTION_ACCEPT) {
   /*
    * Notify the user that the connection has
    * been accepted. Enable the "disconnect" button
    * and disable the "connect" button.
    */
    XBell(XtDisplay(w), 0);
    connection_accepted = TRUE;
    othermachine = XtNewString(event->xclient.data.b);
    xs_wprintf(msg_field, "Connected to %s", othermachine);
    XtSetSensitive(connect_button, FALSE);
    XtSetSensitive(disconnect_button, TRUE);
  } else if(event->xclient.message_type == DISCONNECT_NOTIFY) {
   /*
    * Close the remote display and reset
    * all command buttons to their initial state.
    */
    XBell(XtDisplay(w), 0);
```

```
      if(remote_display)
        XCloseDisplay(remote_display);
      remote_display = NULL;
      connection_accepted = FALSE;
      othermachine = NULL;
      xs_wprintf(msg_field, "%s", "Disconnected");
      XtSetSensitive(connect_button, TRUE);
      XtSetSensitive(disconnect_button, FALSE);
   }
}
```

When **xtalk** receives a connection request, the **accept_button** widget is enabled. If the user then selects the **accept_button** widget, the **accept_callback()** function is invoked. This function attempts to open the remote display and retrieve the window ID of the remote **xtalk**'s listen pane. If successful, the function sends an **XtNconnectionAccepted** client message to indicate that the connection has been accepted. The function also disables the **connect_button** and **accept_button** widgets and enables the **disconnect_button**.

```
void
accept_callback(w, client_data, call_data)
  Widget    w;
  XtPointer client_data, call_data;
{
  int       format, fail;
  unsigned long  nitems, left;
  unsigned char  *retdata;
  Atom      type, REMOTE_XTALK_WINDOW;
  Arg       wargs[10];

  /*
   * Make sure there really is another machine.
   */
  if(strlen(othermachine) > 0 ) {
   /*
    * Attempt to open the remote display.
    */
    if((remote_display = XOpenDisplay(othermachine)) == NULL) {
        xs_wprintf(msg_field, "%s", "Connection Failed");
        return;
    }
    /*
     *  Get the window ID of the remote xtalk program
     */
    REMOTE_XTALK_WINDOW  =
                XInternAtom(remote_display, XtNtalkWindow, 0);
    if(XGetWindowProperty(remote_display,
                         DefaultRootWindow(remote_display),
                         REMOTE_XTALK_WINDOW,
```

```
                              0, 4, FALSE, XA_WINDOW,
                              &type, &format, &nitems, &left,
                              &retdata) == Success &&
              type ==  XA_WINDOW) {
      connection_accepted = TRUE;
      remote_talker_window = *(Window *)retdata;
      /*
       * Notify the remote xtalk that we accept the connection.
       */
      connection_accepted = TRUE;
      xs_send_message(remote_display, remote_talker_window,
                      XtNconnectionAccept, my_displayname);
      xs_wprintf(msg_field, "Connected to %s", othermachine);

      XtSetSensitive(accept_button, FALSE);
      XtSetSensitive(connect_button, FALSE);
      XtSetSensitive(disconnect_button, TRUE);
    } else
      disconnect_callback(disconnect_button, NULL, NULL);
  }
}
```

Once each program has established a connection to the other, each user can type into his or her talk pane. The event handler **send_to_remote()** is invoked when any key or mouse event occurs in the talk pane. This event handler uses **XSendEvent()** to send the event to the remote **xtalk** program, where it is treated just as if the remote user had typed the text into the window. The result is that everything typed in the talk pane of the local **xtalk** program is echoed in the listen pane of the remote **xtalk** program.

```
void
send_to_remote(w, client_data, event)
  Widget     w;
  XtPointer  client_data;
  XEvent     *event;
{
  XEvent newevent;

  if(remote_display && remote_talker_window && connection_accepted) {
    newevent.xkey.type = event->xkey.type;
    newevent.xkey.subwindow = event->xkey.subwindow;
    newevent.xkey.time = event->xkey.time;
    newevent.xkey.x = event->xkey.x;
    newevent.xkey.y = event->xkey.y;
    newevent.xkey.display = remote_display;
    newevent.xkey.window = remote_talker_window;
    newevent.xkey.state = event->xkey.state;
    newevent.xkey.keycode = event->xkey.keycode;
    XSendEvent(remote_display, remote_talker_window,
```

```
                    TRUE, (unsigned long)0, &newevent);
      XFlush(remote_display);
  }
}
```

The TextEdit widget does not provide a way to prevent the user from typing into the listen pane of the **xtalk** window. The TextEdit widget does not distinguish between events generated by the local keyboard and those sent by the remote **xtalk**. This could be confusing to the user, because text typed into the listen pane is echoed in the local listen pane, but is not sent to the remote **xtalk** program. Although we cannot intercept events generated by the keyboard, we can add an event handler that is called in addition to the one defined by the TextEdit widget. The event handler **warn_wrong_pane()** rings the terminal bell whenever the user types into the listen text pane to warn the user that he or she is using the wrong pane. This event handler examines the **send_event** member of each event to determine if the event was sent using **XSendEvent()**

```
void
warn_wrong_pane(w, client_data, event)
  Widget     w;
  XtPointer  client_data;
  XEvent     *event;
{

  /*
   * Just beep if the user types into the wrong pane.
   */
  if (!event->xany.send_event)
    XBell(XtDisplay(w), 0);
}
```

When a conversation has ended, either user can close the connection by activating the **disconnect_button**, invoking the callback function **disconnect_callback()**. This callback resets the state of the buttons and variables used by the program to their initial state, after sending an **XtNdisconnect** client message to notify the remote **xtalk** of the disconnection. Finally, **XCloseDisplay()** closes the connection to the remote display.

```
void
disconnect_callback(w, client_data, call_data)
  Widget          w;
  XtPointer       client_data, call_data;
{
  Arg wargs[10];

  /*
   * Send a disconnect notice and close the display.
   */
  if(remote_display) {
    connection_accepted = FALSE;
    xs_send_message(remote_display, remote_talker_window,
```

```
                              XtNdisconnect, my_displayname);
        XCloseDisplay(remote_display);
        xs_wprintf(msg_field, "%s", "Disconnected");
        othermachine = NULL;
        remote_display = NULL;
        XtSetSensitive(connect_button, TRUE);
        XtSetSensitive(disconnect_button, FALSE);
    }
}
```

The connection is also broken when either user exits the **xtalk** program. Therefore the **quit_callback()** function, invoked when the user activates the window manager's Quit button, also sends an **XtNdisconnect** client message to notify the remote **xtalk** that the connection is about to be closed. This function also deletes the **XTALK_WINDOW** property, to prevent remote **xtalk**s from attempting to connect to a non-existent window.

```
void
quit_callback(w, client_data, call_data)
  Widget          w;
  XtPointer       client_data, call_data;
{
  Display *dpy = XtDisplay(w);
  OlWMProtocolVerify *olwmpv = (OlWMProtocolVerify *)call_data;

  if(olwmpv->msgtype == OL_WM_DELETE_WINDOW) {
    /*
     * Inform the remote connection that we are shutting down.
     */
    if(remote_display && remote_talker_window) {
      connection_accepted = FALSE;
      xs_send_message(remote_display, remote_talker_window,
      XtNdisconnect, my_displayname);
    }
    /*
     * Clean up.
     */
    XDeleteProperty(dpy, DefaultRootWindow(dpy), XTALK_WINDOW);
    exit(0);
  }
}
```

11.4 THE X SELECTION MECHANISM

Most window systems support some mechanism for transferring information between windows. This is often referred to as "cut and paste," because the user deletes ("cuts") an object or section of text from one window and then transfers ("pastes") it into another window. Because all X applications in the user's environment do not necessarily run on the same machine, X implements "cut and paste" via an interclient communication mechanism, using the X server as a central communications point.[5]

The client messages discussed in the previous section allow applications to define their own communication protocols and provides a flexible way to exchange information. These facilities are useful when two or more programs need to define a particular style of communication, as demonstrated by the **xtalk** example. However, for this approach to work, every application involved must respond to the same types of client messages. Requiring every application to define and decipher client messages to do a simple "copy and paste" data transfer places an unacceptable burden on application programmers. On the other hand, a flexible facility that allows arbitrary data types to be copied between applications is highly desirable.

X provides several events and functions that work together to implement a flexible "copy and paste" mechanism. This section first discusses the basic concepts of this mechanism as provided by Xlib, and then demonstrates the concepts with two simple examples using some higher-level functions provided by the Xt Intrinsics.

11.4.1 Basic Concepts

X supports data exchange between applications through the *selection* mechanism. Applications can define the contents of a selection and also request the contents of the selection from another application. Selections are owned and maintained by applications, but do not necessarily represent any existing data. Some applications may choose to generate the data represented by a selection only when another application requests a copy of the selection. Multiple selections can exist at once, each uniquely identified by different selection atoms. X predefines two selection atoms: **XA_PRIMARY**, and **XA_SECONDARY**; applications can also define additional selection atoms.

Any application can claim ownership of a selection by calling the Xlib function:

```
XSetSelectionOwner(display, atom, window, time)
```

This function informs the X server that the specified window claims ownership of the selection corresponding to the given atom. The **time** argument is used to eliminate potential race conditions and should be set to the current server time. Applications can obtain the current server time from most X events. Since most applications grab ownership in response to a user action, the timestamp in the corresponding event can be used to set the time. When an application claims ownership of a selection, the X server sends a **SelectionClear** event to the previous owner to notify it that it has lost the selection.

An application can ask for the ID of the window that currently owns a selection. The function

```
XGetSelectionOwner(display, atom)
```

returns the window ID of the current owner of the selection named by **atom**. Applications should call **XGetSelectionOwner()** after they request ownership of the selection to determine if the

---

[5]   A variation on this technique is often used. Instead of deleting the object from the first window, it could just be copied. This should be referred to as "copy and paste," but often the phrase "cut and paste" is used loosely (although incorrectly) to apply to both techniques. This section actually describes "copy and paste."

request succeeded. Once ownership of the selection is confirmed, most applications visually indicate the selection, often by displaying the region in inverse-video.

The function

```
XConvertSelection(display, atom, type, target_atom, window, time)
```

allows applications to request the data corresponding to a selection. This function requests that the selection identified by the argument **atom** be stored in a property specified by the **target_atom** on the given window. In addition, the **type** argument is an atom that specifies the desired form of the selection. For example, one application might request a selection as a string, while another might request the bitmap image of the region containing the selection. When **XConvertSelection()** is called, the server sends a **SelectionRequest** event to the current owner of the selection. The owner of the selection is responsible for converting the contents of the selection to the requested type, and storing the result in the given property of the requestor's window. Afterwards, the selection owner is expected to send a **SelectionNotify** event to the requesting application to inform it that the data has been stored. The requestor is expected to retrieve the data and then delete the property.

The server reports **SelectionRequest** events using an **XSelectionRequestEvent** structure, which, in addition to the information included in all events, includes the members:

```
Window        owner;
Window        requestor;
Atom          selection;
Atom          target;
Atom          property;
Time          time;
```

This event reports the window ID of the owner of the selection and also the ID of the requestor. Three members of the event structure are atoms. The first, **selection**, identifies the name of the requested selection, while the second, **target**, specifies the data type desired by the requestor. The **property** atom contains the name of a property on the requestor's window where the data is to be stored.

After the owner of the selection converts the selection to the requested type and stores it on the given property of the requestor window, the selection owner is expected to send a **Selection-Notify** event back to the requestor. This event uses an **XSelectionEvent** structure, which includes the members:

```
Window        requestor;
Atom          selection;
Atom          target;
Atom          property;
Time          time;
```

If the selection owner is able to provide the requested type of data, the owner sets the **target** atom to the requested data type. Otherwise the owner sets the atom to the constant **None**. The **selection** member indicates the name of the selection and the **property** specifies the name of the property in which the selection is stored.

When a client requests ownership of a selection, the X server sends the current owner a `SelectionClear` event to notify the application that it has lost the selection. This event uses the `XSelectionClearEvent` event structure, which includes the members

```
Atom            selection;
Time            time;
```

The `selection` atom indicates the name of the selection that has been lost, while `time` indicates the server time at which the event occurred.

We can summarize the X selection process by looking at the sequence of steps that occur in a typical exchange. Assume there are two windows, "Window A" and "Window B," and that "Window A" currently owns a selection. If "Window B" requests the value of that selection, the sequence shown in Figure 11.4 takes place.

Window B:	Calls `XConvertSelection()` to ask for selection contents.
Window A:	Receives a `SelectionRequest` event.
Window A:	Converts the selection data to the type requested by Window B.
Window A:	Stores data on a property of Window B.
Window A:	Sends a `SelectionNotify` event to Window B.
Window B:	Receives `SelectionNotify` event.
Window B:	Retrieves data from property.
Window B:	Deletes property.

Figure 11.4 Exchanging data using selections.

Now let's assume that Window B claims ownership of the selection currently owned by Window A. The sequence in Figure 11.5 traces the steps that should occur when Window B calls `XSetSelectionOwner()`.

Window B:	Calls `XSetSelectionOwner()` to grab the selection.
Window A:	Receives a `SelectionClear` event.
Window A:	Unhighlights selection.
Window B:	Calls `XGetSelectionOwner()`.
Window B:	Highlights selection if Window B is the owner.

Figure 11.5 Gaining ownership of a selection.

11.4.2   Selections With The Xt Intrinsics

The discussion in Section 11.4.1 is a little simplistic and ignores several issues. For example, to transfer large amounts of data efficiently, applications must break up the transfer into several smaller transfers. The complete selection mechanism is defined by the InterClient Communications Conventions Manual (ICCCM). Implementing the selection mechanism as described in this manual can be quite complex. Fortunately the Xt Intrinsics provide several functions that handle most of the details and allow applications to use a much simpler interface. In addition to being simpler to use, the Xt Intrinsics allow application to view all selection transfers as being atomic. The Intrinsics break up large data transfers into smaller ones automatically and transparently.

The Intrinsics define three primary selection functions. The first of these is used to claim ownership of a selection, and has the form:

```
XtOwnSelection(widget, selection, time, convert, lose, done)
```

The first argument to this function specifies the widget that claims ownership of the atom. The second argument is an atom that specifies the selection, usually **XA_PRIMARY** or **XA_SECONDARY**. The third argument is the current server time. As defined by the ICCCM, this time should not be the constant **CurrentTime,** but instead should be obtained from the user event responsible for claiming the selection. The last three arguments specify procedures that must be defined by the application. The first specifies a procedure that the Intrinsics can call when another application requests the value of the selection. The second is a procedure to be called when the application loses the selection. The third is a procedure to be called when a requesting application has actually received the data from a request. This procedure is optional and can be given as **NULL**. **XtOwnSelection()** returns **TRUE** if the caller has successfully gained ownership of the selection.

The **convert** procedure must have the form:

```
Boolean convert_proc(widget, selection, target,
                     type, value, length, format)
    Widget          widget;
    Atom            *selection;
    Atom            *target;
    Atom            *type;
    XtPointer       *value;
    unsigned long   *length;
    int             *format;
```

All parameters except the widget are pointers. The **selection** argument is a pointer to the requested selection atom. The **target** argument is a pointer to an atom that specifies the requested type, while **type** is a pointer to the type actually returned by this procedure. The **value** parameter is a pointer to the data returned by this procedure, while **length** and **format** indicate the size of the data pointed to by **value**. If the application registers a **done** procedure, the application owns the data in **value**, and should use the **done** procedure to free it, if necessary. If the application does not register a **done** procedure, it does not own the storage associated with **value**. The **convert_proc()** callback must return **TRUE** if it successfully converted the selection and **FALSE** if it could not fulfill the request.

The **lose** procedure must have the form:

```
lose_proc(widget, selection)
    Widget  widget;
    Atom    *selection;
```

Here, **widget** is the widget that lost the selection, and **selection** points to an atom specifying the selection type.

The **done** procedure must have the form:

```
done_proc(widget, selection, target)
    Widget    widget;
    Atom      *selection;
    Atom      *target;
```

The **widget** argument is the widget that owns the selection, **selection** points to an atom indicating the selection, and **target** points to an atom indicating the type of the transferred selection.

To request a selection, an application can call the function:

```
XtGetSelectionValue(widget, selection, target, callback,
                      client data, time)
```

Here, **widget** indicates the widget requesting the selection value, **selection** is an atom indicating the selection name, and **target** is an atom indicating the requested type of the data. The **callback** argument must specify a function defined by the application. The Intrinsics invoke this function when it obtains the selection value. The form of this function must be:

```
selection_callback(widget, client_data, selection, type,
                     value, length, format)
    Widget          widget;
    XtPointer       client_data;
    Atom            *selection;
    Atom            *type;
    XtPointer       value;
    unsigned long   *length;
    int             *format;
```

The **client_data** parameter contains the client data specified by the application when registering the callback. The other parameters correspond to the data returned by the selection owner.

11.4.3 Adding Selection Capability to memo

The next two sections demonstrate the X selection mechanism using two simple programs. This section extends the **memo** program from Chapter 2 to grab ownership of the **XA_PRIMARY** selection when the user presses a mouse button in the message window. This version of memo uses a ControlArea widget to manage the message window. Like the earlier version, the message area is implemented using a StaticText widget. The application registers an event handler to be invoked when a button is pressed in the message widget. The event handler claims ownership or the selection when Button2 has been pressed. Any other button press is ignored.

```
/***********************************************
 *  memo.c: Selection Version
 **********************************************/
#include <X11/Intrinsic.h>
```

```
#include <X11/StringDefs.h>
#include <Xol/OpenLook.h>
#include <Xol/StaticText.h>
#include <Xol/ControlAre.h>
#include <X11/Xatom.h>
#include "libXs.h"

void        grab_selection();
Boolean     convert_selection();
void        lose_selection();

main(argc, argv)
  int         argc;
  char        *argv[];
{
  Widget      toplevel, msg_widget, con;
  Arg         wargs[1];
  int         n;
  String      message;

  toplevel = OlInitialize(argv[0],"Memo", NULL, 0,
                          &argc, argv);
  con = XtCreateManagedWidget("con", controlAreaWidgetClass,
                              toplevel, NULL, 0);
  /*
   * Get the contents of the command line and display it in
   * the message window.
   */
  n = 0;
  if ((message = xs_concat_words(argc-1, &argv[1])) != NULL){
        XtSetArg(wargs[n], XtNstring, (XtArgVal) message); n++;
  }
  msg_widget = XtCreateManagedWidget("message",
                                     staticTextWidgetClass,
                                     con, wargs, n);
  XtAddEventHandler(msg_widget, ButtonPressMask,
                    FALSE, grab_selection, NULL);
  /*
   * Realize all widgets and enter the event loop.
   */
  XtRealizeWidget(toplevel);
  XtMainLoop();
}
```

The **grab_selection()** event handler claims ownership of the **XA_PRIMARY** selection when Button2 is pressed by calling **XtOwnSelection()**. It confirms that it owns the selection before calling **xs_invert_widget()** to highlight the selected text. Because

xs_invert_widget() toggles the colors of the message widget when it is called, we must ensure that the widget is not accidently unhighlighted while we still own the selection. We can do this by setting the widget's sensitivity to **FALSE**, to prevent the user from selecting the widget again.

```
void
grab_selection(w, client_data, event, continue_to_dispatch)
  Widget    w;
  XtPointer client_data;
  XEvent    *event;
  Boolean   *continue_to_dispatch;
{
  /*
   * Claim ownership of the PRIMARY selection.
   */

  if(event->xbutton.button == Button2) {
    if(XtOwnSelection(w, XA_PRIMARY,
                      XtLastTimestampProcessed(XtDisplay(w)),
                      convert_selection,  /* handle requests */
                      lose_selection,     /* Give up selection*/
                      (XtSelectionDoneProc) NULL) == TRUE) {
      xs_invert_widget(w);
      XtSetSensitive(w, FALSE);
    }
  }
}
```

The function **xs_invert_widget()** retrieves the current background and fontColor colors of a widget and reverses them. This is a generally useful function that we can place in the libXs library.

```
/***************************************************************
 * invert.c: utility function for inverting a widget's color.
 ***************************************************************/
#include <X11/Intrinsic.h>
#include <X11/StringDefs.h>
#include <Xol/OpenLook.h>

xs_invert_widget(w)
  Widget  w;
{
  Arg  wargs[3];
  int  fc, bg;

  /*
   * Get the widget's current colors.
   */
  XtSetArg(wargs[0], XtNfontColor, &fc);
```

```
   XtSetArg(wargs[1], XtNbackground, &bg);
   XtGetValues(w, wargs, 2);
   /*
    * Reverse them and set the new colors.
    */
   XtSetArg(wargs[0], XtNfontColor, bg);
   XtSetArg(wargs[1], XtNbackground, fc);
   XtSetValues(w, wargs, 2);
}
```

The Intrinsics call the callback function **convert_selection()** whenever **memo** receives a request for the value of the selection. This callback function checks the requested type to be sure it is a type it can handle. In this example, **memo** can only handle requests for type **XA_STRING**. More sophisticated programs might convert to other data types before returning. If the request type is **XA_STRING**, this callback function sets the return parameters to the values corresponding to the selection and returns **TRUE**. Otherwise it returns **FALSE**.

```
Boolean
convert_selection(w, selection, target, type, value, length, format)
   Widget        w;
   Atom          *selection, *target, *type;
   XtPointer     *value;
   unsigned long *length;
   int           *format;
{
   Arg wargs[10];
   String str;
   static String savestr = NULL;

   if (*target == XA_STRING) {
     if(savestr == NULL) {
         XtSetArg(wargs[0], XtNstring, &str);
         XtGetValues(w, wargs, 1);
         savestr = XtNewString(str);
     }
     *type   = XA_STRING;
     *value  = (XtPointer)savestr;
     *length = strlen(*value);
     *format = 8;
     return(TRUE);
   } else
     return(FALSE);
}
```

The Intrinsics call the callback function **lose_selection()** when the message widget loses the selection. This function simply inverts the widget to its normal state and then restores the message widget's sensitivity.

```
void
lose_selection(w, selection)
  Widget    w;
  Atom      *selection;
{
  xs_invert_widget(w);
  XtSetSensitive(w, TRUE);
}
```

We can use this version of **memo** to see how the selection mechanism allows applications to take ownership of a selection. Try running several instances of **memo** at once and click Button2 in each of the windows. As you select each window, the message changes to inverse-video, while the previously selected window reverts to normal video.

11.4.4 A Simple Clipboard

The second part of the selection example is a program named `clipboard` that copies and displays the value of the current **PRIMARY** selection upon request. A clipboard provides a temporary place to save data. The user can select the contents of the clipboard, in the same way as the **memo** program, to allow the data in the clipboard to be transferred to another client. The main portion of the program is similar to **memo**, but rather than extracting the message from the command line, the string displayed by the clipboard is obtained from the owner of the current selection. Like **memo** from the previous section, this program creates a ControlArea widget that manages the message window. The user copies the contents of the current selection to the clipboard by selecting an OblongButton widget labeled "getselection".

```
/************************************************************
 * clipboard.c: A simple clipboard using X selections
 ************************************************************/
#include <X11/Intrinsic.h>
#include <X11/StringDefs.h>
#include <Xol/OpenLook.h>
#include <Xol/StaticText.h>
#include <Xol/OblongButt.h>
#include <Xol/ControlAre.h>
#include <X11/Xatom.h>
#include "libXs.h"

void      grab_selection();
void      request_selection();
Boolean   convert_selection();
void      lose_selection();
void      show_selection();
void      toggle_type();

main(argc, argv)
    int               argc;
```

```
    char               *argv[];
{
  Widget    toplevel, selection, request, con, toggle, quit;

  toplevel = OlInitialize(argv[0], "Clipboard", NULL,
                          0, &argc, argv);
  con = XtCreateManagedWidget("con", controlAreaWidgetClass,
                              toplevel, NULL, 0);

  /*
   * Create a button used to request the selection and
   * a text widget to display it.
   */
  request = XtCreateManagedWidget("getselection",
                                  oblongButtonWidgetClass,
                                  con, NULL, 0);

  selection = XtVaCreateManagedWidget("currentselection",
                                      staticTextWidgetClass, con,
                                      XtNstring, "staticText",
                                      NULL);

  XtAddCallback(request, XtNselect, request_selection, selection);
  XtAddEventHandler(selection, ButtonPress, FALSE,
                    grab_selection, NULL);

  XtRealizeWidget(toplevel);
  XtMainLoop();
}
```

This example defines an event handler and several callbacks. The **grab_selection()** function, registered as an **ButtonPress** event handler for the **selection** widget, is identical to the function of the same name defined for **memo** in the previous section. This function registers the functions **lose_selection()** and **convert_selection()**, also identical to those described in the previous section. Together, these functions claim ownership of the selection for the clipboard's selection widget and handle converting selection requests.

The **request_selection()** callback requests the value of the **XA_PRIMARY** selection when the user presses the "getselection" button. This function simply calls **XtGetSelection-Value()** and is defined as:

```
void
request_selection(w, client_data, call_data)
  Widget    w;
  XtPointer client_data, call_data;
{
  XtGetSelectionValue(w, XA_PRIMARY, XA_STRING,
```

```
                          show_selection, client_data,
                          XtLastTimestampProcessed(XtDisplay(w)));
}
```

Notice that the **time** argument to **XtGetSelectionValue()** is obtained by calling **XtLastTimestampProcessed()**.

XtGetSelectionValue() registers a callback function, **show_selection()**, to be called when the Intrinsics obtain the value of the requested selection. It checks the type of the data received, and if it is a string, uses **xs_wprintf()** to display the data. Notice that the **selection** widget is passed as client data.

```
void
show_selection(w, client_data, selection, type, value, length, format)
  Widget         w;
  XtPointer      client_data;
  Atom           *selection, *type;
  XtPointer      value;
  unsigned long  *length;
  int            *format;
{
  Arg wargs[2];
  if (*type == XA_STRING){
    xs_wprintf(client_data, "%s", value);
  }
}
```

Now we can combine the clipboard program with the **memo** example to experiment with transferring selections between applications. Figure 11.6 shows several instances of **memo**, and a **clipboard**. Clicking on any **memo** window causes that application to grab ownership of the selection. Selecting the **clipboard**'s "getselection" button retrieves and displays the contents of the selection. The contents of the **clipboard** can also be selected and transferred to other clipboards or any other X client that uses the selection mechanism.

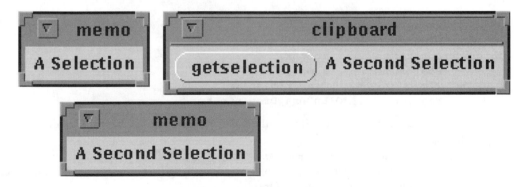

Figure 11.6 Retrieving a selection.

11.5 THE OLIT DRAG AND DROP MECHANISM

The OLIT drag and drop mechanism is built on the Intrinsics selection mechanism. The objective of the drag and drop mechanism is to allow the user to move data between applications by means of the mouse. The source application allows the user to select an object by pressing the mouse button. The user then *drags* the object to the destination application and *drops* the object by releasing the mouse button over a specified drop site. The source and destination drop sites can also exist on the same application.

The following sections describe the drag and drop transaction method and give two complete examples of both a source and destination application.

11.5.1   Dragging from the Source

The process involved in a drag operation requires several steps. First, the application must grab the pointer with

```
OlGrabDragPointer(widget, cursor, window)
```

which grabs control of the pointer. The **widget** argument is the widget associated with the drag operation, **cursor** specifies the cursor that is to be displayed, and **window** specifies the window to which the cursor should be confined. If cursor confinement is not required, set **window** to **None**.

After the cursor is grabbed the application is ready to begin the drag and drop operation by calling:

```
OlDnDDragAndDrop(widget, window, x, y, rootinfo, animate, client_data)
```

This function grabs the keyboard and handles all event processing while the user has the mouse button pressed. When the user releases the mouse button, **OlDnDDragAndDrop()** returns. This is referred to as "the drop". **OlDnDDragAndDrop()** returns TRUE unless an error occurred. The **window, x, y**, and **rootinfo** parameters are all pointers to variables that return useful information. The **window, x**, and **y** parameter specify the window and the position in that window in which the drop took place. The **rootinfo** parameter is of type **OlDnDDragDropInfoPtr** which is defined as:

```
typedef struct _ol_dnd_root_info {
        Window          root_window;
        Position        root_x;
        Position        root_y;
        Time            drop_timestamp;
} OlDnDDragDropInfo, *OlDnDDragDropInfoPtr;
```

This structure provides the root window ID and the x and y coordinates of the root window where the drop took place.

The **animate** parameter specifies the *animate notify* callback. This procedure is called when the application passes over a drop site. This is usually used to change the cursor when it passes over a drop site. The animate notify callback has the form:

```
AnimateNotify(widget, eventcode, time, sensitivity, closure)
```

The **widget** argument is the widget passed to **OlDnDDragAndDrop()**. The **eventcode** argument specifies what type of event invoked the procedure and can be either **EnterNotify** or **LeaveNotify**. The **time** argument specifies the time at which the event occurred, the **sensitivity** argument indicates whether the drop site is sensitive or not, and **closure** is the client data which was set in the **OlDnDDragAndDrop()** call.

When a drop occurs, the source application must claim ownership of the selection with:

```
OlDnDOwnSelection(widget, selection, time, convert, lose, done,
                  state_cb, client_data)
```

This function is similar to **XtOwnSelection()**. If it successfully claimed ownership of the selection, TRUE is returned. The first six arguments are identical to the arguments of **XtOwnSelection()** discussed in Section 11.4.2. The form of the **convert**, **lose**, and **done** callbacks are identical to those described previously. The last two arguments are new. The **state_cb** parameter specifies the transaction state callback that is invoked as the result of a drag and drop protocol event during the drag and drop selection transaction. The **state_cb** procedure must have the form:

```
TransactionStateCallback(widget, selection, state, time, client_data)
```

The arguments are the same as we have seen before: the widget that owns the selection, the selection atom, the time stamp, and client data. The third argument, **state**, specifies the event that has occurred and is of type **OlDnDTransactionState** which can take on the values of:

```
OlDnDTransactionBegins               OlDnDTransactionEnds
OlDnDTransactionDone                 OlDnDTransactionRequestorError
OlDnDTransactionRequestorWindowDeath
```

Next, a trigger message is sent to the destination application by calling:

```
OlDnDDeliverTriggerMessage(widget, root, x, y, selection,
                           operation, time)
```

The **widget** parameter is the widget that owns the selection. The **root**, **x**, **y**, and **time** parameters specify the root window, x and y position on the root window, and the time at which the drop took place. The **rootinfo** parameter returned by **OlDnDDragAndDrop()** contains the fields that are used for these arguments. The **selection** parameter is the selection atom sent to the destination application. The **operation** parameter must be either **OlDnDTriggerCopyOp** or **OlDnDTriggerMoveOp** which specifies either a copy or move operation.

The selection atom specified in the **OlDnDDeliverTriggerMessage()** can be a well known atom such as **XA_PRIMARY** or a dynamically allocated a transient atom. Transient atoms are allocated by calling

```
OlDnDAllocTransientAtom(widget)
```

which returns the newly allocated atom. When finished with the operation, the application should free the transient atom by calling:

```
OlDnDFreeTransientAtom(widget, transient)
```

where **transient** is the atom allocated by **OlDnDAllocTransientAtom()**.

When the selection transfer is completed, the selection owner should disown the selection by calling:

```
OlDnDDisownSelection(widget, selection, time)
```

The **widget** argument is the widget that owns the selection. The **selection** argument is the selection atom, and **time** is a time stamp.

Finally, the pointer should be *ungrabbed* by calling

```
OlUngrabDragPointer(widget)
```

The only argument is the widget which was passed to **OlGrabDragPointer()**.

11.5.2 Dropping on the Destination

The operation of receiving a drop requires that a drop site be registered. The drop site can be associated with either a widget or a window. A drop site is registered by calling either:

```
OlDnDRegisterWidgetDropSite(widget, preview_hints, sites, num_sites,
                            tm_notify, pm_notify, on_interest,
                            client_data)
```

to register a drop site with a widget, or

```
OlDnDRegisterWindowDropSite(dpy, window, preview_hints, sites,
                            num_sites, tm_notify, pm_notify,
                            on_interest, client_data)
```

to register a drop site with a window. A widget must be realized before a drop site can be associated with it.

The first argument to **OlDnDRegisterWidgetDropSite()** specifies the widget with which to associate the drop site. The first two arguments to **OlDnDRegisterWindowDropSite()** specify the display and window with which to associate the drop site. The remainder of the arguments to the two functions are the same. The **preview_hints** argument is of type **OlDnDSitePreviewHints** which can take on the values:

OlDnDSitePreviewNone	OlDnDSitePreviewEnterLeave
OlDnDSitePreviewMotion	OlDnDSitePreviewBoth
OlDnDSitePreviewDefaultSite	OlDnDSitePreviewForwarded
OlDnDSitePreviewInsensitive	

These values can be OR'd together and determine which event or events this drop site is interested in receiving during a drag across it. This is used in conjunction with the preview notify function (**pm_notify**) which is usually used to alter the appearance of the drop site when the drag cursor crosses over it. The **sites** argument is a list of **OlDnDSiteRect**s which is defined as:

```
typedef XRectangle OlDnDSiteRect, *OlDnDSiteRectPtr;
```

Recall from Section 10.3 that the **XRectangle** structure includes an x and y position, and a width and height. The **num_sites** argument specifies the number of rectangles in this drop site. The **tm_notify** argument is the *trigger notify* function. The trigger notify function is called when the source application calls **OlDnDDeliverTriggerMessage()** with the appropriate arguments to specify the destination application's drop site. The **pm_notify** argument is the *preview notify* function. When the application receives the events specified by the **preview_hints** argument, the preview notify function is called. The **on_interest** argument should be set to TRUE to indicate that the drop site is *interested* in receiving a drop. If set to FALSE the drop site will not receive a drop. Finally, the **client_data** argument is client data that is passed to both the **pm_notify** and **tm_notify** functions.

The trigger notify function must have the form:

```
TriggerMessageNotifyProc(widget, window, x, y, selection, time,
                    dropsiteid, operation, send_done,
                    forwarded, client_data)
```

The **widget** and **window** arguments specify the widget and window which own the drop site. **x** and **y** represent the x and y position, relative to the root window, where the drop occurred. The **selection** argument is the selection atom, **time** is the time stamp of the trigger message, and **dropsiteid** is the id of the drop site on which the drop occurred. The **operation** argument will be one of **OlDnDTriggerCopyOp** or **OlDnDTriggerMoveOp** which specifies either a copy or move operation. This corresponds to the **operation** parameter passed to **OlDnDDeliverTriggerMessage()** by the source. The **send_done** parameter is a Boolean which indicates whether the source application expects to be notified when the drag and drop transaction has completed. If true, **OlDnDDragNDropDone()** should be called. The **forwarded** parameter is a Boolean which indicates that the drop has been forwarded from another drop site. An example of a drop site being forwarded is when the drop site's preview hints are set to **OlDnDSitePreviewDefaultSite**. This identifies the drop site as the default drop site. If a drop occurs on the application when it is iconified, the drop is forwarded to the default drop site and the **forwarded** argument is TRUE.

The preview notify function must have the form:

```
PreviewMessageNotifyProc(widget, window, x, y, detail, time,
                    dropsiteid, forwarded, client_data)
```

The arguments are the same as the trigger notify function's arguments with the exception of the **detail** argument which specifies the type of event for which the function was called, namely, **EnterNotify** or **LeaveNotify**.

When the **send_done** argument from the trigger notify function is true, **OlDnDDragNDropDone()** should be called to notify the source that the transaction has completed. The **OlDnDDragNDropDone()** function can be called at the end of every drag and drop operation without consequence. Even when the **send_done** flag is FALSE, it is recommended that **OlDnDDragNDropDone()** be called.

```
OlDnDDragNDropDone(widget, selection, time, proc, client_data)
```

The **proc** argument is the *protocol action* callback function.

11.5.3 Adding Drag Capability to coloredit

In this section the `coloredit` program from Chapter 6 is extended to add dragging capability. A new widget is added, `display_color`, which is used to display the currently selected color and acts as the widget from which to drag. Several of the functions from the original `coloredit` program are unchanged. Only the functions that have been modified or added to the original `coloredit` program are shown here. The new program is `coloreditDnD`.

The main portion of the program is similar to the original `coloredit` with a few additional features to handle dragging. The new widget, `display_color`, has an event handler associated with it. The drag operation begins in the event handler associated with `display_color`.

```
/****************************************************************
 * coloreditDnD.c: Demonstrate "dragging"
 ****************************************************************/
#include "coloredit.h"
#include <X11/Xatom.h>
#include <Xol/OlDnDVCX.h>

static Widget display_color;
static char *supported[] = {"TARGETS", "STRING" };

main(argc, argv)
  int    argc;
  char   *argv[];
{
  Colormap  top_colormap;
  XColor    *Colors;
  int       i;
  Arg       wargs[1];
  Visual    *visual;
  void      start_drag();

 /*
  * Initialize the Intrinsics and save pointer to the display.
  */
  toplevel = OlInitialize(argv[0], "ColoreditDnD", NULL, 0,
                          &argc, argv);
  dpy = XtDisplay(toplevel);
  visual = OlVisualOfObject(toplevel);
  /*
   * If the application's colormap is readonly then
   * inform the user and exit
   */
  switch(visual->class) {
  case StaticGray:
  case StaticColor:
  case TrueColor:
```

```
    printf("Coloredit's colormap is non-writable, Exiting...\n");
    exit(1);
}
/*
 * Determine the number of colors to be edited.
 */
ncells = visual->map_entries;
if(ncells > MAXCOLORS)
  ncolors = MAXCOLORS;
else
  ncolors = ncells;
/*
 * Create a base Form widget to hold everything.
 */
form = XtCreateManagedWidget("base", formWidgetClass,
                                  toplevel, NULL, 0);
/*
 * Create the widget to display the choosen color
 */
display_color = XtCreateManagedWidget("display_color",
                                        staticTextWidgetClass,
                                        form, NULL, 0);
/*
 * Create a grid of buttons, one for each
 * color to be edited.
 */
create_color_bar(form);
/*
 * Create a Form widget containing three Sliders,
 * and three StaticTexts, one for each color component.
 */
sliders = XtCreateManagedWidget("sliderpanel", formWidgetClass,
                                  form, NULL, 0);
red_text    = make_text("redtext", sliders);
red_slider  = make_slider("red", sliders, RED);
green_text  = make_text("greentext", sliders);
green_slider = make_slider("green", sliders, GREEN);
blue_text   = make_text("bluetext", sliders);
blue_slider = make_slider("blue",  sliders, BLUE);
/*
 * Get the ID of toplevel's colormap.
 */
top_colormap = OlColormapOfObject(toplevel);
Colors = (XColor *) XtMalloc(ncells * sizeof(XColor));
for( i = 0; i < ncells; i++ ) {
  Colors[i].pixel = i;
  Colors[i].flags = DoRed | DoGreen | DoBlue;
```

```
    }
    XQueryColors(dpy, top_colormap, Colors, ncells);
    my_colormap = XCreateColormap(dpy,
                        RootWindowOfScreen(XtScreenOfObject(toplevel)),
                        visual, AllocAll);
    XStoreColors(dpy, my_colormap, Colors, ncells);
    /*
     * Initialize the pixel member of the global color struct
     * To the first editable color cell.
     */
    current_color.pixel = 0;
    XtSetArg(wargs[0], XtNcolormap, my_colormap);
    XtSetValues(toplevel, wargs, 1);

    XtAddEventHandler(display_color, ButtonPress, False,
                        start_drag, NULL);
    XtRealizeWidget(toplevel);
    XtMainLoop();
}
```

The **start_drag()** function is the event handler that is invoked when the user presses a mouse button over the **display_color** widget. The substance of the drag operation is contained in this function. A transient atom is allocated, the new cursor is created, the pointer grabbed, and then the drag begins. When the user releases the mouse button the function claims ownership of the selection and delivers a trigger message to the destination application. Finally, the pointer is ungrabbed.

```
    void
    start_drag(w, client_data, event, continue_to_dispatch)
      Widget    w;
      XtPointer client_data;
      XEvent    *event;
      Boolean   *continue_to_dispatch;
    {
      Atom              atom;
      Window            drop_window;
      Position          x, y;
      OlDnDDragDropInfo rinfo;
      Boolean           ConvertSelection();
      void              CleanupTransaction();
      Cursor            DragCursor;

      atom = OlDnDAllocTransientAtom(w);
      DragCursor = OlGetDuplicateCursor(display_color);
      OlGrabDragPointer(w, DragCursor, None);
      if(OlDnDDragAndDrop(w, &drop_window, &x, &y, &rinfo, NULL, NULL)) {
        if(OlDnDOwnSelection(w, atom,
                    XtLastTimestampProcessed(XtDisplay(w)),
```

```
                    ConvertSelection,
                    NULL, NULL, CleanupTransaction, NULL) == FALSE) {
         OlUngrabDragPointer(w);
         return;
      }
      OlDnDDeliverTriggerMessage(w, rinfo.root_window, rinfo.root_x,
                         rinfo.root_y, atom, OlDnDTriggerCopyOp,
                         rinfo.drop_timestamp);
   }
   OlUngrabDragPointer(w);
}
```

The **ConvertSelection()** function is invoked in response to the destination application calling **XtGetSelectionValue()**. **coloreditDnD** supports two targets: **TARGETS** and **STRING**. The **XtConvertAndStore()** function is used to convert the supported Strings to Atoms. If the destination application requests the **TARGETS** atom, a list of supported targets is returned. If the request is for **STRING** then a hexadecimal number representing the selected color is returned.

```
Boolean
ConvertSelection(w, selection, target, type, value, length, format)
   Widget w;
   Atom *selection, *target, *type;
   XtPointer *value;
   unsigned long *length;
   int *format;
{
   XrmValue source, dest;
   Atom targets_atom;
   char hexcolor[8];
   int  i;
   Boolean first = TRUE;
   static Atom *targets;

   if(first) {
      targets = (Atom *) XtMalloc(XtNumber(supported) * sizeof(Atom));
      for(i=0;i<XtNumber(supported);i++) {
         source.size = strlen(supported[i])+1;
         source.addr = supported[i];
         dest.size = sizeof(Atom);
         dest.addr = (char *)&targets[i];
         XtConvertAndStore(w, XtRString, &source, XtRAtom, &dest);
      }
      first = FALSE;
   }
   if(*target == targets[0]) {
      *type = XA_ATOM;
      *value = (XtPointer)targets;
```

```
      *length = XtNumber(supported);
      *format = 32;
      return(TRUE);
   }
   if(*target == targets[1]) {    /* XA_STRING */
     *type = XA_STRING;
     sprintf(hexcolor, "#%02x%02x%02x",
                current_color.red/256,
                current_color.green/256,
                current_color.blue/256);
     *value = (XtPointer)hexcolor;
     *length = 7;
     *format = 8;
     return(TRUE);
   }
   return(FALSE);
}
```

The `CleanupTransaction()` is called when a state transaction event occurs. This is usually the result of the destination application calling `OlDnDDragNDropDone()`. If the transaction is done or an error occurred, the transient atom is freed and the selection disowned.

```
void
CleanupTransaction(w, selection, state, timestamp, closure)
  Widget                  w;
  Atom                    selection;
  OlDnDTransactionState   state;
  Time                    timestamp;
  XtPointer               closure;
{
  switch (state) {
    case OlDnDTransactionDone:
    case OlDnDTransactionRequestorError:
    case OlDnDTransactionRequestorWindowDeath:
      OlDnDFreeTransientAtom(w, selection);
      OlDnDDisownSelection(w, selection,
                           XtLastTimestampProcessed(XtDisplay(w)));
      break;
    case OlDnDTransactionBegins:
    case OlDnDTransactionEnds:
      break;
  }
}
```

The other functions are identical to the `coloredit` example shown in Section 6.2.2. The one exception is the `set_current_color()` function which is the event handler invoked when the user clicks on one of the colors. The additional code sets the background color of the `display_color` widget to match the color selected by the user. These two lines are added to the end of the **set_current_color()** function.

```
XtSetArg(wargs[0], XtNbackground, number);
XtSetValues(display_color, wargs, 1);
```

11.5.4 Adding a Drop Site to draw

In this section the **draw** program from Chapter 10 is extended to add a drop site. A new widget is added, **drop_color**, which is used as the drop site. When a color is dragged from the source application (**coloreditDnD**)[6] and dropped on the drop site, the color of the drop site changes to match the color dropped on it. Objects in the drawing area will be drawn in that color. Several of the functions from the original **draw** program are unchanged. Only the functions which have been modified or added to the original **draw** program will be shown here. The new program is **drawDnD**.

The main portion of the program is similar to the original **draw** program with a few additional features to handle the drop site. The new widget, **drop_color**, is registered as the drop site widget by calling **OlDnDRegisterWidgetDropSite()**. When a "drop" occurs on the drop site the **TriggerNotify()** function is called.

```
/****************************************************************
 * drawDnD.c: Demonstrate "dropping"
 ****************************************************************/
#include "draw.h"
#include <Xol/StaticText.h>
#include <Xol/OlDnDVCX.h>
#define DISPLAYHEIGHT 60
#define DISPLAYWIDTH  60

static Widget drop_color;
static Widget lastbutton;
static Boolean SendDone;
static WidgetList *buttons;
static Atom TARGETS, STRING;

main(argc, argv)
  int    argc;
  char *argv[];
{
  Widget         toplevel, canvas, framework, command, tiles;
  graphics_data data;
  int            n;
  Arg            wargs[10];
  OlDnDSiteRect rect;
  Pixel          fg_color;
  Boolean        TriggerNotify();
```

---

[6] Sun's colorchooser program can also act as the source application.

```
toplevel = OlInitialize(argv[0], "DrawDnD", NULL, 0, &argc, argv);
framework = XtCreateManagedWidget("framework", formWidgetClass,
                                  toplevel, NULL, 0);
/*
 * Create the column to hold the commands.
 */
n = 0;
XtSetArg(wargs[n], XtNlayoutType, OL_FIXEDCOLS);n++;
XtSetArg(wargs[n], XtNmeasure, 1);n++;
XtSetArg(wargs[n], XtNsameSize, OL_NONE);n++;
command = XtCreateManagedWidget("command",
                                controlAreaWidgetClass,
                                framework, wargs, n);
/*
 * Create the drawing surface and add the
 * rubber banding callbacks.
 */
canvas = XtCreateManagedWidget("canvas", drawAreaWidgetClass,
                               framework, NULL, 0);
XtAddCallback(canvas, XtNexposeCallback, refresh, &data);

XtAddEventHandler(canvas, ButtonPressMask, FALSE,
                  start_rubber_band, &data);
XtAddEventHandler(canvas, ButtonMotionMask, FALSE,
                  track_rubber_band, &data);
XtAddEventHandler(canvas, ButtonReleaseMask, FALSE,
                  end_rubber_band, &data);
n = 0;
XtSetArg(wargs[n], XtNyAttachBottom, TRUE);n++;
XtSetArg(wargs[n], XtNyVaryOffset,  FALSE);n++;
XtSetArg(wargs[n], XtNyResizable,   TRUE);n++;
XtSetArg(wargs[n], XtNxAttachRight, TRUE);n++;
XtSetArg(wargs[n], XtNxVaryOffset,  FALSE);n++;
XtSetArg(wargs[n], XtNxResizable,   TRUE);n++;
XtSetArg(wargs[n], XtNxRefWidget,   command);n++;
XtSetArg(wargs[n], XtNxAddWidth,    TRUE);n++;
XtSetValues(canvas, wargs, n);
/*
 * Initialize the graphics buffer and other data.
 */
init_data(canvas, &data);
/*
 * Add the drawing command panel.
 */
create_drawing_commands(command, &data);
/*
```

```
    * Add a palette of fill patterns.
    */
    tiles = xs_create_pixmap_browser(command, bitmaps,
                                     XtNumber(bitmaps),
                                     set_fill_pattern, &data,
                                     &buttons);
    n = 0;
    XtSetArg(wargs[n], XtNforeground, &fg_color);n++;
    XtGetValues(canvas, wargs, n);
    /*
    * Add the drop site and initialize it to the foreground color
    */
    n = 0;
    XtSetArg(wargs[n], XtNwidth, DISPLAYWIDTH);n++;
    XtSetArg(wargs[n], XtNheight, DISPLAYHEIGHT);n++;
    XtSetArg(wargs[n], XtNrecomputeSize, FALSE);n++;
    XtSetArg(wargs[n], XtNbackground, fg_color);n++;
    drop_color = XtCreateManagedWidget("drop_color",
                                       staticTextWidgetClass,
                                       command, wargs, n);
    TARGETS = OlInternAtom(XtDisplay(toplevel), "TARGETS");
    STRING  = OlInternAtom(XtDisplay(toplevel), "STRING");
    XtManageChild(tiles);
    XtRealizeWidget(toplevel);
    /*
    * Establish a passive grab on the drawing canvas window.
    */
    XGrabButton(XtDisplay(canvas), AnyButton, AnyModifier,
                XtWindow(canvas), TRUE,
                ButtonPressMask | ButtonMotionMask |
                ButtonReleaseMask,
                GrabModeAsync, GrabModeAsync,
                XtWindow(canvas),
                XCreateFontCursor(XtDisplay(canvas),
                                  XC_crosshair));
    rect.x = rect.y = 0;
    rect.width = DISPLAYWIDTH;
    rect.height = DISPLAYHEIGHT;
    OlDnDRegisterWidgetDropSite(drop_color, OlDnDSitePreviewDefaultSite,
                                &rect, 1,
                                (OlDnDTMNotifyProc)TriggerNotify,
                                (OlDnDPMNotifyProc)NULL,
                                TRUE, &data);
    XtMainLoop();
}
```

The **TriggerNotify()** function saves a copy of the **send_done** argument in the global variable **SendDone**. This will be checked later to determine if **OlDnDDragNDropDone()** should be called. The **TARGETS** atom is interned and its selection value is requested from the source application. The **get_targets()** function is registered as the selection callback procedure.

```
Boolean
TriggerNotify(wid, win, x, y, selection, timestamp,
                 drop_site, operation, send_done, forwarded, closure)
  Widget wid;
  Window win;
  Position x, y;
  Atom selection;
  Time timestamp;
  OlDnDDropSiteID drop_site;
  OlDnDTriggerOperation operation;
  Boolean send_done;
  Boolean forwarded;
  XtPointer closure;
{
  void get_targets();

  /*
   * Store send_done in SendDone for later retrieval
   */
  SendDone = send_done;
  XtGetSelectionValue(wid, selection, TARGETS, get_targets, closure,
                      timestamp);
}
```

The **get_targets()** function is invoked by the Intrinsics when the value of the requested selection is available. The function searches the list of supported targets for **STRING**. If it is found the selection value of the **STRING** target is requested via **XtGetSelectionValue()**. If the **STRING** target is not supported and the **SendDone** flag is true, **OlDnDDragNDropDone()** is called; otherwise, **OlDnDDragnNDropDone()** is called in the **get_string()** selection callback if **SendDone** is true.

```
void
get_targets(wid, client_data, selection, type, value, length, format)
  Widget wid;
  XtPointer client_data;
  Atom *selection;
  Atom *type;
  XtPointer value;
  unsigned long * length;
  int *format;
{
  Atom *supported_atoms = (Atom *)value;
  graphics_data *data = (graphics_data *)client_data;
```

```
    void get_string();
    Boolean string_target = FALSE;
    int i;

    for(i=0;i<*length;i++) {
      if(STRING == supported_atoms[i])
        string_target = TRUE;
    }
    /*
     * If the selection owner supports the STRING target then
     * request the selection value and handle the
     * OlDnDDragNDropDone() call in the convert proc (get_string)
     * Otherwise, call OlDnDDragNDropDone() now.
     */
    if(string_target)
      XtGetSelectionValue(wid, *selection, STRING, get_string,
                          client_data,
                          XtLastTimestampProcessed(XtDisplay(wid)));
    /*
     * Inform the selection owner that we are done
     */
    else if(SendDone)
      OlDnDDragNDropDone(wid, *selection,
                        XtLastTimestampProcessed(XtDisplay(wid)),
                        NULL, NULL);
}
```

The **get_string()** function is invoked when the **STRING** selection value is available. It uses the value of the "dropped" color to set the color of the **drop_color** widget. Then the background color of the **drop_color** widget is retrieved. This is done because we need the color in pixel format. We could have alternatively used **XtConvertAndStore()** to get the pixel value directly from the color. For the new color to take effect on the next drawing operation, it is necessary to call the **set_fill_pattern()** callback procedure because that is where the GC is created that will use the new foreground color. To keep track of which button is currently selected, a new global variable, **lastbutton**, is updated each time **set_fill_pattern()** is called. It is used here to invoke the correct callback via **XtCallCallbacks()**.

```
void
get_string(wid, client_data, selection, type, value, length, format)
  Widget wid;
  XtPointer client_data;
  Atom *selection;
  Atom *type;
  XtPointer value;
  unsigned long * length;
  int *format;
{
```

```
        Arg wargs[1];
        int n;
        Pixel bg_color;
        graphics_data *data = (graphics_data *)client_data;

        n = 0;
        /*
         * We use the varargs version of SetValues here because
         * it is easier to handle the color conversion
         */
        XtVaSetValues(drop_color,
                    XtVaTypedArg, XtNbackground, XtRString,
                    value, strlen(value)+1,
                    NULL);
        /*
         * Get the pixel value so we can set the GC value
         */
        XtSetArg(wargs[0], XtNbackground, &bg_color);
        XtGetValues(drop_color, wargs, 1);
        data->foreground = bg_color;
        /*
         * The callback must be called when a color gets dropped on
         * the drop site to update the GC.
         */
        if(lastbutton)
          XtCallCallbacks(lastbutton, XtNselect, NULL);
        else
          XtCallCallbacks(buttons[0], XtNselect, NULL);
        /*
         * Inform the selection owner that we are done
         */
        if(SendDone)
          OlDnDDragNDropDone(wid, *selection,
                            XtLastTimestampProcessed(XtDisplay(wid)),
                            NULL, NULL);
    }
```

The **set_fill_pattern()** is identical to the one described in Section 10.4 except for the addition on one line which stores the selected RectButton widget in **lastbutton**.

```
lastbutton = w;
```

Figure 11.7 shows the **coloreditDnD** and **drawDnD** programs. The resources for the **drawDnD** program are unchanged from those set for the **draw** program in Section 10.4. The **coloreditDnD** program requires a few extra resources to achieve the layout shown in Figure 11.7. All the resource described in the original coloredit program in Section 6.2.3 are still required. These additional resources are also required to achieve the layout shown in Figure 11.7.

```
! Position the display_color widget
!
ColoreditDnD*display_color.width:             60
ColoreditDnD*display_color.height:            60
ColoreditDnD*display_color.recomputeSize:     FALSE
ColoreditDnD*display_color.xRefName:          base
ColoreditDnD*display_color.xOffset:           4
ColoreditDnD*display_color.yRefName:          base
ColoreditDnD*display_color.yOffset:           4
ColoreditDnD*colorpanel.xRefName:             display_color
ColoreditDnD*colorpanel.xAddWidth:            TRUE
```

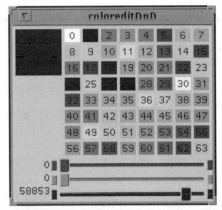

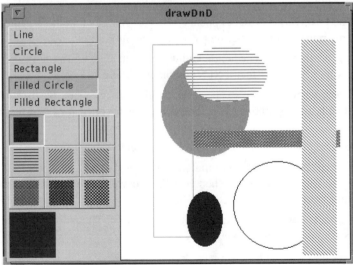

Figure 11.7 The Drag and Drop versions of coloredit and draw

11.5.5 The Drop Target Widget

The DropTarget widget automatically handles much of the drag and drop mechanism discussed thus far in this section. For example, rather than explicitly calling `OlDnDDragAndDrop()` or `OlDnDDeliverTriggerMessage()`, the DropTarget widget makes these and other drag and drop function calls. Callback functions are registered by setting resources such as `XtNdndTriggerCallback` to provide the trigger notify function.

Included here is a description of some of the DropTarget resources:

- `XtNbusyPixmap`: The pixmap to display when the DropTarget widget is busy.
- `XtNdndAcceptCursor`: The animation cursor used when the pointer crosses over a sensitive drop site.
- `XtNdndAnimateCallback`: The animate callback list. This callback list is invoked when the pointer enters a drop site.
- `XtNdndCopyCursor`: The cursor to use for a copy operation.
- `XtNdndMoveCursor`: The cursor to use for a move operation.
- `XtNdndPreviewCallback`: The callback list invoked when the destination application receives a preview notify message.
- `XtNdndPreviewHints`: The preview characteristics that the drop site is interested in receiving.
- `XtNdndRejectCursor`: The animation cursor used when the pointer crosses over an insensitive drop site.
- `XtNdndTriggerCallback`: The callback list invoked when the destination application receives a trigger notify message.
- `XtNfull`: The DropTarget widget appears *full*. This implies that there is data associated with the widget. This must be TRUE before a drag can be initiated.
- `XtNheight, XtNwidth`: The height and width of the widget. Explicitly setting the widget's height and width only takes effect if `XtNrecomputSize` is FALSE.
- `XtNownSelectionCallback`: The callback list invoked when the user releases the mouse button as part of a drag operation. This callback list is invoked for the drag initiator or source application.
- `XtNpixmap`: The pixmap to display in the DropTarget widget.
- `XtNrecomputeSize`: The size computation policy. When TRUE (default) the size of the widget reverts to the default size. When FALSE the size of the widget will be based on the `Xtheight` and `XtNwidth` resources.
- `XtNselectionAtom`: The atom to use for the selection. The atom specified by this resource is the atom used to deliver the trigger notify message.

Each callback provides an identical `call_data` parameter when the callback function is invoked. The `call_data` is a pointer to a `OlDropTargetCallbackStruct` which is defined as:

```
typedef struct {
        int                    reason;
        Widget                 widget;
        Window                 window;
        Position               root_x;
        Position               root_y;
        Atom                   selection;
        Time                   time;
        OlDnDDropSiteID        dropsiteid;
        OlDnDTriggerOperation  operation;
        Boolean                send_done;
        Boolean                forwarded;
        int                    eventcode;
        Boolean                sensitivity;
} OlDropTargetCallbackStruct;
```

The **reason** field indicates the reason the callback was invoked and may be one of:

OL_REASON_NONE	OL_REASON_DND_PREVIEW
OL_REASON_DND_TRIGGER	OL_REASON_DND_OWNSELECTION
OL_REASON_DND_ANIMATE	

The **widget** and **window** fields represent the widget and window associated with the "DropTarget event". The **root_x** and **root_y** fields indicate the x and y position of the cursor at the time the event occurred. The **selection** field represents the selection atom. The **time** field gives the time the event occurred. The **dropsiteid** field uniquely identifies the drop site. The **operation** field specifies whether the operation is a copy or move and must be one of **OlDnDTriggerCopyOp** or **OlDnDTriggerMoveOp**. The **send_done** field indicates that the destination application should complete the drag and drop transaction by calling **OlDnDDragNDropDone()**. The **forwarded** field is set to TRUE is the drop was forwarded from another drop site. The **eventcode** field indicates either an **EnterNotify** of **LeaveNotify** event occurred. The **sensitivity** field indicates whether the drop site is sensitive. A drop site that is sensitive means that it is ready to receive a drop.

Not all of the fields are valid for all callback functions. Only the ones that apply to that particular callback should be used.

The following two sections describe two applications which use the DropTarget widget to implement a drag and drop mechanism.

11.5.6 The Drag Operation with the DropTarget Widget

This section demonstrates the *drag* portion of the drag and drop transaction. The minimum steps required for an application to provide a drag are:

- Create a DropTarget widget.
- Register an *own selection* procedure with the **XtNownSelectionCallback** resource. This procedure is called to claim ownership of the selection.

- Set the **XtNfull** resource to TRUE. A drag operation cannot commence without this set to TRUE.
- Within the own selection procedure
  - Set the **XtNselectionAtom** resource to set the selection atom.
  - Call **OlDnDOwnSelection()** to own the selection. Specify the *convert selection* procedure.
- Define the convert selection procedure.

We demonstrate the drag operation by modifying the **scrollinglist** program from Section 4.3.5.5. The new application, **dragfile**, is identical in operation to **scrollinglist** with the addition of a DropTarget widget.

The object of the program is to select a file from the list and drag it. When an item from the list has been set, the drop target's **XtNfull** resource is set to true. This changes its appearance to show that it is ready for a drag operation. Pressing the SELECT mouse button over the drop target begins the drag and drop transaction. The DropTarget widget grabs the pointer and calls **OlDnDDragAndDrop()**. Releasing the SELECT button over a drop site begins the selection transaction. The deliver trigger message is sent automatically by the widget, but owning the selection is the responsibility of the application. The **XtNownSelectionCallback** specifies the function to call to claim ownership of the selection. This function is called whenever the user releases the mouse button as part of the drag operation.

The **XtNdndAcceptCursor** resource specifies the cursor to use for animation. This cursor is displayed when the pointer passes over a sensitive drop site. The cursor specified by **XtNdndRejectCursor** is displayed when the pointer passes over an insensitive drop site.

The **dragfile** program supports four targets: **TARGETS**, **STRING**, **FILE_NAME**, and **DELETE**.

```
/*****************************************************************
 * dragfile.c: Demonstrate "dragging" with the DropTarget widget.
 *****************************************************************/
#include <X11/Intrinsic.h>
#include <X11/StringDefs.h>
#include <Xol/OpenLook.h>
#include <Xol/RubberTile.h>
#include <Xol/FooterPane.h>
#include <Xol/ScrollingL.h>
#include <Xol/ControlAre.h>
#include <Xol/OblongButt.h>
#include <Xol/DropTarget.h>
#include <X11/Xatom.h>
#include <sys/dirent.h>
#include <sys/fcntl.h>
#include <sys/dir.h>

OlListToken (*AddItem)();
void        (*DeleteItem)();
```

```
void        (*TouchItem)();
void        (*UpdateView)();
void        (*ViewItem)();

typedef struct File {
  String       filename;
  OlListToken  token;
  struct File *next;
} file;

Widget      remove;
file        *head = NULL;      /* head of the list */
OlListToken lasttoken = NULL;
char        *supported[] = {"TARGETS", "FILE_NAME", "STRING", "DELETE" };
String      directory = NULL;
enum { TARGETS, FILE_NAME, STRING, DELETE };

main(argc, argv)
  int argc;
  char *argv[];
{
  int         n;
  Arg         wargs[10];
  Widget      toplevel, fp, form, sl, dt, ca, findcurrent;
  void        initList(), current_callback(), delete_callback();
  void        findcurrent_callback();
  void        dropsite_callback();
  Cursor      AcceptCursor, RejectCursor;

  toplevel = OlInitialize(argv[0], "Dragfile", NULL, 0, &argc, argv);
  /*
   * Get the command line argument, if any
   */
  directory = argv[1];
  /*
   * Create the FooterPanel and Form widgets.
   */
  fp = XtCreateManagedWidget("fp", footerPanelWidgetClass,
                             toplevel, NULL, 0);
  form = XtCreateManagedWidget("form", formWidgetClass,
                               fp, NULL, 0);
  /*
   * Create the DropTarget widget.
   */
  AcceptCursor = OlGetDupeDocDropCursor(form);
  RejectCursor = OlGetDupeDocNoDropCursor(form);
  n = 0;
```

```
    XtSetArg(wargs[n], XtNdndAcceptCursor, AcceptCursor); n++;
    XtSetArg(wargs[n], XtNdndRejectCursor, RejectCursor); n++;
    dt = XtCreateManagedWidget("dt", dropTargetWidgetClass,
                                form, wargs, n);
    /*
     * Create the ScrollingList widget
     */
    n = 0;
    XtSetArg(wargs[n], XtNviewHeight, 6); n++;
    XtSetArg(wargs[n], XtNselectable, FALSE); n++;
    sl = XtCreateManagedWidget("sl", scrollingListWidgetClass,
                                form, wargs, n);
    n = 0;
    XtSetArg(wargs[n], XtNapplAddItem,    &AddItem); n++;
    XtSetArg(wargs[n], XtNapplTouchItem,  &TouchItem); n++;
    XtSetArg(wargs[n], XtNapplUpdateView, &UpdateView); n++;
    XtSetArg(wargs[n], XtNapplDeleteItem, &DeleteItem); n++;
    XtSetArg(wargs[n], XtNapplViewItem,   &ViewItem); n++;
    XtGetValues(sl, wargs, n);
    XtAddCallback(sl, XtNuserMakeCurrent, current_callback, dt);
    /*
     * Create the ControlArea and Buttons
     */
    ca = XtCreateManagedWidget("ca", controlAreaWidgetClass,
                                fp, NULL, 0);
    remove = XtCreateManagedWidget("remove", oblongButtonWidgetClass,
                                    ca, NULL, 0);
    findcurrent = XtCreateManagedWidget("current",
                                            oblongButtonWidgetClass,
                                            ca, NULL, 0);
    initList(sl, directory);
    XtAddCallback(remove, XtNselect, delete_callback, sl);
    XtAddCallback(findcurrent, XtNselect, findcurrent_callback, sl);
    XtAddCallback(dt, XtNownSelectionCallback, dropsite_callback, NULL);
    /*
     * Realize the widgets and enter the event loop.
     */
    XtRealizeWidget(toplevel);
    XtMainLoop();
}
```

The **current_callback()** function has the same purpose as it did with the **scrollinglist** example. In addition, the **XtNfull** resource is set to true when an item in the list is selected and false when no item is selected. This changes the appearance of the DropTarget widget and allows it to be *draggable*.

```
void
current_callback(w, client_data, call_data)
  Widget w;
  XtPointer client_data, call_data;
{
  OlListToken token = (OlListToken)call_data;
  OlListItem *newItem = OlListItemPointer(token);
  OlListItem *lastItem;
  Widget      dt = (Widget)client_data;
  Arg         wargs[1];

  if(lasttoken == token) {        /* unset current choice */
    newItem->attr &= ~OL_LIST_ATTR_CURRENT;
    (*TouchItem)(w, token);
    lasttoken = NULL;
    XtSetArg(wargs[0], XtNfull, FALSE);
    XtSetValues(dt, wargs, 1);
    return;
  }

  if(lasttoken) {
    lastItem = OlListItemPointer(lasttoken);
    if(lastItem->attr & OL_LIST_ATTR_CURRENT)
      lastItem->attr &= ~OL_LIST_ATTR_CURRENT;
    (*TouchItem)(w, lasttoken);
  }
  newItem->attr |= OL_LIST_ATTR_CURRENT;
  (*TouchItem)(w, token);
  lasttoken = token;
  XtSetArg(wargs[0], XtNfull, TRUE);
  XtSetValues(dt, wargs, 1);
}
```

The **dropsite_callback()** callback is called when the drag operation is in process and the user releases the mouse button. If the **reason** field in the **OlDropTarget-CallbackStruct** indicates that the reason the function was invoked was as a result of an own selection action then **OwnSelection()** is called. This function would be easily expandable to support multiple "reasons" by adding other cases to the switch statement. The **dropsite_callback()** could then be registered as the callback for each of these "reasons".

```
void
dropsite_callback(w, client_data, call_data)
  Widget w;
  XtPointer client_data, call_data;
{
  void OwnSelection();
  OlDropTargetCallbackStruct *cd =
      (OlDropTargetCallbackStruct *)call_data;
```

```
switch (cd->reason) {
case OL_REASON_DND_OWNSELECTION:
  OwnSelection(cd);
  break;
default:
  break;
}
}
```

`OwnSelection()` allocates a transient atom and sets the `XtNselectionAtom` resource of the DropTarget widget to that atom. The `XtNselectionAtom` specifies the atom used internally by the widget. It is used as the `atom` argument to `OlDnDDeliverTriggerMessage()`. `OwnSelection()` then calls `OlDnDOwnSelection()` and specifies `Cleanup-Transaction()` as the transaction state callback.

```
void
OwnSelection(cd)
  OlDropTargetCallbackStruct *cd;
{
  Atom      atom;
  Boolean   ConvertSelection();
  void      CleanupTransaction();
  Arg       wargs[1];

  atom = OlDnDAllocTransientAtom(cd->widget);
  XtSetArg(wargs[0], XtNselectionAtom, atom);
  XtSetValues(cd->widget, wargs, 1);
  OlDnDOwnSelection(cd->widget, atom, cd->time, ConvertSelection,
                    NULL, (XtSelectionDoneProc)NULL,
                    CleanupTransaction,
                    (XtPointer)NULL);
}
```

The `ConvertSelection()` function is where much of the real work takes place. This function is called as the result of the destination application requesting a value via `XtGetSelectionValue()`. This function is very similar to the `ConvertSelection()` function shown in Section 11.5.1. The difference is the type of conversion that is done. In this example, the application is interested in providing either the file name or file contents of the selected file from the list.

The `dragfile` program supports four targets: **TARGETS**, **FILE_NAME**, **STRING**, and **DELETE**. We have already discussed the purpose of the **TARGETS** target. The **FILE_NAME** target is used to pass the name of the file. This is the preferred method since it requires only a small amount of data to pass through the server. The **STRING** target is used to deliver the entire contents of the specified file.

The **DELETE** target has a special purpose. The source application does not deliver any information back to the requestor when it receives the **DELETE** target. It is simply a message from the destination that gives the source application the "go ahead" to delete the selection. This is a common practice if the source application is doing a move rather than a copy operation. If for some reason the destination application was unable to receive the selection, then it should not request the **DELETE** target so that the source application will not delete the selection.

If the **DELETE** target is received, then the **remove** widget's callback function is invoked by calling **XtCallCallbacks()**. This invokes the **delete_callback()** function which deletes the item from the list. This does not actually remove the file from the file system, though the application could easily be modified to accomplish this if desired.

```
Boolean
ConvertSelection(w, selection, target, type, value, length, format)
  Widget w;
  Atom *selection, *target, *type;
  XtPointer *value;
  unsigned long *length;
  int *format;
{
  XrmValue source, dest;
  file *current, *findset();
  static Atom *targets;
  String file_contents, complete_path;
  String get_file_contents(), get_pathname();
  struct stat info;
  Boolean first = TRUE;
  int  i;
  long size;

  if(first) {
    targets = (Atom *)XtMalloc(XtNumber(supported) * sizeof(Atom));
    for(i=0;i<XtNumber(supported);i++) {
      source.size = strlen(supported[i])+1;
      source.addr = supported[i];
      dest.size = sizeof(Atom);
      dest.addr = (char *)&targets[i];
      XtConvertAndStore(w, XtRString, &source, XtRAtom, &dest);
    }
    first = FALSE;
  }
  if(*target == targets[TARGETS]) {      /* TARGETS */
    *type = XA_ATOM;
    *value = (XtPointer)targets;
    *length = XtNumber(supported);
    *format = 32;
    return(TRUE);
  }
  if(*target == targets[FILE_NAME]) {   /* FILE_NAME */
    current = findset();
```

```
      if(current == NULL)
        return(FALSE);
      complete_path = get_pathname(directory, current->filename);
      if(stat(complete_path, &info) != 0) {  /* make sure file exists */
        perror(complete_path);
        return(FALSE);
      }
      *type = targets[STRING];
      *value = (XtPointer)complete_path;
      *length = strlen(complete_path);
      *format = 8;
      return(TRUE);
    }
    if(*target == targets[STRING]) {    /* STRING */
      current = findset();
      if(current == NULL)
        return(FALSE);
      complete_path = get_pathname(directory, current->filename);
      file_contents = get_file_contents(complete_path, &size);
      if(file_contents == NULL)
        return(FALSE);
      *type = targets[STRING];
      *length = size;
      *value = (XtPointer)file_contents;
      *format = 8;
      return(TRUE);
    }
    if(*target == targets[DELETE]) {    /* DELETE */
      /*
       * Remove the item from the list
       */
      XtCallCallbacks(remove, XtNselect, NULL);
      *type = targets[DELETE];
      *length = NULL;
      *value = (XtPointer)NULL;
      *format = 8;
      return(TRUE);
    }
    return(FALSE);
}
```

The **CleanupTransaction()** is identical to the one used in the **coloreditDnD** example in Section 11.5.3.

The **findset()** function traverses the linked list of the **file** structures to determine which item in the list is set. It returns a pointer to the set **file** structure.

```
file *
findset()
{
  file       *filep;
  OlListItem *fileItem;

  filep = head;
  while(filep) {
    fileItem = OlListItemPointer(filep->token);
    if(fileItem->attr & OL_LIST_ATTR_CURRENT)
      return(filep);
    else
      filep = filep->next;
  }
  return((file *)NULL);
}
```

The **get_pathname()** function concatenates **directory** and **filename** and returns a pointer to the concatenated name.

```
String
get_pathname(directory, filename)
  String directory, filename;
{
  static char complete_path[1024];        /* Long enough, hopefully */

  if(directory)
    sprintf(complete_path, "%s/%s", directory, filename);
  else
    sprintf(complete_path, "%s", filename);
  return(complete_path);
}
```

The **get_file_contents()** function opens the file specified by **path** and reads in its contents. The size of the file is returned in the **size** parameter. Since a selection done procedure was not specified when ownership of the selection was claimed the storage allocated by **XtMalloc()** is freed automatically by the Intrinsics. The function returns a pointer to the file contents.

```
String
get_file_contents(path, size)
  String path;
  long *size;
{
  int retval;
  struct stat info;
  String file_contents;
  int fd;
```

```
    retval = stat(path, &info);
    if(retval != 0) {
      perror(path);
      return(NULL);
    }

    /*
     * Since we don't have a done_proc the Intrinsics will
     * free this storage
     */
    file_contents = (String)XtMalloc(info.st_size);
    if((fd = open(path, O_RDONLY)) < 0) {
      perror(path);
      return(NULL);
    }
    retval = read(fd, file_contents, info.st_size);
    if(retval != info.st_size) {
      perror(path);
      return(NULL);
    }
    *size = (long)info.st_size;
    return(file_contents);
  }
```

11.5.7 Registering a Drop Site with the DropTarget Widget

This section demonstrates the *drop* portion of the drag and drop transaction. The minimum steps required to receive a drop are:

- Create a DropTarget widget.
- Register a *trigger notify* procedure with the **XtNdndTriggerCallback** resource. This procedure is invoked when a drop is received.
- Within the trigger notify procedure call **XtGetSelectionValue()** to get the selection value from the source.

We demonstrate the drop operation by using the **scrolledwindow** program from Section 4.3.5.4. The new application, **dropedit**, contains a TextEdit widget within a ScrolledWindow widget just as did **scrolledwindow**. Rather than having a TextField widget to enter the name of the file to load into the TextEdit widget, **dropedit** provides a DropTarget widget. The DropTarget widget will receive a "drop" from another application and insert the data it receives into the TextEdit widget.

The main body of the program initializes the Intrinsics and creates the widgets.The program maintains a **SelectionClientData** structure which contains key information that is passed among various callback procedures. After creating the widgets and initializing the **SelectionClientData** structure, the application registers **dropsite_callback()** as the

XtNdndTriggerCallback callback function. This resource specifies the trigger notify function that is called when the source application delivers a trigger message. Every time a "drop" occurs over the DropTarget widget, **dropsite_callback()** will be called.

```
/*****************************************************************
 * dropedit.c: Demonstrate "dropping" with the  DropTarget widget.
 *****************************************************************/
#include <X11/Intrinsic.h>
#include <X11/StringDefs.h>
#include <X11/Shell.h>
#include <Xol/OpenLook.h>
#include <Xol/TextEdit.h>
#include <Xol/Form.h>
#include <Xol/DropTarget.h>
#include <Xol/CheckBox.h>
#include <Xol/ScrolledWi.h>
#include <stdio.h>

typedef struct {
  Boolean                send_done;
  Boolean                delete;
  Widget                 toplevel;
  Widget                 te;
  OlDnDTriggerOperation operation;
} SelectionClientData;

static Atom TARGETS, STRING, FILE_NAME, DELETE;

main(argc, argv)
int argc;
char *argv[];
{
  Widget  toplevel, form, te, sw, dt;
  Arg     wargs[10];
  int     n;
  void    dropsite_callback();
  Boolean delete;
  SelectionClientData scd;

  n = 0;
  toplevel = OlInitialize(argv[0], "Dropedit", NULL, 0,
                          &argc, argv);
  /*
   * Create the Form widget.
   */
  form = XtCreateManagedWidget("form", formWidgetClass,
                               toplevel, wargs, n);
```

```
    /*
     * Create the DropTarget widget.
     */
    n = 0;
    XtSetArg(wargs[n], XtNdndPreviewHints,
             OlDnDSitePreviewDefaultSite); n++;
    dt = XtCreateManagedWidget("dt", dropTargetWidgetClass,
                                    form, wargs, n);
    /*
     * Create ScrolledWindow and TextEdit widgets.
     */
    n = 0;
    sw = XtCreateManagedWidget("sw", scrolledWindowWidgetClass,
                                    form, wargs, n);
    XtSetArg(wargs[n], XtNwrapMode, OL_WRAP_OFF); n++;
    XtSetArg(wargs[n], XtNsourceType, OL_DISK_SOURCE); n++;
    te = XtCreateManagedWidget("te", textEditWidgetClass,
                                    sw, wargs, n);
    scd.send_done = FALSE;
    scd.te        = te;
    scd.toplevel  = toplevel;
    scd.delete    = FALSE;
    /*
     * Intern the required atoms
     */
    STRING    = OlInternAtom(XtDisplay(toplevel), "STRING");
    FILE_NAME = OlInternAtom(XtDisplay(toplevel), "FILE_NAME");
    DELETE    = OlInternAtom(XtDisplay(toplevel), "DELETE");
    TARGETS   = OlInternAtom(XtDisplay(toplevel), "TARGETS");
    /*
     * This is required to make the drop site "droppable"
     */
    XtAddCallback(dt, XtNdndTriggerCallback, dropsite_callback, &scd);
    /*
     * Realize the widgets and enter the event loop.
     */
    XtRealizeWidget(toplevel);
    XtMainLoop();
}
```

The callback we have defined, **dropsite_callback()**, only supports one **reason** but it could easily be expanded to handle multiples "DropTarget events". The **dropsite_callback()** callback checks the reason field from the **OlDropTarget-CallbackStruct** structure. If the reason the function was called was because it received a trigger message, then it saves the **send_done** and **operation** fields from the **OlDropTarget-CallbackStruct** structure in the application defined **SelectionClientData** structure and invokes the trigger notify procedure, **TriggerNotify()**.

```
void
dropsite_callback(w, client_data, call_data)
  Widget w;
  XtPointer client_data, call_data;
{
  void TriggerNotify();
  SelectionClientData *scd = (SelectionClientData *)client_data;
  OlDropTargetCallbackStruct *cd =
      (OlDropTargetCallbackStruct *)call_data;

  switch (cd->reason) {
  case OL_REASON_DND_TRIGGER:
    scd->send_done = cd->send_done;
    scd->operation = cd->operation;
    TriggerNotify(cd, scd);
    break;
  default:
    break;
  }
}
```

The **TriggerNotify()** function calls **XtGetSelectionValue()** to request the **TARGETS** target from the selection owner. The **get_targets()** function is registered as the selection callback procedure which is called when the application obtains the selection value.

```
void
TriggerNotify(cd, scd)
  OlDropTargetCallbackStruct *cd;
  SelectionClientData *scd;
{
  void get_targets();

  XtGetSelectionValue(cd->widget, cd->selection, TARGETS,
                      get_targets, scd, cd->time);
}
```

The **get_targets()** function is invoked as a result of the selection owner returning the targets that it supports. The list of supported targets is checked. This application is interested in three targets: **FILE_NAME**, **STRING**, and **DELETE**. The **FILE_NAME** target is preferred over the **STRING** target, though the application can accept either. If the selection owner can pass the name of the file, the destination application can read in the file directly and save the server the expense of sending the entire contents of the file via the selection mechanism.[7] **XtGetSelectionValue()** is called with either **get_file_name()** or **get_string()** as the selection callback procedure.

---

[7] This approach will not work in all cases. For example, if the selection owner application is running on a remote system, the file name passed by the **FILE_NAME** target may be meaningless to the receiver because the two applications are running on different hosts.

The **delete** field of the **SelectionClientData** structure is updated to reflect whether the selection owner supports the **DELETE** target.

```
void
get_targets(wid, client_data, selection, type, value, length, format)
  Widget wid;
  XtPointer client_data;
  Atom *selection;
  Atom *type;
  XtPointer value;
  unsigned long *length;
  int *format;
{
  Atom *supported_atoms = (Atom *)value;
  int i;
  void get_file_name(), get_string();
  Boolean string_target, file_name_target, delete_target;
  SelectionClientData *scd = (SelectionClientData *)client_data;

  string_target = file_name_target = delete_target = FALSE;
  for(i=0;i<*length;i++) {
    if(FILE_NAME == supported_atoms[i])
      file_name_target = TRUE;
    else if(STRING == supported_atoms[i])
      string_target = TRUE;
    else if(DELETE == supported_atoms[i])
      delete_target = TRUE;
  }
  scd->delete = delete_target;
  /*
   * Prefer to get the FILE_NAME target if available.
   * If not available get STRING target.
   */
  if(file_name_target) {
    XtGetSelectionValue(wid, *selection, FILE_NAME, get_file_name,
                        scd, XtLastTimestampProcessed(XtDisplay(wid)));
  } else if(string_target) {
    XtGetSelectionValue(wid, *selection, STRING, get_string,
                        scd, XtLastTimestampProcessed(XtDisplay(wid)));
  } else
    OlWarning("source does not support STRING or FILE_NAME\n");
}
```

The **get_file_name()** function is invoked as a result of the destination application returning the value of the selection for the **FILE_NAME** target. The **type** field represents the type of data the source application sent. **get_file_name()** accepts a type of **FILE_NAME** or **STRING**. If either of these matches the type, the function sets the **XtNsource** resource of the TextEdit widget to ***value**.

```
void
get_file_name(wid, client_data, selection, type, value, length, format)
  Widget wid;
  XtPointer client_data;
  Atom *selection;
  Atom *type;
  XtPointer value;
  unsigned long * length;
  int *format;
{
  Arg wargs[4];
  int n;
  void handle_done();
  SelectionClientData *scd = (SelectionClientData *)client_data;

  if(*length) {
    /*
     * The source may elect to specify that the filename they
     * are returning is of type STRING, so check of FILE_NAME
     * and STRING
     */
    if(*type == FILE_NAME || *type == STRING) {
      /*
       * Set the cursor and display positions to 0 before loading file
       */
      n = 0;
      XtSetArg(wargs[n], XtNcursorPosition, 0); n++;
      XtSetArg(wargs[n], XtNdisplayPosition, 0); n++;
      XtSetValues(scd->te, wargs, n);
      n = 0;
      XtSetArg(wargs[n], XtNsource, value); n++;
      XtSetValues(scd->te, wargs, n);
      n = 0;
      XtSetArg(wargs[n], XtNtitle, value); n++;
      XtSetValues(scd->toplevel, wargs, n);
    } else {
        OlWarning("get_data: not FILE_NAME or STRING\n");
    }
  }
  handle_done(wid, selection, scd);
}
```

The **get_string()** function is invoked as a result of the destination application returning the value of **STRING**. The function invokes **OlTextEditInser()** with ***value** as the buffer argument.

```
void
get_string(wid, client_data, selection, type, value, length, format)
  Widget wid;
  XtPointer client_data;
  Atom *selection;
  Atom *type;
  XtPointer value;
  unsigned long * length;
  int *format;
{
  Arg wargs[4];
  void handle_done();
  int n;
  SelectionClientData *scd = (SelectionClientData *)client_data;

  if(*length) {
    if(*type == STRING) {
      OlTextEditInsert(scd->te, value, (int)*length);
    } else {
      OlWarning("unsupported type returned by source\n");
    }
  }
  handle_done(wid, selection, scd);
}
```

Both **get_file_name()** and **get_string()** call **handle_done()**. This function determines if the **DELETE** target should be requested. Requesting the **DELETE** target does not actually return any data to this application; it informs the selection owner that the deletion of the selected data can be performed. Two conditions must be checked: the selection owner must support the **DELETE** target and the operation must be a "move" rather than a "copy" event. If both these conditions are true, the application requests the **DELETE** target with **DoneCallback()** registered as the selection callback procedure.

Back in the **dropsite_callback()** callback we saved the value of **send_done** from **OlDropTargetCallbackStruct**. Now we examine its value to determine if **OlDnDDragNDropDone()** should be called. **send_done** is set to **TRUE** by OLIT when a transient atom is being used. If it is true, we call **OlDnDDragNDropDone()** either here in **handle_done()** or in **DoneCallback()** depending on whether the **DELETE** target is requested.

```
void
handle_done(wid, selection, scd)
  Widget                 wid;
  Atom                   *selection;
  SelectionClientData *scd;
{
  void DoneCallback();

  /*
```

```
   * Only send the DELETE is it was a move operation and the
   * owner of the selection supports DELETE
   */
  if(scd->delete && (scd->operation == OlDnDTriggerMoveOp))
    XtGetSelectionValue(wid, *selection, DELETE, DoneCallback,
                        scd, XtLastTimestampProcessed(XtDisplay(wid)));
  else if(scd->send_done)
    OlDnDDragNDropDone(wid, *selection,
                       XtLastTimestampProcessed(XtDisplay(wid)),
                       NULL, NULL);
}
```

The **DoneCallback()** function invokes **OlDnDDragNDropDone()** if **send_done** is
TRUE.

```
void
DoneCallback(w, client_data, selection, type, value, length, format)
  Widget          w;
  XtPointer       client_data;
  Atom            *selection;
  Atom            *type;
  XtPointer       value;
  unsigned long   *length;
  int             *format;
{
  SelectionClientData *scd = (SelectionClientData *)client_data;

  if(scd->send_done)
    OlDnDDragNDropDone(w, *selection,
                       XtLastTimestampProcessed(XtDisplay(w)),
                       NULL, NULL);
}
```

Figure 11.8 shows the **dragfile** and **dropedit** programs. The layout shown is achieved
by setting the following resources for the two programs:

```
! DROPEDIT
Dropedit*te.background:                 white
Dropedit*te.font:                       lucidasans-typewriter
Dropedit*sw.yRefName:                   dt
Dropedit*sw.yAddHeight:                 TRUE
Dropedit*sw.xAttachRight:               TRUE
Dropedit*sw.xResizable:                 TRUE
Dropedit*sw.xVaryOffset:                FALSE
Dropedit*sw.yAttachBottom:              TRUE
Dropedit*sw.yResizable:                 TRUE
Dropedit*sw.yVaryOffset:                FALSE
!
Dropedit*dt.xAttachRight:               TRUE
```

```
Dropedit*dt.xVaryOffset:                          TRUE
!
! DRAGFILE
Dragfile*dt.xAttachRight:                         TRUE
Dragfile*dt.xVaryOffset:                          TRUE
!
Dragfile*sl.yRefName:                             dt
Dragfile*sl.yAddHeight:                           TRUE
Dragfile*sl.xAttachRight:                         TRUE
Dragfile*sl.xResizable:                           TRUE
Dragfile*sl.xVaryOffset:                          FALSE
Dragfile*sl.yAttachBottom:                        TRUE
Dragfile*sl.yResizable:                           TRUE
Dragfile*sl.yVaryOffset:                          FALSE
```

Figure 11.8 Drag and Drop between dragfile and dropedit

11.6 SUMMARY

This chapter discussed several features of X that allow applications to communicate with each other. Atoms provide an efficient way to compare strings between applications. The server assigns an identifier to a string, which is shared by applications that use the same server. Among other things, atoms can be used to identify properties, property types, and types of client messages.

Properties are collections of data, stored in the server. Every property has a name and also an associated atom that identifies the type of the data stored in the property. The X server does not interpret the data in a property, allowing applications to store and retrieve any series of bytes. Because properties are stored in the server, applications can retrieve data stored by other clients. This provides one way to share typed data between applications.

Client messages allow applications to define new event types, which applications use to communicate directly with other applications. Client messages are typed using atoms, and applications that use client messages must agree on the format and meaning of the messages.

X also provides support for exchanging typed data, using selections. Applications can claim ownership of a selection or request the owner to convert the selection to a particular type and transfer it. The server automatically handles notifications between the owner of the selection and applications requesting its contents, or applications seeking to become the owner of the selection.

OLIT provides a drag and drop mechanism built on the Intrinsics selection mechanism. Data is transferred between applications by dragging from one and dropping on another. The sophisticated protocol is simplified by means of the DropTarget widget which handles much of the drag and drop transaction for the user.

12

CREATING NEW WIDGETS

Earlier chapters discussed ways to build user interfaces by combining suitable widgets from the OLIT widget set, defining a few callbacks and event handlers, and occasionally using Xlib functions. However, many programmers eventually find that they need a component not supplied by any existing widget set. In this case, the programmer can use the architecture defined by the Xt Intrinsics to create a new widget class.

After a brief overview of the internal architecture of a widget, this chapter presents some examples that illustrate how to create new widget classes. Widgets fall into three major categories. This chapter examines the simplest type of widget: those used primarily to display information. Chapter 13 presents an example of a composite widget that manages other widgets, and Chapter 14 discusses constraint widgets, which control the geometry of their children according to some additional information associated with each child.

12.1 THE ARCHITECTURE OF A WIDGET

The Xt Intrinsics defines the basic architecture of a widget. This architecture allows widgets built by different programmers to work together smoothly. For example, the programs in this book mix the basic widgets provided by the Xt Intrinsics and the OLIT widget set. These widgets can coexist peacefully in a single application because they share the same architecture. For the same reason, it is usually possible to mix widgets from other widget sets as well.[1]

---

[1] Although this is true in theory, conflicts may arise in practice because each widget set defines its own user interface style and policy. Although the programmer *may* be able to mix different widget sets without many *programmatic* problems, inconsistencies in the interaction style and appearance between widget sets may cause a problem for the user. Many widget sets, including the OLIT widget set, define a particular style of user interface. Programmers should be aware of the human factors involved in designing a good user interface and mix widgets from different widget sets with caution.

The Xt Intrinsics defines an object-oriented architecture that organizes widgets into classes. From a widget programmer's viewpoint, a class consists of some private data structures and a set of procedures that operate on that data. Using object-oriented terminology, these procedures are referred to as *methods*.

Every widget consists of two basic components, a *class part* and an *instance-specific part*. Each of these components is implemented as a C structure containing data and pointers to methods. The Intrinsics defines the organization of each structure. All widgets belonging to the same class share a single copy of the data and methods in the class part, while each individual widget has its own copy of the data in the instance-specific part.

The structure that contains the class part of a widget is known as the *class record*, while the structure that contains the instance-specific part is referred to as the *instance record*. A widget's class record is usually allocated and initialized statically at compile time, while a unique copy of the instance record is created at run time for each individual widget. The following sections discuss the organization and purpose of each of these widget components.

12.1.1 The Widget Class Record

A widget's class record contains data and methods that are common to all widgets of the class. Since all widgets that belong to the same class share the same class record, the class record must contain only static data that does not relate directly to the state of an individual widget. For example, every widget's class record includes a field that contains the widget's class name. The class record also contains methods that define the appearance and behavior of all widgets in the class. Although most of these methods operate on the data in the widget's instance record, the methods themselves are shared by all widgets in a class.

All widget classes are subclasses of the Core widget class. This means, among other things, that the components of the Core widget's class record and instance record are included in the corresponding records of all other widget classes. The Core widget's class record is defined as

```
typedef struct {
    CoreClassPart    core_class;
} WidgetClassRec, *WidgetClass, CoreClassRec, *CoreWidgetClass;
```

where **CoreClassPart** is a structure defining the class data provided by the Core widget class. The widget class pointer for Core is declared as a pointer to the Core widget's class record:

```
WidgetClass widgetClass;
```

This is the class pointer that applications use as the **class** argument to **XtCreateWidget()** when creating a Core widget.

The Core widget's class record contains a single field, **core_class**, which is also a structure, **CoreClassPart**. The Core widget defines this structure as:

```
typedef struct _CoreClassPart {
    WidgetClass      superclass;
    String           class_name;
    Cardinal         widget_size;
```

```
    XtProc              class_initialize;
    XtWidgetClassProc   class_part_initialize;
    XtEnum              class_inited;
    XtInitProc          initialize;
    XtArgsProc          initialize_hook;
    XtRealizeProc       realize;
    XtActionList        actions;
    Cardinal            num_actions;
    XtResourceList      resources;
    Cardinal            num_resources;
    XrmClass            xrm_class;
    Boolean             compress_motion;
    XtEnum              compress_exposure;
    Boolean             compress_enterleave;
    Boolean             visible_interest;
    XtWidgetProc        destroy;
    XtWidgetProc        resize;
    XtExposeProc        expose;
    XtSetValuesFunc     set_values;
    XtArgsFunc          set_values_hook;
    XtAlmostProc        set_values_almost;
    XtArgsProc          get_values_hook;
    XtAcceptFocuProc    accept_focus;
    XtVersionType       version;
    XtPointer           callback_private;
    String              tm_table;
    XtGeometryHandler   query_geometry;
    XtStringProc        display_accelerator;
    XtPointer           extension;
} CoreClassPart;
```

We can divide the fields in this structure into two basic categories: class data and pointers to methods. The data fields include:

- **superclass**. A pointer to the class record defined by the widget's *superclass*.

- **class_name**. A string indicating the name of this class, used by the resource manager when retrieving a widget's resources. For the Core widget class, the **class_name** is initialized to "Core".

- **widget_size**. The size of the widget's instance record structure. This is usually determined using **sizeof()**.

- **class_inited**. An XtEnum value that indicates whether this class structure has been initialized. A widget's class structure is initialized only once. The widget programmer must always initialize this flag to **FALSE**.

- **actions**. A list of actions supported by this widget class, used by the translation manager.

- **num_actions**. The length of the **actions** list.

- **resources**. The list of resources used by all widgets of this class. The resource manager uses this list to initialize each widget's instance record at run time.
- **num_resources**. The length of the resource list.
- **xrm_class**. A private data field containing a representation of the widget's class name used by the resource manager.
- **compress_motion**. A Boolean that indicates whether the Intrinsics should compress mouse motion events for this widget.
- **compress_exposure**. An XtEnum value that indicates whether the Intrinsics should compress **Expose** events for this widget. Possible values are:

```
XtExposeNoCompress          XtExposeCompressSeries
XtExposeCompressMultiple  XtExposeCompressMaximal.
```

These values can also be OR'd with any combination of the following flags, which determine how the Intrinsics treats graphics exposures and NoExpose events for this widget:

```
XtExposeGraphicsExpose   XtExposeGraphicsExposeMerged
XtExposeNoExpose
```

- **compress_enterleave**. A Boolean value that indicates whether **EnterNotify** and **LeaveNotify** events should be reported to this widget if there are no other events between them.
- **visible_interest**. A Boolean value that indicates whether the widget wants to know when it is visible.
- **version**. The version of the Xt Intrinsics. This is usually set to the constant **XtVersion**. The Intrinsics checks this field at run time to ensure that the widget's and the Intrinsics' versions match. Widget writers who are sure their widgets will work with multiple versions of the Intrinsics can set this field to **XtVersionDontCheck**.

Section 12.2.3 discusses the initialization of the data in this structure in more detail, as we discuss the implementation of an example widget. The remaining members of the Core class record are pointers to the methods that determine the behavior of the Core widget class. These members include:

```
class_initialize          class_part_initialize
initialize                initialize_hook
realize                   destroy
resize                    expose
set_values                set_values_hook
set_values_almost         get_values_hook
accept_focus              query_geometry
```

Every widget class must define these methods in one way or another. They are often inherited from the widget's superclass, and some may also be specified as **NULL** if the widget class does not require the particular method. We will discuss each of these methods in Section 12.2.3 as we build a simple widget.

12.1.2 The Instance Record

Each individual widget has its own copy of a structure known as an instance record. The instance record contains the current state of the widget. For example, every widget's instance record contains the window ID of the widget's window, and also the size and location of the window. The instance record also contains a pointer to the widget's class record. Figure 12.1 illustrates this architecture, showing the relationship between the class record and instance records of several widgets belonging to the Core widget class.

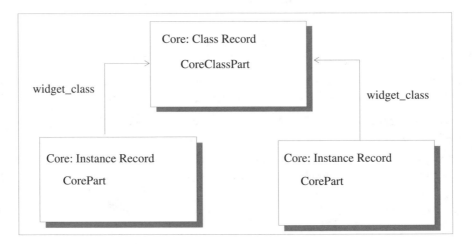

Figure 12.1 Class architecture of a widget.

The Core widget's instance record is defined as:

```
typedef struct {
    CorePart core;
} WidgetRec, *Widget, CoreRec, *CoreWidget;
```

From this definition, we might guess that when an application declares a variable of type **Widget**, it is declaring the variable as a pointer to the widget's instance record. This is true, but applications do not have access to this exact definition, because the Intrinsics uses the data abstraction techniques discussed in Section 12.1.4. The **Widget** type used by applications is declared as a pointer to an undefined structure:

```
typedef struct _WidgetRec *Widget;
```

The function **XtCreateWidget()** returns a pointer to an instance record allocated based on the **widget_size** field of the class record. The Core widget's instance record contains one member, whose type is **CorePart**. Every widget contains its own copy of this **CorePart** data structure in its instance record. In addition to general information needed by the Intrinsics to manipulate the widget, this structure caches some information about the widget's window, to reduce the need to query the server for this information. The information in the **CorePart** structure includes:

- **self**. A pointer to this instance record. The **self** member is of type **Widget**.
- **widget_class**. A pointer to the class record for this widget class.
- **parent**. A pointer to the instance record of this widget's parent.
- **name**. A string containing the name of this particular widget.
- **screen**. The **Screen** structure used by this widget.
- **colormap**. The ID of the colormap associated with the widget's window.
- **window**. The ID of the X window used by the widget.
- **x, y, width, height**. The position and dimensions of the widget's window. The type of **x** and **y** is **Position**, while the type of **width** and **height** is **Dimension**.
- **depth**. The depth of the window.
- **border_width**. The width of the window's border, declared as type **Dimension**.
- **border_pixel** and **border_pixmap**. The pixel index and tiling pattern used for the window border.
- **background_pixel** and **background_pixmap**. The pixel index and tiling pattern used for the window background.
- **event_table**. A private structure used to maintain the event mask and event handlers used by the window.
- **constraints**. A pointer to a constraints structure. This field is NULL unless the widget is a child of a constraint widget. If so, the contents of the **constraints** structure is defined by the widget's parent. (See Chapter 14).
- **visible**. If the **visible_interest** member of the widget's class record is set to **TRUE**, this flag is guaranteed to be **TRUE** when the widget's window is visible. The flag may be **FALSE** if the window is not visible, but this is not guaranteed.
- **sensitive**. If this flag is **TRUE**, the widget responds to events (i.e., the Intrinsics invoke its event handlers). If it is **FALSE**, device events are ignored, although **Expose**, **ConfigureNotify** and some other events are still processed.
- **ancestor_sensitive**. **TRUE** if the widget's parent is sensitive to events. If a widget is insensitive, its children are also insensitive.
- **managed**. **TRUE** if the widget is managed by another widget.
- **mapped_when_managed**. If **TRUE**, Xt automatically maps the widget's window whenever the widget is managed and unmaps it when it is unmanaged.
- **being_destroyed**. Widgets are destroyed in two phases. The first phase sets the **being_destroyed** flag to prevent other functions from operating on the widget while it is being destroyed.
- **destroy_callbacks**. A list of callbacks to be invoked when the widget is destroyed.
- **popup_list**. Xt allows popups to be attached to any widget. If a widget has a popup associated with it, the popup widget is listed here.
- **num_popups**. The length of the **popup_list**.

12.1.3 Inheritance

Inheritance is a powerful feature of many object-oriented systems, including the Xt Intrinsics. Inheritance allows new classes to be created that automatically have most or all the characteristics of another class, but with a few additional or different features. Inheritance allows a programmer to create a new widget class without having to program every detail of the new widget. Often, a widget programmer can design a new widget class by specifying only how the new class differs from its superclass.

Many object-oriented languages provide inheritance as part of the language. However, the Xt Intrinsics are written in the C language, which does not directly support object-oriented programming. In the Xt Intrinsics, inheritance is implemented by including the components of the class record and the instance record from each of the widget's superclasses in the new widget's class and instance records. Each widget class in the inheritance hierarchy contributes one component to these structures.

For example, suppose we want to create a new widget class whose class name is Basic. Assume that we would like this new Basic widget class to be identical to the Core widget class except that we need the Basic widget class to support a foreground pixel and a graphics context, neither of which are provided by the Core widget class. To create this new widget class, we must first define a class record for the new widget class.

```
typedef struct {
    CoreClassPart    core_class;
    BasicClassPart   basic_class;
} BasicClassRec, *BasicWidgetClass;
```

The new widget class record contains two members. The first is the same **CoreClassPart** structure used by the Core widget class. The second is the additional class part for the new widget class. The Basic widget class doesn't require any additional class resources and therefore the structure **BasicClassPart** is defined as a dummy structure:

```
typedef struct {
    int    ignore;
} BasicClassPart;
```

Next, we can define the Basic widget's class pointer as:

```
BasicWidgetClass basicWidgetClass;
```

The Basic widget's instance record consists of the **CorePart** structure defined by the Core widget class, followed by a structure defined by the Basic widget. The instance record is defined as:

```
typedef struct {
    CorePart    core;
    BasicPart   basic;
} BasicRec, *BasicWidget;
```

The structure **BasicPart** defines the new instance-specific resources needed by the Basic widget:

```
typedef struct {
    int    foreground;
    GC     gc;
} BasicPart;
```

Internally, the Basic widget's methods can refer to the **foreground** and **gc** members by accessing the **basic** field of the widget's instance record, for example:

w->basic.foreground

These methods can also access the resources defined by the Core widget class through the **core** member of the instance record, for example:

w->core.background_pixel

Figure 12.2 shows the architecture of the new Basic widget class, including the superclass pointer to the Core widget class.

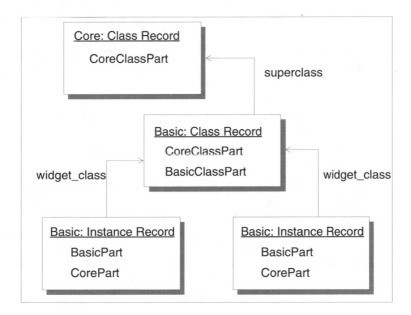

Figure 12.2 Inheriting from the Core widget class.

New widget classes inherit the resources defined by their superclass by specifically including the definition of the superclass structure in the definition of the new class. However, the Xt Intrinsics also provide a mechanism for inheriting the methods defined by a superclass. This is done in two ways. The first mechanism is referred to as *chaining*. When a method is chained, the Intrinsics invoke the method defined by each of the widget's superclasses first, before invoking the widget's method. This allows a widget to inherit part of the behavior of its superclass. The Core widget methods that are chained are:

```
ClassInitialize()              ClassPartInitialize()
InitializeHook()               SetValuesHook()
GetValuesHook()                Initialize()
SetValues()
```

For example, if an application were to create an instance of the Basic widget described in the previous section, the Intrinsics would invoke the Core widget's `Initialize()` method first, and then the Basic widget's `Initialize()` method. If needed, the Basic widget's `Initialize()` method can override any resources in the `CorePart` set by the Core widget's `Initialize()` method. If the Basic widget class requires no initialization beyond that done by the Core `Initialize()` method, the widget programmer can set the `initialize` field of its class record to NULL. In this example, the Basic widget's `Initialize()` method must create a graphics context based on the foreground color in the `BasicPart` structure and the background color found in the `CorePart` structure.

The Xt Intrinsics also provide a mechanism for inheriting methods that are not chained. This is done by using special symbols to specify the methods in the widget's class record. Each symbol is defined by the superclass that adds the method to the widget's class record. For example, the Core widget class defines the following symbols for its methods:

```
XtInheritTranslations          XtInheritRealize
XtInheritResize                XtInheritExpose
XtInheritSetValuesAlmost       XtInheritAcceptFocus
XtInheritQueryGeometry
```

These symbols can be used by any subclass of the Core widget class. They do not have to be redefined by each widget class. Only those classes that contribute new methods to the class record need to define new symbols. For example, the Composite widget class defines symbols for its new methods, including:

```
XtInheritGeometryManager       XtInheritChangeManaged
XtInheritInsertChild           XtInheritDeleteChild
```

When a widget class specifies one of these symbols in the class record, Xt copies the corresponding method used by the widget's superclass into the widget's class structure at class initialization time.[2]

12.1.4 Data Abstraction

The Xt Intrinsics use a data abstraction technique to hide the implementation of a widget from applications that use the widget. This technique involves maintaining both a private, complete definition of each widget structure, and a public, incomplete definition. Applications that use a widget see only the incomplete definition of the widget, and therefore cannot directly access fields in the widget structure. Applications declare all widgets as type **Widget**, which is known as an *opaque type*. This means the application has a pointer to the widget structure, but does not have access to the real definition of the data that it represents. Therefore it cannot access the contents of the data structure.[3]

---

[2]   These symbols are just macros that coerce the symbol _XtInherit to the appropriate procedure type.

To implement this style of data abstraction, the widget programmer must organize the widget implementation into several different files. Each widget implementation consists of one or more private header files, a public header file, and one or more C source files. The private header file contains the real definitions used internally by the widget, while the public header file contains only those definitions required by applications that use the widget.

12.1.4.1   The Private Header File

Every widget class has at least one private header file containing the complete definitions of the widget class record and instance record. Most widget classes have only a single private header file whose name, by convention, ends with the letter "P". For example, the name of the Core widget's private header file is CoreP.h. This file contains the true definitions of the **CoreClassPart** structure and the **CorePart** structure. Finally, the private header file can contain definitions of any other private data structures or variables used by the widget.

It is customary to enclose widget header files within pairs of **#ifdef/endif** statements to prevent problems if the header file is included in an application more than once. Using this convention, the Basic widget's private header file would have the form:

```
#ifndef BASICP_H
#define BASICP_H

/* Declarations go here */

#endif /* BASICP_H */
```

12.1.4.2   The Public Header File

The public header file for most widget classes is very simple and declares any public information exported by the widget. At a minimum, it contains an external declaration of a pointer to the widget class record, used by applications as an argument to **XtCreateWidget()**. For example, the Core widget class's public file, Core.h, contains only the declaration of a pointer to the widget class:

```
extern WidgetClass widgetClass;
```

The public header also often contains definitions of resource strings used by the program. Like the private header file, a widget's public header should also be enclosed within **#ifdef/endif** statements to prevent multiple definitions. By convention, the Basic widget's public header file would have the form:

```
#ifndef BASIC_H
#define BASIC_H

/* Declarations go here */

#endif /* BASIC_H */
```

---

[3]   To say that the contents of the structure cannot be accessed is really wishful thinking. In C, it is always possible to compromise the integrity of such schemes using pointer arithmetic.

12.1.4.3   The Widget Source File

The source files for most widgets have a similar structure. Each file includes both the widget class's public and private header files as well as the public and private Intrinsic header files. The file then declares forward references to the methods and other internal functions used by the widget, followed by a resource list used by the resource manager to initialize the widget's resources and a list of the actions used by the translation manager. Next, the widget's class record is statically initialized, and finally the widget's methods are defined. These methods are usually declared as static so that they are not visible to applications.

12.2 A SIMPLE WIDGET: THE DIAL WIDGET

Although at first exposure the widget architecture may seem to be complex and confusing, it is simple to use in practice. Much of the code for a widget class is "boiler plate", and is quite similar from class to class. This section provides a practical look at the widget architecture by creating a new widget class, which we will name the Dial widget class. A Dial widget displays a rotary dial, similar in appearance to an analog clock, that can be used as a gauge or valuator. An indicator, similar to a clock hand, indicates the relative value displayed by the dial. The Dial widget can display information between a range specified by any two integers.

The Dial widget defines resources that allow users and applications to control the number of markers between the minimum and maximum values, and also the position of the indicator. The Dial widget also defines a callback list that allows an application to register a function which the widget invokes when the user "selects" the widget. The widget is "selected" by invoking an action procedure through the translation manager. Figure 12.3 shows a Dial widget.

Figure 12.3 A Dial widget.

The widgets described in this and the following chapters are simple examples of typical widgets, designed specifically for this book. They are not part of the OLIT widget set nor any vendor's widget set. To avoid confusion, the names of all widgets presented in Chapter 12, 13, and 14 begin with the prefix "Xs" to indicate the X-sample widget set. Otherwise, the naming and capitalization used in the examples follow the conventions normally used by the Xt Intrinsics and OLIT widgets, as described in Chapter 2. Following widget conventions, names of widget methods have the same names as the corresponding member of the widget class record, except that the method name uses mixed case. For example, the method corresponding to the **set_values** member of a widget's core part is usually named **SetValues()**.

12.2.1 The Private Header File: DialP.h

We will begin the discussion of the Dial widget class by examining the contents of the private header file, DialP.h. We must first define a structure containing the Dial widget's contribution to the class record.

```
typedef struct _XsDialClassPart {
        int ignore;
} XsDialClassPart;
```

Even when a widget class has nothing significant to add to the class record, each widget class is expected to add a member to the class record. The Dial widget inherits directly from the Core widget class. Therefore, we can define the Dial widget's full class record as:

```
typedef struct _XsDialClassRec {
   CoreClassPart      core_class;
   XsDialClassPart  dial_class;
} XsDialClassRec;

extern XsDialClassRec XsdialClassRec;
```

The resources used by the Dial widget class are defined in the instance record. The structure **XsDialPart** defines the resources added by the Dial widget.

```
typedef struct _XsDialPart {
     Pixel     indicator_color;  /* Color of the          */
     Pixel     foreground;       /*  indicator and markers */
     int       minimum;          /* minimum value          */
     int       maximum;          /* maximum value          */
     int       markers;          /* number of marks        */
     Dimension marker_length;    /* in pixels              */
     Position  position;         /* indicator position     */
     Position  indicator_x;      /* x,y position of tip    */
     Position  indicator_y;      /*    of the indicator    */
     Position  center_x;         /* coordinates of the     */
     Position  center_y;         /*    dial center         */
     Position  inner_diam;       /* inside of markers      */
     Position  outer_diam;       /* outside of markers     */
     GC        dial_GC;          /* assorted gc's          */
     GC        indicator_GC;
     GC        inverse_GC;
```

```
    XSegment      segments[MAXSEGMENTS];
    XtCallbackList select;      /* callback list              */
} XsDialPart;
```

This structure maintains the current state of each Dial widget, and includes such things as the relative position of the indicator and the color of the markers. Some of the members of this structure (the maximum and minimum dial settings, for example) can be accessed by an application using the Intrinsics functions **XtSetValues()** and **XtGetValues()**. The widget programmer must define corresponding resources in the widget's resource list.

Other fields in the **XsDialPart** are strictly for internal use. The widget's **Initialize()** method derives some of these fields from other resource values. For example, the graphics contexts are derived from the widget's foreground and background colors. The **segments** member is an array of points that define the line segments used to draw the face of the dial. The size of this array must be defined earlier in the file. For example, here it is defined as:

```
#define MAXSEGMENTS 200
```

Having defined the **XsDialPart** data structure, we can define the Dial widget's instance record by combining the **CorePart** structure defined by the Core widget class and the **XsDial-Part**.

```
typedef struct _XsDialRec {
    CorePart            core;
    XsDialPart          dial;
} XsDialRec;
```

This completes the Dial widget class's private header file.

12.2.2 The Public Header File: Dial.h

The Dial widget's public header file defines the Dial widget's class pointer and also defines some strings used to specify resources. Widgets that define new resource names should make these names available to applications by including them in the public header file.

```
/******************************************************
 * Dial.h: Public header file for Dial Widget Class
 ******************************************************/
#ifndef  DIAL_H
#define  DIAL_H

extern WidgetClass XsdialWidgetClass;
typedef struct _XsDialClassRec * XsDialWidgetClass;
typedef struct _XsDialRec       * XsDialWidget;
/*
 * Define resource strings for the Dial widget.
 */
#define XtNselectCallback "selectCallback"
#define XtNmarkers        "markers"
```

```
#define XtNminimum          "minimum"
#define XtNmaximum          "maximum"
#define XtNindicatorColor   "indicatorColor"
#define XtNposition         "position"
#define XtNmarkerLength     "markerLength"

#define XtCMarkers          "Markers"
#define XtCMin              "Min"
#define XtCMax              "Max"
#define Xs_SELECTED         1

typedef struct {
  XEvent *event;
  int     position;
} xsdialCallbackStruct;

#endif /* DIAL_H */
```

12.2.3 The Dial Widget Source File: Dial.c

The file Dial.c contains the declaration and static initialization of the Dial widget's class record, and also contains the widget's methods. Dial.c begins by including the Intrinsics's private header file, IntrinsicP.h, the private header file of the Dial widget's superclass, CoreP.h, and the Dial widget's public and private header files. In addition, the first part of the file defines several convenient macros used by the widget, and declares the widget's methods. Notice that these methods are declared as static, making them private to this file and effectively hiding them from applications that use the widget.

```
/**********************************************************
 * Dial.c: The Dial Widget Methods
 **********************************************************/
#include <stdio.h>
#include <math.h>
#include <X11/IntrinsicP.h>
#include <X11/Intrinsic.h>
#include <X11/StringDefs.h>
#include <X11/CoreP.h>
#include "DialP.h"
#include "Dial.h"

#define   RADIANS(x)   (M_PI * 2.0 * (x) / 360.0)
#define   DEGREES(x)   ((x) / (M_PI * 2.0) * 360.0)
#define   MIN_ANGLE    225.0
#define   MAX_ANGLE    270.0
#define   MIN(a,b)     (((a) < (b)) ? (a) :  (b))

static void   select_dial ();
```

```
static void      Initialize();
static void      Redisplay();
static void      Resize();
static void      Destroy();
static Boolean   SetValues();
```

The next section of the source file defines an action list and a translations list used by the translation manager to map between a user action and a function to be invoked when the action occurs. These statements specify that, by default, the "select()" action is invoked in response to a <Btn1Down> action. An array of type **XtActionsRec** maps the "**select()**" action to a function, **select_dial()**, defined later:

```
static char defaultTranslations[] = "<Btn1Down>: select()";
static XtActionsRec actionsList[] = {
  { "select",    (XtActionProc) select_dial},
};
```

Next, we must define a resource list used by the resource manager to initialize the widget's instance record when an application creates a Dial widget. The resources are automatically stored in the appropriate fields of the instance record. The Dial widget's resource list is defined as:

```
static XtResource resources[] = {
  {XtNmarkers, XtCMarkers, XtRInt, sizeof (int),
    XtOffset(XsDialWidget, dial.markers), XtRString, "10"  },
  {XtNminimum, XtCMin, XtRInt, sizeof (int),
    XtOffset(XsDialWidget, dial.minimum), XtRString, "0"   },
  {XtNmaximum, XtCMax, XtRInt, sizeof (int),
    XtOffset(XsDialWidget, dial.maximum), XtRString, "100" },
  {XtNindicatorColor, XtCColor, XtRPixel, sizeof (Pixel),
    XtOffset(XsDialWidget, dial.indicator_color),
    XtRString, "Black"                                     },
  {XtNposition, XtCPosition, XtRPosition, sizeof (Position),
    XtOffset(XsDialWidget, dial.position), XtRString, "0"  },
  {XtNmarkerLength,XtCLength,XtRDimension,sizeof (Dimension),
    XtOffset(XsDialWidget, dial.marker_length),
    XtRString, "5"                                         },
  {XtNforeground, XtCForeground, XtRPixel, sizeof (Pixel),
    XtOffset(XsDialWidget, dial.foreground),
    XtRString, "Black"                                     },
  {XtNselectCallback,XtCCallback,XtRCallback,sizeof(XtPointer),
    XtOffset (XsDialWidget, dial.select),
    XtRCallback, NULL                                      },
};
```

Notice that only new resources added by the Dial widget class are included in this list. The Dial widget also inherits the resources defined by the **CorePart** of the widget's instance record from the Core widget class. The resource manager initializes the resources inherited from the Core widget class before retrieving the resources defined by the Dial widget. A widget can override the default values for resources defined by its superclass if necessary. However, the Dial widget does not need to override any Core resources.

12.2.3.1 The Class Record

The next step is to define the contents of the Dial widget's class record, which is initialized at compile time by declaring the contents of the structure statically in the source code.

```
XsDialClassRec  XsdialClassRec = {
    /* CoreClassPart */
  {
   (WidgetClass) &widgetClassRec,    /* superclass             */
   "Dial",                           /* class_name             */
   sizeof(XsDialRec),                /* widget_size            */
   NULL,                             /* class_initialize       */
   NULL,                             /* class_part_initialize  */
   FALSE,                            /* class_inited           */
   Initialize,                       /* initialize             */
   NULL,                             /* initialize_hook        */
   XtInheritRealize,                 /* realize                */
   actionsList,                      /* actions                */
   XtNumber(actionsList),            /* num_actions            */
   resources,                        /* resources              */
   XtNumber(resources),              /* num_resources          */
   NULLQUARK,                        /* xrm_class              */
   TRUE,                             /* compress_motion        */
   XtExposeCompressMaximal,          /* compress_exposure      */
   TRUE,                             /* compress_enterleave    */
   TRUE,                             /* visible_interest       */
   Destroy,                          /* destroy                */
   Resize,                           /* resize                 */
   Redisplay,                        /* expose                 */
   SetValues,                        /* set_values             */
   NULL,                             /* set_values_hook        */
   XtInheritSetValuesAlmost,         /* set_values_almost      */
   NULL,                             /* get_values_hook        */
   NULL,                             /* accept_focus           */
   XtVersion,                        /* version                */
   NULL,                             /* callback private       */
   defaultTranslations,              /* tm_table               */
   NULL,                             /* query_geometry         */
   NULL,                             /* display_accelerator    */
   NULL,                             /* extension              */
  },
      /* Dial class fields */
  {
   0,                                /* ignore                 */
```

```
    }
};
```

```
WidgetClass XsdialWidgetClass = (WidgetClass) &XsdialClassRec;
```

Writing a new widget primarily consists of filling in this structure with appropriate values and then writing the methods that define the appearance and behavior of the widget. The following section examines the purpose of each member of the class record in the context of the Dial example, and discusses each of the Dial widget's methods.

The structure of the first part of the Dial class record is inherited from the Core widget class. However, the Dial widget is responsible for initializing this data. The first line indicates that the Dial widget inherits from the Core widget class by specifying a pointer to the Core class record. The next line specifies the class name of the widget, "Dial". `XtCreateWidget()` uses the `widget_size` member of the class record to allocate a new instance of the widget. The `widget_size` member must be set to the size, in bytes, of the Dial widget's instance record.

In addition to the static initialization of the class record, some classes must be initialized dynamically when the first widget belonging to the class is created. The `class_initialize()` and `class_part_initialize()` members allow the widget programmer to define methods to initialize the widget's class record at run time. Because the Dial widget's class record requires no run-time initialization, these members are set to **NULL**. Regardless of whether or not the widget requires dynamic initialization, every widget must initialize the `class_inited` field to **FALSE**.

The next member of the Dial class structure points to the widget's actions list, followed by the length of the actions list. If the widget adds no actions to those defined by its superclasses, the `actions` member can be set to **NULL**, and the `num_actions` field can be set to zero.

Similarly, the `resource` member points to the widget's resource list, if the widget has one, and `num_resource` indicates the length of the list. The translation manager merges the actions list and the resources of a widget with those supplied by its superclasses.

The next four fields of the class structure define how the widget wishes to have events reported to it. The Dial widget specifies that the Intrinsics should compress all events.

The Dial widget must compute the location of the indicator on the face of the dial and draw the indicator whenever its position changes. It is therefore useful to know if the widget is visible, to avoid redrawing the indicator unnecessarily. Therefore we will set the `visible_interest` field to **TRUE**, requesting the Intrinsics to keep the `visible` member of the Dial widget's instance record up to date.

The Dial widget does not use the `dial` part of the class record and initializes its dummy member to **NULL**.

12.2.3.2   Methods

A widget's methods determine its behavior. All methods are private to the Dial widget, and the application programmer can not invoke them directly. Instead, the Intrinsics invoke a widget's methods when events occur or when an application calls the interface functions provided by the Intrinsics. For example, applications use the function `XtCreateWidget()` to create a Dial widget, the function `XtRealizeWidget()` to realize the widget, `XtManageWidget()` and `XtUnmanageWidget()` to manage and unmanage the widget, and so on. Users can also customize the Dial widget using the resource manager, and applications can use the functions **XtSetValues()** and **XtGetValues()** to set and retrieve the widget's resources. These Intrinsics functions call the appropriate methods based on the class of each particular widget.

Not every widget class defines every method in the class structure. For example, the Dial widget does not define several methods in the class record, including:

`ClassInitialize()`	`ClassPartInitialize()`
`InitializeHook()`	`SetValuesHook()`
`GetValuesHook()`	`QueryGeometry()`

The Dial widget initializes the members of the class record corresponding to these methods to **NULL**.

The Dial widget class inherits the **Realize()** and **SetValuesAlmost()** methods from its superclass by specifying **XtInheritRealize** and **XtInheritSetValuesAlmost** for these methods. The remaining methods are defined by the Dial widget class. These methods are:

`Initialize()`	`Destroy()`
`Resize()`	`Redisplay()` (expose)
`SetValues()`	

The following sections present each of the methods used by the Dial widget.

The Initialize() Method

While the class record of most widgets can be initialized at compile time, the instance record of each widget must be initialized at run time. When a new widget is created, the Intrinsics call the widget's **Initialize()** method specified in the widget's class record. This method requires two parameters, each of which are versions of the widget's instance record. The **new** parameter is the real widget, the other is a copy. Every **Initialize()** method has the form:

```
static void Initialize (request, new)
    Widget request, new;
```

Each resource in the **request** widget is set to the original value obtained from defaults in the widgets resource list, taken from values specified by the application when creating the widget, or taken from the user's resource files. By the time this method is called, the **new** structure has potentially been modified by each of the widget's superclasses' **Initialize()** methods.

In this example, Xt calls the Core widget's **Initialize()** method before it calls the Dial widget's **Initialize()** method. A widget's **Initialize()** method may therefore rely on the widget's superclasses to initialize the inherited resources in the instance record. Each widget class needs to initialize only those resources it adds.

The **Initialize()** method can also check any of the resources defined by its superclasses that it cares about and recalculate them if necessary. For example, the Dial widget's **Initialize()** method checks the size of the widget and adjusts the values if they are not acceptable. Unless the application or the user sets the size of the widget's window, it will have zero height and width at this point. The X server will generate an error if a widget attempts to create a zero width or height window, so every widget should make sure its window will have acceptable dimensions.

When changing values set by a superclass, the widget must consider both the values in **new** widget structure and the original values provided by the resource manager, found in the **request** parameter, and resolve any differences. All changes must be made to the **new** structure.

The Dial widget's **Initialize()** method is defined as:

```
static void Initialize (request, new)
  XsDialWidget request, new;
{
  XGCValues values;
  XtGCMask  valueMask;
  /*
   * Make sure the window size is not zero. The Core
   * Initialize() method doesn't do this.
   */
  if (request->core.width == 0)
    new->core.width = 100;
  if (request->core.height == 0)
    new->core.height = 100;
  /*
   * Make sure the min and max dial settings are valid.
   */
  if (new->dial.minimum >= new->dial.maximum) {
    XtWarning ("Maximum must be greater than the Minimum");
    new->dial.minimum = new->dial.maximum - 1;
  }
  if (new->dial.position > new->dial.maximum) {
    XtWarning ("Position exceeds the Dial Maximum");
    new->dial.position =  new->dial.maximum;
  }
  if (new->dial.position < new->dial.minimum) {
    XtWarning ("Position is less than the Minimum");
    new->dial.position =  new->dial.minimum;
  }
  /*
   * Allow only MAXSEGMENTS / 2 markers
   */
  if(new->dial.markers > MAXSEGMENTS / 2){
    XtWarning ("Too many markers");
    new->dial.markers = MAXSEGMENTS / 2;
  }
  /*
   * Create the graphics contexts used for the dial face
   * and the indicator.
   */
  valueMask = GCForeground | GCBackground;
  values.foreground = new->dial.foreground;
  values.background = new->core.background_pixel;
```

```
    new->dial.dial_GC = XtGetGC (new, valueMask, &values);

    values.foreground = new->dial.indicator_color;
    new->dial.indicator_GC = XtGetGC (new, valueMask,&values);

    valueMask = GCForeground | GCBackground;
    values.foreground = new->core.background_pixel;
    values.background = new->dial.indicator_color;
    new->dial.inverse_GC = XtGetGC (new, valueMask, &values);

    Resize (new);
}
```

This method begins by checking the size of the widget's window. If the user or the application specifies a size, the resource manager sets the window size before this method is called. Otherwise, we must ensure that the window width and height are greater than zero. The `Initialize()` method also checks the value of other parameters, such as the maximum and minimum dial settings, to be sure they are reasonable, and initializes derived data fields, such as the graphics contexts used by the widget.

The resource manager initializes the widget structure, using the widget's resource list, before the `Initialize()` method is called. Therefore, we can base the graphics contexts on the foreground color in the `dial_part` of the instance record, and the background color in the `core_part` of the instance record. The Dial widget's `Initialize()` method also calls the widget's `Resize()` method, which calculates the initial position of the dial markers and indicator.

The Realize() Method

The function `XtRealizeWidget()` invokes a widget's `Realize()` method, which is responsible for creating the window used by the widget. Since this method is almost always the same for each widget class, most widget classes inherit their superclass's `Realize()` method. Unlike the `Initialize()` method, the `Realize()` method is not chained. The Dial widget inherits its superclass's `Realize()` method by specifying the symbol `XtInheritRealize` in the class record. The `realize` field of the widget's class record cannot be set to **NULL** unless the widget class is never realized. Realizing a widget whose `Realize()` method is **NULL** generates a fatal error.

The Destroy() Method

Before a widget is destroyed, Xt invokes the widget's `Destroy()` method. This method is chained, although the calling order is reversed with respect to other chained methods. The function `XtDestroyWidget()` calls each widget's `Destroy()` method before its superclass's `Destroy()` method. Each widget class is expected to clean up the resources it has created. For example, the Dial widget class creates three graphics contexts and also defines a callback list that should be removed before the widget is destroyed. A widget's `Destroy()` method must not free the widget structure itself; this is done by the Intrinsics. The Dial widget's `Destroy()` method is defined as:

```
static void Destroy (w)
  XsDialWidget w;
{
  XtReleaseGC (w, w->dial.indicator_GC);
  XtReleaseGC (w, w->dial.inverse_GC);
  XtReleaseGC (w, w->dial.dial_GC);
  XtRemoveAllCallbacks (w, XtNselectCallback, w -> dial.select);
}
```

The Resize() Method

The Intrinsics call a widget's `Resize()` method whenever the widget's window is reconfigured in any way. The `Resize()` method should examine the members of the widget structure and recalculate any derived data that is dependent on the configuration of the widget's window. The Dial widget must recalculate the center of the window, the size of the indicator, and the line segments used to draw the face of the dial.

Because the X server generates an **Expose** event if the contents of a window are lost because of resize, the `Resize()` method only updates the data needed to allow the `Redisplay()` method to redraw the widget correctly and does not actually redraw the window. This method generates a set of line segments that defines the circular face of the dial, centered in the widget window. The Dial widget's `Resize()` method is defined as:

```
static void Resize (w)
  XsDialWidget w;
{
  double     angle, cosine, sine, increment;
  int        i;
  XSegment   *ptr;
  /*
   * Get the address of the first line segment.
   */
  ptr = w->dial.segments;
  /*
   * calculate the center of the widget
   */
  w->dial.center_x = w->core.width/2;
  w->dial.center_y = w->core.height/2;
  /*
   *  Generate the segment array containing the
   *  face of the dial.
   */
  increment = RADIANS(MAX_ANGLE) /(float)(w->dial.markers -1);
  w->dial.outer_diam = (Position)MIN(w->core.width, w->core.height)/ 2;
  w->dial.inner_diam=w->dial.outer_diam-w->dial.marker_length;
  angle = RADIANS(MIN_ANGLE);

  for (i = 0; i < w->dial.markers;i++){
```

```
        cosine = cos(angle);
        sine   = sin(angle);
        ptr->x = w->dial.center_x + w->dial.outer_diam * sine;
        ptr->y = w->dial.center_y - w->dial.outer_diam * cosine;
        ptr->x = w->dial.center_x + w->dial.inner_diam * sine;
        ptr->y = w->dial.center_y - w->dial.inner_diam * cosine;
        ptr++;
        angle += increment;
    }
  calculate_indicator_pos(w);
}
```

The auxiliary function `calculate_indicator_pos()` calculates the coordinates of the end point of the indicator, based on the indicator position and the size of the window. It is defined as

```
static calculate_indicator_pos(w)
    XsDialWidget w;
{
    double    normalized_pos, angle;
    Position indicator_length;
    /*
     * Make the indicator two pixels shorter than the
     * inner edge of the markers.
     */
    indicator_length=w->dial.outer_diam-w->dial.marker_length-2;
    /*
     * Normalize the indicator position to lie between zero
     * and 1, and then convert it to an angle.
     */
    normalized_pos = (w->dial.position - w->dial.minimum)/
                     (float)(w->dial.maximum - w->dial.minimum);
    angle = RADIANS(MIN_ANGLE + MAX_ANGLE  * normalized_pos);
    /*
     * Find the x,y coordinates of the tip of the indicator.
     */
    w->dial.indicator_x = w->dial.center_x +
                                  indicator_length * sin(angle);
    w->dial.indicator_y = w->dial.center_y -
                                  indicator_length  * cos(angle);
}
```

The Redisplay() Method

A widget's **Redisplay()** method is responsible for redrawing any information in the widget's window when an **Expose** event occurs.[4] A widget's **expose** member can be set to **NULL** if the widget does not need to display anything. The Dial widget's **Redisplay()** method draws the face of the dial, using the line segments calculated by the **Resize()** method, and draws the dial indicator at its current position.

The **Redisplay()** method is invoked with three parameters: the widget instance to be redisplayed, a pointer to an **Expose** event, and a **Region**. Unless the **compress_exposures** member of the widget's class structure is initialized to **XtExposeNoCompress**, the **Region** contains the sum of the rectangles reported in all **Expose** events, and the **event** parameter contains the bounding box of the region. If **compress_exposures** is **XtExposeNoCompress**, the **region** parameter is always **NULL**.

The Dial widget requests that **Expose** events be compressed, so we could use the **region** argument as a clip mask for the graphics contexts to eliminate redrawing the dial face unnecessarily. However, in this example, the graphics contexts have been created using **XtGetGC()**, which creates GCs that may be shared by others. Therefore we must not alter the GC in any way, or at least we must undo any changes immediately. For this example we will take the easy way out and simply not use the information in the **region** argument, redrawing the entire face of the dial instead.

Notice that the **Redisplay()** checks the **visible** member of the **CorePart** of the widget's instance record and redraws the dial face only if the widget is visible. The Dial widget's Redisplay method is defined as:

```
static void Redisplay (w, event, region)
   XsDialWidget   w;
   XEvent         *event;
   Region         region;
{
   if(w->core.visible){
     /*
      * Draw the markers used for the dial face.
      */
     XDrawSegments(XtDisplay(w), XtWindow(w),
                   w->dial.dial_GC,
                   w->dial.segments,
                   w->dial.markers);
     /*
      * Draw the indicator at its current position.
      */
     XDrawLine(XtDisplay(w), XtWindow(w),
               w->dial.indicator_GC,
               w->dial.center_x,
               w->dial.center_y,
               w->dial.indicator_x,
               w->dial.indicator_y);
   }
}
```

---

[4] Notice that this is one case where we cannot simply use a mixed case version of the name of the class record member as the method name. The symbol Expose is defined in X.h as an event type, using a C #define statement:

   #define Expose 12

Therefore, the C pre-processor would replace any method named Expose() by 12().

The SetValues() Method

The **SetValues()** method allows a widget to be notified when one of its resources is set or changed. This can occur when the resource manager initializes the widget's resources, or when an application calls **XtSetValues()**. The **SetValues()** methods are chained, and are invoked in superclass to subclass order.

The **SetValues()** method takes three arguments, each a version of the widget's instance record. The form of every **SetValues()** method is:

```
static Boolean SetValues (current, request, new)
     Widget current, request, new;
```

The **current** parameter contains the previous, unaltered state of the widget. The **request** parameter contains the values requested for the widget by a combination of the user's resource files, the widget default resources and the application. The **new** parameter contains the state of the widget after all superclass's **SetValues()** methods have been called. Like the **Initialize()** method, the **SetValues()** method must resolve any differences between these parameters and may override any values that it wishes. All changes must be made to the **new** widget. Notice that at this point the Intrinsics layer has already changed the requested values in the **new** widget. The **SetValues()** method's primary task is to generate any data derived from parameters that have changed and check that all requested values are acceptable.

The **SetValues()** method returns a Boolean value indicating whether the widget should be redrawn. If this value is **TRUE**, the Intrinsics cause an **Expose** event to be generated for the entire window. Because the **SetValues()** method can be invoked at any time, it must not assume that the widget is realized. Therefore, this method must not perform any graphics operations on the widget's window (which might not exist yet) unless the widget is realized.

The Dial widget's **SetValues()** method checks the minimum and maximum values of the dial to ensure that they are reasonable, and resets the values if they are out of range. If the foreground or background colors have changed, we must create new graphics contexts. Last, if the dial position has changed, the method calls the auxiliary function **calculate_indicator_pos()** to calculate the new position of the indicator. If only the position of the indicator has changed, and the redraw flag is still **FALSE**, the old indicator is erased by drawing it with the inverse GC, and then displayed at the new position by drawing it with the normal GC. Notice that when erasing the indicator both the old position and the old graphics context are obtained from the **current** widget, in case the indicator moves and changes color at the same time.

The Dial widget's **SetValues()** method is defined as:

```
static Boolean SetValues (current, request, new)
  XsDialWidget current, request, new;
{
  XGCValues   values;
  XtGCMask    valueMask;
  Boolean     redraw = FALSE;
  Boolean     redraw_indicator = FALSE;

  /*
```

```
     * Make sure the new dial values are reasonable.
     */
    if (new->dial.minimum >= new->dial.maximum) {
      XtWarning ("Minimum must be less than Maximum");
      new->dial.minimum = 0;
      new->dial.maximum = 100;
    }
    if (new->dial.position > new->dial.maximum) {
      XtWarning("Dial position is greater than the Maximum");
      new->dial.position = new->dial.maximum;
    }
    if (new->dial.position < new->dial.minimum) {
      XtWarning("Dial position is less than the Minimum");
      new->dial.position = new->dial.minimum;
    }
    /*
     * If the indicator color or background color
     * has changed, generate the GC's.
     */
  if(new->dial.indicator_color!=current->dial.indicator_color||
   new->core.background_pixel !=current->core.background_pixel){
      valueMask = GCForeground | GCBackground;
      values.foreground = new->dial.indicator_color;
      values.background = new->core.background_pixel;
      XtReleaseGC(new, new->dial.indicator_GC);
      new->dial.indicator_GC = XtGetGC(new, valueMask,&values);
      values.foreground = new->core.background_pixel;
      values.background = new->dial.indicator_color;
      XtReleaseGC(new, new->dial.inverse_GC);
      new->dial.inverse_GC = XtGetGC(new, valueMask, &values);
      redraw_indicator = TRUE;
    }
    /*
     * If the marker color has changed, generate the GC.
     */
    if (new->dial.foreground != current->dial.foreground){
      valueMask = GCForeground | GCBackground;
      values.foreground = new->dial.foreground;
      values.background = new->core.background_pixel;
      XtReleaseGC(new, new->dial.dial_GC);
      new->dial.dial_GC = XtGetGC (new, valueMask, &values);
      redraw = TRUE;
    }
    /*
     * If the indicator position has changed, or if the min/max
     * values have changed, recompute the indicator coordinates.
     */
```

```
    if (new->dial.position != current->dial.position ||
        new->dial.minimum != current->dial.minimum ||
        new->dial.maximum != current->dial.maximum){
      calculate_indicator_pos(new);
      redraw_indicator = TRUE;
    }
    /*
     * If only the indicator needs to be redrawn and
     * the widget is realized, erase the current indicator
     * and draw the new one.
     */
    if(redraw_indicator && ! redraw &&
       XtIsRealized(new) && new->core.visible){
      XDrawLine(XtDisplay(current), XtWindow(current),
                current->dial.inverse_GC,
                current->dial.center_x,
                current->dial.center_y,
                current->dial.indicator_x,
                current->dial.indicator_y);
      XDrawLine(XtDisplay(new), XtWindow(new),
                new->dial.indicator_GC,
                new->dial.center_x,
                new->dial.center_y,
                new->dial.indicator_x,
                new->dial.indicator_y);
    }
    return (redraw);
}
```

12.2.3.3   Defining Action Procedures

The last procedure defined by the Dial widget is not a method, but is specified in the list of actions defined at the beginning of the file. This list associates an action named "**select()**" with a function **select_dial()**. By default, the "**select()**" action is bound to the user event <**Btn1Down**>. The actions provided by a widget are entirely up to the widget programmer. The Dial widget assumes that the "**select()**" action is the result of a mouse button event, and calculates the position of the indicator based on the coordinates of the mouse event. The position is then used in the **call_data** argument to the **XtNselectCallback** list. This callback list is defined in the Dial widget's instance record. The **select_dial()** procedure uses **XtCallCallbacks()** to invoke any **XtNselectCallback** functions registered by the application programmer. The **select_dial()** function is defined as:

```
    static void select_dial (w, event, args, n_args)
      XsDialWidget   w;
      XEvent         *event;
      char           *args[];
      int            n_args;
```

```
{
    Position    pos;
    double      angle;
    xsdialCallbackStruct cb;

    pos = w->dial.position;
    if(event->type == ButtonPress ||
           event->type == MotionNotify){
      /*
       * Get the angle in radians.
       */
      angle=atan2((double)(event->xbutton.y - w->dial.center_y),
                  (double)(event->xbutton.x - w->dial.center_x));
      /*
       * Convert to degrees from the MIN_ANGLE.
       */
      angle = DEGREES(angle) - (MIN_ANGLE - 90.0);
      if (angle < 0)
        angle = 360.0 + angle;
      /*
       * Convert the angle to a position.
       */
      pos = w->dial.minimum + (angle /
                MAX_ANGLE * (w->dial.maximum - w->dial.minimum));
   }
   /*
     * Invoke the callback, report the position in the call_data
     * structure
     */
   cb.event     = event;
   cb.position = pos;
   XtCallCallbacks (w, XtNselectCallback, &cb);
}
```

This concludes the implementation of our first widget. Because the Dial widget uses the architecture and follows the basic conventions of the Xt Intrinsics, it can be combined freely with other widgets in applications. The following section looks at an example program that exercises the Dial widget.

12.2.4 Using The Dial Widget

In this section, we will look at an application of the Dial widget described in the previous section. This simple example creates a single Dial widget and defines a callback that moves the dial indicator to the position of the pointer when the user clicks the mouse within the Dial window.

Every application that uses the Dial widget must include the Intrinsic.h header file and also the Dial widget's public header file, Dial.h. After initializing the Intrinsics, the program creates a Dial widget using **XtCreateManagedWidget()**, and adds a function to the widget's **XtNselect-Callback** list. After realizing the toplevel widget, the application enters the main event loop. At this point, a single Dial widget, similar to the image in Figure 12.3, should appear on the screen.

```
/********************************************************
 * dial.c : test the Dial widget class
 ********************************************************/
#include <X11/Intrinsic.h>
#include <Xol/OpenLook.h>
#include "Dial.h"

void select_callback();

main(argc, argv)
  int    argc;
  char *argv[];
{
  Widget toplevel, dial;

  /*
   * Initialize the Intrinsics.
   */
  toplevel = OlInitialize(argv[0], "DialTest", NULL, 0, &argc, argv);
  /*
   * Create a dial widget and add a select callback.
   */
  dial = XtCreateManagedWidget("dial", XsdialWidgetClass,
                                toplevel, NULL, 0);
  XtAddCallback(dial, XtNselectCallback,
                select_callback, NULL);
  XtRealizeWidget(toplevel);
  XtMainLoop();
}
```

The callback function **select_callback()** uses **XtSetValues()** to reposition the dial indicator. The Dial widget's **XtNselectCallback** provides the position of the indicator corresponding to the location of the pointer in the **call_data** argument, but does not move the indicator. The application can use **XtSetValues()** to move the Dial widget's indicator to the position reported in the call data, if desired. The **select_callback()** function is defined as:

```
void
select_callback(w, client_data, call_data)
  Widget     w;
  XtPointer  client_data;
  XtPointer  call_data;
{
  Arg wargs[1];
  xsdialCallbackStruct *cb = (xsdialCallbackStruct *)call_data;
```

```
    XtSetArg(wargs[0], XtNposition, cb->position);
    XtSetValues(w, wargs, 1);
}
```

12.2.5 Compiling the Dial Widget Example

Since we may want to use the Dial widget in many applications, it is useful to place the widget in the libXs library where it can be linked with applications that use it. We can add the Dial widget to the library in the same way as any other functions.

```
cc -c Dial.c
ar ruv libXs.a Dial.o
```

Then the **dial** example can be compiled and linked with the command:

```
cc -o dial dial.c -lXs -lXt -lX11 -lm
```

12.3 USING INHERITANCE: THE SQUAREDIAL WIDGET

Programmers often find that they need a widget similar to, but not exactly like, an existing widget. In this case, it is often easiest to create a new widget class by inheriting from the existing, similar widget class. We used inheritance in the previous section (the Dial widget class inherits from the Core widget class), but it is possible to go further and inherit from any widget that meets our needs, not just the meta classes provided by the Xt Intrinsics and OLIT.

Let's illustrate this with a simple example. Suppose the Dial example of this chapter is almost what we need, except that we would like markers on the dial face to be square instead of round. We could, of course, write a whole new widget class that creates the square dial face. This new class would also have to duplicate everything the Dial class already does. It is much faster and simpler to inherit from the Dial class and reuse some of the work we did in the Dial widget.

12.3.1 The Private Header File: SquareDialP.h

As with any widget class, we must create a new private header file containing the definition of the SquareDial widget's class record and instance record. The file SquareDialP.h defines a dummy SquareDial class part.

```
typedef struct _XsSquareDialClassPart {
    int ignore;
} XsSquareDialClassPart;
```

The class record for the new class is defined by adding the SquareDial class part to the Core and Dial widget class parts.

```
typedef struct _XsSquareDialClassRec {
   CoreClassPart           core_class;
   XsDialClassPart         dial_class;
   XsSquareDialClassPart   square_dial_class;
} XsSquareDialClassRec;

extern XsSquareDialClassRec XssquareDialClassRec;
```

The SquareDial widget class's contribution to the instance record is also a dummy structure, because we are only going to change the way the new widget displays information and no new resources are required. This dummy structure is added to the instance record after the Dial widget's contribution to the instance record.

```
typedef struct _XsSquareDialPart {
   int ignore;
} XsSquareDialPart;

typedef struct _XsSquareDialRec {
   CorePart          core;
   XsDialPart        dial;
   XsSquareDialPart  squaredial;
} XsSquareDialRec;
```

12.3.2 The Public Header File: SquareDial.h

The public header file contains the public declarations of the SquareDial widget class, and defines the same strings used by the Dial widget class. If we were creating a entire set of widgets, we could define these resources in a header file shared by all widgets in the set. For now, it is easier to just include the file Dial.h.

```
/*******************************************************
 * SquareDial.h:The SquareDial widget public header file.
 *******************************************************/
#ifndef  SQUAREDIAL_H
#define  SQUAREDIAL_H
#include "Dial.h"

extern WidgetClass XssquareDialWidgetClass;

typedef struct _XsSquareDialClassRec *XsSquareDialWidgetClass;
typedef struct _XsSquareDialRec       *XsSquareDialWidget;

#endif /* SQUAREDIAL_H */
```

12.3.3 The Source File: SquareDial.c

The source file of the new widget class must initialize the class record of the new widget class and
define any new methods used by the widget. The SquareDial widget class only defines two methods,
the `Initialize()`, and `Resize()` methods. The `Initialize()` method is called in addition
to the Dial widget's `Initialize()` method, while the `Resize()` method is called instead of the
Dial widget's `Resize()` method. The SquareDial class inherits the Dial widget class's
`Redisplay()` method and also its translations. Notice that SquareDial.c includes the Dial widget's private header file. The initial declarations and class initialization of the SquareDial widget
class is done as follows:

```
/******************************************************
 * SquareDial.c: A subclass of the Dial widget class
 ******************************************************/
#include <stdio.h>
#include <X11/IntrinsicP.h>
#include <X11/Intrinsic.h>
#include <X11/StringDefs.h>
#include <X11/CoreP.h>
#include "DialP.h"
#include "Dial.h"
#include "SquareDialP.h"
#include "SquareDial.h"
#define   MIN(a,b)    (((a) < (b)) ? (a) :   (b))
static void Resize();
static void Initialize();

XsSquareDialClassRec  XssquareDialClassRec = {
/* CoreClassPart */
  {
    (WidgetClass) &XsdialClassRec,    /* superclass          */
    "SquareDial",                     /* class_name          */
    sizeof(XsSquareDialRec),          /* widget_size         */
    NULL,                             /* class_initialize    */
    NULL,                             /* class_part_initialize */
    FALSE,                            /* class_inited        */
    (XtWidgetProc) Initialize,        /* initialize          */
    NULL,                             /* initialize_hook     */
    XtInheritRealize,                 /* realize             */
    NULL,                             /* actions             */
    0,                                /* num_actions         */
    NULL,                             /* resources           */
    0,                                /* num_resources       */
    NULLQUARK,                        /* xrm_class           */
    TRUE,                             /* compress_motion     */
    XtExposeCompressMaximal,          /* compress_exposure   */
    TRUE,                             /* compress_enterleave */
```

```
   TRUE,                              /* visible_interest    */
   NULL,                              /* destroy             */
   (XtWidgetProc) Resize,             /* resize              */
   XtInheritExpose,                   /* expose              */
   NULL,                              /* set_values          */
   NULL,                              /* set_values_hook     */
   XtInheritSetValuesAlmost,          /* set_values_almost   */
   NULL,                              /* get_values_hook     */
   XtInheritAcceptFocus,              /* accept_focus        */
   XtVersion,                         /* version             */
   NULL,                              /* callback private    */
   XtInheritTranslations,             /* tm_table            */
   NULL,                              /* query_geometry      */
   NULL,                              /* display_accelerator */
   NULL                               /* extension           */
   },
      /* Dial class fields */
   {
   0,                                 /* ignore              */
   },
      /* Square Dial class fields */
   {
   0,                                 /* ignore              */
   }
};


WidgetClass XssquareDialWidgetClass =
        (WidgetClass) &XssquareDialClassRec;
```

The SquareDial **Initialize()** method simply calls the SquareDial widget's **Resize()** method to override some of the calculations done by the Dial widget class's **Initialize()** method.

```
static void Initialize(request, new)
  XsSquareDialWidget      request, new;
{
  Resize(new);
}
```

Finally, the SquareDial widget class defines its own **Resize()** method. **Resize()** recomputes the line segments that represent the face of the dial as a square rather than a circle. We can rely on the inherited **Redisplay()** method to actually draw the segments.

```
static void Resize(w)
  XsSquareDialWidget      w;
{
  int          marks_per_side, h_increment, v_increment, i;
  XSegment *ptr;
```

```
    /*
     * Get the address of the segment array.
     */
    ptr = w->dial.segments;
    /*
     * Calculate the center of the window.
     */
    w->dial.center_x = w->core.width / 2;
    w->dial.center_y = w->core.height / 2;

    w->dial.outer_diam = (Position)MIN(w->core.width, w->core.height) /
2;
    w->dial.inner_diam = (Position)w->dial.outer_diam - w-
>dial.marker_length;
    /*
     * Position the marks up the left side, across the top,
     * and down the right side of the window.
     */
    marks_per_side  = w->dial.markers / 3;
    w->dial.markers = marks_per_side * 3;
    h_increment = (int)w->core.width / (marks_per_side + 1);
    v_increment = (int)w->core.height / (marks_per_side + 1);
    /*
     * Do the left side.
     */
    for(i=0;i<marks_per_side;i++){
      ptr->x1 = 0;
      ptr->y1 = w->core.height - i * v_increment - v_increment;
      ptr->x2 = w->dial.marker_length;
      ptr->y2 = w->core.height - i * v_increment - v_increment;
      ptr++;
    }
    /*
     * Do the top.
     */
    for(i=0;i<marks_per_side;i++){
      ptr->x1  = h_increment + i * h_increment;
      ptr->y1  = 0;
      ptr->x2  = h_increment + i * h_increment;
      ptr->y2  = w->dial.marker_length;
      ptr++;
    }
    /*
     * Do the right side.
     */
    for(i=0;i<marks_per_side;i++){
      ptr->x1 = w->core.width - w->dial.marker_length;
```

```
      ptr->y1 = w->core.height - i * v_increment - v_increment;
      ptr->x2 = w->core.width;
      ptr->y2 = w->core.height - i * v_increment - v_increment;
      ptr++;
   }
}
```

This completes the implementation of the SquareDial widget class. By inheriting the behavior of the Dial class, we were able to create the new SquareDial class by writing fewer lines of code than if we had designed the new widget class from scratch. The Dial widget class consists of 336 uncommented lines of code, while the SquareDial widget class required only 121. In addition, it is not necessary (in theory) to have access to the Dial widget's source code in order to inherit from it. In practice, we were able to create a new class easily because we had detailed information about how the Dial class works. Because we know how the dial face was drawn, and that the line segments used for the dial are computed in the Dial widget's `Resize()` method, we were able to make the desired changes by redefining only that method. This would be more difficult without access to the source code.

12.3.4 Using The SquareDial Widget Class

The new SquareDial class is used in exactly the same way as the Dial widget class. We can simply change the header file and the widget class specified to `XtCreateWidget()` in the `dial` test program we used earlier to produce the file sqdial.c.

```
/*******************************************************
 * sqdial.c : Test of the Square Dial widget class
 *******************************************************/
#include <X11/Intrinsic.h>
#include <Xol/OpenLook.h>
#include "SquareDial.h"

main(argc, argv)
  int    argc;
  char *argv[];
{
  void select_callback();
  Widget toplevel, dial;

  /*
   * Initialize the Intrinsics.
   */
  toplevel = OlInitialize(argv[0], "DialTest", NULL, 0, &argc, argv);
  /*
   * Create a square dial widget and assign a callback.
   */
  dial = XtCreateManagedWidget("dial",
                               XssquareDialWidgetClass,
```

```
                             toplevel, NULL, 0);
    XtAddCallback(dial, XtNselectCallback,
                 select_callback, NULL);
    XtRealizeWidget(toplevel);
    XtMainLoop();
}
```

The callback function, **select_callback()**, is defined exactly as in the earlier example. This program produces the display shown in Figure 12.4.

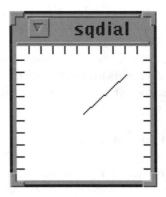

Figure 12.4 A SquareDial widget.

12.4 META-CLASSES

In the previous section we saw how inheritance can simplify the task of writing a new widget. Often this task can be made even easier by carefully structuring new widget classes. It is often possible to extract some general functionality from two or more new widget classes and create a meta-class. Remember that in the Xt Intrinsics, a meta-class is a class that is not intended to be instantiated directly, but serves as a superclass for other similar widgets. For example, in addition to the two types of dials discussed in this chapter, we can probably think of other types of dials or gauges that share some of the characteristics of the Dial and SquareDial widget classes.

We might consider restructuring the widget classes in this chapter by defining a Dial meta-class that includes those components common to all dials. This meta-class might include the creation of graphics contexts, the management of minimum and maximum values, and so on. Using this approach, the two widget classes discussed in this chapter might become the RoundDial and SquareDial classes, which could both be subclasses of the Dial widget class. Figure 12.5 shows how this widget hierarchy might look.

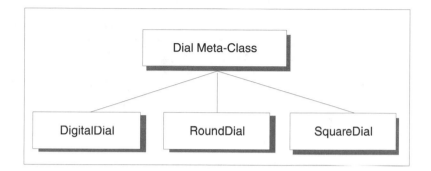

Figure 12.5 Organization of a Dial meta-class.

When creating a complete new widget set, it is often useful to create a hierarchy of meta-classes. With this approach, the top meta-class in the hierarchy defines elements that all widget classes in the set have in common, while each subclass becomes more and more specialized. Such an organization allows the widget programmer to create new widget classes with the least amount of effort, although there is some extra initial effort required to design and create the meta classes.

12.5 SUMMARY

This chapter discussed the architecture of a widget class and created a simple widget class that inherits from the Core widget class. Widgets consist of two basic parts, a class record and an instance record. The class record contains components shared by all widgets of a class, for example, the widget's class name, resource list and methods. Methods are private procedures that operate on the data in the widget's instance record. Each widget has its own copy of the instance record. This structure records the state of the specific widget: the size and position of the widget's window, the colors it uses, and so on.

The implementation of a widget uses a data abstraction technique that uses a private header file containing the true definition of the widget and a public file containing an incomplete definition. Applications see only the incomplete definition, and use Intrinsics functions to create and manipulate the widget.

When creating a new widget, programmers can often reuse parts of a similar widget by inheriting from that widget. To do this, the programmer includes the superclass's class record and instance record in the new widget's definition. Special symbols also allow the programmer to specify that the Intrinsics should copy some of the superclass's methods into the new widget's class record. Other methods are chained, so that the superclass's methods are called first. This provides another way to inherit part of the behavior of another widget.

13

CREATING COMPOSITE WIDGETS

In the previous chapter, we built some simple widgets that defined their own appearance and style of interaction. This chapter presents a more complex type of widget known as a composite widget. These widgets are subclasses of the Composite meta-class, which is defined by the Xt Intrinsics and is a subclass of the Core widget class. The Composite class inherits all the characteristics of the Core widget class, and adds the ability to manage child widgets. Widgets belonging to subclasses of the Composite widget class are referred to as composite widgets. Composite widgets are used primarily as containers for other widgets and are responsible for managing the geometry of their children.

A managed widget is never permitted to resize or move itself directly. Instead, it must request its parent to make the changes. The parent widget considers the request and allows the change, disallows the change, or suggests a compromise, depending on its management policy. Although they do not usually have display semantics, composite widgets are an important part of any widget set because they allow the application programmer to combine other widgets to create a complete user interface.

OLIT container widget classes never inherit directly from the Composite widget class, but rather are subclasses of Manager. The Manager widget class provides several important features that are used by all OLIT container classes. However, it is easier to discuss the features provided by each meta-class if we examine the class individually. So, the widget discussed in this chapter is not completely representative of the way OLIT does a container widget, but is similar in principle. This chapter first discusses the general architecture of the Composite widget class, and then presents an example composite widget.

13.1 ARCHITECTURE OF A COMPOSITE WIDGET

The Composite widget class, along with the Xt Intrinsics, defines the basic mechanism for managing children. Every composite widget's class record contains the methods that implement the widget's management policy. The first two members of every composite widget's class record includes both the Core widget class's **CoreClassPart** structure and a new **CompositeClassPart** structure. For example, the Composite widget class's class record is defined as:

```
typedef struct _CompositeClassRec {
    CoreClassPart        core_class;
    CompositeClassPart   composite_class;
} CompositeClassRec;
```

The **CompositeClassPart** structure contains pointers to the methods that manage children. This structure is defined as:

```
typedef struct _CompositeClassPart {
    XtGeometryHandler   geometry_manager;
    XtWidgetProc        change_managed;
    XtWidgetProc        insert_child;
    XtWidgetProc        delete_child;
    XtPointer           extension;
} CompositeClassPart, *CompositePartPtr;
```

Each composite widget class must supply these methods in one form or another. Section 13.2.3 discusses each of these methods in the context of an example composite widget.

Each composite widget's instance record includes the **CorePart** structure defined by the Core widget class, followed by a **CompositePart** structure. The Composite widget class's instance record is defined as:

```
typedef struct _CompositeRec {
    CorePart        core;
    CompositePart   composite;
} CompositeRec;
```

The **CompositePart** structure is defined in the Composite widget's private header file as:

```
typedef struct _CompositePart {
    WidgetList   children;
    Cardinal     num_children;
    Cardinal     num_slots;
    XtOrderProc  insert_position;
} CompositePart, *CompositePtr;
```

The first member of this structure, **children**, is a list of all widgets managed by the composite widget, while the second member, **num_children**, indicates the number of children on this list. The field **num_slots** is set to the maximum size of the list, and is used by the widget to alter the size of the children list dynamically. The last member of the **CompositePart** structure is a pointer to a method that must return an integer index into the **children** array. This index determines the position in the **children** list where the next child is to be inserted. Most widget classes inherit this method from the Composite widget class, but they can choose to redefine this method to control the order in which widgets are kept on the **children** list.

13.2 A COMPOSITE WIDGET: THE ROW WIDGET

The easiest way to understand how a composite widget works is to look at an example. This section creates a new composite widget class, which we will name the Row widget class.

Every composite widget implements its own management policy that determines how its children are positioned. The Row widget's management policy is simple. It places all managed children in a single row, evenly separated by any remaining space. The Row widget determines the position of each child widget; children may not move themselves. The Row widget honors all resize requests from children as long as there is enough room or if the Row widget itself can grow to accommodate the request. The Row widget serves only as a container for other widgets and therefore has no display semantics itself. Figure 13.1 shows a Row widget managing several button widgets.

Figure 13.1 The Row widget.

Like all widgets, composite widgets consist of private header files, a public header file, and one or more source files. The following sections describe the contents of each of the Row widget's files.

13.2.1   The Private Header File: RowP.h

The Row widget's private header file contains the definitions of the Row widget's class record and the instance record. The Row widget inherits directly from the Composite widget class. It defines its class record by adding its own class part structure to the class parts defined by the Core and Composite widget classes. Because the Row widget uses no additional class data, its class part is a dummy structure.

```
typedef struct _XsRowClassPart {
     int    ignore;
} XsRowClassPart;
```

The Row widget's complete class record can now be defined as:

```
typedef struct _XsRowClassRec {
    CoreClassPart        core_class;
    CompositeClassPart   composite_class;
```

```
      XsRowClassPart        row_class;
} XsRowClassRec;
```

```
extern XsRowClassRec XsrowClassRec;
```

The next step in creating a widget is to define the instance record. The Row widget requires no additional data in its instance record, so its contribution to the instance record is also a dummy structure, defined as:

```
typedef struct {
      int empty;
} XsRowPart;
```

The Row widget's complete instance record is defined as:

```
typedef struct _XsRowRec {
    CorePart        core;
    CompositePart   composite;
    XsRowPart       row;
} XsRowRec;
```

13.2.2 The Public Header File: Row.h

The Row widget's public header file is similar to the public header file for all widgets and consists of only a few public definitions:

```
#ifndef ROW_H
#define ROW_H
extern WidgetClass XsrowWidgetClass;
typedef struct _XsRowClassRec *XsRowWidgetClass;
typedef struct _XsRowRec       *XsRowWidget;
#endif /* ROW_H */
```

Applications use the class pointer, **XsrowWidgetClass**, as an argument to **XtCreateWidget()** to create a Row widget.

13.2.3 The Source File: Row.c

The file Row.c contains the static definition of the Row widget class record, as well as the Row widget's methods. The source file includes the Composite widget class's header files in addition to the private and public Intrinsic header files. It also includes the private and public Row widget header files.

```
/***************************************************
 * Row.c: Methods for the Row widget
 ***************************************************/
#include    <X11/IntrinsicP.h>
#include    <X11/Intrinsic.h>
#include    <X11/Composite.h>
```

```
#include      <X11/CompositeP.h>
#include      "RowP.h"
#include      "Row.h"
```

Next, the methods and other functions used by the Row widget are declared as static, making these functions private to the file. **MAX()** and **MIN()** are useful macros that determine the larger and smaller of two numbers, respectively.

```
#define MAX(a,b) ((a) > (b) ? (a) : (b))
#define MIN(a,b) ((a) < (b) ? (a) : (b))

static void             Initialize();
static void             Resize();
static void             ChangeManaged();
static Boolean          SetValues();
static XtGeometryResult GeometryManager();
static XtGeometryResult PreferredSize();
static XtGeometryResult try_layout();
```

13.2.3.1   The Class Record

The Row widget's class record is initialized entirely at compile time. Because the Row widget has no display semantics of its own and provides no actions or resources, it does not use many of the methods defined by the Core class part. For example, there is no need for a **SetValues()** method or an **Expose()** method. However, we must define several new methods that allow the Row widget to manage its children. The class record is initialized as:

```
XsRowClassRec XsrowClassRec = {
  {
    /* core_class members       */
    (WidgetClass) &compositeClassRec, /* superclass          */
    "Row",                            /* class_name          */
    sizeof(XsRowRec),                 /* widget_size         */
    NULL,                             /* class_initialize    */
    NULL,                             /* class_part_init     */
    FALSE,                            /* class_inited        */
    Initialize,                       /* initialize          */
    NULL,                             /* initialize_hook     */
    XtInheritRealize,                 /* realize             */
    NULL,                             /* actions             */
    0,                                /* num_actions         */
    NULL,                             /* resources           */
    0,                                /* num_resources       */
    NULLQUARK,                        /* xrm_class           */
    TRUE,                             /* compress_motion     */
    XtExposeCompressMaximal,          /* compress_exposure   */
    TRUE,                             /* compress_enterleave*/
    FALSE,                            /* visible_interest    */
```

```
            NULL,                              /* destroy            */
            Resize,                            /* resize             */
            NULL,                              /* expose             */
            NULL,                              /* set_values         */
            NULL,                              /* set_values_hook    */
            XtInheritSetValuesAlmost,          /* set_values_almost  */
            NULL,                              /* get_values_hook    */
            NULL,                              /* accept_focus       */
            XtVersion,                         /* version            */
            NULL,                              /* callback_private   */
            NULL,                              /* tm_table           */
            PreferredSize,                     /* query_geometry     */
            NULL,                              /* display_accelerator*/
            NULL,                              /* extension          */
        },
        {
          /* composite_class members */
          GeometryManager,                     /* geometry_manager   */
          ChangeManaged,                       /* change_managed     */
          XtInheritInsertChild,                /* insert_child       */
          XtInheritDeleteChild,                /* delete_child       */
          NULL,                                /* extension          */
        },
        {
          /* Row class members */
          0,                                   /* empty              */
        }
};
WidgetClass XsrowWidgetClass = (WidgetClass) &XsrowClassRec;
```

The superclass member of the class record specifies a pointer to **compositeClassRec**, the Composite widget class's class structure. The Row widget requires no run time initialization of the class structure, so the **class_initialize** and **class_part_initialize** members are set to **NULL**. Because there are no actions or settable resources, the **actions** and **resource** members are also set to **NULL**. The Row widget sets the **visible_interest** member of the class record to **FALSE** because it does not display anything itself, and does not care if it is visible.

13.2.3.2   Methods

The Row widget defines three core part methods similar to those defined by the simple Dial widget in Chapter 12. However, the most interesting aspect of any composite widget class is the way it manages its children. The Row widget defines several methods and auxiliary functions that allow the Row widget to control the geometry of its children and also negotiate the geometry of the Row widget with its parent. The following sections discuss each of the Row widget's methods, beginning with the basic methods that all widget classes must provide before discussing the methods added by the Composite widget class.

The Initialize() Method

Because the Row widget defines no additional resources of its own, the Row widget's **Initialize()** method is simple. Every widget's **Initialize()** method should check that the width and height of its window are greater than zero. The **Initialize()** method is defined as:

```
static void Initialize(request, new)
  XsRowWidget request, new;
{
  if (request -> core.width <= 0)
    new -> core.width = 5;
  if (request -> core.height <= 0)
    new -> core.height = 5;
}
```

The Realize() Method

Like most widgets, the Row widget class inherits the basic method defined by the Core widget class to create its window. The Row widget sets the **realize** member of its class record to the symbol **XtInheritRealize** to inherit the **Realize()** method used by the Composite widget class. In turn, the Composite widget class inherits its **Realize()** method from the Core widget class.

The InsertChild() Method

Every composite widget must have an **InsertChild()** method, which is responsible for adding new child widgets to the composite widget's list of children. **XtCreateWidget()** calls this method when it creates a widget as a child of a composite widget. Most composite widgets inherit the basic method defined by the Composite widget by specifying the symbol **XtInheritInsertChild** for the **insert_child** member of the class record. The Composite widget's **InsertChild()** method adds new children to the children list, enlarging the list using **XtRealloc()**, if needed. It calls the widget's **InsertPosition()** method to determine the next available position in the **children** array. If this procedure is not defined, the default is to append the child to the end of the list. The list of children contains all widgets created as a child of the composite widget, regardless of whether or not they are currently managed. A composite widget can discover whether a particular child widget is managed by examining the **managed** field of the child's core part.

The DeleteChild() Method

Every composite widget must provide a method to remove widgets from its list of children. Most widgets, including the Row widget, inherit this method from the Composite class, by setting the **delete_child** member of the widget's class record to the symbol **XtInheritDeleteChild**.

The Resize() Method

The Row widget bases the layout of its children on its own size. When a widget's size changes, the Intrinsics invoke its **Resize()** method. The Row widget's **Resize()** method simply calls an auxiliary function, **do_layout()**, to recalculate the layout of its children.

```
static void Resize(w)
  XsRowWidget    w;
{
  do_layout(w);
}
```

The function **do_layout()** determines the position of each managed child. It iterates twice over the list of children found in the composite part of the instance record. On the first pass it computes the sum of the widths of all managed children, to determine how much space, if any, it can place between each widget. The second pass positions each managed child, evenly separated, in a single row.

```
do_layout(parent)
  XsRowWidget parent;
{
  Widget      child;
  int         i;
  Dimension   childwidth = 0;
  Position    xpos = 0;
  Dimension   pad = 0;
  int     n_managed_children = 0;

  /*
   * Compute the total width of all managed children and
   * determine how many children are managed.
   */
  for (i = 0; i < parent -> composite.num_children; i++) {
    child = parent -> composite.children[i];
    if(child->core.managed) {
      n_managed_children++;
      childwidth += child->core.width + child->core.border_width * 2;
    }
  }
  /*
   *  Divide any remaining space by the number
   *  of children.
   */
  if((n_managed_children > 1) &&
          (parent->core.width > childwidth))
    pad = (int)(parent->core.width - childwidth) /
                                  (n_managed_children - 1);
  /*
```

```
 * Position all children.
 */
for (i = 0; i < parent -> composite.num_children; i++) {
  child = parent -> composite.children[i];
  if(child->core.managed) {
     XtMoveWidget (child, xpos, 0);
     xpos += pad + child->core.width +
                         child->core.border_width * 2;
  }
 }
}
```

The QueryGeometry() Method

Managing the geometry of a widget's children often requires a series of negotiations between the composite widget, its parent and its children. While a composite widget has complete control over the geometry of its children, it has no control over its own geometry. Often, a widget that manages the layout of multiple children must alter the size or position of one or more widgets to fulfill its particular layout policy within the constraints mandated by its own size. In this situation, it is often useful for the widget to be able to determine the preferred size of each of its children.

Every widget contains a pointer to a `QueryGeometry()` method in its Core class part. This method is invoked by the Intrinsics function:

```
XtQueryGeometry(widget, &intended, &preferred)
```

A composite widget that intends to change the size or position of one of its children can call this function to determine the child's preferred geometry. The `intended` and `preferred` parameters are structures of type `XtWidgetGeometry`, which contains the members:

```
XtGeometryMask request_mode;
Position       x, y;
Dimension      width, height, border_width;
Widget         sibling;
int            stack_mode;
```

The `request_mode` member of this structure indicates which members of the structure contain valid information and must be set using the masks:

CWX	CWY	CWWidth
CWHeight	CWBorderWidth	CWSibling
CWStackMode		

Before calling `XtQueryGeometry()`, the parent widget indicates the changes it plans to make in an `XtWidgetGeometry` structure and uses it as the `intended` argument. If the child widget has no `QueryGeometry()` method, `XtQueryGeometry()` fills in the `preferred` geometry structure with the child widget's current geometry. Otherwise it invokes the child's `QueryGeometry()` method. If the proposed changes are acceptable to the child widget, its `QueryGeometry()` method should return the constant `XtGeometryYes`. If the changes are unacceptable, or if the child's current geometry is identical to the child's preferred geometry, the method should return **XtGeometryNo**. If some of the proposed changes are acceptable, but others are not, the method can fill in the **preferred** structure with its preferred geometry and return the constant **XtGeometryAlmost**.

A parent widget is under no obligation to a child to maintain the child's preferred geometry, and may choose to ignore the information returned by **XtQueryGeometry()**. The Row widget bases its preferred geometry on the maximum height and the total width of its managed children. Although this is simple in principle, the method that computes the Row widget's preferred geometry is a bit long because there are many cases to test. The Row widget's **QueryGeometry()** method is defined as:

```
static XtGeometryResult PreferredSize(w, request, preferred)
  XsRowWidget w;
  XtWidgetGeometry *request, *preferred;
{
  Widget child;
  int i;

  /*
   * If no changes are being made to width or height, just agree.
   */
  if(!(request->request_mode & CWWidth) &&
     !(request->request_mode & CWHeight))
    return (XtGeometryYes);
  /*
   * Calculate our minimum size.
   */
  preferred->width = 0;
  preferred->height = 0;
  for (i = 0; i < w -> composite.num_children; i++) {
    child = w -> composite.children[i];
    if(child->core.managed) {
      preferred->width += child->core.width +
                              child->core.border_width * 2;
      if(preferred->height < (Dimension)(child->core.height +
              child->core.border_width * 2))
        preferred->height = child->core.height +
                              child->core.border_width * 2;
    }
  }
  preferred->request_mode = CWWidth | CWHeight;
  /*
   * If both width and height are requested.
   */
  if((request->request_mode & CWWidth) &&
     (request->request_mode & CWHeight)) {
    /*
     * If we are to be the same or bigger, say ok.
```

```
     */
    if(preferred->width <= request->width &&
            preferred->height <= request->height) {
      preferred->width  = request->width;
      preferred->height = request->height;
      return (XtGeometryYes);
    }
    /*
     * If both dimensions are too small, say no.
     */
    else
      if(preferred->width > request->width &&
         preferred->height > request->height)
       return (XtGeometryNo);
    /*
     * Otherwise one must be right, so say almost.
     */
      else
        return (XtGeometryAlmost);
  }
  /*
   * If only the width is requested, either it's
   * OK or it isn't. Same for height.
   */
  else
    if(request->request_mode & CWWidth) {
      if(preferred->width <= request->width) {
        preferred->width = request->width;
         return (XtGeometryYes);
      }
      else
        return (XtGeometryNo);
    }
    else if(request->request_mode & CWHeight) {
      if(preferred->height <= request->height) {
         preferred->height = request->height;
         return (XtGeometryYes);
      }
      else
        return (XtGeometryNo);
    }
    return (XtGeometryYes);
}
```

Notice that this method does not help the Row widget manage its children, but rather assists the parent of a Row widget in managing the Row widget itself. Ideally, every widget should define this method to make it easier for its parent to manage the widget's geometry. Geometry management of multiple widgets is a process of negotiation that requires some give and take between all widgets involved. This negotiation is more likely to succeed if every widget defines a **QueryGeometry()** method that provides accurate information about the best size of the widget. Widgets that always claim that their current geometry is the preferred geometry (by specifying the **query_geometry** member as **NULL**) do little to help the negotiation process.

The GeometryManager() Method

As mentioned previously, a widget should never attempt to alter its size or location directly, because the geometry of every widget is the responsibility of the widget's parent. Geometry requests are made using the function:

```
XtMakeGeometryRequest(widget, &request, &reply)
```

This function takes an **XtWidgetGeometry** structure as an argument and returns one of the constants:

XtGeometryYes   **XtGeometryNo**

XtGeometryAlmost   **XtGeometryDone**

XtMakeGeometryRequest() invokes the **GeometryManager()** method belonging to the parent of the given widget. If the parent allows the request, this method returns the constant **XtGeometryYes**, and **XtMakeGeometryRequest()** makes the requested changes. If the **GeometryManager()** method fulfills the request itself, it should return **XtGeometryDone**. The parent's **GeometryManager()** method can also disallow the request by returning **XtGeometryNo** or suggest a compromise by returning the constant **XtGeometryAlmost**.

The Row widget's **GeometryManager()** method begins by checking for and rejecting any changes to the position of a child widget. If the request involves a change in width or height, the method saves the child widget's original size and temporarily sets the widget to the requested size. Next, the Row widget's **GeometryManager()** method calls the auxiliary function **try_layout()** to determine if the new size is acceptable. The **try_layout()** function returns a result of type **XtGeometryResult**, and also a mask containing information about which dimension, if any, is unacceptable.

If the result of **try_layout()** is **XtGeometryNo**, the **GeometryManager()** method restores the widget's original dimensions and returns **XtGeometryNo**. If the result of **try_layout()** is **XtGeometryAlmost**, the **GeometryManager()** method restores the original values for the unacceptable dimensions and returns **XtGeometryAlmost**. In this case, the child widget can choose to use the compromise suggested by the Row widget and call **XtMakeGeometryRequest()** a second time using the suggested values, or it can abort the request and keep its original geometry. Finally, if **try_layout()** returns **XtGeometryYes**, **GeometryManager()** calls **do_layout()** to reposition the children before returning the value **XtGeometryYes**.

```
static XtGeometryResult GeometryManager(w, request, reply)
     Widget              w;
     XtWidgetGeometry    *request;
     XtWidgetGeometry    *reply;
```

```
{
  XsRowWidget        rw = (XsRowWidget) w -> core.parent;
  Mask               mask;
  XtGeometryResult result;
  Dimension          wdelta, hdelta;

  /*
   * If the widget wants to move, just say no.
   */
  if ((request->request_mode & CWX && request->x != w->core.x) ||
      (request->request_mode & CWY && request->y != w->core.y))
    return (XtGeometryNo);
  /*
   *  Otherwise, grant all requests if they fit.
   */
  if (request->request_mode & (CWWidth | CWHeight | CWBorderWidth)) {
    /*
     * Save the original widget size, and set the
     * corresponding widget fields to the requested sizes.
     */
    Dimension savewidth       = w->core.width;
    Dimension saveheight      = w->core.height;
    Dimension saveborderwidth = w->core.border_width;

    if (request->request_mode & CWWidth)
      w->core.width  = request->width;
    if (request->request_mode & CWHeight)
      w->core.height = request->height;
    if (request->request_mode & CWBorderWidth)
      w->core.border_width = request->border_width;
    /*
     * See if we can still handle all the children
     * if the request is granted.
     */
    result = try_layout(rw, &mask, &wdelta, &hdelta);
    /*
     * If the children won't fit, restore the widget to its
     * original size, and return no.
     */
    if(result == XtGeometryNo) {
      w->core.width  = savewidth;
      w->core.height = saveheight;
      w->core.border_width = saveborderwidth;
      return (XtGeometryNo);
    }
    /*
     * If only one dimension fits, restore the one that
```

```
       * doesn't fit and return "almost".
       */
      if(result == XtGeometryAlmost) {
        reply->request_mode = request->request_mode;
        if(!(mask & CWWidth)) {
        reply->width = w->core.width = savewidth;
         reply->border_width  = saveborderwidth;
         w->core.border_width = saveborderwidth;
        }
        if(!(mask & CWHeight))
          reply->height = w->core.height = saveheight;

        return (XtGeometryAlmost);
      }
      /*
       *  If we got here, everything must fit, so reposition
       *  all children based on the new size, and return "yes".
       */
      do_layout(rw);
      return (XtGeometryYes);
    }
    return (XtGeometryYes);
  }
```

The function **try_layout()** calculates the Row widget's minimum width and height, based on the current size of its managed children. If all children fit, the function returns **XtGeometryYes**. Otherwise, the Row widget issues a resize request to its parent in an attempt to accommodate the new size of its children. In this case, **try_layout()** returns the value returned by this request. If the Row widget's parent suggests a compromise geometry, **do_layout()** sets the **mask** argument to indicate which dimension was disallowed and calculates the difference between the requested width and height and the allowed width and height. This information is used by the **ChangeManaged()** method described in the next section.

```
    static XtGeometryResult
    try_layout(parent, mask, w_delta, h_delta)
      XsRowWidget parent;
      Mask        *mask;
      Dimension   *w_delta, *h_delta;
    {
      int   i;
      Dimension total_width = 0, max_height = 0;

      /*
       * Get the bounding width and height of all children.
       */
      for (i = 0; i < parent -> composite.num_children; i++) {
        Widget    child;
```

```
    Dimension width, height;

  child  = parent -> composite.children[i];
  if(child->core.managed) {
    height = child->core.height + child->core.border_width * 2;
    width  = child->core.width + child->core.border_width * 2;
    total_width += width;
    max_height = MAX(max_height, height);
  }
}
/*
 *  If everyone doesn't fit, ask if we can grow. Return the
 *  result, after setting the mask to indicate which (if
 *  any) dimension is ok.
 */
if(total_width > parent->core.width ||
    max_height > parent->core.height) {
  XtGeometryResult result;
  Dimension replyWidth, replyHeight;
  Dimension width  = MAX(total_width, parent->core.width);
  Dimension height = MAX(max_height, parent->core.height);

  result = XtMakeResizeRequest (parent, width, height,
                                &replyWidth, &replyHeight);
  *mask = NULL;
  if(total_width == replyWidth)
    *mask  = CWWidth;
  if(max_height == replyHeight)
   *mask |= CWHeight;

  if(result == XtGeometryAlmost)
    XtMakeResizeRequest (parent, replyWidth, replyHeight, NULL, NULL);
  *w_delta = total_width - parent->core.width;
  *h_delta = max_height - parent->core.height;
  return (result);
}
/*
 * If everybody fits, just return yes.
 */
*mask = CWWidth | CWHeight;
return (XtGeometryYes);
}
```

These two functions, **GeometryManager()** and **try_layout()**, illustrate several aspects of the process of negotiating geometry. The Row widget completely controls the geometry of its children and tries its best to accommodate their preferred sizes. However, the Row widget cannot control its own size; that is controlled by its parent. The Row bases its preferred size on the sum of its children's sizes, and attempts to grow if necessary to contain its managed children. If all widgets cooperate, this negotiation process works smoothly. However, this process fails if any widget in an application's widget tree does not negotiate.

The ChangeManaged() Method

A composite widget's **ChangeManaged()** method is invoked whenever one of its children changes between being managed or unmanaged. Composite widgets generally use this method to recalculate the layout of their children when the set of managed widgets changes. The Row widget's **ChangeManaged()** method first calls **try_layout()** to determine whether all children still fit. Remember that **try_layout()** attempts to increase the size of the Row widget if all children do not fit. If **try_layout()** fails, it returns a delta indicating the difference between the size of the Row widget and the size needed to contain all the children. In this case, **ChangeManaged()** reduces the width of each widget by its share of the width delta, and reduces each widget's height to the height of the Row widget if necessary. Once the children's sizes have been adjusted, **ChangeManaged()** calls **do_layout()** to position each child.

```
static void ChangeManaged(w)
  XsRowWidget w;
{
  XtGeometryResult result;
  Dimension        width, height, delta;
  int              i;
  Mask             mask;
  Widget           child;

  /*
   * See if all children fit.
   */
  result = try_layout(w, &mask, &width, &height);
  /*
   * If they don't, resize all children to be smaller.
   */
  if(result != XtGeometryYes) {
    if(w->composite.num_children > 0) {
      delta = width / w->composite.num_children;
      for(i=0;i<w->composite.num_children;i++) {
        child = w->composite.children[i];
        height = MIN(child->core.height,
               (Dimension)(w->core.height-child->core.border_width));
        if(child->core.managed)
          XtResizeWidget(child,
                      child->core.width - delta,
                      height,
                      child->core.border_width);
      }
    }
```

```
    }
    /*
     * Move all children to their new positions.
     */
    do_layout(w);
}
```

Notice that this method resizes all children equally if the total size of all managed children exceeds the available space. This method could be improved by adding calls to `XtQueryGeometry()` to check each child's preferred geometry, in case one child is more willing than others to have its size reduced.

13.2.4 USING THE ROW WIDGET

This section describes a simple program, **rowtest**, that tests the Row widget's management capabilities. The program uses a Row widget to manage four button widgets. Several callbacks allow the buttons to request size changes, and also to add and delete buttons.

```
/***********************************************
 * rowtest.c: Program to test the Row widget
 ***********************************************/
#include <X11/StringDefs.h>
#include <X11/Intrinsic.h>
#include <Xol/OpenLook.h>
#include <Xol/OblongButt.h>
#include "Row.h"

void    grow ();
void    unmanage();
void    manage();

char *names[] = {"Button1", "Button2", "Button3", "Button4"};

main(argc, argv)
  int     argc;
  char    *argv[];
{
  Widget toplevel, row, buttons[4];
  Arg     wargs[2];
  int     i;

  /*
   * Initialize the Intrinsics.
   */
  toplevel = OlInitialize(argv[0], "Rowtest", NULL, 0, &argc, argv);
  /*
   * Create a Row widget.
```

```
 */
row = XtCreateManagedWidget("row", XsrowWidgetClass,
                            toplevel, NULL, 0);
/*
 * Add children to the Row widget.
 */
for(i=0;i<XtNumber(names);i++)
  buttons[i] = XtCreateWidget(names[i], oblongButtonWidgetClass,
                              row, NULL, 0);

XtAddCallback(buttons[0], XtNselect, grow , NULL);
XtAddCallback(buttons[1], XtNselect, unmanage, NULL);
XtAddCallback(buttons[2], XtNselect, manage, buttons[1]);
XtAddCallback(buttons[3], XtNselect, grow , NULL);

XtManageChildren(buttons, XtNumber(buttons));
XtRealizeWidget(toplevel);
XtMainLoop();
}
```

Figure 13.1 shows the initial layout of the buttons produced by this program.

The **rowtest** program defines three callback functions that demonstrate and test the Row widget's geometry manager. The first callback, **grow()**, is registered as a **XtNselect** function for the widgets **Button1** and **Button4**. Each time the user activates one of these buttons, this callback function requests the Row widget to increase the width and height of the button by 10 pixels.

```
void grow (w, client_data, call_data)
  Widget      w;
  XtPointer   client_data;
  XtPointer   call_data;
{
  Arg         wargs[3];
  Dimension   width, height;

  /*
   *  Get the current width and height of the widget.
   */
  XtSetArg(wargs[0], XtNwidth,  &width);
  XtSetArg(wargs[1], XtNheight, &height);
  XtGetValues(w, wargs, 2);
  /*
   * Increment the width and height by 10 pixels before
   * setting the size.
   */
  width  +=10;
  height +=10;
  XtSetArg(wargs[0], XtNwidth, width);
  XtSetArg(wargs[1], XtNheight, height);
```

```
    XtSetArg(wargs[2], XtNrecomputeSize, FALSE);
    XtSetValues(w, wargs, 3);
}
```

Figure 13.2 shows the layout of the **rowtest** example after this function has been called several times.

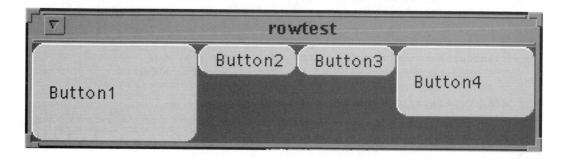

Figure 13.2 Handling resize requests.

A second **XtNselect** function is registered for **Button2**. The **unmanage()** function calls **XtUnmanageChild()**, and causes the Row widget's **ChangeManaged()** method to be invoked to recompute the widget layout. This function is defined as:

```
void
unmanage(w, client_data, call_data)
  Widget      w;
  XtPointer   client_data;
  XtPointer   call_data;
{
  XtUnmanageChild(w);
}
```

The last **XtNselect** function is registered with **Button3**. This function calls **XtManageChild()** to add **Button2** back to the Row widget's managed list.

```
void
manage(w, client_data, call_data)
   Widget      w;
   XtPointer   client_data;
   XtPointer   call_data;
{
  Widget button = (Widget)client_data;

  XtManageChild(button);
}
```

Figure 13.3 shows the how the Row widget adjusts the layout when **Button2** is unmanaged.

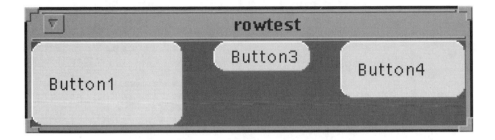

Figure 13.3 Row widget after unmanaging Button2.

13.3 SUMMARY

This chapter introduced the architecture of a composite widget. All composite widgets are subclasses of the Composite widget class. The distinguishing feature of a composite widget is that it can manage other widgets. Composite widgets are primarily responsible for managing the geometry of its children. Widgets can never resize or move themselves directly; instead, they must request their parent to do it for them. Composite widgets define several methods solely for the purpose of managing children.

An understanding of how composite widgets are implemented and how they negotiate and control widget geometries can help an application programmer to choose the best widget for a given task. This chapter explored composite widgets by building a simple example, the Row widget class. We can see from this example that the widget programmer has a large amount of latitude in determining the management policy of its children. The layout policy used by the Row widget is completely arbitrary, and others can easily be imagined. For example, instead of denying resize requests when no more room is available, the Row widget could allow the request, but reduce the size of all other children to create the extra space. Different policies regarding spacing between children are also possible. Many manager widgets provide resources that allow the application programmer to alter the layout policy of a composite widget. This makes the widget much more flexible, but increases the complexity of the widget.

The next chapter discusses the Constraint widget class, a powerful subclass of the Composite widget class.

14

CREATING CONSTRAINT WIDGETS

In the last chapter, we saw how composite widgets manage the layout of other widgets. Composite widgets usually apply their management policy uniformly without regard to any special characteristics of their children. The Constraint widget class is a subclass of the Composite widget class that manages its children based on additional information associated with each child. The class name comes from the fact that this information often takes the form of some constraint. For example, one might like to impose the constraint, "The ScrollBar widget must always be to the left of the Text widget."

A constraint widget has all the responsibilities of a composite widget, but must also manage the constraints imposed on each widget. This chapter discusses the Constraint widget class and presents an example of a constraint widget whose children represent nodes of an acyclic hierarchical graph.

14.1 ARCHITECTURE OF CONSTRAINT WIDGETS

The Constraint widget class's architecture is similar to that of the Composite widget class. However, the Constraint widget class adds methods and resources used to handle constraints. Every constraint widget includes the `CoreClassPart`, the `CompositeClassPart`, and the `ConstraintClassPart` as the first components of its class record.

```
typedef struct _ConstraintClassRec {
    CoreClassPart       core_class;
    CompositeClassPart  composite_class;
    ConstraintClassPart constraint_class;
} ConstraintClassRec;
```

The **ConstraintClassPart** structure contains information and methods used by every constraint widget.

```
typedef struct _ConstraintClassPart {
    XtResourceList   resources;
    Cardinal         num_resources;
    Cardinal         constraint_size;
    XtInitProc       initialize;
    XtWidgetProc     destroy;
    XtSetValuesFunc  set_values;
    XtPointer        extension;
} ConstraintClassPart;
```

In addition to the basic resource list contained in the Core class part of every widget class, the **ConstraintClassPart** of a constraint widget's class record contains a constraint resource list. The resource manager uses this resource list to initialize the constraints structure attached to each child widget. Every widget has a pointer to a constraint structure in the **CorePart** of its instance record (See Chapter 12). This pointer is set to **NULL** unless the child is managed by a constraint widget. When a widget is managed by a constraint widget, Xt allocates space for a constraint structure, the size of which is determined by the **constraint_size** member of the parent's **ConstraintClassPart** structure. The **ConstraintClassPart** structure also contains pointers to three new methods that initialize and manage the constraints of the composite widget's children.

The Constraint widget class's instance record is defined as:

```
typedef struct _ConstraintRec {
    CorePart       core;
    CompositePart  composite;
    ConstraintPart constraint;
} ConstraintRec, *ConstraintWidget;
```

The Constraint widget class requires no additional fields in its instance record, so **ConstraintPart** is defined as a dummy structure.

```
typedef struct _ConstraintPart {
    XtPointer   mumble;
} ConstraintPart;
```

Each constraint widget must also define the constraint structure attached to each of its children. This structure is specific to each particular type of constraint widget and the policy it supports. The example in the following section shows how this is done.

14.2 A CONSTRAINT WIDGET: THE TREE WIDGET

The rest of this chapter presents an example of a constraint widget, the Tree widget class. A Tree widget organizes its children as a hierarchical graph according to a constraint that specifies each child widget's position in the tree.[1] Applications can use the resource manager to specify this constraint when the widget is created. The following sections look at the public and private header files used by the Tree widget and then discuss the Tree widget's methods.

14.2.1 The Tree Private Header File: TreeP.h

The Tree widget's private header file defines the class record, the instance record, and the constraint record attached to each widget managed by the Tree widget. The Tree widget does not require any additional resources in the class record, so its contribution is a dummy structure.

```
typedef struct _XsTreeClassPart {
   int           ignore;
} XsTreeClassPart;
```

The Tree widget's complete class record is defined as:

```
typedef struct _XsTreeClassRec {
   CoreClassPart        core_class;
   CompositeClassPart   composite_class;
   ConstraintClassPart  constraint_class;
   XsTreeClassPart      tree_class;
} XsTreeClassRec;


extern XsTreeClassRec XstreeClassRec;
```

The Tree widget's instance record contains auxiliary information used to position the nodes in the tree and draw connecting lines. This information includes the minimum and maximum spacing between nodes of the tree, the foreground color and graphics context used to draw lines connecting the nodes, and some auxiliary data used by the methods that calculate the position of each widget. The instance record also includes a member that points to a widget used as the root of the tree. The tree widget creates this **tree_root** widget to guarantee that every child widget has a super node. This simplifies the tree layout calculations. The **XsTreePart** structure is defined as:

```
typedef struct {
   Dimension      h_min_space;
   Dimension      v_min_space;
   Pixel          foreground;
   GC             gc;
   TreeOffsetPtr  horizontal;
```

---

1 We have already used many of the terms associated with trees to refer to the X window and widget hierarchies, as well as the inheritance relationship between widget classes. Therefore, in the following discussion each element of the tree is referred to as a node. Each node, except for the root of the tree, has a super node and can also have subnodes.

```
    TreeOffsetPtr    vertical;
    Widget           tree_root;
} XsTreePart;
```

The type **TreeOffsetPtr** is a pointer to an auxiliary structure used by the functions that compute the tree layout. This structure is defined as:

```
typedef struct {
    Dimension   *array;
    int          size;
} TreeOffset, *TreeOffsetPtr;
```

The Tree widget's complete instance record is defined as:

```
typedef struct _XsTreeRec {
    CorePart        core;
    CompositePart   composite;
    ConstraintPart  constraint;
    XsTreePart      tree;
} XsTreeRec;
```

We must also define the constraint structure that the Tree widget attaches to its children. This structure is defined as

```
typedef struct _TreeConstraintsRec {
    TreeConstraintsPart tree;
} TreeConstraintsRec, *TreeConstraints;
```

where the **TreeConstraintsPart** structure is defined as:

```
typedef struct _TreeConstraintsPart {
    Widget          super_node;
    WidgetList      sub_nodes;
    long            n_sub_nodes;
    long            max_sub_nodes;
    Position        x, y;
} TreeConstraintsPart;
```

This structure contains the child's super node, a list of the child's subnodes, and also records the current length and maximum size of the subnode list. The tree layout algorithm uses the **x** and **y** members when calculating each widget's position. Defining the constraint record as a structure within a structure allows us to inherit constraints by adding in each superclasses constraint part, in the same way as we inherit the class parts and instance record parts.

Since we will often be retrieving the constraint record from a child of the Tree widget, it is convenient to define a macro to extract the **constraints** member of the child widget and coerce it to the proper type. This can be done as:

```
#define TREE_CONSTRAINT(w) \
                ((TreeConstraints)((w)->core.constraints))
```

14.2.2 The Tree Public Header File: Tree.h

The Tree widget's public header file is straightforward and similar to the examples in previous chapters. In addition to the type declarations, the header file defines the resource strings that refer to resources defined by the Tree widget.

```
/*************************************************************
 * Tree.h: Public header file for the Tree widget
 *************************************************************/
#ifndef TREE_H
#define TREE_H

extern WidgetClass  XstreeWidgetClass;

typedef struct _XsTreeClassRec *XsTreeWidgetClass;
typedef struct _XsTreeRec       *XsTreeWidget;

#define XtNhorizontalSpace    "horizontalSpace"
#define XtNverticalSpace      "verticalSpace"
#define XtCPad                "Pad"
#define XtNsuperNode          "superNode"
#define XtCSuperNode          "SuperNode"

#endif /* TREE_H */
```

14.2.3 The Tree Widget Source File: Tree.c

The file Tree.c contains the declaration of the class record and the Tree widget's private methods. The file begins by including the Xt Intrinsics private header file, the Core, Composite, and Constraint widget's private header files, and also the public and private Tree widget header files.

```
/*****************************************************
 * Tree.c: The Tree Widget Source File
 *****************************************************/
#include  <X11/Intrinsic.h>
#include  <X11/IntrinsicP.h>
#include  <X11/StringDefs.h>
#include  <X11/CoreP.h>
#include  <X11/CompositeP.h>
#include  <X11/ConstrainP.h>
#include  "Tree.h"
#include  "TreeP.h"
#define   MAX(a,b) ((a) > (b) ? (a) : (b))
```

Forward declarations of the methods and other functions used by the Tree widget come next, followed by the Tree widget's resource lists. This resource list allows applications and users to use the resource manager to control the minimum horizontal and vertical space between nodes and also the foreground color used to draw lines between nodes.

```
static void             Initialize();
static void             ConstraintInitialize();
static void             ConstraintDestroy();
static Boolean          ConstraintSetValues();
static Boolean          SetValues();
static XtGeometryResult GeometryManager();
static void             ChangeManaged();
static void             insert_new_node();
static void             delete_node();
static void             new_layout();
static void             Redisplay();
static TreeOffsetPtr    create_offset();
static int              compute_positions();
static void             shift_subtree();
static void             set_positions();
static void             reset();
static Position         current_position();
static void             set_current_position();
static Position         sum_of_positions();

static XtResource resources[] = {
  {XtNhorizontalSpace,XtCSpace,XtRDimension,sizeof(Dimension),
    XtOffset(XsTreeWidget, tree.h_min_space), XtRString,"15" },
  {XtNverticalSpace,XtCSpace, XtRDimension,sizeof (Dimension),
    XtOffset(XsTreeWidget, tree.v_min_space), XtRString,"5"  },
  {XtNforeground, XtCForeground, XtRPixel, sizeof (Pixel),
    XtOffset(XsTreeWidget, tree.foreground), XtRString,"Black"},
};
```

Constraint widgets usually specify an additional resource list used by the resource manager to set the values in the constraint part of each child widget. The Tree widget's constraint resource list allows applications to use **XtSetValues()** to specify each widget's super node.

```
static XtResource treeConstraintResources[] = {
  {XtNsuperNode, XtCSuperNode, XtRPointer, sizeof(Widget),
    XtOffset(TreeConstraints, tree.super_node),
    XtRPointer, NULL},
};
```

14.2.3.1   The Class Record

Like each of the examples in previous chapters, the Tree widget's class record is initialized entirely at compile time, as follows:

```
XsTreeClassRec XstreeClassRec = {
  {
    /* core_class fields  */
    (WidgetClass) &constraintClassRec,/* superclass       */
    "Tree",                           /* class_name       */
    sizeof(XsTreeRec),                /* widget_size      */
    NULL,                             /* class_init       */
    NULL,                             /* class_part_init  */
    FALSE,                            /* class_inited     */
    Initialize,                       /* initialize       */
    NULL,                             /* initialize_hook  */
    XtInheritRealize,                 /* realize          */
    NULL,                             /* actions          */
    0,                                /* num_actions      */
    resources,                        /* resources        */
    XtNumber(resources),              /* num_resources    */
    NULLQUARK,                        /* xrm_class        */
    TRUE,                             /* compress_motion  */
    XtExposeCompressMaximal,          /* compress_exposure */
    TRUE,                             /* compress_enterleave*/
    TRUE,                             /* visible_interest */
    NULL,                             /* destroy          */
    NULL,                             /* resize           */
    Redisplay,                        /* expose           */
    SetValues,                        /* set_values       */
    NULL,                             /* set_values_hook  */
    XtInheritSetValuesAlmost,         /* set_values_almost */
    NULL,                             /* get_values_hook  */
    NULL,                             /* accept_focus     */
    XtVersion,                        /* version          */
    NULL,                             /* callback_private */
    NULL,                             /* tm_table         */
    NULL,                             /* query_geometry   */
    NULL,                             /* display_accelerator*/
    NULL,                             /* extension        */
  },
  {
    /* composite_class fields */
    GeometryManager,                  /* geometry_manager */
    ChangeManaged,                    /* change_managed   */
    XtInheritInsertChild,             /* insert_child     */
    XtInheritDeleteChild,             /* delete_child     */
    NULL,                             /* extension        */
  },
  {
    /* constraint_class fields */
   treeConstraintResources,           /* subresources     */
```

```
  XtNumber(treeConstraintResources),/* subresource_count   */
  sizeof(TreeConstraintsRec),        /* constraint_size     */
  ConstraintInitialize,              /* initialize          */
  ConstraintDestroy,                 /* destroy             */
  ConstraintSetValues,               /* set_values          */
  NULL,                              /* extension           */
  },
{
  /* Tree class fields */
  0,                                 /* ignore              */
}
};
```

The Tree class pointer is declared internally as a pointer to this `XstreeClassRec` structure:

```
WidgetClass XstreeWidgetClass = (WidgetClass) &XstreeClassRec;
```

14.2.3.2   Methods

The primary difference between a constraint widget and a composite widget is the additional methods that initialize and set the values of the resources in each child widget's constraint record. The `Initialize()` and `SetValues()` methods manage the constraint widget's resources, while the `ConstraintInitialize()` and `ConstraintSetValues()` methods manage the constraints attached to each child widget.

The Initialize() Method

The Intrinsics invokes the Tree widget's `Initialize()` method when the Tree widget is created. The `Initialize()` method first checks that the width and height of the widget are greater than zero, and then creates a graphics context used to draw the lines connecting the nodes of the tree. Next it creates a widget that serves as the root of the tree. This widget is created, but never managed. It is not visible to the user and only exists to simplify the tree layout calculations. Finally, the horizontal and vertical fields of the Tree widget's instance record are initialized. We will discuss the use of these fields and the function `create_offset()` along with the tree layout algorithm.

```
static void Initialize(request, new)
  XsTreeWidget request, new;
{
  Arg        wargs[2];
  XGCValues values;
  XtGCMask  valueMask;
  /*
   * Make sure the widget's width and height are
   * greater than zero.
   */
  if (request->core.width <= 0)
    new->core.width = 5;
```

```
    if (request->core.height <= 0)
      new->core.height = 5;
    /*
     * Create a graphics context for the connecting lines.
     */
    valueMask = GCForeground | GCBackground;
    values.foreground = new->tree.foreground;
    values.background = new->core.background_pixel;
    new->tree.gc = XtGetGC (new, valueMask, &values);
    /*
     * Create the hidden root widget.
     */
    new->tree.tree_root = (Widget) NULL;
    XtSetArg(wargs[0], XtNwidth, 1);
    XtSetArg(wargs[1], XtNheight, 1);
    new->tree.tree_root =
            XtCreateWidget("root", widgetClass, new, wargs, 2);
    /*
     * Allocate the tables used by the layout
     * algorithm.
     */
    new->tree.horizontal = create_offset(10);
    new->tree.vertical   = create_offset(10);
  }
```

The ConstraintInitialize() Method

Every constraint widget also has a `ConstraintInitialize()` method. The Intrinsics invoke this method each time a child of the Tree widget is created, to initialize the child's constraint record. The arguments **request** and **new** are versions of a child of the Tree widget, not the Tree widget itself. The **request** parameter is copy of the widget with all resources as originally requested by a combination of command line arguments, the contents of the resource database and widget defaults. The **new** parameter is the widget after it has been processed by all superclasses's `Constrain`-`tInitialize()` methods.

The Tree widget's `ConstraintInitialize()` method sets the **n_sub_nodes** and **sub_nodes** members of each child's constraint record to zero and **NULL**, respectively, and checks to see if the widget has a super node. If so, the child widget is added to the super node widget's list of subnodes. Otherwise, the widget becomes a subnode of the **tree_root** widget created by the Tree widget. Notice the test to determine whether the **tree_root** widget exists. This prevents the **tree_root** widget from attempting to add itself recursively to its own list of subnodes when it is created.

```
    static void ConstraintInitialize(request, new)
      Widget request, new;
    {
      TreeConstraints tree_const = TREE_CONSTRAINT(new);
      XsTreeWidget tw = (XsTreeWidget) new->core.parent;
```

```
  /*
   * Initialize the widget to have no sub-nodes.
   */
  tree_const->tree.n_sub_nodes = 0;
  tree_const->tree.max_sub_nodes = 0;
  tree_const->tree.sub_nodes = (WidgetList) NULL;
  tree_const->tree.x = tree_const->tree.y = 0;
  /*
   * If this widget has a super-node, add it to that
   * widget' sub-nodes list. Otherwise make it a sub-node of
   * the tree_root widget.
   */
  if(tree_const->tree.super_node)
    insert_new_node(tree_const->tree.super_node, new);
  else
    if(tw->tree.tree_root)
      insert_new_node(tw->tree.tree_root, new);
}
```

The SetValues() Method

The **SetValues()** method is called when a Tree widget resource is altered. The Tree widget's **SetValues()** method must check the values of three resources. If the Tree widget's foreground color is altered, a new graphics context is created and the **redraw** flag is set to **TRUE**. If either of the horizontal or vertical space resources is modified, **SetValues()** calls the auxiliary functions **new_layout()** to reposition all children. Finally, **SetValues()** returns the value of the **redraw** flag, which indicates whether or not the Intrinsics should force the window to be redrawn.

```
static Boolean SetValues(current, request, new)
  XsTreeWidget current, request, new;
{
 int        redraw = FALSE;
 XGCValues values;
 XtGCMask  valueMask;
 /*
  * If the foreground color has changed, redo the GC's
  * and indicate a redraw.
  */
 if (new->tree.foreground != current->tree.foreground ||
     new->core.background_pixel !=
                          current->core.background_pixel){
   valueMask        = GCForeground | GCBackground;
   values.foreground = new->tree.foreground;
   values.background = new->core.background_pixel;
   XtReleaseGC(new, new->tree.gc);
   new->tree.gc    = XtGetGC (new, valueMask, &values);
   redraw = TRUE;
```

```
    }
    /*
     * If the minimum spacing has changed, recalculate the
     * tree layout. new_layout() does a redraw, so we don't
     * need SetValues to do another one.
     */
    if (new->tree.v_min_space != current->tree.v_min_space ||
        new->tree.h_min_space != current->tree.h_min_space){
      new_layout(new);
      redraw = FALSE;
    }
    return (redraw);
}
```

The ConstraintSetValues() Method

The Intrinsics invoke a widget's **ConstraintSetValues()** method when a child's constraint resource is altered. The only resource in the Tree widget's constraint resource list is the **XtNsuperNode** resource. If this resource has changed, the Tree widget calls the function **delete_node()** to remove the affected child widget from the subnode list of the widget's current super node. Then the method **insert_node()** is called to add the widget to the new super node's list of subnodes.

Notice that the **new** widget structure is passed to both of these methods. This is important because each of these methods stores a pointer to the widget in a list. The **new** structure is the actual widget. The other arguments are temporary copies of the widget's instance record, created by the Intrinsics before calling the **ConstraintSetValues()** method. Finally, **ConstraintSetValues()** calls the auxiliary function **new_layout()** to recalculate the position of each child widget.

```
    static Boolean ConstraintSetValues(current, request, new)
      Widget current, request, new;
    {
     TreeConstraints newconst = TREE_CONSTRAINT(new);
     TreeConstraints current_const = TREE_CONSTRAINT(current);
     XsTreeWidget tw = (XsTreeWidget) new->core.parent;
     /*
      * If the super_node field has changed, remove the widget
      * from the old widget's sub_nodes list and add it to the
      * new one.
      */
     if(current_const->tree.super_node !=
                                     newconst->tree.super_node){
       if(current_const->tree.super_node)
         delete_node(current_const->tree.super_node, new);
       if(newconst->tree.super_node)
         insert_new_node(newconst->tree.super_node, new);
       /*
```

```
     * If the Tree widget has been realized,
     * compute new layout.
     */
    if(XtIsRealized(tw))
      new_layout(tw);
  }
  return (False);
}
```

The auxiliary functions **insert_node()** and **delete_node()** are responsible for managing the **sub_nodes** list in each child's constraint record. Each time a new subnode is added, the **insert_node()** function checks whether the list is large enough to contain another widget. If not, the list must be enlarged using **XtRealloc()**. Then the function adds the widget to the end of the list and increments the **n_sub_nodes** index.

```
static void insert_new_node(super_node, node)
  Widget super_node, node;
{
  TreeConstraints super_const = TREE_CONSTRAINT(super_node);
  TreeConstraints node_const = TREE_CONSTRAINT(node);
  int index = super_const->tree.n_sub_nodes;

  node_const->tree.super_node = super_node;
  /*
   * If there is no more room in the sub_nodes array,
   * allocate additional space.
   */
  if(super_const->tree.n_sub_nodes ==
                       super_const->tree.max_sub_nodes){
    super_const->tree.max_sub_nodes +=
                  (super_const->tree.max_sub_nodes / 2) + 2;
    super_const->tree.sub_nodes =
      (WidgetList) XtRealloc(super_const->tree.sub_nodes,
                       (super_const->tree.max_sub_nodes) *
                        sizeof(Widget));
  }
  /*
   * Add the sub_node in the next available slot and
   * increment the counter.
   */
  super_const->tree.sub_nodes[index] = node;
  super_const->tree.n_sub_nodes++;
}
```

The function **delete_node()** performs the opposite operation, removing a widget from the list of subnodes, closing any gap in the list caused by the removal of an entry, and decrementing the **n_sub_nodes** counter.

```
static void delete_node(super_node, node)
    Widget  super_node, node;
{
  TreeConstraints node_const = TREE_CONSTRAINT(node);
  TreeConstraints super_const;
  int             pos, i;
  /*
   * Make sure the super_node exists.
   */
  if(!super_node) return;

  super_const = TREE_CONSTRAINT(super_node);
  /*
   * Find the sub_node on its super_node's list.
   */
  for (pos = 0; pos < super_const->tree.n_sub_nodes; pos++)
    if (super_const->tree.sub_nodes[pos] == node)
      break;
  if (pos == super_const->tree.n_sub_nodes) return;
  /*
   * Decrement the number of sub_nodes
   */
  super_const->tree.n_sub_nodes--;
  /*
   * Fill in the gap left by the sub_node.
   * Zero the last slot for good luck.
   */
  for (i = pos; i < super_const->tree.n_sub_nodes; i++)
    super_const->tree.sub_nodes[i] =
                         super_const->tree.sub_nodes[i+1];
 super_const->tree.sub_nodes[super_const->tree.n_sub_nodes]=0;
}
```

The ConstraintDestroy() Method

The **ConstraintDestroy()** method is called whenever a managed child of a constraint widget
is destroyed. It provides the constraint widget the opportunity to make any adjustments required by
the deletion of a child widget. The method is called with only one argument, which indicates the widget being destroyed. For example, the Tree widget needs to remove any pointers to the widget from
other children's constraint records, and relocate any subnodes of the widget being destroyed. The
tree widget simply moves these subnodes to the **sub_nodes** list of the super node of the widget
being destroyed, and triggers a new layout.

```
static void ConstraintDestroy(w)
    Widget w;
{
  TreeConstraints tree_const = TREE_CONSTRAINT(w);
```

```
    int i;
 /*
  * Remove the widget from its parent's sub-nodes list and
  * make all this widget's sub-nodes sub-nodes of the parent.
  */
 if(tree_const->tree.super_node) {
    delete_node(tree_const->tree.super_node, w);
    for(i=0;i< tree_const->tree.n_sub_nodes; i++)
      insert_new_node(tree_const->tree.super_node,
                      tree_const->tree.sub_nodes[i]);
  }
  new_layout(w->core.parent);
}
```

The Constraint Tree

Now that we have introduced the functions used to initialize and modify the constraint records of the Tree widget's children, let's pause and look closer at the structure created by these constraints. The following small code segment creates a Tree widget that manages three children.

```
tree = XtCreateManagedWidget("TreeTest", XstreeWidgetClass,
                             toplevel, NULL, 0);
widg1 =  XtCreateManagedWidget("One", widgetClass,
                               tree, NULL, 0);
XtSetArg(wargs[0], XtNsuperNode, widg1);
widg2 =  XtCreateManagedWidget("Two", widgetClass,
                               tree, wargs, 1);
XtSetArg(wargs[0], XtNsuperNode, widg1);
widg3 =  XtCreateManagedWidget("Three", widgetClass,
                               tree, wargs, 1);
```

Let's consider the contents of the constraint record of each of these widgets and also the dummy **tree_root** widget created by the Tree widget at the point after **widg3** has been created. The **tree_root** widget's **super_node** field is **NULL**, and its **sub_nodes** list contains a single widget, **widg1**. The **super_node** field of **widg2**'s constraint record contains a pointer to the **tree_root** widget, and its **sub_nodes** list contains two widgets, **widg2**, and **widg3**. The **sub_nodes** fields of **widg2** and **widg3** contain a pointer to **widg1**, and their **sub_nodes** list is empty. Figure 14.1 shows how these pointers create a hierarchical graph.

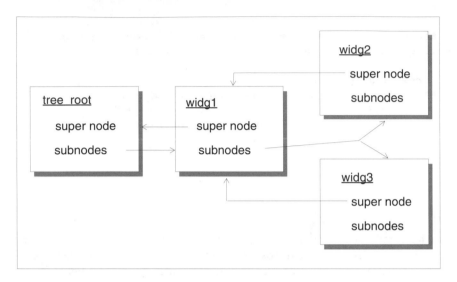

Figure 14.1 A hierarchical constraints structure.

The GeometryManager() Method

The Intrinsics call the Tree widget's **GeometryManager()** method when a child of the Tree widget makes a geometry request. The Tree widget's management policy does not allow a child to change its position, because the tree layout algorithm determines the position of every widget. However, the geometry manager grants all size requests without question. **GeometryManager()** calls the auxiliary function, **new_layout()**, to recompute and redraw the tree layout before returning **XtGeometryYes**.

```
static XtGeometryResult GeometryManager(w, request, reply)
  Widget                w;
  XtWidgetGeometry      *request;
  XtWidgetGeometry      *reply;
{

  XsTreeWidget tw = (XsTreeWidget) w->core.parent;
  /*
   * No position changes allowed!.
   */
  if ((request->request_mode & CWX && request->x!=w->core.x)
      ||(request->request_mode & CWY && request->y!=w->core.y))
    return (XtGeometryNo);
  /*
   * Allow all resize requests.
   */
  if (request->request_mode & CWWidth)
```

```
    w->core.width = request->width;
  if (request->request_mode & CWHeight)
    w->core.height = request->height;
  if (request->request_mode & CWBorderWidth)
    w->core.border_width = request->border_width;
  /*
   *  Compute the new layout based on the new widget sizes;
   */
  new_layout(tw);
  return (XtGeometryYes);
}
```

The ChangeManaged() Method

The Intrinsics invoke the Tree widget's ChangeManaged() method whenever the Tree widget's set of managed children changes. **ChangeManaged()** simply calls **new_layout()** to calculate the desired position of all children.[2]

```
static void ChangeManaged(tw)
  XsTreeWidget tw;
{
  new_layout(tw);
}
```

The Redisplay() Method

The **Redisplay()** method is called whenever an **Expose** event occurs within in Tree widget's window. This method is also called by some other Tree widget methods to redraw the lines connecting the nodes of the tree. This method loops through each child on the Tree widget's list of children, drawing a line from the right edge to the left edge of each of the widget's subnodes.

```
static void Redisplay (w, event, region)
  XsTreeWidget    w;
  XEvent          *event;
  Region          region;
{
  int                i, j;
  TreeConstraints tree_const;
  Widget          child;
  /*
   * If the Tree widget is visible, visit each managed child.
   */
```

---

2 In most constraint widgets, this method should also update the constraint records of all affected widgets when a widget is managed or unmanaged. However, this brings up several sticky issues in the Tree widget (for example, what should be done with a widget's subnodes when the widget is unmanaged, but the subnodes are still managed?), and complicates the Tree widget example beyond the scope of this example. Therefore, this example treats managed and unmanaged children in exactly the same way.

```
      if(w->core.visible)
        for (i = 0; i < w -> composite.num_children; i++){
          child = w -> composite.children[i];
          tree_const = TREE_CONSTRAINT(child);
          /*
           * Draw a line between the right edge of each widget
           * and the left edge of each of its sub_nodes. Don't
           * draw lines from the fake tree_root.
           */
          if(child != w->tree.tree_root &&
             tree_const->tree.n_sub_nodes)
            for (j = 0; j < tree_const->tree.n_sub_nodes; j++)
              XDrawLine(XtDisplay(w), XtWindow(w),
                      w->tree.gc,
                      child->core.x + child->core.width,
                      child->core.y + child->core.height / 2,
                      tree_const->tree.sub_nodes[j]->core.x,
                      tree_const->tree.sub_nodes[j]->core.y +
                  tree_const->tree.sub_nodes[j]->core.height/2);
        }
      }
```

14.2.3.3   The Tree Layout Procedures

The previous sections presented each of the Tree widget's methods. The remaining functions are auxiliary functions used to determine the position of each child widget. The layout algorithm uses a few simple rules of thumb, intended to produce an aesthetically pleasing tree layout. The basic rules, worded to apply to trees that are laid out horizontally, are:

- The overall tree should be as narrow, top to bottom, as possible.
- Each node should be placed as close as possible to its siblings.
- Each node should be centered to the left of its subnodes.
- Nodes at the same level should begin at the same horizontal position.
- The shape of any given subtree should be independent of its position in the tree.

The concept of the tree layout algorithm is simple. The first node of each level is initially positioned at y coordinate 0, and each successive node on the same level is placed below its neighbor. After the positions of all nodes within a particular branch are determined, the super node of the branch is centered to the left of its subnodes. If this position is less than the next available position on the super node's level, we must shift the entire subtree. The offset necessary to move the super node to the next available position at its level is calculated and the entire sub-tree is shifted. This function establishes the y coordinate of each widget. To determine the x position of each widget, we store the maximum width of all nodes at each level. Once the y position of each widget has been computed, this information is used to determine the final x position of each widget.

The function **new_layout()** provides the top-level interface to the layout algorithm. The function resets the auxiliary tables used to store temporary information, then calls other functions to do the real work.

```
static void new_layout(tw)
  XsTreeWidget   tw;
{
  /*
   *  Reset the auxiliary tables.
   */
  reset(tw->tree.vertical);
  reset(tw->tree.horizontal);
  /*
   * Compute each widget's x,y position
   */
  compute_positions(tw, tw->tree.tree_root, 0);
  /*
   * Move each widget into place.
   */
  set_positions(tw, tw->tree.tree_root, 0, 0);
  /*
   * Trigger a redisplay of the lines connecting nodes.
   */
  if(XtIsRealized(tw))
    XClearArea(XtDisplay(tw), XtWindow(tw), 0, 0, 0, 0, TRUE);
}
```

The function **reset()** initializes two data structures that store the next available position in the vertical direction and the maximum width of the widgets on each level in the horizontal direction. We will look at this data structure and its related functions shortly.

The main portion of the tree layout algorithm is handled by the auxiliary function **compute_positions()**.

```
static int compute_positions(tw, w, level)
  XsTreeWidget tw;
  Widget       w;
  long         level;
{
  Position       current_hpos, current_vpos;
  int            i, depth = 0;
  TreeConstraints tree_const = TREE_CONSTRAINT(w);
  /*
   * Get the current positions for this level.
   */
  current_hpos = current_position(tw->tree.horizontal, level);
  current_vpos = current_position(tw->tree.vertical, level);
  /*
   * Set the current horizontal width to the max widths of all
```

```
            * widgets at this level.
            */
           set_current_position(tw->tree.horizontal, level,
                              MAX((Dimension)current_hpos, w->core.width));
           /*
            * If the node has no sub_nodes, just set the vertical
            * position to the next available space.
            */
           if(tree_const->tree.n_sub_nodes == 0) {
             tree_const->tree.y = current_vpos;
           } else {
             Widget           first_kid, last_kid;
             TreeConstraints const1, const2;
             Position         top, bottom;
             /*
              * If the node has sub_nodes, recursively figure the
              * positions of each sub_node.
              */
             for(i = 0; i < tree_const->tree.n_sub_nodes; i++)
               depth = compute_positions(tw,
                                      tree_const->tree.sub_nodes[i],
                                      level + 1);
             /*
              * Now that the vertical positions of all children are
              * known, find the vertical extent of all sub_nodes.
              */
             first_kid= tree_const->tree.sub_nodes[0];
             last_kid =
               tree_const->tree.sub_nodes[tree_const->tree.n_sub_nodes-1];
             const1   = TREE_CONSTRAINT(first_kid);
             const2   = TREE_CONSTRAINT(last_kid);
             top      = const1->tree.y + first_kid->core.height / 2;
             bottom   = const2->tree.y + last_kid->core.height / 2;
             /*
              * Set the node's position to the center of its sub_nodes.
              */
             tree_const->tree.y = (top + bottom)/2 - (w->core.height/ 2);
             /*
              * If this position is less than the next available
              * position, correct it to be the next available
              * position, calculate the amount by which all sub_nodes
              * must be shifted, and shift the entire sub-tree.
              */
             if(tree_const->tree.y < current_vpos) {
               Dimension offset = current_vpos - tree_const->tree.y;
               for(i = 0; i < tree_const->tree.n_sub_nodes; i++)
                 shift_subtree(tree_const->tree.sub_nodes[i], offset);
```

```
      /*
       * Adjust the next available space at all levels below
       * the current level.
       */
      for(i = level + 1; i <= depth; i++) {
        Position pos = current_position(tw->tree.vertical, i);
        set_current_position(tw->tree.vertical, i, pos+offset);
      }
      tree_const->tree.y = current_vpos;
    }
  }
  /*
   * Record the current vertical position at this level.
   */
  set_current_position(tw->tree.vertical, level,
                       tw->tree.v_min_space +
                       tree_const->tree.y + w->core.height);
  return (MAX(depth, level));
}
```

The function **shift_subtree()** moves the given widget's entire subtree by an integer offset.

```
static void shift_subtree(w, offset)
  Widget     w;
  Dimension  offset;
{
  int                i;
  TreeConstraints tree_const = TREE_CONSTRAINT(w);
  /*
   * Shift the node by the offset.
   */
  tree_const->tree.y += offset;
  /*
   * Shift each sub-node into place.
   */
  for(i=0; i< tree_const->tree.n_sub_nodes; i++)
    shift_subtree(tree_const->tree.sub_nodes[i], offset);
}
```

Once the layout of all widgets has been determined, the function **set_positions()** sets the *x* position of each widget and calls **XtMoveWidget()** to move each widget into place. If all children don't fit in the Tree widget, this function makes a geometry request to the Tree widget's parent to attempt to enlarge the Tree widget.

```
static void set_positions(tw, w, level)
  XsTreeWidget tw;
  Widget       w;
  int          level;
```

```
{
  int              i;
  Dimension        replyWidth = 0, replyHeight = 0;
  XtGeometryResult  result;

  if(w){
    TreeConstraints tree_const = TREE_CONSTRAINT(w);
    /*
     * Add up the sum of the width's of all nodes to this
     * depth, and use it as the x position.
     */
    tree_const->tree.x = (level * tw->tree.h_min_space) +
                  sum_of_positions(tw->tree.horizontal, level);
    /*
     * Move the widget into position.
     */
    XtMoveWidget (w, tree_const->tree.x, tree_const->tree.y);
    /*
     * If the widget's position plus its width or height doesn't
     * fit in the tree, ask if the tree can be resized.
     */
    if(tw->core.width <
                (Dimension)(tree_const->tree.x + w->core.width) ||
        tw->core.height <
                (Dimension)(tree_const->tree.y + w->core.height)){
      result =
        XtMakeResizeRequest(tw, MAX(tw->core.width,
                                (Dimension)(tree_const->tree.x +
                                w->core.width)),
                               MAX(tw->core.height,
                                (Dimension)(tree_const->tree.y +
                                w->core.height)),
                            &replyWidth, &replyHeight);
      /*
       * Accept any compromise.
       */
      if (result == XtGeometryAlmost)
        XtMakeResizeRequest (tw, replyWidth, replyHeight,
                             NULL, NULL);
    }
    /*
     * Set the positions of all sub_nodes.
     */
    for(i=0; i< tree_const->tree.n_sub_nodes;i++)
      set_positions(tw, tree_const->tree.sub_nodes[i], level+1);
  }
}
```

The remaining functions store and retrieve a value from a dynamically resizable array. The layout functions use these functions to store the next available position and the maximum width of each level. The function **create_offset()** allocates an array of the given size.

```
static TreeOffsetPtr create_offset(size)
  long size;
{
  TreeOffsetPtr  offset = (TreeOffsetPtr) XtMalloc(sizeof(TreeOffset));
  offset->size = size;
  offset->array = (Dimension *) XtMalloc(size * sizeof(Dimension));
  return (offset);
}
```

The **reset()** function zeroes all entries in a table.

```
static void reset(offset)
  TreeOffsetPtr offset;
{
  long i;
  for(i=0; i< offset->size; i++)
    offset->array[i] = 0;
}
```

The function **current_position()** returns the value in an given position in a table. If the requested position is greater than the size of the table, the function returns zero.

```
static Position current_position(offset, position)
  TreeOffsetPtr  offset;
  long           position;
{
  if(position >= offset->size)
    return (0);
  return (offset->array[position]);
 }
```

The function **set_current_position()** stores a value in a table at a given index position. If the index is larger than the size of the table, the table is enlarged using **XtRealloc()**.

```
static void set_current_position(offset, index, value)
  TreeOffsetPtr offset;
  int           index;
  Dimension     value;
{
  if(index >= offset->size){
    offset->size = index + index / 2;
    offset->array =
      (Dimension *) XtRealloc(offset->array,
                              offset->size * sizeof(Dimension));
```

```
    }
    offset->array[index] = value;
}
```

The **sum_of_positions()** function returns the sum of all values in a table up to the given position.

```
static Position sum_of_positions(offset, index)
   TreeOffsetPtr   offset;
   long            index;
{
  int     i;
  Position  sum  = 0;
  long        stop = index;
  if(index > offset->size)
    stop = offset->size;
  for (i=0;i < stop; i++)
    sum += offset->array[i];
  return (sum);
}
```

This completes the implementation of the Tree widget. The next section discusses an example that uses the Tree widget.

14.2.4 Using The Tree Widget

This section shows how an application can use the Tree widget to display a tree. In this example, the Tree widget is managed by a ScrolledWindow widget to allow the tree to display an area larger than the screen if necessary. The program, named **sort**, reads a list of integers from standard input and displays them in a binary sort tree.[3] A binary sort tree is a tree in which the value of the key in each left subnode is less than the value of its super node's key, and the value of the key in each right subnode is greater than its super node's key. The header includes the various header files and defines a structure used to store the sorted tree.

```
/*************************************************************
 * sort.c: Display a binary sort tree using the tree widget.
 *************************************************************/
#include <stdio.h>
#include <X11/StringDefs.h>
#include <X11/Intrinsic.h>
#include <Xol/OpenLook.h>
#include <Xol/OblongButt.h>
#include <Xol/StaticText.h>
#include <Xol/Form.h>
#include <Xol/ScrolledWi.h>
#include "Tree.h"
```

---

3 Notice that although this example uses the Tree widget to display a binary tree, the Tree widget is not limited to binary trees.

```
/*
 * Define the structure for a node in the binary sort tree.
 */
typedef struct _node {
  int           key;
  struct _node  *left;
  struct _node  *right;
} node;

extern node *insert_node();
extern node *make_node();
```

The body of the program creates the Tree widget, and then inserts numbers read from standard input into a binary sorted tree of **node** structures. Once the tree is built, the function **show_tree()** creates a widget for each node of the tree.

```
main(argc, argv)
  int argc;
  char **argv;
{
  Widget    toplevel, form, sw, tree;
  int       i;
  node      *head = NULL;
  int       digit;
  Arg       wargs[10];
  int       n;

  toplevel = OlInitialize(argv[0], "Sort", NULL, 0, &argc, argv);
  /*
   * Scrolled Window behave better when the child of a ControlArea
   */
  form = XtCreateManagedWidget("form", formWidgetClass,
                                  toplevel, NULL, 0);
  /*
   * Put the tree in a scrolled window, to handle large trees.
   */
  n = 0;
  XtSetArg(wargs[n], XtNxAttachRight, TRUE); n++;
  XtSetArg(wargs[n], XtNyAttachBottom, TRUE); n++;
  XtSetArg(wargs[n], XtNxResizable, TRUE); n++;
  XtSetArg(wargs[n], XtNyResizable, TRUE); n++;
  sw = XtCreateManagedWidget("swindow", scrolledWindowWidgetClass,
                                  form, wargs, n);
  /*
   * Create the tree widget.
   */
  tree = XtCreateManagedWidget("tree", XstreeWidgetClass,
```

```
                                 sw, NULL, 0);
  /*
   * Create a binary sort tree from data read from stdin.
   */
  while(scanf("%d", &digit) != EOF)
    head = insert_node(digit, head);
  /*
   * Create the widgets representing the tree.
   */
  show_tree(tree, head, NULL);

  XtRealizeWidget(toplevel);
  XtMainLoop();
}
```

The function **insert_node()** inserts an integer into the appropriate node of a tree. If the tree doesn't exist, an initial node is allocated and the given key becomes the root of the sort tree. Otherwise, this function follows the branches of the tree until a leaf is found. The new key is inserted at the leaf. At each node, the branch that is followed depends on whether the key in that node is less than or greater than the new key.

```
node *
insert_node(key, head)
  int    key;
  node *head;
{
  node *prev, *ptr  = head;
  /*
   * If the tree doesn't exist, just create and
   * return a new node.
   */
  if(!head)
    return (make_node(key));
  /*
   * Otherwise, find a leaf node, always following the
   * left branches if the key is less than the value in each
   * node, and the right branch otherwise.
   */
  while(ptr != NULL){
    prev = ptr;
    ptr = (key < ptr->key) ? ptr->left : ptr->right;
  }
  /*
   * Make a new node and attach it to the appropriate branch.
   */
  if (key < prev->key)
    prev->left = make_node(key);
  else
```

```
      prev->right = make_node(key);
   return (head);
}
```

The function **make_node()** creates a new node structure, stores the integer key, and initializes the node's subnode pointers to **NULL**.

```
node *
make_node(key)
   int    key;
{
   node   *ptr = (node *) malloc(sizeof(node));

   ptr->key  = key;
   ptr->left = ptr->right = NULL;

   return (ptr);
}
```

Once the tree has been sorted, the function **show_tree()** performs a pre-order traversal of
the nodes, and creates widgets for each node. The function also sets the **XtNsuperNode** constraint
for each widget to point to the widget previously created for the super node in the binary tree.

```
show_tree(parent, branch, super_node)
   Widget   parent;
   node     *branch;
   Widget   super_node;
{
   Widget   w;
   Arg      wargs[3];
   int      n = 0;
   /*
    * If we've hit a leaf, return.
    */
   if(!branch) return;
   /*
    * Create a widget for the node, specifying the
    * given super_node constraint.
    */
   n = 0;
   XtSetArg(wargs[n], XtNsuperNode, super_node); n++;
   w  = XtCreateManagedWidget("node", staticTextWidgetClass,
                                       parent, wargs, n);
   xs_wprintf(w, "%d", branch->key);
   /*
    * Recursively create the subnodes, giving this node's
    * widget as the super_node.
    */
```

```
    show_tree(parent, branch->left,  w);
    show_tree(parent, branch->right, w);
}
```

We can try this program by creating a sample data file containing some numbers.

```
% cat tree.data
50 21 72 10 15 17 19 11 14 80 60
90 83 91 65 52 79 25 67 63 68 66
```

Then we can run the sort program with this data to produce the tree in Figure 14.2.

```
% sort < tree.data
```

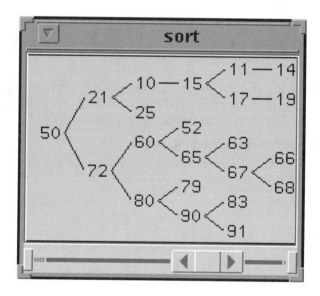

Figure 14.2 A binary sort tree.

14.3 SUMMARY

This chapter presented the architecture and construction of a Constraint widget. The Constraint widget class is a subclass of the Composite widget class that uses additional information attached to its children to determine how the children are managed. Each constraint widget attaches a constraint record to its children to store this additional information, and often provides additional resources for the child widget. The constraint resources allow the application programmer or the user to specify the corresponding values in the constraint record, and influence the layout of each individual widget. Constraint widgets define additional methods to initialize and manage changes to its children's constraint record.

APPENDIX A

OLIT CLASS TREE

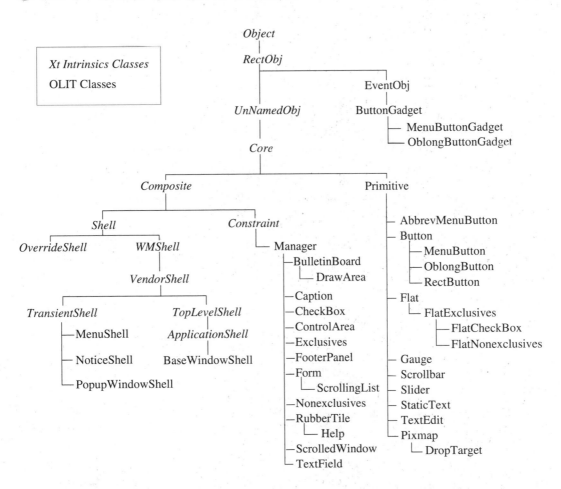

APPENDIX B

OLIT WIDGET REFERENCE

This appendix is a mini-reference guide to the OLIT widgets and various utility functions supported by OLIT. The appendix begins with a table that lists the application resources.The next section describes each widget in the OLIT widget set. There are three parts to each listing. The first part is a brief synopsis that describes the header files that must be included to use the widget. The synopsis section also includes a brief example of how the widget is created. For each widget, the synopsis section is followed by a table that lists the resources used by that widget. Finally, any structures associated with the widget are listed following the resource listing.

The last section of this reference lists many of the utility function supported by OLIT. For each function, there is a brief description, which is followed by the function declaration.

Application Resources

Name	Type	Default	Access
XtNbackground	Pixel	XtDefaultBackground	G
XtNbeep	OlDefine	OL_BEEP_ALWAYS	G
XtNbeepVolume	int	0	G
XtNcontrolName	String	"Ctrl"	G
XtNdragRightDistance	Dimension	20 (pixels)	G
XtNgrabPointer	Boolean	TRUE	G
XtNgrabServer	Boolean	FALSE	G
XtNhelpModel	OlDefine	OL_POINTER	G
XtNinputFocusColor	Pixel	XtDefaultForeground	G
XtNkeyRemapTimeOut	Cardinal	2	G
XtNlockName	String	"Lock"	G
XtNmenuMarkRegion	Dimension	10 (pixels)	G
XtNmnemonicPrefix	Modifiers	Alt	G
XtNmod1Name	String	"Alt"	G
XtNmod2Name	String	"Mod2"	G
XtNmod3Name	String	"Mod3"	G
XtNmod4Name	String	"Mod4"	G
XtNmod5Name	String	"Mod5"	G
XtNmouseDampingFactor	Boolean	8 (points)	G
XtNmouseStatus	Boolean	TRUE	G
XtNmultiClickTimeout	Cardinal	500 (millisec)	G
XtNscaleMap	String	NULL	G
XtNselectDoesPreview	Boolean	TRUE	G
XtNshiftName	STring	NShift	G
XtNshowAccelerators	OlDefine	OL_DISPLAY	G
XtNshowMnemonics	OlDefine	OL_UNDERLINE	G
XtNthreeD	Boolean	TRUE	G

Access: S=XtSetValues   G=XtGetValues   I=inittime   O=otheraccess

AbbrevMenuButton

Synopsis

```
#include <X11/Intrinsic.h>
#include <X11/StringDefs.h>
#include <Xol/OpenLook.h>
#include <Xol/AbbrevMenu.h>
  . . .
Widget                  abbrevmenubutton,  parent;
String                  name;
ArgList                 args;
Cardinal                num_args;
abbrevmenubutton = XtCreateWidget(name, abbrevMenuButtonWidgetClass,
                                  parent,  args,  num_args);
  . . .
Widget                  menupane ;
XtSetArg(args[0], XtNmenuPane, (XtArgVal)menupane);
XtGetValues(abbrevmenubutton, args, 1);
Widget                  menu_item;
WidgetClass             item_class;
String                  item_name;
menu_item = XtCreateWidget(item_name,  item_class,  menupane,  args,  num_args);
```

AbbrevMenuButton Resources

Name	Type	Default	Access
XtNaccelerator	String	NULL	SGI
XtNacceleratorText	String	Dynamic	SGI
XtNancestorSensitive	Boolean	TRUE	GO
XtNbackground	Pixel	White	SGI
XtNbackgroundPixmap	Pixmap	(none)	SGI
XtNbusy	Boolean	FALSE	SGI
XtNconsumeEvent	XtCallbackList	NULL	SGI
XtNdestroyCallback	XtCallbackList	NULL	SI
XtNforeground	Pixel	Black	SGI
XtNheight	Dimension	(calculated)	SGI
XtNinputFocusColor	Pixel	Red	SGI
XtNmappedWhenManaged	Boolean	TRUE	SGI
XtNmenuPane	Widget	(none)	G
XtNmnemonic	unsignedchar	NULL	SGI
XtNpreviewWidget	Widget	NULL	SGI
XtNreferenceName	String	NULL	SGI
XtNreferenceWidget	Widget	NULL	SGI
XtNset	Boolean	FALSE	SGI

AbbrevMenuButton Resources (Continued)

Name	Type	Default	Access
XtNscale	int	12	SGI
XtNsensitive	Boolean	TRUE	GIO
XtNtraversalOn	Boolean	TRUE	SGI
XtNuserData	XtPointer	NULL	SGI
XtNwidth	Dimension	(calculated)	SGI
XtNx	Position	0	SGI
XtNy	Position	0	SGI

Access: S=XtSetValues   G=XtGetValues   I=inittime   O=otheraccess

BulletinBoard

Synopsis

```
#include <X11/Intrinsic.h>
#include <X11/StringDefs.h>
#include <Xol/OpenLook.h>
#include <Xol/BulletinBo.h>
. . .
Widget          bulletinboard, parent;
String          name;
ArgList         args;
Cardinal        num_args;
bulletinboard = XtCreateWidget(name, bulletinBoardWidgetClass,
                      parent, args, num_args );
```

BulletinBoard Resources

Name	Type	Default	Access
XtNancestorSensitive	Boolean	TRUE	GO
XtNbackground	Pixel	White	SGI
XtNbackgroundPixmap	Pixmap	(none)	SGI
XtNborderColor	Pixel	Black	SGI
XtNborderPixmap	Pixmap	(none)	SGI
XtNborderWidth	Dimension	0	SGI
XtNconsumeEvent	XtCallbackList	NULL	SG
XtNdepth	int	(parent's)	GI
XtNdestroyCallback	XtCallbackList	NULL	SI
XtNheight	Dimension	(calculated)	SGI
XtNinputFocusColor	Pixel	Red	SGI
XtNlayout	OlDefine	OL_MINIMIZE	SGI
XtNmappedWhenManaged	Boolean	TRUE	SGI
XtNsensitive	Boolean	TRUE	GIO
XtNuserData	XtPointer	NULL	SGI
XtNwidth	Dimension	(calculated)	SGI
XtNx	Position	0	SGI
XtNy	Position	0	SGI

```
Access:    S=XtSetValues    G=XtGetValues    I=inittime    O=otheraccess
```

Caption

Synopsis

```
#include <X11/Intrinsic.h>
#include <X11/StringDefs.h>
#include <Xol/OpenLook.h>
#include <Xol/Caption.h>
 . . .

Widget          caption,  parent;
String          name;
ArgList         args;
Cardinal        num_args;
caption =  XtCreateWidget(name,  captionWidgetClass,
                          parent,  args,  num_args);
```

Caption Resources

Name	Type	Default	Access
XtNalignment	OlDefine	OL_CENTER	SGI
XtNancestorSensitive	Boolean	TRUE	GO
XtNcaptionWidth	OlDefine	(calculated)	SGI
XtNconsumeEvent	XtCallbackList	NULL	SG
XtNdepth	int	(parent's)	GI
XtNdestroyCallback	XtCallbackList	NULL	SI
XtNfont	XFontStruct	(OPENLOOKfont)	SI
XtNfontColor	Pixel	Black	SGI
XtNheight	Dimension	(calculated)	SGI
XtNlabel	String	NULL	SGI
XtNmnemonic	unsigned char	NULL	SGI
XtNmappedWhenManaged	Boolean	TRUE	SGI
XtNposition	OlDefine	OL_LEFT	SGI
XtNrecomputeSize	Boolean	TRUE	SGI
XtNsensitive	Boolean	TRUE	GIO
XtNspace	Dimension	4	SGI
XtNtraversalOn	Boolean	TRUE	SGI
XtNuserData	XtPointer	NULL	SGI
XtNwidth	Dimension	(calculated)	SGI
XtNx	Position	0	SGI
XtNy	Position	0	SGI

Access: S=XtSetValues   G=XtGetValues   I=inittime   O=otheraccess

CheckBox

Synopsis

```
#include <X11/Intrinsic.h>
#include <X11/StringDefs.h>
#include <Xol/OpenLook.h>
#include <Xol/CheckBox.h>
. . .
Widget           checkbox, parent;
String           name;
ArgList          args;
Cardinal         num_args;
checkbox = XtCreateWidget(name, checkBoxWidgetClass,
                          parent, args, num_args);
```

CheckBox Resources

Name	Type	Default	Access
XtNaccelerator	String	NULL	SGI
XtNacceleratorText	String	Dynamic	SGI
XtNancestorSensitive	Boolean	TRUE	GO
XtNconsumeEvent	XtCallbackList	NULL	SGI
XtNdepth	int	(parent's)	GI
XtNdestroyCallback	XtCallbackList	NULL	SI
XtNdim	Boolean	FALSE	SGI
XtNfont	XFontStruct *	(OPENLOOK font)	SI
XtNfontColor	Pixel	Black	SGI
XtNforeground	Pixel	Black	SGI
XtNheight	Dimension	(calculated)	SGI
XtNinputFocusColor	Pixel	Red	SGI
XtNlabel	String	(classname)	SGI
XtNlabelImage	XImage *	(classname)	SGI
XtNlabelJustify	OlDefine	OL_LEFT	SGI
XtNlabelTile	Boolean	FALSE	SGI
XtNlabelType	OlDefine	OL_STRING	SGI
XtNmappedWhenManaged	Boolean	TRUE	SGI
XtNmnemonic	unsignedchar	NULL	SGI
XtNposition	OlDefine	OL_LEFT	SGI
XtNrecomputeSize	Boolean	TRUE	SGI
XtNreferenceName	String	NULL	SGI
XtNreferenceWidget	Widget	NULL	SGI
XtNscale	int	12	SGI
XtNselect	XtCallbackList	NULL	SI
XtNsensitive	Boolean	TRUE	GIO

CheckBox Resources (Continued)

Name	Type	Default	Access
XtNset	Boolean	TRUE	SGI
XtNtraversalOn	Boolean	TRUE	SGI
XtNunselect	XtCallbackList	NULL	SI
XtNuserData	XtPointer	NULL	SGI
XtNwidth	Dimension	(calculated)	SGI
XtNx	Position	0	SGI
XtNy	Position	0	SGI

Access: S=XtSetValues   G=XtGetValues   I=inittime   O=otheraccess

ControlArea

Synopsis

```
#include <X11/Intrinsic.h>
#include <X11/StringDefs.h>
#include <Xol/OpenLook.h>
#include <Xol/ControlAre.h>
. . .
Widget          controlarea, parent;
String          name;
ArgList         args;
Cardinal        num_args;
controlarea = XtCreateWidget(name, controlAreaWidgetClass,
                        parent, args, num_args);
```

ControlArea Resources

Name	Type	Default	Access
XtNalignCaptions	Boolean	FALSE	SGI
XtNancestorSensitive	Boolean	TRUE	GO
XtNbackground	Pixel	White	SGI
XtNbackgroundPixmap	Pixmap	(none)	SGI
XtNborderColor	Pixel	Black	SGI
XtNborderPixmap	Pixmap	(none)	SGI
XtNborderWidth	Dimension	0	SGI
XtNcenter	Boolean	FALSE	SGI
XtNconsumeEvent	XtCallbackList	NULL	SG
XtNdepth	int	(parent's)	GI
XtNdestroyCallback	XtCallbackList	NULL	SI
XtNhPad	Dimension	4	SGI
XtNhSpace	Dimension	4	SGI
XtNheight	Dimension	(calculated)	SGI
XtNlayoutType	OlDefine	OL_FIXEDROWS	SGI
XtNmappedWhenManaged	Boolean	TRUE	SGI
XtNmeasure	int	1	SGI
XtNsameSize	OlDefine	OL_COLUMNS	SGI
XtNsensitive	Boolean	TRUE	GIO
XtNtraversalManager	Boolean	FALSE	SGI
XtNuserData	XtPointer	NULL	SGI
XtNvPad	Dimension	4	SGI
XtNvSpace	Dimension	4	SGI
XtNwidth	Dimension	(calculated)	SGI
XtNx	Position	0	SGI
XtNy	Position	0	SGI

DrawArea

Synopsis

```
#include <X11/Intrinsic.h>
#include <X11/StringDefs.h>
#include <Xol/OpenLook.h>
#include <Xol/DrawArea.h>
. . .
Widget          drawarea, parent;
String          name;
ArgList         args;
Cardinal        num_args;
drawarea = XtCreateWidget(name, drawAreaWidgetClass,
                    parent, args, num_args);
```

DrawArea Resources

Name	Type	Default	Access
XtNancestorSensitive	Boolean	TRUE	G
XtNbackground	Pixel	White	SGI
XtNbackgroundPixmap	Pixmap	(none)	SGI
XtNborderColor	Pixel	Black	SGI
XtNborderPixmap	Pixmap	(none)	SGI
XtNborderWidth	Dimension	0	SGI
XtNcolormap	Colormap	(parent's)	SGI
XtNconsumeEvent	XtCallbackList	NULL	SG
XtNdepth	int	(parent's)	GI
XtNdestroyCallback	XtCallbackList	NULL	SI
XtNexposeCallback	XtCallbackList	NULL	SGI
XtNforeground	Pixel	XtDefaultForeground	SGI
XtNgraphicsExposeCallback	XtCallbackList	NULL	SGI
XtNheight	Dimension	(calculated)	SGI
XtNinputFocusColor	Pixel	Red	SGI
XtNlayout	OlDefine	OL_MINIMIZE	SGI
XtNmappedWhenManaged	Boolean	TRUE	SGI
XtNresizeCallback	XtCallbackList	NULL	SGI
XtNsensitive	Boolean	TRUE	GIO
XtNuserData	XtPointer	NULL	SGI
XtNvisual	Visual *	(parent's)	GI
XtNwidth	Dimension	(calculated)	SGI
XtNx	Position	0	SGI
XtNy	Position	0	SGI

Access: S=XtSetValues   G=XtGetValues   I=inittime   O=otheraccess

Associated Data Structures

```
typedef struct
{
        int             reason;
        XEvent          *event;
        Position        x;
        Position        y;
        Dimension       width;
        Dimension       height;
} OlDrawAreaCallbackStruct;
```

DropTarget

Synopsis

```
#include <X11/Intrinsic.h>
#include <X11/StringDefs.h>
#include <Xol/OpenLook.h>
#include <Xol/DropTarget.h>
. . .
Widget              droptarget, parent;
String              name;
ArgList             args;
Cardinal            num_args;
droptarget = XtCreateWidget(name, dropTargetWidgetClass,
                        parent, args, num_args);;
```

DropTarget Resources

Name	Type	Default	Access
XtNaccelerator	String	NULL	SGI
XtNacceleratorText	String	Dynamic	SGI
XtNbackground	Pixel	White	SGI
XtNbackgroundPixmap	Pixmap	(none)	SGI
XtNbusyPixmap	Pixmap	XtUnspecifiedPixmap	SGI
XtNcolormap	XtCallbackList	NULL	SGI
XtNconsumeEvent	XtCallbackList	NULL	SGI
XtNdepth	int	(parent's)	GI
XtNdestroyCallback	XtCallbackList	NULL	SI
XtNdndAcceptCursor	Cursor	NULL	SGI
XtNdndAnimateCallback	Callback	NULL	SGI
XtNdndCopyCursor	Cursor	DefaultCopyCursor	SGI
XtNdndMoveCursor	Cursor	DefaultMoveCursor	SGI
XtNdndPreviewCallback	Callback	NULL	SGI
XtNdndPreviewHints	OlDnDSitePreviewHints	OlDnDSitePreviewNone	SGI
XtNdndRejectCursor	Cursor	NULL	SGI
XtNdndTriggerCallback	Callback	NULL	SGI
XtNfont	XFontStruct *	(OPEN LOOK font)	SI
XtNfontColor	Pixel	Black	SGI
XtNforeground	Pixel	Black	SGI
XtNfull	Boolean	FALSE	SGI
XtNheight	Dimension	(calculated)	SGI
XtNinputFocusColor	Pixel	Red	SGI
XtNmappedWhenManaged	Boolean	TRUE	SGI
XtNmnemonic	unsigned char	NULL	SGI

DropTarget Resources (Continued)

Name	Type	Default	Access
XtNownSelectionCallback	Callback	NULL	SGI
XtNpixmap	Pixmap	DefaultPixmap	SGI
XtNrecomputeSize	Boolean	FALSE	SGI
XtNreferenceName	String	NULL	SGI
XtNreferenceWidget	Widget	NULL	SGI
XtNselectionAtom	Atom	NULL	SGI
XtNsensitive	Boolean	TRUE	GIO
XtNtraversalOn	Boolean	TRUE	SGI
XtNuserData	XtPointer	NULL	SGI
XtNwidth	Dimension	(calculated)	SGI
XtNx	Position	0	SGI
XtNy	Position	0	SGI

Access: S=XtSetValues   G=XtGetValues   I=inittime   O=otheraccess

Associated Data Structures

```
typedef struct
{
        int                     reason;
        Widget                  widget;
        Window                  window;
        Position                root_x;
        Position                root_y;
        Atom                    selection;
        Time                    time;
        OlDnDDropSiteID         dropsiteid;
        OlDnDTriggerOperation   operation;
        Boolean                 send_done;
        Boolean                 forwarded;
        int                     eventcode;
        Boolean                 sensitivity;
} OlDropTargetCallbackStruct;
```

Exclusives

Synopsis

```
#include <X11/Intrinsic.h>
#include <X11/StringDefs.h>
#include <Xol/OpenLook.h>
#include <Xol/Exclusives.h>
. . .
Widget          exclusive, parent;
String          name;
ArgList         args;
Cardinal        num_args;
exclusive = XtCreateWidget(name, exclusivesWidgetClass,
                        parent, args, num_args);
```

Exclusives Resources

Name	Type	Default	Access
XtNancestorSensitive	Boolean	TRUE	GO
XtNconsumeEvent	XtCallbackList	NULL	SG
XtNdepth	int	(parent's)	GI
XtNdestroyCallback	XtCallbackList	NULL	SI
XtNheight	Dimension	(calculated)	SGI
XtNlayoutType	OlDefine	OL_FIXEDROWS	SGI
XtNmappedWhenManaged	Boolean	TRUE	SGI
XtNmeasure	int	1	SGI
XtNnoneSet	Boolean	FALSE	SGI
XtNreferenceName	String	NULL	GI
XtNreferenceWidget	Widget	NULL	GI
XtNsensitive	Boolean	TRUE	GIO
XtNtraversalOn	Boolean	TRUE	SGI
XtNuserData	XtPointer	NULL	SGI
XtNwidth	Dimension	(calculated)	SGI
XtNx	Position	0	SGI
XtNy	Position	0	SGI

Access: S=XtSetValues   G=XtGetValues   I=inittime   O=otheraccess

FlatCheckbox

Synopsis

```
#include <X11/Intrinsic.h>
#include <X11/StringDefs.h>
#include <Xol/OpenLook.h>
#include <Xol/FCheckBox.h>
. . .
Widget          flatcheckbox, parent;
String          name;
ArgList         args;
Cardinal        num_args;
flatcheckbox = XtCreateWidget(name, flatCheckBoxWidgetClass,
                        parent, args, num_args);
```

FlatCheckBox Resources

Name	Type	Default	Access
XtNaccelerator	String	NULL	SGI
XtNacceleratorText	String	Dynamic	SGI
XtNancestorSensitive	Boolean	TRUE	G
XtNbackground	Pixel	XtDefaultBackground	SGI
XtNbackgroundPixmap	Pixmap	None	SGI
XtNborderWidth	Dimension	0	SGI
XtNclientData	XtPointer	NULL	SGI
XtNconsumeEvent	XtCallbackList	NULL	SGI
XtNdefault	Boolean	FALSE	SGI
XtNdepth	Cardinal	(parent's)	GI
XtNdim	Boolean	FALSE	SGI
XtNfont	XFontStruct *	(OPEN LOOK font)	SI
XtNfontColor	Pixel	XtDefaultForeground	SGI
XtNforeground	Pixel	XtDefaultForeground	SGI
XtNgravity	int	CenterGravity	SGI
XtNhPad	Dimension	0	SGI
XtNhSpace	Dimension	(calculated)	SGI
XtNheight	Dimension	(calculated)	SGI
XtNinputFocusColor	Pixel	Red	SGI
XtNitemFields	String *	NULL	GI
XtNitemGravity	int	NorthWestGravity	SGI
XtNitemMaxHeight	Dimension	OL_IGNORE	SGI
XtNitemMaxWidth	Dimension	OL_IGNORE	SGI
XtNitemMinHeight	Dimension	OL_IGNORE	SGI
XtNitemMinWidth	Dimension	OL_IGNORE	SGI
XtNitems	XtPointer	NULL	SGI

FlatCheckBox Resources (Continued)

Name	Type	Default	Access
XtNitemsTouched	Boolean	FALSE	SG
XtNlabel	String	NULL	SGI
XtNlabelImage	XImage *	NULL	SGI
XtNlabelJustify	OlDefine	OL_LEFT	SGI
XtNlabelTile	Boolean	FALSE	SGI
XtNlayoutHeight	OlDefine	OL_MINIMIZE	SGI
XtNlayoutType	OlDefine	OL_FIXEDROWS	SGI
XtNlayoutWidth	OlDefine	OL_MINIMIZE	SGI
XtNmanaged	Boolean	TRUE	SGI
XtNmappedWhenManaged	Boolean	TRUE	SGI
XtNmeasure	int	1	SGI
XtNmnemonic	unsigned char	NULL	SGI
XtNnoneSet	Boolean	FALSE	SGI
XtNnumItemFields	Cardinal	0	SGI
XtNnumItems	Cardinal	0	SGI
XtNposition	OlDefine	OL_LEFT	SGI
XtNreferenceName	String	NULL	SGI
XtNreferenceWidget	Widget	NULL	SGI
XtNsameHeight	OlDefine	OL_ALL	SGI
XtNsameWidth	OlDefine	OL_COrLUMNS	SGI
XtNselectProc	XtCallbackProc	NULL	SGI
XtNsensitive	Boolean	TRUE	SGI
XtNset	Boolean	FALSE	SGI
XtNtraversalOn	Boolean	TRUE	SGI
XtNunselectProc	XtCallbackProc	NULL	SGI
XtNuserData	XtPointer	NULL	SGI
XtNvPad	Dimension	0	SGI
XtNvSpace	Dimension	(calculated)	SGI
XtNwidth	Dimension	(calculated)	SGI
XtNx	Position	0	SGI
XtNy	Position	0	SGI

Access: S=XtSetValues   G=XtGetValues   I=inittime   O=otheraccess

Associated Data Structures

```
typedef struct {
        Cardinal        item_index;     /* sub-object initiating callb. */
        XtPointer       items;          /* sub-object list              */
        Cardinal        num_items;      /* number of sub-objects        */
        String *        item_fields;    /* key of fields for list       */
```

```
        Cardinal        num_item_fields;/* number of item fields      */
        Cardinal        num_fields;     /* number of item fields      */
} OlFlatCallData;
```

FlatExclusives

Synopsis

```
#include <X11/Intrinsic.h>
#include <X11/StringDefs.h>
#include <Xol/OpenLook.h>
#include <Xol/FExclusive.h>
. . .
Widget          flatexclusive, parent;
String          name;
ArgList         args;
Cardinal        num_args;
flatexclusive = XtCreateWidget (name, flatExclusivesWidgetClass,
                        parent, args, num_args);
```

FlatExclusives

Name	Type	Default	Access
XtNaccelerator	String	NULL	SGI
XtNacceleratorText	String	Dynamic	SGI
XtNancestorSensitive	Boolean	TRUE	G
XtNbackground	Pixel	XtDefaultBackground	SGI
XtNbackgroundPixmap	Pixmap	None	SGI
XtNborderWidth	Dimension	0	SGI
XtNclientData	XtPointer	NULL	SGI
XtNconsumeEvent	XtCallbackList	NULL	SGI
XtNdefault	Boolean	FALSE	SGI
XtNdepth	Cardinal	(parent's)	GI
XtNdim	Boolean	FALSE	SGI
XtNfont	XFontStruct *	(OPEN LOOK font)	SI
XtNfontColor	Pixel	XtDefaultForeground	SGI
XtNforeground	Pixel	XtDefaultForeground	SGI
XtNgravity	int	CenterGravity	SGI
XtNhPad	Dimension	0	SGI
XtNhSpace	Dimension	(calculated)	SGI
XtNheight	Dimension	(calculated)	SGI
XtNinputFocusColor	Pixel	Red	SGI
XtNitemFields	String *	NULL	GI
XtNitemGravity	int	NorthWestGravity	SGI
XtNitemMaxHeight	Dimension	OL_IGNORE	SGI
XtNitemMaxWidth	Dimension	OL_IGNORE	SGI
XtNitemMinHeight	Dimension	OL_IGNORE	SGI
XtNitemMinWidth	Dimension	OL_IGNORE	SGI
XtNitems	XtPointer	NULL	SGI

FlatExclusives (Continued)

Name	Type	Default	Access
XtNitemsTouched	Boolean	FALSE	SG
XtNlabel	String	NULL	SGI
XtNlabelImage	XImage *	NULL	SGI
XtNlabelJustify	OlDefine	OL_LEFT	SGI
XtNlabelTile	Boolean	FALSE	SGI
XtNlayoutHeight	OlDefine	OL_MINIMIZE	SGI
XtNlayoutType	OlDefine	OL_FIXEDROWS	SGI
XtNlayoutWidth	OlDefine	OL_MINIMIZE	SGI
XtNmanaged	Boolean	TRUE	SGI
XtNmappedWhenManaged	Boolean	TRUE	SGI
XtNmeasure	int	1	SGI
XtNmnemonic	unsigned char	NULL	SGI
XtNnoneSet	Boolean	FALSE	SGI
XtNnumItemFields	Cardinal	0	SGI
XtNnumItems	Cardinal	0	SGI
XtNposition	OlDefine	OL_LEFT	SGI
XtNreferenceName	String	NULL	SGI
XtNreferenceWidget	Widget	NULL	SGI
XtNsameHeight	OlDefine	OL_ALL	SGI
XtNsameWidth	OlDefine	OL_COLUMNS	SGI
XtNselectProc	XtCallbackProc	NULL	SGI
XtNsensitive	Boolean	TRUE	SGI
XtNset	Boolean	FALSE	SGI
XtNtraversalOn	Boolean	TRUE	SGI
XtNunselectProc	XtCallbackProc	NULL	SGI
XtNuserData	XtPointer	NULL	SGI
XtNvPad	Dimension	0	SGI
XtNvSpace	Dimension	(calculated)	SGI
XtNwidth	Dimension	(calculated)	SGI
XtNx	Position	0	SGI
XtNy	Position	0	SGI

Access: S=XtSetValues   G=XtGetValues   I=inittime   O=otheraccess

Associated Data Structures

```
typedef struct {
        Cardinal        item_index;     /* sub-object initiating callb. */
        XtPointer       items;          /* sub-object list              */
        Cardinal        num_items;      /* number of sub-objects        */
        String *        item_fields;    /* key of fields for list       */
```

```
        Cardinal           num_item_fields;/* number of item fields        */
        Cardinal           num_fields;      /* number of item fields        */
} OlFlatCallData;
```

FlatNonexclusives

Synopsis

```
#include <X11/Intrinsic.h>
#include <X11/StringDefs.h>
#include <Xol/OpenLook.h>
#include <Xol/FNonexclus.h>
. . .
Widget          flatnonexclusive, parent;
String          name;
ArgList         args;
Cardinal        num_args;
flatnonexclusive = XtCreateWidget(name, flatNonexclusivesWidgetClass,
                                  parent, args, num_args);
```

FlatNonexclusives Resources

Name	Type	Default	Access
XtNaccelerator	String	NULL	SGI
XtNacceleratorText	String	Dynamic	SGI
XtNancestorSensitive	Boolean	TRUE	G
XtNbackground	Pixel	XtDefaultBackground	SGI
XtNbackgroundPixmap	Pixmap	None	SGI
XtNborderWidth	Dimension	0	SGI
XtNclientData	XtPointer	NULL	SGI
XtNconsumeEvent	XtCallbackList	NULL	SGI
XtNdefault	Boolean	FALSE	SGI
XtNdepth	Cardinal	(parent's)	GI
XtNdim	Boolean	FALSE	SGI
XtNfont	XFontStruct *	(OPEN LOOK font)	SI
XtNfontColor	Pixel	XtDefaultForeground	SGI
XtNforeground	Pixel	XtDefaultForeground	SGI
XtNgravity	int	CenterGravity	SGI
XtNhPad	Dimension	0	SGI
XtNhSpace	Dimension	(calculated)	SGI
XtNheight	Dimension	(calculated)	SGI
XtNinputFocusColor	Pixel	Red	SGI
XtNitemFields	String *	NULL	GI
XtNitemGravity	int	NorthWestGravity	SGI
XtNitemMaxHeight	Dimension	OL_IGNORE	SGI
XtNitemMaxWidth	Dimension	OL_IGNORE	SGI
XtNitemMinHeight	Dimension	OL_IGNORE	SGI
XtNitemMinWidth	Dimension	OL_IGNORE	SGI
XtNitems	XtPointer	NULL	SGI

FlatNonexclusives Resources (Continued)

Name	Type	Default	Access
XtNitemsTouched	Boolean	FALSE	SG
XtNlabel	String	NULL	SGI
XtNlabelImage	XImage *	NULL	SGI
XtNlabelJustify	OlDefine	OL_LEFT	SGI
XtNlabelTile	Boolean	FALSE	SGI
XtNlayoutHeight	OlDefine	OL_MINIMIZE	SGI
XtNlayoutType	OlDefine	OL_FIXEDROWS	SGI
XtNlayoutWidth	OlDefine	OL_MINIMIZE	SGI
XtNmanaged	Boolean	TRUE	SGI
XtNmappedWhenManaged	Boolean	TRUE	SGI
XtNmeasure	int	1	SGI
XtNmnemonic	unsigned char	NULL	SGI
XtNnoneSet	Boolean	FALSE	SGI
XtNnumItemFields	Cardinal	0	SGI
XtNnumItems	Cardinal	0	SGI
XtNposition	OlDefine	OL_LEFT	SGI
XtNreferenceName	String	NULL	SGI
XtNreferenceWidget	Widget	NULL	SGI
XtNsameHeight	OlDefine	OL_ALL	SGI
XtNsameWidth	OlDefine	OL_COLUMNS	SGI
XtNselectProc	XtCallbackProc	NULL	SGI
XtNsensitive	Boolean	TRUE	SGI
XtNset	Boolean	FALSE	SGI
XtNtraversalOn	Boolean	TRUE	SGI
XtNunselectProc	XtCallbackProc	NULL	SGI
XtNuserData	XtPointer	NULL	SGI
XtNvPad	Dimension	0	SGI
XtNvSpace	Dimension	(calculated)	SGI
XtNwidth	Dimension	(calculated)	SGI
XtNx	Position	0	SGI
XtNy	Position	0	SGI

Access: S=XtSetValues   G=XtGetValues   I=inittime   O=otheraccess

Associated Data Structures

```
typedef struct {
        Cardinal        item_index;     /* sub-object initiating callb. */
        XtPointer       items;          /* sub-object list              */
        Cardinal        num_items;      /* number of sub-objects        */
        String *        item_fields;    /* key of fields for list       */
```

```
        Cardinal           num_item_fields;/* number of item fields         */
        Cardinal           num_fields;       /* number of item fields        */
} OlFlatCallData;
```

FooterPanel

Synopsis

```
#include <X11/Intrinsic.h>
#include <X11/StringDefs.h>
#include <Xol/OpenLook.h>
#include <Xol/FooterPane.h>
. . .
Widget          footerpanel, parent;
String          name;
ArgList         args;
Cardinal        num_args;
footerpanel = XtCreateWidget(name, footerPanelWidgetClass,
                             parent, args, num_args);
```

FooterPanel Resources

Name	Type	Default	Access
XtNancestorSensitive	Boolean	TRUE	GO
XtNdepth	int	(parent's)	GI
XtNdestroyCallback	XtCallbackList	NULL	SI
XtNheight	Dimension	(calculated)	SGI
XtNmappedWhenManaged	Boolean	TRUE	SGI
XtNsensitive	Boolean	TRUE	GIO
XtNtraversalManager	Boolean	FALSE	SGI
XtNuserData	XtPointer	NULL	SGI
XtNwidth	Dimension	(calculated)	SGI
XtNx	Position	0	SGI
XtNy	Position	0	SGI

Access: S=XtSetValues   G=XtGetValues   I=inittime   O=otheraccess

Form

Synopsis

```
#include <X11/Intrinsic.h>
#include <X11/StringDefs.h>
#include <Xol/OpenLook.h>
#include <Xol/Form.h>
. . .
Widget          form, parent;
String          name;
ArgList         args;
Cardinal        num_args;
form = XtCreateWidget(name, formWidgetClass,
                      parent, args, num_args);
```

Form Resources

Name	Type	Default	Access
XtNancestorSensitive	Boolean	TRUE	GO
XtNbackground	Pixel	White	SGI
XtNbackgroundPixmap	Pixmap	(none)	SGI
XtNborderColor	Pixel	Black	SGI
XtNborderPixmap	Pixmap	(none)	SGI
XtNborderWidth	Dimension	0	SGI
XtNconsumeEvent	XtCallbackList	NULL	SG
XtNdepth	int	(parent's)	GI
XtNdestroyCallback	XtCallbackList	NULL	SI
XtNheight	Dimension	(calculated)	SGI
XtNmappedWhenManaged	Boolean	TRUE	SGI
XtNsensitive	Boolean	TRUE	GIO
XtNtraversalManager	Boolean	FALSE	SGI
XtNuserData	XtPointer	NULL	SGI
XtNwidth	Dimension	(calculated)	SGI
XtNx	Position	0	SGI
XtNy	Position	0	SGI

```
Access:     S=XtSetValues    G=XtGetValues    I=inittime    O=otheraccess
```

Form Child Constraint Resources

Name	Type	Default	Access
XtNxAddWidth	Boolean	FALSE	SGI
XtNxAttachOffset	int	0	SGI

Form Child Constraint Resources (Continued)

Name	Type	Default	Access
XtNxAttachRight	Boolean	FALSE	SGI
XtNxOffset	int	0	SGI
XtNxRefName	String	NULL	SGI
XtNxRefWidget	Widget	(form)	SGI
XtNxResizable	Boolean	FALSE	SGI
XtNxVaryOffset	Boolean	FALSE	SGI
XtNyAddHeight	Boolean	FLASE	SGI
XtNyAttachBottom	Boolean	FALSE	SGI
XtNyAttachOffset	int	0	SGI
XtNyOffset	int	0	SGI
XtNyRefName	String	NULL	SGI
XtNyRefWidget	Widget	(form)	SGI
XtNyResizable	Boolean	FALSE	SGI
XtNyVaryOffset	Boolean	FLASE	SGI

Access: S=XtSetValues   G=XtGetValues   I=inittime   O=otheraccess

Gauge

Synopsis

```
#include <X11/Intrinsic.h>
#include <X11/StringDefs.h>
#include <Xol/OpenLook.h>
#include <Xol/Gauge.h>
. . .
Widget          gauge, parent;
String          name;
ArgList         args;
Cardinal        num_args;
gauge = XtCreateWidget(name, gaugeWidgetClass,
                    parent, args, num_args);
```

Gauge Resources

Name	Type	Default	Access
XtNancestorSensitive	Boolean	TRUE	G
XtNaccelerator	String	NULL	SGI
XtNacceleratorText	String	Dynamic	SGI
XtNbackground	Pixel	White	SGI
XtNbackgroundPixmap	Pixmap	(none)	SGI
XtNconsumeEvent	XtCallbackList	NULL	SGI
XtNdestroyCallback	XtCallbackList	NULL	SI
XtNfont	FontStruct *	(OPENLOOK default)	SGI
XtNfontColor	Pixel	foreground	SGI
XtNforeground	Pixel	Black	SGI
XtNheight	Dimension	(calculated)	SGI
XtNgranularity	int	1	SGI
XtNinputFocusColor	Pixel	Red	SGI
XtNmappedWhenManaged	Boolean	TRUE	SGI
XtNminLabel	String	NULL	SGI

Access: S=XtSetValues   G=XtGetValues   I=inittime   O=otheraccess

MenuButton

Synopsis

```
#include <X11/Intrinsic.h>
#include <X11/StringDefs.h>
#include <Xol/OpenLook.h>
#include <Xol/MenuButton.h>
. . .
Widget          menubutton, parent;
String          name;
ArgList         args;
Cardinal        num_args;
menubutton = XtCreateWidget(name, menubuttonWidgetClass,
                            parent, args, num_args);

OR

menubutton = XtCreateWidget(name, menubuttonGadgetClass,
                            parent, args, num_args);
. . .
Widget          menupane;
XtSetArg(args[0], XtNmenuPane, (XtArgVal)menupane);
XtGetValues(menubutton, args, 1);
Widget          menu_item;
WidgetClass     item_class;
String          item_name;
menu_item = XtCreateWidget(item_name, item_class, menupane, args, num_args);
```

MenuButton Resources

Name	Type	Default	Access
XtNaccelerator	String	NULL	SGI
XtNacceleratorText	String	Dynamic	SGI
XtNancestorSensitive	Boolean	TRUE	GO
XtNbackground	Pixel	White	SGI
XtNbackgroundPixmap	Pixmap	(none)	SGI
XtNconsumeEvent	XtCallbackList	NULL	SGI
XtNdefault	Boolean	FALSE	SGI
XtNdepth	int	(parent's)	GI
XtNdestroyCallback	XtCallbackList	NULL	SI
XtNfont	XFontStruct *	(OPEN LOOK font)	SI
XtNfontColor	Pixel	Black	SGI
XtNforeground	Pixel	Black	SGI
XtNheight	Dimension	(calculated)	SGI
XtNinputFocusColor	Pixel	Red	SGI
XtNlabel	String	(class name)	SGI

MenuButton Resources (Continued)

Name	Type	Default	Access
XtNlabelJustify	OlDefine	OL_LEFT	SGI
XtNMappedWhenManaged	Boolean	TRUE	SGI
XtNmenuMark	OlDefine	(calculated)	SGI
XtNmenuPane	Widget	(none)	G
XtNmnemonic	unsigned char	NULL	SGI
XtNrecomputeSize	Boolean	TRUE	SGI
XtNreferenceName	String	NULL	SGI
XtNreferenceWidget	Widget	NULL	SGI
XtNscale	int	12	ISG
XtNsensitive	Boolean	TRUE	GIO
XtNuserData	XtPointer	NULL	SGI
XtNwidth	Dimension	(calculated)	SGI
XtNx	Position	0	SGI
XtNy	Position	0	SGI

Access: S=XtSetValues   G=XtGetValues   I=inittime   O=otheraccess

MenuShell

Synopsis

```
#include <X11/Intrinsic.h>
#include <X11/StringDefs.h>
#include <Xol/OpenLook.h>
#include <Xol/Menu.h>
. . .
Widget            menu, parent;
String            name;
ArgList           args;
Cardinal          num_args;
menu = XtCreatePopupShell(name, menuShellWidgetClass,
                               parent, args, num_args);

. . .
Widget            menupane;
XtSetArg(args[0], XtNmenuPane, (XtArgVal)menupane);
XtGetValues(menu, args, 1);
Widget            menu_item;
WidgetClass       item_class;
String            item_name;

menu_item = XtCreateWidget(item_name, item_class, menupane, args, num_args);
```

MenuShell Resources

Name	Type	Default	Access
XtNallowShellResize	Boolean	TRUE	SGI
XtNancestorSensitive	Boolean	TRUE	G
XtNbackground	Pixel	White	SGI
XtNbackgroundPixmap	Pixmap	(none)	SGI
XtNconsumeEvent	XtCallbackList	NULL	SGI
XtNcreatePopupChildProc	XtCreatePopupChildProc	NULL	SGI
XtNdepth	int	(parent's)	GI
XtNdestroyCallback	XtCallbackList	NULL	SI
XtNfocusWidget	Widget	NULL	SGI
XtNheight	Dimension	(calculated)	SGI
XtNheightInc	int	-1	SGI
XtNinput	Boolean	FALSE	G
XtNmaxAspectX	Position	-1	SGI
XtNmaxAspectY	Position	-1	SGI
XtNmaxHeight	Dimension	OL_IGNORE	SGI
XtNmaxWidth	Dimension	OL_IGNORE	SGI
XtNmenuAugment	Boolean	TRUE	GI

MenuShell Resources (Continued)

Name	Type	Default	Access
XtNmenuPane	Widget	(none)	G
XtNminAspectX	Position	-1	SGI
XtNminAspectY	Position	-1	SGI
XtNminHeight	Dimension	OL_IGNORE	SGI
XtNminWidth	Dimension	OL_IGNORE	SGI
XtNpopdownCallback	XtCallbackList	NULL	SI
XtNpopupCallback	XtCallbackList	NULL	SI
XtNpushpin	OlDefine	OL_NONE	GI
XtNpushpinDefault	Boolean	FALSE	GI
XtNsaveUnder	Boolean	FALSE	SGI
XtNsensitive	Boolean	TRUE	GIO
XtNtitle	String	(widget's name)	SGI
XtNuserData	XtPointer	NULL	SGI
XtNwidth	Dimension	(calculated)	SGI
XtNwidthInc	int	-1	SGI

Access: S=XtSetValues   G=XtGetValues   I=inittime   O=otheraccess

NonExclusives

Synopsis

```
#include <X11/Intrinsic.h>
#include <X11/StringDefs.h>
#include <Xol/OpenLook.h>
#include <Xol/Nonexclusi.h>
. . .
Widget          nonexclusive, parent;
String          name;
ArgList         args;
Cardinal        num_args;
nonexclusive = XtCreateWidget (name, nonexclusivesWidgetClass,
                        parent, args, num_args);
```

NonExclusives Resources

Name	Type	Default	Access
XtNancestorSensitive	Boolean	TRUE	GO
XtNconsumeEvent	XtCallbackList	NULL	SG
XtNdepth	int	(parent's)	GI
XtNdestroyCallback	XtCallbackList	NULL	SI
XtNheight	Dimension	(calculated)	SGI
XtNlayoutType	OlDefine	OL_FIXEDROWS	SGI
XtNmappedWhenManaged	Boolean	TRUE	SGI
XtNmeasure	int	1	SGI
XtNreferenceName	String	NULL	GI
XtNreferenceWidget	Widget	NULL	GI
XtNsensitive	Boolean	TRUE	GIO
XtNtraversalOn	Boolean	TRUE	SGI
XtNuserData	XtPointer	NULL	SGI
XtNwidth	Dimension	(calculated)	SGI
XtNx	Position	0	SGI
XtNy	Position	0	SGI

Access: S=XtSetValues   G=XtGetValues   I=inittime   O=otheraccess

Notice

Synopsis

```
#include <X11/Intrinsic.h>
#include <X11/StringDefs.h>
#include <Xol/OpenLook.h>
#include <Xol/Notice.h>
. . .
Widget            notice, parent;
String            name;
ArgList           args;
Cardinal          num_args;
notice = XtCreatePopupShell(name, noticeShellWidgetClass,
                            parent, args, num_args);
. . .
Widget            textarea,  controlarea;
XtSetArg(args[0], XtNtextArea, (XtArgVal)textarea);
XtSetArg(args[1], XtNcontrolArea, (XtArgVal)controlarea);
XtGetValues(notice, args, 2);
Widget            control_item;
WidgetClass       item_class;
String            item_name;
control_item = XtCreateWidget(item_name, item_class, controlarea, args, num_args);
XtPopup(notice_item, XtGrabExclusive);
```

Notice Resources

Name	Type	Default	Access
XtNallowShellResize	Boolean	TRUE	SGI
XtNancestorSensitive	Boolean	TRUE	GO
XtNbackground	Pixel	White	SGI
XtNbackgroundPixmap	Pixmap	(none)	SGI
XtNborderColor	Pixel	White	SGI
XtNborderPixmap	Pixmap	(none)	SGI
XtNconsumeEvent	XtCallbackList	NULL	SGI
XtNcontrolArea	Widget	(none)	G
XtNcreatePopupChildProc	XtCreatePopupChildProc	NULL	SGI
XtNdepth	int	(parent's)	GI
XtNdestroyCallback	XtCallbackList	NULL	SI
XtNemanateWidget	Widget	(parent's)	SGI
XtNfocusWidget	Widget	NULL	SGI
XtNgeometry	String	NULL	GI
XtNheight	Dimension	(calculated)	SGI
XtNpopdownCallback	XtCallbackList	NULL	SI
XtNpopupCallback	XtCallbackList	NULL	SI

Notice Resources (Continued)

Name	Type	Default	Access
XtNsaveUnder	Boolean	FALSE	SGI
XtNsensitive	Boolean	TRUE	GIO
XtNtextArea	Widget	(none)	G
XtNuserData	XtPointer	NULL	SGI
XtNwidth	Dimension	(calculated)	SGI
XtNx	Position	0	SGI
XtNy	Position	0	SGI

Access: S=XtSetValues   G=XtGetValues   I=inittime   O=otheraccess

OblongButton

Synopsis

```
#include <X11/Intrinsic.h>
#include <Xol/OpenLook.h>
#include <X11/StringDefs.h>
#include <Xol/OblongButt.h>
. . .
Widget          oblongbutton, parent;
String          name;
ArgList         args;
Cardinal        num_args;
oblongbutton = XtCreateWidget(name, oblongButtonWidgetClass,
                        parent, args, num_args);
OR

oblongbutton = XtCreateWidget(name, oblongButtonGadgetClass,
                        parent, args, num_args);
```

OblongButton Resources

Name	Type	Default	Access
XtNaccelerator	String	NULL	SGI
XtNacceleratorText	String	Dynamic	SGI
XtNancestorSensitive	Boolean	TRUE	GO
XtNbackground	Pixel	White	SGI
XtNbackgroundPixmap	Pixmap	(none)	SGI
XtNbusy	Boolean	FALSE	SGI
XtNconsumeEvent	XtCallbackList	NULL	SGI
XtNdefault	Boolean	FALSE	SGI
XtNdepth	int	(parent's)	GI
XtNdestroyCallback	XtCallbackList	NULL	SI
XtNfont	XFontStruct *	(OPEN LOOK font)	SI
XtNfontColor	Pixel	Black	SGI
XtNforeground	Pixel	Black	SGI
XtNheight	Dimension	(calculated)	SGI
XtNinputFocusColor	Pixel	Red	SGI
XtNlabel	String	(class name)	SGI
XtNlabelImage	XImage *	NULL	SGI
XtNlabelJustify	OlDefine	OL_LEFT	SGI
XtNlabelTile	Boolean	FALSE	SGI
XtNlabelType	int	OL_STRING	SGI
XtNmappedWhenManaged	Boolean	TRUE	SGI
XtNmnemonic	unsigned char	NULL	SGI

OblongButton Resources (Continued)

Name	Type	Default	Access
XtNrecomputeSize	Boolean	TRUE	SGI
XtNreferenceName	String	NULL	SGI
XtNreferenceWidget	Widget	NULL	SGI
XtNscale	int	12	SGI
XtNselect	XtCallbackList	NULL	SI
XtNsensitive	Boolean	TRUE	GIO
XtNtraversalOn	Boolean	TRUE	SGI
XtNuserData	XtPointer	NULL	SGI
XtNwidth	Dimension	(calculated)	SGI
XtNx	Position	0	SGI
XtNy	Position	0	SGI

Access: S=XtSetValues   G=XtGetValues   I=inittime   O=otheraccess

PopupWindowShell

Synopsis

```
#include <X11/Intrinsic.h>
#include <X11/StringDefs.h>
#include <Xol/OpenLook.h>
#include <Xol/PopupWindo.h>
. . .
XtCallbackRec  applycalls [] = {
   { ApplyCallback,  client_data },
   { NULL, NULL },
};
. . .

XtSetArg(args[0], XtNapply, (XtArgVal)applycalls);
String          name;
Widget          control;
ArgList         args;
Cardinal        num_args;
popup = XtCreatePopupShell(name, popupWindowShellWidgetClass,
                          parent, args, num_args);
. . .
Widget          lower_area, upper_area, footer;
XtSetArg(args[0], XtNupperControlArea, (XtArgVal)upper_area);
XtSetArg(args[1], XtNlowerControlArea, (XtArgVal)lower_area) ;
XtSetArg(args[2], XtNfooterPanel, (XtArgVal)footer);

XtGetValues(popup, args, 3);

Widget          upper_item, lower_item  footer_item;
WidgetClass     upper_class, lower_class, footer_class;
String          upper_name, lower_name, footer_name;

upper_item = XtCreateWidget(upper_name, upper_class, upper_area, args, num_args)
lower_item = XtCreateWidget(lower_name, lower_class, lower_area, args, num_args);
footer_item = XtCreateWidget(footer_name, footer_class, footerarea, args, num_args);
XtPopup(popup, XtGrabNone);
```

PopupWindowShell

Name	Type	Default	Access
XtNallowShellResize	Boolean	TRUE	SGI
XtNancestorSensitive	Boolean	TRUE	GO
XtNapply	XtCallbackList	NULL	I
XtNapplyButton	Widget	NULL	G
XtNbackground	Pixel	White	SGI

PopupWindowShell (Continued)

Name	Type	Default	Access
XtNbackgroundPixmap	Pixmap	(none)	SGI
XtNborderColor	Pixel	Black	SGI
XtNborderPixmap	Pixmap	(none)	SGI
XtNborderWidth	Dimension	0	SGI
XtNconsumeEvent	XtCallbackList	NULL	SGI
XtNcreatePopupChildProc	XtCreatePopupChildProc	NULL	SGI
XtNdepth	int	(parent's)	GI
XtNdestroyCallback	XtCallbackList	NULL	SI
XtNfocusWidget	Widget	NULL	SGI
XtNfooterPanel	Widget	(none)	G
XtNgeometry	String	NULL	GI
XtNheight	Dimension	(calculated)	SGI
XtNheightInc	int	-1	SGI
XtNinput	Boolean	FALSE	G
XtNlowerControlArea	Widget	(none)	G
XtNmaxAspectX	int	-1	SGI
XtNmaxAspectY	int	-1	SGI
XtNmaxHeight	int	OL_IGNORE	SGI
XtNmaxWidth	int	OL_IGNORE	SGI
XtNminAspectX	int	-1	SGI
XtNminAspectY	int	-1	SGI
XtNminHeight	int	OL_IGNORE	SGI
XtNminWidth	int	OL_IGNORE	SGI
XtNpopdownCallback	XtCallbackList	NULL	SI
XtNpopupCallback	XtCallbackList	NULL	SI
XtNpushpin	OlDefine	OL_OUT	GI
XtNreset	XtCallbackList	NULL	I
XtNresetButton	Widget	NULL	G
XtNresetFactory	XtCallbackList	NULL	I
XtNresetFactoryButton	Widget	NULL	G
XtNresizeCorners	Boolean	True	SGI
XtNsaveUnder	Boolean	FALSE	SGI
XtNsensitive	Boolean	TRUE	GIO
XtNsetDefaults	XtCallbackList	NULL	I
XtNsetDefaultsButton	Widget	NULL	G
XtNtitle	String	NULL	SGI
XtNupperControlArea	Widget	(none)	G
XtNuserData	XtPointer	NULL	SGI
XtNverify	XtCallbackList	NULL	I
XtNwidth	Position	(calculated)	SGI

PopupWindowShell (Continued)

Name	Type	Default	Access
XtNwidthInc	Position	-1	SGI
XtNx	Position	0	SGI
XtNy	Position	0	SGI

Access: S=XtSetValues   G=XtGetValues   I=inittime   O=otheraccess

RectButton

Synopsis

```
#include <X11/Intrinsic.h>
#include <X11/StringDefs.h>
#include <Xol/OpenLook.h>
#include <Xol/RectButton.h>

. . .
Widget          rectbutton, parent;
String          name;
ArgList         args;
Cardinal        num_args;
rectbutton = XtCreateWidget(name, rectButtonWidgetClass,
                            parent, args, num_args);
```

RectButton Resources

Name	Type	Default	Access
XtNaccelerator	String	NULL	SGI
XtNacceleratorText	String	Dynamic	SGI
XtNancestorSensitive	Boolean	TRUE	GO
XtNbackground	Pixel	White	SGI
XtNbackgroundPixmap	Pixmap	(none)	SGI
XtNconsumeEvent	XtCallbackList	NULL	SGI
XtNdefault	Boolean	FALSE	SGI
XtNdepth	int	(parent's)	GI
XtNdestroyCallback	XtCallbackList	NULL	SI
XtNdim	Boolean	FALSE	SGI
XtNfont	XFontStruct *	(OPEN LOOK font)	SI
XtNfontColor	Pixel	Black	SGI
XtNforeground	Pixel	Black	SGI
XtNheight	Dimension	(calculated)	SGI
XtNinputFocusColor	Pixel	Red	SGI
XtNlabel	String	(class name)	SGI
XtNlabelImage	XImage *	NULL	SGI
XtNlabelJustify	OlDefine	OL_LEFT	SGI
XtNlabelTile	Boolean	FALSE	SGI
XtNlabelType	int	OL_STRING	SGI
XtNmappedWhenManaged	Boolean	TRUE	SGI
XtNmnemonic	unsigned char	NULL	SGI
XtNreferenceName	String	NULL	SGI
XtNreferenceWidget	Widget	NULL	SGI
XtNrecomputeSize	Boolean	TRUE	SGI
XtNscale	int	12	SGI

RectButton Resources (Continued)

Name	Type	Default	Access
XtNselect	XtCallbackList	NULL	SI
XtNsensitive	Boolean	TRUE	GIO
XtNset	Boolean	TRUE	SGI
XtNtraversalOn	Boolean	TRUE	SGI
XtNunselect	XtCallbackList	NULL	SI
XtNuserData	XtPointer	NULL	SGI
XtNwidth	Dimension	(calculated)	SGI

Access: S=XtSetValues   G=XtGetValues   I=inittime   O=otheraccess

RubberTile

Synopsis

```
#include <X11/Intrinsic.h>
#include <X11/StringDefs.h>
#include <Xol/OpenLook.h>
#include <Xol/RubberTile.h>
. . .
Widget           rubbertile, parent;
String           name;
ArgList          args;
Cardinal         num_args;
rubbertile = XtCreateWidget(name, rubberTileWidgetClass,
                  parent, args, num_args ),
```

RubberTile Resources

Name	Type	Default	Access
XtNancestorSensitive	Boolean	TRUE	GO
XtNbackground	Pixel	White	SGI
XtNbackgroundPixmap	Pixmap	(none)	SGI
XtNborderColor	Pixel	Black	SGI
XtNborderPixmap	Pixmap	(none)	SGI
XtNborderWidth	Dimension	0	SGI
XtNconsumeEvent	XtCallbackList	NULL	SG
XtNdepth	int	(parent's)	GI
XtNdestroyCallback	XtCallbackList	NULL	SI
XtNheight	Dimension	(calculated)	SGI
XtNinputFocusColor	Pixel	Red	SGI
XtNmappedWhenManaged	Boolean	TRUE	SGI
XtNorientation	OlDefine	OL_VERTICAL	SGI
XtNsensitive	Boolean	TRUE	GIO
XtNuserData	XtPointer	NULL	SGI
XtNwidth	Dimension	(calculated)	SGI
XtNx	Position	0	SGI
XtNy	Position	0	SGI

Access: S=XtSetValues   G=XtGetValues   I=inittime   O=otheraccess

RubberTile Child Constraint Resources

Name	Type	Default	Access
XtNrefName	String	NULL	SGI
XtNrefWidget	Widget	NULL	SGI
XtNspace	Dimension	0	SGI
XtNweight	Dimension	1	SGI

Access: S=XtSetValues   G=XtGetValues   I=inittime   O=otheraccess

Scrollbar

Synopsis

```
#include <X11/Intrinsic.h>
#include <X11/StringDefs.h>
#include <Xol/OpenLook.h>
#include <Xol/Scrollbar.h>
.  .  .
Widget              scrollbar, parent;
String              name;
ArgList             args;
Cardinal            num_args;
scrollbar = XtCreateWidget(name, scrollbarWidgetClass,
                           parent, args, num_args);

.  .  .
Widget              menupane;
XtSetArg(args[0], XtNmenuPane, (XtArgVal)menupane);
XtGetValues(scrollbar, args, 1);
Widget              menu_item;
WidgetClass         item_class;
String              item_name;
menu_item = XtCreateWidget(item_name, item_class, menupane, args, num_args);
```

Scrollbar Resources

Name	Type	Default	Access
XtNaccelerator	String	NULL	SGI
XtNacceleratorText	String	Dynamic	SGI
XtNancestorSensitive	Boolean	TRUE	GO
XtNbackground	Pixel	White	SGI
XtNbackgroundPixmap	Pixmap	(none)	SGI
XtNconsumeEvent	XtCallbackList	NULL	SGI
XtNcurrentPage	int	1	SGI
XtNdestroyCallback	XtCallbackList	NULL	SI
XtNdragCBType	OlDefine	OL_CONTINUOUS	SGI
XtNforeground	Pixel	Black	SGI
XtNgranularity	int	1	SGI
XtNheight	Dimension	(calculated)	SGI
XtNinputFocusColor	Pixel	Black	SGI
XtNinitialDelay	int	500	SGI
XtNmappedWhenManaged	Boolean	TRUE	SGI
XtNmenuPane	Widget	(none)	G
XtNmnemonic	unsigned char	NULL	SGI
XtNorientation	OlDefine	OL_VERTICAL	GI

Scrollbar Resources (Continued)

Name	Type	Default	Access
XtNproportionLength	int	(variable)	SGI
XtNreferenceName	String	NULL	SGI
XtNreferenceWidget	Widget	NULL	SGI
XtNrepeatRate	int	100	SGI
XtNsensitive	Boolean	TRUE	GIO
XtNshowPage	OlDefine	OL_NONE	SGI
XtNsliderMax	int	100	SGI
XtNsliderMin	int	0	SGI
XtNsliderMoved	XtCallbackList	NULL	SI
XtNsliderValue	int	0	SGI
XtNstopPosition	OlDefine	OL_ALL	SGI
XtNtraversalOn	Boolean	TRUE	SGI
XtNuserData	XtPointer	NULL	SGI
XtNuseSetValCallback	Boolean	FALSE	SGI
XtNwidth	Dimension	(calculated)	SGI
XtNx	Position	0	SGI
XtNy	Position	0	SGI

Access: S=XtSetValues   G=XtGetValues   I=inittime   O=otheraccess

Associated Data Structures

```
typedef struct OlScrollbarVerify {
        int     new_location;
        int     new_page;
        Boolean ok;
        int     slidermin;
        int     slidermax;
        int     delta;
        Boolean more_cb_pending;
} OlScrollbarVerify;
```

ScrolledWindow

Synopsis

```
#include <X11/Intrinsic.h>
#include <X11/StringDefs.h>
#include <Xol/OpenLook.h>
#include <Xol/ScrolledWi.h>
. . .
Widget          scrolledwindow,  parent;
String          name;
ArgList         args;
Cardinal        num_args;
scrolledwindow = XtCreateWidget(name, scrolledWindowWidgetClass,
                            parent,  args,  num_args);
. . .
Widget          h_controlarea,   v_controlarea;
XtSetArg(args[0], XtNhMenuPane, (XtArgVal)h_controlarea);
XtSetArg(args[1], XtNvMenuPane, (XtArgVal)v_controlarea);
XtGetValues(scrolledwindow, args, 1);
Widget          h_area_item,  h_area_parent,  v_area_item,  v_area_parent;
WidgetClass     h_item_class,  v_item_class;
String          h_item_name,  v_item_name;
h_area_item = XtCreateWidget(h_item_name,  h_item_class,  h_parent,  args,  num_args);
v_area_item = XtCreateWidget(v_item_name,  v_item_class,  v_parent,  args,  num_args);
```

ScrolledWindow Resources

Name	Type	Default	Access
XtNalignHorizontal	int	OL_BOTTOM	SGI
XtNalignVertical	int	OL_RIGHT	SGI
XtNancestorSensitive	Boolean	TRUE	GO
XtNborderColor	Pixel	Black	SGI
XtNborderPixmap	Pixmap	(none)	SGI
XtNcomputeGeometries	Function	Null Function	SGI
XtNconsumeEvent	XtCallbackList	NULL	SG
XtNcurrentPage	int	1	SGI
XtNdepth	int	(parent's)	GI
XtNdestroyCallback	XtCallbackList	NULL	SI
XtNforceHorizontalSB	Boolean	FALSE	SGI
XtNforceVerticalSB	Boolean	FALSE	SGI
XtNforeground	Pixel	Black	SGI
XtNhAutoScroll	Boolean	TRUE	SGI
XtNheight	Dimension	(calculated)	SGI
XtNhInitialDelay	int	500	SGI
XtNhMenuPane	Widget	(none)	G

ScrolledWindow Resources (Continued)

Name	Type	Default	Access
XtNhRepeatRate	int	100	SGI
XtNhScrollbar	Widget	(none)	G
XtNhSliderMoved	XtCallbackList	NULL	SI
XtNhStepSize	int	1	SGI
XtNinitialX	Position	0	GI
XtNinitialY	Position	0	GI
XtNinputFocusColor	Pixel	Red	SGI
XtNmappedWhenManaged	Boolean	TRUE	SGI
XtNrecomputeHeight	Boolean	TRUE	SGI
XtNrecomputeWidth	Boolean	TRUE	SGI
XtNreferenceName	String	NULL	GI
XtNreferenceWidget	Widget	NULL	GI
XtNsensitive	Boolean	TRUE	GIO
XtNshowPage	OlDefine	OL_NONE	SGI
XtNtraversalOn	Boolean	TRUE	SGI
XtNuserData	XtPointer	NULL	SGI
XtNvAutoScroll	Boolean	TRUE	SGI
XtNviewHeight	Dimension	0	SGI
XtNviewWidth	Dimension	0	SGI
XtNvInitialDelay	int	500	SGI
XtNvMenuPane	Widget	(none)	G
XtNvRepeatRate	int	100	SGI
XtNvScrollbar	Widget	(none)	G
XtNvSliderMoved	XtCallbackList	NULL	SI
XtNvStepSize	int	1	SGI
XtNwidth	Dimension	(calculated)	SGI
XtNx	Position	0	SGI
XtNy	Position	0	SGI

Access: S=XtSetValues   G=XtGetValues   I=inittime   O=otheraccess

Associated Data Structures

```
typedef struct _OlSWGeometries
    {
    Widget              sw;
    Widget              vsb;
    Widget              hsb;
    Dimension           bb_border_width;
    Dimension           vsb_width;
    Dimension           vsb_min_height;
    Dimension           hsb_height;
    Dimension           hsb_min_width;
```

```
Dimension              sw_view_width;
Dimension              sw_view_height;
Dimension              bbc_width;
Dimension              bbc_height;
Dimension              bbc_real_width;
Dimension              bbc_real_height;
Boolean                force_hsb;
Boolean                force_vsb;
} OlSWGeometries;
```

ScrollingList

Synopsis

```
#include <X11/Intrinsic.h>
#include <X11/StringDefs.h>
#include <Xol/OpenLook.h>
#include <Xol/ScrollingL.h>
```

. . .

Widget   *scrollinglist*, *parent*;
String   *name*;
ArgList   *args*;
Cardinal   *num_args*;
scrollinglist = XtCreateWidget(*name*, scrollingListWidgetClass,
                          parent, *args*, *num_args*);

. . .

Widget   *textfield*;
XtSetArg(*args*[0], XtNtextField, (XtArgVal)*textfield*);
XtGetValues(*scrollinglist*, *args*, 1);

ScrollingList Resources

Name	Type	Default	Access
XtNancestorSensitive	Boolean	TRUE	G
XtNapplAddItem	OlListToken(*)()	(n/a)	G
XtNapplDeleteItem	void(*)()	(n/a)	G
XtNapplEditClose	void(*)()	(n/a)	G
XtNapplEditOpen	void(*)()	(n/a)	G
XtNapplTouchItem	void(*)()	(n/a)	G
XtNapplUpdateView	void(*)()	(n/a)	G
XtNapplViewItem	void(*)()	(n/a)	G
XtNbackground	Pixel	White	SGI
XtNbackgroundPixmap	Pixmap	(n/a)	SGI
XtNborderColor	Pixel	Black	SGI
XtNborderPixmap	Pixmap	(n/a)	SGI
XtNconsumeEvent	XtCallbackList	NULL	SG
XtNdepth	int	(parent's)	GI
XtNdestroyCallback	XtCallbackList	NULL	SI
XtNfont	XFontStruct *	(OPEN LOOK font)	SI
XtNfontColor	Pixel	Black	SGI
XtNforeground	Pixel	Black	SGI
XtNheight	Dimension	(calculated)	SGI
XtNinputFocusColor	Pixel	Black	SGI
XtNmappedWhenManaged	Boolean	TRUE	SGI
XtNprefMaxWidth	Dimension	0	SGI

ScrollingList Resources (Continued)

Name	Type	Default	Access
XtNprefMinWidth	Dimension	0	SGI
XtNrecomputeWidth	Boolean	TRUE	SGI
XtNreferenceName	String	NULL	GI
XtNreferenceWidget	Widget	NULL	SGI
XtNresizeCallback	XtCallbackList	NULL	SGI
XtNselectable	Boolean	TRUE	SGI
XtNsensitive	Boolean	TRUE	GIO
XtNtextField	Widget	(none)	G
XtNtraversalOn	Boolean	TRUE	SGI
XtNuserData	XtPointer	NULL	SGI
XtNuserDeleteItems	XtCallbackList	NULL	SI
XtNuserMakeCurrent	XtCallbackList	NULL	SI
XtNviewHeight	Dimension	(none)	SI
XtNwidth	Dimension	(calculated)	SGI
XtNx	Position	0	SGI
XtNy	Position	0	SGI

Access: S=XtSetValues   G=XtGetValues   I=inittime   O=otheraccess

Associated Data Structures

```
typedef struct _OlListItem {              /* OPEN LOOK list item */
    OlDefine            label_type;
    XtPointer           label;
    XImage *            glyph;
    OlBitMask           attr;
    XtPointer           user_data;
    unsigned char       mnemonic;
} OlListItem;


typedef struct _OlListDelete {            /* XtNuserDelete call_data */
    OlListToken *       tokens;
    Cardinal            num_tokens;
} OlListDelete;
```

Slider

Synopsis

```
#include <X11/Intrinsic.h>
#include <X11/StringDefs.h>
#include <Xol/OpenLook.h>
#include <Xol/Slider.h>
. . .
Widget          slider, parent;
String          name;
ArgList         args;
Cardinal        num_args;
slider = XtCreateWidget(name, sliderWidgetClass,
                        parent, args, num_args);
```

Slider Resources

Name	Type	Default	Access
XtNaccelerator	String	NULL	SGI
XtNacceleratorText	String	Dynamic	SGI
XtNancestorSensitive	Boolean	TRUE	G
XtNbackground	Pixel	White	SGI
XtNbackgroundPixmap	Pixmap	(none)	SGI
XtNconsumeEvent	XtCallbackList	NULL	SGI
XtNdestroyCallback	XtCallbackList	NULL	SI
XtNdragCBType	OlDefine	OL_CONTINUOUS	SGI
XtNendBoxes	Boolean	TRUE	SGI
XtNfont	FontStruct *	(OPEN LOOK default)	SGI
XtNfontColor	Pixel	foreground	SGI
XtNforeground	Pixel	Black	SGI
XtNgranularity	int	1	SGI
XtNheight	Dimension	(calculated)	SGI
XtNinitialDelay	int	500	SGI
XtNinputFocusColor	Pixel	Black	SGI
XtNmappedWhenManaged	Boolean	TRUE	SGI
XtNminLabel	String	NULL	SGI
XtNmaxLabel	String	NULL	SGI
XtNmnemonic	unsigned char	NULL	SGI
XtNorientation	OlDefine	OL_VERTICAL	GI
XtNrecomputeSize	Boolean	FALSE	SGI
XtNreferenceName	String	NULL	SGI
XtNreferenceWidget	Widget	NULL	SGI
XtNrepeatRate	int	100	SGI
XtNscale	int	12	SGI

Slider Resources (Continued)

Name	Type	Default	Access
XtNuseSetValCallback	Boolean	FALSE	SGI
XtNsensitive	Boolean	TRUE	GI
XtNsliderMax	int	100	SGI
XtNsliderMin	int	0	SGI
XtNsliderMoved	XtCallbackList	NULL	SI
XtNsliderValue	int	0	SGI
XtNspan	Dimension	OL_IGNORE	SGI
XtNstopPosition	OlDefine	OL_ALL	SGI
XtNticks	int	0	SGI
XtNtickUnit	OlDefine	OL_NONE	SGI
XtNtraversalOn	Boolean	TRUE	SGI
XtNuserData	XtPointer	NULL	SGI
XtNwidth	Dimension	(calculated)	SGI
XtNx	Position	0	SGI
XtNy	Position	0	SGI

Access: S=XtSetValues   G=XtGetValues   I=inittime   O=otheraccess

StaticText

Synopsis

```
#include <X11/Intrinsic.h>
#include <X11/StringDefs.h>
#include <Xol/OpenLook.h>
#include <Xol/StaticText.h>
. . .
Widget          statictext, parent;
String          name;
ArgList         args;
Cardinal        num_args;
statictext = XtCreateWidget(name, staticTextWidgetClass,
                            parent, args, num_args);
```

StaticText Resources

Name	Type	Default	Access
XtNaccelerator	String	NULL	SGI
XtNacceleratorText	String	Dynamic	SGI
XtNalignment	OlDefine	OL_LEFT	SGI
XtNancestorSensitive	Boolean	TRUE	GO
XtNbackground	Pixel	White	SGI
XtNbackgroundPixmap	Pixmap	(none)	SGI
XtNborderColor	Pixel	Black	SGI
XtNborderPixmap	Pixmap	(none)	SGI
XtNborderWidth	Dimension	0	SGI
XtNconsumeEvent	XtCallbackList	NULL	SGI
XtNdepth	int	(parent's)	GI
XtNdestroyCallback	XtCallbackList	NULL	SI
XtNfont	XFontStruct *	(OPEN LOOK font)	SI
XtNfontColor	Pixel	(see below)	SGI
XtNforeground	Pixel	Black	SGI
XtNgravity	OlDefine	CenterGravity	SGI
XtNheight	OlDefine	(calculated)	SGI
XtNinputFocusColor	Pixel	Red	SGI
XtNlineSpace	int	0	SGI
XtNmappedWhenManaged	Boolean	TRUE	SGI
XtNmnemonic	unsigned char	NULL	SGI
XtNrecomputeSize	Boolean	TRUE	SGI
XtNreferenceName	String	NULL	SGI
XtNreferenceWidget	Widget	NULL	SGI
XtNsensitive	Boolean	TRUE	GIO
XtNstring	String	NULL	SGI

StaticText Resources (Continued)

Name	Type	Default	Access
XtNstrip	Boolean	TRUE	SGI
XtNtraversalOn	Boolean	FALSE	SGI
XtNuserData	XtPointer	NULL	SGI
XtNwidth	Dimension	(calculated)	SGI
XtNwrap	Boolean	TRUE	SGI
XtNx	Position	0	SGI
XtNy	Position	0	SGI

Access: S=XtSetValues   G=XtGetValues   I=inittime   O=otheraccess

Stub

Synopsis

```
#include <X11/Intrinsic.h>
#include <X11/StringDefs.h>
#include <Xol/OpenLook.h>
#include <Xol/Stub.h>
. . .
Widget          stub, parent;
String          name;
ArgList         args;
Cardinal        num_args;
stub = XtCreateWidget(name, stubWidgetClass,
                      parent, args, num_args);
```

Stub Resources

Name	Type	Default	Access
XtNacceptFocusFunc	XtRFunction	NULL	SGI
XtNaccelerator	String	NULL	SGI
XtNacceleratorText	String	Dynamic	SGI
XtNactivateFunc	Function	NULL	SGI
XtNancestorSensitive	Boolean	TRUE	G
XtNbackground	Pixel	White	SGI
XtNbackgroundPixmap	Pixmap	(none)	SGI
XtNborderColor	Pixel	Black	SGI
XtNborderWidth	Dimension	0	SGI
XtNconsumeEvent	XtCallbackList	NULL	SGI
XtNdepth	Cardinal	(parent's)	GI
XtNdestroy	Function	NULL	SGI
XtNdestroyCallback	XtCallbackList	NULL	I
XtNexpose	Function	NULL	SGI
XtNgetValuesHook	Function	NULL	SGI
XtNheight	Dimension	0	SGI
XtNhighlightHandlerProc	XtRFunction	NULL	SGI
XtNinitialize	Function	(private)	GI
XtNinitializeHook	Function	NULL	GI
XtNinputFocusColor	Pixel	Red	SGI
XtNmappedWhenManaged	Boolean	TRUE	SGI
XtNmnemonic	unsigned char	NULL	SGI
XtNqueryGeometry	Function	NULL	SGI
XtNrealize	Function	(private)	SGI
XtNreferenceName	String	NULL	SGI
XtNreferenceStub	Widget	NULL	GI

Stub Resources (Continued)

Name	Type	Default	Access
XtNreferenceWidget	Widget	NULL	SGI
XtNregisterFocusFunc	XtRFunction	Null	SGI
XtNresize	Function	NULL	SGI
XtNsensitive	Boolean	TRUE	GI
XtNsetValues	Function	NULL	SGI
XtNsetValuesAlmost	Function	(superclass)	SGI
XtNsetValuesHook	Function	NULL	SGI
XtNtraversalHandlerFunc	Function	NULL	SGI
XtNtraversalOn	Boolean	FALSE	SGI
XtNuserData	XtPointer	NULL	SGI
XtNwidth	Dimension	0	SGI
XtNwindow	Window	NULL	GI
XtNx	Position	0	SGI
XtNy	Position	0	SGI

Access: S=XtSetValues   G=XtGetValues   I=inittime   O=otheraccess

TextEdit

Synopsis

```
#include <stdio.h>
#include <Xol/buffutil.h>
#include <Xol/textbuff.h>
#include <X11/Intrinsic.h>
#include <Xol/OpenLook.h>
#include <Xol/TextEdit.h>
. . .
Widget          textedit, parent;
String          name;
ArgList         args;
Cardinal        num_args;
textedit = XtCreateWidget(name, textEditWidgetClass,
                          parent, args, num_args);
```

TextEdit Resources

Name	Type	Default	Access
XtNaccelerator	String	NULL	SGI
XtNacceleratorText	String	Dynamic	SGI
XtNancestorSensitive	Boolean	DYNAMIC	G
XtNbackground	Pixel	XtDefaultBackground	SGI
XtNbackgroundPixmap	Pixmap	Unspecified	SGI
XtNblinkRate	Int	1000	SGI
XtNborderColor	Pixel	XtDefaultForeground	SGI
XtNborderPixmap	Pixmap	Unspecified	SGI
XtNborderWidth	Dimension	0	SGI
XtNbottomMargin	Dimension	4	SGI
XtNbuttons	Callback	NULL	SGI
XtNcharsVisible	Int	50	GI
XtNcolormap	Pointer	DYNAMIC	G
XtNconsumeEvent	XtCallbackList	NULL	SGI
XtNcursorPosition	Int	0	SGI
XtNdepth	Int	DYNAMIC	GI
XtNdisplayPosition	Int	0	SGI
XtNeditType	OlEditType	OL_TEXT_EDIT	SGI
XtNfont	FontStruct	OPEN LOOK Font	SGI
XtNfontColor	Pixel	Black	SGI
XtNheight	Dimension	0	SGI
XtNinputFocusColor	Pixel	Red	SGI
XtNinsertTab	Boolean	TRUE	SGI
XtNkeys	Callback	NULL	SGI

TextEdit Resources (Continued)

Name	Type	Default	Access
XtNleftMargin	Dimension	4	SGI
XtNlinesVisible	Int	16	GI
XtNmappedWhenManaged	Boolean	TRUE	SGI
XtNmargin	Callback	NULL	SGI
XtNmnemonic	unsigned char	NULL	SGI
XtNmodifyVerification	Callback	NULL	SGI
XtNmotionVerification	Callback	NULL	SGI
XtNpostModifyNotification	Callback	NULL	SGI
XtNreferenceName	String	NULL	SGI
XtNreferenceWidget	Widget	NULL	SGI
XtNrightMargin	Dimension	4	SGI
XtNscreen	Pointer	DYNAMIC	G
XtNselectEnd	Int	0	SGI
XtNselectStart	Int	0	SGI
XtNsensitive	Boolean	TRUE	GI
XtNsource	String	NULL	SGI
XtNsourceType	OlSourceType	OL_STRING_SOURCE	SGI
XtNtabTable	Pointer	NULL	SGI
XtNtopMargin	Dimension	4	SGI
XtNtraversalOn	Boolean	TRUE	SGI
XtNuserData	XtPointer	NULL	SGI
XtNwidth	Dimension	0	SGI
XtNwrapMode	OlWrapMode	OL_WRAP_WHITE_SPACE	SGI
XtNx	Position	0	SGI
XtNy	Position	0	SGI

Access: S=XtSetValues   G=XtGetValues   I=inittime   O=otheraccess

Associated Data Structures

```
typedef struct
   {
   Boolean           ok;
   TextPosition      current_cursor;
   TextPosition      new_cursor;
   TextPosition      select_start;
   TextPosition      select_end;
   } OlTextMotionCallData, *OlTextMotionCallDataPointer;

typedef struct
   {
   Boolean           ok;
   TextPosition      current_cursor;
```

```
    TextPosition         select_start;
    TextPosition         select_end;
    TextPosition         new_cursor;
    TextPosition         new_select_start;
    TextPosition         new_select_end;
    char *               text;
    int                  text_length;
    } OlTextModifyCallData, *OlTextModifyCallDataPointer;


typedef struct
    {
    Boolean              requestor;
    TextPosition         new_cursor;
    TextPosition         new_select_start;
    TextPosition         new_select_end;
    char *               inserted;
    char *               deleted;
    TextLocation         delete_start;
    TextLocation         delete_end;
    TextLocation         insert_start;
    TextLocation         insert_end;
    TextPosition         cursor_position;
    } OlTextPostModifyCallData, *OlTextPostModifyCallDataPointer;

typedef enum
    { OL_MARGIN_EXPOSED, OL_MARGIN_CALCULATED } OlTextMarginHint;

typedef struct
    {
    OlTextMarginHint  hint;
    XRectangle *      rect;
    } OlTextMarginCallData, *OlTextMarginCallDataPointer;
```

TextField

Synopsis

```
#include <X11/Intrinsic.h>
#include <X11/StringDefs.h>
#include <Xol/OpenLook.h>
#include <Xol/TextField.h>
. . .
Widget          textfield, parent;
String          name;
ArgList         args;
Cardinal        num_args;
textfield = XtCreateWidget(name, textFieldWidgetClass,
                          parent, args, num_args);
```

TextField Resources

Name	Type	Default	Access
XtNancestorSensitive	Boolean	TRUE	GO
XtNbackground	Pixel	White	SGI
XtNbackgroundPixmap	Pixmap	(none)	SGI
XtNcharsVisible	int	0	GI
XtNconsumeEvent	XtCallbackList	NULL	SG
XtNdepth	int	(parent's)	GI
XtNdestroyCallback	XtCallbackList	NULL	SI
XtNfont	XFontStruct *	(OPEN LOOK font)	SI
XtNfontColor	Pixel	Black	SGI
XtNforeground	Pixel	Black	SGI
XtNheight	Dimension	(calculated)	SGI
XtNinputFocusColor	Pixel	Red	SGI
XtNinitialDelay	int	500	SGI
XtNinsertTab	Boolean	FALSE	SGI
XtNmappedWhenManaged	Boolean	TRUE	SGI
XtNmaximumSize	int	0	SGI
XtNreferenceName	String	NULL	GI
XtNreferenceWidget	Widget	NULL	GI
XtNrepeatRate	int	100	SGI
XtNscale	int	12	SGI
XtNsensitive	Boolean	TRUE	GIO
XtNstring	String	NULL	SGI
XtNtextEditWidget	Widget	NULL	G
XtNtraversalOn	Boolean	TRUE	SGI
XtNuserData	XtPointer	NULL	SGI
XtNverification	XtCallbackList	NULL	SGI

TextField Resources (Continued)

Name	Type	Default	Access
XtNwidth	Dimension	(calculated)	SGI
XtNx	Position	0	SGI
XtNy	Position	0	SGI

Access: S=XtSetValues   G=XtGetValues   I=inittime   O=otheraccess

Associated Data Structures

```
typedef struct
    {
    String              string;
    Boolean             ok;
    OlTextVerifyReason reason;
    } OlTextFieldVerify, *OlTextFieldVerifyPointer;
```

OLIT Utility Functions

AllocateTextBuffer()

Allocate a TextBuffer.

```
#include <Xol/textbuff.h>
. . .
extern TextBuffer *
AllocateTextBuffer(
        char *filename,
        TextUpdateFunction f,
        XtPointer d);
```

BackwardScanTextBuffer()

Scan the TextBuffer backward.

```
#include <Xol/textbuff.h>
. . .
extern ScanResult
BackwardScanTextBuffer(
        TextBuffer *text,
        char *exp,
        TextLocation *location);
```

CopyTextBufferBlock()

Copy a text block from the TextBuffer.

```
#include <Xol/textbuff.h>
. . .
extern int * CopyTextBufferBlock(
        TextBuffer *text,
        char *buffer,
        TextLocation start_position,
        TextLocation end_position,);
```

EndCurrentTextBufferWord()

Locate end of word in TextBuffer.

```
#include <Xol/textbuff.h>
. . .
extern TextLocation
EndCurrentTextBufferWord(
        TextBuffer *textBuffer,
        TextLocation current,);
```

ForwardScanTextBuffer()

Scan the TextBuffer forward.

```
#include <Xol/textbuff.h>
. . .
extern ScanResult
ForwardScanTextBuffer(
        TextBuffer *text,
        char *exp,
        TextLocation *location);
```

FreeTextBuffer()

Free the text buffer.

```
#include <Xol/textbuff.h>
. . .
extern void FreeTextBuffer(
        TextBuffer *text,
        TextUpdateFunction f,
        XtPointer d);
```

rGetTextBufferBlock()

Retrieve a text block from a TextBuffer.

```
#include <Xol/textbuff.h>
. . .
extern char *GetTextBufferBlock(
        TextBuffer *text,
        TextLocation start_location,
        TextLocation end_location);
```

GetTextBufferBuffer()

Retrieve a pointer to the Buffer stored in a TextBuffer.

```
#include <Xol/textbuff.h>
. . .
extern Buffer *GetTextBufferBuffer(
        TextBuffer *text,
        TextLine line);
```

GetTextBufferChar()

Retrieve a character stored in a TextBuffer.

```
#include <Xol/textbuff.h>
. . .
int GetTextBufferChar(
        TextBuffer *text,
        TextLocation location);
```

GetTextBufferLine()
Retrieve the contents of a line from a TextBuffer.
```
#include <Xol/textbuff.h>
. . .
extern char *GetTextBufferLine(
        TextBuffer *text,
        TextLine lineindex);
```

GetTextBufferLocation()
Retrieve a location from a TextBuffer.
```
#include <Xol/textbuff.h>
. . .
extern char *GetTextBufferLocation(
        TextBuffer *text,
        TextLine line_number,
        TextLocation *location);
```

IncrementTextBufferLocation()
Increment a TextBuffer location.
```
#include <Xol/textbuff.h>
. . .
extern TextLocation
IncrementTextBufferLocation(
        TextBuffer *text,
        TextLocation location,
        TextLine line,
        TextPosition offset);
```

LastTextBufferLocation()
Returns the last location in a TextBuffer.
```
#include <Xol/textbuff.h>
. . .
extern TextLocation
LastTextBufferLocation(
        TextBuffer *text);
```

LastTextBufferPosition()
Returns the last position in a TextBuffer.
```
#include <Xol/textbuff.h>
. . .
extern TextPosition
LastTextBufferPosition(
        TextBuffer *text);
```

LineOfPosition()
Translates a position in a TextBuffer to a line index.
```
#include <Xol/textbuff.h>
. . .
extern int LineOfPosition(
        TextBuffer *text,
        TextPosition position);
```

LocationOfPosition()
Translates a position in a TextBuffer to a location.
```
#include <Xol/textbuff.h>
. . .
extern TextLocation
LocationOfPosition(
        TextBuffer *text,
        TextPosition position);
```

NextLocation()
Returns the next location.
```
#include <Xol/textbuff.h>
. . .
extern TextLocation NextLocation(
        TextBuffer *textBuffer,
        TextLocation current);
```

NextTextBufferWord()
Locate the beginning of the next word.
```
#include <Xol/textbuff.h>
. . .
extern TextLocation
NextTextBufferWord(
        TextBuffer *textBuffer,
        TextLocation current);
```

OlActivateWidget()
Programmatically activate a widget.
```
#include <Xol/OpenLook.h>
. . .
Boolean OlActivateWidget(
        Widget widget,
        OlVirtualName activate_type,
        XtPointer data);
```

OlAssociateWidget()

Associate a widget with another widget.

```
#include <Xol/OpenLook.h>
. . .
Boolean OlAssociateWidget(
        Widget leader,
        Widget follower,
        Boolean disable_traversal)
```

OlCallAcceptFocus()

Assign focus to a specified widget.

```
#include <Xol/OpenLook.h>
. . .
Boolean OlCallAcceptFocus(
        Widget w,
        Time time);
```

OlCallDynamicCallbacks()

Call the procedures on the dynamic callback list.

```
#include <Xol/OpenLook.h>
. . .
extern void OlCallDynamicCallbacks(
void )
```

OlCanAcceptFocus()

Determine if a widget can accept focus.

```
#include <Xol/OpenLook.h>
. . .
Boolean OlCanAcceptFocus(
        Widget w,
        Time time);
```

OlColormapOfObject()

Returns the colormap associated with the specified object.

```
#include <Xol/OpenLook.h>
. . .
extern Colormap OlColormapOfObject(
        Widget w);
```

OlCreatePackedWidgetList()

Create a widget tree in one call.

```
#include <X11/Intrinsic.h>
#include <X11/StringDefs.h>
#include <Xol/OpenLook.h>
. . .
Widget OlCreatePackedWidgetList(
        OlPackedWidgetList *pl,
        Cardinal num_pw);
```

OlDepthOfObject()

Returns the depth of the specified object.

```
#include <Xol/OpenLook.h>
. . .
extern int OlDepthOfObject(
        Widget w);
```

OlDnDAllocTransientAtom()

Allocate a transient atom.

```
#include <Xol/OpenLook.h>
#include <Xol/OlDnDVCX.h>
. . .
Atom OlDnDAllocTransientAtom(
        Widget w);
```

OlDnDBeginSelectionTransaction()

Begin the drag and drop selection transaction.

```
#include <Xol/OpenLook.h>
#include <Xol/OlDnDVCX.h>
. . .
void OlDnDBeginSelectionTransaction(
        Widget widget,
        Atom selection,
        Time timestamp,
        OlDnDProtocolActionCbP acp,
        XtPointer closure);
```

OlDnDChangeDropSitePreviewHints()

Change drop site preview hints.

```
#include <OpenLook.h>
. . .
Boolean
OlDnDChangeDropSitePreviewHints(
        OlDnDDropSiteID dropsiteid;
        OlDnDSitePreviewHints ph);
```

OlDnDClearDragState()

Clears the drag state.

```
#include <Xol/OpenLook.h>
#include <Xol/OlDnDVCX.h>
. . .
void OlDnDClearDragState(
        Widget widget);
```

OlDnDDeliverPreviewMessage()

Deliver a preview message.

```
#include <Xol/OpenLook.h>
#include <Xol/OlDnDVCX.h>
. . .
Boolean OlDnDDeliverPreviewMessage(
        Widget widget,
        Window root,
        Position root_x,
        Position root_y,
        Time timestamp);
```

OlDnDeliverTriggerMessage()

Deliver a trigger message.

```
#include <Xol/OpenLook.h>
#include <Xol/OlDnDVCX.h>
. . .
Boolean OlDnDDeliverTriggerMessage(
        Widget widget,
        Window root,
        Position root_x,
        Position root_y,
        Atom selection,
        OlDnDTriggerOperation op,
        Time timestamp);
```

OlDnDDestroyDropSite()

Destroys a drop site.

```
#include <Xol/OpenLook.h>
#include <Xol/OlDnDVCX.h>
. . .
void OlDnDDestroyDropSite(
        OlDnDDropSiteID dropsiteid);
```

OlDnDDisownSelection()

Relinquishes the selection ownership.

```
#include <Xol/OpenLook.h>
#include <Xol/OlDnDVCX.h>
. . .
Boolean OlDnDDisownSelection(
        Widget widget,
        Atom selection,
        Time timestamp);
```

OlDnDDragAndDrop()

Initiate a drag and drop operation.

```
#include <Xol/OpenLook.h>
#include <Xol/OlDnDVCX.h>
. . .
void OlDnDDragAndDrop(
        Widget widget,
        Window *window,
        Position *x,
        Position *y);
```

OlDnDDragNDropDone()

Notify the selection owner that the drag and drop operation is completed.

```
#include <Xol/OpenLook.h>
#include <Xol/OlDnDVCX.h>
. . .
void OlDnDDragNDropDone1(
        Widget widget,
        Atom selection,
        Time timestamp,
        OlDnDProtocolActionCallbackProc
            proc,
        XtPointer closure);
```

OlDnDEndSelectionTransaction()

End the drag and drop selection transaction.

```
#include <Xol/OpenLook.h>
#include <Xol/OlDnDVCX.h>
. . .
void OlDnDEndSelectionTransaction(
        Widget widget,
        Atom selection,
        Time timestamp,
        OlDnDProtocolActionCbP acp,
        XtPointer closure);
```

OlDnDErrorDuringSelectionTransaction()

Notify the selection owner that an error has occurred.

```
#include <Xol/OpenLook.h>
#include <Xol/OlDnDVCX.h>

. . .
void
OlDnDErrorDuringSelectionTransactio
n(
        Widget widget,
        Atom selection,
        Time timestamp,
        OlDnDProtocolActionCbP acp,
        XtPointer closure);
```

OlDnDFreeTransientAtom()

Frees transient atoms.

```
#include <Xol/OpenLook.h>
#include <Xol/OlDnDVCX.h>

. . .
void OlDnDFreeTransientAtom(
        Widget widget,
        Atom transient);
```

OlDnDGetCurrentSelectionsForWidget()

Returns a list of atoms currently held as drag and drop selections for *widget*.

```
#include <Xol/OpenLook.h>
#include <Xol/OlDnDVCX.h>

. . .
Boolean
OlDnDGetCurrentSelectionsForWidget(
        Widget widget,
        Atom **atoms,
        Cardinal *num_atoms);
```

OlDnDGetDropSitesOfWidget()

Returns the registered list of drop sites for *widget*.

```
#include <Xol/OpenLook.h>
#include <Xol/OlDnDVCX.h>

. . .
OlDnDDropSiteID
*OlDnDGetDropSitesOfWidget(
        Widget widget,
        Cardinal *num_sites_return);
```

OlDnDGetDropSitesOfWindow()

Returns the registered list of drop sites for *window*.

```
#include <Xol/OpenLook.h>
#include <Xol/OlDnDVCX.h>

. . .
OlDnDDropSiteID
*OlDnDGetDropSitesOfWindow(
        Display *dpy,
        Window window,
        Cardinal *num_sites_return);
```

OlDnDGetWidgetOfDropSite()

Returns the widget associated with a drop site.

```
#include <Xol/OpenLook.h>
#include <Xol/OlDnDVCX.h>

. . .
Widget OlDnDGetWidgetOfDropSite(
        OlDnDDropSiteID dropsiteid);
```

OlDnDGetWindowOfDropSite()

Returns the window associated with a drop site.

```
#include <Xol/OpenLook.h>
#include <Xol/OlDnDVCX.h>

. . .
Window OlDnDGetWindowOfDropSite(
        OlDnDDropSiteID dsid);
```

OlDnDInitializeDragState()

Initialize the drag state.

```
#include <Xol/OpenLook.h>
#include <Xol/OlDnDVCX.h>

. . .
Boolean OlDnDInitializeDragState(
        Widget widget);
```

OlDnDOwnSelection()

Claims ownership of the drag and drop selection.

```
#include <Xol/OpenLook.h>
#include <Xol/OlDnDVCX.h>
. . .
Boolean OlDnDOwnSelection(
    Widget widget,
    Atom selection,
    Time timestamp,
    XtConvertSelectionProc convert_proc,
    XtLoseSelectionProc lose_proc,
    XtSelectionDoneProc done_proc,
    OlDnDTransactionStateCallback
        state_cb,
    XtPointer closure);
```

OlDnDOwnSelectionIncremental()

Claim ownership of the drag and drop selection incrementally.

```
#include <Xol/OpenLook.h>
#include <Xol/OlDnDVCX.h>
. . .
Boolean
OlDnDOwnSelectionIncremental(
  Widget widget,
  Atom selection,
  XtConvertSelectionIncrProc
      convert_incr_proc,
  XtLoseSelectionIncrProc
      lose_incr_proc,
  XtSelectionDoneIncrProc
      done_incr_proc,
  XtCancelConvertSelectionProc
      cancel_proc,
  XtPointer client_data,
  OlDnDTransactionStateCallback
      state_cb);
```

OlDnDPMNotifyProc()

The function prototype for the preview message notify procedure.

```
#include <Xol/OlDnDVCX.h>
. . .
typedef
OlDnDPreviewMessageNotifyProc
(*OlDnDPMNotifyProc)(
        Widget widget,
        Window window,
        Position root_x,
        Position root_y,
        Atom selection,
        Time time,
        OlDnDDropSiteID dropsiteid,
        OlDnDTriggerOperation operation,
        Boolean send_done,
        Boolean forwarded,
        XtPointer closure);
```

OlDnDProtocolActionCbP()

The function prototype for the protocol action callback procedure.

```
#include <Xol/OpenLook.h>
#include <Xol/OlDnDVCX.h>
. . .
typedef
OlDnDProtocolActionCallbackProc
(*OlDnDProtocolActionCbP)(
        Widget widget,
        Atom selection,
        OlDnDProtocolAction action,
        Boolean ack_ok,
        XtPointer closure);
```

OlDnDQueryDropSiteInfo()

Retrieves information about a particular drop site.

```
#include <Xol/OpenLook.h>
#include <Xol/OlDnDVCX.h>

. . .

Boolean OlDnDQueryDropSiteInfo(
        OlDnDDropSiteID dropsiteid,
        Widget *widget,
        Window *window,
        OlDnDSitePreviewHints
            *preview_hints,
        OlDnDSiteRectPtr *site_rects,
        unsigned int *num_rects,
        Boolean *on_interest);
```

OlDnDRegisterWidgetDropSite()

Creates a drop site associated with *widget*.

```
#include <Xol/OpenLook.h>
#include <Xol/OlDnDVCX.h>

. . .

OlDnDDropSiteID
OlDnDRegisterWidgetDropSite(
        Widget widget,
        OlDnDSitePreviewHints
            preview_hints,
        OlDnDSiteRectPtr sites,
        unsigned int num_sites,
        OlDnDTMNotifyProc tm_notify,
        OlDnDPMNotifyProc pm_notify,
        Boolean on_interest,
        XtPointer closure);
```

OlDnDRegisterWindowDropSite()

Create a drop site associated with *window*.

```
#include <Xol/OpenLook.h>
#include <Xol/OlDnDVCX.h>

. . .

OlDnDDropSiteID
OlDnDRegisterWindowDropSite(
        Display dpy,
        Window window,
        OlDnDSitePreviewHints
            preview_hints,
        OlDnDSiteRectPtr site,
        unsigned int num_sites,
        OlDnDTMNotifyProc tm_notify,
        OlDnDPMNotifyProc pm_notify,
        Boolean on_interest,
        XtPointer closure);
```

OlDnDTMNotifyProc()

The function prototype for the trigger message notify procedure.

```
#include <Xol/OlDnDVCX.h>

. . .

typedef Boolean
(*OlDnDTMNotifyProc)(
        Widget widget,
        Window window,
        Position root_x,
        Position root_y,
        Atom selection,
        Time time,
        OlDnDDropSiteID dropsiteid,
        OlDnDTriggerOperation
            operation,
        Boolean send_done,
        Boolean forwarded,
        XtPointer closure);
```

OlDnDTransactionStateCallback()

The transaction state callback procedure.

```
#include <Xol/OpenLook.h>
#include <Xol/OlDnDVCX.h>

. . .

typedef void
OlDnDTransactionStateCallback(
        Widget widget,
        Atom selection,
        OlDnDTransactionState state,
        Time timestamp);
        XtPointer closure);
```

OlDnDUpdateDropSiteGeometry()

Alters the grometry of a drop site.

```
#include <Xol/OpenLook.h>
#include <Xol/OlDnDVCX.h>

. . .

Boolean OlDnDUpdateDropSiteGeometry(
        OlDnDDropSiteID dropsiteid,
        OlDnDSiteRectPtr site_rects,
        unsigned int num_sites);
```

OlDnDUpdateSitePreviewHints()

Updates a drop site's preview hints.

```
#include <Xol/OpenLook.h>
#include <Xol/OlDnDVCX.h>

. . .

Boolean OlDnDUpdateSitePreviewHints(
        OlDnDDropSiteID dropsiteid,
        OlDnDSitePreviewHints
            preview_hints);
```

OlError()

Writes a string to stderr and exits.

```
#include <X11/Intrinsic.h>
#include <Xol/OpenLook.h>

. . .

void OlError(
        String msg);
```

OlErrorHandler()

The routine to handle errors.

```
#include <X11/Intrinsic.h>
#include <Xol/OpenLook.h>

. . .

typedef void (*OlErrorHandler)(
        String msg);
```

OlFlatCallAcceptFocus()

Assign focus to the specefied item.

```
#include <Xol/OpenLook,h>

. . .

Boolean OlFlatCallAcceptFocus(
        Widget widget,
        Cardinal index,
        Time time);
```

OlFlatGetFocusItem()

Returns the item that has focus.

```
#include <Xol/OpenLook,h>

. . .

Cardinal OlFlatGetFocusItem(
        Widget widget);
```

OlFlatGetItemGeometry()

Return the width and height of an item relative to its flattened widget container.

```
#include <Xol/OpenLook,h>

. . .

void OlFlatGetItemGeometry(
        Widget widget,
        Cardinal index,
        Position *x_ret,
        Position *y_ret,
        Dimension *w_ret,
        Dimension *h_ret);
```

OlFlatGetItemIndex()

Returns the item that contains the given x and y co-ordcinates.

```
#include <Xol/OpenLook,h>

. . .

Cardinal OlFlatGetItemIndex(
        Widget widget,
        Position x,
        Position y);
```

OlFlatGetValues()

Similar to XtGetValues() for flat widgets.

```
#include <Xol/OpenLook,h>
. . .
void OlFlatGetValues(
        Widget widget,
        Cardinal index,
        ArgList args,
        Cardinal num_args);
```

OlFlatSetValues()

Similar to XtSetValues() for flat widgets.

```
#include <Xol/OpenLook,h>
. . .
void OlFlatSetValues(
        Widget widget,
        Cardinal index,
        ArgList args,
        Cardinal num_args);
```

OlGet50PercentGrey()

Obtain the ID of a 50 percent grey Pixmap for *screen*.

```
#include <Xol/OlCursors.h>
. . .
extern Pixmap OlGet50PercentGrey(
        Screen *screen);
```

OlGet75PercentGrey()

Obtain the ID of a 75 percent grey Pixmap for *screen*.

```
#include <Xol/OlCursors.h>
. . .
extern Pixmap OlGet75PercentGrey(
        Screen *screen);
```

OlGetApplicationValues()

Retrieve the application resources.

```
#include
. . .
void OlGetApplicationValues(
        Widget widget,
        ArgList args,
        Cardinal num_args);
```

OlGetCurrentFocusWidget()

Returns the widget that currently has the focus.

```
#include <Xol/OpenLook.h>
. . .
Boolean OlGetCurrentFocusWidget(
        Widget w);
```

OlGetBusyCursor()

```
#include <Xol/Cursors.h>
. . .
extern Cursor OlGetBusyCursor(
        Widget widget),
```

OlGetDnDDocCursor()

```
#include <Xol/Cursors.h>
. . .
extern Cursor OlGetDnDDocCursor(
        Widget widget);
```

OlGetDnDDocStackCursor()

```
#include <Xol/Cursors.h>
. . .
extern Cursor
OlGetDnDDocStackCursor(
        Widget widget);
```

OlGetDnDDropCursor()

```
#include <Xol/Cursors.h>
. . .
extern Cursor OlGetDnDDropCursor(
        Widget widget);
```

OlGetDnDDupeBoxCursor()

```
#include <Xol/Cursors.h>
. . .
extern Cursor OlGetDnDDupeBoxCursor(
        Widget widget);
```

OlGetDnDDupeDocCursor()

```
#include <Xol/Cursors.h>
. . .
extern Cursor OlGetDnDDupeDocCursor(
        Widget widget);
```

OlGetDnDDupeDocDragCursor()

```
#include <Xol/Cursors.h>
. . .
extern Cursor
OlGetDnDDupeDocDragCursor(
        Widget widget);
```

OlGetDnDDupeDocDropCursor()

```
#include <Xol/Cursors.h>
. . .
extern Cursor
OlGetDnDDupeDocDropCursor(
        Widget widget);
```

OlGetDnDDupeDocNoDropCursor()

```
#include <Xol/Cursors.h>
. . .
extern Cursor
OlGetDnDDupeDocNoDropCursor(
        Widget widget);
```

OlGetDnDDupeStackCursor()

```
#include <Xol/Cursors.h>
. . .
extern Cursor
OlGetDnDDupeStackCursor(
        Widget widget);
```

OlGetDnDDupeStackDragCursor()

```
#include <Xol/Cursors.h>
. . .
extern Cursor
OlGetDnDDupeStackDragCursor(
        Widget widget);
```

OlGetDnDDupeStackDropCursor()

```
#include <Xol/Cursors.h>
. . .
extern Cursor
OlGetDnDDupeStackDropCursor(
        Widget widget);
```

OlGetDnDDupeStackNoDropCursor()

```
#include <Xol/Cursors.h>
. . .
extern Cursor
OlGetDnDDupeStackNoDropCursor(
        Widget widget);
```

OlGetDnDMoveBoxCursor()

■

```
#include <Xol/Cursors.h>
. . .
extern Cursor OlGetDnDMoveBoxCursor(
        Widget widget);
```

OlGetDnDMoveDocCursor()

```
#include <Xol/Cursors.h>
. . .
extern Cursor OlGetDnDMoveDocCursor(
        Widget widget);
```

OlGetDnDMoveDocDragCursor()

```
#include <Xol/Cursors.h>
. . .
extern Cursor
OlGetDnDMoveDocDragCursor(
        Widget widget);
```

OlGetDnDMoveDocDropCursor()

```
#include <Xol/Cursors.h>
. . .
extern Cursor
OlGetDnDMoveDocDropCursor(
        Widget widget);
```

OlGetDnDMoveDocNoDropCursor()

```
#include <Xol/Cursors.h>
. . .
extern Cursor
OlGetDnDMoveDocNoDropCursor(
        Widget widget);
```

OlGetDnDMoveStackCursor()

```
#include <Xol/Cursors.h>
. . .
extern Cursor
OlGetDnDMoveStackCursor(
        Widget widget);
```

OlGetDnDMoveStackDragCursor()

```
#include <Xol/Cursors.h>
. . .
extern Cursor
OlGetDnDMoveStackDragCursor(
        Widget widget);
```

OlGetDnDMoveStackDropCursor()

```
#include <Xol/Cursors.h>
. . .
extern Cursor
OlGetDnDMoveStackDropCursor(
        Widget widget);
```

OlGetDnDMoveStackNoDropCursor()

```
#include <Xol/Cursors.h>
. . .
extern Cursor
OlGetDnDMoveStackNoDropCursor(
        Widget widget);
```

OlGetDnDNoDropCursor()

```
#include <Xol/Cursors.h>
. . .
extern Cursor OlGetDnDNoDropCursor(
        Widget widget);
```

OlGetDnDTextDupeBoxCursor()

```
#include <Xol/Cursors.h>
. . .
extern Cursor
OlGetDnDTextDupeBoxCursor(
        Widget widget);
```

OlGetDnDTextDupeDragCursor()

```
#include <Xol/Cursors.h>
. . .
extern Cursor
OlGetDnDTextDupeDragCursor(
        Widget widget);
```

OlGetDnDTextDupeDropCursor()

```
#include <Xol/Cursors.h>
. . .
extern Cursor
OlGetDnDTextDupeDropCursor(
        Widget widget);
```

OlGetDnDTextDupeNoDropCursor()

```
#include <Xol/Cursors.h>
. . .
extern Cursor
OlGetDnDTextDupeNoDropCursor(
        Widget widget);
```

OlGetDnDTextMoveBoxCursor()

```
#include <Xol/Cursors.h>
. . .
extern Cursor
OlGetDnDTextMoveBoxCursor(
        Widget widget);
```

OlGetDnDTextMoveDragCursor()

```
#include <Xol/Cursors.h>
. . .
extern Cursor
OlGetDnDTextMoveDragCursor(
        Widget widget);
```

OlGetDnDTextMoveDropCursor()

```
#include <Xol/Cursors.h>
. . .
extern Cursor
OlGetDnDTextMoveDropCursor(
        Widget widget);
```

OlGetDnDTextMoveNoDropCursor()

```
#include <Xol/Cursors.h>
. . .
extern Cursor
OlGetDnDTextMoveNoDropCursor(
        Widget widget);
```

OlGetDnDTextMoveInsertCursor()

```
#include <Xol/Cursors.h>
. . .
extern Cursor
OlGetDnDTextMoveInsertCursor(
        Widget widget);
```

OlGetDnDTextDupeInsertCursor()

```
#include <Xol/Cursors.h>
. . .
extern Cursor
OlGetDnDTextDupeInsertCursor(
        Widget widget);
```

OlGetDuplicateCursor()

```
#include <Xol/Cursors.h>
. . .
extern Cursor OlGetDuplicateCursor(
        Widget widget);
```

OlGetMoveCursor()

```
#include <Xol/Cursors.h>
. . .
extern Cursor OlGetMoveCursor(
        Widget widget);
```

OlGetPanCursor()

```
#include <Xol/Cursors.h>
. . .
extern Cursor OlGetPanCursor(
        Widget widget);
```

OlGetQuestionCursor()

```
#include <Xol/Cursors.h>
. . .
extern Cursor OlGetQuestionCursor(
        Widget widget);
```

OlGetStandardCursor()

```
#include <Xol/Cursors.h>
. . .
extern Cursor OlGetStandardCursor(
        Widget widget);
```

OlGetTargetCursor()

```
#include <Xol/Cursors.h>
. . .
extern Cursor OlGetTargetCursor(
        Widget widget);
```

OlGrabDragPointer()

Grag the mouse pointer.

```
#include <Xol/OpenLook.h>
. . .
extern void OlGrabDragPointer(
        Widget w,
        Cursor cursor,
        Window window);
```

OlHasFocus()

Determine is the specified widget has the focus.

```
#include <Xol/OpenLook.h>
. . .
Boolean OlHasFocus(
        Widget w);
```

OlInitialize()

The initialization routine.

```
#include <X11/Xlib.h>
#include <Xol/OpenLook.h>
. . .
Widget OlInitialize(
        String shell_name,
        String application_class,
        XrmOptionDescRec *options,
        Cardinal num_options,
        Cardinal *argc,
        String argv[]);
```

OlMenuPopup()

Programmatically pop up a menu.

```
#include <Xol/OpenLook.h>
. . .
void OlMenuPopup(
        Widget menu,
        Widget emanate,
        Cardinal item_index,
        OlDefine state,
        Boolean *set_position;
        Position x,
        Position y,
        OlMenuPositionProc
            pposition_proc);
```

OlMenuPost()

Programmatically pop up a menu.

```
#include <Xol/OpenLook.h>
. . .
void OlMenuPost(
        Widget menu);
```

OlMenuPopdown()

Programmatically pop down a menu.

```
#include <Xol/OpenLook.h>
. . .
void OlMenuPopdown(
        Widget menu,
        Boolean dismiss_pinned);
```

OlMenuUnpost()

Programmatically pop down a menu.

```
#include <Xol/OpenLook.h>
. . .
void OlMenuUnpost(
        Widget menu);
```

OlQueryAcceleratorDisplay()

Query the display state of accelerators.

```
OlDefine OlQueryAcceleratorDisplay(
        Widget w);
```

OlQueryMnemonicDisplay()

Query the display state of mnemonics.

```
OlDefine OlQueryMnemonicDisplay(
        Widget w);
```

OlRegisterDynamicCallback()

Add a function to the list of dynamic callbacks.

```
#include <Xol/OpenLook.h>
. . .
extern void
OlRegisterDynamicCallback(
        OlDynamicCallbackProc
            CB,
        XtPointer data);
```

OlRegisterHelp()

Associate help information with an object.

```
#include <X11/Intrinsic.h>
#include <Xol/OpenLook.h>
. . .
void OlRegisterHelp(
        OlDefine id_type,
        XtPointer id,
        String tag,
        OlDefine source_type,
        XtPointer source);
```

OlSetErrorHandler()

Set the function used to handle errors.

```
#include <X11/Intrinsic.h>
#include <Xol/OpenLook.h>
. . .
OlErrorHandler OlSetErrorHandler(
        OlErrorHandler handler);
```

OlSetInputFocus()

Set the input focus to the specified widget.

```
#include <Xol/OpenLook.h>
. . .
Boolean OlSetInputFocus(
        Widget w);
```

OlSetVaDisplayErrorMsgHandler()

Set the function to handle errors.

```
#include <X11/Intrinsic.h>
#include <Xol/OpenLook.h>
. . .
OlVaDisplayErrorMsgHandler
OlSetVaDisplayErrorMsgHandler(
        OlVaDisplayErrorMsgHandler
            handler);
```

OlSetVaDisplayWarningMsgHandler()

Set the function to handle warnings.

```
#include <X11/Intrinsic.h>
#include <Xol/OpenLook.h>
. . .
OlVaDisplayWarningMsgHandler
OlSetVaDisplayWarningMsgHandler(
        OlVaDisplayWarningMsgHandler
            handler);
```

OlSetWarningHandler()

Set the function to handle warnings.

```
#include <X11/Intrinsic.h>
#include <Xol/OpenLook.h>
. . .
OlWarningHandler
OlSetWarningHandler(
        OlWarningHandler handler);
```

OlSetGaugeValue()

The the value of a gauge.

```
extern void OlSetGaugeValue(
        Widget w,
        int value);
```

OlTextEditClearBuffer()

Delete all text associated with a TextEdit widget.

```
#include <Xol/buffutil.h>
#include <Xol/textbuff.h>
#include <Xol/TextEdit.h>
. . .
extern Boolean
OlTextEditClearBuffer(
        TextEditWidget ctx);
```

OlTextEditCopyBuffer()

Retrieve a copy of the TextBuffer associated with the TextEdit widget.

```
#include <Xol/buffutil.h>
#include <Xol/textbuff.h>
#include <Xol/TextEdit.h>
. . .
extern Boolean OlTextEditCopyBuffer(
        TextEditWidget ctx,
        char **buffer);
```

OlTextEditCopySelection()

Copy of cut the text currently selected in the TextEdit widget.

```
#include <Xol/buffutil.h>
#include <Xol/textbuff.h>
#include <Xol/TextEdit.h>
. . .
extern Boolean
OlTextEditCopySelection(
        TextEditWidget ctx,
        int delete);
```

OlTextEditGetCursorPosition()

Get the current cursor position in the TextEdit widget.

```
#include <Xol/textbuff.h>
#include <Xol/TextEdit.h>
. . .
extern Boolean
OlTextEditGetCursorPosition(
        TextEditWidget ctx,
        TextPosition *start,
        TextPosition *end,
        TextPosition *cursorPosition);
```

OlTextEditGetLastPosition()

Retrieve the position of the last character in the TextEdit widget.

```
#include <Xol/buffutil.h>
#include <Xol/textbuff.h>
#include <Xol/TextEdit.h>
. . .
extern Boolean
OlTextEditGetLastPosition(
        TextEditWidget ctx,
        TextPosition *position);
```

OlTextEditInsert()

Insert *buffer* in the TextEdit widget.

```
#include <Xol/buffutil.h>
#include <Xol/textbuff.h>
#include <Xol/TextEdit.h>
. . .
extern Boolean OlTextEditInsert(
        TextEditWidget ctx,
        String buffer,
        int length);
```

OlTextEditPaste()

Paste the contents of the CLIPBOARD into the TextEdit widget.

```
#include <Xol/buffutil.h>
#include <Xol/textbuff.h>
#include <Xol/TextEdit.h>
. . .
extern Boolean OlTextEditPaste(
        TextEditWidget ctx);
```

OlTextEditReadSubString()

Retrieve a copy of a sub string from the TextEdit widget.

```
#include <Xol/buffutil.h>
#include <Xol/textbuff.h>
#include <Xol/TextEdit.h>
. . .
extern Boolean
OlTextEditReadSubString(
        TextEditWidget ctx,
        char **buffer,
        TextPosition start,
        TextPosition end);
```

OlTextEditRedraw()

Redraw the TextEdit widget.

```
#include <Xol/buffutil.h>
#include <Xol/textbuff.h>
#include <Xol/TextEdit.h>
. . .
extern Boolean OlTextEditRedraw(
        TextEditWidget ctx);
```

OlTextEditSetCursorPosition()

Set the cursor position in the TextEdit widget.

```
#include <Xol/textbuff.h>
#include <Xol/TextEdit.h>
. . .
extern Boolean
OlTextEditSetCursorPosition(
        TextEditWidget ctx,
        TextPosition start,
        TextPosition end,
        TextPosition cursorPosition);
```

OlTextEditTextBuffer()

Retrieve the TextBuffer associated with the TextEdit widget.

```
#include <Xol/buffutil.h>
#include <Xol/textbuff.h>
#include <Xol/TextEdit.h>
. . .
extern TextBuffer
*OlTextEditTextBuffer(
        TextEditWidget ctx);
```

OlTextEditUpdate()

Set the update state of the TextEdit widget.

```
#include <Xol/buffutil.h>
#include <Xol/textbuff.h>
#include <Xol/TextEdit.h>
. . .
extern Boolean OlTextEditUpdate(
        TextEditWidget ctx,
        Boolean state);
```

OlTextFieldCopyString()

Copy a string associated with the TextField widget.

```
#include <Xol/buffutil.h>
#include <Xol/textbuff.h>
#include <Xol/TextField.h>
. . .
extern int OlTextFieldCopyString(
        TextFieldWidget tfw,
        char *string);
```

OlTextFieldGetString()

Get a new copy of the string associated with the Text-Field widget.

```
#include <Xol/buffutil.h>
#include <Xol/textbuff.h>
#include <Xol/TextField.h>
. . .
extern char *OlTextFieldGetString(
        TextFieldWidget tfw,
        int *size);
```

OlToolkitInitialize()

Initialize the OPEN LOOK toolkit. Not to be called in conjuction with OlInitialize().

```
#include <X11/Xlib.h>
#include <Xol/OpenLook.h>
. . .
Widget OlToolkitInitialize(
        XtPointer NULL);
```

OlUnassociateWidget()

Disassociate widgets that are associated.

```
#include <Xol/OpenLook.h>
. . .
void OlUnassociateWidget(
        Widget follower);
```

OlUngrabDragPointer()

Relinquish the pointer grab.

```
#include <Xol/OpenLook.h>
#include <Xol/Dynamic.h>
. . .
extern void OlUngrabDragPointer(
        Widget w);
```

OlUnregisterDynamicCallback()

Remove a function from the dynamic callback list.

```
#include <Xol/OpenLook.h>
. . .
extern int
OlUnregisterDynamicCallback(
        void *CB
        XtPointer data);
```

OlUpdateDisplay()

Process all pending exposure events immediately.

```
#include <Xol/OpenLook.h>
. . .
void OlUpdateDisplay(
        Widget w)
```

OlVaDisplayErrorMsg()

Write an error to stderr and exit.

```
#include <X11/Intrinsic.h>
#include <Xol/OpenLook.h>
. . .
void OlVaDisplayErrorMsg(
        Display *dpy,
        String name,
        String type,
        String class,
        String default_msg,);
```

OlVaDisplayErrorMsgHandler()

Function to handle error messages.

```
#include <X11/Intrinsic.h>
#include <Xol/OpenLook.h>
. . .
typedef void
(*OlVaDisplayErrorMsgHandler)(
        Display *dpy,
        String name,
        String type,
        String class,
        String default_msg,
        va_list ap);
```

OlVaDisplayWarningMsg()

Write an error to stderr and return.

```
#include <X11/Intrinsic.h>
#include <Xol/OpenLook.h>
. . .
void OlVaDisplayWarningMsg(
        Display *dpy,
        String name,
        String type,
        String class,
        String default_msg,);
```

OlVaDisplayWarningMsgHandler()

Function to handle warning messages.

```
#include <X11/Intrinsic.h>
#include <Xol/OpenLook.h>
. . .
typedef void
(*OlVaDisplayWarningMsgHandler)(
        Display *dpy,
        String name,
        String type,
        String class,
        String default_msg,
        va_list ap);
```

OlVaFlatGetValues()

Varargs version of OlFlatGetValues().

```
#include <Xol/OpenLook,h>
. . .
void OlVaFlatGetValues(
        Widget widget,
        Cardinal index,);
```

OlVaFlatSetValues()

Varargs version of OlFlatSetValues().

```
#include <Xol/OpenLook,h>
. . .
void OlVaFlatSetValues(
        Widget widget,
        Cardinal index);
```

OlVisualOfObject()

Returns the visual of the specified object.

```
#include <Xol/OpenLook.h>
. . .
extern Visual *OlVisualOfObject(
        Widget object);
```

OlWMProtocolAction()

Simulate a response to the window manager's protocol.

```
#include
void OlWMProtocolAction(
        Widget w,
        OlWMProtocolVerify *st,
        OlDefine action)
```

OlWarning()

Print a warning message and return.

```
#include <X11/Intrinsic.h>
#include <Xol/OpenLook.h>
. . .
void OlWarning(
        String msg);
```

OlWarningHandler()

The function to handle warning messages.

```
#include <X11/Intrinsic.h>
#include <Xol/OpenLook.h>
. . .
typedef void (*OlWarningHandler)(
        String msg);
```

PositionOfLine()

Translate a line index in a TExtBuffer to a TextPosition.

```
#include <Xol/textbuff.h>
. . .
extern TextPosition PositionOfLine(
        TextBuffer *text,
        TextLine lineindex);
```

PositionOfLocation()

Translate a location in a TextBuffer to a TextPosition.

```
#include <Xol/textbuff.h>
. . .
extern TextPosition
PositionOfLocation(
        TextBuffer *text,
        TextLocation location);
```

PreviousLocation()

Returns the location which precedes the current location in the TextBuffer.

```
#include <Xol/textbuff.h>
. . .
extern TextLocation
PreviousLocation(
        TextBuffer *textBuffer,
        TextLocation current);
```

PreviousTextBufferWord()

Returns the location of the beginning of the current word in the TextBuffer.

```
#include <Xol/textbuff.h>
. . .
extern TextLocation
PreviousTextBufferWord(
        TextBuffer *textBuffer,
        TextLocation current);
```

ReadFileIntoTextBuffer()

Reads a file in a TextBuffer.

```
#include <Xol/textbuff.h>
. . .
extern TextBuffer
*ReadFileIntoTextBuffer(
        char *filename,
        TextUpdateFunction f,
        XtPointer d);
```

ReadStringIntoTextBuffer()

Reads a string into a TextBuffer.

```
#include <Xol/textbuff.h>
. . .
extern TextBuffer
*ReadStringIntoTextBuffer(
        char *string,
        TextUpdateFunction f,
        XtPointer d);
```

ReplaceBlockInTextBuffer()

Replace a block of text in a TextBuffer.

```
#include <Xol/textbuff.h>
. . .
extern EditResult
ReplaceBlockInTextBuffer(
        TextBuffer *text,
        TextLocation *startloc,
        TextLocation *endloc,
        char *string,
        TextUpdateFunction f,
        XtPointer d);
```

ReplaceCharInTextBuffer()

Replace a character in a TextBuffer.

```
#include <Xol/textbuff.h>
. . .
extern EditResult
ReplaceCharInTextBuffer(
        TextBuffer *text,
        TextLocation *location,
        int c,
        TextUpdateFunction f,
        XtPointer d);
```

SaveTextBuffer()

Save a TextBuffer to a file.

```
#include <Xol/textbuff.h>
. . .
extern SaveResult SaveTextBuffer(
        TextBuffer *text,
        char *filename);
```

StartCurrentTextBufferWord()

Locates a word in a TextBuffer.

```
#include <Xol/textbuff.h>
. . .
extern TextLocation
StartCurrentTextBufferWord(
        TextBuffer *textBuffer,
        TextLocation current);
```

APPENDIX C

KEY AND BUTTON BINDINGS

Key	Abbreviation
Alt key	a
Ctrl key	c
no modifier	n
Shift key	s

Button Bindings

Name	Default Value	Virtual Event
adjustBtn	n<Button2>	OL_ADJUST
constrainBtn	s<Button1>	OL_CONSTRAIN
duplicateBtn	c<Button1>	OL_DUPLICATE
menuBtn	n<Button3>	OL_MENU
menuDefaultBtn	c<Button3>	OL_MENUDEFAULT
panBtn	a<Button1>	OL_PAN
selectBtn	n<Button1>	OL_SELECT

Key Bindings

Name	Default Value	Virtual Event
adjustKey	a<Insert>	OL_AJUSTKEY
cancelKey	n<Escape>	OL_CANCEL
charBakKey	<Left>, c<b>	OL_CHARBAK

Key Bindings (Continued)

Name	Default Value	Virtual Event
charFwdKey	\<Right\>, c\<f\>	OL_CHARFWD
copyKey	n\<F16\>	OL_COPY
cutKey	n\<F20\>	OL_CUT
defaultActionKey	\<Return\>,c\<Return\>	OL_DEFAULTACTION
delCharBakKey	\<BackSpace\>,\<Delete\>	OL_DELCHARBAK
delCharFwdKey	s\<BackSpace\>,c\<d\>	OL_DELCHARFWD
delLineBakKey	c\<BackSpace\>,c\<u\>	OL_DELLINEBAK
delLineFwdKey	c\<Delete\>,c\<k\>	OL_DELLINEFWD
delLineKey	m\<BackSpace\>,m\<Delete\>	OL_DELLINE
delWordBakKey	c s\<BackSpace\>,c\<w\>	OL_DELWORDBAK
delWordFwdKey	c s\<Delete\>	OL_DELWORDFWD
docEndKey	c\<R13\>	OL_DOCEND
docStartKey	c\<R7\>	OL_DOCSTART
downKey	\<Down\>	OL_MOVEDOWN
helpKey	n\<Help\>	OL_HELP
horizSBMenuKey	a\<h\>	OL_HSBMENU
leftKey	\<Left\>	OL_MOVELEFT
lineEndKey	n\<R13\>, c\<e\>	OL_LINEEND
lineStartKey	n\<R7\>, c\<a\>	OL_LINESTART
menuDefaultKey	c\<space\>	OL_MENUDEFAULTKEY
menuKey	a\<space\>	OL_MENUKEY
multiDownKey	c\<Down\>	OL_MULTIDOWN
multiLeftKey	c\<Left\>	OL_MULTILEFT
multiRightKey	c\<Right\>	OL_MULTIRIGHT
multiUpKey	c\<Up\>	OL_MULTIUP
nextFieldKey	n\<Tab\>,c\<Tab\>	OL_NEXT_FIELD
pageDownKey	a\<R15\>	OL_PAGEDOWN
pageLeftKey	a c\<R9\>	OL_PAGELEFT
pageRightKey	a c\<R15\>	OL_PAGERIGHT
pageUpKey	a\<R9\>	OL_PAGEUP
paneEndKey	c s\<R13\>	OL_PANEEND
paneStartKey	c s\<R7\>	OL_PANESTART
pasteKey	n\<F18\>, c\<y\>	OL_PASTE
prevFieldKey	s\<Tab\>,c s\<Tab\>	OL_PREV_FIELD
propertiesKey	n\<F13\>	OL_PROPERTY
returnKey	\<Return\>	OL_RETURN
rightKey	\<Right\>	OL_MOVERIGHT
rowDownKey	\<Down\>, c\<n\>	OL_ROWDOWN
rowUpKey	\<Up\>, c\<p\>	OL_ROWUP
scrollBottomKey	a c\<R13\>	OL_SCROLLBOTTOM

Key Bindings (Continued)

Name	Default Value	Virtual Event
scrollDownKey	a\<Down\>	OL_SCROLLDOWN
scrollLeftEdgeKey	a\<R7\>	OL_SCROLLLEFTEDGE
scrollLeftKey	a\<Left\>	OL_SCROLLLEFT
scrollRightEdgeKey	a\<R13\>	OL_SCROLLRIGHTEDGE
scrollRightKey	a\<Right\>	OL_SCROLLRIGHT
scrollTopKey	a c\<R7\>	OL_SCROLLTOP
scrollUpKey	a\<Up\>	OL_SCROLLUP
selCharBakKey	s\<Left\>, s c\<b\>	OL_SELCHARBAK
selCharFwdKey	s\<Right\>, s c\<f\>	OL_SELCHARFWD
selLineBakKey	s\<R7\>, s c\<p\>	OL_SELLINEBAK
selLineFwdKey	s\<R13\>, s c\<n\>	OL_SELLINEFWD
selLineKey	c a\<Left\>	OL_SELLINE
selWordBakKey	c s\<Left\>	OL_SELWORDBAK
selWordFwdKey	c s\<Right\>	OL_SELWORDFWD
selectKey	n\<space\>	OL_SELECTKEY
stopKey	n\<F11\>	OL_STOP
togglePushpinKey	c\<t\>	OL_TOGGLEPUSHPIN
undoKey	n\<F14\>	OL_UNDO
upKey	\<Up\>	OL_MOVEUP
vertSBMenuKey	a\<v\>	OL_VSBMENU
wordBakKey	c\<Left\>	OL_WORDBAK
wordFwdKey	c\<Right\>	OL_WORDFWD

APPENDIX D

LibXs.h

```
#define XtRVerlevel "Verlevel"

typedef enum {
   LEVEL1,
   LEVEL2,
   LEVEL3,
   LEVEL4,
} verlevel;

typedef struct _bitmap_struct {
   unsigned char *bitmap;
   Dimension width;
   Dimension height;
} xs_bitmap_struct;

extern Widget    xs_create_button ();
extern void      xs_invert_widget ();
extern String    xs_concat_words ();
extern Boolean   xs_cvt_str_to_verlevel();
extern XImage    *xs_create_image ();
extern Widget    xs_create_pixmap_button ();
extern Widget    xs_create_pixmap_browser ();
extern void      xs_insert_string();
extern GC        xs_create_xor_gc();
```

APPENDIX E

PIXMAPS

```
#define solid_width 32
#define solid_height 32
static unsigned char solid_bits[] = {
    0xff, 0xff, 0xff, 0xff, 0xff, 0xff, 0xff, 0xff, 0xff, 0xff, 0xff, 0xff,
    0xff, 0xff, 0xff, 0xff, 0xff, 0xff, 0xff, 0xff, 0xff, 0xff, 0xff, 0xff,
    0xff, 0xff, 0xff, 0xff, 0xff, 0xff, 0xff, 0xff, 0xff, 0xff, 0xff, 0xff,
    0xff, 0xff, 0xff, 0xff, 0xff, 0xff, 0xff, 0xff, 0xff, 0xff, 0xff, 0xff,
    0xff, 0xff, 0xff, 0xff, 0xff, 0xff, 0xff, 0xff, 0xff, 0xff, 0xff, 0xff,
    0xff, 0xff, 0xff, 0xff, 0xff, 0xff, 0xff, 0xff, 0xff, 0xff, 0xff, 0xff,
    0xff, 0xff, 0xff, 0xff, 0xff, 0xff, 0xff, 0xff, 0xff, 0xff, 0xff, 0xff,
    0xff, 0xff, 0xff, 0xff, 0xff, 0xff, 0xff, 0xff, 0xff, 0xff, 0xff, 0xff,
    0xff, 0xff, 0xff, 0xff, 0xff, 0xff, 0xff, 0xff, 0xff, 0xff, 0xff, 0xff,
    0xff, 0xff, 0xff, 0xff, 0xff, 0xff, 0xff, 0xff, 0xff, 0xff, 0xff, 0xff,
    0xff, 0xff, 0xff, 0xff, 0xff, 0xff, 0xff, 0xff
};
#define clear_width 32
#define clear_height 32
static unsigned char clear_bits[] = {
    0x00, 0x00, 0x00, 0x00, 0x00, 0x00, 0x00, 0x00, 0x00, 0x00, 0x00, 0x00,
    0x00, 0x00, 0x00, 0x00, 0x00, 0x00, 0x00, 0x00, 0x00, 0x00, 0x00, 0x00,
    0x00, 0x00, 0x00, 0x00, 0x00, 0x00, 0x00, 0x00, 0x00, 0x00, 0x00, 0x00,
    0x00, 0x00, 0x00, 0x00, 0x00, 0x00, 0x00, 0x00, 0x00, 0x00, 0x00, 0x00,
    0x00, 0x00, 0x00, 0x00, 0x00, 0x00, 0x00, 0x00, 0x00, 0x00, 0x00, 0x00,
    0x00, 0x00, 0x00, 0x00, 0x00, 0x00, 0x00, 0x00, 0x00, 0x00, 0x00, 0x00,
    0x00, 0x00, 0x00, 0x00, 0x00, 0x00, 0x00, 0x00, 0x00, 0x00, 0x00, 0x00,
    0x00, 0x00, 0x00, 0x00, 0x00, 0x00, 0x00, 0x00, 0x00, 0x00, 0x00, 0x00,
    0x00, 0x00, 0x00, 0x00, 0x00, 0x00, 0x00, 0x00, 0x00, 0x00, 0x00, 0x00,
    0x00, 0x00, 0x00, 0x00, 0x00, 0x00, 0x00, 0x00, 0x00, 0x00, 0x00, 0x00,
    0x00, 0x00, 0x00, 0x00, 0x00, 0x00, 0x00, 0x00
```

```
};
#define vertical_width 32
#define vertical_height 32
static unsigned char vertical_bits[] = {
   0x88, 0x88, 0x88, 0x88, 0x88, 0x88, 0x88, 0x88, 0x88, 0x88, 0x88, 0x88,
   0x88, 0x88, 0x88, 0x88, 0x88, 0x88, 0x88, 0x88, 0x88, 0x88, 0x88, 0x88,
   0x88, 0x88, 0x88, 0x88, 0x88, 0x88, 0x88, 0x88, 0x88, 0x88, 0x88, 0x88,
   0x88, 0x88, 0x88, 0x88, 0x88, 0x88, 0x88, 0x88, 0x88, 0x88, 0x88, 0x88,
   0x88, 0x88, 0x88, 0x88, 0x88, 0x88, 0x88, 0x88, 0x88, 0x88, 0x88, 0x88,
   0x88, 0x88, 0x88, 0x88, 0x88, 0x88, 0x88, 0x88, 0x88, 0x88, 0x88, 0x88,
   0x88, 0x88, 0x88, 0x88, 0x88, 0x88, 0x88, 0x88, 0x88, 0x88, 0x88, 0x88,
   0x88, 0x88, 0x88, 0x88, 0x88, 0x88, 0x88, 0x88, 0x88, 0x88, 0x88, 0x88,
   0x88, 0x88, 0x88, 0x88, 0x88, 0x88, 0x88, 0x88, 0x88, 0x88, 0x88, 0x88,
   0x88, 0x88, 0x88, 0x88, 0x88, 0x88, 0x88, 0x88, 0x88, 0x88, 0x88, 0x88,
   0x88, 0x88, 0x88, 0x88, 0x88, 0x88, 0x88, 0x88
};
#define horizontal_width 32
#define horizontal_height 32
static unsigned char horizontal_bits[] = {
   0xff, 0xff, 0xff, 0xff, 0x00, 0x00, 0x00, 0x00, 0x00, 0x00, 0x00, 0x00,
   0x00, 0x00, 0x00, 0x00, 0xff, 0xff, 0xff, 0xff, 0x00, 0x00, 0x00, 0x00,
   0x00, 0x00, 0x00, 0x00, 0x00, 0x00, 0x00, 0x00, 0xff, 0xff, 0xff, 0xff,
   0x00, 0x00, 0x00, 0x00, 0x00, 0x00, 0x00, 0x00, 0x00, 0x00, 0x00, 0x00,
   0xff, 0xff, 0xff, 0xff, 0x00, 0x00, 0x00, 0x00, 0x00, 0x00, 0x00, 0x00,
   0x00, 0x00, 0x00, 0x00, 0xff, 0xff, 0xff, 0xff, 0x00, 0x00, 0x00, 0x00,
   0x00, 0x00, 0x00, 0x00, 0x00, 0x00, 0x00, 0x00, 0xff, 0xff, 0xff, 0xff,
   0x00, 0x00, 0x00, 0x00, 0x00, 0x00, 0x00, 0x00, 0x00, 0x00, 0x00, 0x00,
   0xff, 0xff, 0xff, 0xff, 0x00, 0x00, 0x00, 0x00, 0x00, 0x00, 0x00, 0x00,
   0x00, 0x00, 0x00, 0x00, 0xff, 0xff, 0xff, 0xff, 0x00, 0x00, 0x00, 0x00,
   0x00, 0x00, 0x00, 0x00, 0x00, 0x00, 0x00, 0x00
};
#define slant_right_width 32
#define slant_right_height 32
static unsigned char slant_right_bits[] = {
    0x88, 0x88, 0x88, 0x88, 0x11, 0x11, 0x11, 0x11, 0x22, 0x22, 0x22, 0x22,
    0x44, 0x44, 0x44, 0x44, 0x88, 0x88, 0x88, 0x88, 0x11, 0x11, 0x11, 0x11,
    0x22, 0x22, 0x22, 0x22, 0x44, 0x44, 0x44, 0x44, 0x88, 0x88, 0x88, 0x88,
    0x11, 0x11, 0x11, 0x11, 0x22, 0x22, 0x22, 0x22, 0x44, 0x44, 0x44, 0x44,
    0x88, 0x88, 0x88, 0x88, 0x11, 0x11, 0x11, 0x11, 0x22, 0x22, 0x22, 0x22,
    0x44, 0x44, 0x44, 0x44, 0x88, 0x88, 0x88, 0x88, 0x11, 0x11, 0x11, 0x11,
    0x22, 0x22, 0x22, 0x22, 0x44, 0x44, 0x44, 0x44, 0x88, 0x88, 0x88, 0x88,
    0x11, 0x11, 0x11, 0x11, 0x22, 0x22, 0x22, 0x22, 0x44, 0x44, 0x44, 0x44,
    0x88, 0x88, 0x88, 0x88, 0x11, 0x11, 0x11, 0x11, 0x22, 0x22, 0x22, 0x22,
    0x44, 0x44, 0x44, 0x44, 0x88, 0x88, 0x88, 0x88, 0x11, 0x11, 0x11, 0x11,
    0x22, 0x22, 0x22, 0x22, 0x44, 0x44, 0x44, 0x44
};
```

```
#define slant_left_width 32
#define slant_left_height 32
static unsigned char slant_left_bits[] = {
    0x44, 0x44, 0x44, 0x44, 0x22, 0x22, 0x22, 0x22, 0x11, 0x11, 0x11, 0x11,
    0x88, 0x88, 0x88, 0x88, 0x44, 0x44, 0x44, 0x44, 0x22, 0x22, 0x22, 0x22,
    0x11, 0x11, 0x11, 0x11, 0x88, 0x88, 0x88, 0x88, 0x44, 0x44, 0x44, 0x44,
    0x22, 0x22, 0x22, 0x22, 0x11, 0x11, 0x11, 0x11, 0x88, 0x88, 0x88, 0x88,
    0x44, 0x44, 0x44, 0x44, 0x22, 0x22, 0x22, 0x22, 0x11, 0x11, 0x11, 0x11,
    0x88, 0x88, 0x88, 0x88, 0x44, 0x44, 0x44, 0x44, 0x22, 0x22, 0x22, 0x22,
    0x11, 0x11, 0x11, 0x11, 0x88, 0x88, 0x88, 0x88, 0x44, 0x44, 0x44, 0x44,
    0x22, 0x22, 0x22, 0x22, 0x11, 0x11, 0x11, 0x11, 0x88, 0x88, 0x88, 0x88,
    0x44, 0x44, 0x44, 0x44, 0x22, 0x22, 0x22, 0x22, 0x11, 0x11, 0x11, 0x11,
    0x88, 0x88, 0x88, 0x88, 0x44, 0x44, 0x44, 0x44, 0x22, 0x22, 0x22, 0x22,
    0x11, 0x11, 0x11, 0x11, 0x88, 0x88, 0x88, 0x88
};

#define fg25_width 32
#define fg25_height 32
static unsigned char fg25_bits[] = {
    0xdd, 0xdd, 0xdd, 0xdd, 0xee, 0xee, 0xee, 0xee, 0xbb, 0xbb, 0xbb, 0xbb,
    0x77, 0x77, 0x77, 0x77, 0xdd, 0xdd, 0xdd, 0xdd, 0xee, 0xee, 0xee, 0xee,
    0xbb, 0xbb, 0xbb, 0xbb, 0x77, 0x77, 0x77, 0x77, 0xdd, 0xdd, 0xdd, 0xdd,
    0xee, 0xee, 0xee, 0xee, 0xbb, 0xbb, 0xbb, 0xbb, 0x77, 0x77, 0x77, 0x77,
    0xdd, 0xdd, 0xdd, 0xdd, 0xee, 0xee, 0xee, 0xee, 0xbb, 0xbb, 0xbb, 0xbb,
    0x77, 0x77, 0x77, 0x77, 0xdd, 0xdd, 0xdd, 0xdd, 0xee, 0xee, 0xee, 0xee,
    0xbb, 0xbb, 0xbb, 0xbb, 0x77, 0x77, 0x77, 0x77, 0xdd, 0xdd, 0xdd, 0xdd,
    0xee, 0xee, 0xee, 0xee, 0xbb, 0xbb, 0xbb, 0xbb, 0x77, 0x77, 0x77, 0x77,
    0xdd, 0xdd, 0xdd, 0xdd, 0xee, 0xee, 0xee, 0xee, 0xbb, 0xbb, 0xbb, 0xbb,
    0x77, 0x77, 0x77, 0x77, 0xdd, 0xdd, 0xdd, 0xdd, 0xee, 0xee, 0xee, 0xee,
    0xbb, 0xbb, 0xbb, 0xbb, 0x77, 0x77, 0x77, 0x77
};
#define fg50_width 32
#define fg50_height 32
static unsigned char fg50_bits[] = {
    0x55, 0x55, 0x55, 0x55, 0xaa, 0xaa, 0xaa, 0xaa, 0x55, 0x55, 0x55, 0x55,
    0xaa, 0xaa, 0xaa, 0xaa, 0x55, 0x55, 0x55, 0x55, 0xaa, 0xaa, 0xaa, 0xaa,
    0x55, 0x55, 0x55, 0x55, 0xaa, 0xaa, 0xaa, 0xaa, 0x55, 0x55, 0x55, 0x55,
    0xaa, 0xaa, 0xaa, 0xaa, 0x55, 0x55, 0x55, 0x55, 0xaa, 0xaa, 0xaa, 0xaa,
    0x55, 0x55, 0x55, 0x55, 0xaa, 0xaa, 0xaa, 0xaa, 0x55, 0x55, 0x55, 0x55,
    0xaa, 0xaa, 0xaa, 0xaa, 0x55, 0x55, 0x55, 0x55, 0xaa, 0xaa, 0xaa, 0xaa,
    0x55, 0x55, 0x55, 0x55, 0xaa, 0xaa, 0xaa, 0xaa, 0x55, 0x55, 0x55, 0x55,
    0xaa, 0xaa, 0xaa, 0xaa, 0x55, 0x55, 0x55, 0x55, 0xaa, 0xaa, 0xaa, 0xaa,
    0x55, 0x55, 0x55, 0x55, 0xaa, 0xaa, 0xaa, 0xaa, 0x55, 0x55, 0x55, 0x55,
    0xaa, 0xaa, 0xaa, 0xaa, 0x55, 0x55, 0x55, 0x55, 0xaa, 0xaa, 0xaa, 0xaa,
    0x55, 0x55, 0x55, 0x55, 0xaa, 0xaa, 0xaa, 0xaa
};
#define cross_width 32
```

```
#define cross_height 32
static unsigned char cross_bits[] = {
   0xcc, 0xcc, 0xcc, 0xcc, 0x33, 0x33, 0x33, 0x33, 0x33, 0x33, 0x33, 0x33,
   0xcc, 0xcc, 0xcc, 0xcc, 0xcc, 0xcc, 0xcc, 0xcc, 0x33, 0x33, 0x33, 0x33,
   0x33, 0x33, 0x33, 0x33, 0xcc, 0xcc, 0xcc, 0xcc, 0xcc, 0xcc, 0xcc, 0xcc,
   0x33, 0x33, 0x33, 0x33, 0x33, 0x33, 0x33, 0x33, 0xcc, 0xcc, 0xcc, 0xcc,
   0xcc, 0xcc, 0xcc, 0xcc, 0x33, 0x33, 0x33, 0x33, 0x33, 0x33, 0x33, 0x33,
   0xcc, 0xcc, 0xcc, 0xcc, 0xcc, 0xcc, 0xcc, 0xcc, 0x33, 0x33, 0x33, 0x33,
   0x33, 0x33, 0x33, 0x33, 0xcc, 0xcc, 0xcc, 0xcc, 0xcc, 0xcc, 0xcc, 0xcc,
   0x33, 0x33, 0x33, 0x33, 0x33, 0x33, 0x33, 0x33, 0xcc, 0xcc, 0xcc, 0xcc,
   0xcc, 0xcc, 0xcc, 0xcc, 0x33, 0x33, 0x33, 0x33, 0x33, 0x33, 0x33, 0x33,
   0xcc, 0xcc, 0xcc, 0xcc, 0xcc, 0xcc, 0xcc, 0xcc, 0x33, 0x33, 0x33, 0x33,
    0x33, 0x33, 0x33, 0x33, 0xcc, 0xcc, 0xcc, 0xcc,
};
```

BIBLIOGRAPHY

Asente, Paul, and Ralph Swick, *The X Window System Toolkit*, Digital Press, 1990

Johnson, Eric F. and Kevin Reichard, *X Window Applications Programming*, MIS Press, 1989

Jones, Oliver, *Introduction to the X Window System*, Prentice-Hall, 1989.

Miller, John David, *An OPEN LOOK at UNIX*, M&T Books, 1990

Nye, Adrian, *The Xlib Programming Manul*, O'Reilly and Associates, 1988.

Nye, Adrian, *The Xlib Reference Manul*, O'Reilly and Associates, 1988.

Rosenthal, David S., "A Simple X.11 Client Program, or, How Hard Can It Really Be to Write 'Hello, World'?," in *Proceedings of the Winter, 1988 USENIX Conference*, pp. 229-235.

Scheifler, Robert W. and Jim Gettys, "The X Window System," *ACM Transactions on Graphics*, vol. 5, no. 2, pp. 79-109, April, 1986.

Scheifler, Robert W., and James Gettys, X *Window System*, Second Edition, Digital Press, 1990.

Sun Microsystems, Inc., *Open Look Graphical User Interface Application Style Guide*, Addison-Wesley, 1990

Sun Microsystems, Inc., *Open Look Graphical User Interface Functional Specification*, Addison-Wesley, 1989

Young, Douglas A., *The X Window System: Programming and Applications with Xt, OSF/Motif Edition*, Prentice Hall, 1990

INDEX

Y